INTRODUCTION TO BLACK STUDIES

ALSO BY MAULANA KARENGA:

Odu Ifa: The Ethical Teachings (1999)

Kwanzaa: A Celebration of Family, Community and Culture (1998)

Million Man March/Day of Absence Mission Statement (1995)

The Book of Coming Forth by Day:
The Ethics of the Declarations of Innocence (1990)

Reconstructing Kemetic Culture:
Papers, Perspectives, Projects (ed.) (1990)

The African American Holiday of Kwanzaa:
A Celebration of Family, Community and Culture (1988)

Kemet and the African Worldview:
Research, Rescue and Restoration (ed.) (1986)

Selections From The Husia:
Sacred Wisdom of Ancient Egypt (1984)

Kawaida Theory: An Introductory Outline (1980)

Essays on Struggle: Position and Analysis (1978)

Kwanzaa: Origins, Concepts, Practice (1977)

Kawaida: A Communitarian African Philosophy (2002)

Maat, The Moral Ideal in Ancient Egypt:
A Study in Classical African Ethics (forthcoming)

Race, Ethnicity and Multiculturalism:
Issues in Domination, Resistance and Diversity (forthcoming)

INTRODUCTION TO BLACK STUDIES

MAULANA KARENGA

THIRD EDITION

UNIVERSITY OF SANKORE PRESS
LOS ANGELES

2002

FRONT COVER:

The Classical Period - Right to Left: Maiy, Werer, Ancient Egypt, 18th Dynasty

The Holocaust of Enslavement - Right to Left: Harriet Tubman, Frederick Douglass

The Reaffirmation of the 60's - Right to Left: Ella Baker, Eleanor Holmes Norton, Fannie Lou Hamer (forefront); Kwame Ture (rear)

COVER DESIGN:

Mark Tangulifu, Graphic Designer
University of Sankore Press Collective

For information address:
The University of Sankore Press
2560 West 54th Street
Los Angeles, CA 90043.

ISBN 0-943412-23-4

To:

Fannie Lou Hamer who taught us the morality of remembrance, saying there are two things we all should care about – never to forget where we came from and always praise the bridges that carried us over;

Malcolm X who taught us the instructiveness of history, saying, "Of all our studies, history is best prepared to reward our research;"

Mary McLeod Bethune who taught us our mission in education, saying we must discover the dawn and share it with the masses and bring the benefits of science and knowledge to those who need it most;

Paul Robeson who taught us that "The battlefront is everywhere; there is no sheltered rear;"

Anna Julia Cooper who taught us that what we do must be done together as male and female, saying, "There is a female as well as male side to truth: and those who do not honor it do damage to both female and male;"

Amilcar Cabral who taught us the challenge and protracted nature of struggle, saying, "Mask no difficulties, tell no lies and claim no easy victories;"

Lady Ta Aset who taught us the cardinal virtue of reciprocity, saying, "Doing good is not difficult. In fact, just speaking good is a monument to one who does it. For those who do good for others are at the same time doing it for themselves;"

Orunmila, teacher of the transcendent, who taught us, "Let's do things with joy. For surely humans have been chosen to bring good into the world" and this is the fundamental meaning and mission of human life;

and *Kheti* who taught us that "Every day is a donation to eternity and even one hour is a contribution to the future."

Ase, Hotep, Heri

CONTENTS

PREFACE TO THE THIRD EDITION (2002)

In the twenty years since I wrote the first edition of *Introduction to Black Studies*, the developments in the discipline of Black Studies have been numerous and continuous. Moreover, the literature internal to the discipline as well as discipline-related literature has increased tremendously. In this third edition, I have made great effort to keep abreast of this latest, diverse and wide-ranging scholarship. In this regard, I have studied and evaluated a vast amount of materials, making a critical selection of those which were deemed most relevant and useful. Furthermore, I have thoroughly re-examined the second edition, seeking ways to enhance its content and increase its usefulness to faculty, students and the general reader.

Therefore, I have reorganized much of the material, added new headings, pictures, emphasis boxes and more maps, rewritten sections and different portions, expanded the bibliography and included a considerable amount of material which is totally new.

I am acutely aware of the pre-eminent position among introductory texts in the discipline that *IBS* has held since it was first published and its role as an important contribution to the ongoing discussions around the foundation, parameters, content and academic, cultural and social mission of the discipline. I am also equally aware of the value the text has for the African community in providing a framework and data useful for the discussion of critical issues which concern the African American and world African community. And thus, I am constantly attentive to the task of insuring that this work maintains the high level scholarship and usefulness that have earned it its special position within the discipline and the community.

The hieroglyphs which appear at the beginning of each chapter is the ancient Egyptian word, *rhyt* (rekhit) which means both *human* beings and *knowing* beings. It reflects the ancient Egyptian appreciation for knowledge as the fundamental way we understand our humanity, but also the indispensable way by which we realize our humanity in the most meaningful and expansive ways. In an expanded sense, it also suggests their appreciation for knowledge as key to our creating a context of maximum human freedom and human flourishing. This conception parallels the ancient Yoruba conception that knowledge (*imo*) and wisdom (*ogbon*) – moral and practical – are the first criteria for both the existence and creation of a good world. *IBS* embraces this conception and the commitment to knowledge and bringing good in the world which it requires. The hieroglyphic symbol, *rhyt*, is, thus, a reminder and reaffirmation of this.

Finally, I am grateful, as always, to those who have assisted me in the completion of this edition directly and/or indirectly. I am appreciative of my colleagues, other faculty, students and the general readers who choose and use this book and of their valuable suggestions and observations on it, and I have tried to respond appropriately. My profound thanks and appreciation goes also to the members of my Organization Us who have always provided me with a valuable context of intellectual exchange, challenge and support. A special thanks goes also to Mark Tangulifu, our graphic designer for the design of the cover and Tiamoyo Karenga for many of the pictures which appear in this work. I am grateful also to my colleagues for their critical observations and ongoing valuable exchanges: Molefi Asante, Sandra Collins, William Little, La Frances Rodgers-Rose, Amen Rahh, Selasé Williams, Freya Rivers, Reiland Rabaka, Fred Hord, James Naazir Conyers, Errol Henderson, Andrew Smallwood, Theman Taylor and Charles Jones.

I offer thanks to the members of the National Association of Kawaida Organizations (NAKO) and all those who have attended the Kawaida Institute of Pan-African Studies' (KIPAS) annual summer seminar in Social Theory and Practice, for the engaging conversations and insightful exchanges on a myriad of issues, and especially to Segun Shabaka, Maisha Ongoza and Kamau Tyehimba, chairs of NAKO in New York, Philadelphia and Chicago. Asante sana (thanks very much) to the vice-chairs of Us, Tulivu Jadi and Chimbuko Tembo who again relieved me of responsibilities so I could finish this project. Asante sana also to my publishers, Chimbuko Tembo and Limbiko Tembo for a special friendship, constant assistance, support and regular understanding about missed and revised deadlines. And finally, I say to Tiamoyo, my rare and irreplaceable friend, administrative assistant, wife, constant companion in love, work and struggle and in all things good and beautiful - *asante, asante nyingi na baada ya asante, mchanga wa pwani ni haba* – thanks, many thanks and compared to the many times I say thanks, the grains of sand on the seashore are few.

Maulana Karenga
California State University, Long Beach
6241 - January 1 - 2001

PREFACE TO THE SECOND EDITION (1993)

In the ten years since I wrote the first edition of this book, numerous developments have occurred in the discipline of Black Studies accompanied by a new body of literature. Among these developments are the consolidation and expansion of Black Studies professional organizations, the emergence of Afrocentricity as a major intellectual concept, the expansion and growth of Black women's studies, the focus on classical African Studies and the rise and challenge of multiculturalism. These occurrences and the new body of literature have required critical evaluation and inclusion, both to keep abreast with discourse and practice in the discipline and to make a substantive contribution to each. The present edition responds to these challenges.

I am grateful to my colleagues who have made suggestions for this edition and engaged in helpful exchanges with me in various subject areas, especially Molefi Asante, Felix Boateng, Sandra Collins, Roy Garrott, Charles Henry, William Nelson and James Stewart; to my skilled and valuable research assistants, Chimbuko Tembo and Limbiko Tembo, who have assisted me in more ways than I can acknowledge or repay; to Subira Kifano and Tulivu Jadi, who as Vice-Chairs of Us, relieved me of many responsibilities so I could finish this project; and to all the other advocates of my organization, Us, for constant support in these and other endeavors. I am also profoundly and permanently indebted to Tiamoyo, my friend, secretary, administrative assistant, colleague in this project, wife and constant companion in love, work and struggle, and in all things good and beautiful.

Maulana Karenga
Inglewood, California
January, 1993

PREFACE TO THE FIRST EDITION (1982)

This text is essentially a contribution to the efforts to develop a standard body of discipline-specific literature for Black Studies. Its basic aim is to offer a definitive introduction to the discipline. Moreover, as an introductory text, it seeks to provide the student with a concise but substantive intellectual base for a critical understanding and discussion of Black Studies. Although a survey approach is employed, stress is placed on inquiry and analysis as key to building the student's intellectual base in the discipline.

Toward achieving this basic aim, several objectives have guided the preparation of this text: (1) to introduce and define the origins, relevance and scope of Black Studies; (2) to introduce, define and discuss critically the seven core areas of Black Studies, i.e., Black History, Black Religion, Black Social Organization, Black Politics, Black Economics, Black Creative Production and Black Psychology; (3) to introduce and define key concepts in the discipline and each subject area; (4) to delineate fundamental issues and areas for critical discussion in the discipline and its subject areas; (5) to introduce and discuss critically major challenges facing Black Studies; (6) to introduce fundamental literature in the discipline of Black Studies and its core subject areas; and (7) to raise provocative questions about the Black experience which cultivate the use of and on appreciation for inquiry and analysis as indispensable tools to an effective grasp and critical discussion of Black Studies.

This text, then, is structured around these objectives. The first chapter introduces the discipline as a whole through discussion of its origins, relevance and scope. The main body of the text follows and is organized into seven chapters, each of which discusses critically one of the seven core subject areas of Black Studies and thus introduces the student to the basic internal dialogue of each subject area. The final chapter raises includes suggestions of how they might be met. At the end of each chapter are study questions and references aimed at encouraging and facilitating inquiry and analysis by the student.

This enterprise is self-consciously Afrocentric, critical and corrective in response to the internal demands of the discipline itself, whose subject matter and academic and social mission clearly demand this approach. An Afrocentric approach is essentially intellectual inquiry and production centered on and in the image and interest of African peoples. This responds to the early and continuing demands for academic and social relevance of the educational process and its contents. The critical thrust is the advancing of severe and ongoing criticism of the established order of things in order to negate myths, mystifications and insubstantialities of traditional white studies on Blacks, society and the world. And the corrective thrust is the correlative discovery and affirmation of the truth of the Black experience in its current and historical unfolding. It also means posing correctives to problems internal to the discipline of Black studies as well as to those which confront Black people, themselves.

Several other points should be made about the book. First, I have self-consciously used abundant references to introduce the student to the literature in the field and provide him/her with a bibliography which will facilitate research for term papers in Black Studies and its seven core subject areas. Secondly, in citations, I have not used the first names of the authors in hopes that this will encourage use of the bibliography. Thirdly, I have written an admittedly long chapter on Black History in order to give the student a general panoramic view and sense of the origins, challenges and achievements of Black people as a backdrop for the discussions in the particular areas which follow.

Moreover, I tried to deal substantively with vital issues and questions often raised by students but not normally dealt with at length or in a systematic Afrocentric manner by other texts, i.e., resistance in slavery, the DuBois-Garvey conflict, the fall of African societies, Black scientific achievements, and of course the dynamics and legacy of the Sixties. Fourthly, an attempt has been made to avoid negative categories and introduce proactive and positive ones. Therefore, the word "negro" except when it is part of a title is replaced with Black, African, Afro-American, etc. in parenthesis and the text focus is on Black struggle and achievement rather than on victimization.

By way of acknowledgements, I owe a great debt to Tiamoyo, my wife, who lived up to her name "she who inspires." For she inspired, typed, proofread, xeroxed, edited, researched, raised questions, took notes and dictation, and understood and appreciated the limitations on my time during the writing.

Special thanks go to Chimbuko Tembo and Limbiko Tembo who did research, xeroxed, compiled bibliographies and supported the effort in other ways. Thanks goes to Jitahadi Imara, my administrative assistant, who conducted classes, seminars and forums for me while I was writing and to the other Executive Council members of Us, who shared other responsibilities to free me to finish this book. Thanks go to Ralph Tulivu who helped edit and Chanzo Ndoto and Salimu Logan for the long and many hours spent at the libraries on several campuses collecting needed materials for me. Great thanks go to the founders of the Kawaida

Groundwork Committee (Us) who supported my theoretical and practical efforts to preserve and expand the legacy of the 60's out of which this gook grew, i.e., Tiamoyo Karenga, W. Sikivu Kabaila, Mark Tangulifu, Chimbuko Tembo, Subira Kifano, Ujima Goode and Nzinga Ratibisha.

In addition to the founders, I am also grateful to other advocates who critical questions in our regular discussions and at seminars and institutes sponsored by the Institute of Pan-African Studies helped lay the basis for this book. These are Chanzo Ndoto, Brent Mshindaji, Jitahadi Imara, Robert Mpinduzi, Limbiko Tembo, Imani Imara, Gerold Msadiki, Kweli Walker, Robert Tambuzi, Salimu Logan, Haiba Collier, Nyenyekevu Kumbufu, Arnold Kumbufu, Ralph Tulivu, Kamilisha Angalifu, Andrew Angalifu, Jifunza Pinkston, Muhebi James and supporters, Walter Jitahidi and Joel Mjengaji.

I am indebted to the many students who took my classes and listened to my lectures on the many campuses at which I have taught and lectured and who also raised critical questions about Black life, history and struggle which this book seeks to answer. Special thanks to my friend and colleague, Professor Amen Rahh, who Afrocentric stress complements and reinforces mine; to Haki Madhubuti, Kalamu ya Salaam, Segun Shabaka, Mansong Kulubally and Kamau Tyehimba for intellectual exchange and support; to Eunice, my sister and Chestyn my brother, whose support has always been strong and timely; and to Clentine, my sister for whom the finishing of this book was a last aspiration.

I am indebted also to the Black scholars in these pages whose works provide the substance of Black Studies.

But the greatest debt is to Black people whose lives, achievements and aspirations fill this book and give it whatever message and meaning it has.

Maulana Karenga
Inglewood, California
July, 1982

INTRODUCTION

 **INTRODUCTION**

CHAPTER 1

1.1 DEFINING THE DISCIPLINE

DEFINITION

Black Studies is *the critical and systematic study of the thought and practice of African people in their current and historical unfolding.* It is a *critical* study in that it is characterized by careful analysis and considered judgment. And it is *systematic* in that it is structured and methodical in its pursuit and presentation of knowledge. Likewise, stress on the *historical and current unfolding* of African thought and practice is meant to call attention to their *diverse, dynamic* and *constantly developing* character. The word *African* refers here to African peoples on the continent of Africa and those in the Diaspora (Asante, 1997:78-79). The term *Diaspora* means the dispersion or scattering of people with a common origin. Thus, it is used in Black Studies to refer to Black people whose common origin is in Africa, but who have dispersed or been scattered throughout the world, i.e., in the Americas, the Caribbean and other islands of the seas, Europe and Asia.

Because Black Studies began as a self-defined and organized discipline or area of study among African Americans, it tends to focus most heavily on the African American initiative and experience (Conyers, 1997). But from its beginning, Black Studies scholars have always defined and developed the discipline as inclusive of African peoples throughout the world African community (Turner, 1984). This is especially true of the continent of Africa where the history and culture of African peoples have their origin and whose culture and politics still inform and inspire African American activities and interests (Magubane,

1987). But it is also true of African Caribbeans, African Native Americans and African Latinos, i.e., Cubans, Puerto Ricans, Brazilians and others, whose histories overlap and intersect with that of African Americans around such issues as freedom, justice, immigration, religion, cultural exchange and struggle (Asante, 1997; Hine and McLeod, 2001). This thrust to include all Africans as subjects of study is called *pan-African* which literally means *all* Africans (Martin, 1998). It is in the interest of recognizing this *pan-African* scope of Black Studies that some scholars call the discipline "Pan-African Studies" and others call it "Africana Studies". In fact, Africana Studies has become more used as a designation for Black Studies in recent years.

INITIATIVE AND EXPERIENCE

As stated above, Black Studies focuses on the African *initiative* and *experience* in the world. The concept of initiative points to Black Studies stress on Africans' self-understanding and self-assertion in the world. What is important here is to study Africans thinking, acting, producing, creating, building, speaking and problem-solving in their own unique way in the world. This concept which is also called *agency* or the capacity and will to act, is extended to mean the capacity and will to make history, create culture and address critical human concerns in a meaningful and successful manner (Asante, 1990; Karenga, 1997).

In the early years of the development of Black Studies, the phrase "teaching the Black (or African) experience" was used to describe the central focus of the discipline (Young, 1984). At that time, the term "the Black experience" was used to refer to everything African peoples had done and undergone. But as the discipline developed, greater emphasis was increasingly placed on stressing what Africans had done rather than what they had undergone. As a result, the term "experience" began to be used in a more restricted sense as that which was undergone or lived through. The concept of initiative, then, focuses on what Africans have done and do and the concept of experience deals with what Africans have undergone and lived through. For example, Africans emerge as the first humans and experience the wonder, awe and dangers of nature. They take initiative in organizing ways to secure food, clothing, shelter and to build family, community and human culture. Eventually Africans develop some of the basic disciplines of human knowledge and some of the greatest civilizations in ancient times in the Nile Valley, i.e., Egypt, Nubia and Ethiopia.

Moreover, Africans experience the Holocaust of enslavement, but take initiative in resisting enslavement in various ways and creating realms of freedom in an unfree, brutal and dehumanizing situation. Also, they construct a new synthesized culture in which African spirituality, ethics, art, music, literature, dance, family and other cultural forms are both partially retained and reshaped in the crucible of new circumstances (Franklin and Moss, 1999). In the age of segregation or American apartheid, African Americans experience another form of oppression. But they are not passive victims. They seize initiative and wage a struggle which destroys legal segregation, expands the realm of freedom in the country and provides a model and inspiration for other marginalized and oppressed groups and peoples in this country and around the world. Again, the important issue here, as Black Studies stresses, is to offer a dynamic portrait of African life in which Africans are not simply people swept up in the experience of victimization or passive encounter in the world, but rather are active agents of their own life, engaging their environment, each other and other people in unique, meaningful and valuable ways.

1.2   ORIGINS OF THE DISCIPLINE

INTRODUCTION

Some scholars, talking of Black Studies in the general sense, argue that Black Studies began in ancient societies like ancient Egypt, Mali and Songhay which clearly established an intellectual tradition of study of themselves and the world in which they lived. However, if we speak of Black Studies as a self-defined and organized discipline in the university, then we must place its origin in the 1960's. In fact, Black Studies, as an intellectual practice, is rooted in and reflects the social visions and social struggles of this period. The critical concerns in struggles for freedom, justice, equality, power, political and cultural self-determination, educational relevance, and for an expanded sense of human possibility are all reflected in both the vision and practice of Black Studies. And it is from these critical concerns and the struggles which gave concrete expression to them that Black Studies developed its self-understanding as both an area of critical intellectual study and an instrument of social change in the interest of African and human good.

Black Studies, then, began as both a political and academic demand with grounding in both the general student movement and the social struggles of the 60's out of which the Student Movement evolved (Van Deburg, 1993; Pinkney, 1976; Brisbane, 1974; Edwards, 1970; McEvoy and Miller, 1969). The 60's was a time of upheaval and confrontation, and students – both peoples of color and whites – were at the center of the struggles which produced this process. Beginning first off campus in a struggle against the racist structure and functioning of society, students began to see the university as a key institution in the larger system of coercive institutions created by the established order to maintain its power. The university was pictured as a microcosm of society, a small example of how society looked and functioned in terms of race, class and power. It was perceived as racist and unresponsive to peoples of color. Moreover, it was seen by the students as committed to the exploitation and oppression of Blacks, other peoples of color and the poor and to their exclusion from the social knowledge, wealth and power in

Seshat, female divine patron of learning and knowledge, ancient Egypt

U.S. society. The decision then was made to take up the struggle against society at the university, which was seen as society's "brain" and its "intellectual factory" which produced its leaders and followers as well as its cherished social myths (Van Deburg, 1993:63-92; Robinson, Foster and Ogilvie, 1969; McEvoy and Miller, 1969). Thus, Black Studies scholars and students linked knowledge and power, campus and community, student learning with student service and activism in and for community, society and the world.

THE ACTIVIST-INTELLECTUAL TRADITION

Although Black Studies evolves in the context of the social and intellectual struggle of the Sixties, it of necessity draws on the rich resources of the African past, both ancient and modern

models and data. And certainly, one of the most important models it borrows from and builds on is the activist-intellectual tradition of African culture. This tradition extends back to ancient Egypt with its model of the socially conscious and activist intellectual, the sesh, who understood themselves in both moral and social terms and constantly expressed a commitment to using their knowledge and skills in the service of the people. This social service included insuring justice, caring for the vulnerable and the environment, respecting persons as bearers of dignity and divinity, and working for future generations (Karenga, 1994, 1984). Likewise, the sage and teacher (olùkó) Orunmila of Yorubaland taught that the fundamental criterion for a good world and the key instrument in creating the

Amenhotep, son of Hapu, a sage, scribe and minister under Amenhotep III, revered after death for his knowledge and service, 18th Dynasty

good world is effective knowledge of things, a moral wisdom which enables human beings to come together for the purpose of increasing and sustaining good in the world (Karenga, 1999). Therefore, in these and other African societies, the commitment to learning is based on the conception of knowledge which values knowledge not simply for knowledge sake, but rather knowledge for human sake. In a word, knowledge is considered important not simply to enjoy oneself or even simply get a job, but because of its value and role in improving the human condition and enhancing the human prospect or human future.

This activist-intellectual tradition was maintained and further developed in more modern times with activist-intellectuals such as W.E.B. DuBois, Anna Julia Cooper, Ida B. Wells, Mary McLeod Bethune, Malcolm X, Martin Luther King, et al, who used their knowledge and skills to address critical issues of their times in both discourse and social practice. This commitment to knowledge in the service of community, society and humanity is the ground of the African activist-scholar or activist-intellectual tradition. And it is reaffirmed in the self-defined mission of Black Studies which links the academic and social, the quest to learn with the obligation to serve (Crouchett, 1971; Turner and McGann, 1980; Stewart, 1984; Karenga, 1988; Woodyard, 1991). The activist-intellectual tradition then poses as a central task of both Black Studies scholars and students to master, discover, produce and present knowledge in ways that measure up to the highest of standards of intellectual work and then to use that knowledge in the service of community, society and humanity. And it also cultivates appreciation of the value of critical study of African culture and of engaging it as a rich resource for models of excellence in human thought and human practice and as Black Studies' fundamental point of departure for all its work.

SOCIAL STRUGGLES AND THE STUDENT MOVEMENT

The social struggles in the Sixties served as both a context and encouragement for the emergence of a student movement which linked itself to these larger struggles for social change both on-campus and off-campus. There were four basic thrusts in the student movement, each of which aided in creating the context and support for the emergence of Black Studies as a discipline. These are:

1)   the Civil Rights Movement;
2)   the Free Speech Movement;
3)   the Anti-Vietnam War Movement, and
4)   the Black Power Movement.

Although the Civil Rights Movement and Black Power Movement are more directly related to the struggle for Black Studies, the Free Speech Movement and Anti-Vietnam

War Movement on campus indirectly aided the overall thrust. For it helped create a climate of struggle dedicated to challenging university authority, encouraging and demonstrating student power and questioning the content and meaning of educational practices.

Bob Moses, SNCC, teaching volunteers for civil rights work

THE CIVIL RIGHTS MOVEMENT

The first thrust of the Student Movement began in 1960 with Black Students who played a central and indispensable role in the Civil Rights Movement in the South (Forman, 1972; Carson, 1981; Morris, 1984; Williams, 1987; Branch, 1988; Crawford, Rouse and Woods, 1990; Robinett, 1997). Essentially, the Movement sought to: 1) break down the barriers of legal segregation in public accommodations; 2) achieve equality and justice for Blacks; and 3) organize Blacks into a self-conscious social force capable of defining, defending and advancing their interests. The Student Non-Violent Coordinating Committee (SNCC) emerged as a vanguard group in the Civil Rights struggle and especially in the Student Movement. In its role as the preeminent student group in the country, SNCC not only mobilized, organized and politicized thousands of Black students, but also politicized many white students and their leaders through recruiting and training them and bringing them to the South to work in the struggle (McAdam, 1988). As Clay Carson (1981:129) notes, white summer volunteers in Mississippi "who returned home greatly influenced by their experiences...would bring a measure of SNCC radicalism into the student's rights and antiwar movements." This link would prove valuable for joint action later.

THE FREE SPEECH MOVEMENT

The second thrust of the Student Movement began with the Free Speech Movement at UC Berkeley in 1964. It was essentially white student protest against the rigid, arbitrary, restrictive and unresponsive character of the university. In a word, it was a demand for civil rights on campus (Draper, 1965; Lipset and Wolin, 1965; Rorabaugh, 1989). The leadership of the Movement which had served as summer volunteers in Mississippi with SNCC expressed a link between the civil rights struggle on campus and in the larger society. In fact, they posed the Free Speech Movement on UC Berkeley's campus as "another phase of the same struggle," i.e., the civil rights struggle in the larger society and expressed the similarity of suppression of powerless Blacks and students by the established order (Carson, 1981:129).

THE ANTI-WAR MOVEMENT

The third thrust of the Student Movement began in 1965 which was the general student protest against the Vietnam war and university complicity in it through its cooperation with the government in recruitment and research and development programs (McEvoy and Miller, 1969; DeBendetti and Chatfield, 1990). The anti-war movement was launched by New Leftists, especially the Students for a Democratic Society (SDS). SNCC, which inspired leaders of SDS to organized activism, supported this resistance and participated in it. In fact, in 1968 SDS at its annual convention drafted a statement, which acknowl-edged their debt to the Black struggle in the South and SNCC in particular for their new consciousness and activism. Thus, the student protest against the Vietnam war and university complicity in it was initiated by the white Left but was informed and participated in by SNCC and other African American activists.

SNCC and other African American activists participated in the anti-war movement, not only from a student position, but also from a Black and Third World (people of color) position (SNCC, 1968; Taylor, 1973; Hare, 1973; Karenga, 1997). African Americans' opposition to the war in Vietnam was based on their opposition to: 1) the government's war against Third World liberation movements and peoples in general and Vietnam in particular; 2) the threat the draft posed to Blacks and other males of color not covered by student deferment and especially vulnerable in the South, and; 3) fighting an unjust war for a nation depriving Blacks of basic civil and human rights (Taylor, 1973; Terry, 1970). Thus, they forged a link between the Black Freedom struggle, Third World Liberation struggles and their opposition to the war (Carson, 1981:183-185; Karenga, 1997:48). This combined struggle again linked university change to social change and further revealed the university's vulnerability to student power and activism.

THE BLACK POWER MOVEMENT

The final thrust of the Student Movement which led directly to the establishment of Black Studies began in 1965 with the

emergence of the Black Power Movement (Woodard, 1999; Van Deburg, 1997; Pinkney, 1976; Brisbane, 1976). Although the phrase "Black Power" did not evolve until 1966 as a battle cry of SNCC, the beginning of the Black Power Movement is generally set at 1965, the year of the Watts Revolt in Los Angeles. This marked the beginning of a series of revolts across the country

Sisters in Blackness at Spelman College giving the Black Power salute popularized by the Organization Us.

through the latter part of the 60's. The Black Power Movement ushered in a new dialog about relations of power in society and the university, the pervasive character of racism, and the need for struggle to overturn the established order and create a more

Simba Wachanga, The Young Lions, of the Organization Us, holding up text on Kawaida in study session

just society (Carmichael and Hamilton, 1992). Black Power advocates stressed the importance of self-determination – cultural, political and economic, and the need for power in achieving and maintaining it. They also argued for a *relevant education*, an education that was meaningful to the students, useful to the community, and reflective of the realities of society and world (Hare, 1969; 1972).

In addition, Black Power advocates, like the Organization Us and other cultural nationalist organizations, called for a focus on *cultural grounding*, studying and recovering African culture and extracting from it models of excellence and possibility (Karenga, 1980). This was to be done not only to achieve a proper self-consciousness and restructure the university curriculum, but also to rebuild community and society. They also stressed the need for the university and society to recognize the diverse cultures of U.S. society and practice cultural pluralism (the predecessor to multiculturalism today) which respects all people and cultures. Finally, Black Power advocates called on students to engage in struggle in the classrooms, on campus in general and in society not only to improve the quality of education, but also to improve the life of African people and change society itself (Turner, 1970).

Massive student rally for Black Studies at Howard University

THE EMERGENCE OF BLACK STUDIES

THE STRUGGLE AT SAN FRANCISCO STATE UNIVERSITY (SFSU)

In the context of the Black Power Movement's stress on self-determination, cultural grounding, relevant education, cultural pluralism and student activism, Black Studies emerges as a movement and a discipline. It began in 1966 at San Francisco State College (SFSC), now called San Francisco State University, and was again initiated and led by Black students (T'Shaka, 1982; Edwards, 1970; Orrick, 1969). It came at the rising tide of the Black Power Movement and reflected its sense of social mission and urgency. By 1966, the Watts Revolt and the Black Power Movement had ushered in a more racially self-conscious and assertive activism and Black students at SFSC and on other campuses began to respond to this resurgence of nationalist activism. Thus, in 1966, the Negro Students Association changed their name to the Black Student Union (BSU) to indicate a new identity and direction. And in the fall of the same year, the BSU produced a document arguing for and demanding the first Department of Black Studies.

Continuing their thrust, Black students established a Black arts and culture series in the Experimental College which was also created in 1966 and became involved in SFSC's tutorial program for the surrounding community. This and other community service activities signaled the social commitment and service which Black Studies advocates would place at the center of the academic and social mission of Black Studies.

Since the Experimental College was set up with student money, there was no serious resistance to it, but the demand by the BSU for a legitimate Black Studies Department funded by the college and controlled by Black people brought stiff resistance. Moreover, the BSU demanded a special admissions program which would waive entrance requirements for a given number of Black students. This also was resisted, even though Black enrollment had been reduced drastically from over a thousand to a few hundred by the College's tracking system.

By 1968 the situation had escalated to the point where the BSU launched a strike on November 6th around a series of demands including a Black Studies Department, special admissions, financial aid and decisions on personnel. Influenced by the writings of the African revolutionary, Frantz Fanon's (1963) and the emphasis on Third World solidarity by Third World Liberation Movements, other Third World groups joined with the BSU under the umbrella organization, the Third World Liberation Front. These other Third World groups included the Mexican American Student Confederation (MASC), the Asian-American Political Alliance (AAPA), the Intercollegiate Chinese for Social Action (ICSA), the Philippine American Collegiate Endeavor (PACE) and the Latin American Student Organization (LASO). Reflecting a common concern for Third World Students and Third World Studies, they issued fifteen demands which served as a model for other Black Studies struggles. The SDS, Peace and Freedom party and white students from the Experimental College formed a strike support committee and worked to join the struggle of Third World students with the struggle against the war, ROTC on campus and other issues which linked the university with the government. In this student thrust, however, it was Blacks (and other Third World students) who again led the way and the whites supported, as in the first thrust in the early 60's.

In February, 1968, Dr. Nathan Hare was appointed as coordinator of Black Studies and was given the task of formulating an autonomous Black Studies Department. By April, he had completed his proposal which included, not only the structure for the department, but also a program of special admission for Black students, and a B.A. degree in Black Studies. However, the board

of trustees continually delayed
implementation of the program and
it is this which led to the November
6th strike. The school was closed;
students clashed with police; presidents were changed with regularity;
and the community became
involved in the campus struggle in a
way it had never done. Eventually,
the students won at the end of 1968
and San Francisco State became the
first institution to establish a Black
Studies program and department.

Dr. Nathan Hare

OTHER SITES OF STRUGGLE

As Robert Brisbane (1974:228) notes, Black students paid
close attention to the struggle at San Francisco State and were
impressed with the capacity of students to win concessions from
the administration. Thus, already "by fall of 1968, the experiences of San Francisco State were being duplicated on dozens of
campuses throughout the country." On every occasion, these
struggles were seen as linked to the overall struggle for Black liberation and were often led by Black nationalists or Black Power
advocates. Among these were members of SNCC, Us
Organization and other Kawaida formations on the West and
East coasts, the Black Panther Party, Congress of Racial Equality
and smaller local nationalist formations. As Alphonso Pinkney
(1976:177) observed, the struggle for Black Studies was "seen as
a necessary component of Black liberation" and white resistance
seen "as an attempt to preserve (Black) subordinate status in
society. . . ." It became important then to break what was perceived as the white monopoly on knowledge and its use and create a new context for producing and sharing a new knowledge,
directed toward service to the community rather than toward
suppressing it.

Thus, the struggle to win Black Studies coincided with the
general student revolt against the structure and functioning of
the university. And at the beginning it often was supported by
other Third World students and whites. Eventually, however,
the majority of Black students would reject cooperation with

whites and insist on Black self-determination and independence
from alliances with whites. They then went on to launch a series
of struggles and negotiations which forced most of the major colleges and universities to agree to establish some form of Black
Studies by 1969.

The Black Studies struggle extended also to Black colleges
which had prided themselves on being pioneers in teaching the
Black Experience. What they actually taught was "negro history" which both in content and consciousness was different from
the liberational thrust for which Black Studies advocates struggled. Brisbane (1974:238-239) lists three reasons the Black colleges resisted the challenge: 1) alleged financial problems; 2)
assumption that only a militant faction advocated it; and; 3) the
"bourgeois mentality" of the staff which was "committed to
working within the system (and) completely rejected the notion
of Black liberation." However, after a series of struggles and after
"Harvard, Yale and Columbia universities provided 'legitimacy'
by the adoption of such programs," leading Black universities
like Atlanta, Fisk, Howard, Lincoln, Morgan and Tuskegee to
initiate Black Studies Programs by fall of 1969.

1.3   RELEVANCE OF THE DISCIPLINE

THE CONCEPT OF RELEVANCE

One of the most important concepts in the general Student
Movement and especially in the Black Student Movement
which waged the struggle for Black Studies was the concept of a
relevant education, a concept which had both academic and social
dimensions. A relevant education for Black Studies advocates
was an education which was, as stated above, meaningful, useful
and reflective of the realities of society and the world. For Black
Studies and Black Power advocates the central realities were: 1)
the need to solve the pressing problems of the Black community, society and the world and; 2) the revolutionary struggle being
waged to end racist oppression and change society and the world.
To be relevant, education had to address these issues and contribute to these interrelated projects. Thus, Nathan Hare
(1969:42), one of the guiding theorists and founders of the
Movement, argued for an African American education, which

would contribute to solving "the problems of the race" by producing "persons capable of solving problems of a contagious American society." Moreover, he concluded, "a Black education which is not revolutionary in the current day is both irrelevant and useless." It is this stress on academic and social relevance of education that not only gave Black Studies its central self-conception and mission, but also brought it its major opposition.

The push for relevant education in the university was thus joined with a thrust by Black Studies to establish and maintain its own relevance as both an academic and social project. Therefore, in developing a relevant Black Studies, Black Studies advocates expressed two sets of basic concerns, i.e., academic and social ones (Robinson, Foster and Ogilvie, 1969; Blassingame, 1973).

ACADEMIC CONCERNS

On the academic level, they were concerned first with the intellectual inadequacy and injurious nature of traditional white studies. White studies was seen as inadequate and injurious in its omission and/or distortion of the lives and culture of the majority of humankind, especially the fathers and mothers of humankind and human civilization, African people. Secondly, Black Studies advocates perceived white studies for the most part as so much propaganda for the established order which not only posed the white paradigm as the most definitive of human life and society, but also discouraged study and development of models from the cultures of people of color. In a word, it was seen in today's language as essentially *Eurocentric*, i.e., privileging European people and culture at the expense of the culture and lives of the people of color. Also, the Black Studies advocates saw white studies as resistant to social change inquiries and models and thus, supportive of the established order. This they felt could only be countered by a self-conscious and viable discipline of Black Studies which would not only seek to study society and the world, but also to change them. Finally, Black Studies advocates argued for the need to teach Black Studies from "a Black frame of reference" (Karenga, 1969:43ff). This would later become a call for an *Afrocentric* interpretation of the African initiative and experience in the world, i.e., from a position centered within the culture and in which Africans are the subjects of their own history (Asante, 1990; 1998).

SOCIAL CONCERNS

The social concerns of Black Studies centered around the questions of exclusion, treatment on campus, academic conversions and production of a conscious, committed and capable intelligentsia and on what all this meant for the Black community. Black Studies advocates were first concerned with the low number of Blacks on campus which they saw as a racist exclusion to maintain the white monopoly on critical knowledge and to thwart the rise of a Black intelligentsia capable of effectively leading and serving Blacks. Thus, one of their first demands was special admission and recruitment efforts to correct this problem. Secondly, Black Studies advocates were concerned with treatment of Black students on campus. In fact, a key set of grievances and incidents on San Francisco State's campus centered around what was considered racist treatment of Black students in terms of news reports, counseling, instruction, representation on decision-making bodies, etc. The concern was to make Blacks respected and politically effective on campus and in campus politics in the broadest sense of the word (Hare, 1972:33).

Thirdly, Black Studies advocates were concerned about what they conceived as white academic conversion, i.e., transformation of Black students into vulgar careerists with no sense of social commitment. Equally feared was that Black students would become what Frantz Fanon called "obscene caricatures" of Europe, pathetic imitators of their oppressors (Fanon, 1968:255). Finally, Black Studies advocates were concerned with the social problems of the Black community and how Black students and Black Studies could address them.

BASIC OBJECTIVES

It is around these general concerns that Black Studies advocates across the country laid out some basic academic and social objectives which interlocked and mutually reinforced each other (Blassingame, 1973; Hare, 1969; Robinson, 1969). The first and seemingly most urgent objective was *to teach the Black experience* in its historical and current unfolding. As noted above, the category "experience" suggested all that Blacks had encountered, did and endured and sought to reflect the multidimensionality of the process. Moreover, this experience was to be greatly focused on the history and contributions of Blacks who were systematically excluded from history and whose contribution to society and humanity was denied or relegated to minor historical significance. Finally, it was advocated that the data and instruction include both the Continental African and Diasporan African experience, the Diasporan focus treating first African Americans and then all other Africans spread across the world. Although this was the projected scope, in the early years, data and instruction were essentially concentrated on Continental African and African American experience with some curricula offering a few courses on the Caribbean experience.

A second beginning objective of Black Studies was to assemble and create a body of *knowledge which was contributive to intellectual and political emancipation*. Intellectual freedom was posed as a prerequisite to political freedom. In a word, until Black people were able to break beyond the Eurocentric conception of themselves and the world, it was argued, liberation was not only impossible, but unthinkable. For there would be no way to conceive it and thus, no way to carry it out. Political emancipation as a social goal, then, was dependent on intellectual emancipation as an academic goal. These contentions were reflective of Harold Cruse's (1967) and Franklin Frazier's (1973) positions on the crisis and responsibilities of the Black intellectual.

Logically linked to the above objective was a third objective of *creating intellectuals who were dedicated to community service and development* rather than vulgar careerism. Restating W.E.B DuBois' (1961) argument against Booker T. Washington's overstress on vocation at the expense of education for social competence and contribution, Black Studies advocates stressed the need for Black intellectuals who were conscious, capable and committed to Black liberation and a higher level of human life. They argued like DuBois (1969) that the race would be elevated by its best minds, a "Talented Tenth" who would not be seduced by "the system" or established order. On the contrary, liberation would require that these skilled persons recognize their relationship and responsibility to the community and contribute meaningfully to building the community, society and world they wanted to live in. Moreover, it is in the framework of this commitment to the liberation and development of the

African community – nationally and internationally – that they understood Fanon's concept of mission also. One of the most quoted contentions from Fanon's (1963:167) classic work *Wretched of the Earth* by Black activists was his contention that "each generation must...discover its mission, fulfill it or betray it." For Fanon and the Black Studies advocates this mission was the liberation of the people and building of a new world and a new people in and for the world.

Fourthly, Black Studies advocates posed as an early objective the cultivation, maintenance and continuous expansion of a mutually beneficial relationship between the campus and the community. This relationship was best posed in Dr. Nathan Hare's statement which became a slogan and call to action of the Black Studies Movement, "We must bring the campus to the community and the community to the campus." The intent here was to serve and to raise the life-conditions and the consciousness of the community and reinforce the student's relationship with the community through ongoing interaction and service. Thus, the classic alienation between the intellectual and the community would be prevented in an ongoing mutually beneficial exchange, where knowledge is shared and applied in the service of liberation and development of the Black community. (Hare, 1972:33).

Finally, an early (and continuing) objective of Black Studies advocates was to establish and reaffirm its *position in the academy as a discipline essential to the educational project and the conception of a quality education*. This was and remains both an academic and political challenge. The political challenge is one of negotiating successfully with administrations and other departments who are hostile to Black Studies and who reductively translate its relevance and contribution to the educational mission of the academy. The academic challenge is to constantly answer the critics of Black Studies with counter arguments, critical research, solid intellectual production and effective teaching.

There are two basic arguments traditionally put forth against Black Studies. The first is that Black Studies is not a serious discipline. The second is that it is concerned with the social at the expense of the academic. These arguments, however, do not really hold weight given Black Studies' over thirty-five year history of teaching, research, intellectual production and service to students and the university. In fact, Black Studies has enriched intellectual and social discourse and expanded the concept of a quality and comprehensive education. Moreover, Black Studies has rightfully reaffirmed the importance of students cultivating a sense of care and responsibility for the community and world they live in and understanding the value of the acquisition and use of knowledge to improve the human condition and enhance the human future. It is important to note here that the national university system has begun to stress a modified form of Black Studies' historical and ongoing emphasis on linking community and campus and on student social responsibility. It is called "service learning" a project which concedes the importance of social engagement, but unlike Black Studies, does not link it to social change. This difference, of course, is rooted in the different social positions of the advocates of each approach. The university system evolved as a central source to teach and perpetuate the established order. Black Studies emerged as an intellectual and practical critique and corrective of the established order. Unlike the builders and sustainers of the established order, then, Black Studies scholars and advocates pose a concept of service not in the interest of preserving the system, but of changing it in pursuit of a just society and the expanded possibilities of a good world.

THE GROUNDS OF RELEVANCE

Through the practical and theoretical struggle of over thirty-five years to achieve and refine these early objectives, fundamental grounds of relevance of Black Studies have been established which clearly define the academic and social contributions and purpose of Black Studies. The first ground of relevance of Black Studies is that it is a definitive *contribution to humanity's understanding itself*. Black Studies is an important contribution to humanity's understanding itself because African people are the fathers and mothers of both humanity and human civilization. It is in studying African people that we get an idea of the earliest humans beginning to develop language, art, religion, family and other social forms. We also are able to witness and study the development of some of the basic disciplines of human knowledge and some of the greatest civilizations of antiquity in the Nile Valley (Morkot, 2000; Freeman, 1997; Siliotti, 1996;

Wildung, 1997). In this same framework, Black Studies is also important because it is a study of a particular people which aids in the study of humanity as a whole. In other words, to study any people is a contribution to our efforts to understand humanity as a whole. For each people offers its own unique and equally valuable way of being human in the world and thus contributes to our comprehensive understanding of humanity in all its similarity and diversity.

A second ground of relevance of Black studies is found in *its contribution to U.S. society's understanding of itself*. It is not an exaggeration to say that Black and other Ethnic Studies are the most trenchant criticism and most definitive mirror of American society. If it is true that one does not evaluate a society by its public pronouncements but by its social practice, then, the study of the Black experience in the U.S. would obviously give an incisive look at American life, from a race, class and gender perspective. U.S. society claims freedom, justice and equality for all, but Black Studies poses a more definitive view of social wealth and power in the U.S. It is thus to the credit of Black Studies and the social struggles which inform its focus, as I (Karenga, 1977:50) have argued elsewhere, that they "have provided the U.S. with an essential theoretical and practical self-criticism." Furthermore, Black Studies and struggle "have forced the U.S. into a necessary self-knowledge, unmasked its self-indulgent myths and confronted it with internal contradictions so elemental that only a broad and profound social change can resolve them."

Thirdly, and as a logical consequence of the first two contentions, Black Studies has established its relevance as a *contribution to the university's realization of its claim and challenge to teach the whole truth*, or something as close to it as humanly possible. No university can claim universality, comprehensiveness, objectivity or effectiveness in creating a context for the development of a socially competent and aware student, if it diminishes, denies or deforms the role of African peoples in history and society. Wright (1970:366) offered an observation in the early development of Black Studies that retains an essential measure of truth. It is that until the challenge of Black Studies and later other ethnic studies:

> *Higher education in the United States of America has been almost completely under the sway of an illusion*

shared by nearly everybody of European descent since the Middle Ages – the illusion that the history of the world is the history of Europe and its cultural offshoots; that Western interpretations of that experience are sufficient, if not exhaustive and that the resulting value systems embrace everything that matters.

Black Studies scholars, other ethnic studies scholars in this country and Third World scholars in other countries continue to provide an important antidote and alternative to such illusions and the provincialism they produce.

Indeed, such an academic and cultural provincialism can only discredit the university's claim of inclusiveness, objectivity and rigor for its curriculum. It also reflects an image of irreality in a world where Africans, Native Americans, Asians and Latin Americans are stepping back on the stage of human history in both dramatic and unavoidably significant ways and roles. And these initiatives must be on the educational agenda, if any serious claims are made by the university that it offers a comprehensive quality education.

Fourthly, Black Studies has demonstrated its relevance as *a contribution to the rescue and reconstruction of Black history and humanity.* As both an affirmative and negative academic and social project, Black Studies affirms the truth of Black history and humanity and negates the racist myths assembled to deny and deform them. Refusing to answer frivolous racist contentions, it rises to challenge traditional white studies which have intellectualized their biases, omissions and distortions. It realizes the link between history and humanity and is conscious of the fact that Europe denied and deformed Black history in order to deny and diminish Black humanity. Black Studies, then, begins with rigorous research and critical intellectual production in the key social science, history, which yields data and interpretations valuable to all the other fields of Black Studies and offers a more accurate picture of Africans' contribution to human initiative and human achievement in the world.

A fifth ground of relevance of Black Studies is that it is a *critical contribution to a new social science* which will not only benefit Blacks, but also the U.S. and the world. Joyce Ladner's (1973) announcement of "the death of white sociology" can only be answered with the creation of an alternative (affirmative and negative) sociology or more accurately, a new social science which sets a model for others by the standards it sets for itself. Black Studies, as a contribution to that academic project, has already developed along those lines in the light of Harold Cruse's (1967) and Franklin Frazier's (1973) criticism and the challenges posed by students, other departments and the demands of the discipline itself (Karenga, 1986; Conyers, 1997).

As a contribution to a new social science, Black Studies, which is interdisciplinary, becomes a paradigm for the multidimensional approach to social and historical reality. Secondly, it is a model of a holistic social science and an inclusive humanities, not simply focusing on Blacks, but critically including other Third World peoples and whites in appropriate socio-historical periods and places of interaction with Blacks. In a word, it denies no people its relevance, unlike the case of traditional white studies. Thirdly, as a contribution to a new social science, Black Studies is critical and corrective of the inadequacies, omissions and distortions of traditional white studies. In fact, it is its severe and uncompromising critique that so disturbs its traditional critics who cherish the historically exhausted ways of approaching human reality. As a new discipline, Black Studies is not as restricted by old data and methods as white studies. It comes without the burden and baggage of sacred assumptions about society's righteousness and imperviousness to change. Thus, it introduces practices which are corrective of social science and stimulate innovation and deeper inquiry which produce new ideas and new approaches to human reality and human relations.

Black Studies, as both an *investigative* and *applied* discipline poses the paradigm of theory and practice merging into active self-knowledge which leads to positive social change. In a word, it is a discipline dedicated not only to understanding self, society and the world but also to changing them in a positive developmental way in the interest of human history and advancement. In this quest, it challenges the false detachment of traditional white studies which contradicts reality and obscures clarity (Ladner, 1973; Hamilton, 1970).

A sixth ground of the relevance of Black Studies is *its contribution to the development of a socially conscious Black intelligentsia and professional stratum*. Here, Black Studies seeks to cultivate a body of intellectuals who are committed to using their knowledge to improve the human condition and enhance the human future. It is at this point that the academic and social missions of Black Studies merge most definitively and become an expression of knowledge self-consciously placed in the service of community, society and ultimately humankind. It is also an effective response to DuBois' (1969) call in his seminal essay, "The Talented Tenth," for the academic and social cultivation of a body of conscious, capable and committed men and women who would assume leadership of the Black community, set its ideals, direct its thoughts and aspirations and lead its social movements in the struggle for social change. It is also reflective of Mary M. Bethune's (1939:10) call for service oriented professionals and intellectuals who would "discover the dawn and to bring this material within the understanding of. . .the masses of our people." Thus, such stress reaffirms the historical, intellectual and activist thrust of Black education and reflects a vital continuity of thought and practice.

This goal of Black Studies, however, is also reflected in the educational philosophy of American universities which have historically structured curricula and instruction to produce the social servants and leaders society needs. Black Studies, then, as both an investigative and applied social science, follows a similar tradition. However, it focuses more intensely on a particular part of society, the Black community and is concerned with social change rather than maintenance of the established order. And in this focus which seeks to create persons capable of critical thought and problem-solving, Black Studies not only benefits the Black community, but society and the world as well. For in essence, the problems of the Black community are the problems of the larger society and the world, and their collective solution is clearly in the interest of society and humanity as a whole.

A seventh and final ground of relevance of Black Studies is that it is a *vital contribution to the critique, resistance and reversal of the progressive Europeanization of human consciousness and culture* which is one of the major problems of our times. The Europeanization of human consciousness and culture is used here to mean the systematic invasion and effective transformation of the cultural consciousness and practice of the various peoples of the world by Europeans. This is achieved essentially through technology, education, and the media and results in three basic things: 1) the progressive loss and replacement of the historical memories of these people; 2) the progressive disappreciation of themselves and their culture as a result of a conscious and unconscious assessment of themselves using European standards, and; 3) the progressive adoption of a Eurocentric view not only of themselves, but also of each other and the world. This in turn leads to damage and distortion of their own humanity and the increasing degeneration of the cultural diversity and exchange which gave humanity its rich variousness and internal creative challenge.

The established tendency is to use the category "westernization" to express this process of the Europeanization of human consciousness and culture. But in fact, "westernization" is a cultural category that camouflages the fundamental racial reality of European dominance. After all, when one refers to western culture, it is not to indicate Hawaiian or Inuit cultures, the most western of peoples. Nor is it meant to suggest the various other cultures of peoples of color in the western hemisphere, i.e., Native Americans, Africans, Latinos or Asians. What one encounters then is a Eurocentric cultural hegemony camouflaged under a cultural category that hides more than it reveals.

Black Studies challenges both the cultural content of what is called "western" and the definition itself, arguing for a multicultural interpretation of "western" rather than a Eurocentric one. Moreover, Black studies joins with other ethnic studies scholars in creating and posing paradigms for multicultural exchange and possibilities of a just and good society. Such exchange and possibilities, of course, necessitates respect for each people's right and responsibility not only to exist but to speak their own special cultural truth and make their own unique contribution to the forward flow of societal and human history (Karenga, 1988:406ff).

1.4   SCOPE OF THE DISCIPLINE

CORE FIELDS OF BLACK STUDIES

The scope of Black Studies is expressed in its definition and by the parameters it has set for itself as a multidisciplinary or multi-field discipline. In its thrust to study the multidimensional aspects of Black thought and practice in their current and historical unfolding, Black Studies seeks to study phenomena and processes in an inclusive and comprehensive manner or holistically. The thrust of Black Studies, then, is to view each thing in the context of the whole, to always ask historical as well as current questions about it and to study things under investigation from many sides in an attempt to achieve as comprehensive and thorough an understanding as possible.

As a discipline dedicated to a holistic study of Black life, Black Studies contains fields in social science and in humanities. It has also explored the idea of including natural and physical sciences. As James Stewart (1992:54) argues, this inclusion of physical and natural sciences in the realm of Black Studies is vital to the ongoing development of the discipline. The inclusion of these fields, he maintains, does not require the development of a "Black Chemistry" or "Black Physics." Rather, he continues, it requires (1) "the exploration of the potential insights from the new field of 'science, technology and society' into a Black/Africana Studies framework," (2) exploration of the value and use of "new information technologies. . .to accelerate development of the field" as exemplified in Hendrix' et al's (1984) discussion of Black Studies and computer use; and (3) the development by theoretical mathematicians and statisticians of "empirical techniques based on circular rather than linear models."

Stewart is correct to reject a Black science which suggests a biological or racial base. But if he extends the prohibition to include cultural emphasis, then he undermines the very meaning of Black Studies, i.e., to speak African people's special cultural truth and make their own unique contribution to the forward flow of human history. Thus, Black science like Black sociology will, of necessity, reflect a cultural context and conception. A primary task of the Black Studies scientist will be to ask is there a uniquely African as well as general human approach to science? And if so, is it of value today and again, if so, in what ways? In this regard, a beginning task of the Black Studies scientist will be to develop a philosophy of science rooted in and growing out of an African worldview. It will raise not simply questions of knowledge, but equally important ethical ones about the meaning, purpose and use of science. Moreover, a history of African science - Continental and Diasporan - placed in the context of the development of science in the world is also important (Van Sertima, 1983). The point here is that as a multi-field discipline, Black Studies borrows from and builds on invaluable achievements of other disciplines which parallel various fields in Black Studies. But Black Studies must and does bring its own critique, challenge and contribution or it is not a specific discipline only a variant discourse within other disciplines.

Black Studies, then, as a multidisciplinary discipline has seven basic subject areas. These intradisciplinary fields of focus, which at first seem to be disciplines, themselves, are, in fact, separate disciplines when they are outside the discipline of Black Studies. But inside the discipline, they become and are essentially subject areas or fields which contribute to a holistic picture and approach to the Black experience. Moreover, the qualifier Black attached to each area in an explicit or implicit way suggests a more specialized and delimited focus which, of necessity, transforms a broad discipline into a particular field. The seven basic fields of Black Studies then are: Black History; Black Religion; Black Social Organization; Black Politics; Black Economics; Black Creative Production (Black Art, Literature, Music, Dance and other Performing Arts) and Black Psychology.

This volume is structured around these seven fields, for they represent core courses in most Black Studies programs and departments and thus serve as excellent areas of focus for a survey course in Black Studies, i.e., a broad but substantive introduction to the discipline of Black Studies. Furthermore, this conceptual framework is taken from *Kawaida* philosophy, a philosophy of cultural and social change, which has as one of its main propositions the contention that the solution to the problems of Black life demand critiques and correctives in the seven basic areas of culture (Karenga, 1980, 1997). These areas of culture are: spirituality, history, social organization, economic organization, political organization, creative motif and ethos. The categories spirituality, creative motif and ethos were changed to coincide with course titles, but the definition and analysis of these subject areas in this volume are essentially the same.

It should also be noted that Kawaida philosophy "defines culture in the broadest sense to equate it with all the thought and activity of a given people or society" and focuses on the seven areas of culture as core areas of analysis and problem-solving, or in Kawaida terms, of critiques and correctives

(Karenga, 1980:16-17). The Kawaida seven-area focus and definition of culture obviously coincides with the core focus of Black Studies on the totality of Black thought and practice. The similarity would not appear as amazing and coincidental, if we remember Cruse's (1969:6-7) contention that the historical "demand for Black Studies. . .falls under the heading of the movement, tendency (and) ideology of 'Black cultural nationalism.'" "This theoretical and practical thrust of Black cultural nationalism emerged among "young Black intelligentsia, young Black students and young Black activists" and was, as Cruse states, "in response to the feeling that at (that time) there (was) no viable intellectual approach to the problems facing both Blacks and whites in American society." Black Studies was then posed as a critical alternative intellectual approach and as a vital source of the development of critiques and correctives necessary to understanding and changing the Black community and the larger society. These critiques and correctives, Kawaida advocates and other cultural nationalists argued, must be developed from frames of reference rooted in Black culture. Kawaida philosophy then played a central role in defining the Black Studies project as having an indispensable culture component in its overall mission (Karenga, 1997; Pinkney, 1976: Chapter 7).

MISSION AND GOALS OF THE DISCIPLINE

Black Studies advocates, scholars and students, were obviously diverse in both their primary interests and emphases. But out of the diverse discourse that sought to define and develop Black Studies, a broad sense of mission evolved in the midst of intense social struggle and was, of necessity, informed and shaped by this struggle. As both activists in the community and professors and students on campus, Black Studies advocates sought to create a project which would link these two areas of concern and struggle in mutually beneficial ways. To achieve this, the founders of the discipline sought to extend the struggle for social freedom and justice in society to include a struggle for academic freedom and justice in the university. They moved also to bring forth and teach the best of African culture and social practice and pose it as a model of human excellence and human achievement. And finally, they linked knowledge and power, education and the obligation to serve, and student learning with student activism directed toward achieving the good in and for the community, society and the world. Thus, they developed a mission for Black Studies with three basic areas of focus: *cultural grounding, academic excellence and social responsibility.*

CULTURAL GROUNDING

Although the mission has been traditionally posed simply in terms of academic excellence and social responsibility, *cultural grounding* is implicit in the mission and indispensable to it (see Chapter 10 below). For Black Studies as an intellectual and social practice is, of necessity, rooted in African culture – Continental and Diasporan. Indeed, culture is the foundation and framework for Black Studies intellectual and social practice. African culture represents African peoples' unique way of being human in the world and Black Studies seeks to critically explore and teach this paradigm in its varied expressions. Moreover, in putting forth the seven areas of culture as the core areas of the discipline, the discipline's basis in culture is apparent and to talk of an Africa-centered frame of reference is to talk of a frame of reference rooted in African culture. Finally, Black Studies evolves with the central understanding that Black life and culture are worthy of the most careful and detailed study for its models of human excellence, achievement and possibility and that African people have both the right and responsibility to speak their own special cultural truth in the academies of the country and indeed, the world.

ACADEMIC EXCELLENCE

The emphasis on *academic excellence* was/is to reaffirm commitment to the highest level of teaching and intellectual production as Black Studies scholars and a similarly advanced intellectual grounding for students. Especially stressed here is not simply the amassing of data, but below-the-surface thinking and the development of an interpretive capacity to understand and translate the African initiative and experience in the world in varied, depthful and *dignity-affirming* ways.

SOCIAL RESPONSIBILITY

Finally, the emphasis on *social responsibility* is to reaffirm the discipline's commitment to using knowledge to improve the human condition and enhance the human prospect. From its inception, Black Studies understood itself as not only a source of intellectual production and exchange, but also an agency of social change. As noted above, it linked intellectual emancipation with political emancipation and committed itself to both in a single interrelated project. This is logically linked to Black Studies' commitment to critique and corrective which assigns a social activist emancipatory role to both education and the educated.

GOALS

Within the context of these three fundamental foci and commitments of its mission, the Africana Studies project is informed by five overarching goals: (1) the critical and persistent search for truth and meaning in human history and social reality from an African vantage point; (2) a depthful intellectual grasp and appreciation of the ancient, rich, varied and instructive character of the African initiative and experience in the world and of the essential relevance of African culture as a unique and valuable way of being human in the world; (3) a rigorous intellectual challenge and alternative to established-order ways of viewing social and human reality; (4) a moral critique and social policy correctives for social constraints on human freedom and development, especially those rooted in race, class and gender considerations; and (5) cultivation of commitment and contribution to the historical project of creating the truly multicultural, democratic and just society and good world based on mutual respect of the rights and needs of persons and peoples, mutual cooperation for mutual benefit and shared responsibility for building the good world all humans want and deserve to live in as the Odu Ifa (78:1) teaches (Karenga, 1999:228ff).

STUDY QUESTIONS

1. Define Black Studies?
2. How is it critical and systematic?
3. Define Diaspora.
4. Define pan-African. How is Black Studies pan-African?
5. Discuss the activist-intellectual tradition and Black Studies' relationship to it.
6. Discuss the four basic thrusts of the student movement which lead to Black Studies.
7. Discuss the emergence of Black Studies at SFSU. Identify the major groups involved and the contribution of Dr. Nathan Hare.
8. What were the early academic and political concerns of the advocates of Black Studies?
9. What were the early objectives of Black Studies?
10. What are the seven major contributions of Black Studies which establish its academic and socal relevance?
11. What are the seven core fields of Black Studies?
12. Discuss the three basic aspects of the Black Studies mission.
13. Discuss the five overarching goals of the discipline.

REFERENCES

Allen, Robert. (1974) "Politics of the Attack on Black Studies," *The Black Scholar*, 6, 1 (September) 1-7.

Asante, Molefi. (1998) *The Afrocentric Idea*, Philadelphia: Temple University Press.

Asante, Molefi. (1997) "Afrocentricity and the Quest for Method," in James L. Conyers, Jr., (ed.) *Africana Studies: A Disciplinary Quest for Both Theory and Method*, Jefferson, NC: McFarland and Company, Inc.

Asante, Molefi. (1990) *Kemet, Afrocentricity and Knowledge*, Trenton, NJ: Africa World Press.

Bailey, Ronald. (1970) "Why Black Studies?" *The Education Digest*, 35, 9 (May) 46-48.

Bethune, Mary McLeod. (1939) "The Adaptation of the History of the Negro to the Capacity of the Child," *Journal of Negro History*, 24, 9-13.

Blassingame, John. (1973) *New Perspectives on Black Studies*, Chicago: University of Illinois Press.

Branch, Taylor. (1988) *Parting the Waters: America in the King Years, 1954-1963*, New York: Simon & Schuster.

Brisbane, Robert. (1974) *Black Activism*, Valley Forge, PA: Judson Press.

Carmichael, Stokely (Kwame Ture) and Charles V. Hamilton. (1992) *Black Power: The Politics of Liberation in America*, New York: Vintage Books.

Carson, Claybourne. (1981) *In Struggle: SNCC and the Black Awakening of the 60's*, Cambridge: Harvard University Press.

Conyers, James L. (ed.) (1997) *Africana Studies: A Disciplinary Quest for Both Theory and Method*, Jefferson, NC: McFarland and Company, Inc.

Cortada, Rafael. (1974) *Black Studies in Urban and Comparative Curriculum*, Lexington, MA: Xerox College Publishing.

Crouchett, Lawrence. (1971) "Early Black Studies Movements," *Journal of Black Studies*, 2, 2 (December) 189-200.

Cruse, Harold. (1967) *Crisis of the Negro Intellectual*, New York: William Morrow Publishers.

Cruse, Harold. (1969) *Rebellion or Revolution?*, New York: William Morrow Publishers.

Draper, Hal. (1965) *Berkeley: The New Student Revolt*, New York: Grove Press.

DuBois, W.E.B. (1961) *The Souls of Black Folk*, New York: Fawcett Publications, Inc.

DuBois, W.E.B. (1969) "The Talented Tenth" in Ulysses Lee, (ed.), *The Negro Problem*, New York: Arno Press and the New York Times.

Edwards, Harry. (1970) *Black Students*, New York: Free Press.

Fanon, Frantz. (1963) *The Wretched of the Earth*, New York: Grove Press.

Forman, James. (1972) *The Making of Black Revolutionaries*, New York: Macmillan.

Ford, Nick Aaron. (1973) *Black Studies: Threat or Challenge*, New York: Kennikat Press.

Franklin, John Hope and Alfred A. Moss, Jr. (1999) *From Slavery to Freedom: a History of African Americans*, Boston: McGraw-Hill.

Frazier, E. Franklin. (1973) "The Failure of the Negro Intellectual," in *The Death of White Sociology*, Joyce A. Ladner, (ed.), New York: Vintage Books, pp. 52-66.

Freeman, Charles. (1997) *The Legacy of Ancient Egypt*, New York: Facts on File, Inc.

Frye, Charles A. (1978) *Towards a Philosophy of Black Studies*, San Francisco: R & E Research Associates.

Grant, Joanne (ed.) *Black Protest: History, Documents and Analyses, 1619 to the Present*, New York: St. Martin's Press.

Hamilton, Charles. (1970) "The Question of Black Studies," *Phi Delta Kappan*, 57, 7 (March) 362-364.

Hare, Nathan. (1972) "The Battle of Black Studies," *The Black Scholar*, 3, 9 (May) 32-37.

Hare, Nathan. (1973) "It's Time to Turn the Guns the Other Way," in Clyde Taylor, (ed.) *Vietnam and Black America: an Anthology of Protest and Resistance*, Garden City, NY: Anchor/Double Day.

Hare, Nathan. (1969) "What Should be the Role of Afro-American Education in the Undergraduate Curriculum?" *Liberal Education*, 55, 1 (March) 42-50.

Hendrix, Melvin K. et al. (1984) "Computers and Black Studies: Toward the Cognitive Revolution," *Journal of Negro Education*, 53, 3 (Summer) 341-350.

Hine, Darlene Clark and Jacqueline McLeod, (eds.) (2001) *Crossing Boundaries: Comparative History of Black People in Diaspora*, Bloomington: Indiana University Press.

Karenga, Maulana. (1968) "The Black Community and the University: A Community Organizer's Perspective," in Armstead L. Robinson, Craig C. Foster and Donald H. Ogilvie, (eds.), *Black Studies in the University*, New Haven, CT: Yale University Press.

Karenga, Maulana. (1988) "Black Studies and the Problematic of Paradigm: The Philosophical Dimension," *Journal of Black Studies*, 18, 4 (June) 395-414.

Karenga, Maulana. (1977) "Corrective History: Reconstructing the Black Past," *First World*, 1, 3 (May/June) 50-54.

Karenga, Maulana. (1997) *Kawaida. A Communitarian African Philosophy*, Los Angeles: University of Sankore Press.

Karenga, Maulana. (1980) *Kawaida Theory: An Introductory Outline*, Inglewood, CA: Kawaida Publications.

Karenga, Maulana. (1997) "Kwame Ture in the Scales of History: A Legacy of Lessons," *Black Scholar*, 27, 3/4 (Fall/Winter) 46-50.

Karenga, Maulana. (1994) *Maat, The Moral Ideal in Ancient Egypt: A Study in Classical African Ethics*, unpublished dissertation, University of Southern California.

Karenga, Maulana. (1999) *Odu Ifa: The Ethical Teachings*, Los Angeles: University of Sankore Press.

Ladner, Joyce A. (ed.) (1973) *The Death of White Sociology*, New York: Vintage Books.

Lipset, Seymour and S. Wolin (eds.) (1965) *The Berkeley Student Revolt*, New York: Doubleday Anchor.

Magubane, Bernard M.. (1987) *The Ties That Bind: African-American Consciousness of Africa*, Trenton, NJ: Africa World Press.

Martin, Tony. (1998) *The Pan-African Connection: From Slavery to Garvey and Beyond*, Dover, MA: Majority Press.

McEvoy, James and Abraham Miller. (1969) *Black Power and Student Rebellion*, Belmont, CA: Wadsworth Publishing Co.

Morkot, Robert. (2000) *The Black Pharaohs: Egypt's Nubian Rulers*, London: Rubicon Press.

Morris, Aldon D. (1984) *The Origins of the Civil Rights Movement: Black Communities Organizing for Change*, New York: The Free Press.

Orrick, William H. (1969) *Shut It Down! A College in Crisis: San Francisco State College, October 1968-April 1969*, Washington, D.C.: U.S. Government Printing Office.

Pinkney, Alphonso. (1976) *Red, Black and Green: Black Nationalism in the United States*, Cambridge: Cambridge University Press.

Robinson, Armstead, Craig C. Foster and Donald H. Ogilvie, (eds.). (1969) *Black Studies in the University*, New Haven, CT: Yale University Press.

Siliotti, Albert. (1996) *Egypt, Splendors of an Ancient Civilization*, New York: Thames & Hudson.

Stewart, James B. (1979) "Introducing Black Studies: A Critical Examination of Some Textual Materials," *Umoja*, 3, 1, (Spring) 5-17.

Stewart, James B. (1984) "The Legacy of W.E.B. DuBois for Contemporary Black Studies," *Journal of Negro History* 53, 3 (Summer) 296-311.

Stewart, James B. (1992) "Reaching for Higher Ground: Toward an Understanding of Black/Africana Studies," *The Afrocentric Scholar* 1, 1 (May) 1-63.

Student Non-Violent Coordinating Committee. (1968) "Statement on Vietnam, January 6, 1966," in Joanne Grant, (ed.) *Black Protest: History, Documents and Analyses, 1619 to the Present*, New York: St. Martin's Press.

Taylor, Clyde (ed.) (1973) *Vietnam and Black America: An Anthology of Protest and Resistance*, Garden City, NY: Anchor/Double Day.

Terry, Wallace II. (1970) "Bringing the War Home," *The Black Scholar*, 2, 3 (November) 6-18.

T'Shaka, Oba. (1982) "The San Francisco State Strike, A Study of the First Black Student Strike in the U.S.," *Journal of Black Studies*, 1, 1 (Summer) 15-23.

Turner, James. (1984) *The Next Decade: Theoretical and Research Issues in Africana Studies*, Ithaca, NY: Africana studies and Research Center, Cornell University.

Turner, Jams and C. Steven McGann. (1980) "Black Studies as an Integral Tradition in African American Intellectual History," *Journal of Negro Education*, 49, 1 (Winter) 52-59.

Turner, James and C. Steven McGann. (1980) "Black Studies as an Integral Tradition in African American Intellectual History," *Journal of Negro Education*, 49, 1 (Winter) 52-59.

Turner, James and Eric W. Perkins. (1976) "Towards a Critique of Social Science," *The Black Scholar*, 7, 1 (April) 2-11.

Van Deburg, William L. (1993) *New Day in Babylon: The Black Power Movement and African American Culture, 1965-1975*, Chicago: University of Chicago Press.

Van Sertima, Ivan, (ed.). (1983) *Blacks in Science: Ancient and Modern*, New Brunswick: Transaction Books.

Wildung, Dietrich. (1997) *Sudan: Ancient Kingdom of the Nile*, Paris: Flammarion.

Williams, Juan. (1987) *Eyes on the Prize*, New York: Viking Penguin.

Woodard, Komozi. (1999) *A Nation Within A Nation: Amiri Baraka (LeRoi Jones) & Black Power Politics*, Chapel Hill: University of North Carolina Press.

Woodyard, Jeffrey L. (1991) "Evolution of a Discipline: Intellectual Antecedents of African American Studies," *Journal of Black Studies*, 22, 2 (December) 239-251.

Wright, Stephen. (1970) "Black Studies and Sound Scholarship," *Phi Delta Kappan* (March) 356-368.

Young, Carlene, (ed.). (1984) *An Assessment of Black Studies Programs in American Higher Education, Journal of Negro Education*, 53, 3 (Summer).

DEVELOPMENTAL
INITIATIVES

DEVELOPMENTAL INITIATIVES

CHAPTER 2

2.1. INTRODUCTION

If the 60's marked the definitive founding of the discipline of Black Studies, the 70's, 80's and 90's represent a multidimensional thrust toward consolidation and expansion (Young, 1984; Turner, 1984; Aldridge, 1988; Harris, 1990; Anderson, 1990; Harris, Hine and McKay, 1990; Conyers, 1997; Hall, 1999). In this multifaceted process several new developments have occurred which have defined both the course and character of the discipline. Among these are the emergence of and focus on: 1) professional organizations of the discipline; 2) the Afrocentric initiative; 3) Black Women's Studies; 4) Multicultural Studies; and 5) Classical African Studies.

2.2 PROFESSIONAL ORGANIZATIONS OF THE DISCIPLINE

AFRICAN HERITAGE STUDIES ASSOCIATION (AHSA)

The founding of the African Heritage Studies Association evolved in the context of the general thrust toward self-determination of the Freedom Movement in the 60's and the parallel efforts of Black Studies scholars within the Africana Studies movement to do likewise in the academy. The AHSA emerged from a year of discussions within the Black Caucus of the African Studies Association (ASA), the major professional organization of African Studies at that time, and simultaneous negotiations with the leadership of this organization. During the 11th Annual Convention of ASA held in Los Angeles in 1968,

Black members met to discuss grievances against ASA and to list demands for it to change its Eurocentric treatment of both the subject matter of Africa and of them (Rowe, 1970:4). Moreover, they decided to form "a new organization to cater to Black scholars and to correct the teaching of Euro-Africa rather than Africa in U.S. colleges and universities."

In addition to the decision to form a new organization "to serve Black scholars and Black communities," several other decisions were made. Among them was the decision that the new organization act as a clearing house and liaison among Black scholars all around the world, "exchanging information, and establishing networks to correct the present monopoly of information about Black cultures and histories in white hands." Thirdly, it was decided that members of the new organization would "link with Africanists in Africa through embassies." Fourthly, the new organization was to "encourage active participation of its members in all Black conferences at home or abroad." And finally, a decision was made to meet in December of that year in New York to consolidate agreements reached in Los Angeles.

After a follow-up meeting in December 1968, AHSA held its first convention in June 1969 at Federal City College in Washington, D.C. However, AHSA still maintained its links with ASA, defining its relationship with ASA as one "of a symbiotic nature." Thus, at ASA's conference in Montreal, October 1969, its Black Caucus inside petitioned ASA for equal representation in all decision-making committees, an equitable number of ASA fellowships, adequate representation at all national and international conferences relating to African or Black Studies, and encouragement of the involvement of Black scholars in various roles according to their expertise and interests. ASA, however, rejected these requests. John Henrik Clarke (1976:8), the founding president of AHSA, read the rejection as resistance of the white majority to giving Blacks "the means of changing the ideological and structural bases of the African Studies Association." According to AHSA members, ASA had become accustomed to its monopoly on the interpretation of African history and culture, resisted the stress on the pan-Africanist perspective and was threatened by the intellectual and practical challenge posed by African Americans claiming a special relationship with Africa and independent grounding in African Studies.

The Montreal conference was for Black Caucus members of the ASA a decisive point of rupture. They left the conference convinced that the leadership of ASA did not wish collaboration but monopoly and that only a totally independent African organization could do the practical and intellectual work necessary to serve the interests of Black scholars and Black people. Thus, they formed AHSA as an indispensable "association of scholars of African descent...committed to the preservation, interpretation and creative presentation of the historical and cultural heritage of African people, both on the ancestral soil of Africa and in the Diaspora in the Americas and throughout the world" (Clarke, 1976:11).

Within this context, according to Clarke (1976:3ff), the Pan-Africanist scholars and activists set themselves several fundamental goals. Among these were: 1) "to examine every aspect and approach to the history and culture of African people in this country and throughout the world;" 2) "to project (AHSA) influence into every organization that relates to Africans and the people of African descent;" 3) to challenge and question all who claim authority on African life and history; 4) "to use African history to effect a world union of African people;" 5) to establish "a new frame of reference in all matters relating to Africa," i.e., a critical pan-Africanist perspective which stresses especially the inter-relatedness of African peoples and the linkage of the intellectual with the practical; and finally, 6) to define African heritage and "to put components of (this) heritage together to weld an instrument of liberation."

Since its formation, AHSA has essentially served several functions. First, and foremost, it has served as a ground and context for scholarly encounter and exchange. Its annual conferences bring scholars from all over the world African community in fruitful exchanges and creative challenge. Secondly, AHSA has served through its individual members, an organizational role for other professional organizations. In her inaugural presidential address in 1989 titled "Agenda for AHSA: 21st Century," Charshee McIntyre (1989:3) listed several organizations in which AHSA members played a founding role, i.e., TransAfrica, a lobby for African interests, the National Council for Black Studies, the National Association of Black Educators, the Association for the Study of Classical African Civilizations

Dr. Charshee McIntyre

and the National Congress of Black Faculty. Thirdly, AHSA has been an advocacy organization for Black interests in education in general as well as on larger social issues organizing forums, engaging in demonstrations and participating in governmental and institutional policy discussions. It has been also a major participant in the overall thrust to link African peoples intellectually and practically in ongoing projects.

Finally, McIntyre (1989:5ff) has noted several other ongoing projects to which AHSA is committed. These include: 1) focus on transnational and international African world interests and cooperative relations among scholars throughout the African world as outlined in Locksley Edmondson's 1985 memo "Redefining the Role of AHSA;" 2) strengthening and expanding the AHSA student commission to mentor and support young scholars; 3) a publishing project to aid Africana Studies scholars in publishing their work and produce regular organization literature; 4) sustaining and expanding the AHSA newsletter; and 5) building a Pan-African research institute dedicated to the pursuit of truth and the reaffirmation of African heritage.

NATIONAL COUNCIL FOR BLACK STUDIES (NCBS)

The National Council for Black Studies (NCBS) was founded in 1976 and has since become the preeminent discipline organization. The process which led to its founding was initiated in 1975 by Bertha Maxwell, who was then the chair of the Department of Afro-American Studies at the University of North Carolina at Charlotte. Calling on Black scholars around the country to engage in dialog on critical issues of Black Studies, she created the interest and opportunity for the building of NCBS and played a central role in its formation and development. In 1976 at the founding conference, women and men of the discipline developed programs and strategies for organizational and discipline development and Maxwell became NCBS' founding chairperson. She was followed by chairpersons William King, William "Nick" Nelson, Carlene Young, Delores Aldridge, Selasé W. Williams, Charles Henry, William Little and James Stewart. It is important to note here that since its inception

NCBS has not only had a balance of
female and male officers, but also of
the key players in its founding and
development. This has helped produce, as argued below, a positive and
productive male/female dialog and
exchange and has thus expanded and
enriched the organization and the
discipline.

Dr. Bertha Maxwell Roddy

In a paper titled "A Synoptic
History of NCBS and Its Future
Direction" and presented at the
NCBS Summer Faculty Institute in June 1991 at Ohio State
University, then president Selasé Williams outlined the role of
the organization in defining, defending and developing Black
Studies. He (1991:1) noted the unique role of NCBS as a professional organization for a discipline which "always insisted on
the inclusion of both the intellectual and political dimensions of
the Black Experience in its curriculum, its research and other
professional responsibilities." Thus, he (1991:2) calls attention
to Article II of the NCBS Constitution which shows its commitment to both academic excellence and social responsibility,
building on and drawing from not only educators but also students, interested citizens and other professionals. "The purpose
of this Council," the Article reads, "is to promote and strength-
en academic and community programs in the area of Black
Studies. The Council believes that Black Studies academic programs should include any subject area that has the Black experience as the principle object and content of study."

Under successive administrations, NCBS emerged as the
preeminent professional organization of the discipline. Having
established its national office at Indiana University,
Bloomington under the auspices of Herman Hudson, Dean of
Afro-American Studies, it proceeded to produce its organizational voice, *Voices in Black Studies* and to expand its regional
structures. Moreover, it began in the early 80's to produce a
series of documents which defined its goals and informed its
practice. Among these are: *The Black Studies Core Curriculum*,
(The Hall Report) 1981; *The Black Studies 4-Year College and
University Survey* (The Daniel and Zike Report) 1983; and *The
Short-Range and Long-Range Goals Report* (The Williams Report)

1984. In addition, NCBS chairpersons Carlene Young and Delores Aldridge produced special Black Studies issues of journals on the state, future and direction of the discipline. Young (1984) edited a special issue of the *Journal of Negro Education* and Aldridge (1988) edited a special issue of *Phylon*, both of which contributed to the ongoing dialog on the scope ad direction of Black Studies.

Important also to NCBS' development has been its establishment of an accreditation process for Black Studies programs, its creation of specialty caucuses, its workshops on multicultural education and Black women issues, its joint activities with AHSA, the Congressional Black Caucus and other academic, professional and community organizations; and its establishment of its discipline journal, *International Journal of Africana Studies*, which was formerly titled *The Afrocentric Scholar*. Also, among its most significant programs has been the foundation sponsored projects such as the Summer Faculty Institute, the Administrative Training Workshop and curriculum development and data collection. Especially central is the Summer Faculty Institute which introduces new Black Studies faculty to the history, philosophy and varied discourses of the discipline, and provides them with a context of creative challenge and exchange with peers as well as major scholars in the discipline.

Finally, Williams (1991:4) lists as the future direction and goals of NCBS: 1) continued production of discipline literature and organizational documents; 2) ongoing and expanded grant and research proposals for development of projects for the discipline, faculty, students and community; 3) continuing organizational professionalization and reorganization for improved performance and service; and 4) increasing and enriching contexts for discourse and exchange, i.e., conferences, symposia, workshops, etc. In addition to these goals, certainly the pursuit of curriculum development to meet new challenges and expand the discipline to include new discourse and issues, i.e., Black women studies, classical African studies, multicultural studies and international studies, also stand at the core of the NCBS mission (Aldridge, 1992).

2.3   THE AFROCENTRIC INITIATIVE

Dr. Molefi Asante

Clearly one of the most important developments in Black Studies is the Afrocentric initiative, marked by the emergence of Afrocentricity as a major conceptual framework within the discipline. As an intellectual category, *Afrocentricity* is relatively new, emerging in the late 70's and finding its most definitive treatment then in a work by Molefi Asante titled *Afrocentricity: The Theory of Social Change* and published in 1980. With this initial work Asante (1980:66) introduced Afrocentricity as the indispensable perspective of the Black Studies project and initiated a wide-ranging discourse which had both academic and social implications and consequences.

One could argue that the Afrocentric emphasis in Black studies is not new and that it reaches back to much earlier periods in Black intellectual history (Morgan, 1991). For example works on education by W.E.B. DuBois (1975), Anna Julia Cooper (1892) and especially, Carter G. Woodson's (1969) *Miseducation of the Negro* could certainly be called in part or whole Afrocentric works. But it is Asante (1980, 1998, 1990) who provided the category Afrocentricity and an accompanying literature which contributed definitively to establishing the concept as a central element in Black Studies discourse and practice. And it is Asante who energized Black Studies discourse and contributed definitively to the pursuit of new research direction in Black Studies with his insistence on African location or centeredness, African agency, and an African frame of reference in research methodology and intellectual production. Also, his role as the founder of the first Ph.D. program in Black Studies at Temple University gave him a context in which he was able not only to create this new critical discourse, but also to train numerous Ph.D. students from around the world whose contributions helped shape and expand Black Studies discourse and development on an international level.

As the Afrocentric initiative spread beyond the campus to

the African American community, the larger society and the international context, Asante became a much sought after lecturer and commentator, lecturing and appearing regularly in the media to answer questions concerning the meaning and implications of the Afrocentric initiative in the academic and social context. Also other scholars participated fully in this initiative and Afrocentricity began to emerge as both an academic and popular approach to African social and human issues. This latter occurrence caused concern among some Afrocentric scholars that the popular version of Afrocentricity not become the defining understanding of the concept. For in its popular version, Afrocentrism, Afrocentricity included a wide-range of problematic assertions and approaches.

In an important article on the direction of Black Studies and the role of the Afrocentric initiative in it, Stewart (1992:3) pointed out, " a popular Afrocentrism" has emerged which "is being confused increasingly with systematic intellectual approaches in the field." He adds that "this confusion has contributed to a distorted view of the state of the field and is fueling uneasiness in some circles about the intellectual credibility of Black/Africana Studies." Here one can draw a distinction between Afrocentricity and Afrocentrism (Karenga, 1995:44). Afrocentrism appears more often in ideological discourse between Afrocentric advocates and critics especially in popular pieces on the subject. What Stewart is calling attention to is the popular appropriation of the category by some of its advocates, critics and the media who use it for purposes which tend to define it as an ideological posture rather than an intellectual category. Its transformation from Afrocentricity to Afrocentrism is indicative of this. For the use of "ism" tends to suggest that it is seen as more of a political posture than a methodology or orientation in intellectual work.

Afrocentricity is, thus, used in this work rather than Afrocentrism for several reasons (Karenga, 1995:44ff). First, it is to stress its intellectual value as distinct from its ideological use. For in the final analysis, it must prove its value as an intellectual category regardless of the ideological use advocates and critics make of it. Second, Afrocentricity is preferable to Afrocentcism to clearly distinguish it from Eurocentricism. Eurocentrism is defined here as an *ideology and practice of domination and exclusion based on the fundamental assumption that all relevance and value are centered in European culture and peoples and that all other cultures and peoples are at best marginal and at worse irrelevant.* Afrocentricity is not built on or conceived as a denial of worth and values to others. On the contrary, it conceptually includes both a particular (African) and universal (human) dimension as indicated below.

Thirdly, Afrocentricity is preferred to establish it as a quality of thought and practice rather than thought and practice themselves. In a word, it is used to focus on the cultural and human quality of African thought and practice rather than on thought and practice as an ideological conception and conduct. Rejecting the "ism" becomes a way to avoid being labeled as simply another ideological posture. In a similar view, the category *African-centeredness* is also used to escape ideological associations (Keto, 1994).

Having made such distinctions, one is still compelled to concede that there is a rich diversity of approaches to the definition and application of Afrocentricity. Nevertheless, Molefi Asante (1998:2) has given us the essential elements of the definition. He states that "Afrocentricity...means literally, placing African ideals at the center of any analysis that involves African culture and behavior." Clearly the concept of "centeredness" is key to Asante's definition. And by centeredness he (1990:12) means "the groundedness of observation and behavior in one's own historical experiences." Secondly, Asante (1998:44ff) argues that Afrocentricity is a theoretical framework or methodology which stresses African agency. That is to say, it treats Africans as active subjects of history rather than objects or passive victims.

Accepting these insights as a reaffirmation of the Kawaida insistence since its inception on a "Black frame of reference" in Black Studies and social practice (Karenga, 1969:43ff; Asante, 1980:23ff), Afrocentricity is defined here in a similar way. From a Kawaida perspective, *Afrocentricity* is a methodology, orientation or quality of thought and practice rooted in the cultural image and human interest of African people (Karenga, 1988:403; 1995:45). To be rooted in the cultural image of African people is to be anchored in the views and values of African people as well as in the practice which emanates from and gives rise to these views and values. To be rooted in the human interests of African people is to embrace principles and practices which represent the best of what it means to be

African and human in the fullest sense. These include profound concerns for human dignity and freedom, human and environmental justice, truth and the ongoing quest for knowledge in the interest of the Good. Here, one notes that Afrocentricity, as an intellectual concept, contains both a *particular* and *universal* dimension. It self-consciously contributes a valuable particular cultural insight and discourse to the multicultural project and in the process, finds common ground with other cultures which can be cultivated and developed for mutual benefit.

The Afrocentric vision, critically defined and developed, then, demands that Black Studies root itself in African culture and in the worldview which evolves from and informs that culture. However, having rooted itself in African culture, which is the source and substance of its intellectual and social project, Black Studies as a mode of grasping reality, expands outward, to the acquisition of other relevant human knowledge and the knowledge of other humans as DuBois (1975:98) urges. For even as there are lessons for humanity in *African particularity*, there are lessons for Africans in *human commonality*. And African humanity is enriched and expanded by mutually beneficial exchanges with others. Moreover, in understanding human history as a whole, Africans can even more critically appreciate their fundamental role in the origins of humanity and human civilization and in the forward flow of human history.

Afrocentricity as an intellectual conception, then, evolves out of and is based on several fundamental assumptions. First, it is based on the assumption that African culture is not only worthy of study, but critical to understanding society and the human experience, given its key role in each (see the chapter on Black history below). Secondly, Afrocentricity or African-centeredness as a methodological orientation, contends that the most effective and fruitful way of studying and understanding African people is from their own perspective (Karenga, 1988:403-404). Thirdly, Afrocentric theory argues that Black Studies is not simply a body of data but also a way of approaching and interpreting data, i.e., from an African-centered perspective (Asante, 1990:7). Thus, Afrocentricity becomes an indispensable aspect of the Black Studies project and an important measure of the accuracy and value of a given work. And finally, Afrocentric theory is based on the assumption that if an African-centered approach is incorrect or of little value, then so is the discipline of Black Studies which is based on an equally important assumption that the African experience is both a valid and valuable subject of study.

Of course, Afrocentricity has its critics inside and outside the discipline. Often critiques outside the discipline appear more ideological than intellectual (Lefkowitz, 1996; Schlesinger, 1991; Ravitch, 1990) and they have been noted and answered (Asante, 1999, 1991). Internal criticism, however, raises issues that have created an ongoing discourse which is valuable to the discipline's need to constantly question and refine its thought and practice (Hall, 1992; Oyebade, 1990). Among the essential challenges posed by critics and the discipline's own commitment to ongoing self-criticism and self-correction are the challenges to avoid the tendency: 1) to project Afrocentricity as a dogma of authenticity rather than an orientation and methodology; 2) to deny the reality and value of the diversity of perspectives and approaches within the discipline of Black Studies; 3) to promote a static, monolithic and unreal concept of African culture which denies or diminishes its dynamic and diverse character; 4) to over focus on the Continental African past at the expense of recognizing the African American past and present as central to and constitutive of African culture and the Afrocentric enterprise; and 5) overfocus on the academic at the expense of the social dimension of the Black Studies project which requires not only cultural recovery and critiques of domination, but also correctives directed toward improving the human condition and enhancing the human prospect. In this way, Afrocentricity not only contributes to the intellectual enrichment of the Black Studies project, but also to the realization of its mission of expanding the possibilities of knowledge in the service of the free and empowered community, the just society and the good world.

2.4 BLACK WOMEN'S STUDIES

Another major development in Black Studies is the emergence of Black women's studies as a fundamental, even indispensable, part of Black Studies. The lack of adequate scholarly treatment of Black women in Black Studies and in the academy as a whole posed both a serious problematic and challenge for Black Studies since its inception. But as Delores Aldridge (1992:171) notes, "Within the last several years, there has been increasing advocacy for recognition and correction of this failure to deal equitably with Africana women in scholarship and the academy." This development was not automatic nor easily achieved and is still marked by both continuing inattentiveness and outright resistance as well as support and achievement. Several factors have shaped and contributed to the emergence of Black women studies in the discipline of Black Studies.

The first and foremost of these factors is the intellectual and practical struggles waged by Black women in the discipline itself. These efforts have been directed towards creating and sustaining space for teaching and research in Black women studies in particular and gender studies in general. Challenging male-centered interpretations of African and human reality and the relationships which such interpretations cultivated and sustained, Black women scholars produced and insisted on alternative visions. Among some of the early works in the 70's which raised important Black women studies issues are Toni Cade's *The Black Woman* (1970), Joyce Ladner's *Tomorrow's Tomorrow* (1971), Inez Smith-Reid's *"Together" Black Women* (1972), Mary Helen Washington's *Black-Eyed Susans* (1975), Sharon Hurley's and Rosalyn Terborg-Penn's *The Afro-American Woman: Struggles and Images* (1978), and Roseann P. Bell's, Bettye J. Parker's and Beverly Guy-Sheftall's *Sturdy Black Bridges: Visions of Black Women in Literature* (1979). These works raised critical issues of race, gender and class and called for correctives.

In the 80's and 90's early Black women studies literature was built on and expanded in various fields, especially in literature. Among the most notable are LaFrancis Rodgers-Rose's *The Black Woman* (1980); Barbara Christian's *Black Feminist Criticism: Perspectives on Black Women Writers* (1980); Angela Davis' *Women, Race and Class* (1981); Gloria Hull's, Patricia Bell Scott's and Barbara Smith's *All the Women are White, All Blacks are Men, But Some of Us are Brave* (1982); Paula Giddings' *When and Where I Enter: The Impact of Black Women on Race and Sex in America* (1984); Gloria Wade-Gayle's *No Crystal Stair: Visions of Race and Sex in Woman's Fiction* (1984); Margaret Simms' and Julianne Malveaux's *Slipping Through the Cracks: The Status of the Black Woman* (1986); Vivian Gordon's *Black Women, Feminism and Black Liberation* (1987); Hazel Carby's *Reconstructing*

Dr. Vivian Gordon

Womanhood: The Emergence of the Afro-American Woman Novelist (1987); Delores Aldridge's *Black Male-Female Relationships* (1989); bell hooks' many books including *Talking Back: Thinking Feminist, Thinking Black* (1989), *Yearning: race, gender and cultural politics* (1990), *Black Looks: race and representation* (1992); Darlene Clark Hine's multi-volume *Black Women in American History* (1990); Beverly Guy-Sheftall's *Daughters of Sorrow, Attitudes toward Black Women 1880-1920* (1990); Patricia Hill Collins' *Black Feminist Thought* (1991); Clenora Hudson-Weems' *Africana Womanism: Reclaiming Ourselves* (1993); Niara Sudarkasa's *The Strength of Our Mothers: African and African American Women and Families* (1996); Rosalyn Terborg-Penn's and Andrea Benton Rushing's *Women in Africa and the African Diaspora* (1996); and Shirley Logan's *"We Are Coming" The Persuasive Discourse of Nineteenth-Century Black Women* (1999).

A second factor shaping Black women's struggle for space, recognition and egalitarian relationships was the key role Black women played in building and developing the two major professional organizations of the discipline, the African Heritage Studies Association (AHSA) and the National Council for Black Studies (NCBS). In 1968 at the founding of AHSA, women were in the vanguard of the move for self-determination and self-definition in the discipline. They collaborated in both the intellectual and practical construction of the organization and have played a fundamental role in its maintenance, development and leadership. Some of the important pioneers in this process are: Shelby Lewis, Barbara Wheeler, Barbara Sizemore, Charshee McIntyre, Nancy Cortez, and Inez Smith-Reid.

Likewise, it was Bertha Maxwell whose conceptual and organizational initiative led to the founding of NCBS. Calling on Black scholars around the country in 1975 to come to the University of North Carolina to engage in dialog on critical issues in Black Studies, she created the

Dr. Barbara Wheeler

interest and opportunity for building NCBS. Along with other women, she played a central role in its formulation and development and was its first chair in 1976; Maxwell led NCBS well through its beginning years of establishing a national office and regional structures producing its organizational voice, *Voices in Black Studies*, and initiating a conference process. Also, as in AHSA, women not only played leadership roles in the founding and development of NCBS but also in the definition and development of the discipline itself. Among the most noted, in addition to Maxwell, are Delores Aldridge and Carlene Young. These women of NCBS as well as those in AHSA have continuously advanced gender issues in both Black Studies discourse and organizational practice. And in this persistence, they have provided necessary creative tension for positive and productive discourse and change with their male colleagues, thus expanding and enriching the discipline.

A third factor which shaped the construction of Black women studies was the creative tension and discourse between Black womanists and feminists and white feminists and between Black Studies and white women studies in the academy. Especially in the early period of Black women studies, work by Black women tended to stress racial oppression more than gender oppression and to stress a common front of male and female for Black liberation (LaRue, 1970; Cade, 1970; Hare and Hare, 1970; Cooper, 1971; King, 1973). However, even later many Black women stressed the race, as well as gender character of their oppression and the need for white women to recognize the race and class nature of their own feminism, the differences as well as commonalities among women and the privileged position of white women in the racist white patriarchy which worked to Black women's and Black people's disadvantage (Rodgers-Rose, 1980; Gordon, 1987; hooks, 1990; Carby, 1987; Hill-Collins, 1991; Hudson-Weems, 1993). This creative tension helped develop Black womanist and feminist thought and at the same time laid a basis for criticism of sexism in the Black Movement and community—currently and historically.

Thus, a fourth factor which aided in shaping the development of Black women studies is the ongoing inquiry into and criticism of relations in the Black Freedom Movement (hooks, 1981; Hull, Scott and Smith, 1982; Giddings, 1984; Gordon, 1987). The women of SNCC under the leadership of Ruby Doris

Robinson are credited with first raising in written form a serious critique of sexism in the movement (Fleming, 1998). But this criticism became an enlarged discourse with a persistent demand for inclusion and the end of inequality in participation, power and representation (Clark, 1986; Giddings, 1984). In addition to criticism of current and historical practices of the movement by women and men, there are also genuine efforts of many men to be self-critical and self-corrective and a developing literature on the ethical basis for improving male/female relations (Aldridge, 1989; Rodgers-Rose, 1980; Rodgers-Rose and Rodgers, 1985).

As it continues to develop, Black women studies as a subject area of Black Studies faces several challenges. Aldridge (1992:179) outlines the challenges as follows: 1) continued and expanded scholarship by and about Black women "with increased focus in the social and behavioral sciences, the natural sciences, professions and policy studies;" 2) "increased contributions by women to conceptualization of the theoretical and empirical issues of the field in general;" 3) "continued involvement of Africana women with womanist perspectives in leadership positions in the professional bodies for Africana Studies so that programs and policies reflect their perspectives;" 4) "increased attention to developing new and restructuring old curricula to reflect a balance that is inclusive of Africana women;" 5) "increased balancing of speakers and cultural activities on campuses that draw upon both men and women not only from the literary tradition but other orientations;" and 6) "concentrated efforts to search out and quote works of both Africana women and men in the field...".

In addition to these, key to Black women's studies is the continued development of womanist theory so that it cannot only distinguish itself from white feminism but also move beyond its early concentration on oppression rather than agency (Carby, 1987; Gordon, 1987; hooks, 1990). As Carby (1987:16) notes, "Black feminist theory continues to be shaped by tensions apparent in feminist theory in general." These above all include concentration on what men have done rather than what women have done, and can and will do. It is as hooks notes, the struggle between concentrating on victimization or agency.

Moreover, as Gordon argues, much of the literature follows too closely white feminism without recognizing and taking into consideration vital differences. In fact, even when Black women

use the category womanist, there is little theoretical development of its distinctness as a defining characteristic of Black feminist thought. Certainly, Vivian Gordon (1987), Clenora
Hudson-Weems (1993), Niara Sudarkasa (1996), Rosalyn
Terborg-Penn (1997) and Filomena Chioma Steady (1997) have
made a major contribution to this effort, but as these authors
contend, womanism still needs a more developed and distinctive
theory.

Hill-Collins (1991:38-39) contends that "the primary guiding principle of Black feminism is a recurring humanist vision."
She quotes Anna Julia Cooper's classic statement from *A Voice
From the South* (1892) which states "We take our stand on the
solidarity of humanity, oneness of life, and the unnaturalness and
injustice of all favoritism whether of sex, race, country of condition...." She links this with Alice Walker's (1983:xi) concept of
"womanist" and argues that Walker's concept of womanist, as
one who is "committed to the survival and wholeness of an
entire people, male and female," is an expression of the "notion
of the solidarity of humanity." This is clearly part of it, but it also
speaks of the unity of male and female without dominance and
of wholeness, balance and a mutually beneficial togetherness in
love and struggle (Gordon, 1987; Hudson-Weems, 1993;
Sudarkasa, 1996; Terborg-Penn, 1997; Steady, 1997). These are
clearly concepts which offer excellent points of departure for not
only a critical discourse on the reconstruction of womanhood,
but also the reconstruction of male-female relations and society.
And this challenge is, in the final analysis, the most daunting
and promising one.

Finally, directly related to this theoretical challenge of distinctness is the challenge of developing more Black women studies literature in areas other than literature and literary criticism.
As noted above and in Chapter 7 on Black Creative Production,
literature and related areas are well-represented. But as Aldridge
(1992: 178ff) notes in her challenges, this is not so for other
areas. The challenge thus is to develop both theory and major
studies in these other areas which speak Black women's own special truth and serve as their unique contribution to both education and liberation (hooks, 1989).

2.5   MULTICULTURAL STUDIES

Another key development in Black Studies is its varied response to the emergence of multiculturalism as discourse and practice (Asante, 1999; Reed, 1997; Bowser, Jones and Young, 1995). Essentially there have been three responses inside the discipline to it. First, there is a tendency to see it as simply another attempt by the established order to dilute and divert the legitimate claims and demands of African people and maintain the power and worldview of the established order. Secondly, multiculturalism is seen as superficial cultural diversion from more serious issues of wealth and power. In a word, it becomes a preoccupation with cultural symbols rather than with the issue of wealth and power relations which either give or deny cultural substances and maintains white dominance. And finally, multiculturalism is seen by others in the discipline as a continuation of the struggle for a quality education, and a just and good society under another category. It is in this later conception that multiculturalism becomes an important development and challenge to Black Studies (Karenga, 1995).

Seen as a new expression of a continuing struggle for quality education and a just and good society, multiculturalism becomes and is a part of a Black historical tradition in education and society. Marable (1992:15) makes the same determination, linking the political and ethical aspirations of the Black Freedom Movement to multicultural democracy. He states that "multicultural democracy must perceive of itself in this historic tradition, as a critical project which transforms the larger society...restoring humanity and humanistic values to a system which is materialistic, destructive to the environment, and abusive of fellow beings."

Moreover, the struggle for a multicultural education begins in full form in the 60's with the Black Student Movement demanding the end to exclusive white studies instruction. As noted in the Introduction above, the Black students' struggle for Black Studies and the end to the Eurocentric curriculum was joined and aided by Third World groups who formed with Blacks the Third World Liberation Front. Moreover, white progressives formed a support committee for the Front. Thus, this historic struggle for Black Studies was in fact a struggle for a multicultural education as opposed to a Eurocentric one. For it not only broke the Eurocentric monopoly on what was taught as relevant and truth, but it also opened to the door for an even wider challenge. Therefore, other ethnic studies, i.e., Native American, Latino and Asian Studies, and women studies built on this tradition and joined in demanding an education of quality and relevance. It is at this point that quality education unavoidably requires a multicultural content.

The challenge to Black Studies, then, is to recognize its vanguard role in initiating both the discourse and process of multiculturalism (Karenga, 1995; Carruthers, 1990:17). As Delores Aldridge (1991:24) states, "It was African American Studies scholars who dared initiate and embrace a new way of looking at and examining knowledge about the world with a focus upon the experiences of the people of African descent." She states, Black Studies scholars "should take the lead in defining the new multicultural curriculum and indeed the concept itself which is mired in confusion." In a word, she concludes, "Black Studies, then, must lead in resolving the issues and definitions of what is multicultural...."

The challenge to define multiculturalism and rescue it from the established order or the Eurocentric version is a key task. Jacob Carruthers (1990:3) has noted that "even the most carefully developed multicultural curriculum will be unavoidably centered in the culture of the community by or in which the program is developed and taught." He goes on to say that this "means that if nothing else is done in the United States, the curriculum will have a Eurocentric focus." Criticizing Diane Ravitch's (1990) view of multiculturalism, Carruthers (1990:5ff) notes that she refuses to recognize unequal power in society and its effect on the multicultural curriculum, and that it is not simply a question of teaching too little of cultures of the people of color, but also of what is taught, i.e., falsehoods. Moreover, she does not recognize the history of the struggle for a revised curriculum and wishes to pretend progress in this area simply happened. It is these problems and others that make Carruthers conclude, the established order cannot be left to define and impose its own version of multiculturalism.

Molefi Asante (1992, 1999) in his critique of Arthur Schlesinger's (1991) multiculturalism, also reveals problems of Eurocentric versions. First, he (1992:305) points out that Schlesinger's vision of multiculturalism evolves from a conception of "an American rooted in the past, where whites, actually Anglo-Saxon whites, defined the protocols of American society and white culture itself represented the example to which others were forced to aspire." It is thus a multiculturalism with a hegemonic role for European culture, a conceptual blindness to oppression and domination and a studied aversion to Afrocentric theory and practice which reveal flaws in the body politics and the hegemonic position of Euro-Americans in education and society. As a counter, Asante (1992:311) suggests that an Afrocentric conception of multiculturalism "becomes useful for the expansion of dialogue and the widening of discourse-the proper function of education." This, he concludes, would of necessity mean the development of "a curriculum of instruction that affirms all people in their cultural heritages" and the parallel end of "the white self-esteem curriculum now present in most school systems."

As I (Karenga, 1995:41) have argued, "The current debate on the character and content of quality education in a multicultural context offers new possibilities not only for the reconception and reconstruction of public and higher education, but also for the reconception and reconstruction of society itself." This is because "the debate is in essence about power and place, standards of relevance and the quality of relations among various cultural groups which compose U.S. society and indeed the world." This multiculturalism is a critical thought and practice which cannot and should not be left to established order theorists who often reduce it to activities around food, fashion and festival. Conceived in an Afrocentric framework, *multiculturalism* can be defined as thought and practice organized around respect for human diversity. It expresses itself in four basic ways: 1) mutual respect for each people and culture; 2) mutual respect for each people's right and responsibility to speak their own special cultural truth and make their own unique contribution to society and the world; 3) mutual commitment to the constant search for common ground in the midst of our diversity; and 4) mutual commitment to an ethics of sharing in order to build the world we all want and deserve to live in. This ethics of sharing is directed toward a sharing in seven basic areas: 1) shared status; 2) shared knowledge; 3) shared space; 4) shared wealth; 5) shared power; 6) shared interests; and 7) shared responsibility for building the world we all want and deserve to live in – in a word the good world. The ethics of sharing is based on the assumption rooted in African ethical tradition that the greatest goods are shared goods, i.e., freedom, justice, equality, sisterhood, brotherhood, family, friendship, etc.

Black Studies is also challenged to provide a rationale for multicultural education. This rationale will, of necessity, resemble and build on the rationale for Black Studies itself. For again, it is the struggle for Black Studies which laid the ground for multicultural discourse and practice. There are essentially three basic grounds for multicultural education - moral, intellectual and social (President's Task Force Report, 1991:3ff; Karenga, 1995:41ff). The *moral ground* of multicultural education rests in a real respect for the concrete human person in all her/his diversity. In such a conception, the student and teacher are not abstracted from concrete conditions for critical understanding but are engaged and challenged to generate reflective problematics from their own experience. In a word, they speak from their own experience and location in history and culture and thus enrich and expand educational discourse.

The *intellectual ground* of multicultural education is established, as I (President's Task Force Report, 1991:3) have argued elsewhere, in its use and value as 1) "a necessary corrective for the conceptual and content inadequacy of the exclusive curriculum which omits and diminishes the rich (and instructive) variety of human cultures; 2) an equally important corrective for racist, sexist, classist and chauvinistic approaches to knowledge and education which deny, demean or diminish the meaning, experience and voice of the other; and 3) a creative challenge to the established order of things. For multicultural education, especially in its Afrocentric form, comes into being and establishes itself as an uncompromising and relentless critique of the established order. It then joins this critique with correctives pointed toward creating not only a richer and more varied educational experience but also a just and good society.

The *social ground* of multicultural education is established in its function as: 1) a just response to the demand of marginalized and excluded peoples and groups for an education reflective of and relevant to their own life experience; 2) an indispensable preparation of students and teachers for the world in which they live, work, study and exchange; and 3) "part and parcel of the thrust to create a just and good society, to avoid civil strife, and to enhance the quality of social life through cultivation of democratic values."

A third challenge for Black Studies is to construct a model multicultural curriculum at various levels of education. If quality education is at the same time and of necessity multicultural education, then, the challenge here is not to provide an Afrocentric curriculum in schools and universities, but rather to propose an Afrocentric paradigm for a multicultural education. Thus, in a multicultural context, the curriculum cannot be totally Afrocentric or it will become hegemonic as is the current Eurocentric model. On the contrary, the curriculum will and should be multicultural with various cultural visions, including the Afrocentric vision, as fundamental constitutive parts of the educational process. This position in no way suggests that Africana Studies departments and programs should not be Afrocentric. On the contrary, they must be Afrocentric; otherwise the distinctiveness of their contribution to multicultural discourse is called into question and ultimately undermined. What is key here is to create and pose a paradigm which rises from particular African views and values but also reflects the human interests we share with others. And this, of course, is the true meaning of Afrocentric, i.e., a paradigm rooted in the cultural image and human interest of African people.

Finally, multiculturalism confronts Black Studies with the challenge to demonstrate the effective difference and value of Afrocentric or African-centered concepts and practices to the multicultural education and enterprise. At this point, it is important to state that use of the terms African-centeredness and Afrocentric does not intend to suggest any more for the conceptual category "African" than is indicated by the terms "European" (Western), "Asian" (Oriental) or "Latin American." The categories *African* philosophy, worldview, values, etc., simply suggest *shared orientations* born of similar cultural experiences. As Gyekye (1987:x) notes, "(i)t is the underlying cultural unity or identity of the various individual thinkers that justifies references to varieties of thought as wholes, such as Western, European or Oriental philosophy." Therefore, to say African philosophy, worldview or values is to assume certain shared orientations based on similar cultural experiences. Among these shared orientations are: 1) the centrality of community; 2) respect for tradition; 3) a high level spirituality and ethical concern; 4) harmony with nature; 5) the sociality of selfhood; 6) veneration of ancestors; and 7) the unity of being. This is also not to say that there are not other African core values which one could focus on as central to the Afrocentric vision. However, these are a conceptual and indispensable minimum regardless of other additions.

Within the context of an Afrocentric cultural paradigm, then, several conceptual contributions can be offered as an enrichment of multicultural discourse and education. Among these are: 1) centeredness or groundedness and critical insight from one's own culture; (this is also called location or orientation); 2) the holistic approach to knowledge; 3) critique and corrective as a joint project in the educational enterprise; 4) the essentiality of an historical perspective; and 5) the centrality of the ethical dimension to the educational project both in terms of reaffirmation of the worth and dignity of the human person and knowledge in the service of humankind and the just and good society. All of these contributions are interrelated and mutually reinforcing and offer a paradigm of difference as possibility in a multicultural context. They also represent an excellent point of departure for further research and discourse.

2.6   CLASSICAL AFRICAN STUDIES

Finally, one of the most important and challenging developments in Black Studies since the decade of the 60's is the emergence in the 80's of increased intellectual and academic stress on the study of classical African civilizations, especially Egypt. Classes on Egypt in Black Studies departments and programs have increased and include history, culture, art, literature, language, religion and ethical philosophy. Moreover, major conferences and smaller symposia are held regularly around this intellectual focus. Also, works on ancient Egypt and use of ancient Egyptian culture as a major research source have increased. Among the important works on ancient Egypt or with major reference to it which were published during the 80's and 90's are Jacob Carruthers' *Essays in Ancient Egyptian Studies* (1984); Molefi Asante's *Kemet, Afrocentricity and Knowledge,* (1990); Ivan Van Sertima's *Nile Valley Civilizations* (1985) and *Egypt Revisited* (1989); Rkhty Amen Jones' *Medu Neter: The Ancient Egyptian Hieroglyphs* (1990); Wade Nobles', Lawford

Goodard's and William Cavil's *The Km Ebit Husia: Authoritative Utterances of Exceptional Insight for the Black Family* (1985); Maulana Karenga and Jacob Carruthers' *Kemet and the African Worldview* (1986); and Maulana Karenga's *Selections from the Husia: Sacred Wisdom of Ancient Egypt* (1984), *Reconstructing Kemetic Culture* (1990b), *The Book of Coming Forth By Day* (1990a), and his second dissertation, *The Moral Ideal in Ancient Egypt: A Study in Classical African Ethics* (1994).

The works of African Americans like David Walker, Hosea Easton, Martin Delaney and Henry Highland Garnet had exhibited an early interest in Egypt as a classical African civilization (Carruthers, 1992). And later the seminal work of George James, *Stolen Legacy* (1976) first and, then, the works of John Jackson (1972, 1980), Yosef ben-Jochannan (1970, 1971) and Chancellor Williams (1987) represent a continuing interest in Egypt and classical African civilization in general. In 1978 the Kemetic Institute in Chicago, dedicated to the recovery of ancient Egypt's legacy was founded, and in 1979 the Kawaida Institute of Pan-African Studies of Los Angeles also turned its attention to the critical study of Egypt and the rescue and reconstruction of its legacy. Moreover, Black Studies departments and programs have had courses on classical African civilization in general since their inception. However, full-fledged and widespread concern with Egypt as an intellectual development does not occur until the 80's. This period is marked by a flurry of intellectual and practical activity on a national level which lays the groundwork for this expanded and deepened focus.

An important factor in this flowering in the 80's is the planning and organizing by Us Organization of the First Annual Ancient Egyptian Studies Conference under the leadership of Maulana Karenga in February 1984 at Southwest College in Los Angeles which led to the founding of the Association for the Study of Classical African Civilizations (ASCAC). The Kawaida Institute of Pan-African Studies, the research arm of Us, invited scholars and others working on ancient Egypt to come and present their work to the community and exchange among themselves on research in process. The Kemetic Institute under the leadership of Jacob Carruthers lent its name to the conference and joined in calling for a professional organization for those interested in ancient Egyptian studies. This marked the founding of ASCAC and Jacob Carruthers and Maulana

Karenga became founding chair and vice-chair respectively. In its first three years ASCAC published important works, registered a membership of a thousand people which it took to Egypt in 1987, and reached deeply and widely into communities and campuses across the country to establish ancient Egyptian studies as a priority. However afterwards, it seems to have lost its original focus on scholarship and education of the masses and thus, lost its early driving force.

A second major factor shaping the development of classical studies was activities of the Nile Valley Civilization group headed by Ivan van Sertima. It also held a major conference on Nile Valley Civilization in September 1984, seven months after the founding of ASCAC, calling together scholars and ancient Egyptian enthusiasts. But unlike the ASCAC group, they formed no professional organization. However, Ivan van Sertima who founded the *Journal of African Civilization*, built the journal into a major source for publication of critical research on Nile Valley and other classical African civilizations and African presence in civilizations around the world.

Dr. Cheikh Anta Diop

A third factor shaping the flourishing of ancient Egyptian studies was the increasing familiarity with and receptivity to the works of Cheikh Anta Diop (1974, 1976, 1981, 1989, 1991) and to a lesser degree, familiarity with works of his student and colleague, Theophile Obenga (1992, 1972). Because Diop wrote in French, English-speaking Africans, except for scholars, were for the most part not familiar with his work. But as Diop's works were translated, in part or in whole and discussed widely during this period, African American scholars and lay persons became very much influenced by his works.

It is Diop who, in fact, pioneered the African focus on Egypt as a classical African civilization. In his major works, *The African Origin of Civilization* and *Civilization or Barbarism*, he outlined both the basic arguments for the African character of Egypt and its importance to African and world history. Later Martin Bernal (1987), whose work would cause controversy in Eurocentric circles, would support many of Diop's contentions. However, he would not critically discuss Diop's work (Carruthers, 1992) nor reaffirm the African, i.e., Black, character of Egypt when challenged (*Arethusa*, 1989).

Diop presented several arguments for the African or Black character of Egypt. First, he (1989:9) presented the evidence of *physical anthropology*, i.e., iconography, melanin dosage tests, osteological (bone) measurements and blood group tests. And all of these, he argues, reveal a definite Africanness or Blackness to Egypt. Secondly, Diop (1989:20) argues from the *self-definition* of the Egyptians who called themselves *Kmtyw* or *Kemetiu* — Black people — stemming from *km* — the ancient Egyptian word for Black. Eurocentric scholars, he notes, hardly ever mentioned this term and when they do translate it, it is as "the Egyptian" rather than the "Blacks" and they also prefer to use "*Rmṯ Kmt*" which means — people of the country of Black people or people of the Black land, i.e., Black land (fertile) as opposed to Red Land (desert). Thirdly, Diop (1989:161ff) offered *eyewitness reports* of "Greek and Latin writers contemporary with the ancient Egyptians" who describe the Egyptians as having defiant hair, bold lips and thin legs, all characteristic of Africans. These witnesses include Herodotus, Aristotle, Lucian, Apollodorus, Strabo, Diodorus and others. In addition, Diop (1989:22) offers the eyewitness reports of the ancient Israelites who in their sacred text state that "the sons of Ham (were) Cush and Misraim (i.e., Egypt)." The Jews, he asserts, lived side by side with Egyptians and had no interest in misrepresenting their African ethnicity.

Fourthly, Diop (1989:22; 1974) argues that *cultural similarities* prove the African character of Egypt. These include common elements with other African cultures such as circumcision, divine kingship, totemism, matrilineal focus, cosmogonies, architecture, musical instruments and religious practices. Related to cultural similarities, Diop (1989:23) points also to the linguistic affinity of ancient Egyptian with "Wolof, a Senegalese language spoken in the extreme west of Africa on the Atlantic Ocean" which he argues "is perhaps as close to ancient Egyptian as Coptic," the modern form of ancient Egyptian. The kinship with Wolof, he notes, cannot be ignored, especially since ancient Egyptian is not Semitic and displays a "genetic, that is non-accidental relationship" with other African languages.

Also, Diop offers *artistic evidence* presenting Egyptian sculpture and painting to show what is considered prototypical

Africanoid features of the ancient Egyptians and their similarities to some Nubians. It is important to note here, however, that Diop is not obliged to prove that all Egyptians look like a Eurocentric conception of a prototypical West African. For Africa is the home of humanity as well as human civilization and thus would, of necessity, show varied physical features. Zulus, Ethiopians, Yoruba, Somali, Ashanti, Congolese and others resemble and differ at the same time. So it is, in a sense, playing Europe's racial game to concede that Egyptians are white or Asian if they don't look like a Eurocentric version of a West African. Ethiopians and Somalis, perhaps, resemble the ancient Egyptians more than any other peoples and they are, even by Eurocentric standards, African.

Finally, when all else is said, there is the *evidence of geography*. Egypt is in Africa and not in the political construction called the Middle East or Western Asia. Ancient Egypt is, in fact, the only country in history that ever had to justify its geography—that is to say, explain why it's in Africa when it should not be there if racist scholarship is right. For racist scholarship since Hegel has claimed Africa had no history and thus could not be a suitable place for Egypt. In order to maintain this distortion of the historical record, such scholars took Africans out of Egypt, Egypt out of Africa, and then Africa out of human history in their discourse.

It is this removal process, which Diop calls the falsification of history, that leads him to place so much emphasis on the rescue and reconstruction of ancient Egyptian history and culture. Thus, he (1981:12) states that "For us, the return to Egypt in all fields, is the necessary condition" to achieve three basic goals: 1) "to reconcile African civilization with history, (i.e., end the great falsification of African and human history,);" 2) to enable Africans "to build a body of modern human sciences;" and 3) "to renew African culture."

He continues, saying "Far from being a diversion in the past, a look back toward ancient Egypt is the best way to conceive and build our cultural future." For, he concludes, having recovered Egypt, "Egypt will play in a reconceived and renewed African culture the same role that the Greco-Latin ancient past plays in western culture." It is this conception of the role of ancient Egypt in African history and culture that informed and guided the flowering of interest in and activity around the project of Egypt's recovery.

Critics have raised the question of the relevance of ancient history and especially ancient Egypt to the present and future. Not only has Diop answered this, but also it is obviously an ill-considered question, especially from people who read from ancient sacred and secular texts everyday and find meaning and cultural and intellectual grounding in them. Ancient Egyptian sacred and secular texts offer no less.

It is also said that ancient Egypt was a slave-holding society, and thus, is a flawed candidate for a paradigm of Black culture. There are several basic responses to this. First, if the whole of Egyptian culture is discredited and dismissed for slave-holding, so should be the societies of ancient Israel, Greece, Rome and the U.S., since all were, at one time or the other, slave-holding also. Secondly, one should be clear about the difference between religious ideology and historical fact or between a narrative of faith (religion) and a narrative of fact (history). No scholar of any weight argues the biblical interpretation of Egypt as the epitome of oppression. In fact, the image of Egypt as having large-scale slavery or even slavery like Greece, is erroneous (James, 1972:37-38; Ruffle, 1977:36; Bierbrier, 1984:12-13). T.G.H. James (1972:37) asserts that "Herodotus may have been chiefly responsible for the belief that the pyramids were built by slave labor." But actually, the idea has been spread by Judeo-Christian discourse which depends so much on the narrative of oppression, exodus and freedom and thus the demonization of Egypt (Assmann, 1997). However, a more accurate assessment as Bierbrier (1984:12) notes, is that people were conscripted, hired and volunteered for public work projects, such as the pyramids, during the flood season when land was covered with water and agriculture impossible. Recent excavations have shown settlements around the pyramids and patterns of life and payment which do not indicate slavery. On the contrary, there is evidence of a complex community, committed to this public works project, living lives of meaning and purpose and coping with problems characteristic of human life (Hawass, 1999; Hawass and Lehner, 1997). This is not to deny enslavement of some foreign captives in Egypt, especially in its imperial period. In fact, virtually all ancient societies, except communal ones, tended to enslave. And there is no reason for or morality in defending such practices. But claiming that Egypt used slavery to build the pyramids or held a whole nation in captivity does not correspond to historical evidence.

What is required morally, then, is to condemn anti-human practices in all societies. However, it is not required that we indict a whole society because of religious or racial bias and deny its contribution, not only to the world, but also to the very people who so severely and incorrectly indicted it. In fact, as Breasted (1934:xv) noted in his seminal work, *The Dawn of Conscience*, Egypt was a center of moral development and teaching in the ancient world. He states, "It is now quite evident that the ripe social and moral development of mankind in the Nile Valley, which is three thousand years older than that of the Hebrews, contributed essentially to the formation of the Hebrew literature we call the Old Testament." He concludes saying, "Our moral heritage, therefore, derives from a wider *human* past enormously older than the Hebrews, and it has come to us rather *through* the Hebrews than *from* them." This historical fact in no way denies the Hebrews their originality and uniqueness in moral development and teaching. But it is worth noting that Egypt, the society which Judeo-Christian teaching so much associates with oppression, turns out to be a moral society which shared its moral concepts and philosophy with the Hebrews, Christians and the world (see also section on The Egyptian Legacy and Tradition in Chapter 3 and Karenga, 1984, 1989, 1990a, 1994).

The question is also raised of why Egypt and not other African civilizations for the classical paradigm. But it is not a question of one civilization to the exclusion of others. On the contrary, one is compelled to study the classical cultures of Yorubaland, Ashantiland, Ghana, Mali, Songhai, et al as well. Egypt is simply a priority focus for several basic reasons: 1) Egypt's antiquity, allowing for a long view of Africans in history; 2) the abundant availability of documents (books and writings in all forms and on all surfaces, art, architecture, cultural products, etc., thus, the capacity of Egypt to speak its own truth; 3) its level of achievements in so many of the basic disciplines of human knowledge; 4) its meaning to other African societies; and 5) its contribution to the world in the basic disciplines of human knowledge - ethics, science, math, medicine, architecture, literature, astronomy, etc. It is this latter fact that makes it contested terrain but also makes it worthy of the contest and of its paradigm status. The challenge for Black Studies, then, is to rescue and reconstruct this rich ancient heritage and explore Diop's conception of the fertile field of possibilities ancient Egypt offers.

STUDY QUESTIONS

1. Discuss the history and goals of AHSA and NCBS. Stress the role of Black women in their founding and development.
2. Discuss the emergence of the Afrocentric initiative and Molefi Asante's founding role in it. What are the essential elements of an Afrocentric methodology according to Asante?
3. Define Afrocentricity according to *IBS*. What is the difference between Afrocentricity and Afrocentrism?
4. Define Eurocentrism. What is the difference between Afrocentricity and Eurocentrism?
5. What are some tendencies that Afrocentricity must avoid in order to make the most useful contribution to the Black Studies project?
6. What are some factors which have shaped and contributed to the emergence and development of Black Women Studies to the discipline?
7. What are some challenges which confront Black Women Studies as it continues to develop according to Delores Aldridge?
8. What are some of the essential elements of concern and focus important in the continued development of womanist theory?
9. Define and discuss the fundamental aspects of multiculturalism.
10. What is the basic rationale for a multicultural education?
11. What are some conceptual contributions the Afrocentric paradigm can make to enrich and expand multicultural discourse?
12. Discuss the evolution of emphasis on the study of classical civilizations in Black Studies.
13. Discuss the arguments of Cheikh Anta Diop for the African character of Egypt.
14. Discuss the three basic tasks Diop sets for scholars in their critical study of ancient Egyptian history and culture in the effort to conceive and build a new future.
15. Discuss the reasons for the priority given the study of Egypt among all the classical African civilizations.

REFERENCES

Aldridge, Delores. (ed). (1989) *Black Male-Female Relationships: A Resource Book of Selected Materials*, Dubuque, IA: Kendall/Hunt Publishing Co.

Aldridge, Delores. (1991) "An Interview," *Word: A Black Cultural Journal*, 1, 1 (Spring) 19-28.

Aldridge, Delores. (1992) "Womanist Issues in Black Studies: Towards Integrating Africana Women into Africana Studies," *Journal of the National Council for Black Studies*, 1, 1 (May) 167-182.

Aldridge, Delores. (1988) *New Perspectives on Black Studies*, Special Issue, *Phylon*, 49, 1 (Spring).

Anderson, Talmadge. (1990) *Black Studies: Theory, Method and Cultural Perspective*, Pullman, WA: Washington State University Press.

Arethusa. (1989) Special Issue (Fall).

Asante, Molefi. (1980) *Afrocentricity: The Theory of Social Change*, Buffalo: Amulefi Publishing Co.

Asante, Molefi. (1998) *The Afrocentric Idea*, Philadelphia: Temple University Press.

Asante, Molefi. (1990) *Kemet, Afrocentricity and Knowledge*, Trenton, NJ: Africa World Press.

Asante, Molefi. (1991) "Multiculturalism: An Exchange," *The American Scholar* (Spring) 267-271.

Asante, Molefi. (1992) "The Painful Demise of Eurocentrism," *The World & I*, (April) 305-317.

Asante, Molefi. (1999) *The Painful Demise of Eurocentrism: An Afrocentric Response to Critics*, Trenton, NJ: Africa World Press.

Assmann, Jan. (1997) *Moses the Egyptian: The Memory of Egypt in Western Monotheism*, Cambridge, MA: Harvard University Press.

ben-Jochannon, Yosef A.A. (1971) *Africa: Mother of "Western Civilization,"* New York: Alkebulan Books Associates.

ben-Jochannon, Yosef A.A. (1970) *African Origins of the Major "Western Religions,"* New York: Alkebu-lan Books Associates.

Bernal, Martin. (1987) *Black Athena: The Afro-Asiatic Roots of Classical Civilization*, Vol. I, London: Free Association Books.

Bierbrier, Morris. (1984) *The Tomb-Builders of the Pharaohs*, New York: Charles Scribner's Sons.

Bowser, Benjamin, Terry Jones and Gale Auletta Young (eds.). (1995) *Toward the Multicultural University*, Westport, CT: Praeger.

Breasted, James. (1934) *The Dawn of Conscience*, New York: Charles Scribner's Sons.

Cade, (Bambara) Toni. (ed.) (1970) *The Black Woman*, New York: New American Library.

Carby, Hazel. (1987) *Reconstructing Womanhood: The Emergence of the Afro-American Woman Novelist*, New York: Oxford University Press.

Carruthers, Jacob. (1992) "Bernal's Critique of Black Champions of Ancient Egypt," *Journal of Black Studies*, 22, 4 (June) 459-476.

Carruthers, Jacob H. (1990) "The Defenders of Western Civilization and the Battle Over the Multicultural Curriculum," unpublished manuscript.

Carruthers, Jacob H. (1984) *Essays in Ancient Egyptian Studies*, Los Angeles: University of Sankore Press.

Clark, Septima. (1986) *Reading From Within: Septima Clark & the Civil Rights Movements*, New York: Wild Trees Press.

Clarke, John Henrik. (1976) "AHSA: A History," *Issue: A Quarterly Journal of Africanist Opinion*, 6, 1/3 (Summer/Fall).

Conyers, Jr., James (ed.). (1997) *Africana Studies: A Disciplinary Quest for Both Theory and Method*, Jefferson, NC: McFarland and Company, Inc.

Cooper, Anna Julia. (1892) *A Voice from the South: By a Black Woman of the South*, Xenia, OH: Aldine Printing House.

Cooper, Jean. (1971) "Women's Liberation and the Black Woman," *Journal of Home Economics*, 63, (October) 521- 523.

Diop, Cheikh Anta. (1974) *The African Origin of Civilization: Myth or Reality*, Westport, CT: Lawrence Hill & Co.

Diop, Cheikh Anta. (1991) *Civilization or Barbarism: An Authentic Anthropology*, New York: Lawrence Hill Books.

Diop, Cheikh Anta. (1981) *Civilization ou Barbarie*, Paris: Présence Africaine.

Diop, Cheikh Anta. (1976) *The Cultural Unity of Black Africa*, Chicago: Third World Press.

Diop, Cheikh Anta. (1989) "Origin of the Ancient Egyptians," *Journal of African Civilizations*, 10 (Summer) 9-37.

DuBois, W.E.B. (1975) *The Education of Black People: Ten Critiques, 1906-1960*, New York: Monthly Review Press.

Fleming, Cynthia. (1998) *Soon We Will Not Cry: The Liberation of Ruby Doris Smith Robinson*, Lanham, MD: Rowman and Littlefield.

Giddings, Paula. (1984) *When and Where I Enter: The Impact of Black Women on Race and Sex in America*, New York: William Morrow and Co.

Gordon, Vivian. (1987) *Black Women, Feminism and Black Liberation: Which Way?*, New York: William Morrow.

Gyekye, Kwame. (1987) *An Essay on African Philosophical Thought: The Akan Conceptual Scheme*, New York: Cambridge University Press.

Hall, Perry. (1992) "Beyond Afrocentrism: Alternatives for Afro-American Studies," *Western Journal of Black Studies*, 5, 4 (winter) 27-212.

Hall, Perry. (1999) *In the Vineyard: Working in African American Studies*, Knoxville, TN: University of Tennessee Press.

Hare, Nathan. (1969) "What Should be the Role of Afro-American Education in the Undergraduate Curriculum?" *Liberal Education*, 55, 1 (March) 42-50.

Hare, Nathan. (1972) "The Battle of Black Studies," *The Black Scholar*, 3, 9 (May) 32-37.

Hare, Nathan and Julia Hare. (1970) "Black Women 1970," *Transaction*, 8 (November-December) 68, 90.

Harris, Robert. (1990) "The Intellectual and Institutional Development of Africana Studies," in Robert Harris, Darlene Clark Hine and Nellie McKay, (eds.), *Three Essays: Black Studies in the United States*, New York: Ford Foundation.

Harris, Robert, Darlene Clark Hine and Nellie McKay. (1990) *Three Essays: Black Studies in the United States*, New York: Ford Foundation.

Hawass, Zahi. (1999) "Giza, Workmen's Community" in Kathryn A. Bard (ed.), *Encyclopedia of the Archaeology of Ancient Egypt*, London: Routledge, pp. 353-356.

Hawass, Z. and M. Lehner. (1997) "Builders of the Pyramids," *Archaeology*, 50, 1 (31-9)

Hendrix, M. et al. (1984) "Computers and Black Studies: Toward the Cognitive Revolution," *Journal of Negro Education* 53, 341-350.

Hill-Collins, Patricia. (1991) *Black Feminist Thought*, New York: Routledge.

hooks, bell. (1981) *Ain't I A Woman: black women and feminism*, Boston: South End Press.

hooks, bell. (1989) *Talking Back: Thinking Feminist, Thinking Black*, Boston: South End Press.

hooks, bell. (1990) *Yearning: race, gender and cultural politics*, Boston, South End Press.

Hudson-Weems, Clenora. (1993) *Africana Womanism: Reclaiming Ourselves*, Troy, NI: Bedford Publishers.

Hull, Gloria, Patricia Bell Scott and Barbara Smith, (eds.) (1982) *All the Women are White, All the Blacks are Men, but Some of Us are Brave*, Old Westbury, NY: Feminist Press.

Jackson, John. (1980) *Introduction to African Civilizations*, Secaucus, NJ: Citadel Press.

Jackson, John. (1972) *Man, God, and Civilization*, New Hyde Park, New York: University Books.

James, George. (1976) *Stolen Legacy*, San Francisco: Julian Richardson Associates.

James, T.G.H. (1972) *The Archaeology of Ancient Egypt*, New York: Henry Z Walck.

Jones, Rkhty Amen. (1990) *Medu Neter: The Ancient Egyptian Hieroglyphs*, Orange, NJ: Institute of Kemetic Philology.

Karenga, Maulana. (1995) "Afrocentricity and Multicultural Education: Concept, Challenge and Contribution" in Benjamin Bowser, Terry Jones and Gale Auletta Young (eds.), *Toward the Multicultural University*, Westport, CT: Praeger, pp. 42-61.

Karenga, Maulana. (1969) "The Black Community and the University: A community Organizer's Perspective," in Armstead Robinson, Craig C. Foster and Donald H. Ogilvie, (eds.), *Black Studies in the University*, New Haven, CT: Yale University Press, pp. 37-54.

Karenga, Maulana. (1988) "Black Studies and the Problematic of Paradigm: The Philosophical Dimension," *Journal of Black Studies* 18, 4 (June) 395-414.

Karenga, Maulana. (1990a) *The Book of Coming Forth By Day: The Ethics of the Declarations of Innocence*, Los Angeles: University of Sankore Press.

Karenga, Maulana. (1977) "Corrective History: Reconstructing the Black Past," *First World*, 1, 3 (May/June) 50-54.

Karenga, Maulana. (1980) *Kawaida Theory: An Introductory Outline*, Inglewood, CA: Kawaida Publications.

Karenga, Maulana. (1994) *Maat, The Moral Ideal in Ancient Egypt: A Study in Classical African Ethics*, unpublished dissertation, University of Southern California.

Karenga, Maulana. (1990b) *Reconstructing Kemetic Culture*, Los Angeles: University of Sankore Press.

Karenga, Maulana. (1984) *Selections From the Husia: Sacred Wisdom of Ancient Egypt*, Los Angeles: University of Sankore Press.

Karenga, Maulana. (1989) "Towards a Sociology of Maatian Ethics: Literature and Context", in Ivan Van Sertima (ed.), *Egypt Revisited*, New Brunswick, NJ: Transaction Publications.

Keto, C. Tsehloane. (1994) *An Introduction to the Africa Centered Perspective of History*, London/Chicago: Research Associates School Times Publications/Karnak House.

King, Mae C. (1973) "The Politics of Sexual Stereotypes," *The Black Scholar*, 4 (March/April) 12.

King, Richard D. (1990) *African Origin of Biological Psychiatry*, Germantown, TN: Seymour-Smith, Inc.

Ladner, Joyce A. (ed.) (1973) *The Death of White Sociology*, New York: Vintage Books.

LaRue, Linda J.M. (1970) "Black Liberation and Women's Lib," *Transaction*, 8 (November-December) 59-64.

Lefkowitz, Mary R. (1996) *Not Out of Africa: How Afrocentrism Became an Excuse to Teach Myth as History*, New York: Free Press.

Logan, Shirley. (1999) *We are Coming: the Persuasive Discourse of Nineteenth-Century Black Women*, Carbondale: Southern Illinois University Press..

Marable, Manning. (1992) *Black America: Multicultural Democracy in the Age of Clarence Thomas and David Duke*, (Open Magazine Pamphlet Series), Westfield, NJ: Open Media.

McIntyre, Charshee. (1989) "Agenda for AHSA: 21st Century." Unpublished manuscript, State University of New York at Old Westbury.

Morgan, Gordon J. (1991) "Afrocentricity in Social Science," *Western Journal of Black Studies*, 15, 4 (Winter) 197-206.

Nobles, Wade W., Lawford Goddard and William Cavil. (1985) *The Km Ebit Husia: Authoritative Utterances of Exceptional Insight*, Oakland: The Institute for the Advanced Study of Black Family Life and Culture.

Obenga, Théophile. (1992) *Ancient Egypt and Black Africa*, London: Karnak House.

Obenga, Théophile. (1972) *L'Afrique dans L'Antiquité: Egypte pharaonique-Afrique Noire*, Paris: Présence Africaine.

Oyabede, Bayo (1990) "African Studies and The Afrocentric Paradigm: A Critique," *Journal of Black Studies*, 21, 2, 233-238.

President's Task Force Report on Multicultural Education and Campus Diversity. (1991) *The Challenge of Diversity and Multicultural Education*, Long Beach: California State University, Long Beach.

Ravitch, Dianne. (1990) "Multiculturalism," *American Scholar* (Summer).

Reed, Ishmael. (1997) *Multi-America: Essays on Cultural Wars and Cultural Peace*, New York: Viking Penguin.

Robinson, Armstead, et al. (1969) *Black Studies in the University*, New York: Bantam Books.

Rodgers-Rose, La Francis (ed.) (1980) *The Black Woman*, Beverly Hills: Sage Publication.

Rodgers-Rose, La Francis and James T. Rodgers. (1985) *Strategies for Resolving Conflict in Black Male and Female Relationships*, Newark: Traces Institute Publications.

Rowe, Cyprian L. (1970) *Crisis in African Studies: The Birth of the African Heritage Studies Association*, Buffalo: Black Academy Press, Inc.

Ruffle, John. (1977) *The Egyptians: An Introduction to Egyptian Archaeology*, Ithaca, NY: Cornell University Press.

Schlesinger, Arthur. (1991) *The Disuniting of America: Reflections on a Multicultural Society*, Knoxville, TN: Whittle Direct Books.

Simms, Margaret C. and Julianne Malveaux (eds.) (1986) *Slipping Through the Cracks: The Status of Black Women*, New Brunswick, NJ: Transaction.

Steady, Filomena Chioma. (1997) "African Feminism: A Worldwide Perspective" in Rosalyn Terborg-Penn and Andrea Benton Rushing (eds.), *Women in Africa and the African Diaspora*, Washington, DC: Howard University Press.

Stewart, James B. (1979) "Introducing Black Studies: A Critical Examination of Some Textual Materials," *Umoja*, 3, 1, (Spring) 5-17.

Stewart, James B. (1984) "The Legacy of W.E.B. DuBois for Contemporary Black Studies," *Journal of Negro Education*, 53, 296-311.

Stewart, James. (1992) "Reaching For Higher Ground: Toward an Understanding of Black/Africana Studies", *The Afrocentric Scholar*, 1, 1, (May) 1-63.

Sudarkasa, Niara. (1996) *The Strength of Our Mothers, African And African American Women and Families*, Trenton, NJ: Africa World Press.

Terborg-Penn, Rosalyn. (1997) "A Theoretical Approach to the History of Women in the African Diaspora" in Rosalyn Terborg-Penn and Andrea Benton Rushing (eds.), *Women in Africa and the African Diaspora*, Washington, DC: Howard University Press.

Turner, James. (1984) *The Next Decade: Theoretical and Research Issues in Africana Studies*, Ithaca: Africana Studies and Research Center, Cornell University.

Van Sertima, Ivan. (1999) *Egypt Revisited*, Journal of African Civilizations, New Brunswick: Transaction Publishers.

Van Sertima, Ivan. (1985) *Nile Valley Civilizations*, Journal of African Civilizations, New Brunswick: Transaction Publishers.

Walker, Alice. (1983) *In Search of Our Mother's Garden*, New York: Harcourt, Brace and Jovanovich.

Williams, Chancellor. (1987) *The Destruction of Black Civilization: Great Issues of a Race From 4500 B.C. to 2000 A.D.*, Chicago: Third World Press.

Williams, Selase. (1991) "A Synoptic History of NCBS and Its Future," unpublished paper delivered at NCBS Summer Faculty Institute, Ohio State University (June).

Woodson, Carter G. (1969) *The Miseducation of the Negro*, Washington, DC: Associated Publishers Inc.

Woodyard, Jeffrey L. (1991) "Evolution of a Discipline: Intellectual Antecedents of African American Studies," *Journal of Black Studies* 22, 2 (December) 239-251.

Young, Carlene. (1984) "An Assessment of Black Studies Programs in American Higher Education," *Journal of Negro Education*, 53.

BLACK HISTORY:
AFRICAN BACKGROUND

BLACK HISTORY: AFRICAN BACKGROUND

CHAPTER 3

3.1 INTRODUCTION

Black History is engaged here as the first field of study in the introduction to Black Studies for several reasons. First, it is to emphasize the discipline's stress on the indispensability of the historical perspective in understanding social and human reality (Keto, 1994). Black Studies is not equated with history, but it is considered an indispensable area of study in understanding the origins, development and meaning of things. Malcolm X (1965:8) reaffirms the centrality of history to the study of social reality in his statement that "of all our studies history is best prepared to reward our research."

Secondly, beginning with Black History stresses also the importance of the ongoing project of *historical recovery* to every field in Black Studies. This process is called *sankofa*, an *Akan* word which means "to return and recover it." This involves returning to the rich resource of the African past, or history, and using it as a foundation to improve the present and enhance the future. The idea of Sankofa is depicted as a bird reaching back with its beak into is feathers. According to Niangoran-Bouah (1984, Vol. I:210), the Sankofa bird "is a symbol representing the quest for knowledge and the return to the source." This process of returning to the source in the constant quest for valuable and

Sankofa, to return and recover

diverse knowledge of African peoples and African culture has become a central concept and practice in all fields of Black Studies – history, religion, sociology, politics, economics, creative production, psychology, etc.

It is from this ongoing process of *sankofa* that Black Studies scholars discover and recover some of its most important paradigms of African thought and practice. And these data are used not only to constantly develop and expand the discipline, but also as a critical resource to understand and address the major issues of our time.

Finally, Black Studies also begins with Black history because it is relevant, even indispensable to the introduction and development of all the other subject areas. Black history places them in perspective, establishes their origins and development, and thus, aids in critical discussion and understanding of them. Moreover, each of the other subject areas of Black Studies teaches its own particular history which in turn is a part of general Black history. Black history, therefore, offers not only a broad framework for critically viewing and understanding Black people, but also a necessary background perspective for critical insights into other subjects.

3.2   DEFINITION

The understanding and appreciation of Black History begins with the definition of history itself and then uses that definition to define Black history and its relevance. *History is the struggle and record of humans in the process of humanizing the world, i.e., shaping it in their own image and interests.* To shape the world in a human image is to give it a human form and character and to shape it in human interests it to make it serve humans rather than threaten, deform or destroy them. In a word, shaping the world in a human image and in human interests is to make it a context which reflects and insures human defense, development and ultimate self-realization. African or Black history, then, is the struggle and record of Africans in the process of Africanizing the world, i.e., shaping it in their own image and interests. As a particular people, Africans shape the world in a particular way, i.e., they tend to Africanize it, or shape it in their own image and interests. This adds to the richness and beauty of human diversity and contributes to the overall effort of humans to transform the world in ways that improve the human condition and enhance the human future.

Put another way, history reveals itself as a human practice directed in its diversity toward *self-construction, social construction and world construction*. For as a people builds itself, it builds a society it lives and develops in and this effort becomes a contribution to and a vital part of the overall human construction of the world. Thus, as Africans developed agriculture, medicine, science, etc. to defend and develop themselves, they built societies and civilizations which contributed to the overall humanization of the world and to the forward flow of human history (Jackson, 1980; Diop, 1974; 1991).

But history does not just happen nor is it the work of unseen forces. On the contrary, it is a process which is defined by five basic characteristics. First, it is human in the fullest and most diverse sense of the word. Secondly, it is social, by and about people in definite social situations, in a definite society in relation to others, themselves and nature. Third, it is conflictual, that is to say, full of contradictions, i.e., conflicts and struggle to solve conflicts. In fact, the motive force of history is struggle against four major oppositions, nature, society, others and self which will be discussed below. Fourthly, history is fluid and changeable, i.e., in constant movement. Finally, history is manageable, i.e., subject to controlled and directed change. Humans do not always make history as they would like, but only through self-conscious intervention in the social and historical process can history be managed or self-consciously made. Self-conscious intervention in the social and historical process means intervention in the structure and tendencies of society and the world.

The most effective means of intervention is struggle. In fact, the motive force and shaper of history is struggle. Thus to make history, humans must struggle with four major oppositions: (1) nature; (2) society; (3) other humans; and (4) their immediate selves. Even a cursory review of African history shows Africans in the process of solving these fundamental contradictions. The very battle to be human, to separate oneself from the animal kingdom is a struggle with nature. As the first humans, Africans began to humanize the world by controlling various forces of nature and breaking its hold on them (Clark, 1970). Thus, they discover fire, make tools, clothes, shelter, and devise ways to increase food. They collect seeds, learn the seasons, engage in cultivation, harness the Nile and use it for irrigation and call this science agriculture. They study disease and develop cures and call it medicine; they dig in the earth and discover and extract its resources and call it mining; they move beyond basic structures and build large temples and pyramids and create architecture; and they observe the stars, discover patterns and movements, name them and call this astronomy. As they engage in these activities, they reshape themselves, societies and the world, distinguish and distance themselves from the animal world and make true human history a reality.

The second major opposition humans face and must overcome continuously in making history is society or more precisely the limitations it imposes at various historical periods on the defense and development of human life. It is a fundamental paradox that society which is designed and built as a context for human freedom, defense and development often becomes a context for suppression, exploitation and oppression. In the long march toward human freedom, i.e., the absence of restraint and the capacity for rational self-determination, society has both impeded and aided progress toward this goal. In the constant struggle to shape society in a more human, i.e., freer and more positive image, humans have made bold strokes on the canvas of history. The struggle to break the priests' monopoly on knowledge and make it available to the masses, and the struggle against dictatorship and to establish and maintain democracy, the struggle to establish science over and against superstitions are vivid and continuing examples.

In African American history, the struggle against society or more precisely society in its various oppressive forms of enslavement, racism and capitalism has clearly been its motive force. In fact, the periodization of Black history reveals focal points of struggle against social exploitation and oppression. The Holocaust of Enslavement, reversal of Reconstruction and the rise of Jim Crow; lynchings and racism in education, employment and other areas of social life; powerlessness and police brutality are all categories not only of exploitation and oppressive social relations but foci of struggle against them.

But society is only context. Other humans are actors who impose, exploit and oppress in that context. Thus at the heart of history is the struggle against others who threaten human life, freedom and development. Enslavement is imposed by the enslaver, racism by the racist, capitalism and colonialism by the capitalist and colonizer. The ruling ideas and dominant relations in any given society at any historical period are the ideas and relations of those who rule. This social grouping may be a ruling class or a ruling race or as in the USA and pre-independence South Africa (Azania), a ruling race/class, i.e., a ruling class made up of and exclusive to the ruling race in a society. Moreover, "others" could be other smaller social units like ethnic groups, political parties or interest groups who challenge and check, or exploit and oppress them. And "others" could be other nations, whose nationalism deteriorates into pathological forms such as chauvinism, jingoism, apartheid, fascism, nazism, etc.

However, within this array of "others" who pose challenges contributive to making history, the struggle between classes and between nations or peoples are the most definitive struggles of history. Marxists argue that class struggle is the motive force of history (Bober, 1948). Black nationalists argue that it is the struggle of races and nations, two categories which are often used interchangeably (Williams, 1974). It is important to see however, that class struggle may or may not be the key struggle in every socio-historical setting and the same is true of racial or national struggles. Also, in the panoramic vastness of human history, it is, as argued at the outset, not just social struggle in and against society which makes history, but four basic struggles, the four major oppositions we are discussing. In a word, it is struggle in its full diversity which is the motive force of history, although a key struggle (race, class, etc.) tends to express itself in any given socio-historical setting (Rodney, 1974:89).

The final major opposition is the struggle of humans against themselves, with their conception of themselves and their conditions and the possibilities they see in them. That which *is* seems permanent and overwhelming. Thus the human personality is often prone toward submitting to or accepting the immediate. But history is made human when humans collectively and personally break beyond the current concept of self and distinguish between actuality, that which is; potentially, that which can be; and reality, that which ought to be and becomes when a person, people, society or thing realizes itself, i.e., fulfills its inherent potential. The Dogon (Mali) astronomer who discovered Sirius B and C; the ancient Ishongo (Congo) mathematician who devised the abacus; the Egyptian physician Imhotep, who founded the science of medicine and the African American chemurgist, George Washington Carver, who created over 300 synthetic and organic products out of the peanut, all reached beyond the immediate, realized in part the unlimited potential of humankind, and thus, advanced human history. Fundamental to understanding this conception, then, is to see reality not as *being,* but as *becoming* and to see struggle as the motive force of both becoming and history. For human essence is human possibility and history is the process thru which that possibility is expressed and realized.

3.3   PROBLEMS OF STUDY

The history of Black people, humans and human civilization began in Africa (Reader, 1998; Stringer and McKie, 1997; Ki-Zerbo, 1990). Three major factors, however, have combined to obscure this fact and make the study and writing of African history problematic. The first factor is the vastness of the subject. African history is the history of a continent in flux and in contact and exchange with the world, and one can easily assume, especially given the Eurocentric thrust and character of most histories of Africa, that others rather than Africans gave rise to Africa's many contributions to the forward flow of human history. As Williams (1974:33) remarked, "African history is complex and many-sided, and would be so (even) if we were discussing just one nation and not an entire continent." Thus, without the time or inclination to do the necessary research one ends up repeating what was written before in the image and interests of Europeans. An example of this is the tendency to pass along the French and English translations which call the founders of Ghana "white" (Gailey, 1970) although further investigation shows they were referred to as "red" or "reddish-brown" by the people of the region (Fage, 1969:8).

Secondly, the study of African history is complicated by the predominance of oral history in many places as the most definitive African perspective on the subject. That is not to say that Africans did not have several scripts. On the contrary, there were many scripts in Africa, including the three scripts of ancient Egypt — hieroglyphic, hieratic and demotic; the

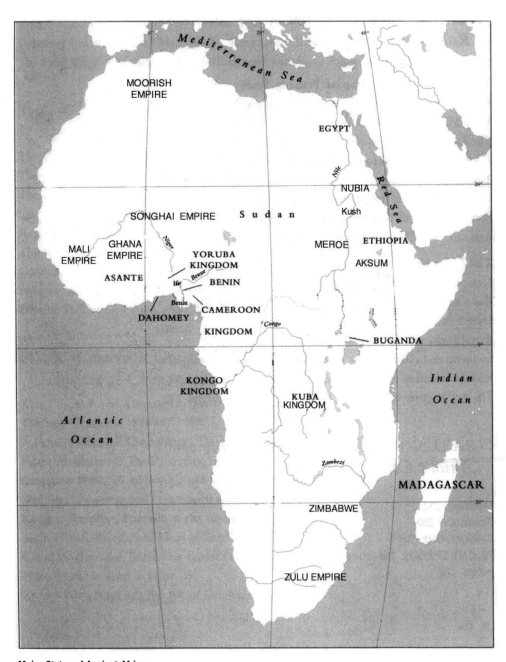

Major States of Ancient Africa

Meroitic and Coptic scripts of Nubia; the Amharic, Sabean and G'eez scripts of Ethiopia; the Berber and Carthaginian scripts of North Africa; the Arabic script of North, Northeastern and Western Africa; the Swahili Perso-Arabic script of the East Coast of Africa; the Nsibidi script of Nigeria; the Mende script of Mali; the Toma and Vai scripts of Liberia; and the Mum script of Cameroun (Obenga, 1972: Chapter X). This long list clearly exceeds Europe which has two main scripts, Greek and Roman, but these scripts do not always have abundant historical literatures of either a given people or larger areas of the continent. Documents, then, were not only few but often lost or destroyed, thus adding to the problem. Moreover, the European and Arab conquests led to much destruction also. However, in most parts of Africa, sources of history were essentially griots, a stratum or group of professional oral historians. It was their task to act as the collective memory of an ethnic group, nation or empire and pass on from generation to generation the history of its people. But whereas it is intellectually impressive to remember hundreds of years of key figures, phenomena and processes, it is also a vulnerable form of record keeping. For this "Heritage of the Ears," as the Hova of Madagascar call it, is subject not only to the problems of retention and repetition, but also to the unexpected deaths of the keepers (McCall, 1969:38-62).

Thirdly, and perhaps the most important of the problems of studying African history, is the European conquest of Africa and all that it meant to African history as both record and process. As suggested above, one cannot deny that Europeans destroyed many documents in Africa as well as other evidences of African presence and achievement (Williams, 1974; Diop, 1974, 1991). Moreover, European scholars often denied the value and authenticity of documents and/or their data, if it did not coincide with what they believed or wanted others and themselves to believe. The record of Egyptologists in this matter has been documented by Cheikh Anta Diop. As Diop (1974:168) states, they operated on this principle, "Given what I've been taught about (Blacks), even if the evidence proves objectively that civilization was created by the said Blacks...it must be wrong."

Finally, with the conquest of Africa by Europe came the attempt also to Europeanize or "Caucasize" all important achievements and deny African presence and accomplishments (Drake, 1987). George James (1976) argues this in his contention that the contribution of Egyptians to Greek philosophy is regularly denied. Diop (1974; 1991) shows how Egypt's entire civilization is claimed by whites thru falsification of history, discounting contrary evidence, and arguing racial and racist theories inapplicable to the ancient world. Also, Jackson (1980) and Van Sertima (1992) show how the Moors who brought a high level of civilization to Europe are Caucasized and Arabized to deny their Blackness. Clearly, the Moors are a mixed people, but often the Black or African component is either denied or minimized. And then there are the useful mythical "Hamites" who are trotted out, whenever others are unavailable, to serve as founders of any civilization when it is important to deny its African origins (Fage, 1969:6-10).

However, in spite of these obstacles, significant evidence of African genius and creativity still shine through and provide us with strong foundations for the rescue and reconstruction of Black history and humanity (Davidson, 1991; Bernal, 1987). Given the vastness of the subject, however, this text can in no way be exhaustive or comprehensive. What it will seek to do then is offer some of the many significant models of African political formations and achievements which tend to counter the racist lies and affirm the world historical achievements and significance of African civilization. More detailed and comprehensive treatment of African history can be found in the books cited as references. The student is thus encouraged to explore them, for the exploration will be most informative and engaging.

3.4   THE ORIGINS IN EAST AFRICA

In spite of religious and secular myths about the origins of humans in Mesopotamia five or six thousand years ago, the reality is that humans originated in Africa (Stringer and McKie, 1997; Ki-Zerbo, 1990; Phillipson, 1985). As J. Ki-Zerbo (1990:313) states, "all evidence suggests that the (African) continent was the first — and indeed the principal-center of human development." Evidence suggests that *Australopithecus* Africanus was the first *hominid*, and "was followed by the Zinjanthrope — from the word Zinj or East Africa — which was the first direct ancestor of modern Man" and lived approximately 1.7 million

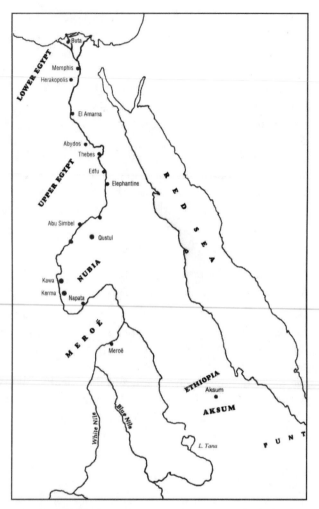

Nile Valley Civilizations

years ago. Homo erectus came next, followed by the Homo sapi-
en type whose features were Africanoid even in Europe. Thus,
"All the links in the chain relating us to the earliest hominids
and pre-hominians are to be found in Africa."

Phillipson (1985:60) notes that "(f)ully modern man H.s.
sapiens (Homo sapiens sapiens) was present, at least in southern
Africa, more than 100,000 years ago," but it was approximately
35,000 years ago, however, that modern humans began to lay the
basis for true human civilization. It is at this point that humans
began to diversify activities from the early total preoccupation

with survival and engage in art and religious reflection. At about 10,000 years ago, humans began to establish cultivation as an alternative to hunting and gathering, thus allowing even more time to lay a basis for expanded cultural development (Curtin, et al, 1990:41). It is estimated that about this time, 8,000 B.C.E. (Before the Common Era), Egypt rose from the waters of the Nile and its lakes and marshes; and thus the basis of habitation and cultivation in the Nile Valley was established (Rice, 1990).

3.5   THE NILE VALLEY CIVILIZATIONS

The flower of ancient African classical civilization originates and flourishes in the Nile Valley civilizations of Nubia, Egypt and Ethiopia. These civilizations represent a complex of cultures which interacted and mutually influenced each other and became a major source and resource of human culture and development.

Diop (1974; 1991), Jackson (1980) and Williams (1974) all argue that Egypt's origin is in Ethiopia, i.e., in the south. DuBois (1965:117ff) agrees stating that "In Ethiopia the sunrise of human culture took place, spreading down into the Nile Valley. Ethiopia, the land of the Blacks, was thus the cradle of Egyptian civilization." In the earliest times, DuBois continues, "the Ethiopians looked upon themselves as the source of Egypt and declared according to Diodorus Siculus that Egyptian laws and custom were of Ethiopian origin. The Egyptians themselves in later days affirmed that their civilization came out of the south." We know now that Ethiopia, like Nubia, was used for all of Africa and also meant the land to the south of Egypt. Nubia was the first of those lands and had a long relationship with Egypt.

NUBIA

It was once argued that Nubia had no civilization which Egypt, her northern neighbor, did not give her. But modern scholarship affirms an indigenous civilization in Nubia that was not only as old if not older than Egypt itself, but also was a rival, equal and ruler of Egypt at various times (Morkot, 2000; Wildung, 1997; Haynes, 1992; Olson and Wegner, 1992; Taylor, 1991).

Delegation of a Nubian princess on a mission to Egypt

The name Nubia seems to have originated from the ancient Egyptian word for gold, *Nub (nbw)* and is first used by the Greek, Strabo, in his Geography "to designate a land which the Greeks called Ethiopia" (Säve-Söderbergh, 1987:14). Nubia was indeed a land of gold, but the Egyptians themselves called it two basic names — *Kash (K3s)* from which we later get Kush and *Ta-Seti,* Land of the Bow, because of the skill and fame of Nubian archers who often served in and fought against the Egyptian army.

Nubia's history stretches back to approximately 3900 B.C.E. and continues in various forms to 1400 C.E. (the Common Era, i.e., this era) (Adams, 1977; Wenig, 1978). The history of Nubia can be divided into four main periods and cultures, all of which except the first period are organized around capital cities. These are the pre-Kerma, the Kerma, the Napatan and the Meroitic periods organized around the capital cities of Kerma, Napata and Meroe respectively.

PRE-KERMA [3900-2500]

The pre-Kerma period of Nubia history and culture begins around 3900 B.C.E. and includes here the peoples anthropologists call A-Group and C-Group. There is evidence to suggest that in this period, Nubia developed a royal dynasty or pharonic kingship system as early as Egypt (Williams, 1989). The pre-Kerma Nubians are farmers, herdspeople and traders. Evidence suggests ongoing contact and trade with Egypt in gold, ivory, ebony, incense, animal skins and pottery.

KERMA [2500-1500]

The Kerma kingdom evolves around 2500 B.C.E. and unites the various peoples into a strong political system. The capital city was a great city distinguished by its defensive fortifications, complex architecture, beautiful courts and gardens, fine pottery and numerous and well-constructed religious and administrative buildings and monuments. The kingdom also plays a key role in a complex trade network which involved exchange north-south and east-west via well-established routes and ports. It is this culture which the Egyptians called and Ta-seti. Nubia is effectively colonized by the Egyptians after almost a century of campaigns in 1500 B.C.E. and they continued to rule it until 1000 B.C.E. Here the Egyptians built temples and tombs, fortresses and trading posts, and exploited Nubia's human and material resources.

NAPATA [900-270]

However, it is the Kingdom of Kush in its Napatan (900-270 B.C.E.) and Meroitic period (270 B.C.E. - 350 C.E.) that is most known in history (Welsh, 1996). From the capital city of Napata, Kushite kings emerged as a powerful political force to unite Nubia and begin to extend their power north to Egypt. The first known leader is King Kashta, father of Piankhi, conqueror of Egypt and founder of the Twenty-Fifth Dynasty of Egypt. Piankhi, also known as Piye, at first simply ruled southern Egypt but upon request of Theban rulers went to Egypt ca. 734 B.C.E.to subdue a local ruler of the Delta, Tefnakht, who had ambitions of ruling all of Egypt. However, he retired to Nubia and left it to his successor to actually rule for approximately a century (756-656 B.C.E.).

He did, however, leave one of Egypt's and Nubia's most impressive pieces of literature, the *Victory Text*, detailing his conquest of Egypt which was discovered in the remains of the Temple of Amen at Napata at the foot of Gebel Barkal, the sacred mountain of Nubia (Schafer, 1905:1-56, Urkunden III). Lichtheim (1980:66) notes that the text reveals that Piankhi was a powerful, intelligent and generous king, "preferred treaties to warfare, and when he fought did not glory in the slaughter of his adversaries in the manner of an Assyrian king."

Passage from King Piankhi's Victory Text (see partial translation below)

A deeply religious man, Piankhi begins saying,

> "Hear what I accomplished, beyond the ancestors. I am a King, the image of God, the living likeness of God, Atum. One who came forth from the womb established as a ruler. One who is shown deference by another greater than he. One whom his father knew and his mother perceived would be a ruler while he was still in the egg. The good divine one, beloved of the divine ones. The Son of Ra. One who acts with his arms." Piankhi, Beloved of God, Amen (Urk.III:4:1-2)."

Moreover, he tells his troops before battle to pray and give praise to Amen Ra. "For there is no strength for the mighty without Amen Ra. He makes the weak armed into the strong armed, so that the multitudes flee from the feeble and one alone takes a thousand captive." Therefore, he continues, "Anoint yourselves with the waters of his altars and bow down to the earth before Him and say make for us a way that we might fight in the shadow of your strong arm. For when young men who you have sent forth launch their attack, the multitudes tremble before them" (Urk.III, 12-14).

Another important king of this period is Shabaka known for copying and preserving "a work of the ancestors" called both "The Memphite Theology" and the "Shabaka Text." In any case, it is the earliest record of creation described as an act of creative thought and speech and prefigures the logos doctrine of Christianity (Breasted, 1934:37; Lichtheim, 1975;51ff; Karenga, 1989:375ff). Here the Creator, conceives creation in his heart/mind (*ib*), as an expression of wisdom or exceptional insight (*Sia*) and through authoritative utterance (*Hu*), brings the world into being.

King Shabaka making offerings to Amen Ra

In Nubia, as in Egypt and other parts of Africa, there is sacred or divine kingship. Moreover, Nubian kings adopted the Egyptian custom of designating themselves as the Son of Ra and the queens followed this custom also. Two notable features of the Nubia kingship and queenship is the emergence of the office of High Priestess of Amen and the strengthening of the role of the Queen Mother. The High Priestess had three different titles — the Divine Wife, the Adorer of God and the Hand of God — and was an office exercised by the King's daughter and passed on through adoption. This gave her equal economic and political power and influence in the government. Her representative was called Chief Steward as in the case of one Harwa, who was an important person in the administration of the country (Lichtheim, 1980:24ff). Harwa says of his patron, Amenirdis, Adorer of God, "My Lady made me great when I was a small boy. She advanced my position when I was a child." He goes on to say he went on missions for the King and his Lady and that "Every

mission on which their majesties sent me, I accomplished it correctly. I never told a lie about it." Speaking of his virtues as a person and civil servant, he says:

"I have done what the people love and God praises. I was one truly venerated and without fault. One who gave bread to the hungry and clothes to the naked. I put an end to pain and erased wrongdoing. I buried the blessed, supported the aged and satisfied the needs of the have-nots. I was a shelter for the child and a helper for the widow." (Karenga, 1984:93; Lichtheim, 1980:27).

The Divine Wife of Amen, Amenirdis, 25th Dynasty

This declaration of virtue reflects the moral standards and quality of leadership the Divine Wife expected.

The second female position of importance in government was that of queen mother. In Meroitic, the word is *Ktke* or *Kdke* or in English Candace or Kandake which became a well-known title in Greco-Roman times. The title transforms from queen mother with power to the office of queen in the second century B.C.E. under queen or Kandake Shanankdekhete (Hakem, 1990:175). Also, as Hakem points out, beginning with Queen Amenirenas in the first century B.C.E., another important development takes place. "This was the close association of the first wife of the king and perhaps their eldest son on so many of the important monuments." Such an association tends to suggest "some degree of coregency since the wife who survived her husband often became the reigning *Candace*."

The end of Kushite rule of Egypt which had lasted 100 years ended with the invasion of Assyrian armies and King Tantumani's retreat to the Nubian capital of Napata in approximately 656 B.C.E. This effectively ended the Twenty-Fifth

Dynasty. However, the Kushite kings continued to use the titles of kingship from Egypt throughout the Meroitic period.

MEROE [195 - 320]

The Meroitic period (270 B.C.E.- 350 C.E.) begins with the shift of the capital to Meroe, a city located further south in Nubia. Meroe was a great city with exquisite palaces, an observatory, magnificent temples, pools and foundations, excellent arts and crafts, and large industrial complexes especially built around a large iron industry. They also engaged in trade and were like other Nubian kingdoms middle men in the trade between the south and the north. The relations with the Greeks, who had conquered Egypt in 332 B.C.E., tended to be mutually respectful, especially in the third century under King Arkamani, and known to the Greeks as Ergamenes, who was said to have had a Greek education. He also joined in temple building projects with the Greek whom he allowed to build temples in the northern part of Lower Egypt and to live and work at his court (Säve-Söderbergh, 1987:39).

Meroe's relations with the Romans were less friendly and "following the Roman conquest of Egypt (30 B.C.E.), the Meroites attacked and sacked Philae and Aswan." And "in triumph, they carried home statues of the (Roman) Emperor Augustus erected at the Roman boundary" and buried at least one head under a palace (Säve-Söderbergh, 1987:39). In retaliation, the Romans sacked Napata in 25 B.C.E., but the Queen (Kandake) of Meroe, possibly Amenirenas, responded, driving the Romans back north and readjusting the borders between Roman-controlled Egypt and Nubia. She thus won back the whole of Nubia, a control which lasted until the conquest of Nubia by Axum in 325 C.E.

Even with the fall of Meroe to Axum, Nubia produced another kingdom called the Ballana culture (350-550 C.E.). By the 6th century C.E. three kingdoms had emerged in Nubia — Nobadia, Makuria and Alwa. In this period the Nubians became Christians and maintained their kingdom until 1400 when the Muslims conquered them. Thus, Nubia has a history of 5300 years from 3900 B.C.E. to 1400 C.E. and a record of noteworthy achievements in the arts, architecture, literature, industry and international relations.

EGYPT

The civilization of Egypt represents the full flowering of African culture in antiquity (Diop, 1991; Siliotti, 1996). As Bruce Trigger (1983:1) states "Through pharaonic Egypt, Africa lays claim to being the cradle of one of the earliest and most spectacular civilizations of antiquity." In fact, one could say Egypt was the greatest civilization in antiquity, for neither Sumer, Babylonia nor any other earlier civilizations equalled her achievement (Trigger, 1983; Gardiner, 1961).

THE CHRONOLOGY

Egypt's chronology is divided into several periods: a "prehistorical" period, a predynastic period and a series of dynastic periods. It is the dynastic periods with which we will concern ourselves. The first period of Egyptian history is called the Early Dynastic period (c.3100-2686 B.C.E.). An important artistic and historical item in this period is the Narmer Palette which shows the King Narmer wearing both the White Crown of Upper Egypt (South) and the Red Crown of Lower Egypt (North), indicating he ruled the two kingdoms of Upper and Lower Egypt. The king came from the south and conquered the north, establishing a unified state approximately 3100 B.C.E., calling it the Two Lands, *Tawy*. Also Egypt was called *Kemet*, Land of the Blacks or the Black Land, and *Ta Meri*, the Beloved Land. In this same period, writing and irrigation are also established. Although the name Narmer is mentioned on this document, Menes or Mena is considered the traditional founder of the First Dynasty. However, it is not known whether Mena is King Narmer or King Aha or both. What is clear is that the state establishes a large bureaucracy and that "in the course of the Early Dynastic Period, artisans and civil servants working for the central government were to fashion the highly sophisticated traditions of art and learning that thereafter were to constitute the basic pattern of Pharaonic civilization" (Trigger, 1983:50).

But it is in the Old Kingdom period (c. 2686-2182 B.C.E.) that Kemetic culture flowers. It is in this period that Imhotep, the master architect, under King Zoser or Djoser, builds the first pyramid, a step-pyramid at Saqqara. Imhotep is the world's first recorded multidimensional man, being, in addition to the royal architect, a philosopher, priest, astronomer, prime minister, engineer, teacher and chief physician to the king. In fact, it can be said he was the father of medicine and his "fame in later times was so great that he was ultimately venerated as a god and equated by the Greeks with Asklepios, their own god of healing" (James, 1979:44).

In the Fourth Dynasty, King Khufu builds the Great Pyramid at Giza which contained over 1,300,000 blocks of stone with an average weight of two and one-half tons a piece. King Khafra (Chephren) builds a smaller pyramid near Khufu's and a Sphinx which is said to be in his image. The Fifth Dynasty sees the emergence of the oldest texts in history, the *Pyramid Texts*, found in the Pyramids of Unas, Teti and Pepi, the last king of the Fifth Dynasty, and the first two of the Sixth Dynasty respectively. Moreover, the *Declarations of Virtues*, statements of career and moral claims, evolve and give a moral portrait of Kemetic life. Already in the *Pyramid Texts*, Unas states that he wishes to be judged in the afterlife by what he has done on earth. And he affirms that "no one alive or dead accuses him and neither does beast or bird" (Lichtheim, 1975:35).

In his *Declarations of Virtue*, Harkuf, a noble, justifies himself before history and heaven saying, "I was one worthy. One beloved of his father, praised by his mother, and one whom all his sisters and brothers loved. I gave bread to the hungry, clothes to the naked and brought the boatless to (dry) land. I was one who spoke justly, who repeated that which was pleasing to hear. I never spoke evilly against any one to his or her superior. For I wished to stand well with God" (Karenga, 1984:94,95). Again, these *Declarations of Virtues* yield an important portrait of the Kemetic concept of morality.

Joined to this type of moral literature is the evolution of the *Sebait* or *Books of Wise Instruction* which also contained Egyptian moral philosophy. In the oldest complete Sebait the Book of Ptah-hotep, we are introduced to the concept of *Maat*, the central moral and spiritual concept in Kemetic society. *Maat* means many things, including truth, justice, propriety, harmony, balance, reciprocity and order — in a word, rightness in the divine, natural and social realms. Ptah-hotep tells us "Maat is great, its value is lasting and it has remained unchanged since the time of the Creator. It lies as a (plain) path even before the uninformed and those who violate its laws are punished. Although wicked-

Imhotep, builder of the first pyramid, architect, prime minister, philosopher-teacher, father of medicine

ness may gain wealth, wrong-doing has never brought its wares to a (safe) port. In the end, it is Maat (the way of truth, justice and righteousness) which lasts and enables one to say it is the legacy of my father (and mother)" (Karenga, 1984:41).

It is this tradition of excellence and achievement which marks the Old Kingdom that continues throughout Egyptian history at varying levels through periods called the First Intermediate Period (c. 2181-2050 B.C.E.); the Middle Kingdom (c. 2050-1786 B.C.E.); the Second Intermediate Period (c. 1786-1567 B.C.E.); the New Kingdom (c. 1567-1085 B.C.E.); and the Late Period (c.1085-332 B.C.E. The Intermediate periods were periods of decentralization and weak central government. And 332 B.C.E. marks the conquest of Egypt by Alexander, the Macedonian Greek. Within this 3000 year period of history, Egypt left an important and impressive legacy for both Africa and the world. And it is to this legacy to which we now turn.

THE LEGACY

The legacy of Egypt is awesome and occurs in several disciplines of human knowledge (Freeman, 1997; Diop, 1987, 1991; Harris, 1971). First, Egypt made a significant contribution in the area of spirituality and ethics, giving the world some of its most important spiritual and ethical concepts (Karenga, 1994; Diop, 1991; Breasted, 1934). These include concepts of resurrection and judgment after death; the immortality of the soul; immortality through righteous living; humans as the image of God; the related concept of humans as bearers of dignity; the equality of men and women; the treatment of the vulnerable and poor as the fundamental measure of the moral quality of a society; and the moral obligation to constantly repair and heal the world (*serudj ta*) making it more beautiful and beneficial than when we inherited it. As mentioned above, Egypt provides a rich, ancient and varied ethical and spiritual literature in which these concepts and others were introduced and developed (see chapter 5 Black Religion).

Secondly, another major contribution which ancient Egyptians made was in the field of agriculture. By 5000 B.C.E., they had transformed the Nile Valley from a food-gathering economy to a food-producing economy laying the basis for a settled life and thus a life of varied intellectual and cultural pursuits. In the field of agriculture, they developed the practice of irrigation and a nilometer to measure and control water levels. Moreover, animal domestication and husbandry were likewise a part of this body of knowledge.

Having gained the capacity for a settled life, the Kemites began to diversify thought and practice and produced various crafts and professions. These included cloth weaving, woodworking, shipbuilding, glass-making, leatherwork, pottery production, metallurgy and mining in gold, silver, and copper as well as its alloys, brass and bronze. Moreover, craftsmanship involved work in precious stones such as turquoise, carnelian, lapis lazuli, feldspar and amethyst. These activities in metal and mineral use required and produced techniques, i.e., forging, casting, riveting, soldering, stamping and hammering, and tools such as mallets, adzes, chisels, saws, drills, etc. These techniques, tools and the products were spread throughout the then known world.

Especially is Egypt known for its excellence in stonemasonry and architecture which included massive works in granite, diorite, limestone, basalt and gneiss. This work, of course, culminates in the masterful construction of the pyramids which are scientific, technical, aesthetic and religious masterpieces dedicated to God, Ra. As an allied field of architecture, the Kemites developed the discipline of engineering, laying out cities, building dams, dikes and canals, pools, ponds, gardens and courtyards, reservoirs, fortresses, and the instruments to measure, shape and complete these projects.

Egypt also contributed to science and math leaving "a valuable legacy in the fields of physics, chemistry, zoology, geology, medicine, pharmacology, geometry and applied mathematics" (El Nadoury, 1990:107). These include the science of mummification, surgery and medicine as outlined and explained in the *Edwin Smith Papyrus*, the *Ebers Papyrus* and the *Berlin Papyrus*. These documents reveal knowledge and treatment of major and minor diseases and disorders. In fact, as Rogers (1972:38-42) notes, the ancient Egyptians had diagnosed, treated and catalogued over 200 diseases and were conducting surgery and auscultation and were aware of blood circulation.

In mathematics, the *Moscow Papyrus* and the *Rhind Papyrus* reveal the Kemite knowledge of arithmetic, algebra and geometry. In fact, ancient Egyptians were credited by the Greeks (Herodotus and Strabo) as having invented geometry. They were knowledgeable of how to calculate a circle, triangle, the volume of a cylinder, a hemisphere and appear to be knowledgeable of *pi*. As shown in the *Carlsberg 1* and *Carlsberg 9 Papyri*, ancient Egyptians had an excellent knowledge of astronomy. They divided the year into 12 months, the day into 24 hours and gave us the 365 day calendar year on which the current calendar year is based.

In the discipline of art, the Kemites left countless examples

The Rhind Mathematical Papyrus of ancient Egypt

Maiy and Werer, a noble couple, 18th Dynasty

of not only architecture of great aesthetic value, especially columns, temples, and palaces, but also fine paintings, reliefs and sculpture. In literature one has in ancient Egypt copies of the oldest books in the world. These include the *Pyramid Texts*, the oldest religious texts in the world; the oldest medical texts, as mentioned above; the oldest social justice text, the *Book of Khun-Anup* (The Eloquent Peasant); and the oldest ethical texts, the *Declarations of Virtues*. In addition, we find various forms of creative literature, poems, plays, narratives and histories. In the area of religion, as noted above, ancient Egypt has the oldest religious and ethical texts and apparently contributed to the formulation of both the Jewish-Christian-Islamic tradition as well as Greek philosophy (Diop, 1991; Bernal, 1991, 1987; James, 1976; Breasted, 1934).

Finally, ancient Egypt contributed both the technique of and the art of writing, using three systems, hieroglyphic, hieratic and demotic and also the paper on which to write. In fact the word paper has its origins in the word *papyrus*, the Greek word for the plant material on which the Egyptians wrote. The ancient Egyptians themselves called the plant by various names (*mnh*, *w3d̲*, etc.); the blank papyrus roll — (*shw*); and one with writing — (*md̲3t*, *t3w*, *sfdw*, etc.) Yet in considering all these achievements, it is important to remember DuBois' (1965:103) contention that the "first great experiment in human civilization" rose out of African problem-solving, out of the need to shape their world in their own image and interest. "The history of civilization which began in Egypt was not so much a matter of dynasties and dates," DuBois states. Rather, "It was an attempt to settle the problems of living together, of government, defense, religion, family, property, science and art." Therefore, to meet the challenges of nature and society, "African Egypt...made the beginning and set the pace...in these seven lines of human endeavor."

Given that the legacy of ancient Kemet is an extensive and

far-reaching one, it has become contested ground. For as Diop observes, its real history reveals a debt to Africa that Eurocentric and racist thinking can neither concede nor accept. And this has led to the falsification of both African and human history. Thus, new research and fresh and fruitful thinking are needed to reverse and end this state of things (Diop, 1991; Bernal, 1987).

ETHIOPIA/AKSUM

Although Ethiopia was a name once used for the whole of Africa, as mentioned above, Ethopia as a country has its own particular and impressive history. Ethiopian history evolves from the formation of the state of Aksum which had its origins in the economic and cultural exchange between Africans and peoples in southwestern Arabia, beginning around 500 B.C.E.(El Mahdi, 1965; Pankhurst, 1967; Shinnie, 1967). The evolving state speaks the classical Ethiopian language of Ge'ez which has its own script and which merged with Cushitic linguistic elements to form modern Amharic, the major language of Ethiopia. Aksum's rapid growth and expansion is linked to two major factors. First, its growth is linked to its developing an extensive trade at the seaport of Adulis which becomes its capital city. It is strategically located between the Red Sea and the Indian Ocean and takes advantage of this position to develop extensive trade with Nubians, Egyptians, Greeks, Persians, Indians and later Romans. The Aksumite exports include ivory, glass, crystal, copper, brass, frankincense and myrrh. Some of their main imports were spices, silks and other fines clothes.

Secondly, their rapid expansion is linked to the development and spread of iron technology which not only enhanced agricultural development, but also military power and practices (Sergev, 1972). Thus, Aksum's expansion into an empire is facilitated by this technology and it begins to conquer principalities around it. Moreover, it went on to conquer Southern Arabia and integrated the kingdom of Saba there into its political system. It is from this history that the legendary Makeda, Queen of Saba (Sheba) emerges (Budge, 1970, Vol. I:193-204).

The Aksumites also farm and herd cattle and sheep, and like the ancient Egyptians and Nubians, develop a high level of skill and artistry in the crafts and trades of metal working, pottery, carving, architecture and stonemasonry. They built **impressive**

An ancient Ethiopian obelisk of Aksum

temples, palaces, tombs and massive stone monuments, usually at the site of a ruler's tomb. These tall and thin monuments of stone are called obelisks or stelae. The tallest of these signature monuments was seven-hundred (700) tons and stood approximately 105 feet high.

Aksum's most famous king and emperor was Ezana (320-350 C.E.) who converted to Christianity and established it as the state religion. He is known for his defeat of Nubia which eventually lead to its decline and transformation into smaller states. Ezana, like Ramsess, the Great, left an extensive treasure of monuments and inscriptions. These inscriptions record his achievements and deeds, especially his military campaigns, and are written in Ge'ez, Sabean, Himyaritic and Greek. Certainly, one of his most important inscriptions is the one recording his defeat of the Noba or Nubians in approximately 325 C.E. It is important not only for the historical record of this defeat of another great African civilization, but also for its reflection of Ezana's ethical conception of rulership and his commitment to rule his people with righteousness and justice (Budge, 1970, Vol. I:252-258).

He begins saying:

> "By the power of the Lord of Heaven, who in heaven and upon earth is mightier than everything which exists, Ezana, the son of Ella Amida, a native of Halen, King of Aksum and of Himyar and of Raydan and of Saba, and of Salhen and of Seyamo, and of Bega and Kasu, King of Kings, the son of Ella Amida, who is invincible to the enemy. By the might of the Lord of Heaven, who has made me lord, who through all eternity, the Perfect One, reigns. Who is invincible to the enemy; no enemy shall stand before me, and after me no enemy shall follow."

He then goes on to relate how he made war of the Noba and defeated them and he ends this long inscription committing himself to rule righteously and justly and calls on the people to protect the throne and the earth on which it is established. He says:

ወተክልኩ | መንበረ | በዝየ | በሡዶ| በጎይ
ለ | እግዚአ | ሰማይ | ዘውእቱ | እርደአኒ | ወወሀበኒ | መንግሥተ | እ
ግዚአ | ሰማይ | የጽንዕ | መንግሥትየ | ወከመ | ዮም | ሞአ ሊተ | ፀርየ [|]
ለይማእ | ሊተ | ወአደ | ሐርኩ | ከመ | ዮም | ሞአ | ሊተ | ወእ ግነየ | ሊተ | ፀ
ርየ | በጽድቅ | ወበርትዕ | እንዘ | ኢኢጌምዕ | እሕዛበ | ወእመሕፀ ኑ | ዘመንበረ | ዘተከልኩ | ለእግዚአ | ሰማይ | ዘአንገሡን | ወለም ድር | ዘይጸውር | ለእመቦ | ዘነቀሉ | ወአግሰና | ወነሡፉ | ውእቱ | ወ

Passage from Emperor Ezana's Victory Text

"I have established this throne here in Shado by the might of the Lord of Heaven, who has helped me and given me sovereignty. May the Lord of Heaven make strong my kingdom. And as he has this day conquered for me my enemy, may he conquer for me wheresoever I go. And as he has this day conquered for me, and overthrown for me my enemy, [I will rule] the people with righteousness and justice and will not oppress them. And may they preserve this throne which I have (established) for the Lord of Heaven who has made me king and the earth which carries it."

Aksum prospered under Ezana and afterward extending its rule to parts of Nubia and Saba as mentioned above. But by the seventh century, it had lost its hold in Saba to the Persians and was weakened in its trading position to both the Persians and Arabs. Also, like Nubia, it suffered from environmental deterioration and eventually lost its position as a major power in the region. Aksum began a slow revival in about 1000 C.E. and began a rapid expansion as a strong state under the Zagwe Dynasty who took power from the rulers of the Aksumite state in about 1150. The Zagwe are known for their rebuilding international relations and building one of the great wonders of the world, eleven churches out of the mountains in the region of their capital Adefa. This region was eventually named after the emperor who commissioned them, Lalibela (1200-1250). The Zagwe rulers were overthrown in 1250 by the Solomonic Dynasty who justified their kingship through the legacy of Aksum and the legendary union of the Hebrew King Solomon and the Sabean Queen Makeda (Tamrat, 1972). It is this line that extended to the last Ethiopian emperor Haile Selassie who was overthrown in 1974.

No other African country holds for African people on the Continent and in the Diaspora, the mystique and meaning that Ethiopia has. It is a special land with religious, cultural and political meaning for Africans everywhere and thus a continuous and core focus in Africana Studies.

3.6   THE WESTERN SUDANIC CIVILIZATIONS

The Sudanic civilizations of Ghana, Mali and Songhai are characterized by continuity and similarity (Osae, Mwabara and Odunsi, 1973: Part One; Davidson, 1977: Chapters 2-5, 7). They follow each other and build on each other's legacy. Moreover, they are heavily influenced by their interaction with the world Islamic community, especially Mali and Songhai. This interaction is expressed in the growth of commerce, scholarship and international relations. Also, they are societies defined by large and powerful armies, able rulers and industrious peoples.

GHANA

Ghana emerged as a state in approximately 300 C.E. It reached its height in the eleventh century and came to an effective political end in 1240. As early as 773-4 C.E., the Muslim author Al-Fazari wrote of Ghana, calling it the Land of Gold. Also, other Muslim authors wrote of Ghana and its wealth and importance to the trans-Saharan trade. Among these were al-Yaqubi in the ninth century, al-Mas'udin and Ibn Hawqal in the

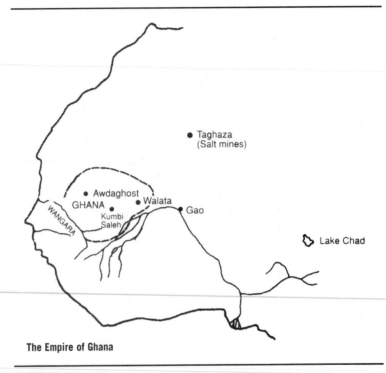

The Empire of Ghana

tenth century. But the most definitive report of the early Muslim writers was *The Description of North Africa* (1067) written by al-Bakri, a Moor who lived in the Moorish empire in Spain and who was also a geographer. However, two West African Muslims, Mahmud Kati who wrote Tarikh al Fattakh (*History of the Seeker After Knowledge*) and Abdul-Rahman as-Sadi who wrote Tarikh as-Sudan (*History of the Sudan*) also wrote on Ghana, as well as on the other Sudanic civilizations.

From al-Bakri's report and other sources, we know that Ghana's wealth was a result of the control of trade in two key items — salt and gold. Strategically located along routes of the trans-Saharan trade, Ghana controlled the flow of trade and levied import and export taxes on the traders. Ghana controlled two main routes which stretched north to Morocco and Libya and West to the Bornu region near Lake Chad which tied in with the Nile Valley trade (Harris, 1987:51). Moreover, the report reveals that Ghana's capital city, Kumbi Saleh, had two sections — one for the King or Tunka and Ghanaian people and the other for the Muslim traders.

Tunka Menin, the king of the time, circa 1065, was an

absolute monarch with an elaborate court of counselors, ministers, interpreters and a treasurer. Much revered, he held court with impressive splendor often ruling on great and small matters. Moreover, he maintained a large standing army of 200,000 and more than 40,000 were bowman. To gauge how impressive and politically powerful this was, one can remember that about this time, the Norman army which conquered England in 1066 was only 15,000 strong. Recognizing the rise of Islam and Muslim popularity in his empire, Tunka Menin showed political and economic wisdom by appointing several Muslims as ministers, treating all Muslims justly and allowing them to practice their religion freely. This not only contributed to peace in the empire, but received the economic benefit of good relations and increased trade with the Muslim North.

The trans-Saharan trade was brisk and varied passing thru towns like Walata, Kumbi Saleh, Tichitl and Awdaghost. From the North, traders brought salt, daggers, silk, jewelry, time pieces and fine cloth. From other parts of the Sudan, they brought bars of iron, gold, leather, cotton, kola nuts, shea butter, millet and sorghum. At the peak of its empire, Ghana contained a population of several million and a territory of about 250,000 square miles. Its imperial might rested on the 200,000 man army, its control of trade and the revenues from it, as well as good political administration which was able to keep revolts at a minimum and put them down when and if they occurred. In 1076, religious reformers called Almoravids led a Berber army which captured Kumbi Saleh. By 1087, however, they had lost control of the empire and Ghana disintegrated into smaller states, laying the basis for the rise of Mali.

MALI

The empire of Mali has its roots in the state of Kangaba, a small state which was part of the Ghana Empire. The first Malian emperor was Sundiata, who defeated his rivals, established his rule in approximately 1230 and reigned until his death in 1255. During this time, he took control of the trans-Saharan trade and set up Niani, his capital as a key trading and financial center. He also turned his attention to agriculture, transforming many of his soldiers, who now had no wars to fight, into farmers.

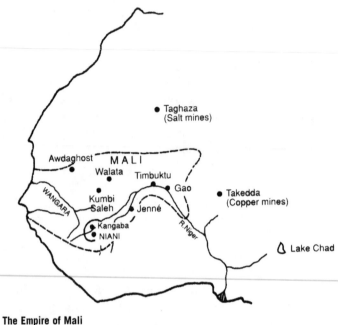

The Empire of Mali

This attention to agriculture paid off in a few years and Mali established itself as one of the richest farming areas in West Africa.

Mali's most illustrious and well-known emperor was Mansa (emperor) Musa who came to the throne in 1312 and ruled until 1332. In his brief reign, he built Mali into one of the world's largest empires and his fame spread throughout the Muslim world and Europe. Conquering most of the major Berber cities of the western desert, Musa extended Mali into what is now Mauritania and southern Algeria in the north, and as far south as northern Nigeria to establish contact with the Hausa states. By the time of his death, he had made Mali twice the size of Ghana with a population of approximately ten million.

Mansa Musa is best known, however, for his famous hajj or pilgrimage to Mecca in 1324. With him he took 60,000 persons, many of them soldiers, baggage men, and royal secretaries to record this momentous trip. Also included were friends, doctors, teachers and local political leaders. To finance the trip, Musa took 80-100 camel loads of gold dust. Passing thru Cairo, he was honored and given royal assistance from the Sultan of Cairo for the remainder of his trip. In Mecca and Medina, he gave gifts generously and on his return trip he passed thru Cairo again giving out so much gold, he depressed the price of gold in Egypt. One writer in the service of the Sultan stated that it took twelve years for the Egyptian economy to recover from Musa's generosity with gold.

Musa went through Cairo, Mecca, Medina and Tripoli and brought back many Muslim scholars, jurists, architects and other skilled men, among them African scholars from the University of Fez, Morocco. This had a tremendous impact on the development of African civilization. Among the many architects who returned with Musa was as-Saheli, a Moor from Granada who was also a poet. as-Saheli constructed many buildings in Mali, especially mosques and a palace for Musa. Most importantly, however, he built the University of Sankore at Timbuktu which became an intellectual center which attracted students and professors from all over the Muslim world. Also Musa encouraged learning, building many Quranic schools which taught reading and writing especially of the Quran. In addition, he sent ambassadors to Egypt and Morocco and representatives to many North African and Sudanic cities and the forest kingdoms near the Coast.

Mansa Musa laid the basis for European recognition and respect of Africa below the Sahara during that time. European scholars and traders were aware of his empire and in 1375 Charles V of France had an atlas drawn showing "Rex Melli" or "Musa Mali" in the area of West Africa wearing robes and a crown and holding a gold nugget in one hand and a scepter in the other. Mansa Musa left a strong impression on the African, Muslim and European world and a strong empire so that even when Mali was in decline in 1494, the Portuguese sought and established diplomatic relations and exchanged ambassadors with Mali. Mali began to decline in 1400 and in 1468, Songhai began its rise.

SONGHAI

The largest and greatest of the Western Sudanic civilizations was Songhai. Songhai's foundation was laid by Sunni (Sonni) Ali Ber who came to the throne in 1464 and recaptured Timbuktu in 1468 from Mali, the year usually fixed as the begin-

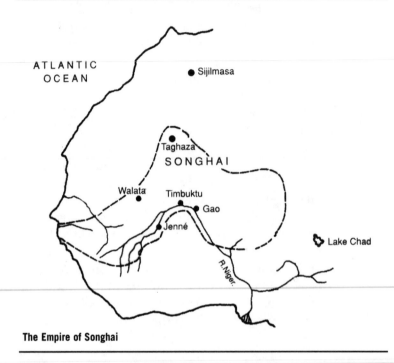

The Empire of Songhai

ning of the Songhai Empire. Sunni Ali was described by as-Sadi, author of Tarikh as-Sudan, (*History of the Sudan*), as a brutal and fierce tyrant. Sunni was the title of Ali's dynasty and Ber means "the Great," a name established thru fierce and uncompromising conquest by this warrior-king. During the twenty-eight years of his reign, he was always at war and on the march, defeating all challengers and strengthening his army thru a systematic build-up of his cavalry. He even drafted soldiers from vassal states and built a navy of war canoes which sailed the Niger. By the time of his death, he had consolidated and greatly expanded his empire and laid the basis for the renowned glories of Songhai.

The most illustrious emperor of Songhai was Muhammad Toure, a distinguished general who served in Sunni Ali's army. Muhammad, who bore the title Askia (general), showed himself an able administrator as well as general. Ruling form 1493-1529, he built an effective army out of POW's and men formerly enslaved whom he freed and put into service to the empire. He based his administration on Islamic law, built a support system among the learned and the wealthy urbanites of Gao, Jenne and Timbuktu and surrounded himself with professionals in law and administration to insure uniform justice in the empire.

It is Askia Muhammad, also called Askia the Great, who built the largest empire in the history of West and Central Africa. DuBois (1975:47-48) states that Askia Muhammad "during his reign conquered and consolidated an empire two thousand miles long by one thousand miles wide at its greatest extent — a territory as large as all Europe." He divided this great empire into a series of provinces and appointed professional administrators as governors. Emulating Mansa Musa of Mali, Askia Muhammad made a spectacular hajj to Mecca in 1495. With him he took 300,000 pieces of gold which he used for expenses, gifts and purchases. At Mecca, he was appointed as Caliph of the Western Sudan by the Sharif of Mecca, who was the spiritual ruler of all Islam. This had both political and religious ramifications, for it give him claim to allegiance of all Muslims westward to the Atlantic. It also put him in a united front of Muslims against the encroaching Christians and cemented his conquests and economic relations with the Muslim world.

Askia Muhammad is also responsible for a flowering of intellectual achievement. In Gao, Jenne and Timbuktu, many universities and schools were established. The universities taught philosophy, medicine, law, government, astronomy, math, literature, ethnography, hygiene, logic, rhetoric, grammar, geography, music and poetry writing. Scholars and students from other parts of Africa, Asia, the Muslim world and Europe visited the universities for study and exchange. One of the famous scholars at the University of Sankore at Timbuktu was professor Ahmad Baba, who was a faculty member, an author of forty books on such diverse fields as astronomy, ethnography, biography and theology, Islamic law, and owner of a library of 1600 volumes (Jackson, 1980:217). So enduring are his works that thirteen of them are still used in part of West Africa. This was also the time of the famous *Tarikhs* (Histories) of Western Sudanic civilization by Mahmud Kati and Abdul-Rahman as-Sadi.

In 1528, Askia the Great, who was now blind, was deposed by his son Musa, ending a brilliant and enlightened reign. The empire saw few dramatic developments after his reign and due to weak leadership, revolts sprang up and continuously increased. Finally, in 1591 a Moroccan army, led by a Spanish Christian who had converted to Islam and composed of captured Christians, Spanish Muslims and Moroccans, set out to attack and sack Songhai. The fire power of the army, which had lost many of its members crossing the Sahara, prevailed and the Songhai troops retreated down the Niger. Although the Moroccans held the main cities, they could not hold the empire, for Songhai troops continuously harassed them with guerilla warfare. Eventually, the empire disintegrated into city states and the Moroccans were assimilated into the indigenous populace. Songhai, the greatest and largest empire of the Western Sudanic civilization had thus come to an end.

3.7   THE MOORISH EMPIRE IN SPAIN

The Moorish empire in Spain represents not only a golden age in Islamic civilization, but also a golden age of civilization for Africa, Europe and ultimately the world (Jayyusi, 2000; Kennedy, 1997). In a era of multiculturalism, scholarly research has begun to concede the major contribution of Moors and Muslims to world civilization, but there is still strong reluctance to recognize and discuss the African component in this multicultural people and civilization of Africans, Arabs and Berbers. Once called "Black-a-Moors" by Europeans to indicate their dark color and African origins in the process of revisionist history, they became more and more simply Muslims and less and less Africans. This falsification of history is challenged by African scholars who have continued to remind the world of African presence in and contribution to Moorish civilization. And they have also reminded us of the Moorish civilization's contribution to Europe in numerous and highly significant ways.

In his *Introduction to African Civilizations*, John Jackson (1980) devotes a chapter to "Africa and the Civilizing of Europe." In it he builds a strong case for Europe's debt to Africans, namely Moors, who raised the Spaniards out of the period (500-1000 C.E.) which Europeans call the "Dark Ages" and gave them a civilization no other country in Europe had at the time, but from which all Europe would eventually borrow. More recently, Ivan Van Sertima (1992) has edited a text titled *Golden Age of the Moors* in which various scholars, including Jackson, offer critical perspectives on this extensive contribution, using the latest data in the field. James Ravell's (1992:407-454) bibliographic essay, titled "Annotated Bibliography of the

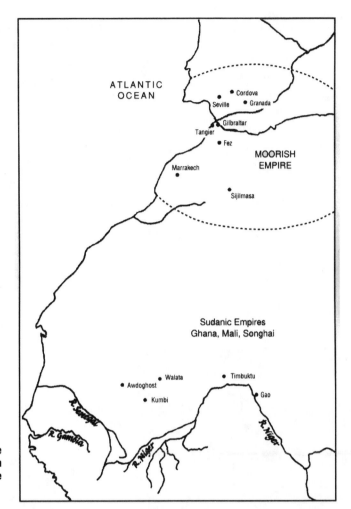

ATLANTIC
OCEAN

● Cordova
Seville ● ● Granada
▲ Gilbraltar
Tangier ●
● Fez

MOORISH
EMPIRE

Marrakech ●

● Sijilmasa

Sudanic Empires
Ghana, Mali, Songhai

● Walata   ● Timbuktu
● Awdoghost
● Kumbi   ● Gao

R. Senegal
R. Gambia
R. Niger
R. Niger

**The
Moorish
Empire**

Moors: 711-1492 A.C." is extensive and extremely useful for further research and reference.

The Moorish conquest and cultural transformation of Spain
began in 711. In that year, Tarik, a Moorish general, landed in
Spain near a cliff later named Jebel Tarik, the Rock or Mountain
of Tarik, i.e. Gibraltar, in his honor. After conquering some
towns near Gibraltar, Tarik met and defeated Roderick, King of
the Visigoths in Spain at the Battle of Xeres. This marked the
beginning of Spain's golden age which she has never since duplicated (McCabe, 1935; Lane-Poole, 1886). The Moors brought
Spain and thus Europe several gifts from African creativity and
inventiveness, including agriculture, engineering, mining,

industry, manufacturing, expanded commerce, beautiful skilled architecture and education and scholarship (Van Sertima, 1992; Burckhardt, 1999; Jayyusi, 2000).

In agriculture, the Moors brought new products, but also skill and literature in the field. They introduced rice, strawberries, cotton, sugar cane, ginger, lemons and dates. Ibn-al-Awam and Abu Zacaria produced scholarly works on agriculture and husbandry. As late as 1802, Ibn-al-Awam's treatise on agriculture was being translated and used in Spain. As first-rate engineers, the Moors built Spain its aqueduct system for irrigation, its reservoirs for water, underground silos for grain, tunnels thru mountains, raised sidewalks, lighted paved streets and dams. They also built a sewer system and artificial lakes to beautify cities. In the areas of mining and manufacturing they mined gold, silver, copper, tin, lead, iron and alum and made luxury and utilitarian items out of these and brass. In addition, the Moors were respected for their fine jewelry mosaics, pottery and glass work, tile and fine silk and cotton products. It

is, in fact, the Moors who introduced cotton manufacture to Europe. Finally, Jackson (1980:188) states that also "the Moors introduced the manufacture of gunpowder in Europe." Given this economic boom, the Moors also engaged in shipbuilding and expanded trade. This maritime commerce on the Mediterranean by the Moors and other Muslims was greater than that of the Christians and maintained its dominance up to the 12th century.

In terms of architecture, the Moors built structures not simply for use, but equally for aesthetic value. Their arches, courtyards and gardens are reflected in the architecture of California and the Southwest with its so-called Spanish motif. Actually, it is

Court of the Lions, Alhambra, Moorish Seat of Government in Spain

Moorish motif passed on thru the Spanish to the Mexicans from which the white Americans borrowed. In Cordova alone in the 10th century, there were 200,000 homes, 10,000 palaces of the wealthy and many royal palaces with exquisitely designed gardens. Also, there were 900 beautiful public baths and many private ones at a time when the rest of Europe considered bathing self-indulgent and a sin.

Finally, in terms of education and scholarship, the Moors were equally impressive in stature and contribution. At a time when even European kings could not read or write, and 99% of Christian Europe was illiterate, the Moors made education universal. And in the 10th and 11th centuries when Europe had no public libraries and only two significant universities, the Moors gave Spain more than 70 public libraries, built Spain seventeen famous universities and established an observatory at Seville. According to Rocker (1937:412) astronomy, physics, chemistry, geometry, philology, geography and math were taught at these universities. Also, artists and scholars formed professional associations and held regular conferences "where the latest achievements of research were announced and discussed which naturally contributed greatly to the spread of scientific thought." Carew (1991) also notes how Moorish scholarship was so respected that for centuries Arabic was seen as key to scholarship.

In addition to the subjects listed above, trigonometry, botany and history were taught in the university where students from Africa, the Middle East and Europe flocked. Lane-Poole (1886) reports that even women were encouraged to engage in serious study and that there were women doctors. Van Sertima (1991:11) notes what he calls "a benign influence" on the way Islam operated in Spain particularly in relationships to women. He also points out that the famous traveller Ibn Battuta had remarked on the freedom of Muslim women in Africa. Thus, in Moorish Spain, Van Sertima states that women "moved freely in public and engaged in various gatherings."

Jackson (1980) and Turner (1997) point out that Moroccan science and scholarship were an integral part of the overall Muslim cultural achievement which produced advances in math, algebra, physics and astronomy. Jackson (1980:181) points out that approximately 400 years before Magellan's trip in 1519 established for Europe that the world was round, Moors taught it in geography classes using a globe. In fact, El Idrisi, a Moor, wrote a book in the mid-twelfth century observing that according to astronomers and other learned men and philosophers, "the world is round as a sphere." He also suggested a concept of gravity, stating in his book that the earth draws "to itself all that is heavy in the same way as a magnet attracts iron."

By 1492, the Moorish empire in Spain came to an end with the fall of Granada. This was almost an 800 year Moorish reign of culture and science which developed as no other European country. For a brief while Spain tried to maintain her cultural standards and progress. Isabella and Ferdinand had used their wealth from Granada to finance Columbus' voyage to America when he found Blacks had already preceded him (Van Sertima, 1976:11). And then there was a push for trade and exploration in the New World which was no doubt aided by Moorish and other Muslim navigational experience and knowledge (Parry, 1966:Chapter 1). But as Lane-Poole (1886:vii-ix) observed, "this was but a last halo about the dying moments of a (once) mighty state." What followed with the vulgarity and unbridled violence of the Christian Inquisition, a condemnation of science, closing of universities and libraries with not one public library in Madrid in the 18th century, the decrease by four-fifths of the number of looms in Seville, destruction of the baths in the hysterical drive against imagined sin, deterioration of the irrigation and decline of agriculture production and decay in general. Jan Carew (1992) writing in *Golden Age of the Moors* confirms this disintegration not only of the economy, but also of the religious tolerance and multiculturalism which so defined the Moorish Empire. Numerous authors in Mann's and Glick's (1992) edited volume on *Convivencia* or coexistence in Muslim dominated Spain, speak to the high level of cultural and religious respect cultivated by the Moors and the multicultural exchanges that evolved in such a context. In this context Muslims, Jews and Christians engaged in productive exchanges in science, math, astronomy, philosophy and religion which contributed greatly to the advance of human culture in the world.

This state of things would quickly change under Christian rule after the defeat of the Moors in 1492. Under the Moorish terms of surrender, the Christian monarchs, Isabella and Ferdinand, promised to respect each religion and culture as did the Moorish rulers of Spain. But as Carew (1992:249) notes,

Isabella's reneging on her commitment to religious tolerance under the terms of the surrender and subsequently expelling and launching attacks on the Moors and Jews established a "precedent...and tradition of treachery and racism that was adopted by all European colonizers...(which) would endure throughout the Columbian era." Given Spain's deterioration, it is interesting to note that after all the commentaries on and claims about the tragedy that would descend on Africans if and when Europeans left Africa, it was a major European state, Spain, that deteriorated after Africans left. Such is the irony and severe instruction of history.

3.8   OTHER STATES AND EMPIRES

There are numerous other states, empire and ethnic-nations which need to be studied by serious students of African history. Among these are the Hausa states and the Kanem-Bornu empire in the Western Sudan (Ajayi and Crowder, 1984; Ajayi and Epsie,1972; Trimmingham, 1962). Secondly, there are the West African states and empires — Ife, Oyo, Benin, Dahomey and the Akan states and empires of Ashanti and Fante (Murdock, 1959; Davidson, 1977). Thirdly, there are Central African states — Kongo, Luba and Lunda (Collins, 1968; Vasina, 1968); and the lake states of Bunyoro and Bunganda (Oliver, 1963; Beattie, 1960). Finally, there are the southeastern and southern states and empires, the Omani Sultanate, the civilization of Zimbabwe (The Mutapa Empire) and the Zulu Empire (Davidson, 1959, 1967; Oliver and Mathews, 1963; Vilakazi, 1962; Omer-Cooper, 1966). These, however, are but selective examples of the rich variousness of African history and the struggle for self-, social and world construction it represents.

3.9   THE DECLINE OF AFRICAN SOCIETIES

Invariably students of Black Studies raise the question of why did Africa with all its glory and achievement fall to the European advance. There are several reasons, but before we treat them, we should put the question in historical perspective with three fundamental observations. First of all, one should know that all civilizations, regardless of how great they are or seem, eventually decline for various internal and external reasons. Egypt, Ethiopia, Rome, Greece, Ghana, Mali, Songhai, and of late the British, French and American empires all suffered this tendency. So it should not be seen as a special weakness or oddity that the civilizations of Africa eventually declined and fell to the onslaught of Europe. Secondly, it should be noted that the conquest and colonization of Africa took over 400 years, from mid 1400's to the end of the 1800's which culminated in the partition of Africa. Throughout this time, Africans continuously resisted and won many battles and wars against the Europeans.

Queen Nzingha of Angola's long war with the Portuguese, Samory Toure of the Western Sudan's ongoing war with the French, the Zulu nation's defeat of the British at the Battle of Isandlwana, 1896; Menelik of Ethiopia's defeat of the Italians at the Battle of Adua, 1898; the Asante's long wars with the British and the Mahdi of Eastern Sudan's victories in the Sudan are but a few examples of African resistance and victories (Ajayi and Espie, 1972; Rogers, 1972 Vol 1). In fact, as suggested above, Europe first came to Africa as an equal and sometimes as an inferior on the cultural and political power level. The exchange of ambassadors between Portugal and Mali, the Moorish domination of Spain and superiority in science and scholarship to all Europe and the tribute and tax paid to kings and local rulers, all show an early deference and often higher level of culture of Africans at that time.

As July (1998:168) points out, the city-states of the Niger Delta offer another strong example of resistance to European penetration and of control of exchange by Africans. Although the Europeans built forts for stability, defense and as a launching base, "at first they gained not more than a minimum foothold for their garrisons remained by sufferance, unable to either exert political authority outside their walls or to enforce their desired trade monopoly." In fact, local leaders "characteristically extracted payment of tariffs, fines and rents while refusing traders access to the interior,...maintaining control over the inland trade." July argues that a typical situation was related by a European agent who reported the authority and power of the Fante who neither the English or Dutch "dare oppose...for fear of being ruined themselves." Finally, July states that perhaps "the degree of tenacity in opposition to European penetration was best exemplified by John Conny," a political leader of Ghana

(Gold Coast) of the early 18th century. He fought off the Dutch for seven years when they attacked to take his fort and negotiated a settlement "only after seven years of combined diplomatic and military pressure."

Finally, to discuss critically the fall of Africa one must realize that Africa did not fall; separate empires, states, nations and ethnic groups were eventually conquered and colonized. To talk of Africa as if it were a self-conscious political unit rather than mostly a geographical fact with various cultural similarities is to obscure the reality and damage clarity. Africa did not fall with the defeat of the Asante and Zulu empires nor with the conquest of the Hausa states or the Sudan. There was no capital or central government for Africa. Africa was a continent in itself, but not self-consciously for itself. Only with the rise of Pan-Africanism did the peoples of Africa begin to see and define themselves as one. This was to Europe's advantage, but still the conquest and colonization of Africa proved to be a 400 year project which ended in great part in less than seventy-years as a result of the African independence struggles. Thus, it might be better to rephrase the question and ask, not why Africa fell, but rather what factors led to Europe's temporary conquest and colonization of African societies?

With these observations in mind, one can begin to answer the question by citing Europe's technological advantage. It is important to note here that Europe at first did not have serious technological advantage over Africa, especially during the Moorish occupation of Spain and up to the end of the 1400's. Also, Rodney (1974:10) states: "in the fifteenth century European technology was not totally superior to that of other parts of the world." In fact, Europeans imported African and Asian cloths and other consumer goods during this period. In terms of Europe's eventual technological advantage, it is also important to recognize that it was not simply the gun which gave Europe the advantage, for Africans and Asians often had guns. What is important to recognize is the complexity of factors of which the gun was only one, even though it was a central factor. In fact, there were three things which Europe possessed which would eventually give them a technological advantage over Africa: 1) guns; 2) long distance ships; and 3) capitalism as a system of production. Both Rodney (1974) and Parry (1966) agree with these, but Parry adds maps as a significant factor in the rise of European hegemony. Also, both give Africans and/or Muslims (Africans, Arabs, Persians, et al) credit for most of the basic knowledge which led to maritime science and capability.

The gun and the monopoly on it gave Europeans the capacity to impose; ships gave them the capacity to collect and synthesize technique and other knowledge from around the world, as well as control, block or bombard the African coast, and capitalism gave them the capacity to mass produce, monopolize and expand technology in great strides. Thus, by the colonial era in the 1800's Europe was able to: 1) conquer cities, states and empires thru force of arms; 2) dictate political developments in Africa; 3) force abandonment of productive processes like clothing manufacture and iron-smelting, and therefore encourage loss of technique and scientific inquiry necessary for technological advancement; and 4) refuse to share its borrowed and synthesized technology with Africans in spite of request. This process not only increased Europe's technological advantage, it also contributed to technological arrest in Africa.

A second factor which increased Europe's ability to conquer and impose its will on Africa was its economic advantage. In fact, the technological advantage and economic advantage are linked. Europe's ships which gave them capacity for long-distance travel and trade and valuable military capability, its guns which gave them the capacity to conquer and impose, and capitalism which gave them the capacity to mass produce and outproduce others clearly had both a technological and economic dimension. Therefore, with this combined power, they were able to: 1) graft African economies into the capitalist system; 2) disrupt African trade routes and relations as the Portuguese did in Upper Guinea with the cotton trade, in Angola with salt and in Kongo with cowries; 3) reduce African economies to a one-product or low number product economy, i.e., slaves, kola nuts, etc. to satisfy European demands; 4) force consumption of European goods; and 5) continue the European stranglehold on African consumer markets. Moreover, as Rodney (1974:106) points out, "the lines of economic activity attached to foreign trade were either destructive as enslavement was, or at best extractive like ivory hunting and cutting comwood trees." This too produced developmental arrest and vulnerability.

Directly related to the economic and technological advantages was the holocaust of enslavement which deprived Africa of conditions for development and made security a priority over development. Furthermore, this trade deprived Africa of her youth, the major source of inventiveness and inquiry. Caught in a vicious cycle of needing to give Europeans what they demanded in order to get the guns Europeans had given their enemies, African rulers more and more got bogged down in the commerce in enslaved persons which not only cost Africans many millions, but also created a context for insecurity, fear and lowered internal productivity. As July (1998:170) states, "no doubt an economy based on slaving was based insecurely, while nations devoted to slave mongering became brutalized and unproductive."

A fourth factor which led to the decline of African societies and their eventual conquest was internal and external problems of the various societies at given times of European penetration. Often they were too small for effective resistance to large well-armed European armies or contingents. Certainly, small ethnic groups were little match for states. And in fact the African states and empires put up a more effective resistance. Secondly, they might have been at war with various neighboring states or peoples, thus making them and their neighbors more vulnerable to European manipulation thru arms supplies. Thirdly, the class divisions and antagonisms in African societies were often played on where they existed and created where they did not. In this regard an example is the rise of mulatto strata or classes throughout Africa which acted as buffers, agents and middle men for Europeans. Also with the rise of the European imposition of the commerce in enslaved Africans, a new class of enslaved persons was developed by the late 18th century in parts of West Africa where once there were none. This further divided African societies in terms of class and color given Europe's fixation on race.

Finally, African societies found themselves culturally vulnerable to European penetration and conquest on several levels. First, except for Islamic societies, they lacked a unifying ideology which cut across the various socio-political formations to which they belonged. The Europeans had Christianity, capitalism and racism and though they often rivalled each other, these ideological focuses were also points of unity against the so-called Black heathen. Thus, "Pope Alexander VI issued a papal bull in 1493 giving, by the grace of an understanding god, the people of color of the world (all considered heathen) and especially their resources to Portugal and Spain" (Karenga, 1978:55). This had the effect of turning their immediate attention from killing each other to killing, enslaving and exploiting the so-called swarthy heathen.

Moreover, African vulnerability was increased by the communalistic character of African societies. This included a tendency toward xenophilia rather than xenophobia as with the European, the non-aggressive approach toward nature and thus, the likelihood of being technologically unable to meet the challenges of a society literally out to conquer and fully exploit nature. Such a people dedicated to the conquest of nature and others is more likely to be prepared for war than those deeply spiritual and deferential to nature and concerned with living in harmony with it rather than conquering it.

Even now such a cultural emphasis remains a problem for the development and defense of African and other Third World peoples. For the needed thrust to control and utilize nature often clashes with cultural values which are more spiritual than material. The question is raised here of how to synthesize the need and growth of science and technology with the need for human sensitivity and morality or how to humanize nature without denaturalizing and dehumanizing humans? Europe by its own admission had failed in this project. It now falls on Africans and other Third World people to demonstrate its possibility.

CONCLUSION

As stated in the Introduction, a comprehensive and detailed treatment of African history is not possible in this work. What was attempted was some definitive examples of African genius, creativity and historical struggles to shape the world in their own image and interests. Egypt, Nubia, and Ethiopia were chosen because they represent the flowering of ancient African civilization in the Nile Valley and because Egypt is especially high achieving, important to the history of world civilization and contested terrain; the Western Sudanic civilization because of its high level of achievement and its being the source of many Africans brought to the New World; and the Moorish empire in Spain because, it like Egypt, shows Europe's immense debt to Africa and African peoples although they, through racial or racist immodesty, often mistakenly assume that African people owe them everything real and worth mentioning.

STUDY QUESTIONS

1. What is the project of sankofa? What are its goals?
2. Define history discussing five characteristics of it.
3. Discuss the four major oppositions with which humans struggle in making history.
4. What are some factors which complicate the study of African history? Discuss them.
5. What are the roles and accomplishments of the Nubian pharaohs Piankhi and Shabaka, the Divine Wife of Amen Amenirdis and the Kandake Amenirenas?
6. What is the importance of the Shabaka Text or Memphite Theology?
7. Discuss the ancient Egyptian ethical and spiritual concept of Maat. What are the Seven Cardinal Virtues of Maat?
8. Discuss the rich legacy of ancient Egypt, Kemet, to world civilization.
9. Discuss the similarities in the development and basis of the strength of the Western Sudanic civilizations, i.e., commerce, just and able administration, scholarship and education, military might.
10. What are some of the major contributions of the Moorish empire to European and world civilization?
11. Discuss the rise of Ethiopia in Aksum, its international trade and relations.
12. Discuss Emperor Ezana's victory text and its stating of his commitment to rule justly and righteously.
13. What are some basic factors contributive to the decline and fall of African societies?

REFERENCES

Adams, William Y. (1977) *Nubia: Corridor to Africa*, Princeton: Princeton University Press.

Ajayi, J.F.A. and Ian Espie (eds.) (1972) A *Thousand Years of West African History*, New York: Humanities Press.

Ajayi, J.F.A. and Michael Crowder, (eds.) 1984) *History of West Africa*, 3rd Ed., 2 Vols., Burnt Hill, UK: Longman

Beattie, John. (1960) *Bunyoro, An African Kingdom*, New York: Holt, Reinhart, Winston.

ben-Jochannon, Yosef A.A. (1971) *Africa: Mother of "Western Civilization,"* New York: Alkebu-Lan Books Associates.

ben-Jochannon, Yosef A.A. (1970) *African Origins of the Major "Western Religions,"* New York: Alkebu-Lan Books Associates.

Bernal, Martin. (1991) *Black Athena: The AfroAsiatic Roots of Classical Civilization*, Vol. II, New Brunswick, NJ: Rutgers University Press.

Bernal, Martin. (1987) *Black Athena: The AfroAsiatic Roots of Classical Civilization,* Vol. I, New Brunswick, NJ: Rutgers University Press.

Billington, Ray A. (ed.) (1981) *The Journal of Charlotte Forten: A Free Negro in the Slave Era,* New York: W. W. Norton.

Bober, M.M. (1948) *Karl Marx' Interpretation of History,* NewYork: W.W. Norton & Co.

Bracey, John H. et. al. (1970) *Black Nationalism in America,* New York: Bobbs-Merrill Co.

Breasted, James. (1934) *The Dawn of Conscience,* New York: University Books.

Budge, E.A. Wallis (transl.). (1960) *The Book of the Dead,* New York: University Books.

Budge, E.A. Wallis. (1970) *A History of Ethiopia: Nubia and Abyssinia,* Vol. 1, Oosterhout N.B., Netherlands: Anthropological Publications.

Burckhardt, Titus. (1999) *Moorish Culture in Spain,* Lahore: Suhail Academy.

Carew, Jan. (1992) "Moorish Culture-Bringers: Bearers of Enlightenment," *Journal of African Civilizations,* II (Fall) 248-277.

Clark, J. Desmond. (1970) *The Prehistory of Africa,* New York: Praeger Publishers.

Collins, Robert O. (1968) *Problems in African History,* Englewood Cliffs: Prentice Hall, Inc.

Conrad, Earl. (1943) *Harriet Tubman,* Washington, D.C.: Associated Publishers, Inc.

Curtin, Philip et al. (1990) *African History,* London: Longman.

Davidson, Basil. (1991) *African Civilizations Revisited,* Trenton, NJ: Africa World Press.

Davidson, Basil. (1967) *East and Central Africa to the Late Nineteenth Century,* Nairobi: Longmans, Green & Co.

Davidson, Basil. (1966) *A History of East Africa to the Nineteenth Century,* Garden City, N.Y.: Doubleday & Co.

Davidson, Basil. (1977) *A History of West Africa, 1000-1800,* London: Longman.

Davidson, Basil. (1959) *The Lost Cities of Africa,* Boston: Little, Brown & Co.

DeGraft-Johnson, John C. (1966) *African Glory,* New York: Walker & Co.

Diop, Cheikh Anta. (1974) *The African Origin of Civilization: Myth or Reality,* Westport, CT: Lawrence Hill & Co.

Diop, Cheikh Anta. (1991) *Civilization or Barbarism: An Authentic Anthropology,* New York: Lawrence Hill Books.

Diop, Cheikh Anta. (1981) *Civilization ou Barbarie,* Paris: Présence Africaine.

Diop, Cheikh Anta. (1978) *The Cultural Unity of Black Africa,* Chicago: Third World Press.

Diop, Cheikh Anta. (1987) *Pre-Colonial Black Africa,* Westport, CT: Lawrence Hill & Company.

Drake, St. Clair. (1987) *Black Folk Here and There: An Essay in History and Anthropology,* Los Angeles, Center for Afro-American Studies, University of California.

DuBois, W.E.B. (1975) *Black Folk: Then and Now*, New York: Kraus-Thomson.

DuBois, W.E.B. (1965) *The World and Africa*, New York: International Publishers.

El Mahdi, Mandour. (1965) *A Short History of the Sudan*, London: Oxford University Press.

El Nadoury R. (1990) "The Legacy of Pharaonic Egypt," in G. Mokhtar (ed.) *General History of Africa, Vol. II, Ancient Civilizations of Africa* , Berkeley: University of California Press.

Fage, J.D. (1969) *A History of West Africa*, London: Cambridge University Press.

Forbes, Jack. (1980) *Black Africans and Native Americans*, Cambridge, MA: Blackwell.

Freeman, Charles. (1997) *The Legacy of Ancient Egypt*, New York: Facts on File Inc.

Gailey, Harry A. (1970) *History of Africa From Earliest Times to 1800*, New York: Holt, Rinehart and Winston.

Gardiner, A.H. (1961) *Egypt of the Pharaohs: An Introduction*, New York: Oxford University Press.

Garvey, Amy Jacques (ed.) (1977) *Philosophy & Opinions of Marcus Garvey, I & II*, New York: Atheneum.

Hakem, A.A. (1990) "The Civilization of Napata and Meroe," in G. Mokhtar (ed.) *General History of Africa, Vol II, Ancient Civilizations of Africa*, Berkeley: University of California Press, pp, 172-202.

Harris, J.R. (ed.). (1971) *The Legacy of Egypt*, Oxford: Oxford University Press.

Harris, Joseph. (1987) *Africans and Their History*, New York: New American Library.

Haynes, Joyce L. (1992) *Nubia: Ancient Kingdoms of Africa*, Boston: Museum of Fine Arts.

Jackson, John G. (1980) *Introduction to African Civilizations*, Secaucus, N.J.: Citadel Press.

James, George. (1976) *Stolen Legacy*, San Francisco: Julian Richardson Associates.

James, T.G.H. (1979) *An Introduction to Ancient Egypt*, New York: Harper & Row.

Jayyusi, Salma Khadra, (ed.). (2000) *The Legacy of Muslim Spain*, Weisbaden: Brill Academic Publishers.

Johanson, Donald D. and Maitland A. Edey. (1981) Lucy: *The Beginnings of Humankind*, London: Granada.

July, Robert W. (1970) *A History of the African People*, New York: Charles Scribner's Sons.

July, Robert W. (1998) *A History of the African People*, 5th Edition, Prospect Heights, IL: Waveland.

Karenga, Maulana. (1977) "Corrective History," *First World*, 1,3 (May/June) 50-54.

Karenga, Maulana. (1978) *Essays on Struggle: Position and Analysis*, San Diego: Kawaida Publications.

Karenga, Maulana. (1980) *Kawaida Theory: An Introductory Outline*, Inglewood, CA: Kawaida Publications.

Karenga, Maulana. (1994) *Maat, The Moral Ideal in Ancient Egypt: A Study in Classical African Ethics*, unpublished dissertation, University of Southern California.

Karenga, Maulana. (1984) *Selections From the Husia: Sacred Wisdom of Ancient Egypt*, Los Angeles: University of Sankore Press.

Karenga, Maulana. (1989) "The Sociology of Maatian Ethics: Literature and Context," *Journal of African Civilizations*, 10 (Summer) 352-398.

Kennedy, Hugh. (1997) *Muslim Spain and Portugal: A Political History of Al Andalus*, Reading, MA: Addison-Wesley Publishing Co.

Keto, C. Tsehloane. (1994) *An Introduction to the Africa-Centered Perspective of History*, London/Chicago: Research Associates School Times Publications/Karnak House.

Ki-Zerbo, J. (ed.) (1990) *General History of Africa, I: Methodology and African Prehistory*, CA: UNESCO.

Kling, Susan. (1979) *Fannie Lou Hamer*, Chicago: Women For Racial and Economic Equality.

Lane-Poole, Stanley. (1886) *The Story of the Moors in Spain*, New York: G.P. Putnam's Sons.

Lichtheim, Miriam. (1975) (1976) (1980) *Ancient Egyptian Literature: A Book of Readings, Vol. I, Vol. II, Vol. III*, Los Angeles: University of California Press.

Malcolm X. (1965) *Malcolm X Speaks*, New York: Merit Publishers.

Mann, Vivian B. And Thomas Glick, (eds.). (1992) *Convivencia: Jews, Muslims and Christians in Medieval Spain*, New York: G. Braziller.

Massie, Dorothy C. (1974) *The Legacy of Mary McLeod Bethune*, Washington, D.C.: National Education Association.

McCabe, Joseph. (1935) *The Splendour of Moorish Spain*, London: Watts and Co.

McCall, Daniel F. (1969) *Africa in Time-Perspective*, New York: Oxford University Press.

Morkot, Robert. (2000) *The Black Pharaohs: Egypt's Nubian Rulers*, London: Rubicon Press.

Murdock, G.P. (1959) *Africa: Its People and Their Culture History*, New York: McGraw Hill.

Murphy, E. Jefferson. (1972) *History of African Civilization*, New York: Dell Publishing Company.

National Education Association. (1974) *Mary McLeod Bethune*, New York: National Educational Association.

Niangoran-Bouah, G. (1984) *The Akan World of Gold Weights: Abstract Design Weights*, Volume I, Abidjan, Ivory Coast: Les Nouvelles Editions Africaines.

Obenga, Théophile. (1992) *Ancient Egypt and Black Africa*, London: Karnak House.

Obenga, Theophile. (1972) *L'Afrique Dans L'Antiquité: Egypte Pharonique-Afrique Noire*, Paris: Presénce Africaine.

Oliver, Roland and G. Matthews. (1963) *History of East Africa, I*, Oxford: Clarendon Press.

Olson, Stacie and Josef Wegner. (1992) *Ancient Nubia: Egypt's Rival in Africa*, Philadelphia: University Museum of Archeology and Anthropology, University of Pennsylvania.

Omer-Cooper, John D. (1966) *The Zulu Aftermath*, London: Longmans.

Osae, T.A. and S.N. Nwabara, et al. (1973) *A Short History of West Africa*. New York: Hill and Wang.

Pankhurst, Richard Keir. (1967) *The Ethiopian Royal Chronicles*, Addis Ababa: Oxford University Press.

Parry, J. H. (1966) *The Establishment of the European Hegemony*, New York: Harper & Row.

Petry, Ann. (1955) *Harriet Tubman*, New York: Robert Books.

Phillipson, David W. (1985) *African Archaeology*, Cambridge: Cambridge University Press.

Ravell, James. (1992) "An Annotated Bibliography of the Moors: 711-1492 A.C.," in Ivan Van Sertima (ed.) *Golden Age of the Moors, Journal of African Civilizations*, II (Fall) 407-454.

Reader, John. (1998) *Africa: A Biography of the Continent*, New York: Knopf.

Rice, Michael. (1990) *Egypt's Making: The Origins of Ancient Egypt, 500-2000 B.C.*, New York: Routledge.

Rocker, Rudolph. (1937) *Nationalism and Culture*, New York: Couici-Friede.

Rodney, Walter. (1974) *How Europe Underdeveloped Africa*, Washington, D.C.: Howard University Press.

Rogers, J.A. (1972) *World's Great Men of Color, Vol. I*, New York: Macmillian Publishing Co.

Säve-Söderbergh, Torgny (ed.) (1987) *Temples and Tombs of Ancient Nubia*, New York: Thames and Hudson Inc.

Schafer, Heinrich. (1905) *Urkunden der altern Äthiopenkonige*, Leipzig: J.D. Hinrichs'sche Buchhandlung.

Sergew, Hable Selassie. (1972) *Ancient and Medieval Ethiopian History to 1270*, Addis Ababa: United Printers.

Shinnie, Peter L. (1967) *Meroe: A Civilization of the Sudan*, New York: Frederick A. Praeger, Inc.

Siliotti, Albert. (1996) *Egypt, Splendors of an Ancient Civilization*, New York: Thames & Hudson.

Stringer, Christopher and Robin McKie. (1997) *African Exodus: The Origins of Modern Humanity*, New York: Henry Holt.

Tamrat, Taddesse. (1972) *Church and State in Ethiopia, 1250-1527*, Oxford: Clarendon Press.

Taylor, John H. (1991) *Egypt and Nubia*, Cambridge: Harvard University Press.

Thorpe, Earl. (1971) *Black Historians*, New York: William Morrow.

Trigger, B.G. et al. (1983) *Ancient Egypt: A Social History*, New York: Cambridge University Press.

Trimingham, John S. (1962) *A History of Islam in West Africa*, London: Oxford University Press.

Turner, Howard. (1997) *Science in Medieval Islam: An Illustrated Introduction*, Austin: University of Texas Press.

Van Sertima, Ivan. (1992) *Golden Age of the Moors*, New Brunswick: Transaction Publishers.

Van Sertima, Ivan. (1976) *They Came Before Columbus*, New York: Random House.

Vasina, Jan. (1968) *Kingdoms of the Savanna*, Madison: University of Wisconsin Press.

Vilakazi, Absolam. (1962) *Zulu Transformations, Natal*, S.A.: University of Witwatersrand Press.

Welsby, Derck. (1996) *The Kingdom of Kush: The Napatan and Meroitic Empires*, London: British Museum Press.

Wenig, S. (1978) *Africa in Antiquity, Vol. II, Arts of Ancient Nubia and Sudan*, New York: The Brooklyn Museum.

Wildung, Dietrich. (1997) *Sudan: Ancient Kingdoms of the Nile*, Paris: Flammarion.

Williams, Bruce. (1989) "The Last Pharaohs of Nubia," *Journal of African Civilizations*, 10 (Summer) 90-104.

Williams, Chancellor. (1974) *The Destruction of Black Civilization*, Chicago: Third World Press.

BLACK HISTORY:
AFRICANS IN AMERICA

BLACK HISTORY:
AFRICANS IN AMERICA

CHAPTER 4

4. 1 INTRODUCTION

It is important to restate here some of the basic concerns listed in the section on African Background. First, this section, as the one on Continental African history, will not seek to be an exhaustive treatment of African American history. The intention is rather to acquaint the student with major issues, processes, events and historical figures which have shaped the course and character of Black history. Secondly, in achieving this, focus will be placed more on modal experiences than on establishing neat chronological periods in which these experiences took place. By modal experience, I mean major experiences which defined Black life with Blacks in the roles of both producers and products of history, those who make and are made by these historical experiences (Asante and Mattson, 1992).

Thirdly, stress will be placed on Blacks as historical actors rather than the object of historical action, struggling to define, defend and develop their interests rather than their being imposed on by others. The interest here is in the rich diversity of proactive responses Blacks had to life in a new and hostile land. It, thus, will not be a litany of lost battles, a dirge of endless defeats or a chronicle of simple survival. Rather this section will seek to show Blacks as they were and are, meeting major challenges with impressive adaptive vitality, durability and achievement. It will show them then, not simply surviving, but more importantly, self-consciously developing, a process which carries with it both the assumption and insurance of survival.

Finally this section will seek to present concise, critical summaries of major issues, events and processes so that the student can grasp the essence of each rather than get bogged down in insubstantial or less relevant data. The attempt here is to isolate and present the core and kernel of major phenomena and processes in Black History. The detailed presentations are in the general and specific works in the field. This, in a word, is a critical and concise introduction.

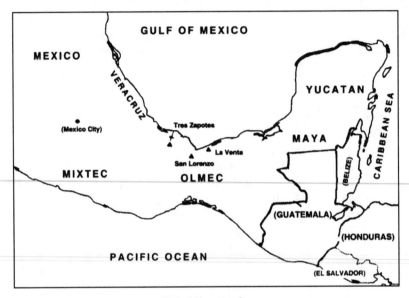

Map of Mesoamerica

4. 2 EGYPT, MALI AND THE OLMECS

There is significant evidence that Africans did not come to America first on enslavement ships or as crew members and pilots on European ships, but on their own ships perhaps as early as 1200 B.C.E. followed by voyages between 800-700 B.C.E. and again in 1311 and 1312 C.E. This is obviously a contested contention but there is a sufficient body of evidence which invites serious consideration. However, if Europeans could reach America by accident, why couldn't Africans reach it by design and skill? Easily the seminal and most definitive work on African presence in ancient American is Ivan Van Sertima's (1976), *They Came Before Columbus*. In this major and controversial work, Van Sertima argues not only that Africans were here before Columbus but that they helped build the Olmec civiliza-

Olmec Head

tion, the parent civilization for all subsequent ones in Mesoamerica (Clark and Pye, 2000; Coe, 1996, 1962).

Since publication of his first work, Van Sertima (1992, 1998) has published new data to substantiate his claims. In an edited text, *African Presence in Early America,* other scholars join him in critical exploration of this contention. Among these is Alexander Von Wuthenau, author of *Unexpected Faces* in America who has done extensive work on the multicultural character of ancient America which supports Van Sertima's contentions of African presence in ancient America. In fact, Von Wuthenau provided Van Sertima with new sculptures as evidence. In his text, *Early America Revisited* (1998), Van Sertima answers some of his critics and reaffirms his original position. In both texts, Van Sertima gives an overview of what he feels has transpired in the years since the publication of his work in 1976. He explains that more evidence has been unearthed to substantiate his contentions: more Olmec heads, especially one at Tres Zapotes showing Ethiopian type braids; more clay sculptures of African types which reflect the coloration and texture of African hair; reaffirmation of skeletal evidence; new evidence from ancient maps; new comparisons of African and South American pyramids; and further discussion on dating of the voyages to America. In conclusion, he maintains, his earlier stance is fortified with new evidence.

The Olmec civilization, in which Van Sertima finds African presence, is the parent civilization of Mesoamerica informing the development of many subsequent ones. As Bernal (1979:9) informs us, it "marks the dawn of civilization and the formation for the cultural areas of Mesoamerica." It is a civilization known for its magnificent temples and pyramids, ceremonial plazas, colonnaded courts for religious rituals, its reverence for the jaguar, its elegant and exquisitely carved figures in jade and other stones. It is also known for its hieroglyphic writing and calendar "which was used throughout early Mesoamerican history and represents an advanced knowledge of astronomy and mathematics, including knowledge of zero." But the most extraordinary and discussed monuments to and of Olmec artistic and technical skill are a series of eleven colossal heads in Southwest Mexico carved out of basalt, each standing nine feet tall and weighing about fifteen tons (Miller, 2001; Benson and La Fuente, 1996). Emmerich (1963:53) points out that these heads "portray men with characteristic Olmec features: thick, heavy lips, full cheeks, broad nostrils, almost swollen eyelids and a peculiar close-fitting headdress or helmet."

This helmet is not "peculiar" to Van Sertima. For he sees them as typical helmets used by Nubian soldiers of the 25th Dynasty of Egypt whom he argues came here and contributed to the building of the Olmec civilization. Moreover, nor are the bold features an unsolvable mystery, for they too show an unmistakable Africanoid character and origin.

In his earliest work, Van Sertima (1976) offers and documents two main contentions to develop his thesis that Blacks did in fact come to ancient America. First, he argued that they came as Nubians from the 25th Dynasty of Egypt (751-656 B.C.E.) to the Olmec Heartland. This, he stated, would put them here in time to be at the founding of Olmec civilization. In his latest work, following the estimation of Rafique Jairazbhoy, Van Sertima (1992, 1998) says new evidence indicates that the Egyptians came earlier in the Ramesside period between 1305-1080 B.C.E. In this work, he sets this date as 1200 B.C.E.

Secondly, he posits that Africans also came to America from the Mali empire. In 1310, Malian Emperor Abubakari II sent a fleet of 200 master ships and 200 supply ships into the Atlantic Ocean toward America. Only one ship returned, but could not report the fate of the others which seemed to be swept away by ocean currents which drive anything in them inevitably to America. In 1311 Abubakari, undeterred from exploring the possibilities of a trans-Atlantic voyage, led a fleet of 2,000 ships to America, and never returned, leaving his brother Mansa Musa in authority. In a chapter titled "The Mandingo Voyages," in *Early America Revisited*, Van Sertima (1998) offers an expanded discussion of these voyages.

Some of the major evidence supporting African presence, influence and achievement before the coming of Columbus, especially in Olmec civilization, which Van Sertima cites is as follows. First, he shows cultural and artistic influence, providing over thirty plates to show Africanoid heads, masks, symbols, shields and similarity in phallic cults in Egypt and Mexico. Secondly, Van Sertima demonstrates similarity in socio-religious beliefs and practices showing the Egyptian gods Sokar and Aken in Mexico, similar burial customs such as mummification, the Horus burial jar, golden mummy masks, and the bird-serpent motif in coats of arms and royal diadems. In fact, he (1998:55) argues that it was primarily for religious motives, the Nubian-Egyptian came to early America in a kind of pilgrimage to the West, Amenta, the place of the hereafter in Kemetic theology (see also his (1998:97ff) section on "ritual correpondences." He (1992b:72) also argues that there was "a cluster of...royal traits shared by ruling circles in both civilizations, i.e., the double crown, the royal flail, the sacred bark, the use of purple, the artificial beard, etc." Thirdly, he (1976:155-156) contends that the step pyramid or ziggurat is a distinctive religious structure and that it is significant that "the very first American pyramid or stepped temple appears at La Venta, the site of the colossal (Africanoid) heads..." Moreover, he continues, not "only are the shape and religious function the same" for the Olmec pyramid and its presumed Egyptian prototype, "but also the astronomical and spatial relationships."

A fourth kind of proof, Van Sertima offers, is the similarities of plants in Africa and Mexico. Among those listed which appear to have been transplanted, he lists the banana, bottle gourd, cotton, Jack bean, yams and tobacco. Fifthly, linguistic evidence is offered in the form of similarities in Egyptian and Mexican words respectively like Ra for sun in both, and kuphi and copal for sacred incense. Moreover, Van Sertima also shows West African and Mexican word similarities. A sixth form of evidence offered for African presence and influence is observation and reports by European travelers as well as documents of East and West Africa reporting voyages to the West. In fact, he states (1992:29) in his address to the Smithsonian Institute that Columbus was the first person from Europe to suggest that there were Africans already in America. Afterwards, many other Europeans reported seeing them.

Also, Van Sertima presents a further proof, skeletal evidence, from studies by craniologist Andrzej Weircinski which reveal a clear presence of Africanoid skulls from Olmec B.C.E. sites. He also notes that 13.5% were evident in the pre-classic period and only 4.5% in the classic period indicating the fusion of Africans in the native population. Finally Van Sertima, argues the technological possibility in support of his thesis. He cites Thor Heyerdal's Atlantic crossing to prove the possibility of Egyptians' crossing the Atlantic, argues that both East and West Africans had the capacity for trans-Atlantic travel and makes the point that Africans navigated the Atlantic before the Christian era and conquered a part of Ireland in an early period. In further proof of the technical possibility, Van Sertima publishes an article by Joan Covey (1992:13ff) in which she argues that "the ancient Egyptian had the requisite mapping skills" to come to America.

Van Sertima (1976, 1992, 1998) has clearly shown the African presence and legacy in ancient America and thus, has given an alternative image and period of African arrival here. In a word, he has demonstrated that Africans came first to America, not as enslaved persons, but as explorers, traders, visitors and built with the Native Americans a great civilization that fortunately could not be erased by Europeans' wholesale book burning and vandalism in Mexico. In doing this, he has made a significant contribution to the rescue and reconstruction of Black history and humanity.

4.3   THE HOLOCAUST OF ENSLAVEMENT

It is clear from all historical evidence that the massive European enslavement and its accompanying violence, destruction and commercial aspect was one of the most catastrophic events in the history of humankind. If one objectively calculates the costs to Africa and Africans in terms of the 50 to 100 million lives lost thru mass murder, war, the forcible transfer of populations, and the brutal rigors of the Middle Passage and of enslavement as well as the attendant dehumanization and cultural destruction, one cannot help but conclude that of all the holocausts of history, none surpasses this one. By the use of the word *holocaust* in relation to the process of enslavement, I mean to introduce and stress the *moral* dimension of the tragedy as distinct from its *commercial* aspect. For the stress on the commercial aspect of enslavement often denies, ignores or diminishes the moral monstrousness that this massive destruction of human life, human culture and human possibility represents. As argued below, the severity of the violence undermines the use of the category trade as we usually think of it. What we will describe here is a holocaust. And a *holocaust is a morally monstrous act of genocide that is not only against a people themselves but also against humanity.*

The Holocaust of enslavement, then, is holocaust which expressed itself in three basic ways as: 1) a morally monstrous destruction of human life – millions of persons killed, whole peoples destroyed; 2) a morally monstrous destruction of human culture – cities, towns, villages, great works of art and literatures; 3) the morally monstrous destruction of human possibility – the destruction of life-chances and the grounds for human aspiration, freedom, dignity and human solidarity with others. It is, in a word, the transformation of people into things and thus engineering their *social death* (Patterson, 1982).

What is intended here is to engage in a discussion using a language that constantly reminds us we are talking about real people, real lives destroyed and disrupted. Moreover, to use the category "slave" without a cultural, ethnic or national qualifier is to suggest the person has no identity outside of being enslaved, that s/he is a "slave" by nature not by social imposition. But to use the designation *enslaved African* is to affirm cultural identity and indicate that the African was enslaved not simply a slave by birth or being. In a word, it is to begin to resurrect the enslaved Africans from the *social death* imposed on them. Finally, to say simply "slave" suggests a permanent and natural condition, but to say "enslaved" suggests an imposition and thus, the possibility of it being challenged and ended. To further discuss the basis for the contention we can begin by clearing up some of the basic misconceptions about African enslavement. Secondly, we will discuss its impact in more detail to demonstrate the toll it took in Africa and on African peoples.

MISCONCEPTIONS

First, as Rodney (1974:95) contends, the category "trade" does not reveal the reality of the process and practice. In fact, although there were transactions between Europeans and Africans which would be called commerce in enslaved persons, "on the whole the process by which captives were obtained on

African soil was not trade at all." On the contrary, "it was through warfare, trickery, banditry and kidnapping." Thus, Rodney concludes, "when one tries to measure the effect of European slave trading on the African continent, it is essential to realize that one is measuring the effect of social violence rather than trade in the normal sense."

Secondly, Europeans do not escape moral indictment by blaming Arabs and Africans for participation in the process of enslavement, including its commercial aspect. In terms of the Arabs, when the so-called Arab slave trade in East Africa was at its height in the 18th century and early 19th century, it was still tied to and controlled by Europeans (Rodney, 1974:97). For the destination of most of those captured by the Arabs "was the European-owned plantation economies of Mauritius, Reunion and Seychelles — as well as the Americas, via Cape of Good Hope." Moreover, in the same centuries Africans who were enslaved in certain Arab countries "were all ultimately serving the European capitalist system which set up the demand for slave grown products such as the cloves grown in Zanzibar under the supervision of Arab masters."

Furthermore, "as European political and economic influence in North Africa increased from the 1870's, the northern slave entrepots of the trans-Saharan and Nile valley were drawn into the European orbit..."(Harris, 1972:78). Thus, one discovers that what looked like an Arab-controlled "trade" was in fact a European dominated "trade" with Europeans using Arabs as middle men. None of this is to deny Arab involvement or even the involvement of some East Indians, but rather to focus the bulk of responsibility for the ultimate and greatest demand, and the wholesale destruction and depopulation of Africa where it belongs - squarely on the shoulders of Europeans. Moreover, granted Arabs had enslaved persons before Europeans demanded them for their labor systems, Arab enslavement was domestic and escapable. In fact, there are many examples of servants or persons enslaved by Arabs who rose to power and social and political achievement in the world of Islam.

In terms of African involvement, it is true also that Africans enslaved others before the coming and demands of the European. But three other facts must be added to this statement to give a holistic picture. First, African enslavement was in no way like European enslavement. It was servitude which usually occurred "through conquest, capture in war or punishment for a crime" (Davidson, 1968:181). It could also resemble serfdom as in Medieval Europe where peasants were tied to the land and a lord for protection. They were thus obligated to provide certain goods and services. Moreover, they "were not outcasts in the body politics" as in European chattel slavery. They often lived as members of the family, married their masters' daughters and rose to political and economic prominence and did not face the brutalization and dehumanization which defined European chattel slavery.

Secondly, it is the European demand which forced Africans into a system whose implications few Africans realized at first. This forcing came from among other methods: 1) using their knowledge of local African politics to foment factionalism, launch war and thus get captives; 2) supplying arms to kings or local leaders to raid enemies' cities or villages in exchange for war prisoners; 3) demanding captives for guns from a king who needed them to counter an armed rival king; 4) hiring and launching raiding parties; 5) demanding captives in order to continue providing military supplies to given societies; 6) obtaining some African laborers under false pretenses and enslaving them afterwards; and 7) beginning in one kind of commerce and then demanding enslaved persons at a point when failure to comply would destroy a merchant's business.

Thirdly, it must be remembered that Africans also resisted this commerce in enslaved persons. In fact as Harris (1972:79) points out, "Resistance marked the whole endeavor from initial raid to sale abroad." Queen Nzinga of the Angolan state of Matamba fought fiercely for approximately thirty years against the Portuguese and their imposition of enslavement and its commerce until isolated and overwhelmed and forced back into the European economic orbit. The same is true of the political leader, Tomba, of the Baga people who lived in what is present-day Guinea. About 1720, he tried to build an alliance against the commerce in human persons, but was defeated by an alliance of Europeans, mixed persons and Africans involved in the traffic in persons and forced also back into the system. King Nzenga Meremba (Alfonso) of the Congo also resisted Portuguese trafficking in persons vigorously, and is often cited as a strong example of African opposition to enslavement. Even King Agaja Trudo of Dahomey, a state known for enslavement later, sent armies to capture and destroy centers of commerce in enslaved persons on the coast in 1724, but was also forced into the system by superior arms and economic pressures. But as Harris notes, "Agaja, like Alfonso and other Kings in Futa Toro, Benin and elsewhere, all lacked local and international power to change the situation." Thus, they were forced into a system imposed from outside and the tragedy and loss were incalculable.

IMPACT OF THE ENSLAVEMENT

The impact of the violence and destruction of European enslavement of Africans expressed itself in various tragic ways. First and most easily perceived is the depopulation through mass murder, societal disruption and destruction, and forced transfer of populations, especially in Angola and parts of West Africa. Estimates run as high as 50 to 100 million persons lost to Africa. Secondly, the Holocaust of enslavement caused the loss of youth and skilled personnel, thus affecting the scientific, technological and cultural progress of Africa. The youth were key, for it is among them that the thrust toward scientific inquiry and inventiveness is greatest. And loss of skilled people could only blunt and in some cases eliminate development and induce technical arrest.

Thirdly, the Holocaust of enslavement affected economic activity. It not only interrupted and destroyed markets and industries, but grafted African economies on and subordinated them to the commerce and violence of enslavement, leaving other branches of the economic activity under-attended or unattended. This meant Africans entered into a vicious cycle of dependence and severely diminished ability to produce and provide for themselves and to continue the battle to harness and utilize nature. Fourthly, as a source of constant war and violence, it created and sustained patterns of destruction of life and material achievements as well as conditions of uncertainty and insecurity which accompanied them. Finally, the European imposition of enslavement led directly to the underdevelopment of Africa and overdevelopment of Europe. In fact, Rodney (1974) points out, underdevelopment in Africa is dialectically linked to overdevelopment in the European society — Continental and Diasporan. Eric Williams (1966) systematically shows how the Holocaust of enslavement and its commerce in persons led to vast capital formation and expanded industries in shipbuilding, textiles, sugar refining, metal, insurance and banking in Europe. This exploitation, oppression and appropriation of the vast human and material resources of Africa for their use in the European West, unavoidably led to an interruption and deformation of Africa's development.

Moreover, it represented the combination of these two economic processes, underdevelopment and development, into a single system, capitalist imperialism. This system was/is characterized by the tendency to concentrate wealth at the European center and impose poverty in the so-called marginal areas, i.e., the Third World. It is further defined by an internal logic of competitiveness which pushes it to seek control of markets, raw materials and profitable fields of investment in less developed countries. Colonization grew to secure these necessary factors for capitalist growth and was possible because of the colonial power and wealth Europe had amassed at the expense of Africa and the rest of the Third World.

Thus, when one raises the question of why Africa is not where she was during the Egyptian or Mali Empire, in relation to Europe, one must focus on the period of the Holocaust of enslavement by Europeans which interrupted African history and development, drained it of its human and material resources and thus, imposed the pattern of underdevelopment and poverty we witness in Africa today. Of course, the reasons Europe was able to do this which are explained in Chapter 3 in the section entitled "The Fall of African Societies" can be argued. But it is impossible to deny that European exploitation and oppression of Africa, beginning in the 1400's, marks a clear turning point in African and world history at the expense of Africa and its peoples as well as other peoples of color.

4.4 ENSLAVEMENT: BASIS AND SYSTEM

THE BASIS OF ENSLAVEMENT

The American system of enslavement had its basis in three major sets of factors: 1) its profitability; 2) its practicality; and 3) its justifiability in European racist thought. The profitability of enslavement and commerce in persons was alluded to above. Williams (1966), in his often quoted work, *Capitalism and Slavery*, has shown clearly the contribution of the system and the "trade" to capital accumulation and economic development by England. Some of these areas were: 1) shipbuilding, 2) rise of seaport towns and connected manufacturing centers, 3) banking and insurance houses like Barclay's and Lloyd's; 4) the textile industry; 5) sugar refineries; and 6) metal industries. This was true for other European countries as well.

The United States profited from the system of enslavement and its commerce in persons both as a colony and as a free interdependent part of the world capitalist system. In the USA, the enslaved African was profitable on three basic levels: 1) as a commodity to be sold; 2) as an object of labor to be rented; and 3) as a producer of cash products such as cotton, sugar, tobacco and rice. Around the economic process, commercial and industrial areas grew up, first in New England and New York and then the South. That growth led DuBois (1969) to conclude in his seminal work that this economic process, involving merchants and planters, became "the very life of the colonies." In fact, up to the mid-19th century, American economic development rested mainly on foreign commerce with enslavement and products grown by enslaved Africans at the center of the process.

Enslavement also had its basis in the practicality of the process. As Bennett (1975) states, forced labor was first tried on the Native American and then on indentured whites. But several factors made the enslavement of these groups unattractive and the enslavement of Africans more practical. The first factor was Africa's closeness to the Caribbean where plantations were set up early and where Africans were "seasoned," i.e., made manageable, and then re-exported. Secondly, Africans already had experience in large-scale agriculture with their own fields and European plantations in Africa, unlike the Native Americans who mainly hunted and gathered their food. Thirdly, Africans had relative immunity to European diseases due to long-term contact, whereas the Native Americans did not and were decimated at first by this.

Fourthly, the practicality of African enslavement rested in their low escape possibilities, as opposed to Native Americans and whites, due to unfamiliarity with the land, high social visibility and lack of a nearby home base. Fifthly, there were no major political repercussions for the enslavement of Africans, unlike the Native Americans who had people here to retaliate and the whites whose enslavement would challenge the tenets of Christianity and the age of enlightenment and reason on which Europe prided itself (Bennett, 1975:65).

Finally, the basis of the American system of enslavement was in its justifiability in European racist thought. Although the enslavement of Africans was based in economic reasons, it also rested in racism as a ideology (Davis, 1966; Jordan, 1968). Racism as an ideology became a justification and encouragement for African enslavement. It expresses itself in religious absurdities, biological absurdities and cultural absurdities. Thus, religiously, it was argued God ordained whites to conquer, civilize and christianize the African "heathen" and of course, take his/her wealth in the process. Moreover, the biological absurdities included redefinition of Africans out of the human race, denying their history and humanity and giving them animal characteristics to suit their bestial treatment by whites. And finally, the cultural absurdities revolved around claims of white cultural superiority and social Darwinist claims of having both the natural right and responsibility to conquer and use the human and material resources of "lesser" peoples for the advancement of the more "noble and advanced" ones. Although Rodney (1974:88-89) at first argues that Africans were enslaved for economic rather than racists reasons, he later concedes the dialectical relation between the two. He correctly concludes that "oppression of African people on purely racial grounds accompanied, strengthened and became indistinguishable from oppression for economic reasons." Moreover, he maintained that "by the nineteenth century white racism had become so institutionalized in the capitalist world (and notably in the USA) that it sometimes ranked above the maximization of profit as a motive for oppressing Black people."

THE SYSTEM OF ENSLAVEMENT

The American system of enslavement has been classified in several ways. Phillips (1963) a major apologist for enslavement, calls it benign and civilizing. Stampp (1965) classifies it as peculiar, cruel and brutal. Genovese (1974) describes it as paternalistic. Elkins (1966) sees it as infantilizing. And cliometricians Fogel and Engerman (1974) think it was simply efficient. It is obvious that the first of the above descriptions are more apologetic than critical and that regardless of the various other descriptions, the system was brutal and defined by the domination, exploitation and oppression which permeate all systems of enslavement (Campbell and Rice, 1991; Hurmence, 1990; Kolchin, 1993; Berlin, 1998).

American enslavement as a system, then, can be defined by: 1) the extent of its brutality; 2) its cultural genocide; and 3) its machinery of control. The brutality of enslavement expresses itself on the physical, psychological and sexual level. Physically, it included violence in various forms — whippings, mutilations, torture, murder, overworking and deprivation of food, clothing and shelter. Psychological brutality included daily humiliation, denial and deformation of African history and humanity.

It was, in fact, an objectification of the enslaved African, reducing him/her to an object of labor, and using his "race" as proof and assignment of human worth and social status. Sexual brutality was imposed on enslaved African women, men and children. Each was subjected to the sexual lust and exploitation of the master and his family. "Breeding" and rape became the two principal forms of sexual abuse and brutality which they all suffered, but especially the women (White, 1991; Jacobs, 1987; White, 1985: Chapter 2).

It is here that we see the implications of Patterson's (1982:1-14) definition of enslavement as "the permanent, violent domination of natally alienated and generally dishonored persons." He points out the need to concretely and symbolically dishonor the enslaved person and to humiliate and undermine the sense of self and connectedness with others and one's own community.

Harriet Jacobs (1987:77) one of the few enslaved African women to write a narrative of her life in enslavement noted that "slavery is terrible for men, but it is far more terrible for women." For "Super added to the burden common to all, they have wrongs, and sufferings and mortifications peculiarly their own." And these peculiar forms of sufferings were sexual exploitation as well as racial and class oppression (Gaspar and Hine, 1996; Morton, 1996). They also included the burden of motherhood and being a wife in a system that devalued Black women, and allowed white men to rape, beat and sell mother, child and husband with impunity. As Deborah White (1991:102-103) points out, various aspects of the Black woman's life was seen in sexual terms and used against her; scarce clothing because of poverty, bending over to work, or lifting one's dress to keep it clean from dirt and water were seen by the slaveholder in sexual terms. In fact, she notes even "some whippings had sexual overtones." Enslaved Africans report beatings stripped naked and masters delighting in it in special ways. As Henry Bibb (1969:120) reports in his narrative as an enslaved African, his master stated that "he had rather paddle a female than eat when hungry." Jacqueline Jones (1985:37) concludes that generally speaking "the sexual violation of Black women by white men rivaled the separation of families as the foremost provocation injected into the Black family life by slaveholders...." And although they had few options in this situation and were brutally punished for resisting, still "Black women often struggled to resist and their fathers, sons and husbands, often struggled to protect them" (see modes of resistance below).

The second major aspect of the American system of enslavement was its cultural genocide against Africans. By cultural genocide is meant, the wholesale intentional destruction of a people's culture and cultural identity and their capacity to produce, reproduce and expand themselves. It includes the destruction of: 1) political identities and ethnic units and identities; 2) families; and 3) cultural leaders. These were all units of the preservation and transmission of African culture. But they were also units of real and potential resistance — on the cultural and physical level and thus, the enslaver sought to destroy them. As Patterson (1982) again notes, one aspect of social death is natal alienation from one's culture and community, one's ancestors and relatives. Thus Africans were systematically deculturalized and cultivated to be totally dependent and marginal.

Finally, the American system of enslavement can be defined and discussed in terms of its machinery of control (Jones, 1990). This machinery of control was one of the most brutal and extensive in the history of enslavement. Basically, it involved five mechanisms of control: 1) laws; 2) coercive bodies; 3) the church; 4) politically divisive strategies; and 5) plantation punishments. The "slave laws" were directed toward defining Africans as property and depriving them of any legal or human right or personality (McIntyre, 1992: Chapter 4). Under these laws or Slave Codes, the enslaved African could not make a contract, could not testify against anyone except another African, could not strike a white man even in self-defense, could not leave a plantation without authorization; could not possess firearms; cold not visit whites, free Africans or entertain them in their quarters; could not assemble without whites; could not learn or be taught to read or write; and could not even beat drums or blow horns (Franklin, 1974:140-141).

The coercive bodies include first, local, county, state and federal armed bodies, soldiers and militias, patrols and vigilante committees dedicated to enforcing the laws even against whites who dared defy them, as in the case of teaching or allowing Africans to learn to read and write or fraternizing with them. Also the Church, as Bennett (1975:73) states was "an integral part of the governing mechanism" and thus, a part of the machinery of control. It was directly involved in upholding the law, buying and selling enslaved Africans and teaching doctrines supportive of the subordination and dehumanization of Africans.

A fourth aspect of the machinery of control was the use of politically divisive strategies to split consciousness and disrupt and deny unity among enslaved Africans. These included strategies to develop "class" or rather stratum divisions among enslaved Africans who worked in the house, yard and field and to develop a collaborator corps that spanned all strata and was used to stifle dissent, spread disinformation and mostly nip revolts in the bud.

Finally, the machinery of control included brutal plantation punishments. Stampp (1965:171-191) in his chapter "To Make Them Stand In Fear", lists some of the viciously ingenious ways whites punished Africans who would not accept or broke the laws and rules of the system of enslavement. Those included: demotions for the house Africans, foremen or drivers to field work; denials of food, clothing, shelter or recreation; splitting up families; imprisonment in private plantation jails; placing in stocks; brandings; whippings; torture; mutilation; and murder. Some of the most heinous and savage punishments were washing wounds in salt, purposely allowing dogs to maul rebels, boiling them alive, skinning them alive, burying them alive and quartering them by tying the legs and arms to one horse each and pulling them apart in four directions. None of this is said to shock or indulge in victimization history, but to clearly depict the system as it was. It is also presented to lay the basis for discussing the resistance of enslaved Africans. For in depicting in stark detail the obstacles enslavement posed to initiative and resistance, one can better appreciate the strength and depth of human will and spirit which led Africans to resist even in the most brutal and controlled situations.

4.5 RESISTANCE TO ENSLAVEMENT

African resistance to enslavement began in Africa, as argued above, and continued in America throughout the period of enslavement (McKivigan and Harrold, 1999). In spite of works which question the equality or extent of African resistance to enslavement, there is ample evidence to demonstrate real and unrelenting resistance to enslavement by both enslaved and free African women and men (Morton, 1996; McIntyre, 1992; Yee, 1992). Given that enslavement threatened and affected even free Africans and that they were thus constantly defending themselves as well as trying to liberate enslaved Africans, African resistance will be treated as a single process, even though more stress will be placed on the resistance activities of the enslaved. There are many works which discuss and analyze various forms for resistance, but no single volume deals thoroughly or extensively with all the ones listed below (Aptheker, 1968, 1943; Quarles, 1969; Mullin, 1972; Price, 1973; Sorin, 1973; Genovese, 1981; Dillon, 1990; McKivigan and Harrold, 1999). But the problem and truth are not that African Americans resisted less, but rather that interpretations of their resistance were less critical and often failed to take into consideration the different circumstances and variables involved. Thus, their comparative analyses were deficient and could not but make Black resistance in the U.S. look likewise.

Variables to take in account when comparing African resistance in the U.S. with African resistance in other societies in the Western hemisphere are: 1) the smaller population size; 2) the existence of less nearby unsettled regions for Maroon or independent societies of escaped Africans; 3) the isolated character of the U.S. plantations which hampered organized unified efforts; 4) the harsh winters which made survival in maroon societies more difficult to maintain as opposed to tropical areas where food and shelter were less a problem; 5) the drastic decline of importation of large numbers of new Africans after

1807 with the federal prohibition of trafficking in enslaved persons, thus depriving enslaved Africans of a vital source of revitalization and rebellion; 6) the greater balance between the sexes and division into family units in the U.S. which often dampened male rebellion and flight in consideration for their family; and finally 7) the pervasive severity of the system which was not content to dominate physically but engaged in the most brutal and racist deculturalization process in the Western hemisphere. This process, as shown above, did not destroy all culture or cultural resistance, but joined to the fact of reduced and halted revitalization from newly imported Africans, the toll it took was significant.

Still, evidence reveals that resistance among African Americans was strong and continuous. But given the arguments surrounding resistance, it is necessary to define it as a preface to discussion of its forms. Resistance here then can be defined as any and all personal and collective acts designed to: 1) deny support to, challenge or overturn the established order; 2) deny, diminish or eliminate its hold; 3) force changes in its structure and functioning and/or; 4) escape its control and jurisdiction. From this definition and available evidence, free and enslaved Africans engaged in five basic forms of resistance to slavery: 1) cultural; 2) day-to-day; 3) abolitionism, 4) emigrationism, and 5) armed struggle.

CULTURAL RESISTANCE

Undoubtedly the most impressive and inclusive book on cultural resistance by enslaved Africans is Blassingame's *The Slave Community*. In this work Blassingame (1979:6) argues that the personality and initiative of the African in enslavement was determined not simply by the impositions of the enslaver, "but rather the interaction between certain universal elements of West African culture, the institutionalized demands of plantation life, the process or enslavement and (the African's) creative response to enslavement." Berlin (1998) and Kolchin (1993) reaffirm the enslaved Africans' adaptive vitality and creative ability to shape lives of meaning and value in the midst of the most inhuman conditions.

Among the forms of cultural resistance, Blassingame lists the following: 1) cultural retention and synthesis; 2) cultural creation; and 3) maintenance and development of a family against all odds. Blassingame observes that most distinctive survivals or retentions are dances, moral narratives, music, magic and language patterns and spiritual beliefs (Holloway, 1990; Webber, 1978). Synthesis took place in these same areas especially in religion and music where, as Blassingame (1979:20-21) notes, "in the process of acculturation, the slaves made European forms serve African functions."

Cultural creation was a form of cultural resistance in that the European sought not only to destroy the African's past but to limit and control his/her future. But the Africans carved out space for themselves wherever and whenever they could and proved that "however oppressive or dehumanizing the plantation was, the struggle for survival was not severed enough to crush the slave's creative instincts" (Blassingame, 1979:105).

A third form of cultural resistance was building and maintaining the African family against all odds (White, 1991; Jacobs, 1987; Jones, 1985; Gutman, 1976). The slaveholder's sexual abuse of African women, his division and selling of family members, his breeding practices, and the denial and restriction of the African man's ability to protect, provide for and exercise authority in his family, all militated against a viable and durable Black family. Yet not only did the Black family survive, but it developed and performed the basic functions of socialization and care all families provide. However, it was not only "an important buffer (and) refuge from the rigors of slavery," but also a space where values of resistance were taught, where the trust needed for successful resistance was found and where active support for resistance was often available (Blassingame 1979:191).

DAY-TO-DAY RESISTANCE

Most literature on resistance to enslavement focuses on day-to-day resistance as the definitive form but as this section shows, there were equally important other forms which deserve critical study. Day-to-Day resistance was, however, very important to the resistance process (Jones, 1990; Bauer and Bauer, 1942). Its regularity and pervasiveness are suggested by the category used to define it, i.e., "day-to-day." This form of resistance reflects the daily refusal and challenge with which Africans confronted the enslavement system and include sabotage, i.e., breaking tools and destroying crops, shamming illness or ignorance, taking property, spontaneous and planned strikes, work slow-downs, self-mutilation, arson, attacks on whites and poisoning of slave-holders and their families. Also, this form included suicide and infanticide which was designed to prevent life in enslavement of both parents and children and then deny the slaveholder both the profit and the perverse pleasure of domination and commerce of enslaved persons. A final form of day-to-day resistance was flight. Although many writers list flight as distinct from day-to-day resistance, I included it because of its regularity and the daily preoccupation with it (Mullin, 1972). All these forms, however, not only prove the real and unrelenting daily presence of resistance, but also disproves the image of the docile enslaved African that Phillips (1963) and Elkins (1966) contrived.

ABOLITIONISM

This form of resistance includes all efforts dedicated to abolishing enslavement conducted by both free Africans and formerly enslaved Africans like Harriet Tubman, Frederick Douglass and Sojourner Truth, Maria Stewart, Frances Ellen Watkins Harper, William Wells Brown, Ellen and William Craft and others (Painter, 1996; Reed, 1994; Yee, 1992; Blackett, 1983; Quarles, 1969). As early as 1797, African fugitives from enslavement petitioned Congress to consider "our relief as a people." And in 1800, a group of Philadelphian Africans petitioned Congress to revise federal laws concerning the enslavement of Africans and fugitive enslaved Africans and to adopt measures for eventual emancipation. By 1830 free Africans had organized fifty anti-enslavement societies dedicated to abolition of the system of enslavement and aid to enslaved Africans in escaping and to those who escaped or were freed by purchase or other means. They also were founding members of multi-racial anti-enslavement societies, such as the American Anti-Slavery Society and the New England Anti-Slavery Society and were 400 of the 450 original subscribers to William

Sojourner Truth

Garrison's famous anti-enslavement paper, the Liberator (Quarles, 1969).

Frederick Douglass

The diversity and intensity of the activities of the Black abolitionist are extremely impressive. Among these activities were: 1) fundraising efforts for purchase, aid and legal defense of enslaved Africans and anti-enslavement literature; 2) provision of security forces for defense and anti-enslavement rallies and to prevent kidnappings of fugitive and free Africans by former holders and catchers of enslaved Africans; 3) a massive publication effort including at its height major narratives of enslaved Africans, anti-enslavement books and 17 newspapers, including the first Black paper in the U.S., *Freedom's Journal*, 1827; 4) establishment of a distinguished speakers bureau of both formerly enslaved and free Africans to disseminate information and call for support in the struggle in the U.S., Canada and throughout Europe; 5) boycott efforts against products which though largely unsuccessful were significant as an expression of exhausting all avenues; 6) establishment of legal committees to defend free and enslaved Africans against enslavement and return; 7) establishment of vigilance committees, self-help and mutual aid societies to aid formerly enslaved Africans in adjusting to freedom; and 8) the building and maintenance of the Underground Railroad, a system of freeing, transporting and placing formerly enslaved Africans in the North or Canada.

It is important to stress two of the activities above. First, the publication efforts also included such works as *David Walker's Appeal* (1820) which was a severe and famous criticism of the system of enslavement, a call for revolt by the enslaved Africans and for aid by the free; George Moses Horton's *Hope of Liberty* (1829), and Robert Young's *Ethiopian Manifesto* (1829); Maria Stewart's *Meditations from the Pen of Mrs. Maria W. Stewart* (1832), Mary Prince's *The History of Mary Prince, A West Indian Slave* (1831), Lucy Delaney's *From Darkness Cometh the Light or Struggles for Freedom* (n.d.), Henry Highland Garnett's *Address* (1843), Frederick Douglass' *Narrative of My Life* (1845); Harriet Jacob's *Incidents in the Life of a Slave Girl* (1861) and Frances

E.W. Harper's *Poems on Miscellaneous Subjects* (1854) among others. Secondly, the Underground Railroad represented in "a most dramatic way the determination of the abolitionists to destroy slavery" (Franklin, 1974:198). For it was a direct act against the system of enslavement, depriving it of its key units, its objects of labor and inspiring in them thoughts of freedom and a sense of possibility. Both the fear and effectiveness of this underground effort to free enslaved Africans are expressed in a governor of Mississippi's claim that "between 1810 and 1850 the South lost 100,000 slaves valued at more than $30 million" (Franklin, 1974:203).

Although, it had many distinguished "conductors" or group leaders, none was as outstanding in legend and reality as Harriet

Harriet Tubman

Tubman (Conrad, 1943). Freeing herself, she also freed her children, her sister and mother and father as well as hundreds of others. With the largest bounty ever on the head of an enslaved African, she went South at least 19 times, defying death and capture, and refusing to let any enslaved African turn back under penalty of death. She was also an excellent lecturer and raised funds for the cause, setting an example of the determination of the enslaved to be free and their dedication to freeing others they had left behind. Moreover, as Franklin and Moss (1988:170) report, Tubman was so dedicated to the struggle for freedom that she "would take several months off whenever she was running low in funds and hire herself out as a domestic servant in order to raise money for conveying (enslaved Africans) to freedom."

Also, it is important to stress the role of the numerous Black women abolitionists who often were not given due recognition and credit for their work. Yee (1992) offers a valuable portrait of Black women who gave their lives to the cause of freedom. Confronting both the racism of the white women's movement and the sexism of the abolitionist movement they nevertheless worked for freedom with untiring energy (Foster, 1990; Bernard, 1990; Billington, 1981, Richardson, 1987). Explaining this focus on freedom and struggle, Frances Watkins Harper, an active member of the Underground Railroad and one of the first African American women to be employed as an abolitionist lecturer, noted in 1852 that the work of abolitionism was an urgent and collective one. In a word, she said "the condition of our people, the wants of our children, and the welfare our own race demand the aid of every helping hand" (quoted in Sterling, 1984:159). Binding together in networks of friendship and sisterhood, they organized politically, raised money, created intellectual groups for ongoing exchange, lectured and taught and engaged in a myriad of activities that abolitionism required and encouraged. Also, Black women formed the first female anti-enslavement society, the Salem Female Antislavery Society in 1832. Through these activities they established models of sisterhood and struggle which informed and inspired subsequent women and men activists.

EMIGRATIONISM

Another key form of African resistance to enslavement was emigrationism, the push to emigrate back to Africa or go elsewhere where Africans could be free and self-determining. As early as 1773, a group of enslaved Africans in Massachusetts petitioned colonial officials for permission to work in order to earn money for transportation to "some part of the coast of Africa where we propose a settlement" (Aptheker, 1951:8). Also, in 1787, "a group of eighty Boston Blacks petitioned the state legislature to assist them in getting to Africa, providing them money to pay passage and buy land" (Quarles, 1976:96). These Africans were members of the African Society which was dedicated to encouraging emigration to establish a self-determining, self-reliant African nation on the West Coast of Africa. Paul Cuffee, a Black Quaker, was also one of the early advocates of emigrationism and used his own money to repatriate 38 Africans to Sierra Leone in 1815 (Harris, 1972). He also petitioned the U.S. President and Congress for aid in this project in 1814 but to no avail. It is in light of this that he used his own money and urged others to help to repatriate as many Africans as he could before he died in 1817.

In 1817 the Negro Convention Movement was organized in Philadelphia and became in time a source for the ardent advocacy of emigrationism. The Convention Movement was abolitionist and emigrationist and though it focused on sending Blacks to Canada, at an 1854 convention, it met to consider emigration to other areas including Africa, the Caribbean and Central America. Some of its best known members were Martin Delaney, who argued for the indispensability of Black nationhood; James Holly, who stressed the need to go to Haiti and develop it; and Daniel Payne and Alexander Crummell, giants of the African Methodist Episcopal Church. Also, Mary Ann Shadd Cary actively advocated emigration to Canada. In 1852 she wrote an essay titled *A Plea for Emigration or Notes of Canada West, in its Moral, Social and Political Aspect.* The first African American female editor and publisher, Shadd used her *Provincial Freeman* to advocate self-reliance.

Although only some members of the Convention Movement advocated emigrationism, all of them opposed the

Martin Delaney

colonization schemes of the American Colonization Society. This was essentially a white initiated and dominated organization which had supported the founding of Liberia and advocated that all Blacks including free Blacks return to Africa. The free Africans opposed this wholesale immigration for four basic reasons: 1) they saw it as a way to get rid of free Blacks to better secure slavery; 2) they considered it their duty to stay and fight for emancipation; 3) they assumed it would give weight to the arguments of Black inferiority and inability to cope with "civilization;" and 4) they reasoned that they were as much Americans as whites in terms of their contribution and birth. Given these strong positions and fear of emigrationist sentiments being manipulated by racists wanting to get rid of all Blacks, emigrationism lost much of its appeal and appeared strongest at times of extreme oppression and anti-Black agitation.

ARMED RESISTANCE

Obviously, the ultimate criticism of and resistance to a society is armed action against it, and enslaved Africans engaged in this form of resistance (Genovese, 1981; Dillon, 1990; McKivigan and Harrold, 1999). Although much of the literature on armed resistance focuses on revolts, there were other forms. In addition to revolts, four other basic forms stand out: ship mutinies, guerilla warfare, Afro-Mexican alliance and struggle, and Afro-Native American alliance and struggle.

REVOLTS

Over 250 revolts are recorded in the U.S., but only a few have been researched and written on at length (Aptheker, 1943; Carroll, 1938). Among the most notable and most written on are: 1) the New York City Revolt in 1712; 2) the Stono, South Carolina revolt in 1739; 3) the southern Louisiana revolt in 1811; 4) the Nat Turner revolt in 1831. In addition, two planned revolts or conspiracies are also well-written about and well-discussed, i.e., the Gabriel and Nana Prosser conspiracy in 1800 and the Denmark Vesey conspiracy in 1822 (Egerton, 1993; Sidbury, 1998; Egerton, 1999; Robertson, 1999; Pearson, 1999).

The importance of these and other revolts or attempted revolts lies not so much in their military effectiveness, for a revolt by definition is an unsuccessful revolution, i.e., an unsuccessful armed uprising which does not end in seizure of state power. Rather their significance lies in: 1) what is revealed about the rebels, especially their leaders; 2) the chilling effect they had on the slaveholders; and 3) the effect they had on the other enslaved Africans and eventually their descendants.

The major revolts reveal rebel leaders conscious of and prone toward use of religion as an instrument of unity and struggle. Both historical African religion and Africanized Christianity were used to call the rebels to arms, to justify the moral right to rebellion and freedom, and steel them against overwhelming odds. Moreover, the rebel leaders, especially the Prossers, Vesey and Turner were aware of and sought to use current political realities to their advantage. The Prossers expected French help in their struggle; Vesey looked to Haiti for inspiration and support, and Turner saw in the internal debates on enslavement a good omen reinforced by the religio-political visions he had of war and liberation. Each having taught himself to read and write, kept up with the news and used the concepts and arguments for freedom and rights in the Declaration of Independence, the Constitution and the Rights of Man, demonstrating a grasp of the ideologies of the Age of Revolution. Finally, one is struck by the dedication, determination and audaciousness of these rebels, risking all to be free even though being as knowledgeable as they were, they knew the overwhelming odds. Given these odds, as Genovese (1981:50) notes, "only the most heroic souls, even as measured by the highest standards of revolutionary self sacrifice could contemplate such a course..."

The effect those rebels and revolts had on whites is clear from the record. The reactions of the enslavers and other whites were invariably reflective of bloodthirsty hysteria. The bloodletting they engaged in and the stringent laws they passed after each revolt showed their fear and tended to erode their contrived image of invincibility. Often they imagined revolts and conspiracies where there were none, showing a respect for Blacks they would never admit and even many historians fail to observe. Thus, in spite of their writings about the docile, happy enslaved African, they could not easily deny their own deaths at the hands of African rebels. They could and did often hide these realities, but they knew them and were thus forced to face the constant fact and threat of revolt throughout the period of enslavement. What Franklin (1974:160) noted about the result of the Prosser conspiracy can be said of other conspiracies and revolts, "The large numbers (at least a thousand), together with the disregard the slaves seemed to have for their own lives caused the whites to shudder." Moreover, "the 'high ground' they took in maintaining silence added to the *stark terror of the situation*" (emphasis mine).

The effect these rebels and revolts had on the other enslaved Africans was strong and positive. Although some may argue that their capture, death and lack of success discouraged other enslaved Africans, this is only partly true. For as some were discouraged, as in the case of revolts of the enslaved throughout the world and throughout history, many were also encouraged by the audaciousness and determination shown by the rebels. One cannot but be impressed by the rebels' willingness to risk their lives and those of their loved ones against such overwhelming odds. One is also unavoidably impressed by the political commitment and political awareness of an enslaved African in 1800 slaveholding America, informing his captors who asked what he had to say during the "trial" that:

I have nothing more to offer than what General Washington would have had to offer, had he been taken

by the British officers and put to trial by them. I have
ventured my life in endeavoring to obtain the liberty of
my countrymen, and am a willing sacrifice to their
cause; and I ask a favour, that I may be immediately led
to execution. I know that you have predetermined to shed
my blood. Why then all this mockery of a trial?

The witnesses to this bold and well-presented statement and
stand were not only the captors but other enslaved Africans who
undoubtedly felt admiration and respect.

Nat Turner reports an exchange between himself and a newcomer to his group of rebels which indicates a similar political
commitment to the freedom struggle. He reports that he:

...asked Will (the newcomer) how he came there? He
answered (that) his life was worth no more than others,
and his liberty as dear to him. I asked him if he meant to
obtain it? He said he would or lose his life.

Again, this commitment was recognized and respected by
other enslaved Africans. A strong evidence of this recognition
and respect is found in the following popular song praising Nat
Turner and noting the vulnerability of the enslaver and the system of enslavement:

You might be rich as cream
And drive you a coach and four-horse team.
But you can't keep de world from movin' round
Nor Nat Turner from gainin ground.
And your name it might be Caesar for sure.
And got you a canon that can shoot a mile or more,
But you can't keep de world from movin' round
Nor Nat Turner from gaining ground.
(following Stuckey: 1973:141).

It is this legacy also which has: 1) inspired the descendants
of the once enslaved Africans, 2) negated the lies their oppressors have told them about their foreparents' resistance, 3) taught
possibilities of struggle and the strength to endure and prevail
based on historical precedence and models; and 5) demonstrated
to the enslavers, the enslaved Africans, their descendants, and

the world, the impossibility of destroying the will and thrust of African peoples to resist and be free.

SHIP MUTINIES

Ship mutinies constituted a second form of armed struggle to enslavement (Harding, 1981:Chapter 1). These struggles also stand out for overcoming the obstacles placed in their way to prevent them. Greene (1944:347) reports that "every possible precaution was taken to prevent the slaves from revolting." Not only were the crews well armed with canons, guns and knives, but guards stood on constant watch. Also the enslaved Africans — men, women and children — were chained in compartments only three feet three inches and sometimes no more than 18 inches to prevent their sitting erect. Forced to lie spoon fashion to increase carrying capacity and prevent any defiance, the enslaved Africans often were rubbed raw by rolling ships, caught all kinds of diseases and died of suffocation.

But in spite of this oppressive and restrictive Middle Passage ride, the enslaved Africans although weakened by confinement and ship-contracted disease, often rebelled and attempted to seize the ship and return to Africa. From evidence, ship mutinies seemed to have been more successful than revolts on land. Among the many successful mutinies were those on the Little George (1730), the Jolly Bachelor (1740) and the Amistad (1839). In the case of the Little George, the ship had sailed from the Guinea Coast in 1730 with ninety-six enslaved Africans. Freeing themselves from shackles, they put the crew to flight in the cabin below. They guided the ship into Sierra Leone River, removed all the women and children and left the ship. The Jolly Bachelor which was carrying captives down the Sierra Leone River in 1740 was attacked and captured by Africans who freed the enslaved Africans and stripped the ship of its sails and rigging and then disembarked.

Perhaps the most famous ship mutiny in African American history, however, is the Amistad mutiny in 1839. In this mutiny, a group of Africans, led by Joseph Cinque, an African prince, seized the ship, killed their captors and attempted to return to Africa. Intercepted by a U.S. naval vessel, they were captured and brought to trial. Abolitionists hired John Quincy Adams to defend them and they were freed and allowed to return to Africa.

Again, this form of armed resistance proves the will and spirit to be free among enslaved Africans and contributes definitively to an important legacy.

GUERRILLA WARFARE

A third form of armed resistance to enslavement was guerrilla warfare conducted by members of Maroon or independent communities. Although attention and credit have been given to Maroon societies and struggles in other parts of the Western Hemisphere, comparatively little has been written on Maroon societies and warfare in the U.S. (Price, 1973; Aptheker, 1968; Mullin, 1972).

There is evidence of the establishment of at least fifty Maroon communities between 1672-1864 with varying life-spans. These communities existed in the forest, mountain and swampy regions of several states, i.e., Virginia, North Carolina, South Carolina, Georgia, Louisiana, Mississippi, Alabama and Florida. However, the most notable and largest communities existed in the Dismal Swamp, along the Virginia-North Carolina border and in Florida in union with the Seminole Native Americans which will be discussed under Afro-Native American alliance and struggle. These Maroons sought in varying ways to duplicate the African societies from which they came. They built communal agricultural societies, raised crops and animals and fowl, maintained families with African kinship patterns and even engaged in trade with whites in certain areas.

The significance of the Maroon communities as a source of resistance, expressed itself on five basic levels. First, they represented a reality and possibility of self-determination and power to other enslaved Africans. Both their existence and their victories against search-and-destroy expeditions and successful attacks on plantations reaffirmed this reality and possibility. Secondly, they were sources of asylum for fugitives daring enough to escape and reach them. Thirdly, they were bases from which to launch attacks on plantations for supplies or in retaliation and thus, on the system of enslavement itself, even if only in a minor and isolated way. Fourthly, they often raided plantations to free enslaved Africans. Fifthly, they often provided leadership and inspiration for revolts among the enslaved. Thus, although isolated, limited means of subsistence and regular search-destroy measures reduced the Maroon communities' capacity to expand and consolidate and wage a more effective guerilla warfare, the contribution they did make to the overall process and legacy of resistance stands out and must be recognized and respected.

AFRO-MEXICAN ALLIANCE AND STRUGGLE

Afro-Mexican alliance and struggle offers a fourth form of armed resistance by Africans against enslavement. Enslaved Africans began to go to Mexico early in the 1800's to seek freedom. This was due to three basic reasons. First, Mexico was close to the South, especially close to Texas, Louisiana and Florida from which most came. Secondly, local Mexicans would often protect them from pursuing Anglos whom they resented or hated. Thirdly, the Mexican government was favorable toward enslaved Africans, having abolished enslavement in 1824 and put it in the Constitution in 1857, the same year, the U.S. Supreme Court ruled in the Dred Scott decision that Blacks had no rights whites were bound to respect (Schwartz, 1975).

Mexico's anti-enslavement position was both humanitarian and political. In its war with Spain, it had raised the cry of freedom for all and took it seriously. In terms of its political position, it saw Africans as barriers against Anglo invasion and encroachment on their lands. Thus, they offered Africans and Native Americans land on the border in states such as Tamaulipas and Coahuila where Blacks who have not totally merged with the indigenous population still live today. In the early 1850's hundreds of Seminoles (Afro-Native Americans) migrated from Oklahoma to Coahuila forming military colonies and buffers against Anglo soldiers and slave-raiders. Other Blacks received land in the state of Vera Cruz for development and were exempted from all taxes and from military service, barring foreign invasions.

AFRO-NATIVE AMERICAN ALLIANCE AND STRUGGLE

A fifth and final form of armed resistance by enslaved Africans to enslavement was Afro-Native American alliances and struggle (Twyman, 1999; Foster, 1935; Littlefield, 1977; Bennett, 1975). Africans and Native Americans have a close history in community and struggle which reaches back to the Holocaust of enslavement and the common ground they found first in struggle (hooks, 1992; Katz, 1986; Forbes, 1980). One of the earliest known examples of Africans and Native Americans allied in resistance and war was in an uprising in Hartford, Connecticut in 1657 (Bennett, 1975:89). From 1657 on, Bennett reports a continuous series of plots, insurrections and armed actions against Europeans by Afro-Native American joint action. In fact, in the New York City rebellion of 1712, Native Americans fought jointly with Africans. These alliances and joint actions were rooted in their association as fellow enslaved persons, their common mistreatment by the European, their intermixture and need to defend themselves from the threat of conquest and enslavement.

Easily, the most clear and impressive example of Afro-Native American alliance is the Afro-Seminole Alliance in Florida. In no other Native American nation or ethnic group were Africans treated with such deference and did they rise to such leadership roles in politics and war. As early as 1738, enslaved Africans began to regularly escape from South Carolina taking refuge among the Creeks or Seminoles in Florida.

The Seminoles were a group of Creeks whose name in Creek means runaways and who in 1750 seceded from the Creek Nation and went to a territory in Florida. There they settled near African Maroons and began to build a strong bond. In fact, it can be argued that the Seminole Nation developed early into an Afro-Native American nation controlled and run by Africans. Even though Porter (1932:326) refers to enslavement among the Seminoles, he has to admit that "not only were the Seminole slaves not slaves in the usual sense of the word; they might even lay claim to being the *true rulers of the nation*" (emphasis mine). Porter attributes this rise to political leadership by Africans among the Seminole to four basic factors: 1) Africans' knowledge of the European and his culture and thus their value in war and peace exchanges; 2) their indispensability as negotiators, guides and interpreters, often speaking French, Spanish and English; 3) their agricultural skills and thus value in creating and sustaining agricultural economies; 4) their courage and skill in war. Therefore, he concludes, the Africans were valued as allies and associates and accepted as equals and later, leaders in war and politics.

Moreover, in the Seminole wars, Africans were both generals and often most of the soldiers. They fought fiercely, won many victories and would not often surrender because of the certainty of re-enslavement. They also used their key political and military positions in the Seminole Nation to refuse emigration to Oklahoma Territory suggested by the U.S. Government and prolonged the struggle to avoid re-enslavement and maintain self-determination. This is why Gen. Jessup, a U.S. commander in the war, argued that Seminole wars were "an (African) not a (Native American) war which if not quickly put down would affect the enslaved African population."

4.6 CIVIL WAR AND RECONSTRUCTION

The road to Civil War was most definitively laid in the stormy 1850's (Franklin, 1974:208ff; McPherson, 1988). In this decade, a series of events made war almost inevitable. First, was the passage of the 1850 Fugitive Slave Law which made the fugitive guilty until proven innocent, denied his/her testimony and was retroactive (Collison, 1998; Von Frank, 1998). It gave the abolitionists another opportunity to expose the viciousness and recalcitrance of enslavers and enslavement advocates. Secondly, in 1854 Congress passed the Kansas-Nebraska Act which repealed the Missouri Compromise of 1850 which prohibited enslavement in the Kansas-Nebraska Territory. This increased the bloody struggle in the territory and foreshadowed larger battles. Thirdly, the U.S. Supreme Court ruled in the Dred Scott case (1857) that neither free nor enslaved Africans were citizens and had no rights whites were bound to respect. Fourthly, John Brown, a white radical abolitionist attacked Harper's Ferry in 1859 to gain arms for at least 500 enslaved Africans and wage a war in the South. Although Black abolitionists like Frederick Douglass and Harriet Tubman thought correctly that this move was premature and unwise, he became a martyr of the abolitionist movement and foreshadowed the coming war. The final straw came with the election of Abraham Lincoln whom the South hated and whose election they saw as an abolitionist vote.

CIVIL WAR

The Civil War began with the Confederate attack on Fort Sumner, S.C. in April 1861. Although many factors can be cited as causes of the Civil War, the question of enslavement and by extension the question of the future of Africans in America stand at the core of its causes. The Civil War is important in African American history not only because it led to their emancipation, but even more important, because they fought heroically and in great numbers in the war and played other significant roles in it (Williams, 1888). As Quarles (1969:296) states, African Americans "took stock in the adage that they who would be free must themselves strike the blow." Thus, they took up arms and became self-conscious agents of their own liberation.

At first the whites resisted the idea of Blacks serving in the army, feeling that: 1) to call and depend on Blacks implied their inadequacies; 2) arming Blacks meant arming potential rebels; 3) serving in the armed forces would change the social attitude and status of Blacks and thus pose a problem for white rule and power. They also pretended to doubt the fighting qualities of Blacks, but this was irrational and based more on racist ego-needs than evidence as the war would prove. By the summer of 1862, after a series of military defeats by Union forces, Congress passed the Confiscation Act and Militia Act which opened the way for free and freed Africans to aid the war effort. Moreover, Lincoln, seeing the indispensability of African American participation in the war, if it were to be won, issued in the same year the Emancipation Proclamation.

The Proclamation was not a blanket declaration of freedom for all enslaved Africans, only for enslaved Africans in states and parts of states in rebellion against the U.S. government. Loyal slave states like Missouri, Kentucky, Maryland and Delaware were exempt. Moreover, it did not grant freedom; it only "declared" it—a declaration totally unenforceable. For the proclamation was declaring freedom for enslaved Africans in the Confederacy, a land which had already rejected U.S. jurisdiction and was at war with it to defend its decision. Its value was as a propaganda document to appease abolitionists and Radical Republicans, give the war the moral character it lacked and contribute further to the rebellion and flight among enslaved

Africans which had already reached a high level (Quarles, 1953:117).

Africans, anxious to fight for freedom, respect and better status and role in society, enlisted in large numbers and served in various capacities. In addition to serving as regular soldiers and sailors, they served as guides, scouts, intelligence agents, engineers, nurses, surgeons, chaplains, construction workers, teamsters, cooks, carpenters, miners, farmers, commandos and recruiters. An estimated 186,000 Africans participated as soldiers and 29,000 as sailors accounting for 25% of U.S. sailors. The real number of participants is probably much higher but was disguised by many racially mixed people being registered as whites. Moreover, Blacks served in every theater of operations, fought in 449 engagements, thirty-nine of which were major battles and won seventeen Congressional Medals of Honor on land and four on sea. These achievements were made in spite of vicious racism exhibited in treatment, pay and time differentials, poor equipment, bad medical care, excess fatigue details, reckless and hasty assignments and the no-quarter policy of the South against Black soldiers.

The Civil War ended April 9, 1865 with the surrender of Gen. Robert E. Lee to Gen. Ulysses S. Grant. The end of the war and the Union victory was important to both African Americans and the nation as a whole. For African Americans, it was an end to enslavement which had lasted almost 250 years. Secondly, it represented a victory won only as a result of their entry and heroic participation in the struggle which was not only to free them but win respect and a new status in society. Thirdly, it meant the beginning of a new struggle to secure economic and political rights which did not automatically come with emancipation. For the nation, the victory meant the federal government had clearly established its sovereignty over the states, freed the South from a morally indefensible and politically and economically backward system and thus opened for the South and the nation a new era of economic growth and political change — as well as the problems which accompanied this process.

RECONSTRUCTION

The period of Reconstruction (1865-1877) represented for African Americans "the best of times and the worst of times" (Berlin and Rowlands, 1997). It was a time of great leaps forward and hope and great disappointment and betrayal (Logan, 1954). For the U.S., it represented a time of great possibility to realize its ideals of freedom, justice and equality for all. But after a strong start it betrayed its own ideals and failed in solving the problems the post-war period posed, i.e., the problems of Reconstruction. These problems were essentially: 1) rebuilding the South's economy on the basis of free labor and its industrialization and reintegration in the national economy; 2) politically subduing and transforming the South; and 3) integration of the freed Africans into the social fabric, especially in the South and protecting them from re-enslavement, exploitation and abuse. Out of these problems, only the reintegration of the South economically and politically were really achieved. This took place on the South's own terms and included the betrayal and sacrifice of the African American (Harding, 1981).

However, early events seemed to suggest an alternative outcome. The Freedman's Bureau was established by Congress in 1865 to guide and protect the freed Africans. It was to: 1) set up schools for them; 2) provide medical services, 3) write, supervise and enforce their contracts; 4) manage, lease and sell them confiscated and abandoned lands; 5) resettle them; and 6) provide them legal assistance and protection. Moreover, Congress passed three cornerstone Amendments directed toward integration of Blacks in the social fabric on the basis of equality, i.e., the Thirteenth, Fourteenth and Fifteenth Amendments. Essentially, the Thirteenth freed them; the Fourteenth made them citizens, and the Fifteenth gave them the right to vote. Also, Congress passed the 1866 Civil Rights Act (CRA) declaring Blacks citizens again; the 1870 Civil Rights Act to expand and strengthen the 1866 CRA; and the 1871 CRA which sought to establish equal rights in the public facilities and jury duties. Congress also passed the 1871 Enforcement Act which outlawed white terrorist societies like the Ku Klux Klan.

However, economically, Congress did not give Blacks the support they needed and they were essentially reintegrated back into the southern economy under semi-enslaved conditions as sharecroppers. Whites, never accepting the freedom and equali-ty of African Americans, passed Black Codes, patterned after the antebellum Slave Codes which made "the control of Blacks by white employers...about as great as that which slaveholders exer-cised" (Franklin, 1988:206). In spite of the general assumption among Blacks that the federal government would give them lots of forty acres, and the tacit encouragement given this assump-tion by the creation of the Freedman's Bureau, the government never did, thus posing one of the main problems of Black eco-nomic adjustment. For with no land of their own, the majority of freed Africans slowly but inevitably returned to the plantation more or less at the mercy of their employers.

Moreover, those who did go to urban areas were met with crippling discrimination and severe exploitation. Black carpen-ters, bricklayers, painters, blacksmiths and other skilled workers were strongly opposed by white artisans in their employment efforts. Skilled and unskilled workers were denied union mem-bership and white employers often used Blacks to break union strikes thus, splitting the labor movement and casting Blacks as essentially strikebreakers and ones who would work for the low-est wages. In 1869 African Americans created two unions, the National Labor Convention of Colored Men and the National Negro Labor Union, and sought affiliation with white labor unions, but to no avail. By 1874, due to this exclusion and other factors, these Black labor union thrusts were effectively ended.

The Reconstruction period, however, did provide some political gains for African American although they were short-lived. During this period 22 African American served in Congress. Two served in the Senate, Hiram Revels and Blanche K. Bruce, both from Mississippi and 20 served in the House. In spite of the racist claims that they were uneducated, ten had gone to college and five had degrees. Moreover, most had some political experience before going to Congress as delegates to constitutional conventions and as local and state officials and state senators and representatives. Although African American legislators were unable to pass much legislation in Congress, at the state levels they were able to achieve much more. They expanded suffrage, instituted free public education, improved the tax system, reorganized the judicial system and repealed imprisonment for debt laws as well as negative labor laws of 1865 and 1866 which were part of the Black Codes.

Eventually, however, the efforts to reconstruct the life of the African American and the South on the basis of freedom, justice and equality, failed for several reasons. (Harding, 1981:Chapter 16). These included: 1) the failure of the federal government to give Blacks land and equipment, thus forcing them into semi-enslaved status; 2) the return of Southerners to status of respect represented by the repeal of the loyalty oath requirement for re-entering national political life; 3) the rise of the white terrorist societies like the KKK and the Camelias in spite of the 1870 and 1871 laws against such societies; 4) the Supreme Court's eroding constitutional and legislative gains for Blacks through rulings favorable to the South; 5) the disintegration of the old coalition of abolitionists, Radical Republicans and northern industrialists through fatigue, retirement, disenchantment and the push for social peace in the South which would allow economic growth; and finally, 6) the Hayes-Tilden Compromise in 1877 which saw President Hayes grant the South federal troop withdrawal, assistance in internal improvements and better representation in Congress for its electoral votes. In 1878, federal troops were withdrawn leaving Blacks at the mercy of racist governments and terrorist societies. In 1894 federal marshals were withdrawn and in 1896 the Supreme Court issued its Plessy vs. Ferguson decision, the "separate but equal" doctrine that lasted until 1954 with the Brown vs. the Board of Education decision.

4.7   THE GREAT MIGRATIONS AND URBANIZATION

The end of the Civil War brought migrations in three basic directions, i.e., to the southern cities, southwestward to Arkansas, Oklahoma, Texas and Kansas and to the northern cities (Trotter, 1991; Marks, 1989). The Kansas migration in 1879 was the largest southwest movement and included over 7,000 Blacks going to Kansas with lesser numbers to Missouri, Iowa and Nebraska (Painter, 1977). But the greatest migrations were to the northern and southern cities — and between 1890 — 1910, the urbanization of Blacks moved from 20 to 27 percent. At first the southern cities received the majority of Black migrants, but by the 1900's the tide was turning in favor of the northern cities. Thus, by 1903 DuBois noted that "the most significant economic change among (Blacks) in the last ten or twenty years had been their influx into northern cities."

The Great Migration of the World War I era was due to several factors. First, it was due to the dissatisfaction with and determination to escape the oppressive and exploitative race relations in the South (Litwack, 1998). Secondly, it was prompted by the depressed economic situation in the South which included crop failures, the ravage of the boll weevil and natural disasters like the 1915 floods in Alabama and Mississippi which had disastrous results on the agricultural economies. A third factor was the growth of industry in the North, especially with increased semi-skilled and unskilled labor demands due to World War I. Fourthly, the world war had cut off immigration from Europe and with it its pool of unskilled laborers and domestic servants. And finally, there were intense efforts by manufacturing companies who sent recruiting agents in the South to solicit Black labor as well as by Black newspapers who induced Blacks to come North for greater opportunities (Quarles, 1969:193-194).

But the North was not the heaven promised. On the contrary, racial violence, discrimination and abuse continued in the

Ida B. Wells-Barnett

North. As Drake and Cayton (1962, Vol. 1:174) noted, the migration led to the rise of the ghetto or "Black Belt," a segregated residential area "whose inhabitants can neither scatter as individuals nor expand as a group..." Moreover, it was defined by its dilapidated houses, overcrowdedness, poor health, high mortality rate, police brutality and other social ills. Secondly, Blacks encountered continued white terrorism and violence evidenced in lynchings and racial riots by whites (Tolnay and Beck, 1995; Patterson, 1998). In the summer of 1919, often called the "Red Summer," there were twenty incidents of white mob violence of riots, against Blacks in the North and South. Ida B. Wells-Barnett (1990), a journalist, author and anti-lynching activist, played an important role in exposing this white terrorism and unmasking the self-serving sexual ideologies of white racists (Carby, 1987:110ff; Duster, 1977). In her autobiography, *Crusade for Justice* she recounts in detail the vicious practices of lynching and her tireless crusade against it under daily threat to her life. Her pamphlets against lynching, *Southern Horror* (1892), *Red Record* (1895) and *Mob Rule* in New Orleans (1900) were important in providing both statistical and literary witness to the terror and a critical analysis of race and gender relations in the U.S. at this time. In the first year of the century, there were a hundred lynchings and by 1914, there were more than 1,100. Although most occurred in the South, as with the riots, the North had its share. Finally, the Black migrant met worsening conditions of the labor market. After the war, employment declined rapidly due to the decrease in government contracts with industry, the return of 4,500,000 soldiers and traditional discrimination which made Blacks the "last hired and first fired."

4.8 ORGANIZATION FOR SOCIAL JUSTICE AND SOCIAL SERVICE

BLACK WOMEN'S NATIONAL CLUB MOVEMENT

Black women's national club movement emerged among African American women during the 1890's. It rose out of African cultural traditions which stressed collective concern and responsibility to family and community (Sudarkasa, 1996) and this led to free Black women and men establishing numerous mutual aid societies during the period of enslavement and afterwards. Some of the earliest female societies would include the Benevolent Daughters (1796), the Daughters of Africa (1812), and the American Female Bond Benevolent Society of Bethel (1817).

After the Holocaust of enslavement, the national Black women's club movement, which was broader and more organized than these early mutual aid societies, formed as Black women became more urbanized, developed more organizations, and had greater access to education. As racial oppression intensified after Reconstruction, they turned greater attention to the struggle for social justice (Logan, 1999; White, 1999; Neverdon-Morton, 1998; Terborg-Penn, 1998; Carby, 1987; Giddings, 1984). In 1896, the First National Conference of the Colored Women of America convened and established the National Association of Colored Women (NACW) with Mary Church Terrell as its first president. It was the merger of two broad coalitions, the Colored Women's League founded in 1892 and the National Federation of African American Women founded in 1895, representing 113 and 85 organizations respectively. The concerns of the NACW can be summed up in its model "Lifting as we climb" and included issues and activities around: 1) education; 2) lynching of Black men, women and children; 3) white sexual abuse and attacks on the moral character of the Black woman; 4) health care; 5) child care services and housing for orphans; 6) care for the elderly; 7) job training; and 8) the broad struggle for social justice and equal rights.

Within twenty years of its founding, NACW represented over 1,000 clubs and 100,000 Black women. Some of the major figures in this movement were Mary Church Terrell, Ida B. Wells-Barnett, Anna Julia Cooper, Charlotte Brown, Fannie Barrier Williams, Margaret Murray Washington and Mary McLeod Bethune. Working within the NACW as its president, Mary McLeod Bethune (1924-1929), had a vision of a larger and more powerful organization, The National Council of Negro Women (NCNW), which she organized and founded in 1935.

Dr. Mary McLeod Bethune

"We need an organization to open new doors for our young women (which) when (it) speaks its power will be felt" she proposed (quoted in Giddings, 1984:212). Expressing her commitment to vision and the development of women, she stated "I am interested in women and I believe in their possibilities. We need vision for larger things, for the unfolding and reviewing of worthwhile things" (Giddings, 1984:214). But Bethune was also for the welfare of the masses of Black people and she directed the development of the NCNW toward service to Black people. And she worked tirelessly in the areas of race, women, education and youth (Giddings, 1984:215).

THE NIAGARA MOVEMENT, NAACP AND URBAN LEAGUE

In addition to the Black women's club movement, other organizations were formed to fight discrimination and oppression. These included the Niagara Movement, the NAACP and the Urban League. The Niagara Movement was formed in 1905 by W.E.B. DuBois and others to fight against injustice. It demanded the right to justice, the vote, education, the abolition of Jim Crow, equal treatment in the armed forces and enforcement of the 13th, 14th and 15th amendments. This militant organization gave way to the National Association for the Advancement of Colored People which was formed by 1909 by African Americans and white liberals (Kellog, 1967). The NAACP, which absorbed many of the Niagara Movement's members including W.E.B. DuBois adopted much of the Movement's philosophy but was not as militant, due to the whites that controlled its executive board. In fact, DuBois was the only African American among its original executive officers. However, the NAACP went on to launch and win effective campaigns against lynching and Jim Crowism, and to secure the vote. Also, the Urban League was founded in 1911 and dedicated itself to social welfare programs (Weiss, 1974). Like the NAACP, white liberals controlled it and it devoted itself to social service programs for jobs, housing, recreation facilities and health clinics, etc., shunning politics and the social struggles of African Americans.

4.9 ACCOMMODATIONISM, CONFRONTATION AND BLACK NATIONALISM

In the wake of the failure of Reconstruction, African Americans were confronted more and more with discrimination and mob violence. By the end of the century, Jim Crowism, the racist system based on the separate-but-equal doctrine and the political, economic and social subordination of Blacks, was firmly in place. Most of the Southern states had passed such discriminatory laws and in 1896 in the *Plessy v. Ferguson* case, the Supreme Court had upheld and enshrined such practices, a ruling that would last until the 1954 Brown Decision. In the areas of politics, economics and justice, African Americans were excluded from voting, jobs and unions, and jury duty. And white terrorist societies rose to ensure such exclusion and subordination.

Moreover, Southern patterns of race relations and racist ideology were shaping public opinion in the North and West. The doctrine of African inferiority was supported by most white anthropologists, and historians and political scientists reinterpreted Reconstruction in the interest of whites. Social Darwinism, which advocated the right and responsibility of the assumed strong to conquer and use the assumed weak for their own more noble ends, not only served as a justification for Blacks subjugation in the U.S., but also for American imperialism against other Third World peoples. In this precarious context, three major leaders rose to pose related but different ways to achieve freedom and justice for African people. Separately and through their ideological struggles with each other they established political tendencies which even today serve as models and points of debate concerning the future and struggle of Blacks in the U.S. These leaders were Booker T. Washington, W.E.B. DuBois and The Hon. Marcus Garvey.

BOOKER T. WASHINGTON

The career of Booker T. Washington was indisputably an impressive one (Washington, 1968; Harlan, 1972, 1983). Having been born in enslavement in Virginia, he rose to national and international fame and was accepted in the North and South as the major Black leader of his time. In 1903, even DuBois (1969:79), his major opposition, was compelled to state that "Easily the most striking thing in the history of the American (Black) since 1876 is the ascendancy of Mr. Booker T. Washington." Washington's base was at Tuskegee where he arrived in 1881 to found a school which would serve as a model of the vocational education he saw as the way for Blacks to raise themselves and gain the respect and tolerance of whites.

Booker T. Washington

Washington's thought and practice were molded and informed by four major factors: 1) his experience in enslavement; 2) his education at Hampton Institute; 3) the tasks before him at Tuskegee; and 4) his reading of the socio-historical setting in which he operated. The system of enslavement taught him the viciousness, violence and power of whites; Hampton taught him the need to conciliate whites in order to get necessary resources and stay operating; and his reading of the times brutally suggested that protest in the South was counterproductive and extremely dangerous (Washington, 1968).

The core contentions of Washington's philosophy were advanced in his famous Atlanta Exposition Speech in 1895 (Washington, 1968:218-224). In it he advanced propositions which he would repeat and expand on throughout his life. First, he argued that vocational education was the key to Black economic success and urged Blacks to get into practical occupations such as agriculture, mechanics, commerce, domestic service and the professions. Secondly, he advanced the concept of social separation with economic integration in his famous statement "In all things that are purely social we can be as separate as the fingers, yet one as the hand in all things essential to mutual progress."

Thirdly, Washington suggested Black accommodation to social inequality and disenfranchisement, arguing that "agitation of questions of social equality is the extremist folly" and that not "artificial forcing" but productive labor and business would end discrimination. "No race that has anything to contribute to the markets of the world, " he stated, "is long in any degree ostracized." Fourthly, he asserted the essentiality of Black-white cooperation in social progress with whites as superior benefactors and Blacks as a subordinate pliant work force and the "most patient, faithful, law-abiding and unresentful people."

In later interviews, speeches and writings, Washington expanded on these themes (Thornbrough, 1969). He also argued that economic progress was both a way to and substitute for equality and political rights. Moreover, he stated that economic progress could not only raise Blacks but make "the white man partly dependent on (Blacks) instead of all the dependence being on the other side." Stressing economic self-help and racial solidarity, he urged Blacks to pull themselves up by their own bootstraps and not let grievances blind them to opportunities. Finally, he emphasized the need for moral regeneration of Blacks, i.e., the cultivation of virtues and values which would destroy laziness, immorality and wastefulness and other vices which he felt were a legacy of enslavement.

However, Washington's policy of accommodation was contradicted by his private efforts against racism (Meier, 1957). He was deeply involved in the struggle against disenfranchisement and other forms of discrimination. He not only lobbied in the background against disenfranchisement and other forms of discrimination, he also raised money to pay lobbyists and fight court cases against racism. Moreover, he was for Black economic power and built the National Negro Business League to advance Black economic interests. Furthermore, he was an expert politician himself, and in spite of his talk against political participation, ran the Black Republican campaign for Roosevelt and was instrumental in both the appointment and rejection of Blacks in high office and employment throughout the country.

Although Black leaders like W.E.B. DuBois, Ida B. Wells-Barnett and Monroe Trotter strenuously opposed Washington for his open accommodationism, he nevertheless maintained his power until his death in 1915. Washington's success was obviously rooted in his mastery and manipulation of three major socio-political and economic tendencies, i.e., capitalism, racism and Christianity. His stress on vocational education, pliant industrial and agricultural workers and social peace provided capitalism with its supply of cheap, non-striking and apolitical workers. His stress on separateness, his disinterest in political and civil rights and his promise to be loyal to whites, not compete with them, and start at the bottom, satisfied the demands of racism.

Finally, his emphasis on the need for the Black moral regeneration and putting behind the assumed moral negatives developed in enslavement appealed to the Christian mentality. Thus, he spoke to the spirit and motion of the times, much of which was accepted by Blacks as well as whites. For many middle class Blacks had recognized the problems of political participation, accepted literary and property qualifications if equally applied to both races, saw the economic realm as the key area of advancement and advocated self-help, racial solidarity and the cultivation of middle class virtues.

W.E.B. DuBois

Washington's foremost critic was W.E.B. DuBois, an impressive leader in his own right whose rise to national and international fame was based not on white patronage, but on his own intellectual genius and role as an activist-scholar (Lewis, 2000; 1993). DuBois studied at Fisk University and the University of Berlin, received three degrees from Harvard and became in 1895

Dr. W.E.B. DuBois

the first African American to receive a Ph.D. An historian and sociologist, DuBois' doctoral dissertation, *The Suppression of the African Slave Trade*, was the first published work in the Harvard Historical Studies and his *Black Reconstruction*, a monumental and voluminous work, as well as his *Philadelphia Negro* became classic studies of Blacks.

Washington had been understandably impressed with DuBois' scholarly achievement and at first tried to enlist him as an aid, but intellectual achievement, self-conception as a leader and his opposite political approach to social struggle all militated against such a relationship. In 1903 in his classic work, *Souls of Black Folk*, DuBois (1969) wrote an essay "Of Mr. Booker T. Washington and Others" in which he offered the core points of his opposition to Washington. Through his ideological struggle with Washington, he repeated and expanded on these with the severe and incisive criticism which so characterized his writings.

DuBois said that Washington's leadership was not so original as it was reflective of the times. He called Washington's Atlanta Exposition speech the "Atlanta Compromise," criticized him for silencing his critics in unprincipled ways and trying to maintain a monopoly on Black leadership. He defined three basic kinds of historical Black leadership and response to oppression — revolt, accommodation, and self-realization and self-development. Nat Turner and David Walker represent the first kind; Washington represented the second; and Frederick Douglass whom he called "the greatest of American (Black) leaders" represented the third.

Washington, DuBois argued, had not only assumed and advocated "the old attitude of adjustment and submission," but in catering to the times, had introduced "a gospel of Work and

Money to such an extent as apparently almost complete to over-shadow the higher aims of life." Moreover, he criticized Washington for not only catering to triumphant capitalism, but also to Southern racism which demand Black subordination. He cited three basic paradoxes of Washington's program: 1) advocacy of Black business and ownership of property and denunciation of struggles for political rights to defend them: 2) insistence on thrift and self-respect yet counseling "a silent submission to civil inferiority...bound to sap the manhood of any race...;" and 3) advocacy of common schools and industrial training and disappreciation of institutions of higher learning from which teachers for his industrial and common schools came.

DuBois rejected Washington's demand that Blacks give up "political power, insistence on civil rights and higher education." He noted he did not oppose industrial training, only the exclusive emphasis on it; he did not oppose reconciliation in the South, only "the industrial slavery and civil death" of Blacks which it demanded. And he complimented Washington's practical achievement in open and behind-the-scenes efforts against racism and oppression, but he opposed his apologies for injustice, support of the caste system and opposition to higher education.

DuBois, however, did not simply oppose Washington, he offered his own form of confrontation and agitational leadership (Lewis, 1993; Broderick, 1969; Moon, 1972; Weinberg, 1970). First he argued for a "Talented Tenth," an intellectual and political vanguard which would lead Black people to freedom and a higher level of human life. Secondly, he advocated a multidimensional education which would enable Blacks to grasp, confront and be effective in society and the world. He abhorred the vulgar careerism which reduced education to money-making at the expense of an effective social competence and social commitment. Thirdly, he advocated a cultural nationalism and pluralism, which stressed pride in Black heritage and unity yet a full and effective membership in American society.

Fourthly, DuBois insisted on confrontational activities in the struggle for social, political and economic rights and gains. He also saw political rights as the basis for economic opportunities and defense of economic gains. Moreover, he too argued for self-help and racial solidarity. Fifthly, DuBois advocated Pan-Africanism and called and presided over four of the five pre-independence Congresses from 1919 to 1945. He recognized and advocated the unity and common interests and struggle of all Africans and the world historical importance of Africa. In his later years, he went to live in Africa and died in 1963 at the age of 95 in Ghana working on the Encyclopedia Africana. Finally, DuBois proposed cooperative economics for the community at first and later advocated socialism for the country. In this, he saw socialism as an alternative to capitalism's unequal distribution of wealth, enslavement of labor and reduction of human aspiration to material pursuits.

MARCUS GARVEY

Born in Jamaica, Marcus Garvey arrived in Harlem in 1916, an ardent Pan-Africanist dedicated to the liberation of Africa

and building a nation-state in Africa that would demand the rights and respect of Africans everywhere (Martin, 1976). He had admired and written to Booker T. Washington and expected to see him when he arrived in the U.S., but Washington died a year earlier. It might seem strange to some that Garvey, the father of modern Black Nationalism, would admire Washington, the assumed paradigm of Tomism. But, as argued earlier, a one-dimensional portrait of Washington is not an accurate one. Garvey admired Washington's stress on social separateness, racial solidarity, economic self-help and self-sufficiency and institution building.

Hon. Marcus Garvey

Moreover, Garvey, while condemning whites' denial of Black rights, did not see Blacks' political salvation in the U.S., but in Africa and thus, like Washington, put no real emphasis on political struggles in the U.S. However, he did not reject politics as Washington and he argued that "If Washington had lived he would have had to change his program." For the problem of Black power "must be solved not by the industrial leader only, but by the political and military leaders as well." In a word, the new leader must recognize that the New African "does not seek industrial opportunity alone, but a political voice" (Garvey, 1977, Vol. 1:56).

Garvey and DuBois clashed openly in their struggle for leadership preeminence. Garvey criticized DuBois for a year in his paper The Negro World before DuBois responded. He accused DuBois of being equivocal and unvigorous in his criticism of imperialism. Agreeing with A. Phillip Randolph, he argued that DuBois was controlled by the white capitalists on the NAACP's board. Also, he criticized DuBois' elitism, his theorizing while Garvey was acting, and his focus on integration.

DuBois' first public response to Garvey was in the Crisis, his NAACP organ, in December 1920. He called Garvey an "extraordinary leader of men" and acknowledged that Garvey was "essentially an honest and sincere man with a tremendous vision, great dynamic force, stubborn determination and unselfish desire to serve." But he also thought him a "dictatorial, domineering man" and without any real business sense. He also criticized him for introducing the Jamaican Black-mulatto division, alienating the British whom he needed for his international trade, alienating Liberia where he hoped to establish his base and unnecessarily antagonizing and attacking other Black leaders. Eventually, they both began to argue ad hominem, questioning each other's sanity and sincerity.

The source of their conflict was both their different philosophies and their struggle for leadership preeminence. Garvey was a global Pan-Africanist engaged in the practical redemption of Africans everywhere, posing a liberated Africa as a base. DuBois focused on continental Pan-Africanism and stressed continental self-determination. Garvey was an effective mass leader, organizing over six million Blacks (working class and petty-bourgeoisie) in the Universal Negro Improvement Association (UNIA), whereas DuBois was elitist and by his own analysis unable to reach the masses. His concept of the Talented Tenth was both positive and problematic. Garvey was a man of action, an institution builder; DuBois was more the theoretician and scholar. Garvey argued for race purity and race first; DuBois was for integration. Finally, Garvey advocated statehood and state power for Blacks while DuBois stressed political participation within the U.S. system.

Garvey, however, advanced a larger strategy for liberation and a higher level of life for Blacks. As the father of modern Black Nationalism, he wrote and spoke extensively on all four emphases of nationalism — economics, politics, religion and culture — and thus laid the theoretical bases for all subsequent nationalist assertions. Likewise, his practice — politics, organization and institution building — has served as models for all subsequent practical nationalist thrusts (Garvey, 1977, Vols. I & II).

Economically, he advocated economic autonomy, arguing that "A race that is solely dependent upon others for its economic existence sooner or later dies." Thus, there is a need for factories, businesses and commerce based on self-help and self-reliance. Moreover, he saw class struggles and revolution as a fundamental feature in the rise and fall of nations, and argued for checks on corporate ownership to prevent monopoly and the rule of the few at the expense of the masses.

Politically, Garvey posited "Race First" as a principle of theory and practice, i.e., an Afrocentric approach to the definition, defense and development of Black interests. He used nation and race interchangeably and thus argued for a global Pan-Africanism which sought to free "Africa for the Africans at home and abroad." His Pan-Africanism stressed anti-imperialism, global unity of Blacks and liberation and reconstruction of the African continent. He sought to establish a national power base to defend African interests all over the world, to raise the level of the African masses and return an effective number of Diasporan African pioneers to start and sustain the project. Garvey also advocated armed struggle in the liberation of Africa stating that "any sane man, race or nation that desires freedom must first of all think in terms of blood, " i.e., costly struggle.

On the question of religion, Garvey advocated a race-specific God. It is only human, he stated, to see God through one's own eyes, thus Black people must see God in their own image and interests. He criticized the bankruptcy and hypocrisy of white Christianity, attacking white Christian control of Africa through mass murder and brutality and Christians preaching brotherhood while everywhere killing Third World people. A forerunner of Black liberational theology, he posited the need for religion to be socially rooted and socially relevant. Thus, he too posed Jesus as a social reformer, organized and used ceremonies to reinforce nation-building, painted Jesus and Mary Black and posed God as a warrior God whose assertive defense of his rights humans should emulate. Moreover, he gave humans the central role after creation in building the world. "Man is supreme lord of creation," he contended, and in him "lies the power of mastery of all creation."

Finally, Garvey advocated cultural nationalism, a bold redefinition of reality in Black images and interests. This thrust, he contended, should begin with a rescue and reconstruction of Black history, for little can be expected from whites who "have tried to rob the Black man of his proud past." Blacks, he said, "have a beautiful history of their own and none of any other race can truly write it but themselves." Moreover, he urged encouragement of Black authors "who are loyal to the race" and exhibit race pride and severe criticism for those who prostitute their skills for white patrons and allies. Also, he urged an education that was socially relevant, i.e., applicable and inspirational in the struggle of Blacks to free themselves and rebuild the world in their own image and interests. To do this, Garvey called for a Black Vanguard, "men and women who are able to create, originate and improve, and thus make an independent racial contribution to the world and civilization."

4.10 BLACK SCIENCE AND INVENTIONS

One of the most important factors contributing to the rapid industrialization of the U.S. was the increase in inventions. Between the period of 1860 and 1890 which transformed the U.S. from an agricultural to an industrial nation, hundreds of thousands of patents were registered. Some of the most important inventions contributing to this industrialization process were by African Americans (Diggs, 1975; Adams, 1979; Carwell, 1977; Hayden, 1972; Haber, 1970; Klein, 1971). By 1913, Blacks had patented an estimated one thousand inventions, especially in the fields of electricity, transportation and industrial machinery, and the records showed that more than twenty of the approximately 190 Black inventors were Black women.

Before the Civil War, Black inventions were hardly recognized or known due to the fact that enslaved Africans could not patent their inventions. In fact in 1858, the U.S. Attorney General ruled that since an enslaved person was not a citizen and a patent was a contract between the government and a citizen inventor, an enslaved person could not make a contract with the government or assign the invention to his enslaver.

Nevertheless, reports are numerous of enslaved Africans inventing useful devices. At first the inventions centered on household and agricultural devices, but eventually the field of Black inventions widened to include achievements in nearly all branches of industrial inventions.

The first African American to receive a U.S. patent was Henry Blair who in 1834 registered a seed planter and in 1836 registered a corn harvester. In 1846, one of the most important inventions by an African American was patented. In that year, Norbert Rillieux patented the revolutionary multiple-effect vacuum evaporation process for refining sugar. Today, his basic technique is not only used in manufacturing sugar, but also condensed milk, gelatin, glue, soap, etc.

After the Civil War, the most significant inventors near the turn of the century were Lewis Latimer, Jan Matzeliger, Elijah McCoy, Garret Morgan and Granville T. Woods. Lewis Latimer invented the first electric lamp with a carbon filament, an inexpensive production technique for making carbon filaments for lamps, and the cotton thread filament which made electric light bulbs practical and inexpensive. Thus, although Edison is credited with inventing the bulb, it is important to note that this bulb continuously burnt out quickly, and it was Latimer's inventions which made it last and become a useable item. Latimer also drew designs for Alexander Bell's telephone patent, worked for Thomas Edison, General Electric and Westinghouse and in 1890 wrote the first book on the electrical lighting system.

Jan Matzeliger, revolutionized the shoe industry with his invention of the shoe lasting machine in 1891. Within the first twenty years of Matzeliger's invention, the shoe industry doubled its production in dollars from $220,000,000 to $442, 631,000 and shoes became 50% cheaper and of much better quality. Elijah McCoy's most important invention was the automatic lubricator for use on locomotive engines in 1872. This drip cup eliminated the need to stop and restart engines in order to lubricate them. His product was so respected, the phrase "the Real McCoy" was used to question or confirm the genuineness of his and other products.

Garret Morgan invented a belt fastener for sewing machines in 1921, the smoke inhalator in 1914 and the automatic traffic light in 1923. His smoke inhalator was a lifesaver used by fire departments and was transformed into a gas mask in World War

I to protect soldiers. His automatic traffic light was sold to General Electric for $40,000. The most productive inventor was Granville T. Woods who patented over one hundred inventions. His first patent was in 1884 for an improved steam boiler furnace. In 1887, he patented his most important invention, the Induction Telegraphy System which permitted communications between moving trains and between them and the stations, and thus made rail travel safer. Thomas Edison attempted twice to claim priority in this invention but Woods won both cases and was certified by the U.S. patent office as the real inventor. His other inventions include a telephone transmitter (1884); an apparatus for transmission of telephone and electric messages (1885) which was bought by the American Bell Telephone; an electro-mechanical brake and apparatus (1904-1905) both of which were sold to Westinghouse Electric Company, and an electric railway (1901) which was sold to the General Electric Company of Thomas Edison. Edison tried to hire him, but he remained independent forming his own company, Woods Electric Company.

There were, of course, other significant inventors and inventions during this period among which were John Parker, a screw for tobacco presses, 1884; William Purvis, over a dozen inventions in machinery for making paper bags; J.A. Burr, a lawn mower, 1899; G. Grant, the golf tee, 1899; J. Winters, a fire escape ladder, 1878; J. Standard, a refrigerator, 1891; and A. Miles, an elevator, 1887. The importance of these inventions lies not only in their value to industrial growth, but also in their being a model of achievement under the most severe discrimination and oppression.

Finally, it is important to mention the significant contribution of Afro-America's most distinguished scientist, George Washington Carver, even though most of his work was done after the major period of industrialization. Carver was a chemurgist, i.e., a chemist pioneer in the field before it become a recognized science. Determined to free the South from overdependence on cotton, he encouraged farmers to grow peanuts, sweet potatoes and soybeans and developed hundreds of products from them. In his small ill-equipped laboratory at Tuskegee, he made over 300 synthetic products from the peanut, over 100 from the sweet potato and over 75 from the pecan. Some of his synthetic products were adhesives, axle grease, bleach, facial cream, dyes, fuel briquettes, ink, insulating board, linoleum, metal polish mucilage paper, rubbing oils, soil conditioner, shampoo, shoe polish, shaving cream, synthetic rubber, wood stain, wood filler, buttermilk, cheese, flour, instant coffee, mayonnaise, meal, meat tenderizer, milk flakes, sugar and worcester sauce.

He also developed dehydrated foods and the U.S. army used his sweet potato flour during WWI. Although Thomas Edison and Henry Ford offered him large sums to come to their laboratories, he stayed at Tuskegee. He never patented any of his discoveries, refused to profit from them and instead donated them all to humanity.

4.11 CRISIS AND THE NEW DEAL

The decade of the great depression was especially difficult for African Americans (Sullivan, 1996; Walters, 1974). The New Deal, under President Franklin Roosevelt, held out hope and relief for Blacks through its focus on social welfare and public work programs. Blacks recognizing the importance of this new focus shifted dramatically from their traditional Republican voting to support Roosevelt and the Democratic party by 1936. Also, the New Deal marked a significant turning point in Black-white relations for the better. This was due to the continuous struggle of Blacks for equality and the end of discrimination as well as to the humanitarian focus of the administration.

Through the initiative of the NAACP and the Urban League, several social activist organizations established the Joint Committee on National Recovery (JCNR) to oversee federal government policy and oppose discriminatory aspects of it. The JCNR exposed unequal wage rates, lobbied for race relation advisors in major federal departments and generally fought for federal respect and defense of Black rights. Blacks were also successful in getting the Public Works Administration to stipulate numerical goals for Blacks in slum clearance projects. The Civilian Conservation Corps, and the Works Progress Administration (WPA) were valuable to the employment of Blacks during this period. The Federal Arts Project which was a branch of the WPA employed many Black actors and writers. In addition, the National Youth Administration had a Black division headed by Mary McLeod Bethune.

The New Deal passed two major Acts which were of great importance to Blacks. The first was the Social Security Act of 1935 which not only guaranteed old-age and unemployment insurance for workers, but also provided federal monies for social welfare. Secondly, the Wagner Labor Relations Act of 1935 guaranteed the right of collective bargaining and outlawed company unions. In the same year, the Congress of Industrial Organizations (CIO) was formed, began to organize workers and opened up to Blacks. At first distrustful, based on past discrimination, Blacks urged by the Urban League and other Black organizations, joined and were very instrumental in organizing the steel workers in the Steel Workers Organizing Committee. Moreover, they joined and helped build the Ladies' Garment Workers Union and the Amalgamated Clothing Workers Union, the International Longshoreman's Union and the United Auto Workers. Through these struggles and gains, Black workers penetrated organized labor and thus gained a strong base from which to wage even larger struggles.

Finally, Blacks achieved an increased respectability in the Roosevelt Administration as specialist and advisors in various governmental departments. This marked a change in the Washington model of unofficial advisor whose relationship with the president, more than his skill, fitted him/her for the job. These were highly respected specialist and advisors who were civil servants. They were called the "Black Cabinet" and the "Black Brain Trust" due to their academic and professional achievements.

Among the most notable of this brain trust were Robert Weaver, an economist who served in the Department of Interior and several federal agencies; Mary McLeod Bethune, founder-president of Bethune-Cookman College, National Youth Administration; Eugene Jones, Executive Secretary of the Urban League, Department of Commerce; Ralph Bunche, Department of State; Rayford Logan, Coordinator of Inter-American Affairs; and Abram Harris, economist, National Recovery Administration. Although these positions were not cabinet level, they were a breakthrough in appointment by merit and paved the way for advances in the 60's and afterwards (Egerton, 1994).

4.12 THE REAFFIRMATION OF THE 60'S

The Reaffirmation of the 60's stands, after the classical period and the Holocaust of enslavement, as one of the major modal periods in Black history. As stated above in the Introduction to this chapter, by modal periods is meant periods which defined Black life in profound and enduring ways and speak to the best of what it means to be African and human in the fullest sense. The classical period in the Nile Valley clearly reflected the African commitment to knowledge, moral and spiritual grounding and cultural excellence, introducing some of the basic disciplines of human knowledge, and contributing definitively to the forward flow of human history. The Holocaust of enslavement tested and tempered African people, demonstrated their adaptive vitality, human durability and internal capacity to prevail, and reinforced their commitment to human freedom and human dignity.

The 60's was above all a *Reaffirmation* — a reaffirmation of our *Africanness* and *social justice tradition* which had at its core an uncompromising commitment to struggle. It is in this decade that African Americans not only reaffirmed their identity and dignity as African people, but compelled U.S. society and its academies to recognize and respect the most ancient history and culture of humankind and to teach it in the universities in newly constructed departments, programs and centers. Here we launched a definitive struggle to return to our own history, speak our own special cultural truth to the world and self-consciously make our own unique contribution, as a people, to how this country is reconceived and reconstructed.

Likewise, African Americans reaffirmed our commitment to our social justice tradition, a social justice tradition of rich and ancient origins, reaching back to the ethical teachings of ancient Egypt and continuing in the teachings and struggles through the Holocaust of enslavement and Jim Crowism to the 60's. It is a tradition defined by its commitment to the dignity and rights of the human person, the well-being and flourishing of family and community, the integrity and value of the environment and the reciprocal solidarity and cooperation of humanity for common good. Again, it is in and through struggle on every level that Black people reaffirmed both themselves as Africans and the social justice tradition which is at the core of their self-understanding and self-assertion in the world as a people.

Thus, the Reaffirmation of the 60's stands unquestionably as one of the most definitive and significant decades in the history of Black people in the U.S. Indeed, it is in this decade that the major civil rights and nationalist organizations and personalities reached their height and have not regained a similar status since then. This is also the decade in which Blacks made the most severe and successful theoretical and practical criticism of the structure and content of U.S. society. And it is in this decade that ordinary people did and achieved extraordinary things in the interest of freedom, justice and equality. Through this they and the Black Freedom Movement became models of the struggle for human liberation that inspired other struggles for freedom, justice and equality in this country and around the world. Indeed, other oppressed groups in the U.S. and around the world borrowed from and built on our moral vision and moral vocabulary, sang our songs of freedom and posed our struggle as a model to emulate. Thus, the Reaffirmation of the 60's has become, through its achievements and uncompleted and ongoing tasks, the unavoidable historical referent-both for analysis of the 70's and 80's and 90's and the projections for the future (Carson, 1981; Williams, 1987; Harding, 1987; McAdam, 1983).

To discuss the Reaffirmation of the 60's as a unified process is not to deny that there were varying tendencies and interpretations of what was to be done. There were, in fact, two main tendencies, the integrationist and the nationalist. Chronologically speaking the integrationist tendency reached its height first and through its loss of initiative laid the historical groundwork for the resurgence of nationalism. The logic of the process seems to suggest that only after the integrationist thrust had proved itself unworkable and historically exhausted, was the nationalist alternative able to challenge it successfully and eventually overshadow it (Brisbane, 1974; Sales 1994). Thus, in 1963 and most definitively in the period of 1965-1968 the strategy of non-violence was challenged by the urban revolts and in 1966 SNCC led the move from integrated groups and aspirations to Black groups and Black power. It was also in the mid-Sixties that the "Back to Black" thrust expanded to reach beyond the U.S. to Africa for models and inspiration. Thus, though we speak of the 60's as a unified process on one hand, it is instructive on the other hand to recognize the two basic tendencies which shaped and informed this critical decade (Robinson and Sullivan, 1991).

THE CIVIL RIGHTS MOVEMENT

The Civil Rights Movement, which was essentially integrationist, gave Black people in the U.S. their first major accomplishments of the decade (Robnett, 1997; Powledge, 1991; Morris, 1984). The integrationist thrust, in its political sense, was an effort to break down barriers to full participation in U.S. society and remove the penalties and other negative consequences of racial distinctions. Thus, a major accomplishment of this period and tendency was not only major civil right executive orders and legislation to overcome these negatives, but also the building of a mass

From right to left, Ella Baker (SCLC), Eleanor Holmes Norton (SNCC), Fannie Lou Hamer (MFDP), rear: Kwame Ture (SNCC) and two other members of the MFDP Delegation at the 1964 Democratic National Convention

movement which mobilized and politically educated millions of Black people. It is a significant number of these mobilized and politically educated people who would go beyond the vision and aspirations of civil rights to demand human rights and Black power. Therefore, it can be said that the Civil Rights Movement produced activists and organizations which would prove effective in transforming it into its Black nationalist alternative.

The Civil rights struggle was led by major groups such as SNCC, CORE and SCLC, although countless smaller groups played fundamental and indeed indispensable roles in the civil rights struggle (Garrow, 1986; Farmer, 1985; Carson, 1981; Meir and Rudwick, 1973). Likewise, major personalities like Fannie Lou Hamer, Bob Moses, Ella Baker, Martin Luther King, Jr., Ruby Doris Robinson and Kwame Ture (Stokely Carmichael) were key to the civil rights struggle, but there were countless "unknown soldiers" without whom the struggle could not have begun or been sustained (Lomax, 1962; Clark, 1963; Youth of the Rural Organizing and Cultural Center, 1991; Robinson, 1987; Morris, 1984).

The turning point in the Black civil rights struggle is usually considered to be the winning of the NAACP of the 1954 Supreme Court Decision *Brown v. The Board of Education* (Tushnet, 1994,1987; Kluger, 1976). The decision put a legal end to the "separate but equal" doctrine established in the 1896 Supreme Court decision of *Plessy v. Ferguson*. Even though the decision was hampered in implementation, it gave a necessary psychological boost to the Black struggle and gave legal support to the struggle against segregation.

The beginning of the Montgomery Bus Boycott in 1956 marked another key event in the civil rights struggle (Robinson,

Dr. Martin Luther King, Jr.

1987; Burns, 1997). On December 1, 1955, Rosa Parks, having decided that she was not going to give up her bus seat in servile deference to whites, became the catalyst to a struggle which not only catapulted Dr. Martin Luther King to national fame, but also built a model that Blacks in other Southern cities were soon to emulate. The economic boycott was thus established as an effective instrument of breaking down segregation barriers (King, 1958).

On February 1, 1960, four students from North Carolina

Agricultural and Technical College in Greensboro, N.C., decided they would no longer accept segregation of public facilities and moved to protest and challenge the state of things by sitting down at a lunch counter in a variety store and ordering coffee (Wolff, 1972; Proudfoot, 1962). This marked the beginning of the sit-in movement and a sustained period of Black activism and societal confrontation that would last a decade, only declining with police suppression in the late Sixties and defection in the early Seventies.

In May, 1961, the Congress of Racial Equality (CORE) developed another strategy to force the civil rights issue — the Freedom Rides (Farmer, 1985; 1965; Peck, 1962). CORE, an essentially integrationist group, developed the Freedom Rides to challenge segregationist laws and practices in interstate transportation which forced seating by race. However, the strategy had the spin-off effect of forcing the federal government to take a more vigorous stand on protection of the civil rights guaranteed by the Constitution. The Kennedys (John and Robert, who were in power at the time as President and U.S. Attorney General respectively) were disturbed by the assertiveness of these activists and asked for a cooling-off period. But the activists continued their thrust and forced the Attorney General to dispatch a force of 600 marshals and other federal officers to intervene in a Freedom Ride confrontation in Montgomery.

In 1963, the centennial year of the Emancipation Proclamation, Black people launched a series of massive demonstrations to expose the contradictions in U.S. society and demanded serious social change. One of the most notable of these was the Birmingham Demonstration of April 3, 1963 under the leadership of Martin Luther King and the Southern Christian Leadership Conference (SCLC) (King, 1962; Branch, 1988, Fairclough, 1987; Garrow, 1986). Again, racist violence flared, but the marchers were adamant in their push for fair employment, desegregation of public facilities and dropping of politically motivated charges against the thousands of demonstrators arrested. Easily the largest and most dramatic march was "The March on Washington for Jobs and Freedom," August 28, 1963, which involved over 200,000 participants.

It is important to note here that throughout this period, the Student Non-Violent Coordinating Committee (SNCC) from its inception had been the most effective and largest contributor of freedom fighters to the struggle (Carson, 1981; Forman, 1972; Stoper, 1989; Zinn, 1964). It had participated in great numbers in the major strategies of the Civil Rights Movement — including boycotts, sit-ins, voter registration campaigns, cooperative projects and even political party building. It was SNCC who, along with Fannie Lou Hamer and Bob Moses, organized the Mississippi Freedom Democratic Party (MFDP); and SNCC also built the Lowndes County Freedom Organization which was popularly called the Black Panther Party. Some of SNCC's most important leaders were John Lewis, Ruby Doris Robinson, Kwame Ture and H. Rap Brown. It was also SNCC, as mentioned above, who would lead the movement discussion and organizational move away from one of integration to one of Black power (Carmichael and Hamilton, 1967).

Ruby Doris Robinson

A critical analysis of the civil rights struggle, then, would reveal a series of major accomplishments. As mentioned above, its first and perhaps most important achievement was the increased liberalization of the U.S. system. Through legal, economic and political challenges, Blacks were able to achieve among other things: 1) the 1954 Brown Decision; 2) the Civil Rights Act of 1957; 3) the 1960 Civil Rights Bill; 4) the Interstate Commerce Commission ruling September, 1961, against racial segregation on interstate carriers and terminals; 5) the Civil Rights Act of 1964 which was the most far-reaching and comprehensive civil rights law passed by Congress; 6) mass voter registration; 7) the 1965 Voting Act; and 8) widespread desegregation of public facilities.

Secondly, as mentioned above, the Civil Rights Movement severely exposed the contradictions of the American dream in both the eyes of U.S. society and the world. This uncompromising and fierce exposure contributed to the internationalization of the Black struggle which was another gain for the Movement. It brought world attention to the struggle and won it moral and political allies around the world. The U.S. was thus, forced to operate under the attentive world eye and, therefore, sought to check its excesses against Blacks in a way it was not compelled to do before. Thirdly, the Movement mobilized and politically educated people who before were, in fact, outside the political process. It is significant to note here that King, believing in and teaching the social function of religion, turned religion into a political force for massive social change. King, stressing the social aspect of religion, taught civil disobedience against unjust practices as a moral imperative, gave Blacks boldness by stressing that they were God's soldiers in an unjust world and thus, enabled an otherwise reluctant people to dare take control of their destiny and daily life.

Fourthly, the Civil Rights Movement laid the organizational and political-educational basis for continued struggle in other areas. The mobilized and organized masses did not simply disband at the end of the Civil Rights Movement, but went on to win elections, build co-ops and unions and in general build institutions that housed, defended and expanded their interests. Finally, the Civil Rights Movement, by its uncompleted tasks, the non-attainment of its core and social objectives, the timidity of its methods and its eventual historical exhaustion, laid the historical basis for the rise of its nationalist alternative.

The Civil Rights Movement was thus, limited in its goals and methods for their achievements. Moreover, its Black leadership was unnecessarily concerned with and deferential to the wishes and support of white allies. Whites, through financial contributions and organizational positions, limited the Movement's possibilities and ultimately had to be confronted and rejected for leadership positions. And it is in the process of reassessment of the goals, methods and leadership of the Black Civil Rights Movement that the nationalist alternative appeared, grew and eventually checked and surpassed the thrust toward integration.

It is important at this point, however, to stress that all the gains made during the 60's, both of the Civil Rights and Nationalist Movements, were not the gifts of presidents, Congress or liberal allies, but the result of a people's self-conscious struggle to free and realize themselves. As evident in the case of the liberal Kennedys, Black needs and the political concerns of liberals easily clash. But through the self conscious collective struggle of Blacks to control their destiny and daily lives, presidents, Congress and shaky allies were time and time again forced to act even against their will.

The painful process of reassessment which occurred in the middle 60's produced, perhaps, the most definitive aspect and achievement of the Sixties — the self-conscious decision of Africans in the U.S. to initiate a theoretical and practical thrust to redefine and restructure society in Black images and interests. Even the integrationist wanted Black interests to be recognized and respected. Even they fought for a society which did not penalize Blacks for their color and which would concede to affirmative action to end and compensate for such behavior. But it was the nationalist tendency which redefined both society and the world in Black images and interests.

THE BLACK POWER MOVEMENT

The Black Power Movement began in the midst of the urban rebellions and the decline of the Civil Rights Movement. Its beginning is marked by the Watts Revolt in 1965 and it continues until 1975. Although the call for Black Power was not made until 1966, its history had already begun in the early 60's with the resurgence of the Black nationalist sentiment among African Americans. As Kwame Ture (Carmichael, 1968:64) observed during this period, "the concept of 'Black Power' is not a recent or isolated phenomena: it has grown out of the ferment of agitation and activity by different people and organizations in many Black communities over the years." Certainly, the teachings of the Nation of Islam, especially its national representative Min. Malcolm X (1965), and smaller nationalist organizations in the urban areas of the U.S. can be credited with this evolving political and cultural orientation (Woodard, 1999; Van DeBurg, 1993; Pinkney, 1976; Brisbane, 1974). But it is from SNCC that the call for Black Power emerges and is embraced nationally as a fundamental focus. Willie Ricks first made the call on a SNCC march, but it was Kwame Ture (Stokely Carmichael) who made it a national battle cry. And it is Ture and Charles Hamilton who wrote the essential book on Black Power (Carmichael and Hamilton, 1967, 1992). In their book, Ture and Hamilton stress the need for Black power to overcome racist oppression, making a clear distinction between individual acts of discrimination and racism as an institutional arrangement.

In 1966 Rep. Adam Clayton Powell called a group of leaders to plan a series of National Black Power Conferences in order to develop and carry out agenda to achieve Black Power in the U.S. (Woodard, 1999:85ff). The meeting established a Continuations

**Kwame Ture
(Stokely Carmichael)**

Committee to organize the conferences. Dr. Nathan Wright of Newark was elected chair and Maulana Karenga of Los Angeles was elected vice-chair. The second conference was held in Newark in 1967 and the third in Philadelphia in 1968 (Stone, 1968). Woodard (1999:107-108) reports that "While Dr. Nathan Wright remained in the leadership of the National Black Power Conference Continuations Committee, by 1968, Karenga was recognized as its chief organizer and foremost theoretician." Addressing the issue of the struggle for Black Power, Maulana Karenga asserted that it was a struggle to achieve three fundamental things: *self-determination, self-respect* and *self-defense*. By these goals he meant Black people's control of their communities, destiny and daily life through institutional strength; community control; a sense of expanded self-worth and ability rooted in culture and struggle; and the capacity of Black people to exercise their right to defend themselves against attacks of racism, especially by the police, as Malcolm said, "by any means necessary" (Karenga, 1980; Halisi, 1971:12). He also introduced during the Black Power conferences the concept of operational unity which he defined as "unity in diversity and unity without uniformity" and which became a standard reference and call to unity in the Black Liberation Movement.

As the Black Power Movement developed its conference process, it also engaged in electoral politics and embraced and nurtured the Black Arts Movement and the Black Studies and Black Student Movements (Woodard, 1999; Van DeBurg, 1993). It also launched a massive political and cultural education process linked to the African American struggle with Continental African and Third World liberation struggle and introduced the concept and practice of armed struggle in the urban centers (Cruse, 1967; Barbour, 1968). As an expression of nationalism, the Black Power Movement can be divided into

Black Power Conference. Seated left to right: Maulana Karenga (Us); Rap Brown (SNCC); Ralph Featherstone (SNCC); Jesse Jackson (PUSH). Far Background: Dr. Nathan Wright (with glasses), Chair, The Black Power Conference

three basic tendencies or thrusts: 1) the religious thrust; 2) the cultural thrust; and 3) the political thrust.

THE RELIGIOUS THRUST

The religious thrust was both Islamic and Christian. The Islamic section was personified by the Nation of Islam (NOI) under the leadership of the Honorable Elijah Muhammad (Muhammad, 1965, 1973, 1997). Muhammad posed Islam as a necessary alternative to Christianity, which he saw as the oppressor's religion. Secondly, he argued that Blacks were the chosen people of God, and that God was Black and the devil was white. This reversal of the world order was a bold redefinition of reality and was instrumental in reinforcing the concept of the beauty and creative genius of Blacks. Thirdly, Muhammad contended that separation of Blacks was a divine imperative. This was central in order to escape the degenerative effect of white society and the wrath of Allah who would destroy the U.S., a modern-day Babylon. Muhammad also argued for economic self-help and national racial solidarity in a Black United Front. Finally, he stressed the need for racial and Islamic solidarity throughout the world.

Although the Nation had its beginning in 1930, it reached its height in the early Sixties. Muhammad's achievements, as

Hon. Elijah Muhammad

leader of the NOI, lie in both the area of theory and practice. He broke the monopoly whites had on good and God by revealing an alternative truth and reconstructing reality in Black images and interests. Moreover, he likewise broke the traditional monopoly Arabs and other Asian Muslims had on the doctrinal interpretation of Islam in the U.S. Thirdly, in doing this, he established a socio-historically specific form of Islam for Blacks. And fourthly, through this theological achievement and the building of its practical, organizational and institutional complement, the NOI, he placed himself in the ranks of the most significant Black men in the history of the African American people.

The Christian nationalist focus was best personified by Albert Cleage, the minister of the Shrine of the Black Madonna (Cleage, 1968; 1972). Cleage began this thrust by arguing that the Judeo-Christian heritage was, in fact, Black and needed to be redefined and reappropriated. He portrayed Jesus as a Black revolutionary who led a national liberation struggle against a white power, Rome. Moreover, he argued God is Black and partisan and demands social struggle, not submission. Power, he contended, is a basic aspect of group existence and Blacks can only demand and establish respect and end oppression through unity and power. Cleage finally argues that the church must assume its historical revolutionary role and lead "God's Chosen People" Blacks, to liberation and social reconstruction.

THE CULTURAL THRUST

The cultural thrust during the Sixties was most definitively represented by the Organization Us under the leadership of Maulana Karenga (2002, 1980, 1978). Us, which means simply "Us, us African people," was founded in 1965 and is a social and cultural change organization. Through its organizational activities and its philosophy Kawaida, Us played a leadership role in the major initiatives in the Sixties including the Black Arts, Black Studies, Black Student unions, independent schools and the Black Power Conference movements. Us also organized one of the most important youth organizations in the Sixties, the *Simba Wachanga*, the Young Lions, who worked to organize

Dr. Maulana Karenga

Black student unions in high schools and colleges and community structures and projects, provided community service and served as a community defense unit. Although Us, like many groups, advocated and trained for self-defense of the community following the lead of Min. Malcolm X and Robert Williams, it resisted the draft and was involved in the anti-war movement. Also Us, like many other organizations, including the Nation of Islam, SCLC, the Panthers, the Revolutionary Action Movement (RAM), the Republic of New Africa (RNA), and others, experienced suppression by the government (Federal Bureau of Investigation, 1978). However, Us was not broken and remains active today in cultural, political and educational activities.

Maulana Karenga and the Organization Us are most known for their work to wage a cultural revolution to recover the best of African views, values and practices and use them to enrich and expand the lives of Black people and enhance their capacity to wage and win the struggle for liberation. Us' and Maulana Karenga's most widely known creations in this regard are the pan-African holiday *Kwanzaa* and the *Nguzo Saba* (The Seven Principles) (Karenga, 1998). Created by Karenga in 1966, Kwanzaa was first practiced and nurtured in the supportive context of Us, eventually spread throughout the world African community and is now celebrated by over 28 million persons on every continent in the world. *Kwanzaa is a celebration of family, community and culture* which seeks to raise up and reinforce values and practices which represent the best of what it means to be both African and human in the fullest sense.

Although, the Nguzo Saba are most widely known as the Seven Principles of Kwanzaa, they are in a larger sense the Seven Principles of Kawaida philosophy, a cultural and social change philosophy out of which Kwanzaa and the Nguzo Saba were created (Karenga, 2002, 1998, 1980).

The Nguzo Saba (The Seven Principles) were put forth as a communitarian African value system necessary to build community and serve as social glue and a moral orientation for cultural practice. These principles in Swahili and English are: *Umoja*

Simba Wachanga, The Young Lions of the Organization Us in formation

(Unity), *Kujichagulia* (Self-Determination), *Ujima* (Collective Work and Responsibility), *Ujamaa* (Cooperative Economics), *Nia* (Purpose), *Kuumba* (Creativity), and *Imani* (Faith). Since their introduction in 1965, the Nguzo Saba has become the basis for the cultural grounding and value orientation of many independent schools, rites of passage programs, cooperatives, and various other community and professional organizations and programs. And, of course, they are the fundamental values around which *Kwanzaa* is organized.

Also, Kawaida, as a system of thought, affected in varying degrees the early political development of activists such as Angela Davis, Amiri Baraka, Haki Madhubuti, Kalamu ya Salaam, and Jitu Weusi. In addition, Kawaida and Us laid the ideological and organizational basis out of which grew Black United Fronts like the Black Congress in Los Angeles; the Black Federation in San Diego; Committee for a Unified Newark; the Congress of African Peoples and the National Black Assembly and provided the theoretical framework which shaped the three national Black Power Conferences in the 60's (Baraka, 1972; Madhubuti, 1973; ya Salaam, 1975).

Another definitive cultural achievement of the Sixties was the widespread positive turn toward Africa for revitalization and roots which was fostered by all Black nationalist groups. It was a logical outgrowth of the rejection of white values. It represented a defiant acceptance of Blackness and a search for an

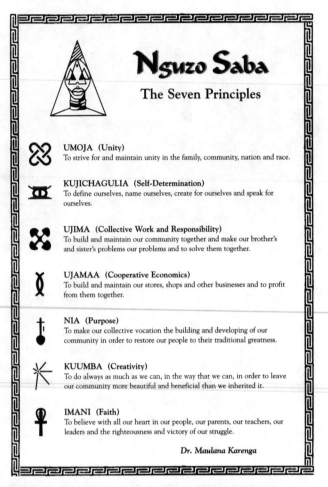

Nguzo Saba

The Seven Principles

UMOJA (Unity)
To strive for and maintain unity in the family, community, nation and race.

KUJICHAGULIA (Self-Determination)
To define ourselves, name ourselves, create for ourselves and speak for ourselves.

UJIMA (Collective Work and Responsibility)
To build and maintain our community together and make our brother's and sister's problems our problems and to solve them together.

UJAMAA (Cooperative Economics)
To build and maintain our stores, shops and other businesses and to profit from them together.

NIA (Purpose)
To make our collective vocation the building and developing of our community in order to restore our people to their traditional greatness.

KUUMBA (Creativity)
To do always as much as we can, in the way that we can, in order to leave our community more beautiful and beneficial than we inherited it.

IMANI (Faith)
To believe with all our heart in our people, our parents, our teachers, our leaders and the righteousness and victory of our struggle.

Dr. Maulana Karenga

Afrocentric perspective and national program. This turn toward Africa was not simply symbolic in terms of dress and hairstyle, but was both cultural and political. It expressed a Pan-Africanism which culminated in the African Liberation Support Committee, the Congress of African Peoples, the Sixth Pan-African Congress and Second World Black and African Festival of Arts and Culture (FESTAC) in the Seventies.

Finally, the cultural thrust was defined by its stress on a new education for Blacks. From this came the Black Students' and Black Studies Movements. SNCC had been at the center and head of the student movement during the Civil Rights Movement and during the Nationalist Movement, SNCC remained vital. It was joined by Us, the

Panthers, CORE and smaller groups in building both Black Student Unions and a climate and structure for the demand and achievement of Black Studies.

It was, thus, during the Sixties that the Black Student Movement came into being, won Black Studies programs and challenged the traditional wisdom and structure of white academia (Robinson, et al, 1969; Edwards, 1970; Hare, 1972). The Black Student Movement and Black Studies Movement stressed the need to bring the campus to the community and the community to the campus. Thus, inherent in their assumptions and aspirations was the thrust toward a new educational process which would be focused not only in established academia, but also in alternative institutions in the community. Some definitive examples were the School of African American Culture of Us, the Ahidiana Work/Study Center, Uhuru Sasa of the East, and the Institute of Positive Education. (Kawaida served as the philosophical base for these new institutions.) These structures sought to define, introduce, and reinforce new Afrocentric values and visions of self, society and the world; and their impact on the African American Freedom Movement was central and continuing.

THE POLITICAL THRUST

The political thrust of the Nationalist Movement was best exemplified by Min. Malcolm X (El-Hajj Malik El-Shabazz) who served as a model, ideologically and personally, for countless nationalist groups and leaders (Malcolm X, 1965; 1966; 1970, 1992). Min. Malcolm X was educated and reached his height in the Nation of Islam. There, he laid the organizational basis for its national

El-Hajj Malik El-Shabazz
(Min. Malcolm X)

al expansion and introduced it to the country and world. Malcolm, however, came into conflict with a changed direction and character of the NOI. He was first suspended in 1963, and then, left to set up his own organizations, Muslim Mosque, Inc. and the Organization of African American Unity, in 1964.

Malcolm advocated several concepts which informed and

Robert Williams

inspired the Movement (Karenga, 1979). Thus, although he was a Muslim, Malcolm reached beyond the religious context, and had a profound effect on the entire Movement. Malcolm, like his former teacher Muhammad, argued that Blacks needed a moral and spiritual regeneration and that it was best achieved through Islam. He stressed also the need for a Black United Front and built the Organization of African American Unity modeled after the Organization of African Unity on the continent. Moreover, Malcolm taught the need for Pan-Africanism and Third World solidarity. He emphasized the values of breaking the "minority mentality" by seeing ourselves as part of the majority in the U.S. and world, i.e., the peoples of color. He, therefore urged a linking of struggles and a worldview of our problems using the spirit and movement of the Bandung conference which urged Third World solidarity as a model (Malcolm X, 1965:ff).

Closely linked with this concept was Malcolm's contention that Blacks needed to redefine the Black struggle from one of civil rights to human rights. This, he argued, would overcome the UN and international prohibition against interference in domestic affairs. He reasoned that the domestic character of civil rights issues prohibits world intervention, but that issues of human rights demanded humanity's intervention both morally and politically in terms of the UN charter.

Finally, Malcolm stressed the right and responsibility of self-defense. Joined to this was the logical extension of the right and responsibility to struggle for freedom by any means necessary. He argued that it was criminal to teach Blacks not to defend themselves and to leave them defenseless in the face of violence. Moreover, he contended, that it was equally criminal and dispiriting to teach Blacks that they do not have the right to win their freedom by struggle — armed and otherwise — like all other peoples in the world. To the end of his life, Malcolm served as a model of audaciousness, defying threats from the system, and travelling to world capitals to gain support for the Black liberation struggle.

That the Sixties witnessed Black people becoming less convinced about the viability of non-violence and daring to explore armed struggle and self-defense against racist violence was not due entirely to Malcolm. Robert Williams (1973), who had been the president of the NAACP in Monroe, North Carolina, had argued in the late Fifties that self-defense against racist violence was a natural and constitutional right (Tyson, 1999). Moreover, he contended that the capacity for self-defense often limited the need to use it. For the attackers would be less likely to attack if they knew swift and effective penalties would follow. To illustrate this in practice, Williams organized a defense group which successfully protected the Black community against Klan attacks and intimidation; and in doing so, he gave Black people a new method and model of struggle. His model produced the Deacons for Defense in Louisiana, which protected civil rights workers in the South and served as inspiration to urban nationalist groups in the North.

Moreover, Williams deserves much credit for helping to internationalize the Black struggle. Fleeing a trumped-up charge (which was later dropped) and death threats, he traveled to

Canada, Cuba, China, and Tanzania, where he wrote extensively on the African American struggle. In China, he succeeded in getting the country's leader, Mao Tse-tung, to issue a statement in support of the African American liberation struggle in 1963 and was asked for comments on a subsequent support statement in 1968.

Members of the Black Panther Party holding banners

The Sixties also saw the founding and transformation of the Black Panther Party for Self-Defense from a nationalist community defense structure to a Marxist-integrationist structure (Jones, 1998; Seale, 1970; Newton, 1972). Founded in Oakland in 1966 by Huey Newton and Bobby Seale, the group took its name from the Black Panther Party of Lowndes County of Alabama which was also called the Lowndes County Freedom Organization. They began to establish a program of monitoring the police in Oakland and stressing the right to bear arms in self-defense.

In 1968 they dropped the word self-defense and began to work with whites in political and community service programs. These programs included providing free breakfasts, health care and drug education in the Oakland and Chicago areas. They also worked in political campaigns with the Peace and Freedom Party in an attempt to win office. However, their constant confrontations with the police and government suppression directed much of their attention to legal defense activities. They also advocated full employment, decent housing, freedom for Black men in prisons and jails and the end to police brutality among other things (Carson et al, 1991:346-47; Jones, 1998).

Finally, the Sixties saw the rise of and focus on the land question. Although the Nation of Islam had stressed the question during the Malcolm period, after '64 it was stressed less. Stokely Carmichael (Kwame Ture) also raised it in the end of the 60's and stressed it in the 70's. However, it was the Republic of New Africa (RNA) under the leadership of Imari Obadele, which pressed it in a political and practical way (Obadele, 1975). Borrowing from Malcolm and Muhammad, Obadele argued that Blacks were not citizens of the U.S. and were due a referendum to choose among three options: 1) U.S. citizenship; 2) nationalism in Africa or a country of choice; 3) building of a nation on this soil. Obadele and the RNA chose this land, declared independence from the U.S. in 1968 and demanded five southern sates (South Carolina, Georgia, Alabama, Louisiana and Mississippi) to construct a Republic of New Africa. Moreover, the RNA demanded reparations from the U.S. to build the nation and solicited world support. The question is still a burning one and is not solved by non-believers dismissing it as utopian.

Dr. Imari Obadele

The nationalist thrust, thus, contributed greatly to the character, course and achievement of the 60's. It included: 1) the building of economic institutions mainly though the NOI; 2) alternative educational institutional constructions; 3) the building of Black Student Unions and a Black Student Movement; 4) the construction of Black Studies Programs; 5) the necessary relinking with the African people on the continent and in the Diaspora; 6) the exploration of armed struggle and self-defense as a right and responsibility; 7) the redefinition of the world in Black images and interests; and 8) laying of the foundations for benefits enjoyed in the 70's.

In conclusion, it is important to note that the Sixties left a fundamental lesson both in the process of its development, as well as in its comparison with the 70's. It is a lesson written in life struggles all over the world, i.e., the liberation of a people depends primarily on its own strength and struggle — regardless of the sincerity or support of its allies. In the final analysis, the Sixties taught Black people that a people that cannot save itself is lost forever. It was in opposition to their erstwhile allies, that Blacks charted a new course and made the new gains listed above. And if one reviews the 70's, 80's and 90's, the lull and the losses they reflect, one cannot help but see the dismantling and weakening of Black structures as a significant factor in that development.

Bakke, Weber, the rise of the vulgar right and the cutback in social welfare gains in the 70's, 80's and 90's point to the structural incapacity of African Americans to check these assaults on previous gains. It was Black structural capacity and struggle which brought Black gains and it was the absence of these which emboldened their adversaries. To paraphrase Frederick Douglass, if you want to know how much a tyrant will impose on a people, find out how much they will take. The misinterpretation of Black history and gains in the Sixties led to faulty reassessments and wholesale defections from the Afrocentric philosophical and practical thrust. This resulted in the structural incapacity to respond to assaults on previous gains and reduced petty bourgeois leadership to making moral denunciations rather than taking concrete political steps to challenge and check such assaults.

Finally, it is important to note that the Reaffirmation of the Sixties with its focus on reaffirming our Africanness and social justice tradition through intensive and ongoing struggle left a lasting legacy for this country and the world. For not only did it expand the realm of freedom in this country, but also it inspired and informed the liberation struggles of other marginalized and oppressed groups and peoples in this country and around the world.

Post-Sixties

The Seventies

The decade began with recovery from the massive suppression and havoc wreaked on the Black Movement by the COINTELPRO or counterintelligence program launched by the FBI in 1968 (Federal Bureau of Investigation, 1968). J. Edgar Hoover, director of the FBI, in a November 1968 memo, asked 41 field officers for hard-hitting ideas to disrupt, discredit and destroy all real and potentially threatening Black leadership. As mentioned above, this included groups such as the Nation of Islam, Black Panthers, Us (especially the leadership and the Simba Wachanga, the Young Lions), CORE, SNCC, RAM and leaders as moderate as Martin Luther King. From this, violent internecine struggles were provoked and sustained as between the Panthers and Us, activists shot and murdered, put in captivity on trumped-up charges or driven into exile, and families as well as organizations disrupted and destroyed (Olsen, 2000; O'Reilly, 1989; Karenga, 1978, 1976; FBI, 1978).

Hoover feared the unity of the Movement and rise of a Messiah who could unify it and create the basis for a real Black revolution. Cautioning the media never to advertise Black activists, especially nationalists, except to discredit them, he created and fed disinformation to them. Using agent-provocateurs, he penetrated organizations, provoked them into internal struggles and violence and adventuristic acts which led to their arrests and deaths. This and other information was revealed through the Senate Select Committee Hearings on Intelligence and the Freedom of Information Act which allows citizens to get copies of files kept on them by intelligence agencies (FBI, 1978).

The violence and shock of the suppression destroyed morale, provoked both critical and uncritical reassessment and made many wonder whether organized activism was any longer a valid strategy for social change. Much of what passed as critical assessment of the Sixties was in fact Black self-condemnation and reflected both a loss of heart and vision of what the 60's were all about and certainly what was achieved. As argued, the 60's was one of the most important decades in Black history and its achievements were substantial. And even though Blacks lost ground during the Seventies, they also made gains.

Easily the greatest gains of African Americans during the Seventies were their penetration and victories in electoral politics. Taking advantage of the Voting Rights Act of 1965, Blacks went to the polls in great numbers, especially in the South. Whereas in 1966, there were only six Blacks in Congress, ninety-seven in state legislatures and no mayors, by 1976, Blacks had elected eighteen Blacks to Congress, several hundred to state legislatures, two lieutenant-governors in California and Colorado and several mayors of major cities, including Los Angeles, Atlanta, Washington, D.C., Newark and Cleveland. Moreover, thousands had been elected to other state and local offices (Conyers and Wallace, 1976).

Also, Blacks sought to build national independent power structures throughout the decade, beginning with the first National Black Political Convention in Gary, Indiana in March 1972 (Smith, 1996). Here over 3,000 delegates and approximately 5,000 alternates and observers passed resolutions, produced an historic document titled *The Black Political Agenda* and created a structure, the Black Assembly, that was posed as both a national body for collective planning and an organizing structure for independent electoral participation. *The Black Political Agenda* called for a new vision and bold and independent politics to meet the challenge of a clear social crisis in the U.S. (Gilliam, 1975:Chapter 6). Although the Agenda criticized the Democratic and Republican parties, it did not call for an independent Black party. Not until August 1980 at the Fourth National Black Assembly Convention in New Orleans was the decision made to form an independent Black party. In November, over 1,300 delegates from various organizations and political tendencies met to form the National Black Independent Political Party (NBIPP) "to advance a new Black politics of social transformation and self-determination" including, organizing, party-building, mobilization and "lobbying around private and public policy" and effectively and independently participating in electoral politics (Holmes, 1999).

The Seventies also brought a resurgence of Pan-Africanism and the formation of two key organizations to advance its principles and practice. The first was the African Liberation Support Committee (ALSC), a united front of Nationalist, Pan-Africanist and Marxist tendencies, dedicated to supporting liberation struggles on the continent of Africa through yearly massive African Liberation Day rallies in May, political education, and raising material and financial resources for the struggles. ALSC was eventually split by the Nationalist/Marxist ideological struggle for hegemony within it and lost the massive support it once had (Salaam, 1974). Still, however, various Pan-Africanist and nationalist groups continue to support the Continental liberation struggle and celebration of African Liberation Day, May 25. The second major organization founded was TransAfrica, an African American lobby for Africa and the Caribbean. It has grown through the years and still monitors legislation and policy concerning Africa and the Caribbean and conducts political education through lectures, conferences and its bulletins. Also, it has developed a journal on U.S. policy toward Africa and the Caribbean.

Affirmative Action was another major issue and struggle in the Seventies. Growing out of Title VII of the 1964 Civil Rights Act, it was extended and reinforced by Executive Orders and the Equal Employment Opportunities Act of 1972. Although there were other cases as the DeFundis and Weber court cases which challenged affirmative action terming it "reverse discrimination," none was so argued and followed as the *Bakke* case. The Bakke case which originated in California over the special admissions policy of U.C. Davis' medical school, brought to head the struggle over the questions of numerical goals vs. quotas, preferential treatment vs. corrective measures for historical injustices and racially-weighted criteria vs. race-conscious criteria for school admission as well as employment.

Blacks parted company with many of their traditional allies among Jews, liberals and labor who felt threatened by the implications of affirmative action. Although moral and philosophical arguments were understandably raised, the basic problem centered around the fact that Black entrance into law, medical and other professional schools and areas of employment meant increase competition and struggle for critical social space with those who traditionally held a monopoly on them. The Supreme Court seemed to straddle and ruled in 1978 that reservation of places for people of color and uncompetitive evaluation was prohibited, but that consideration of race and ethnic origin as one criteria for selection as well as consciously seeking diversity were permissible (Sindler, 1978: Chapter 4).

Key also to the Seventies was the emergence of an open and ongoing discussion among Black men and women on the quality, forms and future of their relationships and the transformation this produced. Major Black journals and magazines like *Black Scholar* and *Black Books Bulletin*, *Essence*, and *Ebony*, regularly carried articles and sometimes dedicated whole issues to the question of Black Male/Female relationships. Books, poems and plays self-consciously concerned themselves with this pressing issue; and debates and discussions on campuses, in the community and on TV and radio were regular occurrences. Moreover, psychologists, Drs. Nathan and Julia Hare started a new journal, *Black Male/Female Relationships*, dedicated entirely to critically discussing, understanding and improving the relationships between Black men and women. The impetus for this reassessment was rooted in three basic factors: 1) the general reassessment of the thought and practices of the Sixties; 2) collective agreement on its urgency; and 3) the influence of the general struggle of women for social equality. Although Black women did not join the Women's Liberation Movement in great numbers, they raised many of its questions, influenced and were influenced by much of its literature and were thus part of the overall struggle to end sexism in social and personal relations.

Finally, Vincent Harding (1980, Chapter 30) lists in addition to the above key issues and events of the Seventies, the prison revolts as at Soledad and Attica, the transformation of the Nation of Islam, and the awesome tragedy of Jonestown. The prison revolts reflected a continuing relationship with the struggles of the Sixties; and the transformation of the NOI represented the loss of an important Black "religiously based challenge to the structures of White American life" and a symbol of defiant Blackness. Jonestown represented the great dangers of unguided and uncritical searches for spiritual community in the context of cynicism, hedonism, materialism, individualism and alienation which marked the Seventies. It also underlined the absence of a Black mass movement which historically served as a base of meaningful relationships, community and hope. As Blacks moved into the 80's, they were keenly aware of the value and urgency of the need to rebuild a self-conscious united and active community which characterized the 60's.

THE EIGHTIES

The decade began with three major challenges to African Americans: 1) the continuing crisis of U.S. society; 2) the rise of the vulgar and "respectable" right; and 3) the continuing struggle to rebuild a Black mass movement and appropriate alliances and coalitions in order to defend Black gains, win new ones and minimize losses. The continuing crisis in U.S. society was marked most definitively by severe economic problems including high level inflation and employment, especially among Blacks, a perennially unbalanced budget, an aging productive structure, resource shortages, large military spending and massive cutbacks and cutoffs of government spending in other areas, especially in social welfare. And it was clearly complicated by self-confessed confusion at the highest levels of government as to how exactly to address these problems (Greider, 1981).

The rise of the right, which continued from the Seventies, expressed itself in the return of violent racist groups like the Klan and other neo-nazi formations, the rise of Christian fundamentalists and perhaps most importantly, Reagan's presidential victory in 1980 and the various successes of right-wing candidates in state and local elections (Dalleck, 1984). With this turn of events came several related occurrences: 1) the tendency to declare social entitlement programs morally wrong and financially too costly; 2) strong and continuing demands for tax cuts, reduced social services, and especially, reduced and more stringently restricted social welfare; 3) the progressive diminishing of the government's role in achieving social justice and equality for Third World peoples and the poor; and 4) the steady reversal of gains of the 60's and 70's.

In addition to the rise of the white right in and out of government, there was a parallel rise of a Black right (Daniels, 1980). These Black conservatives, who were also in and out of government, served the Reagan/Bush Administrations and right-wing thrust by supporting policies and developing arguments against the minimum wage, government intervention to correct injustices for ethnics and the poor, affirmative action, equal opportunity programs, and most other programs and proposals won in the general thrust for civil rights in the 60's and early 70's. This rise of Black conservatism and the challenge it poses for the liberal civil rights approach clearly has its historical parallel in the Washington-DuBois conflict concerning approaches to Black social advancement. Like Washington, the Black conservatives reject Black protest and emphasize vocational education and self-help. On the other hand, the liberals, like DuBois, stress protest, multidimensional education and the obligation of U.S. society to live up to its claims and of government to facilitate and insure this.

In this context, the liberal and radical Black leadership and the mass movement requires national organizations with adequate vision, structure and resources to meet the challenge of leadership and cooperation necessary to form a national Black united front which will stand at the center of the mass movement. Both radical and liberal organizations have attempted to build such a united front formation. The liberal forces created the Black Leadership Forum which was made up of approximately sixteen national organizations. However, it was not well-known and was not visibly engaged in collective planning, organizing the national Black community or confronting the system. Secondly, the liberal forces often use the yearly Congressional Black Caucus (CBC) Legislative Weekend structure as a means to gather, get briefings on the latest governmental policies, decisions and proposals, and to discuss possible defensive and development strategies. But the CBC is not really suited for activist leadership and the Weekends are more for briefings and informal exchanges than for the development of concrete action plans.

The radicals also produced two national structures which they saw as possibly providing an ideological and structural center for the mass movement necessary to define, defend and develop Black interests. Those are the National Black United Front (NBUF) and the National Black Independent Political Party (NBIPP), both of which were formed in 1980, the former in June and the latter in November. NBIPP, as mentioned above, sought to be a genuine party would give Blacks a clear alternative to the two traditional parties. Following in the tradition of other Black political parties, it attempted to point out the inability of the traditional parties to meet Black needs and build a powerful alternative structure to accomplish this (Daniels, 1980; Flewellen, 1981; Holmes, 1999). The Party, however, remained in the formative stages and finally dissolved, having experienced the traditional problems of third parties, i.e., lack of adequate resources, strategy, membership, community legitimacy and electoral success. (Walton, 1972).

NBUF is the largest of the two organizations, more active and more solidly based in the national community with chapters throughout the country (Daughtry, 1981). Although it is essentially a nationalist formation, NBUF's constitution sets for itself the task of "delicately" formulating "the conservative, moderate, reform, radical and nationalist concerns, problems and goals of the carried constituencies in the Black community into a dynamic black agenda, which speaks to our collective interests as a people." However, it has essentially evolved into a single organization instead of an organization of organizations and thus has not realized its expansive early goal.

The problem of alliance and coalition was also a challenge for Blacks in the 80's. For they are a necessary complement to the building of a self-conscious and effective mass movement. Although strains developed in the traditional Black-labor-liberal coalition in the late 60's and 70's, the Black liberal forces continued to see this coalition as vital to defense of gains and the struggle for broad social change and thus, strove to rebuild it. And the radicals, who see alliances with Third World people and labor as necessary political projects, likewise attempted to rebuild and build those and make them active and effective.

The 80's also witnessed a heightened level of electoral political activity among African Americans. In Chicago, Harold Washington waged a brilliant campaign to become mayor. He put together a coalition of Blacks, Latinos, workers, professionals, nationalists, white liberals and leftists to achieve his victory. Key groups in this process were the African Community of Chicago, PUSH (People United to Save Humanity), the Black United Front, and People's College. However, Washington passed suddenly from a heart attack and therefore was not able to realize the promise inherent in his platform and the multicultural coalition he built. Also Jesse Jackson ran in 1984 and 1988 for president, mobilizing and registering millions of voters which were instrumental in getting other Blacks and progressives elected. His campaign in '88 garnered seven million votes and brought into the political process many formerly marginalized groups. Moreover, he raised issues of substance in a context of mediocre political discourse and challenged the country to live up to its highest ideals. Although he did not win office, his campaigns were seen as an important tool for mobilizing, organizing and politically educating Blacks and progressives and building the Rainbow Coalition for the inauguration of a new progressive politics (Karenga, 1984; Morris, 1990; Henry, 1991).

In 1989, Douglas Wilder, the first Black governor, was elected governor of the State of Virginia, a former bastion of the Confederacy. This was occasioned by several factors: 1) African

Americans who gave him 96 percent of their vote; 2) women who favored him by 53%; and 3) his moving between moderate and conservative politics. It was a model of crossover politics which would bode ill for Black politics in some analysts opinion, for it seemed to, at times, sacrifice Black interests on the altar of compromise. Also, David Dinkins was elected in 1989 as mayor of New York. He too was the recipient of the support of an active African American community, the Latino community, liberals, Jews and labor. A progressive politician, his greatest challenge was to build a truly interactive and

Rev. Jesse Jackson, Rainbow/PUSH

mutually respecting multicultural city. But as the 90's and the year 2000 would prove, it remains a desirable but difficult goal in the context of the racist legacy of this country's history.

THE NINETIES

The 90's opened with celebrations of the above-mentioned elections of Wilder and Dinkins and appreciation for Jackson's political mobilization. But there were carry-over problems from the 80's that required sober assessment. Among these problems were: 1) the increasing negative attitude of the Supreme Court to racial justice and affirmative action; 2) continuation of hate crimes against African Americans, which tripled in the last seven years (1983-1990); 3) the veto and later passage of the 1991 Civil Rights Act; and 4) the increase in poverty among Blacks and in the country as a whole.

Clearly, among the most significant and dramatic events of the 90's were: The Clarence Thomas-Anita Hill confrontation in October 1991; the Los Angeles Rebellion in April 1992; the Million Man March/Day of Absence on October 16, 1995 in Washington, D.C.; the Million Woman March on October 25,

1997 in Philadelphia; and the Million Youth Marches on September 5, 1998 in New York and September 4-7, 1998 in Atlanta.

THE THOMAS-HILL CONFRONTATION. The Thomas-Hill confrontation revolved around the confirmation hearing of Clarence Thomas for a seat on the Supreme Court. Hill charged him with sexual harassment as her former supervisor and argued with allies that he was unfit to serve. He countered saying the charge was a lie and the interrogation, which began to resemble a trial, was a high-tech lynching. The Black community split around the issues of race and gender and the controversy revealed an ongoing problematic of race and gender relations and the need to constantly confront them (Chrisman and Allen, 1992; Morrison, 1992).

LOS ANGELES REVOLT. The Los Angeles Revolt or Rebellion of April 1992 grew out of smoldering resentment of oppression in the Black and Latino communities (Madhubuti, 1993; Gooding-Williams, 1993). But it was triggered by the acquittal of four white Los Angeles policemen who beat a Black man, Rodney King, mercilessly while he was on the ground and incapacitated. The anger overflowed not only in response to the beating but also, because the beating had been caught on video and the jury seemed to be too racist to concede that it ever happened. Moreover, the verdict appeared to declare that Black men, as Black men, were a real and continuing menace, that they were less deserving of rights and that anything done to restrain and deter them is both understandable and justified. The Rebellion was the most destructive in recent U.S. history, leading to the loss of 58 lives and millions of dollars in property. Rodney King became a symbol of police brutality and the Rebellion became a reminder of the injustice Black people face. It also had a Latino dimension and reflected similar injustices that are suffered by them and that they too will dare to struggle to correct them.

ELECTORAL POLITICS. The 90's also brought many African Americans a measure of political optimism with the election of Bill Clinton to the presidency and the presence of thirty-nine Black members of Congress and one Black Senator, Carol Mosely Braun. However, others remained cautious because in

spite of Clinton's cabinet appointments of Blacks, these ges-
tures do not translate into a substantive programs for the masses of Black people or deal with the challenges of urban life and
politics (Browning et al, 1990). Likewise, the election of new
faces to Congress and one person to the Senate is important,
but they do not equal a critical mass necessary to determine
policy. Moreover, Clinton began to adopt Republican policies
towards social welfare, crime and social policy in general;
Carole Mosely Brawn was defeated in re-election efforts; and
the courts began to make debilitating rulings against the drawing and maintaining of Black districts. Thus, the caution is to
realize that the struggle for a just and good society is a long and
difficult one and, therefore, as Amilcar Cabral, leader of the
Guinea Bissau revolution, says concerning this, one should
"mask no difficulties, tell no lies and claim no easy victories"
(1969:89).

Million Man March/Day of Absence in Washington, D.C.

THE MILLION MAN MARCH/DAY OF ABSENCE. The Million
Man March/Day of Absence (MMM/DOA) was clearly an event
of major importance, not only because of the vast numbers of its
participants but also because of its *social policy* and *social practice*
emphasis and the effect it had on Black men, Black people and
the country (Madhubuti and Karenga, 1996). Called for by Min.
Louis Farrakhan, the leader of the Nation of Islam, the

MMM/DOA was a joint project of hundreds of organizations and was one of the most massive organizing efforts for a demonstration in the history of the country. It brought together Africans from all over the country and world, Africans from all spiritual traditions and involved building local organizing committees in over 300 cities. Held in Washington, D.C. on October 16, 1995, it assembled together over one million persons and was the largest demonstration in the city's history.

The MMM/DOA had started out as essentially a man's project with little or no women's participation. In fact, controversy arose around the NOI's initial request to women to remain home and let men take the lead in the project.

Min. Louis Farrakhan

However, after a meeting of Min. Farrakhan and a select group of nationalist leaders from around the country, a new position was put forward. First, it was agreed that women would not be discouraged from coming, but that men would continue to lead the March since it was called for and directed toward them. In fact, women participated in large numbers in the local and the national organizing committees and many women spoke at the March. A second aspect of the project would be the Day of Absence in which women would take the lead in organizing the communities to stay away from businesses, school and work in support and observance, to register people to vote and to hold teach-ins around social policy initiatives to improve and empower the community (Tembo, 1996; Karenga, T., 1996; Kifano, 1996).

Finally, it was agreed to put forth the Mission Statement which represented the collective position of the leadership of the March, the National Million Man March/Day of Absence Organizing Committee, a broad based leadership group representing various political, religious and economic affiliations and interests. Maulana Karenga (1995) was selected to draft the collective mission statement, pulling together the common grounds for a joint set of policies and initiatives directed toward the community, government, and corporations.

The statement begins registering consciousness "of the critical juncture in which we live and the challenges it poses for us" and "concern about increasing racism and continuing commitment to white supremacy in this country; the deteriorating social conditions, degradation of the environment and the impact of these on our community, the larger society and the world" (p.1) Moreover, the *Mission Statement* noted that African men came to the capital "reaffirming the best values of our social justice tradition which require respect for the dignity and rights of the human person, economic justice, meaningful political participation, shared power, cultural integrity, mutual respect for all peoples and uncompromising resistance to social forces and structures which deny or limit these" (p.2). In this spirit, they also came to "declare our commitment to assume a new and expanded responsibility in the struggle to build and sustain a free and empowered community, a just society and a better world."

In addition to posing challenges to African men and the African American community, it called on the government and corporations to initiate policies which reflect a greater level of responsibility to the people and environment. Among the social policy initiatives called for were reparations, restraint on corporations in their degradation of the environment, affirmative action, affordable housing, repeal of the Omnibus Crime Bill, an economic bill of rights, halt of privatization of public wealth and space, honoring of treaties signed with Native Americans, a sensible and moral foreign policy which would prohibit imposing boycotts on whole peoples (a reference to Cuba and Iraq) and support immigration without race and class discrimination, debt cancellation for former colonies, respect for the right of self-determination of peoples in the Middle East (referring especially to the Palestinians), and respect for the multicultural character of this country. The corporations were called on to exercise corporate responsibility by respecting the dignity and interests of the worker in this country and abroad, halting policies destructive of the environment, eliminating race and gender discrimination and reinvesting profits back in the urban areas to halt and reverse urban decay. The organizers also offered a plan for continued activism including independent politics, economic development, mentoring and family strengthening and standing in solidarity with African peoples and Third World peoples in their liberation struggles (also see Politics chapter).

The MMM/DOA had a tremendous impact on the Black community, creating a sense of possibility and promise. Immediately after the MMM/DOA there were significant

> ... *reaffirming the best values of our social justice tradition which require:*
> - *respect for the dignity and rights of the human person*
> - *economic justice*
> - *meaningful political participation*
> - *shared power*
> - *cultural integrity*
> - *mutual respect for all peoples, and*
> - *uncompromising resistance to social forces and structures which deny or limit these...*
> — THE MILLION MAN MARCH / DAY OF ABSENCE
> MISSION STATEMENT

increases in membership in organizations and institutions, in adoption rates, mentoring programs and social activism. Also, there are empirical data from the Joint Center for Political Studies which show that although overall voter participation dropped dramatically in the 1996 election, nearly 2 million more African Americans voted in the election of whom 1.7 million were Black men. The Joint Center credits this increase to the stimulation of the Million Man March/Day of Absence. Many local organizing committees continued working on local and larger issues and building expanded networks. Also, other groups would later emulate the MMM/DOA in its call for social policy initiatives and activism.

THE MILLION WOMAN MARCH. The Million Woman March (MWM) was held at the Benjamin Franklin Parkway in Philadelphia, October 25, 1997. It grew out of extended discussions among women activists on the need to energize the lives and struggles of Black women in a manner and on a scale similar to Black men in the MMM/DOA. The leading organizers of the March were Philé Chionesu, an entrepreneur and leader in the International Family and Friends of Mumia Abu Jamal Committee, and Asia Coney, a public housing activist and leader in the Tenant's Association. Two other women important in the initial and subsequent organizing efforts were Maisha Ongoza, chair of the Kwanzaa Cooperative of Philadelphia and of the National Association of Kawaida Organizations, who served as an advisor to Chionesu and raised the initial seed money within

Million Woman March in Philadelphia

NAKO for the project; and Pam Africa, chair of the International Family and Friends of Mumia Abu Jamal Committee, who was helpful in international outreach.

Chionesu and Coney, who developed the idea of the March in lengthy discussions, built an expanding circle of local women activists who in turn reached out to a broad spectrum of African women on the local, national and international levels. Through an intense and massive effort, they were able to build a national organizing committee which completed its work in time and with less funding, less public relations and less media coverage than the MMM/DOA.

The organizing committee put forth a Twelve-Point Platform which included a wide-range of immediate and ongoing concerns. These were:

1. National support for…a probe into the CIA's participation and its relation to the influx of drugs into the African American community.
2. The development and completion of Black independent schools.
3. The formation of progressive mechanisms for the development and advancement of Black women leaving the penal system.

4. The development of health facilities for preventive and therapeutic treatment with major emphasis on alternative and traditional medicine.
5. The formation of Rites of Passage centers/academies...
6. The further development of Black women who are or wish to become professionals, entrepreneurs and/or politicians.
7. The further development of mechanisms that will assist Black women in "transitional" experiences.
8. The examination of Human Rights violations of Africans in the Americas and their effects.
9. The development of programming that will bring about a sincere and respectful environment that will foster the necessary interaction with our youth.
10. The formulation of progressive mechanisms to combat homelessness (and related problems).
11. The development of mechanisms to (prevent) gentrification of our neighborhoods.
12. The reclaiming of our elders' rights who are entitled to the development of appropriate programs and support systems that will insure that their quality of life is maintained, enhanced and preserved.

In addition to these stated goals and concerns, the organizers, speakers and general participants emphasized also a need to reaffirm sisterhood, reinforce families, improve and strengthen male/female relations, and recommit themselves and the African community to the ongoing struggle for a just society.

THE MILLION YOUTH MARCH. The idea of Million Youth March (MYM) began with a problematic start. First, it was proposed for New York by Min. Khallid Muhammad of the NOI; and forces in the community who disagreed politically with Min. Khallid proposed an alternative march in Atlanta. Secondly, the mayor of New York tried to suppress the March also, saying it would create a public safety hazard and traffic jam. The March won in the courts and was held on September 5, 1998 in Harlem. Given the division of forces between Harlem and Atlanta and the apprehension concerning possible police intervention at the March, the turn out for the March was not as large as initially projected.

Shaped essentially by its organizer, Min. Khallid, the MYM advanced goals and concerns which are standard for the Black Movement. These include: 1) self-determination for Black people everywhere; 2) reparations; 3) increased youth responsibility and cooperation and the end to internecine youth violence; 4) increased parental responsibility towards youth; 5) end of police abuse and brutality; 6) freedom for political prisoners; and 7) commitment to the struggle for Black liberation everywhere. Like the MMM/DOA and MWM, the MYM was a statement and stimulant for self-consciousness as Black men, Black women and Black youth and the responsibility to community and struggle which this implies and requires.

THE NEW ERA

The new era poses not only a challenge to Blacks, but also to other peoples of color, progressives, and liberals to be actively concerned about what kind of country this should be. Clearly, however, it is in the interest and historical tradition of African Americans to serve again as catalyst and vanguard of the struggle which resists reversals of fundamental humanistic gains and continues to build a society which successfully defends and expands the national ideals of freedom, equality of access and opportunity, and social justice. Symbolic placements in government are not enough. Structures and strategy must be built and put in place. As Harding (1980:231) contends, it is African Americans who must, at "so elemental a time of turning" and coming from such a rich history of social change and leadership, pose the question to themselves and others of "how do we move forward, beyond our best leaders of the past, beyond our best declarations, beyond our best actions, beyond our best dreams, to participate fully in the creation of a fundamentally new reality, in ourselves, in our people, in this nation, and in this world?"

STUDY QUESTIONS

1. What arguments does Van Sertima make to prove African presence in Olmec civilization?
2. Discuss the importance of the category "the Holocaust of African enslavement." Discuss the significance of its moral emphasis versus the traditional commercial emphasis of trade.

3. What are some basic misconceptions about the "slave trade"? Discuss its impact.
4. What was the basis for enslavement and some of its basic aspects?
5. List and discuss the major forms of resistance to enslavement.
6. Discuss Black participation in the Civil War.
7. What were some of the basic reasons for the failure of Reconstruction?
8. What were the reasons for the Great Migration?
9. What were some of the major organizations founded to struggle against injustice? Especially discuss the Black Women's Club Movement.
10. What were some of the major Black inventors and inventions during the period of industrialization?
11. What are some of the major philosophical contentions of Washington, DuBois and Garvey?
12. Discuss the New Deal period.
13. What were the two main tendencies of the 60's and what were their organizations and achievements?
14. What are some major challenges and achievements of the 70's, 80's and 90's?
15. Discuss the Million Person Marches. What were their concerns and effect on the Black community and the Black Movement?

REFERENCES

Adams, Russell L. (1969) *Great Negroes Past and Presents*, Chicago: Afro-Am Publishing Co.

Aptheker, Herbert. (1951) *A Documentary History of the Negro People in the United States*, New York: Citadel Press.

Aptheker, Herbert. (1943) *American Negro Slave Revolts*, New York: International Publishers.

Aptheker, Herbert. (1968) *To Be Free*, New York: International Publishers.

Asante, Molefi and Mark T. Matson. (1992) *The Historical and Cultural Atlas of African Americans*, New York: Macmillan Publishing Co.

Baraka, Imamu Amiri (LeRoi Jones). (1972) *African Congress: A Documentary of the First Modern Pan-African Congress*, New York: William Morrow & Co.

Barbour, Floyd, (ed.) (1968) *The Black Power Revolt*, Boston: Porter Sargent.

Bauer, Raymond and Alice Bauer. (1942) "Day-to-Day Resistance to Slavery," *Journal of Negro History*, 27 (October) 388-419.

Bennett, Lerone. (1975) *The Shaping of Black America*, Chicago: Johnson Publishing Company.

Benson, Elizabeth P. and Beatriz de la Fuente, (eds.) (1996) *Olmec Art of Ancient Mexico*, Washington, D.C. : National Gallery of Art.

Berlin, Ira. (1998) *Many Thousand Gone: The First Two Centuries of Slavery in North America*, Cambridge, MA: Belknap Press.

Berlin, Ira and Leslie Rowland, (eds.) (1997) *Families and Freedom: A Documentary History of African American Kinship in the Civil War Era*, New York: Cambridge University Press.

Bernal, Ignacio. (1979) *Great Sculpture of Ancient Mexico*, New York: William Morrow & Company.

Bernard, Jacqueline. (1990) *Journey Toward Freedom: The Story of Sojourner Truth*, New York: The Feminist Press at the City University of New York.

Berry, Mary Frances and John W. Blassingame. (1982) *Long Memory: The Black Experience in America*, New York: Oxford University Press..

Bibb, Henry. (1969) *Narratives of the Life and Adventures of Henry Bibb, An American Slave, in Puttin' on Ole Massa*, New York.

Billington, Ray A. (1981) *The Journal of Charlotte Forten, A Free Negro in the Slave Era*, New York: W. W. Norton & Co.

Blackett, R.J.M. (1983) *Building an Anti-Slavery Wall: Blacks in the Atlantic Abolitionist Movement, 1830-1860*, Baton Rouge: Southern University Press.

Blassingame, John. (1979) *The Slave Community*, New York: Oxford University Press.

Bracey, John et al. (eds.) (1971) *Blacks in the Abolitionist Movement*, Belmont, CA: Wadsworth Publishing Co.

Branch, Taylor. (1988) *Parting the Waters: America in the King Years, 1954-63*, New York: Simon & Schuster.

Brent, Linda. (1973) [1861] *Incidents in the Life of a Slave Girl*. Edited by Lydia Maria Child, New York: Harcourt Brace Jovanovich. (see Harriet Jacobs)

Brisbane, Robert H. (1974) *Black Activism*, Valley Force, PA: Judson Press.

Broderick, Francis. (1969) *W.E.B. DuBois: Negro Leader in Time of Crisis*, Stanford: Stanford University Press.

Browning, Rufus, et al. (1990) *Racial Politics in American Cities*, NY: Longman's.

Burns, Stewart. (1997) *Daybreak of Freedom: The Montgomery Bus Boycott*, Chapel Hill: University of North Carolina Press.

Cabral, Amilcar. (1969) *Revolution in Guinea*, New York: Monthly Review Press.

Campbell, Edward D., Jr. and Kym S. Rice, (eds.) (1991) *Before Freedom Came: African American Life in the Antebellum South*, Richmond: University of Virginia Press.

Carmichael, Stokely. (1968) "Power and Racism," in Floyd Barbour, (ed.) *The Black Power Revolt*, Boston: Porter Sargent, pp. 61-71.

Carmichael, Stokely and Charles Hamilton. (1967) *Black Power*, New York: Vintage Books.

Carmichael, Stokely and Charles Hamilton. (1992) *The Politics of Liberation in America*, New York: Vintage Books.

Carroll, Joseph. (1938) *Slave Insurrections in the U.S.*, Boston: Little, Brown & Co.

Carby, Hazel. (1987) *Reconstructing Womanhood: The Emergence of the Afro-American Woman Novelist*, New York: Oxford University Press.

Carson, Claybourne. (1981) *In Struggle: SNCC and the Black Awakening of the 1960s*, Cambridge, MA: Harvard University Press.

Carson, Claybourne et al. (1991) *Eyes on the Price Civil Rights Reader*, New York: Viking Penguin.

Carwell, Hattie. (1977) *Blacks in Science*, Hicksville, NY: Exposition Park.

Chrisman, Robert and Robert L. Allen. (eds.) (1992) *Court of Appeal: The Black Community Speaks Out on the Racial and Sexual Politics of Clarence Thomas vs. Anita Hill*, New York: Ballantine Books.

Clark, John E. and Mary E. Pye, (eds.) (2000) *Olmec Art and Archeology in Mesoamerica*, New Haven, CT: Yale University Press.

Clark, Kenneth (ed). (1963) *The Negro Protest*, Boston: Harper Press.

Cleage, Albert. (1972) *Black Christian Nationalism*, New York: William Morrow & Co.

Cleage, Albert. (1968) *The Black Messiah*, New York: Sheed & Ward.

Clegg, III, Claude Andrew. (1997) *An Original Man: The Life and Times of Elijah Muhammad*, New York: St. Martin's Griffin.

Collison, Gary. (1998) *Shadrack Minkins*, Cambridge: Harvard University Press.

Coe, Michael. (1962) *Mexico*, New York: Praeger Publishers.

Coe, Michael. (1996) *The Olmec World: Ritual and Rulership*, Princeton: Art Museum at Princeton.

Conrad, Earl. (1943) *Harriet Tubman*, New York: Paul S. Erikson.

Conyers, James E. and Walter L. Wallace. (1976) *Black Elected Officials*, New York: Russell Sage Foundation.

Covey, Joan. (1992) "African Sea Kings in America: Evidence from Early Maps," in Ivan Van Sertima (ed.) *African Presence in Early America*, New Brunswick: Transaction Publishers.

Crawford, Vickie, Jacqueline Rouse and Barbara Woods. (1990) *Women in the Civil Rights Movement: Trailblazers and Torch-Bearers*, Brooklyn: Carlson Publishing.

Cruse, Harold. (1967) *Crisis of the Negro Intellectual*, New York: William Morrow & Co.

Dalleck, Robert. (1984) *Ronald Reagan: The Politics of Symbolism*, Cambridge, MA: Harvard University Press.

Daniels, Ron. (1980) "The National Black Assembly: Building Independent Black Politics in the 1980's," *Black Scholar*, 11, 4 (March/April).

Daughtery, Herbert. (1981) "An Interview," *The Black Nation*, (Fall) 8-11.

Davidson, Basil. (1977) *Africa in History*, London: Macmillan Company.

Davis, David Brian. (1966) *The Problem of Slavery in the Age of Revolution, 1770-1823*, Ithaca, NY: Cornell University.

De Roo, Peter. (1990) *History of America Before Columbus*, Philadelphia: J.B. Lippincott.

Diggs, Irene. (1975) *Black Innovators*, Chicago: Third World Press.

Dillon, Morton L. (1990) *Slavery Attacked: Southern Slaves and Their Allies (1619-1865)*, Baton Rouge: Louisiana State University Press.

Drake, St. Clair and Horace Cayton. (1962) *Black Metropolis*, New York: Harper & Row.

Drake, W. Avon and Robert D. Holsworth. (1996) *Affirmative Action and the Stalled Quest for Black Progress*, Urbana: University of Illinois Press.

DuBois, W.E.B. (1969) *Souls of Black Folk*, New York: New American Library.

Duster, Alfred A. (ed.). (1970) *Crusade for Justice: The Autobiography of Ida B. Wells*, Chicago: University of Chicago Press.

Edwards, Harry. (1970) *Black Students*, New York: Free Press.

Egerton, Douglas R. (1993) *Gabriel's Rebellion: The Virginia Slave Conspiracies of 1800 and 1802*, Chapel Hill: University of North Carolina Press.

Egerton, Douglas R. (1999) *He Shall Go Out Free: The Lives of Denmark Vesey*, Madison, WI: Madison House.

Egerton, John. (1994) *Speak Now Against the Day: The Generation Before the Civil Rights Movement in the South*, New York: Knopf.

Elkins, Stanley. (1966) *Slavery*, Chicago: University of Chicago Press.

Emmerich, Andre. (1963) *Art Before Columbus*, New York: Simon and Schuster.

Fairclough, Adam. (1987) *To Redeem the Soul of America: The Southern Christian Leadership Conference and Martin Luther King*, Athens: University of Georgia Press.

Farmer, James. (1965) *Freedom Win*, New York: Random House.

Farmer, James. (1985) *Lay Bare the Heart: An Autobiography of the Civil Rights Movement*, New York: Arbor House.

Fauset, Arthur H. (1938) *Sojourner Truth, God's Faithful Pilgrim*, Chapel Hill: University of North Carolina.

Federal Bureau of Investigation. (1978) "Black Nationalist Hate Groups File, 100-448006," Sections 1-23 in COINTELPRO: *The Counter Intelligence Program of the FBI*, [Microfilm], Wilmington: Scholarly Resources.

Flewellen, Kathryn. (1981) "The National Black Independent Political Party: Will History Repeat?" *Freedomways*, 21, 2, pp. 93-105.

Forbes, Jack. (1980) *Black Africans and Native Americans*, Cambridge, MA: Blackwell.

Forman, James. (1972) *The Making of Black Revolutionaries*, New York: Macmillan Co.

Fogel, Robert and Barry Engerman. (1974) *Time on the Cross*, Boston: Little, Brown & Co.

Foster, Frances S. (1990) *A Brighter Coming Day: A Frances Ellen Watkins Harper Reader*, New York: The Feminist Press and the City University of New York.

Foster, Laurence. (1935) *Negro-Indian Relationships in the Southwest*, Philadelphia: AMS Press.

Franklin, John H. and Alfred Moss, Jr. (1988) *From Slavery to Freedom: A History of Negro Americans*, New York: Alfred A. Knopf.

Franklin, John H. (1974) *From Slavery to Freedom*, New York: Alfred A. Knopf.

Garrow, David. (1986) *Bearing the Cross: Martin Luther King Jr. and the Southern Christian Leadership Conference, 1955-1968*, New York: Morrow.

Garvey, Amy Jacques (ed.). (1977) *Philosophy & Opinions of Marcus Garvey, I & II*. New York: Atheneum.

Gaspar, David Barry and Darlene Clark Hine (eds.) (1996) *More Than Chattel: Black Women and Slavery in the Americas*, Bloomington: University of Indiana Press.

Genovese, Eugene. (1981) *From Rebellion to Revolution*, New York: Vintage Books.

Genovese, Eugene. (1974) *Roll, Jordan, Roll*, New York: Pantheon Books.

Giddings, Paula. (1984) *When and Where I Enter: The Impact of Race and Sex in America*, New York: William Morrow & Company.

Gilliam, Reginald E. (1975) *Black Political Development*, Port Washington, NY: Kennikat Press.

Gooding-Williams, Robert. (ed.) (1993) *Reading Rodney King: Reading Urban Uprisings*, New York: Routledge.

Greene, Lorenzo. (1944) "Mutiny on the Slave Ships," *Phylon*, 5 (4th qtr.)

Greider, William. (1981) "The Education of David Stockman," *The Atlantic Monthly*, (December) 27-54.

Gutman, Herbert G. (1976) *The Black Family in Slavery and Freedom, 1750-1925*, New York: Pantheon.

Haber, Louis. (1970). *Black Pioneers of Science and Invention*, New York: Harcourt, Brace and World, Inc.

Hakem, A.A. (1991) "The Civilization of Napata and Meroe," in G. Mokhtar (ed.) *General History of Africa II, Ancient Civilizations of Africa*, London: UNESCO, pp. 172-184,

Halisi, Imamu, (ed.) (1971) *Kitabu: Beginning Concepts in Kawaida*, Los Angeles: The Organization Us.

Harding, Vincent. (1987) *Hope and History: Why We Must Share the Story of the Movement*, Maryknoll, NY: Orbis.

Harding, Vincent. (1980) *The Other American Revolution*, Los Angeles/Atlanta: Center for Afro-American Studies/ Institute of the Black World.

Harding, Vincent. (1981) *There is a River*, New York: Harcourt, Brace Jovanovich.

Hare, Nathan. (1972) "The Battle for Black Studies," *The Black Scholar*, 3, 9 (May) 32-47.

Harlan, Louis R. (1972) *Booker T. Washington: The Making of a Black Leader, 1856-1901*, New York: Oxford University Press.

Harlan, Louis R. (1983) *Booker T. Washington: The Making of a Black Leader, 1901-1915*, New York: Oxford University Press.

Harris, J.R. (ed.). (1971) *The Legacy of Egypt*, Oxford: Oxford University Press.

Harris, Joseph E. (1972) *Africans and Their History*, New York: New American Library.

Hayden, Robert C. (1972) *Eight Black American Inventors*, Reading, MA: Addison-Wesley Co.

Haynes, Joyce L. (1992) *Nubia: Ancient Kingdoms of Africa*, Boston: Museum of Fine Arts.

Henry, Charles. (1991) *Jesse Jackson: The Search for Common Ground*, Oakland: Black Scholar Press.

Holloway, Joseph E. (ed.). (1990) *Africanisms in American Culture*, Bloomington: Indiana University Press.

Holmes, Warren N. (1999) *The National Black Independent Political Party: Political Insurgency or Ideological Conversion*, New York: Garland Publication House.

hooks, bell. (1992) *Black Looks, Race and Representation*, Boston: South End Press.

Hurmence, Belinda (ed.). (1990) *Before Freedom: 48 Oral Histories of Former North and South Carolina Slaves*, New York: A Mentor Book.

Jackson, John G. (1980) *Pagan Origins of the Christ Myth*, San Diego: The Truth Seeker Company.

Jacobs, Harriet A. (1987) *Incidents in the Life of Slave Girl Written by Herself*, Cambridge, MA: Harvard University Press. (See also Linda Brent)

Jairazbhoy, R.A. (1974) *Ancient Egyptians and Chinese in America*, Totowa, NJ: Rowan and Littlefield.

Jones, Charles, (ed.) (1998) *The Black Panther Party (Reconsidered): Reflections and Scholarship*, Baltimore: Black Classic Press.

Jones, Jacqueline. (1985) *Labor of Love, Labor of Sorrow: Black Women, Work, and the Family from Slavery to the Present*, New York: Basic Books.

Jones, Norrece T. (1990) *Born a Child of Freedom, Yet A Slave: Mechanisms of Control and Strategies of Resistance in Antebellum South Carolina*, Middleton, CT: Wesleyan University Press.

Jordan, Winthrop D. (1968) *White Over Black: American Attitudes Toward the Negro, 1550-1812*, Chapel Hill: University of North Carolina Press.

Karenga, Maulana. (1977) "Corrective History," *First World*, 1, 3 (May/June) 50-54.

Karenga, Maulana. (1978) *Essays on Struggle: Position and Analysis*, San Diego: Kawaida Publications.

Karenga, Maulana. (1980) "From Civil Rights to Human Rights: Social Struggles in the Sixties," *Black Collegian*, (February/March) 10-16.

Karenga, Maulana. (1984) "Jesse Jackson and the Presidential Campaign: The Invitation and Oppositions of History," *The Black Scholar*, 15, 5 (September/October, 1984) 57-71.

Karenga, Maulana. (1980) *Kawaida Theory: An Introductory Outline*, Inglewood, CA.: Kawaida Publications.

Karenga, Maulana. (2002) *Kawaida: A Communitarian African Philosophy*, Los Angeles: University of Sankore Press.

Karenga, Maulana. (1998) *Kwanzaa: A Celebration of Family, Community and Culture*, Los Angeles: University of Sankore Press.

Karenga, Maulana. (1997) "Kwame Ture in the Scales of History: A Legacy of Lessons," *Black Scholar*, 27, 3/4 (Fall/Winter) 46-50.

Karenga, Maulana. (1995) *The Million Man March/Day of Absence Mission Statement*, Los Angeles: University of Sankore Press.

Karenga, Maulana. (1978) "A Response to Muhammad Ahmad on the Us/Panther Conflict," *Black Scholar*, 9, 10, (July/August, 1978) 55-57.

Karenga, Maulana. (1976) *The Roots of the Us/Panther Conflict: The Perverse and Deadly Games Police Play*, San Diego: Kawaida Publications.

Karenga, Maulana. (1979) "The Socio-Political Philosophy of Malcolm X," *Journal of Black Studies*, 3, 4 (Winter) 251-262.

Karenga, Tiamoyo. (1996) "A Time of Possibility: Continuing the Historical Legacy" in Haki Madhubuti and Maulana Karenga, (eds.) (1996) *Million Man March-Day of Absence: A Commemorative Anthology*, Chicago/Los Angeles: Third World Press/University of Sankore Press, pp. 75-76.

Katz, William. (1986) *Black Indians*, New York: Macmillan Children's Book Group.

Kellog, Charles. (1967) *NAACP: A History of the National Association for the Advancement of Colored People*, Baltimore: Johns Hopkins University Press.

Kelly, Robin D.G. and Earl Lewis, (eds.). (2000) *To Make Our World Anew: A History of African Americans*, New York: Oxford University Press.

Kifano, Subira Sekhmet. (1996) "The Day of Absence: Its Value and Benefit to Our Struggle," in

Haki Madhubuti and Maulana Karenga, (eds.), *Million Man March-Day of Absence: A Commemorative Anthology*, Chicago/Los Angeles: Third World Press/University of Sankore Press, pp. 100-102.

King, Martin Luther, Jr. (1958) *Stride Toward Freedom*, New York: Harper & Row Publishers.

King, Martin Luther, Jr. (1962) *Why We Can't Wait*, New York: Harper & Row Publishers.

Klein, Aaron E. (1971) *The Hidden Contributions: Black Scientists and Inventors in America*, New York: Doubleday and Co.

Kluger, Richard. (1976) *Simple Justice: The History of Brown v. Board of Education, Black America's Struggle for Equality*, New York: Alfred A. Knopf.

Kolchin, Peter. (1993) *American Slavery, 1619-1877*, New York: Hill and Wang.

Lawrence, Harol. (1962) "African Explorers in the New World," *The Crisis*, (June-July) 321-332.

Lawson, Steven F. (1991) *Running for Freedom: Civil Rights and Black Politics in America Since 1941*, Philadelphia: Temple University Press.

Lewis, David Levering. (1993) *W.E.B. DuBois: Biography of a Race, 1868-1919*, New York: Henry Holt & Co.

Lewis, David Levering. (1993) *W.E.B. DuBois: A Reader*, New York: Henry Holt & Co.

Littlefield, Daniel Jr. (1977) *Africans and Seminoles*, Westport: Greenwood Press.

Litwack, Leon. (1998) *Trouble in Mind: Black Southerners in the Age of Jim Crow*, New York: Alfred A. Knopf.

Logan, Rayford. (1954) *The Negro in American Life and Thought: The Nadir, 1877-1901*, New York: Van Nostrand Reinhold Co.

Logan, Shirley W. (1999) *We Are Coming: The Persuasive Discourse, Nineteenth Century Black Women*, Cardondale: Southern Illinois University Press.

Lomax, Louis E. (1962) *The Negro Revolt*, New York: Signet Books.

McAdam, Doug. (1983) *Political Process and the Development of Black Insurgency 1930-1970*, Chicago: University of Chicago Press.

McIntyre, Charshee C. (1992) *Criminalizing a Race: Free Blacks During Slavery*, Queens, NY: Kayode Publications.

McKivigin, John R. and Stanley Harrold, (eds.) 1999) *Anti-Slavery Violence: Sectional Racial and Cultural Conflict in Antebellum America*, Knoxville: University of Tennessee Press.

McPherson, James. (1988) *Battle Cry of Freedom: The Civil War Era*, New York: Oxford University Press.

Madhubuti, Haki R. (1973) *From Plan to Planet: Life Studies; The Need for Afrikan Minds and Institutions*, Detroit: Broadside Press.

Madhubuti, Haki R. (ed.). (1993) *Why L.A. Happened: Implications of the '92 Los Angeles Rebellion*, Chicago: Third World Press.

Madhubuti, Haki and Maulana Karenga, (eds.) (1996) *Million Man March-Day of Absence: A Commemorative Anthology*, Chicago/Los Angeles: Third World Press/University of Sankore Press.

Malcolm X. (1965) *Autobiography of Malcolm X*, New York: Grove Press.

Malcolm X. (1970) *By Any Means Necessary*, New York: Grove Press.

Malcolm X. (1992) *February 1965: The Final Speeches*, New York: Pathfinder Press.

Malcolm X. (1966) *Malcolm X Speaks*, New York: Grove Press.

Marable, Manning. (1985) *Black American Politics: From Washington Marches to Jesse Jackson*, London: Verso.Marks, Carole. (1989) *Farewell–We're Good and Gone, The Great Black Migration*, Bloomington, IN: University of Indiana Press.

Martin, Tony. (1976) *Race First*, Westport: Greenwood Press.

Meier, August. (1975) "Toward A Reinterpretation of Booker T. Washington," *Journal of Southern History*, 23, pp. 220-227.

Meier, August and Elliot Rudwick. (1973) *CORE: A Study of the Civil Rights Movement, 1942-1968*, New York: Oxford University Press.

Miller, Mary Ellen. (2001) *The Art of Mesoamerica from Olmec to Aztec*, 3rd Ed., London: Thames and Hudson.

Moon, Henry. (1972) *The Emerging Thought of W.E.B. DuBois*, New York: Simon & Schuster.

Morris, Aldon. D. (1984) *The Origins of the Civil Rights Movement*, New York: The Free Press.

Morris, Lorenzo, (ed.) (1990) *The Social and Political Implications of the 1984 Jesse Jackson Presidential Campaign*, Westport, CT: Greenwood.

Morrison, Toni. (1992) *Race-Ing Justice, En-Gendering Power: Essays on Anita Hill, Clarence Thomas, and the Construction of Social Reality*, New York: Pantheon Books.

Morton, Patricia (ed.) (1996) *Discovering Women in Slavery: Emancipatory Perspectives on the American Past*, Athens: University of Georgia Press.

Muhammad, Elijah. (1973) *The Fall of Africa*, Chicago: Muhammad's Temple of Islam, No. 2.

Muhammad, Elijah. (1965) *Message to the Black Man in America*, Chicago: Muhammad's Temple of Islam, No. 2.

Muhammad, Elijah. (1997) *The True History of Elijah Muhammad: Autobiographically Authoritative*, Atlanta: Secretarious Publications.

Mullin, Gerald W. (1972) *Flight and Rebellion*, New York: Oxford University Press.

Neverdon-Morton, Cynthia. (1998) *Afro-American Women of the South and the Advancement of the Race, 1895-1925*, Knoxville: University of Tennessee Press.

Newton, Huey. (1972) *To Die For the People*, New York: Random House.

Niangoran-Bouah, G. (1984) *The Akan World of Gold Weights: Abstract Design Weights*, Vol. I, Abidjan: Les Nouvelles Editiones Africaines.

Obadele, Imari. (1975) *Foundations of the Black Nation*, Detroit: Songhay Press.

Olsen, Jack. (2000) *Last Man Standing: The Tragedy and Triumph of Geronimo Pratt*, New York: Doubleday.

O'Reilly, Kenneth. (1989) *"Racial Matters": The FBI's Secret File on Black America, 1960-1972*, New York: The Free Press.

Painter, Nell Irvin. (1977) *Exodusters: Black Migration to Kansas After Reconstruction*, New York: Alfred A. Knopf.

Painter, Nell Irvin. (1996) *Sojourner Truth: A Life, A Symbol,* New York: Norton.

Patterson, Orlando. (1998) *Rituals of Blood: Consequences of Slavery in Two American Centuries,* Washington, D.C.: Civitas/Counterpoint.

Patterson, Orlando. (1982) *Slavery and Social Death,* Cambridge, MA: Harvard University Press.

Pearson, Edward A. (ed.) (1999) *Designs Against Charleston: The Trial Record of the Denmark Vesey Slave Conspiracy of 1822,* Chapel Hill: University of North Carolina Press.

Peck, James. (1962) *Freedom Ride,* New York: Simon & Schuster.

Phillips, Ulrich B. (1963) "Life and Labor in the Old South," Boston: Little, Brown & Co.

Pinkney, Alphonso. (1976) *Red, Black and Green Black Nationalism in the United States,* Cambridge: Cambridge University Press.

Porter, Kenneth. (1932) "Relations Between Negroes and Indians with the Present Limits of the United States," *Journal of Negro History,* 17 (July) 287-367.

Powledge, Fred. (1991) *Free at Last? The Civil Rights Movement and the People Who Made It,* Boston: Little Brown.

Price, Richard. (1973) *Maroon Societies,* Garden City, NY: Anchor Books.

Proudfoot, Merrill. (1962) *Diary of a Sit-In,* Chapel Hill, NC: University of North Carolina Press.

Quarles, Benjamin. (1969) *Black Abolitionists,* New York: Oxford University Press.

Quarles, Benjamin. (1988) "Harriet Tubman's Unlikely Leadership," *Black Leaders of the Nineteenth Century,* Urbana: University of Illinois Press.

Quarles, Benjamin. (1953) *The Negro in the Civil War,* Boston: Little, Brown & Co.

Quarles, Benjamin. (1976) *The Negro in the Making of America,* New York: Collier Books.

Reed, Harry. (1994) *Platforms for Change: The Foundations of the Northern Free Black Community,* East Lansing, MI: Michigan State University Press.

Richardson, Marilyn. (ed.). (1987) *Maria W. Stewart: America's First Black Woman Political Writer,* Bloomington, IN: University Press.

Robertson, David. (1999) *Denmark Vesey,* New York: Alfred Knopf.

Robinson, Armstead et al (eds). (1969) *Black Studies in the University,* New York: Bantam Books.

Robinson, Armstead and Patricia Sullivan, (eds.) (1991) *New Directions in Civil Rights Studies,* Charlotteville: University Press of Virginia.

Robinson, Jo Ann Gibson. (1987) *The Montgomery Bus Boycott and the Women Who Started It: The Memoir of Jo Ann Gibson Robinson,* Knoxville: University of Tennessee Press.

Robnett, Belinda. (1997) *How Long? How Long? African American Women in the Struggle for Civil Rights,* New York: Oxford University Press.

Rodney, Walter. (1974) *How Europe Underdeveloped Africa*, Washington, D.C.: Howard University Press.

Rogers, J.A. (1961) *Africa's Gift to America*, New York: Helga M. Rogers.

Salaam, Kalamu ya. (1974) "Tell No Lies Claim No Easy Victories," *Black World*, 23, 12 (October) 18-34.

Sales, William, Jr. (1994) *From Civil Rights to Black Liberation: Malcolm X and the Organization of Afro-American Unity*, Boston: South End Press.

Schwartz, Rosalie. (1975) *Across the Rio to Freedom*, El Paso: Texas Western Press.

Seale, Bobby. (1970) *Seize the Time*, New York: Random House.

Shaw, Stephanie. (1995) "Black Club Women and the Creation of the National Association of Colored Women," in Darlene Clark Hine, Wilma King and Linda Reed, (eds.), *We Specialize in the Wholly Impossible: A Reader in Black Women's History*, Brooklyn: Carlson Publishing, Inc., pp. 433-447.

Sidbury, James. (1998) *Plough Shares into Swords: Race Rebellion and Identity in Gabriel's Virginia, 1730-1810*, New York: Cambridge University Press.

Sindler, Allan P. (1978) *Bakke, DeFunis and Minority Admissions*, New York: Longman.

Smith, Robert C. (1996) *We Have No Leaders: African Americans in the Post-Civil Rights Era*, New York: State University Press.

Sorin, Gerald. (1973) *Abolitionism*, New York: Praeger Publishers.

Stampp, Kenneth. (1965) *Peculiar Institution*, New York: Alfred Knopf, Inc.

Sterling, Dorothy. (1984) *We Are Sisters: Black Women in the Nineteenth Century*, New York: W. W. Norton & Co.

Stirling, Matthew, W. (1939) "Discovering the New World's Oldest Dated Work of Man," *National Geographic Magazine*, 76 (August) 183-218.

Stone, Chuck. (1968) "The National Conference on Black Power," in Floyd Barbour, (ed.) *The Black Power Revolt*, Boston: Porter Sargent, pp. 189-198.

Stoper, Emily. (1989) *The Student Nonviolent Coordinating Committee: The Growth of Radicalism in a Civil Rights Organization*, Brooklyn: Carlson Publications.

Stuckey, Sterling. (1973) "Through the Prism of Folklore: the Black Ethos in Slavery," in *American Negro Slavery*, (eds.) Allen Weinstein and Frank Gatell, New York: Oxford University Press, 134-152.

Sudarkasa, Niara. (1996) *Strength of Our Mothers: African and African American Women and Families*, Trenton, NJ: Africa World Press.

Sullivan, Patricia. (1996) *Days of Hope: Race and Democracy in the New Deal Era*, Chapel Hill: University of North Carolina Press.

Tembo, Chimbuko. (1996) "The Million Man March and Day of Absence," in Haki Madhubuti and Maulana Karenga, (eds.) (1996) *Million Man March-Day of Absence: A Commemorative Anthology*, Chicago/Los Angeles: Third World Press/University of Sankore Press, pp. 125-126.

Terborg-Penn, Rosalyn. (1998) *African American Women in the Struggle for the Vote, 1850-1920*, Bloomington: Indiana University Press.

Thornbrough, E.L. (ed.) (1969) *Booker T. Washington*, Englewood Cliffs: Prentice-Hall, Inc.

Van Sertima, Ivan. (1992) *African Presence in Early America*, New Brunswick: Transaction Publishers.

Tolnay, Stewart E. and E.M. Beck, (eds.) (1995) *A Festival of Violence: An Analysis of Southern Lynchings 1882-1903*, Urbana: University of Illinois Press.

Trotter, Jr. Joe William. (ed.) (1991) *The Great Migration in Historical Perspective*, Bloomington: Indiana University Press.

Tushnet, Mark V. (1994) *Making Civil Rights Law: Thurgood Marshall and the Supreme Court, 1936-1961*, New York: Oxford University Press.

Twyman, Bruce E. (1999) *The Black Seminole Legacy and Northern American Polices, 1693-1845*, Washington, D.C.: Howard University Press.

Tyson, Timothy B. (1999) *Radio Free Dixie, Robert F. Williams and the Roots of Black Power*, Chapel Hill: University of North Carolina Press.

Van DeBurg, William. (1993) *New Day in Babylon: The Black Power Movement and African American Culture, 1965-1975*, Chicago: University of Chicago Press.

Van Sertima, Ivan. (1998) *Early America Revisited*, New Brunswick, NJ: Transaction Publishers.

Van Sertima, Ivan. (1992) *Golden Age of the Moor*, New Brunswick: Transaction Publishers.

Van Sertima, Ivan. (1976) *They Came Before Columbus*, New York: Random House.

Von Frank, Albert J. (1998) *The Trials of Anthony Burns*, Cambridge: Harvard University Press.

Von Wuthenau, Alexander. (1969) *The Art of Terracotta Pottery in Pre-Columbian South and Central America*, New York: Free Press.

Walton, Hanes Jr. (1972) *Black Political Parties*, New York: Free Press.

Washington, Booker T. (1968) *Up From Slavery*, New York: Magnum Books.

Webber, Thomas L. (1978) *Deep Like the Rivers: Education in the Slave Quarter Community, 1831-1865*, New York. W. W. Norton & Co.

Weinberg, Meyer. (1970) *W.E.B. DuBois: A Reader*, New York: Harper & Row Publishers.

Weiner, Leo. (1972) *Africa and the Discovery of America*, Philadelphia: Innes and Sons.

Weiss, Nancy. (1974) *The National Urban League, 1910-1940*, New York: Oxford University Press.

Wells-Barnett, Ida B. (1990) *On Lynching: Southern Horrors, A Red Record and Mob Rule in New Orleans*, Salem, NH: Ayer Company.

White, Deborah Gray. (1987) *Ar'n't I A Woman? Female Slaves in the Plantation South*, New York: W. W. Norton & Co.

White, Deborah Gray. (1991) "Female Slaves in the Plantation South," in Edward D.C. Campbell, Jr., (ed.) *Before Freedom Came*, Richmond: The Museum of the Confederacy.

White, Deborah Gray. (1999) *Too Heavy a Load: Black Women in Defense of Themselves*, New York: Norton.

Williams, Eric. (1966) *Capitalism & Slavery*, New York: Capricorn Books.

Williams, George. (1888) *History of Negro Troops in the War of Rebellion*, New York: Harper and Row.

Williams, Juan. (1987) *Eyes on the Prize*, New York: Viking.

Williams, Robert. (1973) *Negroes With Guns*, Chicago: Third World Press.

Wolff, Miles. (1972) *Lunch at the Five and Ten*, New York: Stein & Day Publishers.

Wolters, Raymond. (1974) *Negroes and the Great Depression: The Problem of Economic Recovery*, Westport, CT: Greenwood Publishers Groups, Inc.

Woodard, Komozi. (1999) *A Nation Within A Nation: Amiri Baraka (LeRoi Jones) and Black Power Politics*, Chapel Hill: University of North Carolina Press.

Woodson, Carter G. and Charles H. Wesley. (1972) *The Negro in Our History*, Washington, D.C.: Associated Publishers.

Ya Salaam, Kalamu. (1975) "Afrikan-American Culture," *Nkombo*, 5, 2 (January) 1-4.

Yee, Shirley J. (1992) *Black Women Abolitionists: A Study in Activism, 1828-1860*, Knoxville: University of Tennessee Press.

Youth of the Rural Organizing and Cultural Center. (1991) *Minds Stayed on Freedom: The Civil Rights Struggle in the Rural South, and Oral History*, Boulder: Westview Press.

Zinn, Howard. (1964) *SNCC: The New Abolitionist*, Boston: Beacon Press.

BLACK RELIGION

BLACK RELIGION

CHAPTER 5

5.1   INTRODUCTION

Religion has always been a vital part of Black life in both Africa and the U.S. In Africa, religion was so pervasive that distinctions between it and other areas of life were almost imperceptible (Mbiti, 1970; Zahan, 1979; Morenz, 1984). In the U.S., the extent of Black religiousness is clear and has been well-documented (Wilmore, 1998; Fulop and Raboteau, 1997; Lincoln, 1974a). Although there are numerous definitions for religion, for the purpose of this chapter, *religion can be defined as thought, belief and practice concerned with the transcendent and the ultimate questions of life* (Karenga, 1980:23). Among such questions are those concerning human death, relevance, origin, destiny, suffering and obligations to other humans and in most cases, to a Supreme or Ultimate Being. Within the context of the concern with the ultimate is also the clear division between the sacred, i.e., the set apart and exalted, and the profane, i.e., the common and non-exalted (Hoffmeier, 1985).

The religion of Black people in the U.S. is predominantly Judeo-Christian, but Islam, both Black and orthodox, and ancient African religious and ethical traditions, are growing among African Americans (Wilmore, 1998). Among these other varied traditions are the Black Hebrew tradition (Ben Yehuda, 1975), the Rastafarian tradition (Barrett, 1988; Morrison, 1992) and the Yoruba tradition which is an international tradition including a Continental Yoruba practice (Lucas, 1948; Idowu, 1975; Abimbola, 1976; Awolalu, 1979; Thompson, 1983; Drewal, 1992; Karenga, 1999), a Santería Yoruba practice

(Murphy, 1988; Gonzalez-Wippler, 1982; Gleason, 1975) and a Candomblé Yoruba practice (Bastide, 1978; Richards, 1976). Also in recent years, the Maatian tradition from ancient Egypt has emerged and is discussed below (Karenga, 1984, 1989, 1994).

Given that whites have so shaped the public and scholarly discourse on Judeo-Christianity and its public images are essentially white, the tendency is to see Black religion as "white religion in Black face" (Chapman, 1996). However, as Lincoln (1974a) and Wilmore (1973) contend, such an interpretation is grossly incorrect. For regardless of what external details of white Christianity are similar to Black Christianity, the essence of Black Christianity is different. The essence of a people's religion is rooted in its own social and historical experiences and in the truth and meaning they extract from these and translate into an authentic spiritual expression which speaks specifically to them. Thus, Black religion represents in its essence then, not imitation but "the desire of Blacks to be self-conscious about the meaning of their Blackness and to search for spiritual fulfillment in terms of their understanding of themselves and their experience of history" (Lincoln, 1974a:3).

5.2   ANCIENT AFRICAN TRADITIONS

GENERAL THEMES

Black religion like Black people began in Africa and thus, it is important to discuss its historical forms before turning to its current expressions. The study of traditional African religions is made difficult by Europeans' interpretations which exhibit a need to make Christianity seem superior and African religions primitive (Evans-Pritchard, 1965) and by African Christian interpretations which strive to make African religions more "normal" by making them look more Christian or Abrahamic, i.e., Christian, Jewish, Muslim (Mbiti, 1970). To appreciate African religions, one must admit similarities and differences without seeing the similarities as "less developed" and the differences as evidence of psychological or cultural defectiveness.

Thus, if African stories of creation and divinities are myths, so are Christian, Jewish and Islamic ones. However, a better category for both African and other creation stories would be "narratives." Moreover, Jehovah, Yahweh and Allah are no more arguable than Nkulunkulu, Oludumare and Amma. And the abasom of the Ashanti and the orisha of the Yoruba are no less effective as divine intermediaries than Catholic saints like Jude and Christopher. All non-scientific approaches to the origin of the world and the forces operative in it are vulnerable to challenge. And the choice of one over the other is more a matter of tradition and preference than proof of any particular one's validity. Therefore, my use of Abrahamic religious examples will not be to force comparisons or contrasts, but to demonstrate parallels where appropriate which would tend to lessen a person's tendency to reductively translate African religions in a mistaken assumption of superiority for his/her own.

Although African religious traditions are complex and diverse, there are some general themes which tend to appear in all of them (Mbiti, 1970, 1991; Ray, 1976; Zahan, 1979; Wright, 1984; Gyekye, 1987; Karenga, 1994, 1999b). First, there is the belief in one Supreme God: Oludumare among the Yoruba, Nkulunkulu among the Zulu and Amma among the Dogon, etc. This God is the Father in most societies, but also appears as Mother in matriarchal societies like the Ovambo in Namibia and the Nuba in Kenya. Moreover, in Dogon religion, Amma has both male and female characteristics, reflecting the Dogon concept of binary opposition as the motive force and structure of the universe (Ray, 1976:28-29; Griaule, 1978).

Secondly, in ancient African religious traditions, God is both immanent and transcendent, near and far. In this framework, then, Africans engage in daily interaction with divinities, who are seen as God's intermediaries and assistants (Mbiti, 1970, 1991). These divinities are both similar to and different from Jesus, angels and Catholic saints as intermediaries and assistants to the Supreme Being. It is this deference and exchange with the divinities which made the less critical assume Africans were polytheistic rather than monotheistic. However, evidence clearly argues against this assumption.

Thirdly, African religions stress ancestor veneration. The ancestors are venerated for several reasons which reinforce the concepts of linkage, heritage and spiritual relevance (Richards, 1989:7,8). They "are venerated because they are: 1) a source and symbol of lineage; 2) models of ethical life, service and social achievement to the community; and 3) because they are spiritual intercessors between humans and the Creator" (Karenga, 1988: 20, see also Mbiti, 1970:108, 1991). The Ashanti have a special Day of Remembrance of the Ancestors called *Akwasidae* in which ceremonies focus on linkage between those who have passed, the living and the yet unborn. As Mends (1976:8) notes, by participating in the ceremony to honor ancestors one is stressing "the common bonds of kinship and association which make for solidarity among the people." And it is also a way to reinforce the value and honor due those whose ethical life and service make them worthy members of the community.

Fourthly, ancient African religions stress the necessary balance between one's collective identity and responsibility as a member of society and one's personal identity and responsibility. Like religion itself, a person is defined as an integral part of a definite community, to which she/he belongs and in which she/he finds identity and relevance. Summing up this conception, Mbiti (1970:141) states that "I am because we are, and since we are, therefore I am." The Dinka have captured this stress on the moral ideal of harmonious integration of self with the community in their word *cieng* which means both morality and living together. In this conception, the highest moral ideal is to live in harmony, know oneself and one's duties through others and reach one's fullness in cooperation with and through support from one's significant others (Deng, 1973).

Another key theme in African religions is the profound respect for nature. Because humans live in a religious universe, everything that is has religious relevance (Richards, 1989:6-7). The whole world as God's creation is alive with His/Her symbols and gifts to humans, and bear witness to His/Her power, beauty and beneficence. Thus, there are sacred trees, rivers, mountains and animals (as in Abrahamic religions). Nature is not only respected because of its association with God, but also because of its relevance to humankind. This respect is grounded in the belief that there is an unbreakable bond between the divine, the human and the natural and that therefore damage to one is damage to the other and likewise respect and care for one is respect and care for the other. The stress, then, is to show nature due respect, not abuse it in any way and to live in harmony with it and the universe. Dona Marimba Richards (1989:10) notes that African culture is a "culture that perceives the interrelationships and interdependence of all beings within the universe." Thus, she says the African approach is that "if we take or destroy, we must give or rebuild; for there is one spiritual unity that joins us all...."

Finally, the conception of death and immortality is an important theme in African religions. Death in African religions is seen in several ways. First, it is seen as another stage in human development. Humans are born, live, die and become the ancestors. Death is thus not the end, but a beginning of another form of existence, i.e., as ancestor and spirit. Therefore, it is seen as a transition in life rather than an end to it. After a period of mourning there is celebration for the human conquest of death. For after the funeral, the dead are "revived" in the spirit world and, as ancestors, are close and relevant. Secondly, death is seen as reflective of cosmic patterns, i.e., the rising and setting of the sun, and often graves are dug east and west to imitate this pattern.

Thirdly, death is seen as a transition in life to personal and collective immortality. Personally, one lives after death through five means: 1) children; 2) other relatives; 3) rituals of remembrance; 4) good deeds; and 5) great works. The living remember and speak one's name and deeds, and one's works speak of one's significance throughout time. Thus, without relatives to keep one's memory alive or significant achievements and good deeds, one is what Africans call "utterly dead." Collective immortality is achieved through the life of one's people and through what one means to them. For as long as they live, the person lives and shares in their life and destiny.

THE DOGON TRADITION

INTRODUCTION

One of the most complex and impressive African religious systems is that of the Dogon. The Dogon, who live in Mali, have astounded the world by their astronomical knowledge and impressed it with the logic and intricacy of their thought. So impressive is their knowledge, especially of the Sirius star-system, that some Europeans have argued that the Dogon's knowledge was given to them by space beings (Temple, 1976) or by mysterious Europeans (Sagan, 1979). However, Europeans did not know themselves until the 1800's what the Dogon knew about the Sirius star-system 700 years ago (Adams, 1979).

The socio-religious thought of the Dogon evolves from an elaborate cosmogony and an extremely complex cosmology (Griaule, 1978; Griaule and Dieterlen, 1965). It is these constructions around which the Dogon understand and organize their world and seek to carry out their social and spiritual tasks. For the sake of brevity and clarity, I have tried to reduce the story of creation to its most basic elements while at the same time, trying to remain faithful to its logic and content.

THE CREATION NARRATIVE

In the beginning everything that would be already potentially was. The substances and structure of the universe was in Amma, the Supreme God, who was in the image of an egg and divided into four quarters containing the four basic elements of air, earth, fire and water, and the four cardinal directions-north, south, east and west. Thus, Amma was the egg of the universe, and the universe and Amma were one. As egg, Amma symbolized and was fertility and unlimited creative possibility. Through creative thought, Amma traced within himself the design and developmental course of the universe using 266 cosmic signs which contained the essence, structure and life-principle of all things. Placing the four basic elements and sacred signs and seeds on a flat disk, Amma set the disk revolving between the two cosmic axes. But the spinning disk threw off the water drying up the seeds. The first creation was thus, aborted and Amma began again, deciding that this time he would make humans the preservers of order and life in the world.

Placing a seed at the center of himself, the cosmic egg, he spoke seven creative words. From this, the seed (matter) vibrated seven times unfolding along a spiral path, conserving itself on one hand and transforming itself on the other through alternations between opposites. Thus, the principal of twinness or binary opposition directed its movement and its form and established a pattern for the structure and functioning of the universe, i.e., up/down, man/woman, action/inaction, hot/cold, etc. From the infinitely small (seed, atom), the infinitely large (universe) evolved. The seed, vibrating seven times and turning in a spiral fashion, extended itself in seven directions in the womb of the world, pre-figuring the shape of a human being, i.e., two directions for the head, two for the arms, two for the legs and one for the genital. The world was, thus, created in the image of humans and would later be organized around them.

Transforming the egg into a double placenta, Amma placed two sets of twins, male and female in each, again underscoring the principle of opposites which informs the structure and functioning of the universe. In the twins, He placed the sacred signs, words and seeds of creation. Before gestation was completed, however, one of the male twins, Yurugu (Ogo) feeling lonely and incomplete bursts through the womb to seize his female twin. Unable to acquire his twin, he rebelled against the established order of things. Imposing disorder on a orderly process, Yurugu descended into the void in an attempt to create a world himself. But his knowledge was incomplete and he could not speak the creative words. Then Amma, using the piece of placenta which Yurugu took as he broke from the celestial egg-womb, created the earth. This creation of earth restored the human shape of the world. The celestial egg became the head of man; the lower incomplete placenta, now earth and forming an incomplete circle, became the hips and legs; and the space and lines which divide and connect heaven and earth became the trunk and arms. Binary opposition is thus, again established in that heaven is the head (mind, spirit) and earth, the lower region of the body (the physical). Joined together, they form the structure and essence of humans.

To restore order in the world, Amma scattered Yurugu's male twin, Nommo, i.e., creative word, over the expanse of the universe. Also, He created four other Nommo spirits from Nommo and their offspring became the eight ancestors of the Dogon. Amma then sent Nommo and the eight ancestors down to Earth, with all species of animals and plants, and all the elements of human culture, thus laying the basis for human development and a prosperous earth. Descending, Nommo shouted out the creative words, therefore transmitting the power of creative speech and thought to Earth, making it available to humankind. Through this power, they would be able to push back the boundaries of ignorance and disorder and impose creative order on the world. To punish Yurugu for his disorder and revolt, Amma transformed him into a Pale Fox. Deprived of his female half, the Pale Fox is an incomplete and lonely being wandering though the world in a vain quest for wholeness. But as he wanders, he leaves tracks through the mysteries of life, revealing the dangers humans must avoid. Finally, sending rain to Earth, Amma made the Earth flourish and humans began to cultivate the land and cover it with ever-increasing numbers. Possessing creative intelligence through Nommo, humans walk the way of Yurugu as well, alternating between disorder and order, destruction and creation, rationality and irrationality, conformity and revolt.

THEOLOGICAL INSIGHTS

There are several aspects of this cosmogonical construction which reveal the profundity of Dogon thought and its susceptibility to interesting and expansive interpretations. First, it stresses the binary oppositional character and functioning of the universe, i.e., creation/destruction, order/disorder, male/ female, perfection/imperfection, self-conscious action/ unconscious action, etc. This is essentially an African dialectic, posing opposites necessary to the explanation and functioning of the world. In fact, each opposite explains and necessitates the other. Thus, Yurugu rebels because he feels deprived of his female half which he needs for his wholeness. He fails because he represents action without critical consciousness, and Nommo, who reflects the creative thought and action of Amma, succeeds in establishing order and promoting development. Secondly, the concept of God as the cosmic womb, already containing in the beginning everything that would come into being in Him, suggest a concept of God as the universe and of its already having at the beginning all the building material (matter) for everything in it. This reflects the scientific principle that matter was always and already here, and only its forms changed and change.

Thirdly, the concept of God as egg is reflective of His fertility, productiveness and infinite creative possibilities, as well as the idea of them. As infinite creative possibility in the universe and of the universe, God is infinite in a logical and meaningful way. Fourthly, the Dogon pose God as making a mistake in the first creation and thus, maintain logical consistency even in discussing God. For God is both perfect and imperfect, male and female, thought and action and therefore reflects and reinforces the principle of binary opposition.

Also, there is a clear contention that the world is not perfect either and is in the process of perpetual becoming. This process

again is marked by binary opposition in structure and functioning and strives toward the creative and ongoing harmonizing of
the two opposites. Especially, profound and far-reaching is the
concept that becoming of necessity requires rebellion or oppositional thought and action against the established order. Yurugu
comes into being by breaking through the cosmic egg and thus,
sets up conditions for a new world. Breaking from Amma, God,
he becomes truly human rather than a cosmic baby. In this
action, he reminds one of the young adult leaving his/her parents' house in order to build a world for him/herself. In a word,
independence and development requires a break from the established state of things. And even though Yurugu fails to make the
world, he contributed to its origin and still leaves tracks through
the mysteries of life which humankind can read and from which
they can learn vital lessons.

Finally, Dogon thought is clearly impressive in its stress on
humans as the indispensable element in the world's becoming
and functioning. As noted above, the universe was created in
the image of the human personality; he/she is the world in
microcosm, containing its basic elements, the four cardinal
directions, and the sacred cosmic seeds, signs and words.
Moreover, Amma, God could not make the world without
humans, for not only did the world need man/woman to flourish, but so did God. For if God is idea and creative possibility,
only man/woman can know and appreciate it. Only humans are
capable of creative thought; trees will not pray or praise, and
dogs do not discuss spiritual or social duties. But if God needs
man/woman, the binary oppositional logic of Dogon thought
requires that man/woman also needs God. For if idea and creative possibility (God) cannot exist without man/woman,
man/woman cannot exist without idea and creative possibility
(God).

MAAT: THE ANCIENT EGYPTIAN TRADITION

INTRODUCTION

The contribution of ancient Egypt to human civilization, as
noted in chapter 3, is immense, enduring and well-documented
(Obenga, 1992; Diop, 1991, 1974; Van Sertima, 1989, 1994;
Harris, 1971). However, as I have argued elsewhere, no legacy

left by ancient Egypt is more significant and enduring than its ethical and spiritual legacy, Maat (Karenga, 1999b, 1994, 1990a, 1984). It is Kemet, ancient Egypt, which gave humankind the concepts of humans as the image of God and human dignity which is derived from it, resurrection and judgment after death, preference and care for the poor and vulnerable, care and responsibility toward the environment, the moral essentiality of service, and building for eternity so that we may live for eternity. And it is concepts like these which constitute the profoundly rich and significant contribution of Kemet to the shaping and development of human spiritual and moral understanding and practice (Asante, 2000; Diop, 1991; Breasted, 1934).

There is an abundance of literature on the ancient Egyptian spiritual and ethical tradition, including excellent anthologies of translated texts. The definitive collection in English of Kemetic religious texts is Piankoff's (1954-74) Egyptian Religious Texts and Representations (6 volumes). Other anthologies include a wide-range of literature in addition to religious literature. Among these are Breasted's (1905-1906) Ancient Records of Egypt (5 volumes), Lichtheim's (1973, 1976, 1980) Ancient Egyptian Literature (3 volumes) and her (1988) Ancient Egyptian Autobiographies Chiefly of the Middle Kingdom, Simpson's et al's (1973) The Literature of Ancient Egypt, and more recently Parkinson's (1991) Voices From Ancient Egypt and his (1997) The Tale of Sinuhe and Other Ancient Egyptian Poems, 1940-1640 BC. Even though it is in French, La philosphie africaine de la périod pharaonique, 2780-330 avant notre ère (African Philosophy in the Pharonic Period, 2780-330 CE) merits mention as a major work of original translation and critical commentary by the dean of African and African-centered Egyptologists, Theophile Obenga (1990). Also, Faulkner's (1969) Ancient Egyptian Pyramid Texts (2 volumes) and his (1973-1978) Ancient Egyptian Coffin Texts (3 volumes) and Allen's (1960) The Book of the Dead or Going Forth By Day are also of considerable importance in understanding the spiritual and ethical tradition of ancient Egypt.

The Maatian tradition discussed below is rooted in ancient Egyptian ethical thought and practice, but is clearly shaped by the resurgence of interest and intellectual work in ancient Egyptian spirituality and ethics since the 1980's. Its point of departure is the initiative launched by the Organization Us and others in the 80's, discussed above in chapter 1 to recover the rich and ancient resource of Kemetic culture (Karenga, 1984, 1990a, 1990b, 1990c; Karenga and Carruthers, 1986). The collection, translation and dissemination of the *Husia* (Karenga, 1984) by the Seba Maat (moral teachers) of the Kawaida Temple (Us) and Us' calling of the First Annual Ancient Egyptian Studies Conference in February 1984 in Los Angeles, represented the beginning of a new discourse on Maat, the ancient Egyptian spiritual and ethical tradition, in both the community and academy. And it is this project of recovery and reconstruction which is represented in the teachings of the *Husia* (Karenga, 1984, 1986b) and the critical commentary in *Maat, The Moral Ideal in Ancient Egypt: A Study in Classical African Ethics* (Karenga, 1994) that forms the foundation and framework for the discussion of Maatian tradition here.

MAAT: THE CONCEPT

The starting point for any critical and meaningful discussion of the Maatian tradition is the concept of *Maat* (Karenga, 1994; Lichtheim, 1992; Assmann, 1990; Teeter, 1990; Tobin, 1989; Morenz, 1984). A critical study of is use in Kemetic moral and spiritual literature indicates that Maat has multiple meanings. But essentially Maat means *rightness* in the spiritual and moral sense in three realms: the Divine, the natural and the social. In another sense, it is an *interrelated order of rightness* which requires and is the result of right relations with and behavior towards the Divine, nature and other humans. In this context, Maat is also a *way of rightness* defined by The Seven Cardinal Virtues which will be discussed below: truth, justice, propriety, harmony, balance, reciprocity and order. In the *Husia*, the scared text of the Maatian tradition, the Seba, Ptahhotep says, "Established are those whose standard is Maat, who walk according to its ways. They shall surely prosper thereby" (*The Husia*, 44:X). And Seba Khun-Anup says, "Speak Maat (truth), do Maat (justice) for Maat is mighty, it is great, it endures. Its worth is real and it leads one to blessedness. Wrongdoing does not achieve its goal, but one who is righteous reaches dry land" (*The Husia*, 34:VIII).

Thus, Maat is a path and guide to a more meaningful and rewarding life. In this sense, it becomes a designation and criterion of the ideal world, society and person, i.e., the Maatian world, Maatian society and Maatian person. Finally, Maat is our intimate link with the Ultimate Ideal. For by the practice, promotion and defense of Maat, we come to embody it and in embodying Maat we assimilate the Divine. As Queen Hatshepsut says with regard to God, Amen Ra, "I have exalted Maat which he loves, for I know he lives by it. Also, it is my bread and I drink from its dew. I am of one body with him" (Karenga, 1994:441). Complete harmony or oneness with Maat, then, becomes oneness with the Creative Force of the Universe which is both a blessing and the basis for eternal life.

THE HUSIA

The teachings of the Maatian tradition, as noted above, are found in its sacred text, *The Husia*. Edited and translated by this author, these teachings span the vast body of writings on spirituality and ethics left by the ancient Egyptians. Currently only a brief selection of this immense corpus exists in the text, *Selections From The Husia: Sacred Wisdom of Ancient Egypt* (Karenga, 1984). But a larger text is in process and will include the full forms of the major ethical and spiritual teachings of ancient Egypt. The name of the text, *Husia*, translates as authoritative utterance (*Hu*) of exceptional insight (*Sia*). According to the Maatian creation narrative, these are the two main powers by which Ra, God, created the world. He conceived it in his heart and mind and then spoke the creative words which brought the world into being. Thus, the Divine or sacred texts are called *The Husia*.

BASIC TENETS

Like all spiritual and ethical traditions or religions, Maat has some basic tenets which define the tradition and set the standards for practicing it. This moral and spiritual vision and set of values seeks to cultivate the Maatian person and create and sustain a Maatian world. The Maatian person will strive for rightness in her/his life and relations through right thought, right emotion, right speech and right conduct. And s/he will likewise in this way, constantly work to repair and heal the world, always making it more beautiful and beneficial than it was before.

To focus the presentation, I will quote mostly from *The Husia* as it has been currently compiled and translated. However, I will also draw from the larger body of ancient Egyptian literature which is also a part of the complete *Husia* and which is found in *Maat, The Moral Ideal in Ancient Egypt: A Study in Classical African Ethics* (Karenga, 1994). In the citations from *The Husia*, I use Arabic (Muslim) numerals for the page of the citation and Roman numerals to indicate the chapter.

HUMANS AS THE DIVINE IMAGE OF GOD. Clearly, one of the most important tenets of the Maatian tradition is its concept that humans are in the image of God (*snn Ntr* – senen netcher). This is a key concept in the spiritual and moral development of humankind and represents one of Africa's most important contributions to this process. This conception of the human person is first advanced around 2140 B.C.E. in the Book of Kheti and precedes any other religion's similar conception by hundreds, if not a thousand years.

In *The Husia* in the Book of Kheti (52:VIII), we read: "Well-cared for is humankind who are the flocks of God.... He gave breath of life for their noses. They are *His images* and came from his body" (emphasis mine). It is from this Maatian concept of humans as images of God (*snnw Ntr*) that we get the earliest evidence of the concept of human dignity and its central pillar, the sanctity of life. Thus, humans as images of God have a special moral, even sacred, status and must never be treated by themselves or each other in any way that violates their inherent dignity which is grounded in their identity as images of God.

Also, in *The Husia* in the Book of Prayers and Sacred Praises (21:VII), it says of God: "O' Ra all can turn to you and put their petitions to you. Your ears are open to hear them and you grant what they desire. For you are the Creator who loves those in His image, the shepherd who is fond of his flock." Thus, the sacredness of human beings is established and this lays the basis for an equally important concept, the inherent dignity of humans.

THE DIGNITY OF THE HUMAN BEING. Rooted in and reflective of the Maatian concept of humans as images of God, then, is the concept of the dignity or inherent worthiness of humans. As bearers of divinity, humans are also bearers of dignity, an inherent worthiness which cannot be denied or diminished by social status or any other distinguishing condition. This too is one of

Africa's greatest contributions to the moral development of humankind through ancient Egypt. For it reaffirms the sanctity of human life and makes no distinction between persons because of social or physical differences.

Nowhere is the concept of human dignity and the sanctity of human life more clearly presented than in the Narrative of Djedi (Blackman, 1988). In the Narrative of Djedi, Djedi speaks Maat (truth) to power when he tells Pharaoh Khufu who is about to kill a prisoner that he must not kill or use any person for an experiment. When the king calls for a prisoner to use in a deadly experiment, Djedi tells him: "Not to a human being O' king. Surely it is not permitted to do such a thing to the noble flock of God." His ground for this, of course, is the ancient and sacred Maatian teaching against killing and doing harm to humans. This prohibition is reaffirmed in the Declarations of Innocence which prohibit killing and ordering anyone to kill as well as various other harms to people (*The Husia*, Declarations of Innocence, 110:IX). Finally, to be in the image of God is also to be obligated to act like God (*irt mi Ra*), that is to act in Maat (righteousness). In the Book of Unas, King Unas is told "May you shine like Ra, repressing wrong and causing Maat to stand behind Ra" (Karenga, 1994:84). Thus, as bearers of dignity and divinity, humans are morally obligated to act in ways worthy of such a status.

STANDING WORTHY BEFORE GOD AND THE PEOPLE. In Maatian moral discourse the concept of "standing worthy before God and people" is also central. This is expressed in the obligation to "stand well," "be worthy" and "be loved" found in the sacred texts. Harkhuf (*The Husia*, 94-95:IV) says,

> I was one worthy. One beloved of his father, praised by his mother and one whom all his sisters and brothers loved. I gave bread to the hungry, clothes to the naked and brought the boatless to dry land… For I wished to stand well with the Most High God.

Nefer-Seshem-Ra says, "I have spoke truly and done right (*Maat*). I spoke justly and repeated that which was just… so as to stand well with the people" (*The Husia*, 95:V). And Wennofer says,

I was true hearted, just and trustworthy. One who walked on the water of God (i.e., was devoted to God). I was one praised in his town, generous in his district, kind and compassionate to everyone. I was friendly and one welcomed by others, widely loved...a strong shelter for the needy, one on whom all could lean. I welcomed the stranger and was a helpful adviser and an effective guide (The Husia, 95:VI).

Thus, one who follows these examples and teachings are compelled to strive daily to stand worthy. As the sacred texts teach, "the virtuous person is rewarded for his virtue. And there is love for one who is blameless." The reward is both Divine and social. The Divine reward is love of God and immortality in the next world. The social reward is love, praise and immortal memory in the hearts and minds of the people.

WORTHINESS BEFORE NATURE. As noted above, Maat requires worthiness before the Creator, nature and people. The concept of worthiness before nature in the Maatian tradition evolves out of the understanding that moral worthiness, like existence, is interrelated in every area of life. One thus seeks to be able to claim a Maatian standing in every area of moral consideration and our relation with nature is one of the three major areas. In other words, in the Maatian tradition, one seeks a unity in one's life in every area of moral concern. Maat is the principle and practice that binds all things and beings together. Humans are a part of a Maatian order and belong to each. "In their identity as images and offspring of God, humans belong to the Divine; in their identity as social beings, they belong to society; and in their identity as living beings, they belong to nature" (Karenga, 1994:723). Thus, they must seek to do Maat within each of these areas. Unas' concern to have no accuser within the divine, natural or social realms is expressive of this moral status and requirement.

The Maatian tradition finds several basic grounds for our standing worthy before nature. The first is the sacredness of the world as God's creation and His care for all His creation great and small. The book of Prayers and Sacred Praises says that it is Ra, God, who sustains the people, birds, animals, reptiles and insects, linking all under His divine care and concern. The scared texts say of Ra, He is

The unique one who made all that is...the one who created the herbage that nourishes the animals and the fruit trees for humankind, who makes the fish in the river live and birds under heaven, who gives breath to what is in the egg and nourishes even the young snake, who makes that on which gnats live and likewise worms and flies, who supplies the needs of mice in their holes and nourishes flying things in every tree (The Husia, 15:1; Karenga, 1994:750).

Here and elsewhere humans are placed in the midst of other living things all of which, as well as the world itself is in the loving care of the Creator.

A second ground for our need to stand worthy before nature and for a Maatian environmental ethics is the filial obligation we have as offspring of the Divine to care for His creation which must be done as a loving son or daughter does for one's parent. Thus, Queen Hatshepsut says she is the beloved daughter of Ra, "an effective image of the Lord of all who he chose as guardian of Egypt, protector of the nobles and the masses,...(whom Ra created) so as to have useful offspring on earth for the well-being of humankind" (Karenga, 1994:409-410). This well-being of humankind is, of course, linked with the well-being of the world in which they live. Thus, she states that she repaired the world as a loving daughter. Moreover, King Amenhotep II says, "It was my father (Amen Ra) who commanded that I do it, Amen who created my goodness. He appointed me as shepherd of this land, knowing I would rule it well for him (Karenga, 1994:420).

Also linked to our filial obligation to care for the world for the Creator is our mutual obligation to care for and not damage the shared heritage or inheritance from our Creator. In the Book of Vindication, Ra lists 4 Good Deeds he does for humankind and two of those Good Deeds are gifts of nature. He says: "I made the four winds so that every person might breath therefrom in his or her own time. I made the great flood so that the humble person might benefit from it like the great." The other two Good Deeds or gifts are: 1) equality and free will; and 2) religious consciousness so that we may offer Maat to the Divine. And Maat as offered is above all a daily and social practice of the good.

Likewise, Maatian environmental ethics is based on a moral obligation to protect and preserve the earth for future generations. Nakhtefmut says that he strove daily to do good in the world. "For I knew that the results of a good deed is a storehouse which one's children will find afterwards" (Maat, 750). Finally, central to Maatian ethics in general and in particular for the environment is the moral obligation of *serudj ta* which means to constantly repair, heal and restore the world making it more beautiful than when we inherited it. The Maatian tradition teaches that the world and all in it are constantly being damaged and injured by what we do wrong and fail to do right. Thus, we must constantly recreate the world, repairing and restoring it and making it more beautiful and beneficial than it was before. In the *Declarations of Virtues*, serudj is defined as a moral obligation and practice "to raise up and restore that which is in ruins, to repair that which is damaged, to rejoin that which is severed; to replenish that which is lacking; to strengthen that which is weakened; to set right that which is wrong and to make flourish that which is fragile and undeveloped" (Karenga, 1994:742).

THE PRACTICE OF THE SEVEN CARDINAL VIRTUES OF MAAT. The Maatian person is obligated to practice, defend and promote the Seven Cardinal Virtues (*Ikheru*). These are: truth, justice, propriety, harmony, balance, reciprocity and order. Repeatedly in the Declarations of Virtues, the moral self-presentations of the writers included these virtues. The Maatian project begins with truth and justice. To say Maat is to say truth and justice. Therefore, Ankhsheshonqi says, "speak truth to everyone; let it cling to your speech" (*The Husia*, 66:V). And again, Khun-Anup says, "speak truth and do justice. For Maat is Mighty. It is great. It endures and it leads one to blessedness" (*The Husia*, 34:VIII). Moreover, he says "do Maat (truth, justice and rightness in general) for the Lord of Maat." Propriety requires proper behavior which enhance our relations with each other and the world. Here gentleness of speech and conduct are key. Phebhor says, "Do not make your mouth harsh or speak loudly with your tongue. For a loud voice does damage to members of the body like an illness" (*The Husia*, 69:VI). Living in harmony requires a *sedjemic* person, one who listens, who hears and who is responsive to others. Ptahhotep in speaking to this central virtue of harmony and the role of responsiveness in it says, "hearing (responsiveness) is better than everything for it creates good will" (Karenga, 1994:703). And it teaches reciprocal listening, hearing and responding. For Ptahhotep says, "if hearing enters the listener, the listener becomes a hearer." And he concludes that "it is the heart (moral sensitivity to others) that cause a person to hear or not to hear."

The virtue of balance stresses a measured approach to everything, avoiding excesses of any kind. As *The Husia* says in the Book of Phebhor (67:I): "Those who apply the right measure (balance) in all good things are not blamed. The God of just measure has created a balance in order to establish right measure on earth. He placed the heart deep in the body for the right measure (balance) of its owner. Thus, if those who are learned are not balanced, their learning is of little use and a fool who does not know balance does not escape misfortune. Excessive pride and arrogance are the destruction of the owner. But those who are gentle in character create their own fate." In conclusion, Khun-Anup teaches that "the balancing of the land (or earth) lies in Maat" (*The Husia*: 32:III).

The Cardinal Virtue of reciprocity is also central to Maatian moral practice. Clearly Khun-Anup's stress on reciprocity in our relations is important here. He says, "Desire to live long, for as it is said 'doing Maat is breath to the nose'." Thus, he says, "Answer not good with evil and put not one thing in the place of another." Moreover, he encourages us to initiate reciprocal good by doing good, saying "Do to the doer that he or she may also do" (*The Husia*, 32:II, III) But perhaps the most instructive teaching on reciprocity is in the Book of Lady Ta-Aset which teaches the mutual benefit of doing good in the world with implications for every virtue. She says, "Doing good is not difficult. In fact, just speaking good is a monument for those who do it. Those who do good for others are actually doing it for themselves" (Karenga, 1994:229). For they are building the moral community and world they want and deserve to live in.

> "Doing good is not difficult. In fact, just speaking good
> is a monument for those who do it. Those who do good
> for others are actually doing it for themselves"
> — LADY TA-ASET

The Seventh Cardinal Virtue is order, a disciplined life which aids in the highest degree of development and flourishing. The understanding here is that without discipline there is no development, not in the highest and most meaningful sense. Spiritual and moral discipline undergird and make possible the just and good world. Maat is and insures order; uncontrolled thought, emotion, speech and conduct leads to *isfet*, chaos and evil, the opposite of Maat. Self-mastery and a just social order are inter-linked and mutually productive and supportive of each other. Therefore, the Maatian tradition seeks to cultivate the *geru maa*, the truly self-mastered person.

One of the most impressive moral portraits of this geru-maa is the moral self-presentation of Antef who says in his Declaration of Virtue in *The Husia* (97:X):

> I am self-controlled before the angry, patient with the unlearned in order to quell conflict. I am calm, free from hasty acts, anticipating the outcome, expecting what occurs. I am one who counsels in situations of strife, a person who knows which words incite anger. I am considerate when called upon to those who would tell me their concern. I am self-disciplined, kind, considerate, one who comforts the weeper with good words. I am friendly to those who count on me and one who does good to his peers. I am one who is upright in the house of the Lord, who recognizes flattery when it is spoken. I am pleasant, openhanded, a possessor of food who does not hide his face from those in need. I am a friend of the poor and favorable to the have-nots. I am one who feeds the hungry who are needy and one who is openhanded to those who are destitute. I am one who is informed to those who lack knowledge and one who teaches a person what is useful to him or her. I am upright in the house of the pharaoh, one who knows what should be said in every office. I am a listener, one who listens to Maat and who ponders it in the heart. I am one who is pleasant in the house of his Lord and one who is remembered by reason of his excellent qualities.

THE ESSENTIALITY OF SERVICE, ESPECIALLY TO THE VULNERABLE. Essential to Maatian moral practice is service, especially to the most vulnerable among us. What the ancient Egyptians sought to emphasize here is the value of *other-directedness* as central to our moral and spiritual grounding and to creating a good world. In a word, they taught the indispensable role of our relationships with others in both our self-formation and our self-understanding as moral and good persons. And they taught, as noted above, that our standing worthy before God, nature and others, was not only the grounds for the just society and good and sustainable world, but also the basis for eternal life. Service to others, then, especially to the vulnerable, becomes the fundamental way this is understood and expressed.

Thus, it is a standard moral claim in the Declarations of Virtue, on the moral self-presentations of persons in their auto-biographical writings, that they spoke truth, did justice, and cared for the vulnerable. A typical Declaration of Virtue can be found in the autobiographical text and moral self-presentation of Harwa, the Grand Steward of the Divine Wife Amenirdis. Harwa says:

> "I have done what people love and God praises. I was one...who gave bread to the hungry and clothes to the naked. I put an end to pain and erased wrongdoing. I buried the blessed, supported the aged and satisfied the needs of the have-nots. I was a shelter for the child and help to the widow, one who gave rank even to an infant. I did these things know-ing their value and knowing their reward from the Lord of Maat..." (The Husia, 93:I).

Finally, service, as a moral requirement of Maatian life, is summed up in the Sebait (Instructions) of Seba Ankhsheshonqi (The Husia 64:I) who says: "Serve God that He may protect you. Serve your brothers and sisters that you may enjoy a good repu-tation. Serve a wise person that he or she may serve you. Serve one who serves you. Serve any person that you may benefit from it. And serve your mother and father that you may go forward and prosper."

PRACTICE OF THE DECLARATIONS OF INNOCENCE. These Declarations of Innocence which were often incorrectly called "negative confessions" are at the core of Maatian ethics. In Chapter 125 of the Book of Coming Forth By Day (Karenga, 1990a; The Husia 109-110:IX), we have two lists of offenses that one must affirm before God that s/he has not committed to achieve eternal life - 36 in List A and 42 in List B. Representing moral claims of living a Maatian life, they include declarations of innocence from offenses in thought, emotion, speech and con-duct: such as killing, violent and non-violent injury to others;

blasphemy; adultery and other sexual misconduct, robbery and theft, especially from the vulnerable; the misuse of speech, i.e., lying, slander, loudness; negative emotions such as hot-temperedness, immodesty, ill-temperedness; cheating; deception; harm to animals and misuse of nature. On the day of Judgment, one must be able to declare:

> I come to you O 'Lord. I have bought you righteousness and have done away with Isfet (unrighteousness and the opposite of Maat) for you. I have not done evil against people, blasphemed against God, inflicted pain, committed murder or ordered the killing of anyone, cheated, told lies, stolen, robbed, been angry without cause, dealt deceitfully.... I have not been deaf to truth or been blind to injustice... I have done what men and women request and what pleases God. Therefore, let it be said to me: 'Welcome, come in peace.' (The Husia, 111-112:X).

JUDGMENT, JUSTIFICATION AND IMMORTALITY. The hinge and hub upon which Maatian moral theology turns is the concept of *judgment* which carries with it two interrelated concepts - *justification* and *immortality*. This triple conceptual cluster represents one of ancient Egypt's and thus Africa's most significant and enduring gifts to humanity. This idea of judgment after death passes from Egypt into Christian, Jewish and Islamic texts and expresses itself in debates between Christianity, Judaism and Islam on reward and punishment, individual responsibility and free will and human worthiness. The essential contention is that one will be resurrected and judged after death, that one must stand worthy before heaven and history and be justified by what s/he has done and will receive eternal life or not, based on this moral record. The textual ground for this concept begins in the Book of Unas (*The Pyramid Texts*) in which, as noted above, Unas asked to be judged by what he has done, justifies himself by asserting his innocence of offense to any divine spirit, human, beast or bird and thus asks for eternal life based on this. This justification based on righteousness is called *"maa kheru"*, literally true of voice.

In the Book of Kheti, *The Husia* says, "a person survives after death and his deeds are set beside him as an allotment," and he is judged by them. And "as for one who reaches them (the divine judges) without having done wrong, he will exist in eternity as a divine spirit." Moreover, Kheti says concerning this quest for immortality that "Every day is a donation to eternity and even one hour is a contribution to the future. For God knows who works for him" (Karenga, 1994:304, 305).

Finally, in Chapter 125 of the Book of Coming Forth, the day of judgment is called the "Day of Assessing Characters" and "the Day of Great Reckoning." This emphasis on assessing character points to the Maatian emphasis on virtue and character as expressed in the Declarations of Virtue and the Declarations of Innocence. The resurrected person who reaches the Great Hall of Maati, the Hall of Judgment, as noted above, must declare him- or herself innocent of the 36 and 42 offenses and be justified by what s/he has done. Having declared one's innocence and having had one's heart weighed in the balance and been found innocent, one requests the reward of eternal life (*The Husia*, 109:IX).

In the Declarations of Virtue of Satepihu (Karenga, 1994:294), this concept of judgment, resurrection and reward of eternal life is succinctly stated thus: "A spirit in heaven; a continuing power on earth, justification in God's domain, resurrection after death. These are the rewards of the person without offense. And a righteous (Maatian) person is one who receives them. He will be counted among the ancestors. His name shall endure as a monument. And what he has done on earth will never perish or pass away." This is but a brief summary of the major tenets of the Maatian ethical and spiritual tradition. As it is engaged more as a resource for moral reflection and moral discourse, the rich and complex legacy it represents will constantly become clearer, both in terms of its deeper meaning and its value in engaging the critical issues of our time.

IFA: THE ANCIENT YORUBA TRADITION

INTRODUCTION

The spiritual and ethical tradition of *Ifa* of ancient Yorubaland holds a unique position among African religions (Karenga, 1999a; Abimbola, 1997; Lawal, 1996). First, it is the only African religion that has survived and developed on an international level. Although it appears under numerous names – Lekumi (Santeria) in Cuba, Puerto Rico and the U.S.; Voudun in Haiti, Shango in Cuba, and Candomblé in Brazil or Ifa in Nigeria and the U.S., it is the same tradition rooted in ancient teachings found in the same text, the *Odu Ifa*. Secondly, Ifa, along with *Maat* of ancient Egypt, is one of the only two ancient African religions with organized bodies of texts in which the tradition is rooted and developed.

The Odu Ifa, the sacred text of the spiritual and ethical tradition of Ifa, is one of the great sacred texts of the world and a classic of African and world literature. Like other great scared texts, the *Husia* (Maatian); the *Dhammapada* (Buddhist); the *Popol Vuh* (Mayan); the *Quran* (Muslim); the *Baghavad Gita* (Hindu); the *Torah* (Jewish) and the *Bible* (Christian), it includes a wide range of literary forms and subjects, ranging from poetry and sacred narratives to prescriptions for divination and moral instructions for daily life. It is composed of 256 chapters (*odu*) and innumerable verses (*ese*). Its name *Odu Ifa* is translated in the Kawaida tradition as "Baskets of Sacred Wisdom of Ifa." It gets its name from the Ifa creation Narrative in which Olodumare, God, gives divine ones and humans baskets of sacred wisdom to make the world good (*dara*). Thus, each chapter or Odu is a container of sacred wisdom for the use by humans to make the world and life in it good. Ifa is both the name of the system of knowledge in the text and another name of the sage and master teacher, Orunmila, who taught this sacred wisdom.

The seminal work in translation and commentary has been done by Dr. Wande Abimbola (1997, 1977, 1976, 1975a, 1975b) who is Awise Agbaye or International Spokesman for the Ifa Tradition. But there are also important works of translation by Popoola (1997), Epega and Neimark (1995) and Bascom (1969, 1980) and there is an excellent discussion of Ifa in the context of an impressive study by Lawal (1996) of Gèlèdè, a women's ceremony of power, beauty and social harmony. In addition, Idowu's (1962) definitive work on Yoruba religion remains a very valuable contribution to the critical study of the spiritual and ethical tradition of Ifa. My contribution has been to offer an original translation of a body of ethical teachings of the Odu Ifa in a language of modern moral discourse in a text titled *Odu Ifa: The Ethical Teachings* (1999a). It is from this text that core concepts of the Ifa tradition are discussed and citations made below.

BASIC TENETS

The Odu Ifa's central message revolves around the teachings of the Goodness of and in the world; the chosen status of humans in the world; the criteria of a good world and the requirements for a good world. Although these themes are throughout the Odu Ifa, nowhere are they more explicit than in Odu 78:1. The Odu (chapter) begins by declaring "Let's do things with joy... For surely humans have been chosen to bring good into the world." The verse calls for an approach to life that is joyful and rooted in the self-understanding that we humans are divinely chosen by the Creator to bring good into the world. And this self-understanding becomes, as argued below, the fundamental mission and meaning of human life.

THE GOODNESS OF THE WORLD. The Ifa tradition asserts that at the time of creation Olodumare, God, sent the divine ones, orisha, into the world to make the world good and He gave them the *ase* (pronounced ah-shay), the power, to complete their work and to do it well (*Odu*, 10:2). The word used here for making the world *good* is *dara* which not only means good in the sense of beneficial and suitable to a purpose, but also pleasant and enjoyable. Thus, we are encouraged to "do things with joy," to find good in the world, embrace it, increase it and not let any good be lost. As I have argued "here we have the affirmation of the inherent goodness of the world, an inherent goodness which the Creator ordains at the beginning of creation (Karenga, 1999a:77-78). It is important, however, to note that although the world is essentially good, there is a constant need to "struggle to increase good in the world and not to let any good be lost" (*Odu*, 78:1).

It is obvious here that all is not well with the world, given the poverty, oppression, exploitation and general suffering of people. But inherent in this firm belief in the good that is found in the *Odu Ifa* is the faith that in the midst of the worst of situations there are good people, good will and possibilities for creating good, increasing good and thus constantly expanding the realm of good. This is why the morality of sacrifice is so central to the Ifa tradition, for one must commit to struggle for the good, to give oneself to the project and promise of brining good into the world. Moreover, in addition to human good in the world, even in the worst of times, there is also natural good – earth, heaven, wind, water, other living things, stone and star. And there is also Divine good, a spirit of Goodness that infuses the world and we are to embrace this and use it to ground ourselves and enjoy and carry out the chosen status and role we have been assigned. Again, then, the world is a place to enjoy and realize oneself, but there is still a need to sustain and enhance it. And it is here that the chosen status of humans finds its fundamental meaning and expression.

THE CHOSEN STATUS OF HUMANS. *Odu* 78:1 says we should do things with joy "for surely humans have been chosen (*yan*) to bring good into the world." This joyfulness is advocated then, not only because the world is essentially good, but equally important because we, as human beings, are *chosen* by the Creator. Now, the unique aspect of this chosenness is that it is not a chosenness that belongs to or is granted to one people only, but to all humans. In fact, the essential word for human being or human beings is *eniyan* which literally means *chosen one(s)*.

Moreover, it is not a chosenness based on *preference* for one people over all others. Rather it is a chosenness based on the *assignment* and *power* (*ase*) to complete it given to all people. That assignment is to constantly bring good into the world and it is this special status and assignment to bring good into the world that is the fundamental meaning and mission in human life.

Now the moral superiority of this Ifaic concept of chosenness over those which show preference for one group is obvious. For it reaffirms, without equivocation or exception, the moral teaching of Ifa that all humans are *omo Olodumare*, offspring of the Creator, and that each of us should understand ourselves as special and chosen by the Creator without distinction of nation, race, gender, special religious relationship or promise. It thus poses an ideal many other world religions are still striving to establish as a central moral doctrine.

Also, this moral and spiritual conception of the human person is important because it is a chosenness bestowed by the Creator with all the transcendent and ultimate meaning this brings with it for us as persons, peoples and members of the human community. Indeed, it reinforces the companion concept of the human status as offspring of God and gives augmented grounding to the concept of our being *bearers of dignity and divinity* in the Ifa tradition. The constant concern in the *Odu Ifa* that we treat each other with respect indicates a rich concept of the inherent worthiness of human persons. Clearly, this concept of all humans as divinely chosen is a contribution of considerable value to the moral and spiritual development of humankind. It anticipates and enriches the ethics of multiculturalism which informs the best of modern moral discourse and takes as its fundamental point of departure the shared and equal status of all persons and peoples.

THE RIGHT TO A GOOD LIFE. *Odu* 78:1 also says that no one can reach their highest level of spirituality or rest in heaven until we all achieve the good world "that Olodumare, God, has ordained for every human being." This establishes a *divinely ordained right to a good life* for every human being. But joined to this human right is the obligation of shared responsibility of humans to make the world good so that everyone can enjoy a good life. The important contribution this makes here to theological and social ethics is that it teaches that transcendence in the spiritual and social sense can never be individualistic, but must always include the happiness and well-being of others. It is clearly a unique spiritual and moral claim to make that one cannot escape the limits of recurrent mortal life until all persons have the good life God has ordained for each and every human being. This contrasts starkly with some traditions' claims that the poor will always be with us and that humans can reach heaven and spiritual transcendence by some individualist pursuit of purity. The *Odu Ifa* says all deserve a good life and good world; ultimate transcendence is impossible without it and it is a shared task of all humans to achieve it.

CONDITIONS FOR A GOOD WORLD. The question is, then, posed to the sage and master teacher, Orunmila, of what is a good life and the conditions for the good world. Orunmila answers by saying that the achieving of a good life or good world is defined by several essential things: full knowledge of things; happiness everywhere; freedom from anxiety and fear of hostile others; the end of antagonism with other beings on earth, i.e., animals, reptiles and the like; well-being and the end of forces that threaten it; and finally, freedom from poverty and misery. Now, it is of great significance that the first criteria for good life and good world is *knowledge*. In fact, Orunmila also says that knowledge or rather wisdom is the first criteria or requirement for achieving the good. This points to knowledge or education as a basic human right, necessary not only for our understanding our humanity in its most expansive forms, but also to realize it in the most meaningful and flourishing ways.

Freedom from anxiety and fear of hostile others is the human longing and need for peace in the world and within themselves. The end of fear of and antagonism with other living beings as a criteria of a good life is not only an ancient longing for a sense of safety and peace in the larger natural realm, but also a pointing towards another principle for an environmental ethic which encourages harmony in and with nature. The requirement of well-being lists problems of disease and unnatural death, saying we should be free of fear of these as well as superstitions and evil forces which threaten us. And clearly freedom from want and misery speaks to the human need for material well-being. It thus urges us to link a life of dignity with a decent life in which our status as bearers of dignity and divinity is complemented by a life of good and ultimately the promise and practice of maximum human flourishing.

THE REQUIREMENTS FOR A GOOD WORLD (AYE RERE).

MORAL WISDOM. The first criteria Orunmila lists for achieving a good world, as noted above is wisdom. The text says "wisdom adequate to govern the world." This reaffirms human responsibility for the world and the need to obtain adequate wisdom to carry out this responsibility effectively. *Odu* 33:2 says, "Those whose turn it is to take responsibility for the world, they should do good for the world." It is clear that the wisdom sought here is not simply technical knowledge. On the contrary, "the core wisdom is of necessity moral and spiritual wisdom which conceives the world in its interrelated wholeness, respects its integrity and works constantly to save, renew and expand the good in it" (Karenga, 1999a:238). But in addition, it requires that we know the world in its concreteness and complexity and thus requires human development, pursuit and mastery of all the disciplines of human knowledge and that we use them in the service of humankind.

In fact, the Yoruba word *akoso*, used here to mean govern, means in its most expansive sense to gather people together for the purpose of good. It is a binding together to achieve good ends and thus requires both moral sensitivity and practical knowledge of the world. The sacred teachings say that in this pursuit of the good, we should "Speak truth, do justice. Be kind and do not do evil...For one who is righteous is supported by the Divine" (*Odu*, 33:1). Here we are told the good society must not only be just, but must also be committed to truth. It must, then, not only operate on the principle of fairness, equity and due respect, but also on the principle of openness and transparency, a term of modern currency but of ancient and enduring value.

A MORALITY OF SACRIFICE. Orunmila, the sage and master teacher, taught that humans must move beyond moralities of convenience to a morality of sacrifice, i.e., self-giving in a real meaningful and sustained way. The *Odu Ifa* says that one who makes a small sacrifice will have a small result (*Odu*, 45:1). It says to us "be able to suffer without surrendering and persevere in what you do" (*Odu*, 150). Finally, the Odu teaches that we must work hard and be patient and not be undone by impatience. For it says,

> Uncontrolled emotion does not create anything for anyone.
> Patience is the father of character. A person who is patient
> will become master of all things. She will reach a ripe old age.
> He will live a health life. And she will enjoy life thoroughly
> like a person tasting honey (Odu, 31:1).

CHARACTER. A central moral quest in the Ifa spiritual and ethical tradition is to achieve *iwapele*, a gentle character or *iwarere*, good character which are often interchangeable (Abimbola, 1975a). Orunmila cites this as the third requirement to achieving a good world. "It is gentle character which enables the rope of life to remain strong in our hands" according to *Odu* 119:1. And in *Odu* 39:1, we read that even if we have money, children, a good house and fine clothes, if we do not have character, these good things belong to someone else. In fact, it states "All the good things we have, if we do not have character, these good things belong to someone else. And so, it's character, *iwa*, we are looking for, character." By character is meant here a relatively stable disposition to do good (*ire*). And clearly to bring good into the world in a sustained and consistent manner, this relatively stable disposition toward doing good is indispensable.

LOVE OF DOING GOOD. Orunmila, the sage and master teacher, teaches that another one of the main requirements for achieving the good world is "the love of doing good for all people, especially for those who are in need and those who seek assistance from us." First, this is a call not simply to do good, but *to love doing good*. For it seeks to create a moral community based not on cold calculation of rule and duty, but on the love of doing good and the joy and benefit it brings to the doer and the recipient of the good. *Odu* 141:1 says, "Ofun is giving out goodness everywhere. (But) Ofun does not make noise about it." Indeed, to do things coldly and/or loudly is to diminish the good done. For it is not done for the person and the joy of doing it, but for rule or duty or undue recognition. The *Odu* 146:1 goes on to suggest that "Anyone who wants to do wonderful things should observe the ways of heaven." For heaven gives to all rain, sun, wind and earth equally without the need for undue recognition.

EAGERNESS AND STRUGGLE. The last requirement Orunmila, sage and master teacher, cites as a requirement for creating a good world returns us to the fundamental meaning and mission in human life. He says what is required is "the eagerness and struggle to increase good into the world and not let any good be lost." Again, Orunmila calls for an emotional commitment to the good world, and an ongoing and intense struggle "to increase good in the world and not let any good be lost." Now this stress on struggle is key to life and achievement of the good world. The *Odu Ifa* says, we must stay steadfast in our struggle for a good world until it is achieved. It says "a constant soldier is never unready even once" (*Odu*, 159:1). And it also says, "One who stands ready to act for good is supported by Ogun (the divine spirit of struggle) on the day of battle." The *Odu Ifa* also says, "Struggle brings respect. Struggle brings honor." And, of course, it is through struggle that we create the good world we all want and deserve to live in.

Finally, it is important to note that this passage speaks of *increasing* good in the world and not letting any good be lost. To

increase good in the world implies that there is already good in it
and that constant struggle is necessary to add to and enhance it.
Also, the instruction not to let any good be lost recognizes the ero-
sive forces in the world and on the world and calls on human
beings to struggle constantly to save the good of the world and the
good in the world. For in this they honor their special status by
choosing, even as they are chosen, to bring good into the world.

5.3   THE CHRISTIAN TRADITION

REASONS FOR CONVERSION

It is common knowledge that African Americans were converted to Christianity during enslavement. But what is less
known and less discussed are the reasons for the conversion both
from the point of view of the enslavers and the enslaved
Africans. The enslavers reasons for Christianizing the enslaved
Africans began with their perception of Christianity as a way to
reinforce and maintain dominance. Thus, in 1743, a white minister prepared a book of dialogue for enslavers to teach enslaved
Africans which stressed contentment and thanks for being
enslaved and ended saying "I can't help knowing my duty. I am
to serve God in that state in which he has placed me. I am to do
what my master orders me" (Frazier, 1974:19). As the indoctri-
nation progressed, then, enslavers soon discovered that many of
the most amenable and submissive enslaved Africans were those
who were Christians.

Secondly, the enslavers were equally and at times more so,
interested in uprooting Africans from their own religious heritage, in order to deprive them of cultural distinction and motivation for revolt. As Frazier (1974:17) points out, "whites were
always on guard against African religious practices which could
provide an opportunity for slave revolts, and they outlawed such
practices." Finally, enslavers converted Africans because they
and other whites believed it was their duty to bring light to
"benighted and lost heathens." It was, in a word, based on a culturally chauvinist assumption that their religion was the only
real and correct one and that all others were pagan and an abom-
ination to their intolerant and jealous God.

Although many Africans accepted Christianity, many others

resisted it for a long time, maintaining their commitment to ancient African religions or Islam. Moreover, most of those who accepted Christianity transformed it in their own image and interest (Hopkins, 2000; Coleman 2000; Blassingame,1979; Wilmore,1998). Given the importance of religion to Blacks and the reverence they had for their God, one must raise the question, what compelled them to exchange their God for that of the enslaver? The first reason for African American conversion to Christianity was obviously the conquest and coercion by the enslaver. Alex Haley's (1976) description of the brutally coerced transformation of Kunta Kinte into Christianized Toby in his popular family saga, *Roots*, is representative of the process. Moreover, at one point as Frazier (1974:15) notes, the enslavers and the "Missionaries recognized its difficulty of converting adult Africans and concentrated their efforts on children."

Secondly, Africans began to accept Christianity more as they gradually began to accept the enslavers religious and cultural contentions which posed Christianity and the Christian God as more powerful. This gradual acceptance, was encouraged by the fact of their enslavement, the religious doubt and self-doubt it raised, the gradual loss of historical memory and the end of revivifying contacts from Africa through the end of the enslavement period. Thirdly, Christianity came to be seen as a coping strategy on the social and psychological level. Social acceptance meant avoidance of humiliation, punishment and beatings reserved for recalcitrant "heathens." Psychologically, it meant a transferred hope for deliverance, which the old religions seemed unable to fulfill.

Fourthly, Christianity and the religious meetings it allowed became, even more under severe restriction, a means of establishing and maintaining a sense of community. This was a time for the enslaved Africans to meet, to reinforce bonds between them, discuss hopes, problems and also, as in the Turner, Vesey and Prosser revolts, a time to plan liberation strategies. Finally, after years of forced conversion and tentative and partial acceptance, Christianity became a heritage, and subsequent generations born in a Christian context simply accepted it. However, it is important to stress that in spite of this conversion to Christianity, Africans did not accept it totally in its racist African enslavement-supporting form. In fact, "a distinctive African American form of Christianity — actually a new religion of an oppressed people — slowly took root in the Black community" (Wilmore, 1983:36). This new "Black folk religion carried within its perspectives a definitive moral judgment against African enslavement and a clear legitimation of the enslaved Africans' and later the freedman's struggle against the forces of injustice and inequality."

THE HISTORICAL ROLE OF THE CHURCH

The role of the Black church in African American life has been substantial and enduring since its inception (Woodson, 1945; Wilmore, 1989; Lincoln and Mamiya, 1990; Hopkins, 2000). Although Frazier (1974) divides the church into the "invisible church" in African enslavement and the institutional church which began with the founding of the African Methodist Episcopal Church in 1787 and the first African Baptist Church in 1788, for the purpose of this section and to stress historical continuity, the division will not be made. Moreover, although the Black church has rightly been and continues to be accused of support for the established order at various times (Washington, 1964), it does have a history of social activism and social service of which it can be proud (Lincoln, 1974a; Wilmore, 1998; Paris, 1985). And it is this history which will be stressed.

The Black church obviously began as a spiritual sanctuary and community against the violent and destructive character of the Holocaust of enslavement. And even after enslavement, it remained a wall of defense and comfort against racism and its accompanying attacks on Black dignity, relevance and social worth. Secondly, the Black church served as an agency of social reorientation and reconstruction, providing reinforcement for the old values of marriage, family, morality and spirituality in the face of the corrosive effects of enslavement (Blassingame, 1979; Lincoln and Mamiya, 1990).

Thirdly, the church became a center for economic coopera-tion, pooling resources to buy churches, building mutual aid societies which provided social services for free Blacks purchas-ing and helping resettle enslaved Africans, and setting up busi-nesses for economic development. Fourthly, the church engaged in both public and internal educational projects, setting up schools and training ministers and teachers and raising funds to carry out these projects. Finally, the Black church from its earliest days as an invisible spiritual community, supported social change and struggle, providing leaders and leadership at various points in the struggle for Black liberation and a truly higher level of human life (Best, 1998).

THE SOCIAL ETHICS OF MARTIN LUTHER KING

The death of Bishop Henry M. Turner left the Black community with "no clergyman of his stature who could, by temperament or ideology, assume the leadership role he played in a persistent but unsuccessful attempt to radicalize the Black church" (Wilmore,1973:187). Turner had been an advocate of the social role and responsibility of the church and religion, had engaged in a merciless criticism of U.S. society, and advocated the Blackness of God, draft resistance, armed self-defense and emigrationism (Angell,1992). Not until King did another Black Christian leader rise to his level of relevance and social effectiveness. "It was Martin Luther King," Lincoln (1974a:114) observes, "who made the contemporary church aware of its power to effect change." Moreover, he also revived its tradition of self-conscious social activism and thus, broke it from the moderate accommodating tendency which was also a part of its history and which it had exhibited since the death of Turner.

King developed a theory and practice which combined the best of Black religion with socially-focused concepts borrowed from Ghandi, Thoreau, Hegel, Rauschenbush, Tillich and others (King, 1958, 1963, 1964, 1967; Washington, 1986; Branch, 1988). Within his socio-political philosophy, five key concepts stand at its core. First, King posed Blacks as a people whose suffering and social situation has prepared them for and in fact, gives them a divine historical mission of not only liberating themselves, but also of restructuring and spiritualizing U.S. society.

Secondly, King argued that Blacks had both the moral right and responsibility to disobey unjust laws in their resistance to social evil. This stress, as Walton (1976:44) notes, combines Henry David Thoreau's concept of "the rightfulness of civil disobedience," Jesus' stress on humanity, forgiveness and love, and Ghandi's stress on loving non-violence as a method of social transformation. "Your highest loyalty is to God" King (1963:128) stated, "and not to the mores, or folkways, the state or the nation or any man-made institution." Thus, when any of those "conflict with God's will, it is your Christian duty to oppose it."

Closely related to the above concept is King's contention that it is immoral and cowardly to collaborate in one's own oppression. "To accept passively an unjust system is to cooperate with that system," he (1958:188) maintained. And in doing this, "the oppressed becomes as evil as the oppressor." Moreover, such non-action says "to the oppressor that his actions are morally right." Thus, he (1958:189) concludes, acquiescence to oppression is not only morally wrong and corruptive, "it is (also) the way of a coward."

Fourthly, King posed the necessity of religion having a social as well as spiritual function. Having read Walter Rauschenbush's *Christianity and the Social Crisis*, he (1958:72) developed "a theological basis for the social concern" which he felt religion should have "as a result of his experiences." Therefore, he stressed that true religion was obligated to deal "with the whole man, not only his soul, but his body, not only his spiritual well-being but his social well-being." A final core concept in King's socio-political philosophy was his contention that human nature is perfectible through struggle. He (1958:82) asserted that Hegel's "analysis of the dialectical process...helped me to see that growth comes through struggle." Central to this concept is the emphasis on "creative tension," non-violent struggle which not only changes the oppressor, but also the oppressed in the process.

King's socio-political philosophy was important to Black religion and the Civil Rights Movement in several ways. First, it gave religious sanction to social resistance, although of the non-violent type, and thus spiritually inspired an oppressed people who would not have been moved as deeply by other doctrines in their quest for freedom. Secondly, it made social passivity immoral, an act in contradiction with the will of God and His desire for truth, freedom and justice in the world, and therefore, reinforced the need to resist social evil. Thirdly, it placed on preachers a continuing responsibility and pressure to take an active stand in the Freedom Movement and make religion more socially relevant. And finally, King's socio-political philosophy served as a transition in Black religion which encouraged self-criticism and pointed toward a Black liberation theology.

BLACK LIBERATION THEOLOGY

HISTORICAL BACKGROUND

In July 1966 and in the midst of the period of Black urban revolts, a group of Black clergy met in Harlem to develop a position on the struggle for Black power in the U.S. There, they assumed a position which made a definitive contribution to the emergence of Black liberation theology. Breaking from King's negative position on Black power as "nihilistic," they affirmed the right and need of Black power, criticized the Black church for too often steering "its members away from the reign of God in this world to a distorted and complacent view of an otherworldly conception of God's power" and committed themselves to "use more of the resources of our churches in working for human justice in places of social change and upheaval" where God is truly already at work. This statement and other highly significant Black liberation theology documents appear in Wilmore and Cone's (1979) excellent documentary history of Black Theology from 1966 to 1979. Finally, the body of clergy who began in 1966 as the National Committee of Negro Churchmen changed their name to the National Committee of Black Churchmen (NCBC), and became the practical expression and representative of the new Black liberation theology.

Black liberation theology, however, did not come into being by itself. It evolved from several fundamental sources. Although Hopkins (2000), Hayes (1996) and others find its earliest sources in the liberational aspirations and assertions during the Holocaust of enslavement, its definitive formation as an intellectual discipline is closer to our times. Thus, it was developed in response to the dynamics of the decade of the 60's with its stress on Blackness and social activism and struggle. The 60's demanded a redefinition of the world in Black images and interests and Black religion was no exception. Also, the 60's demanded active engagement in the Black struggle for liberation and a higher level of human life and challenged the church to participate or disband. Secondly, it rose in response to the teachings and theology of the Honorable Elijah Muhammad (1965, 1973, 1992) and Malcolm X (1965a, 1965b) who for the first time problematized Christianity as the religion of Black people by their criticism and thus the demand to justify itself and distinguish itself from the Judeo-Christianity of the oppressor.

Thirdly, Black liberation theology was inspired by both emulation and criticism of King. King's stress on the social relevance and role of religion and on active engagement in the struggle against social evil were accepted and applied, but his stress on non-violence was challenged or played down, his denunciation of Black power rejected, and his emphasis on redemptive suffering translated as redemption through liberating struggle. Fourthly, Black liberation theology evolved from an ongoing internal criticism and push for a more relevant religion in light of the activist tradition of the Black church as well as the temper of the time. This process was given support and intensified by the dynamics of the 60's and forced Black churchmen and women and theologians to redefine the meaning and role of God in history and His relationship to Black oppression and struggle for liberation. Finally, Black liberation theology helped inspire and was in turn inspired by Third World Theology (Cummings, 1993; Wilmore, 1979). Especially key here is Latin American Liberation Theology represented by Gustavo Gutierrez (1974, 1973) and Sergio Torres (1981, 1976) who translate religion in the most socially relevant and demanding ways.

One could argue there is a distinction between Black Theology and Black liberation theology, the former being all forms of Black systematic religious thought and the latter being one particular form of it. However, this distinction will not be made; for the quest for a Black Theology is firmly and clearly rooted in the search for religious answers to the questions of Black liberation (Hopkins, 1999b). Some of the major writers who have sought to pose and answer such questions are Gayraud Wilmore (1973), Major Jones (1971, 1974), William Jones (1973), J. Deotis Roberts (1974, 1971), Joseph Washington (1967), Joseph Johnson (1978, 1971) and Cornel West (1982, 1988). More recently, Will Coleman (2000), Dwight Hopkins (2000, 1999a), Mark Chapman (1996), George Cummings (1993) among others have made significant contributions to this project. Certainly, the new womanist theologians are part of this over-all project, but they have mapped out a special space within this tradition of Black people and are, therefore, treated in distinction and in relationship in a section below.

In addition to the above writers, two others stand out as definitive of the two trends in Black liberation theology, i.e.,

Black nationalist Christianity and Black Christian Nationalism. These are James Cone (1969, 1970, 1975, 1983, 1984, 1999) and Albert Cleage, Jr. (1968, 1972). Moreover, both Cone and Cleage were key to the development of Black liberation theology. James Cone, a professor of systematic theology at Union Theological Seminary, "more than anyone else...set the tone and described the context of Black Theology with the publication of his book *Black Theology and Black Power* in 1969" and helped shape the movement as a practical project (Wilmore and Cone, 1979:77). Albert Cleage, the dean of Black Nationalist Christians and founder and head of the Shrine of the Black Madonna as early as 1963 "was also an active member of the NCBC almost from its inception and took part in the first theological discussions of the new movement of militant Black clergy in 1967" (Wilmore and Cone, 1979:67). Given their relevance to and work in this theoretical and practical thrust, their contentions can serve as a framework for discussion of Black liberation theology in general.

JAMES CONE

As noted above, James Cone is generally considered by religious scholars as the father of Black Theology as an intellectual discipline and systematic discourse (Hopkins, 1999a). His initial works (1969, 1970) not only introduced Black theology as a critical public discourse, but also offered an incisive critique of racist theological traditions within Judeo-Christianity and spoke definitely to the significance of the Black Liberation struggle as an essential and valuable point of departure for doing theology. In fact, establishing the basis for a Black liberation theology in his inaugural work (1969), Cone maintains that it must above all speak to the condition and struggle of Black people. "Black Theology has as its starting point the Black condition," he (1969:18) asserts. "It is a theology which confronts white society as racist Antichrist, communicating to the oppressor that nothing will be spared in the fight for freedom" (1969:135).

Secondly, Cone (1970:120) insists on the Blackness of God and Jesus. "The Blackness of God and everything implied by it in a racist society is the heart of Black Theology's doctrine of God;" for "there is no place for a colorless God in a society (where) people suffer precisely because of their color." Thirdly, Cone

(1970:116) argues that the God of Black liberation theology is and must be "the God of and for the oppressed of the land who makes himself known through their liberation." For Cone (1969:47) then, Black power and Black liberation are "doing God's work in history by righting the wrongs done against his people..." Thus, Blacks become God's covenant community. His later books, *God of the Oppressed* (1975), *My Soul Looks Back* (1983) and *For My People* (1984), reaffirm this stress on God's role in Black life and history as dictated by biblical assertions.

A fourth contention of Cone is the need for vindication of the Black church and the call upon it to recapture its radical tradition in the struggle for freedom, justice and equality. Citing Henry Garnet and Nat Turner as models, he (1969:94) argues that "the Black church was born in protest" and "in this sense, it is the precursor of Black Power." The need, then, is to revive this "heritage of radical involvement in the world." For "this past is a symbol of what is actively needed in the present" (1969:112-113). Fifthly, rejecting non-violence as "a technique of the rich to keep the poor poor," Cone declares that "if the system is evil, then revolutionary violence is both justified and necessary to end it." In fact, "sacrificing love" must be revolutionary love which "may mean joining a violent rebellion" (1969:113).

Moreover, Cone in his later works has been very insistent on the need to address and end sexism in the Black church. In both *My Soul Looks Back* (1983) and *For My People* (1984), Cone devotes a chapter to critically delineating the problematic of sexism in Black theology and the Black church and the urgency of ending it in order to build an egalitarian religious community. Also in his co-edited work with Gayraud Wilmore, *Black Theology* (1979), he has written a chapter which challenged the church to divest itself of sexist ideas and practices negative to the liberation project. In addition, Cone, beginning especially in his *God of the Oppressed* (1975), has consistently stressed the need for a class analysis and class approach to liberation. For him, as his title suggests, God is the God of the oppressed and requires a preferential practice toward the poor and vulnerable. Thus liberation is a freedom won in struggle not only against racism and sexism but also against classism.

Finally, in his latest work, *Risks of Faith: The Emergence of a Black Theology of Liberation, 1968-1998*, Cone (1999), after reviewing developments in Black Theology, argues for an expansion of "the race critique" and the linking of racism with "the ecological crisis" as reflected in "the degradation of the earth." He credits Delores S. Williams, Emilie Townes and other womanist theologians with important intellectual work in this area and urges an expansion of what he calls "the ecological critique" in the Black Liberation Theology Project. In this work, he also reaffirms the importance of an activist theology engaging real-world concerns and calls for critical examination of the teachings of Malcolm X whose incisive critique of white America was essential to the development of Cone's theology as well as Black Theology as whole – both its liberation and orthodox forms.

ALBERT CLEAGE

The theology of Albert Cleage (1968:38) maintains at the outset that the Judeo-Christian heritage is a stolen heritage that must be recaptured. For "the white man captured the religion of a Black Nation (Israel), the revelations of a Black God, the teachings of a Black Messiah (Jesus) and he used them to keep Black men enslaved." This contention already leads Cleage to his second contention that God is and must be Black, as of course, is Jesus. Thirdly, Cleage (1972:3-4) argues for a rejection of the "Pauline perversion" of God's words in the New Testament with its emphasis on loving submission and concentration on the Old Testament's emphasis on struggle and liberation. The need is to make a distinction between salvation (spiritual) and liberation (social), and to struggle to eliminate "oppression, powerlessness and the white man's declaration of Black inferiority through Black unity" within the framework of Black Christian Nationalism.

Fourthly, like Cone, Cleage identifies the church as a key instrument in the liberation of Blacks. Thus, he (1972:xxxiv) calls for Blacks to "rediscover the historic roots of Christianity, strip from them the mystical distortions...bring the Black Christian church into the liberation struggle and make it relevant to the lives of Blacks."

Finally, Cleage (1972:403) argues that there is a dual aspect to the liberation struggle, an internal as well as external dimension. Given Blacks' history of oppression, they "have two beasts to fight: the beast within and the beast without." Externally, their enemy is whites, in fact, white Christians (Cleage,

1968:55). For "...within the system in which we live, we are not only separate, we are in conflict. We seek our freedom in a power struggle against them and in the context of this struggle, they are the enemy." Internally, the struggle is against what white society has made African people, i.e., individualistic, addicted to mysticism about God and using religion as psychic relief rather than inspiration to actively seek liberation.

SUMMARY

In sum then, Black liberation theology is centered around several core contentions which appear in varying and similar forms in most writings on it. Among these are 1) the need for theology to be rooted in and reflective of the Black experience; 2) the need for a God in Black people's own image and interest, i.e., Black and of and for the oppressed; 3) the imperative that religion must reflect the interests of Blacks and concretely and actively benefit them; 4) the recognition of the Black church's radical history and a call for its resuming this role in the liberation struggle of Black people, especially along the lines of race, class and gender; and 5) the indispensability of social struggle to liberate Blacks — socially and spiritually — and realize God's will to bring truth, freedom and justice to society and the world.

BLACK WOMANIST THEOLOGY AND ETHICS

Clearly, one of the most important developments in Black religion in general and in Black Christianity in particular is the emergence of a distinctly Black womanist or feminist discourse. An excellent early corpus of such literature can be found in Wilmore and Cone's *Black Theology* in which several Black women theologians and writers delineate the history and challenge of Black women in the church (Grant, 1979; Hoover, 1979; Murray, 1979). Moreover, much work has been done on these issues by Black women scholars in the context of writing M.A. theses and doctorate dissertations. These include Jualynne Dodson (1983), LaTaunya Marie Bynum (1980), Delores Williams (1975) and Katie G. Cannon (1983), whose dissertation has since been published as a book titled *Black Womanist Ethics*, (1988), and is discussed below. Rita Weems' (1988) *Just A Sister Away* was also an important earlier contribution. More recently womanist theological discourse has expanded widely and rapidly, including works by Douglass (1994, 1999); Cannon (1995); Sanders (1995); Terrel (1998); Townes (1993, 1995), and Williams (1993) among others.

JACQUELYN GRANT

Certainly, one of the most important theologians of this rapidly developing discourse is Jacquelyn Grant (1979, 1989) whose early work helped shape its course and content. Her major work, *White Women's Christ and Black Women's Jesus*, offers an important discussion of womanist issues in theology. Grant is concerned first of all with self-naming, that is to say, giving specific name and voice to Black women in the historical and current church. She seeks to recover the hidden and denied role and relevance of Black women and speak their special truth. To do this she both criticizes and borrows from white feminist theology. It is her contention that white feminist theology cannot and does not adequately address the Black womanist tradition in the faith, for it is both white and racist (Grant, 1989:195ff). Moreover, she criticizes Black male religionists for their having both denied and diminished the vital role and relevance of Black women in the construction and maintenance of the Black religious tradition. However, she also cites both James Cone (1975,1983,1984) and James Evans (1981) for their critique of sexism in theology and the church and their call for corrective measures.

What is needed, she (1989:205) contends, is a Black womanist theology which "begins with the experiences of Black women as its point of departure." This theology will and does respect the tridimensional character of Black women's life, i.e., its vulnerability to racism, classism, and sexism (1989:209). It thus locates itself in the struggle against these forms of oppression and in the struggle to create free space to speak and act in Black women's own terms. Moreover, Black womanist theology challenges Eurocentric and androcentric interpretations of both text and context, scripture and history, building on Black women's experience as both oppositional and contributive.

Secondly, Grant argues for a gender-free Jesus, given the problematic of maleness as a metaphor for oppression and superiority. Thus, she (1989:212) envisions Jesus as "the divine co-sufferer, who empowers them (Black people) in situations of oppression." Here Jesus is both inclusive God and essential human, containing both male and female and also transcendent. Thirdly, Grant argues for a concrete intimacy with Jesus in the womanist tradition. This of course allows her to draw the distinction made in the title and theme of her book between white women's Christ and Black women's Jesus. Again she contends Jesus in the womanist tradition is more intimate and concrete and less transcendental. Thus, he is "my sweet Jesus," friend, healer, hope-giver, co-sufferer and Black women's central religious frame of reference.

Fourthly, Grant (1989:211ff) argues for building on the emancipatory biblical tradition as central to the Black womanist project. She maintains that womanist theology must and does engage in an internal critique of biblical patriarchal views while at the same time brings its narratives to life, extracting their emancipatory possibilities. This means meeting the challenge to "investigate the relationship between the oppression of women and theological symbolism" and then moving to correct and transcend oppressive theological tendencies in the thrust to build an egalitarian theology of human wholeness (Grant, 1989:219ff).

Finally, Grant argues for a constructive Christology and theology that reject racist, sexist and classist interpretations and practices. This theology of necessity, Grant maintains, will be rooted in and rise out of the life, teachings and narratives of the bold, assertive and creative Black women whose lessons of resistance, love, construction and commitment inspire and inform the best of Christian and Black tradition, i.e., Sojourner Truth, Fannie Lou Hamer, Ida B. Wells, Jarna Lee, Mary McLeod Bethune, et al. However, it will not deny the contribution or humanity of Black males, for a theology or Christology which negates Black male humanity is still destructive to the Black community (Grant, 1989:221). What is needed then, she concludes, is a constructive rather than destructive practice, which rejects the unusable past and builds in reconciliation a future which grounds and reflects maximum human flourishing.

KATIE CANNON

Another important early participant in the defining discourse of womanist theology is Katie G. Cannon (1988, 1995).

Her earlier work laid out some of the basic contours of her developing ethical project and merits critical consideration. Cannon's project of developing a Black womanist ethics begins with the privileging of ordinary experience. She (1988:5) wishes to use Black women's literary tradition "to interpret and explain the community's socio-cultural patterns from which ethical values can be gleaned." It will be the development of an ethics by which persons "learn to glean directives for living in the here-and-now" (Cannon, 1988:126). This will in turn "help Black women and others who care to understand and to appreciate the richness of their own moral struggle through the life of the common people and oral tradition" (Cannon, 1988:5). It is thus in Zora Neal Hurston's writings and life that she believes she has discovered a rich source of ethical values and insights.

Secondly, Cannon (1988:6ff) seeks to contextualize her ethics by focusing on "the interrelationship of white supremacy and male superiority which has characterized the Black woman's moral situation." She focuses on the historical context which "generates the conditions for the patterns of ethical behavior and moral wisdom which emerged in the Black female community." This "untangling of the Black woman's history sheds light on the values and virtues" that will undergird and inform a Black womanist ethics. And it also helps "to further understanding of some of the differences between ethics of life under oppression and established moral approaches which take for granted freedom and a wide range of choices" (Cannon, 1988:5-6).

Thirdly, Cannon (1988:104) argues that a womanist ethics is a virtue ethics and she defines virtue in a Hurstonian way as a "feistiness about life that nobody can wipe out no matter how hard they try." This, in a word, is an adaptive vitality and durability under pressure and oppression. For she asserts the moral quality of life of Black women has been defined by "the balancing of complexities in such a way that suffering did not overwhelm and endurance with dignity was possible." This, of course, is a vital element in the definition of "womanist."

Fourthly, Cannon posits the concept of "invisible dignity" or "unshouted courage" as a key virtue in womanist ethics. For her, Hurston and other strong Black women exhibited this quality, demonstrating "a moral wisdom wherein in grace and truth constitute each other" (Cannon, 1988:128). Grace for her is grounding in a situation of struggle, a struggle to survive and develop in two contradictory worlds "one white, privileged and oppressive, the other Black, exploited and oppressed."

Finally, Cannon (1988:159ff) borrows from and builds on three fundamental themes from the works of Howard Thurman and Martin L. King to round out her womanist ethics. This is an important act because it expresses and reaffirms her commitment to the community as a whole—male and female—and to the richness of its various ethical teachings. The first of these themes is the *imago dei* anthropological concept. This concept of being in the image of God undergirds and propels the quest for wholeness and the urgency of freedom. It compels one to reject the oppressor's devaluation of one's humanity and to struggle for the inalienable rights of freedom and justice, etc. Here again, Cannon poses Hurston and other strong Black women as models of this quest for wholeness and struggle for "'living space' carved out of the intricate web of racism, sexism and poverty."

A second theme useful to womanist ethics is the interrelationship of love and justice. A love ethics for both Thurman and King is the basis of community and human relatedness. But whereas Thurman stresses reconciliation, King stresses struggle for justice and the achievement of justice as grounding for reconciliation and community. Thirdly, Cannon poses the centrality of community based on love and justice in both womanist ethics as expressed by Hurston, and in the ethics of Thurman and King. She concludes reaffirming the rich moral resource of the Black religious tradition and the need for it to be transformed to include space and opportunity for Black women's deserved recognition and continued contribution in a context of love, equality and common struggle for the paradigmatic "beloved community."

5.4   THE ISLAMIC TRADITION

The history of Islam in America is a long one, reaching back to the Malian voyages of 1311 and 1312 (Muhammad, 2001; Van Sertima, 1998) and through enslavement (Diouf, 1998). Islam is clearly the largest and most effective religious challenge to Christianity among Blacks. In fact, as Lincoln (1974b:154) contends, "It has an inevitable appeal to Blacks who have difficulty with American Christianity because of its

racism, and with the Black Christian church because of it posture of accommodation." Although Muslims came to America in
the 1300's, Islam was not an established religion in the U.S. until
the early 1900's. Beginning in 1913 with Noble Drew Ali's establishment of the Moorish Science Temple and growing to its
highest point in the early 60's in the context of the Nation of
Islam, headed by the Hon. Elijah Muhammad, Islam has become
a major religion among African Americans. Moreover, it has
served as a creative challenge to Black Christianity in its internal criticism and struggle to create a more socially relevant religion, as expressed in Black liberation theology (McCloud, 1995).

THE MOORISH SCIENCE TEMPLE

In 1913, Noble Drew Ali established the Moorish Science
Temple in Newark, New Jersey and began to teach a synthesized
version of orthodox Islam, Garveyism, Christianity and various
extractions from oriental philosophy (Bontemps and Conroy,
1945:175; Moorish Science Temple, 1991). From Newark, Ali's
teaching spread to the northern cities of Detroit, Harlem,
Chicago, Pittsburgh, Philadelphia and various cities in the
South, eventually embracing an estimated membership of 20-
30,000 (Lincoln, 1961).

The main contentions of Noble Drew Ali's religious nationalism were that: 1) the key to the salvation and liberation of
African people in the U.S. lay in the discovery and acceptance
of their national origin as Moors; 2) Islam was "the only instrument for (Black) unity and advancement;" 3) whites were the
opposite of and negative to Blacks and were soon to be destroyed; 4) the need to obey the law and refrain from radicalism;
and finally, 5) the essentiality of love, harmony and peace in the
world and especially among Blacks. Urging his followers to struggle to be righteous and build a better world, he sums up his teachings saying:

*"In conclusion, I urge you to remember there is work
enough for all to do in helping to build a better world.
The problems of life are largely social and economic. In
a profound sense, they are moral and spiritual. Have
lofty conceptions of your duties to your country and fel-
lowmen in general and especially those with whom you*

deal. This includes such honesty and righteousness as will cause you to put yourself in the other fellow's place. Look for the best in others and give them the best that is in you. Have a deeper appreciation for womanhood. Brighten the hopes of our youth in order that their courage be increased to dare and do wondrous things. Adhere at all times to the principles of love, truth, peace, freedom and justice." (Moorish Science Temple, 1991:52)

As Essien-Udom (1964:76) maintained, Ali's basic contentions and principles laid a basis for the Nation of Islam which came into being afterwards. His stress on name, land and nationality, his division of the world into dark and white peoples, his political conservatism and his conception of divine retribution of Allah on whites all find subsequent expression in the ideology and practice of the Nation of Islam. However, although the Black Islamic tradition owes its origins to Nobel Drew Ali, it realized its most definitive development and recognition under the Hon. Elijah Muhammad and the Nation of Islam.

THE NATION OF ISLAM

The Nation of Islam (NOI) began in 1930 with the splitting into two factions of the Moorish Science Temple, one following a newcomer, W.D. Fard, to Detroit, and the other faction remaining faithful to Noble Drew Ali. Those following Fard eventually embraced him as God in person when he disappeared in 1933 and they became the founding members of the Nation of Islam under the leadership of Messenger Elijah Muhammad (Lincoln, 1961:181-182; Rashad, 1994; Muhammad, 1997; Clegg, 1997). Within the context of building the Nation of Islam, Muhammad developed an oppositional theology which is presented in his three basic works (1965, 1973, 1992).

The first and most fundamental aspect of the socio-religious thought of Muhammad is the posing of Islam as the true religion of Black people and Christianity as the religion of their opposite and enemy, white people. Islam is a Black religion because it means submission to the will of Allah and Black people are submissive to God by nature. Secondly, it is the "religion of freedom, justice and equality" and thus, serves Black people's interest better than Christianity which "is a white man's religion and...contains no salvation for the Black man" (Muhammad, 1973:8,4).

The second aspect of Muhammad's socio-religious philosophy is his contention that Allah (God) is in reality a Black man and the Black man is God (Muhammad, 1992:92ff). As Lincoln (1961:73) observed, "all Black men represent Allah or at least participate in Him for all Black men are divine." Thirdly, Muhammad argues that Black people are a chosen people who are "righteous by creation" and "righteous by nature."

Reversing the religious and world order ideologically in a way no one else had done, Muhammad defines the white man as the devil. By this he meant two things: 1) that logically if God is Black, the devil of dialectical necessity must be white; and 2) that if the devil means the embodiment of evil, the historical record of the white man both exposes and confirms his true identity. Thus, he (1965:134) states, that the white man's claim to be God or the chosen of God is in fact a lie. It is this part of Muhammad's doctrine of deliverance, the God-devil thesis, which has proved the most controversial and, at the same time, the most effective organizing principle (Muhammad, 1992:191ff).

Fifthly, Muhammad argues that separation on the social and political level from whites was a divine imperative. This he (1965:273-275) contended is necessary in order for Blacks to avoid the corruptive influence of white civilization which is "floating in corruption," to avoid the divine destruction Allah has for America, and to establish a nation in their own image and interests. Also, Muhammad stresses the need for economic self-help and racial solidarity. To accomplish this, Muhammad calls for "a united front of Black men of America" who will join hands in a program of economic, political and spiritual uplift-ment of Black people. Lastly, Muhammad stressed the need for racial and Islamic solidarity throughout the world. He argued that all Third World people were original people and that they were destined to unite in spite of the evil influence of the West which divided them.

THE SOCIO-ETHICAL TEACHINGS OF MALCOLM X

Muhammad's message was raised and taught at a national and international level by the NOI's most eminent and competent spokesman, Malcolm X (Al Hajj Malik Shabazz). Malcolm

(1965a, 1965b, 1968, 1970, 1989, 1992) not only translated Muhammad's message into its most trenchant and compelling form, but he also went beyond it to produce and articulate one of the most effective and cogent critiques of domination in U.S. history. It is this severe incisiveness of his analysis, along with his bold stands and organizational ability that made him the most definitive symbol of the Black liberation movement in the 1960's (Clarke, 1969; Karenga, 1979, 1982; Cone, 1991; DeCaro, 1996; Smallwood, 2001).

Malcolm's critique of domination focused on the religious, racial and class restraints on Black and human freedom. He chastised white Christianity for its role in African enslavement, racism and oppression and its hypocrisy in dividing the secular from the sacred. He (1965a:244) states that "the Holy Bible in the white man's hands and his interpretations of it have been the greatest single ideological weapon for enslaving millions of human beings of color." In fact, Malcolm continues, "every country the white man conquered with guns, he has always paved the way and salvaged his conscience by carrying the bible" and using it to justify his dominance and destruction. Having rejected Christianity, he urged moral and spiritual grounding in the colorblind religious community of Islam. As he states, "The teaching of Islam seeks to clear up our morals and (thus) qualify us to enter into this new righteous nation of God" (Lomax, 1963:151). And therefore, one becomes a worthy member of the righteous community, able to stand upright without either vice or shame before both history and heaven.

Secondly, he taught the social rootedness and responsibility of religion, its need to be an instrument and support of social change. His strategy for moral grounding and liberation through struggle for the masses was to "wake them up, clean them up and then stand them up." Malcolm argued for an engaged community that was not simply a witness of history, but rather a midwife of history. Religion for him was a historical practice. Thus he (1970:140) states, "I believe in a religion that believes in freedom." And to any religion that does not respond accordingly to the struggle for freedom, "I say to hell with that religion."

Thirdly, Malcolm taught preference for the human interests of the masses against the narrow class interests of the middle class. For him, the masses were the core and conscience of the movement while the middle class was dedicated to integrationism, tokenism, compromise and self-mutilation. Here, he makes his classic distinction between the slavish behavior of the "house Black" and the resistance behavior of the "field Black." In modern terms, he (1983:95) cites the integrationist Black who "waits to beg white people to accept him or to force himself into white society" and "the new type of Black man who wants to think for himself, stand on his own feet, and walk for himself."

Fourthly, Malcolm argued for an ethics of self-defense. In fact, his famous slogan "freedom by any means necessary" is rooted in his ethics of self-defense. Freedom is constitutive of what it means to be human. As he says, "freedom is essential to life" (Lomax, 1963:150). Thus to deny one freedom is to deny one's life as human. Given this, Malcolm concludes one is justified in using any methods necessary to gain freedom and therefore secure one's humanity. Moreover, direct defense to save one's life is also justified. "We are not for violence in any shape or form" he (1992:46) states, "but believe that the people who have violence committed against them should be able to defend themselves." This, Malcolm (1992:47) clarifies, does not mean that one should "initiate acts of aggression...but where the government fails to protect... (one) is entitled to do it himself." Malcolm bases these contentions on Quranic teachings, constitutional guarantees in the Second Amendment and the Natural law assumption that self-preservation is the first law of nature. The Quran (2:190-191) teaches that one is permitted to "fight in the way of Allah against those who fight against you but be not aggressive (for) Allah loves not the aggressor." Also one should fight because "oppression is worse than death." Finally, the Quran (42:41) teaches that "whoever defends himself from oppression, these it is against whom there is no blame." Thus, Malcolm (1968:175) concludes "I'm for peace, yet I believe any man facing death should be able to go to any length to assure that whoever is trying to kill him has no chance."

Finally, Malcolm saw history as a field for both human and divine action and a need for African and other oppressed people to unite in solidarity and to self-consciously struggle to regain their history and humanity and build a new world. Thus, he (1965:233) notes that the African American struggle is "part of a global rebellion of the oppressed against the oppressor, the exploited against the exploiter." And this was for him God's hand in history on the side of the righteous and truly human.

SCHISM, TRANSFORMATION AND REBUILDING

THE SCHISM

In 1963 the Nation of Islam (NOI) began to show signs of unraveling as evidenced by the underlying reasons for the suspension and eventual ouster/resignation of Malcolm X. His ouster/resignation had a tremendous impact on the NOI and the Black Movement and indicated a series of problems that would eventually lead to factionalization and transformation of the NOI. Although the NOI gave the reason for Malcolm's suspension as his disobeying an order not to comment on the Kennedy assassination, the underlying political basis for it was the conflict between two major tendencies in the NOI, the radicals represented by Malcolm and the conservatives represented by the ruling stratum in charge of daily administration. Each vied for and was dependent on Muhammad's decision and support for victory in the daily battle and the ultimate struggle itself (Carson, 1991; Evanzz, 1992).

As I (1982:5) have argued in a paper on the conflict, four major factors appear to have shaped and fed the conflict. First, the transformation of the NOI from a small marginal group to a multi-million dollar budget and huge bureaucracy changed both its political character and its conception of what was politically acceptable. As Lincoln (1961) predicted and Lomax (1963) reported, the ruling stratum became increasingly conservative in its desire to protect its gains and Malcolm could not adjust to the new conservatism.

Secondly, then, the conflict was shaped by the ruling stratum's fierce opposition to Malcolm. Although they recognized his worth and significance to the NOI, they resented and opposed him because of: 1) his moral posture against the corruptive materialism which permeated the ruling stratum; 2) his unwillingness to moderate his radicalism in the face of changed circumstances; and 3) the likelihood of his succeeding Muhammad and establishing a radical position. Thirdly, the conflict was shaped by the ruling stratum's ability to eventually alienate Muhammad and Malcolm in spite of their prior closeness. This was achieved essentially by their being in the pivotal position of daily administration and, thus, of briefing the Messenger everyday and arguing Malcolm's refusal to moderate his disruptive radicalism and to accept Muhammad's divine authority (Evanzz, 1992).

Having been convinced of these charges, Muhammad suspended Malcolm at first and later denounced him. Malcolm in turn denounced the NOI and Muhammad and the ensuing conditions set the stage for his assassination. Finally, evidence suggest that the FBI had a significant role in provoking and sustaining the leadership struggle within the NOI. For as early as 1959, it had placed people in the leadership stratum. Moreover, documents from the FBI's Counter Intelligence Program (Cointelpro) obtained through the Freedom of Information Act reveal the FBI's decision to divide the NOI and either transform it or destroy it (Evanzz, 1992; Carson, 1991).

TRANSFORMATION

After Muhammad's death in 1975, the NOI underwent a drastic transformation and fragmentation involving severe criticism of Muhammad, rejection of the early Muslim belief on whites, and the introduction of a strong Americanism and orthodox Islam (Muhammad, 1980). This process "has its roots in the unsolved political and economic problems which shaped and fed the conflict between Malcolm and the ruling stratum" (Karenga, 1982:339). In other words, "the non-engagement, isolation and general conservatism which Malcolm fought in the 60's expresses itself in similar forms in the 70's...with the added dimensions of Americanism and orthodox Islam advocated by Muhammad's son, Wallace." In addition to the above factor, four others contributed to the transformation (Karenga, 1981: 339ff). A second factor contributive to the transformation then was the ideology and structure of the Nation itself. The theocratic leadership structure based on divine wisdom and authority allowed for corrupt officials to act without check, denied mass participation in decision-making and debates, and prevented criticism necessary to check the transformation carried to its ultimate by Wallace and the ruling stratum. Also, the ideological tendency toward non-engagement in social struggle, obeying laws and the stress on material acquisition cultivated an appreciation for political conservatism and vulgar materialism of the ruling stratum (Lincoln, 1961; Essien-Udom, 1964).

A third contributing factor was the leadership style and

problems of succession of Imam Wallace Muhammad who succeeded his father. Wallace's leadership style leaned toward
decentralization and orthodox Islam even before his father's
death. Once at the helm, he reshaped the Nation. Also, his problems of succession were ones of establishing his authority; creating a new image of the NOI; and winning new converts and
allies. Thus, he disavowed his father's divine authority and his
God, disbanded the paramilitary arm, the Fruit of Islam, eliminating a possible challenge and changing the military or coercive
image of the NOI. Moreover, he changed the doctrine of the
NOI from religious Black nationalism to Americanism and
orthodox Islam, winning new converts and allies who once
opposed the race-and-earth focused religious doctrine of his
father. Finally, as argued above, there is evidence of the U.S.
government's intervention and role in the process of transformation and fragmentation. From positions at the top, it appears
they not only provoked conflict and helped eliminate the radicals, but encouraged the transformation which insured an
accommodationist religious structure.

THE REBUILDING

Although Minister Louis Farrakhan, the national spokesman
after Malcolm, had at first gone along with the transformation,
he eventually objected. In 1978, he announced publicly that he
could no longer accept in silence the transformation of the
Nation and its members. He listed, among other things, the following which he found intolerable: the ingratitude and disrespect for Messenger Muhammad which the transformed NOI was
exhibiting; its open admission of whites; the deterioration of discipline and the emphasis on orthodox Islam as opposed to a people-specific Islam for Blacks which Muhammad had developed
(Overbea, 1978:9).

To offset the disintegration he perceived in the NOI, which
was then called the World Community of Islam in the West,
Farrakhan moved to rebuild the NOI in its original Black image.
He formed discussion groups around the country, lectured, published and republished the Messenger's works, reproduced tape
recordings of the Messenger and himself, started a newspaper,
The Final Call, and began to rebuild the Mosque structures and
leadership cadres across the country. At the heart of his efforts to

rebuild the NOI was the struggle to rescue and reconstruct the image of Messenger Muhammad. To accomplish this, Farrakhan argued: The truth and currency of Muhammad's message; his moral and material achievement; and the praiseworthiness of his character as a leader (Karenga, 1981:379; Eure and Jerome, 1989). The success of Farrakhan in rebuilding the NOI depended on several factors: 1) his own leadership capacity; 2) his overshadowing and making peace with opposing Islamic groups claiming the Messenger's mantle; 3) his success in building a capable and committed cadre; and finally, 4) his ability to relate positively and effectively to the larger Black community.

In fact, the crowning achievement of his rebuilding the Nation of Islam was the success of the Million Man March/Day of Absence (MMM/DOA). Although, as noted above in chapter 4, the project involved thousands of organizers in local organizing committees in over 300 cities, it is Min. Farrakhan and the NOI who called the March. Moreover, they formed its core body of workers at the national level and was successful in bringing a wide range of organizations into the National Organizing Committee (Madhubuti and Karenga, 1996). The success of the MMM/DOA reaffirmed his major leadership role in the U.S. and also reinforced his position internationally as a leader among Muslims of the world (Alexander, 1998). Recently, Min. Farrakhan has made an important ideological shift toward orthodox Islam. This includes conceding that whites would one day be members of the NOI; stressing a common humanity as he did at the Million Family March in 2000 in which various races, including whites, participated and teaching more from the Quran. The source and significance of this is open to analysis, but it is clear that the shift will affect the way Islam is understood and approached in the U.S.

STUDY QUESTIONS

1. Define religion and list some of the major African American religious traditions.
2. What are some general characteristics and general themes in African religions?
3. Discuss the ideas suggested by Dogon cosmogony.

4. What are some of the basic ethical teachings of the Maatian tradition? Discuss their reasoning and relevance to modern moral issues.

5. Identify and discuss some of the basic tenets of the Ifa tradition in terms of their relevance for modern moral discourse.

6. Why did enslaved Africans convert to Christianity?

7. What has been the historical role of the Black church?

8. Cite some basic tenets of Dr. Martin Luther King's socio-political philosophy and his philosophical impact on Black religion and the Civil Rights Movement.

9. What are some of the basic contentions of Malcolm X's social-ethical philosophy and his philosophical impact on Black religion and the liberation movements of the 1960's?

10. Who are two major Black liberation theologians and what are some of their basic theories?

11. What are the challenges posed by Black womanist theology as argued by Jacqueline Grant? How does she address them?

12. Discuss Katie Cannon's womanist ethics and her use of Black women's literature to develop them.

13. Discuss the contentions and religious legacy of the Moorish Science Temple in relationship to the Nation of Islam.

14. Discuss the philosophy of Messenger Muhammad.

15. What factors contributed to the conflict between Malcolm X and the Nation of Islam?

16. What are some of the factors which contributed to the transformation of the NOI after the death of Messenger Muhammad?

17. What were the challenges posed for Minister Louis Farrakhan in rebuilding the NOI? How has his approach to Islam changed since the MMM/DOA?

REFERENCES

Abimbola, Wande. (1975a) Ìwàpèlè: The Concept of Good Character in Ifá Literary Corpus, in Yoruba Oral Tradition: Poetry in Music, Dance and Drama, Ilé-Ifè, Nigeria: Department of African Languages and Literatures, University of Ifè.

Abimbola, Wande. (1975b) Sixteen Great Poems of Ifá, Washington, D.C.: UNESCO.

Abimbola, Wande. (1976) Ifá: An Exposition of the Ifá Literary Corpus, Ìbàdàn, Nigeria: Oxford University Press.

Abimbola, Wande. (1977) Ifá Divination Poetry, New York: London, Lagos: Nok Publishers.

Abimbola, Wande. (1997) Ifá Will Mend Our Broken Ways: Thoughts on Yoruba Religion and Culture in Africa and the Diaspora, Roxbury, MA: Aim Books.

Adams, Hunter III. (1979) "African Observers of the Universe: The Sirius Question," *Journal of African Civilization*, 1,2 (November) 1-20.

Alexander, Amy (ed.) (1998) *The Farrakhan Factor: African American Writers on Leadership, Nationhood and Minister Louis Farrakhan*, New York: Grove Press.

Allen, Thomas G. (1960) *The Book of the Dead or Going Forth By Day*, Chicago: University of Chicago Press.

Ammi, Ben. (1990) *God, the Black Man and Truth*, Washington D.C.: Communicators Press.

Angell, Stephen W. (1992) *Bishop Henry McNeal Turner and African American Religion in the South*, Knoxville: The University of Tennessee Press.

Asante, Molefi. K. (2000) *The Egyptian Philosophers*, Chicago: African American Images.

Assmann, Jan. (1990) *Ma'at: Gerechtigkeit und Unsterblichkeit im alten Ägypten*, München: Verlag C.H. Beck.

Austin, Allan D. (ed.) (1997) *African Muslims in Antebellum America: Proud Exiles*, London: Routledge.

Awolalu, J.O. (1979) *Yoruba Beliefs and Sacrificial Rights*, London: Longmans.

Barrett, Leonard E. (1988) *The Rastafarians*, Boston: Beacon Press.

Bascom, William R. (1969) *Ifá Divination: Communication between Men and Gods in West Africa*, Bloomington: Indiana University Press.

Bascom. William R. (1980) *Sixteen Cowries: Yoruba Divination from Africa to the New World*, Bloomington: Indiana University Press.

Bastide, Roger. (1978) *The African Religions of Brazil: Towards A Sociology of the Interpretations of Civilizations*, Baltimore: John Hopkins University, Book Associates.

Ben Yehuda, Shaleak. (1975) *Black Hebrew Israelites: From America to the Promised Land*, New York: Vantage Press.

Best, Felton O. (ed.) (1998) *Black Religious Leadership From the Slave Community to the Million Man March*, New York: Mellen.

Blackman, Aylward. (1988) *The Story of King Cheops and the Magicians*, (Berlin Papyrus 3033), Reading, PA: J.V. Books.

Blassingame, John W. (1979) *The Slave Community*, New York: Oxford University Press.

Bontemps, Arna and Jack Conroy. (1945) *They Seek A City*, Garden City, NY: Doubleday, Daran and Company, Inc.

Branch, Taylor. (1988) *Parting The Waters: America in the King Years, 1954-1963*, New York: Simon and Schuster.

Breasted, James. (1934) *The Dawn of Conscience*, New York: Charles Scribner's Sons.

Breasted, James. (1905-1906) *Ancient Records of Egypt*, 5 volumes, Chicago: University of Chicago Press.

Bynum, LaTaunya Marie. (1980) *Black Feminist Theology: A New Word About God.* Unpublished master's thesis, School of Theology, Claremont.

Cannon, Katie G. (1988) *Black Womanist Ethics*, Atlanta: Scholars Press.

Cannon, Katie G. (1995) *Katie's Canon: Womanism and the Soul of the Black Community*, New York: Continuum.

Cannon, Katie G. (1983) *Resources for a Constructive Ethic for Women with Special Attention to the Life and Work of Zora Neale Hurston*, unpublished dissertation, Union Theological Seminary, New York.

Carson, Claybourne. (1991) *Malcolm X: The FBI File*, New York: Carroll and Graf Publishers, Inc.

Chapman, Mark L. (1996) *Christianity on Trial: African American Religious Thought Before and After Black Power*, Maryknoll, NY: Orbis Books.

Clarke, John H. (1969) *Malcolm X: The Man and His Times*, New York: Macmillan.

Cleage, Albert Jr. (1972) *Black Christian Nationalism*, New York: William Morrow and Co.

Cleage, Albert Jr. (1968) *The Black Messiah*, New York: Sheed and Ward.

Clegg, Claude Andrew. (1997) *An Original Man: The Life and Times of Elijah Muhammad*, New York: Secretarious Publications.

Coleman, Will. (2000) *Tribal Talk: Black Theology, Hermeneutics and African American Ways of "Telling the Story,"* University Park: Pennsylvania University Press.

Cone, James. (1969) *Black Theology and Black Power*, New York: Seabury Press.

Cone, James. (1970) *A Black Theology of Liberation*, Philadelphia: Lippincott Co.

Cone, James. (1984) *For My People: Black Theology of the Black Church*, New York: Orbis Books.

Cone, James. (1975) *God of the Oppressed*, New York: Seabury Press.

Cone, James. (1991) *Martin and Malcolm and America: A Dream or A Nightmare*, Maryknoll, New York: Orbis Books.

Cone, James. (1983) *My Soul Looks Back*, Nashville: Abingdon Press.

Cone, James. (1999) *Risks of Faith: The Emergence of a Black Theology of Liberation 1968-1998*, Boston: Beacon Press.

Cummings, George. (1993) *A Common Journey: Black theology (USA) and Latin American Liberation Theology*, Maryknoll, NY: Orbis Books.

DeCaro, Louis A. (1996) *On the Side of My People: A Religious Life of Malcolm X*, New York: New York University Press.

Deng, Francis. (1973) *The Dinka and Their Songs*, Oxford: Clarendon Press.

Diop, Cheikh Anta. (1991) *Civilization or Barbarism: An Authentic Anthropology*, New York: Lawrence Hill Books.

Diop, Cheikh Anta. (1981) *Civilization ou Barbarie*, Paris: Présence Africaine.

Diop, Cheikh Anta. (1974) *The African Origin of Civilization: Myth or Reality*, Westport, CT: Lawrence Hill & Co.

Diouf, Sylviane. (1998) *Servants of Allah: African Muslims Enslaved in the Americas*, New York: University Press.

Dodson, Jualynne. (1983) *Women's Collective Power in the African Methodist Episcopal Church*. Unpublished dissertation, University of California, Berkeley.

Douglas, Kelly Brown. (1994) *The Black Christ*, Maryknoll, NY: Orbis Books.

Douglas, Kelly Brown. (1999) *Sexuality and the Black Church: A Womanist Perspective*, Maryknoll, NY: Orbis Books.

Drewal, Margaret T. (1992) *Yoruba Ritual*, Bloomington, IN: Indiana University Press.

Epega, Afolabi A. and Philip John Neimark. (1995) *The Sacred Ifá Oracle*, San Francisco: Harper Collins Publishers.

Essien-Udom, E.U. (1964) *Black Nationalism*, New York: Dell Publishing Co.

Eure, Joseph and Richard Jerome (1989) *Back Where We Belong: Selected Speeches by Minister Louis Farrakhan*, Philadelphia: DC International Press.

Evans, James. (1981) "Black Theology and Black Feminism," in *Journal of Religious Thought*, 38, Spring/Summer, pp. 43-53.

Evans-Pritchard, E.E. (1965) *Theories of Primitive Religion*, London: Oxford University Press.

Evanzz, Karl (1992) *The Judas Factor: The Plot to Kill Malcolm X*, New York: Thunder Mouth Press.

Faulkner, R.O. (1973) *The Ancient Egyptian Coffin Texts*, Warminister, England: Aris & Phillips, Ltd.

Faulkner, R.O. (1969) *The Ancient Egyptian Pyramid Texts*, Oxford: University of Oxford Press.

Fauset, H. (1944) *Blacks Gods of the Metropolis*, Philadelphia: University of Pennsylvania Press.

Frazier, E. Franklin. (1974) *The Negro Church in America*, New York: Schocken Books, Inc.

Fulop, Timothy and Albert J. Raboteau, (eds.) (1996) *African American Religion: Interpretive Essays in History and Culture*, New York: Routledge.

Gleason, Judith. (1975) *Santería*, Bronx, NY: Atheneum Press.

Gonzales-Wippler, Migene. (1982) *The Santería Experience*, Bronx, New York: Original Publications.

Grant, Jacquelyn. (1979) "Black Theology and The Black Woman," in Gayraud Wilmore and James Cone (eds.) *Black Theology*, New York: Orbis Books.

Grant, Jacquelyn. (1989) *White Women's Christ and Black Women's Jesus: Feminist Christology and Womanist Response*, Atlanta: Scholars Press.

Griaule, Marcel. (1978) *Conversations with Ogotemmeli*, New York: Oxford University Press.

Griaule, Marcel and Germain Dieterlen. (1965) "The Dogon," in Daryll Ford (ed.) *African Worlds*, London: Oxford University Press, pp. 83-110.

Gutierrez, Gustavo. (1974) *The Mystical and Political Dimensions of the Christian Faith*, New York: Hurder & Hurder.

Gutierrez, Gustavo. (1973) *A Theology of Liberation*, Maryknoll, New York: Orbis.

Gyekye, Kwame. (1987) *An Essay on African Philosophical Thought: The Akan Conceptual Theme*, New York: Cambridge University Press.

Haley, Alex. (1976) *Roots*, New York: Dell Publishing Co.

Harding, Vincent. (1969) "The Religion of Black Power," in *The Religious Stratum*, (ed.) Donald Cutler, Boston: Beacon Press.

Harris, J.R. (ed.) (1971) *The Legacy of Egypt*, Oxford: Oxford University Press.

Hayes, Diana. (1996) *And Still We Rise: An Introduction to Black Liberation Theology*, New York: Paulist Press.

Hodges, Graham. (ed.) (1999) *Nation Builders: Female Activism in the Nation of Islam*, New York: Garland.

Hopkins, Dwight. (ed.) (1999a) *Black Faith and Public Talk: Critical Essays on James H. Cone's Black Theology and Black Power*, Maryknoll, NY: Orbis Books.

Hopkins, Dwight. (1999b) *Introducing Black Theology of Liberation*, Maryknoll, NY: Orbis Books.

Hopkins, Dwight. (2000) *Up, Down and Over: Slave Religion and Black Theology*, Minneapolis: Fortress Press.

Hoover, Theressa. (1979) "Black Women and the Churches: Triple Jeopardy" in Gayraud Wilmore and James Cone (eds.) *Black Theology*, New York: Orbis Books.

Idowu, E. Bolaji. (1975) *African Traditional Religion*, Maryknoll, New York: Orbis Books.

Idowu, E. Bolaji. (1962) *Olódùmarè: God in Yoruba Belief*, London: Longman.

Johnson, Joseph. (1978) *Proclamation Theology*, Shreveport: Fourth District Press.

Johnson, Joseph. (1971) *The Souls of the Black Preacher*, Philadelphia: United Church Press.

Jones, Major J. (1971) *Black Awareness*, Nashville: Abingdon Press.

Jones, Major J. (1974) *Christian Ethics for Black Theology*, Nashville: Abindgon Press.

Jones, William R. (1973) *Is God a White Racist?* Garden City, New York: Anchor Press/Doubleday.

Karenga, Maulana. (1981) *Afro-American Nationalism: An Alternative Analysis*, unpublished dissertation, U.S. International University, San Diego.

Karenga, Maulana. (1990a) *The Book of Coming Forth By Day: The Ethics of the Declarations of Innocence*, Los Angeles: University of Sankore Press.

Karenga, Maulana. (1980) *Kawaida Theory: An Introductory Outline*, Los Angeles: Kawaida Publications.

Karenga, Maulana. (1982) "Malcolm and the Messenger: From Psychological Assumptions to Political Analysis," *Western Journal of Black Studies*, 6, 4, (Winter) pp. 193-201.

Karenga, Maulana. (1994) *Maat, The Moral Ideal in Ancient Egypt: A Study in Classical African Ethics*. Unpublished dissertation, University of Southern California, Los Angeles.

Karenga, Maulana. (1999a) *Odu Ifa: The Ethical Teachings*, Los Angeles: University of Sankore Press.

Karenga, Maulana (ed.) (1990b) *Reconstructing Kemetic Culture: Papers, Perspectives, Projects*, Los Angeles: University of Sankore Press.

Karenga, Maulana. (1986b) "Restoration of the Husia: Reviving a Sacred Legacy" in Maulana Karenga and Jacob H. Carruthers (eds.), *Kemet and the African Worldview*, Los Angeles: University of Sankore Press, pp. 83-99.

Karenga, Maulana. (1990c) "The Rescue and Reconstruction of Ancient Egypt: The Spiritual Dimension of the Project" in Maulana Karenga (ed.) *Reconstructing Kemetic Culture: Papers, Perspectives, Projects*, Los Angeles: University of Sankore Press, pp. 181-199.

Karenga, Maulana. (1984) *Selections From the Husia: Sacred Wisdom of Ancient Egypt*, Los Angeles: University of Sankore Press.

Karenga, Maulana. (1979) "The Socio-Political Philosophy of Malcolm X," *Western Journal of Black Studies*, 3, 4 (Winter) 251-262.

Karenga, Maulana. (1999b) "Sources of Self in Ancient Egyptian Autobiographies: A Kawaida Articulation," in James L. Conyers, Jr. (ed.) *Black American Intellectualism and Culture: A Social Study of African American Social and Political Thought*, Stamford, CT: JAI Press, Inc., pp. 37-56.

Karenga, Maulana. (1989) "Towards a Sociology of Maatian Ethics: Literature and Context," *Journal of African Civilizations*, 10, 1, (Fall) 352-395.

Karenga, Maulana and Jacob H. Carruthers, (eds.). (1986a) *Kemet and the African Worldview*, Los Angeles: University of Sankore Press.

King, Martin Luther, Jr. (1963) *Strength To Love*, New York: Harper & Row.

King, Martin Luther, Jr. (1958) *Stride Toward Freedom*, New York: Harper & Row.

King, Martin Luther, Jr. (1964) *Why We Can't Wait*, New York: Harper & Row.

King, Martin Luther, Jr. (1967) *Where Do We Go From Here: Chaos or Community*, New York: Harper & Row.

Lawal, Babatunde. (1996) *The Gèlèdè Spectacle: Art, Gender, and Social Harmony in an African Culture*, Seattle and London: University of Washington Press.

Lichtheim, Miriam. (1988) *Ancient Egyptian Autobiographies Chiefly of the Middle Kingdom*, Fribourg, Switzerland: Biblical Institute, University of Fribourg.

Lichtheim, Miriam. (1973) (1976) (1980) *Ancient Egyptian Literature: A Book of Readings, Vol. I, 1975; Vol. II, 1976; Vol. III, 1980*, Berkeley: University of California Press.

Lichtheim, Miriam. (1992) *Maat in Egyptian Autobiographies and Related Studies*, Fribourg, Göttingen: Universitäts-verlag.

Lincoln, C. Eric and Lawrence H. Mamiya. (1990) *The Black Church in the African American Experience*, Durham, NC: Duke University Press.

Lincoln, C. Eric. (1974a) *The Black Church Since Frazier*, New York: Schocken Books, Inc.

Lincoln, C. Eric. (1974b) *The Black Experience in Religion*, Garden City, New York: Anchor Books.

Lincoln, C. Eric. (1961) *The Black Muslims in America*, Boston: Beacon Press.

Lomax, Louis. (1963) *When The Word Is Given...*, New York: World Publishing Co.

Lucas, J.O. (1948) *The Religion of the Yoruba*, Lagos: C.M.S. Bookshop.

Madhubuti, Haki and Maulana Karenga, (eds.) (1996) *Million Man March/Day of Absence: A Commemorative Anthology*, Chicago/Los Angeles: Third World Press/University of Sankore Press.

Malcolm X. (1965a) *The Autobiography of Malcolm X*, New York: Grove Press.

Malcolm X. (1970) *By Any Means Necessary*, New York: Pathfinder Press.

Malcolm X. (1983) *The End of White Supremacy*, New York: Seavers Books.

Malcolm X. (1992) *February 1965: The Final Speeches*, New York: Pathfinder Press.

Malcolm X. (1965b) *Malcolm X Speaks*, New York: Merit Publishers.

Malcolm X. (1968) *Speeches of Malcolm X at Harvard*, New York: William Morrow & Co.

Malcolm X. (1989) *The Last Speeches*, New York: Pathfinder Press.

Marx, Karl and Frederick Engels. (1964) *On Religion*, New York: Schocken Books, Inc.

Massey, Gerald. (1970) *Egypt Light of the World*, New York: Samuel Weiser, Inc.

Mbiti, John S. (1970) *African Religions and Philosophy*, Garden City, NY: Anchor Books.

Mbiti, John. (1991) *Introduction to African Religion*, (2nd edition), Oxford: Heineman International Literature and Textbooks.

McCloud, Aminah B. (1995) *African American Islam*, New York: Routledge.

Mends, E. H. (1976) "Ritual in the Social Life of Ghanaian Society," in J. M. Assimeng, (ed.) *Traditional Life, Culture and Literature in Ghana*, New York: Cinch Magazine Limited.

Mohammed, Imam W. Deen. (1991) *Al-Islam, Unity and Leadership*, Chicago: The Sense Maker.

Morenz, Siegfried. (1984) *Egyptian Religion*, Ithaca: Cornell University Press.

Moorish Science Temple of America, Inc. (1991) *Moor Sense 2000 Journal: Righting of a Nation Resurrected*, Augusta, WV: Seven Circles Publishing Co.

Morrison, Silburn M. (1992) *Rastafari: The Conscious Embrace*, Bronx, NY: Itality Publishing House.

Muhammad, Amir N. (2001) *Muslims in America: Seven Centuries of History, 1312-2000*, Beltsville, MD: Amana Publications.

Muhammad, Elijah. (1973) *The Fall of America*, Chicago: Muhammad's Temple of Islam No. 2.

Muhammad, Elijah. (1965) *Message to the Black Man in America*, Chicago: Muhammad's Temple of Islam No. 2.

Muhammad, Elijah. (1997) *The True History of Elijah Muhammad: Autobiographically Authoritative*, Atlanta: Secretarius Publications.

Muhammad, Elijah. (1992) *The Theology of Time*, Hampton, VA: U.B. & U.S. Communication Systems, 1992.

Muhammad, Wallace D. (1980) *As the Light Shineth From the East*, Chicago: Wallace D. Muhammad Publishing Company.

Murphy, Joseph. (1988) *Santería: An African Religion in America*, Boston: Beacon Press.

Murray, Pauli. (1979) "Black Theology and Feminist Theology: A Comparative View," in *Black Theology*, (eds.) Gayraud Wilmore and James Cone, New York: Orbis Books.

Obenga, Theopile. (1992) *Ancient Egypt and Black Africa: A Student's Handbook for Study of Ancient Egypt in Philosophy, Linguistics and Gender Relations*, London: Karnak House.

Obenga, Theopile. (1990) *La philosophie africaine de la périod pharaonique, 2780-330 avant notre ère*, Paris: Éditions L'Harmattan.

Overbea, Luix. (1978) "Leader Quits Black Muslims," *Christian Science Monitor* (June 13).

Paris, Peter J. (1985) *The Social Teaching of the Black Churches*, Philadelphia: Fortress Press.

Parkinson, R.B. (1997) *The Tale of Sinuhe and Other Ancient Egyptian Poems, 1940-1640 BC*, Oxford: Clarendon Press.

Parkinson, R.B. (1991) *Voices from Ancient Egypt: An Anthology of Middle Kingdom Writings*, London: British Museum Press.

Piankoff, Alexandre. (1954-74) *Egyptian Religious Texts & Representations*, 6 volumes, Princeton: Princeton University Press.

Popoola, S. Solagbade. (1997) *Practical Ifá, For the Beginner and Professional*, New York: Athelia Henrietta Press.

Rashad, Adib (James Miller). (1994) *Elijah Muhammad & The Ideological Foundation of the Nation of Islam*, Hampton, VA: U.B. & U.S. Communications Systems.

Ray, Benjamin C. (1976) *African Religions*, Englewood Cliffs, N.J.: Prentice-Hall, Inc.

Richards, Dona Marimba. (1976) "A Community of African Descendants; The Afro-Bahian Candomblé, *The Proceedings of the Conference on Yoruba Civilization, 26-31 July*, Ife, Nigeria: University of Ife.

Richards, Dona Marimba. (1989) *Let the Circle Be Unbroken, Implications of African Spirituality in the Diaspora*, New York: Dona Marimba Richards.

Roberts, J. Deotis. (1974) *A Black Political Theology*, Philadelphia: Westminister Press.

Roberts, J. Deotis. (1971) *Liberation and Reconciliation*, Philadelphia: Westminister Press.

Sagan, Carl. (1979) *Broca's Brain-Reflections on the Romance of Science*, New York: Random House.

Sanders, Cheryl J. (ed.) (1995) *Living in the Intersection: Womanism and Afrocentrism in Theology*, Minneapolis: Fortress Press.

Simpson, William et al. (1973) *The Literature of Ancient Egypt: An Anthology of Stories, Instruction and Poetry*, New Haven: Yale University Press.

Smallwood, Andrew. (2001) *An Afrocentric Study of the Intellectual Development, Leadership Praxis & Pedagogy of Malcolm X*, Lewiston: Edwin Mellen Press.

Teeter, Emily. (1990) *The Presentation of Maat: Iconography and Theology of An Ancient Egyptian Offering Ritual*, unpublished Ph.D. dissertation, University of Chicago.

Temple, Robert. (1976) *The Sirius Mystery*, New York: St. Martin's Press.

Terrell, JoAnn. (1998) *Power in the Blood?: The Cross in the African American Experience*. Maryknoll, NY: Orbis Books.

Thompson, Robert F. (1983) *Flash of the Spirit*, New York: Random House.

Tobin, Vincent A. (1989) *Theological Principles of Egyptian Religion*, American University Series VII, Theology and Religion, Volume 59, New York: Peter Lang Publishing, Inc.

Torres, Sergio. (1981) *The Challenge of a Basic Christian Community*, Maryknoll, N.Y.: Orbis Books.

Torres, Sergio. (1976) *Theology in the Americas*, Maryknoll, N.Y.: Orbis Books.

Townes, Emilie M. (1993) *Womanist Justice, Womanist Hope*, Atlanta, GA: Scholars Press.

Townes, Emilie M. (1995) *In a Blaze of Glory: Womanist Spirituality as Social Witness*, Nashville: Abingdon Press.

Turner, Richard B. (1997) *Islam in the African American Experience*, Bloomington: Indiana University Press.

Van Sertima, Ivan. (ed.) (1998) *Early America Revisited*, New Brunswick, NJ: Transaction Publishers.

Van Sertima, Ivan. (ed.) (1994) *Egypt Child of Africa*, New Brunswick, NJ: Transaction Publishers.

Van Sertima, Ivan. (ed.) (1989) *Egypt Revisited*, 2nd edition, New Brunswick, NY: Transaction Publishers

Walton, Hanes Jr. (1976) *The Political Philosophy of Martin Luther King, Jr.* Westport, Conn.: Greenwood Press.

Washington, James M. (ed.) (1986) *A Testament of Hope: The Essential Writings of Martin Luther King, Jr.*, San Francisco: Harper and Row.

Washington, Joseph. (1964) *Black Religion*, Boston: Beacon Press.

Washington, Joseph. (1967) *The Politics of God*, Boston: Beacon Press.

Weems, Renita J. (1988) *Just A Sister Away: A Womanist Vision of Women's Relationship in the Bible*, San Diego: LuraMedia.

West, Cornel. (1982) *Prophesy Deliverance: An Afro-American Revolutionary Christianity*, Philadelphia: Westminster Press.

West, Cornel. (1988) *Prophetic Fragments*, Trenton, NJ: African World Press.

Williams, Delores. (1975) *The Black Woman Portrayed in Selected Black Literature and Some Questions for Black Theology.* Unpublished master's thesis, Columbia University and Union Theological Seminary, Columbia and New York.

Williams, Delores. (1993) *Sisters in the Wilderness: The Challenge of Womanist God-Talk*, Maryknoll, NY: Orbis Books.

Wilmore, Gayraud S. (ed.) (1989) *African American Religious Studies*, Durham, N.C.: Duke University Press.

Wilmore, Gayraud S. (1983) *Black Religion and Black Radicalism*, (2rd Edition), MaryKnoll, N.Y.: Orbis Books.

Wilmore, Gayraud S. (1998) *Black Religion and Black Radicalism*, (3rd Edition), MaryKnoll, N.Y.: Orbis Books.

Wilmore, Gayraud S. (1979) "The Role of Afro-America in the Rise of Third World Theology: A Historical Reappraisal," in *African Theology En Route*, (eds.) Kofi Appiah-Kubi and Sergio Torres, pp. 196-208.

Wilmore, Gayraud S. and James H. Cone (eds.). (1979) *Black Theology*, Maryknoll, N.Y.: Orbis Books.

Woodson, Carter G. (1945) *The History of the Negro Church*, Washington, D.C.: Associated Publishers.

Wright, Richard A. (1984) *African Philosophy: An Introduction*, (3rd edition), New York: University Press of America.

Zahan, Dominique. (1979) *The Religion, Spirituality, and Thought of Traditional Africa*, Chicago: The University of Chicago Press.

BLACK SOCIOLOGY

BLACK SOCIOLOGY

CHAPTER 6

6.1 INTRODUCTION

B lack sociology *is essentially the critical study of the structure and functioning of the Black community as a whole, as well as the various units and processes which compose and define it, and its relations with peoples and forces external to it.* This includes study of family, groups, institutions, views and values, relations of race, class and gender and related subjects. Moreover, Black sociology directs itself to the study of Black social reality from a Black perspective (Conyers and Barnett, 1999; Ladner, 1999; Staples, 1999). This is necessary for two basic reasons. First, it is important to understanding Black social reality from a position internal to the culture so that the voices and interests of the people are valued and considered critically in any research. Secondly, Black sociology, as an intellectual project in the interest of Black people, seeks not only to understand Black social reality, but also to explore the possibilities inherent in it for emancipatory intellectual and social practice. For it understands established order sociology as a project in the interest of oppression. And as Staples (1973:168) argues, "if white sociology is the science of oppression, Black sociology must be the science of liberation."

As an emancipatory social science, Black sociology offers both critiques and correctives. Continuing the tradition of DuBois (1967), Frazier (1957), Cox (1970), and Hare (1965), Black sociology has set for itself several basic aims: 1) to rescue Black life from the racist interpretations which pose it as pathological and pathogenic, and redefine it in its multidimensionality and variousness; 2) to create new concepts, categories, analytical frameworks and bodies of data that enhance understanding of both Black reality and the larger reality of U.S. society; 3) to make ongoing critical analyses of the structure and functioning of U.S. society, especially in terms of race, class and gender; 4) to join severe criticism of internal forces negative to Black progress and liberation with criticism of negative external forces; and 5) to discover, develop and reveal possibilities of social change inherent in both the Black community and the larger society (Ladner, 1999, 1973; Conyers and Barnett, 1999; Staples, 1999, 1976; DuBois, 1975).

Since Black sociology is so inclusive a social science, only a small selection of its concerns can be treated in this chapter. Other major concerns such as politics, economics and social psychology of the Black community will be treated in the other appropriate chapters. The selected concerns which follow are fundamental to understanding Black social organization and are also reflective of issues and problems which are directly related to Black subordination and oppression in U.S. society and Black struggle to end this condition.

6.2   THE PROBLEM OF GHETTOIZATION

The Black community, like other communities is defined by its sharing of common space, experiences, view and value systems, social institutions and self-consciousness. Parts of its common space, however, are bounded areas of living, i.e., ghettos, which not only close Blacks in the community, but simultaneously shuts them out from the access and various opportunities available in the larger society, creating areas of concentrated poverty and isolation (Wilson, 1996, 1978). In *The Truly Disadvantaged* (1989), Wilson had cited some defining features of the ghetto in its more recent form. These included joblessness, social isolation, outmigrations of non-poor Blacks and other ethnic families, and an increase in poverty of those in the area. In his new work, he (1996:42), notes that "additional research on the growth of concentrated poverty suggests another factor: the movement of poor people into a neighborhood (inmigration)." In addition, he stated that still another factor should be added to this mix, changes in the age structure of the community."

Even when Black move beyond the original bounded areas and form what is called "gilded ghettos" in integrated areas, these outskirt communities "also become linked to the central Black area," as whites leave and other Blacks move in (Glasgow, 1981:34). Dudd (1999:145) reaffirms this, stating that "for the most part Black suburbanization does not represent integration; rather it is an extension of racially segregated living patterns in the central cities into close-in suburbs." Moreover, even outside the ghetto physically, Blacks are defined and treated as the majority who are still in the ghetto with allowable variations. Benjamin (1991) argues forcefully that racism, both as an institutional and individual expression, affects the lives of all African Americans regardless of class. She (1991:97) argues that even in the corporate world "there is a sense of ghettoization of Black professionals...."

W.E.B. DuBois (1967) pioneered the scientific study of Black urban life with a major work, *The Philadelphia Negro*, in 1899 and in 1945. In the early 60's, St. Clair Drake and Horace Cayton (1962) published *Black Metropolis*, the first major study which was a systematic and scholarly investigation of the Black ghetto itself. Later in the decade, Kenneth Clark (1965) contributed *Dark Ghetto: Dilemmas of Social Power* which gave an incisive overview of the problems of ghetto life using Harlem as a model.

What appears, then, from DuBois', Drake's and Cayton's, and Clark's analyses, along with others, is a social reality defined by six basic dimensions. First, the ghetto is territorial, i.e., residential, bounded and segregated (Sawyers and Henderson, 2000; Massey and Denton, 1994). In spite of Wilson's (1979) findings of increased suburbanization, Rose (1976) shows that in five major cities, it was simply the expansion of the central city areas or increase in the Black population already in the suburbs. Moreover, Clay (1981:89) reports that suburban migration is limited essentially to the middle class and generally "produces a resegregation pattern where Blacks are concentrated in a few suburban enclaves." Also, racism in housing often blocks even those who might could afford the move from leaving the ghetto (Thomas and Ritzdorf, 1996; Momemi, 1986). Secondly, the ghetto is racial/ethnic, i.e., essentially Black and a product of a racist society which poses race as a central criteria for determining life-chances, opportunities, social status and human worth (Polednak, 1997; Bullard and Feagin, 1991). Thirdly, the ghetto is socio-economic, i.e., marked by what Clark (1965:27ff), in his classic work, *Dark Ghetto*, calls economic and social decay. Clark lists, as symptoms of ghetto life, poor education, poor housing, unemployment, drug addiction and alcoholism, frequent illness and early death, and crime, all accented by "the primary afflic-tion of inferior racial status in a racist society." It is here also that Wilson's (1998, 1996, 1987) concept of the ghetto as an area of concentrated poverty is quite evident and applicable.

Fourthly, the ghetto is institutional, i.e., it has a complex of community institutions, organizations and enterprises which are both a positive and a negative (Spear, 1967). The positive aspect of them is that they are structures necessary for self-determined maintenance and development. But the negative aspect is that they are often not strong enough to fulfill their function or fail to use their strength adequately for social advancement and change (Wilson, 1996: Chapter 3). This becomes even clearer with the loss of a large segment of the middle and working class which built and sustained the institutional base and social net-works (Wilson, 1987:561).

Fifthly, the ghetto is clearly political, i.e., both an expression and product of Black powerlessness to prevent its establishment or end its existence. This relative powerlessness is obviously related to the ghetto's structural incapacity to define, defend and develop its interests as alluded to above. For without strong com-munity structures to resist imposition and advance Black inter-ests, external interests will most likely be imposed. Thus, the ghetto is controlled from outside and it is this external control joined with other factors of ghetto life which led some scholars to argue that it is an internal colony (Cruse, 1968; Clark, 1965). This relative powerlessness is clear in the inner-city's inability to protect itself from what Robert Bullard (1990) calls "environ-mental racism," i.e., turning the ghetto into a toxic waste dump-ing ground, or to direct or benefit fully from some of the most important urban policies put forth, i.e., urban renewal, model cities, etc. (Thomas and Ritzdorf, 1996).

Finally, the ghetto is psycho-cultural, i.e., defined by views, values and self-consciousness negative to its development and transformation into a free, proud and productive community (Poussaint and Alexander, 2000; Carroll, 1998; Wilson, 1992,

1990). Although the psychological aspect will be discussed at length in the chapter on psychology, the cultural dimensions which are directly related will be discussed below. In conclusion, then, it is the reality of ghetto life, the negatives which emerge from it and the solutions posed to correct them and develop a higher level of life that form a significant body of sociological inquiry and prescription concerning the Black community (Tidwell, 2000; Danziger and Gottschalk, 1995).

6.3   THE RACE/CLASS QUESTION

One of the most pressing questions in Black sociology is the significance of race and class in Black life (Clayton, 1996; Hochschild, 1995; West, 1993; Zegeye, et al, 1991. The significance of the question rests not only in its relevance to understanding Black oppression, but also in its relevance in generating strategies for development and liberation. The question of race has become even more pressing in the context of globalization which promises to pose new and difficult challenges for Black people and their ongoing quest for justice and equality and shared power (Lusane, 1997; Persuad and Lusane, 2000). For depending on the weight each or both are given, the Black community correctly or incorrectly grasps the character of its oppression and the theoretical and practical requirements necessary to end it. Since the late Seventies the debate has intensified concerning which is the most important — race oppression or class oppression and how the two interact and relate (Wilson, 1987, 1978; Willie, 1979).

THE CLASS QUESTION

The focus on class as the fundamental unit of social analysis and the key determinant in social life has been provided most definitively by the sociology of Marxism (Bottomore and Rubel, 1964). Marx argued essentially that the shape and functioning of society was determined by its economic foundation and that class, as a socio-economic category, was basic to the understanding of society and history. Furthermore, he contended that productive systems establish given economic roles — farmer, trader, industrialists, worker — and that each group of persons which stands in the same relationship to the means of production (raw materials, factories, machines, etc.) form a class. As a class, each did the same work, had the same basic interests ("real" as opposed to "perceived") and often engage in conflict with other classes. This conflict between classes, he argued, is the motive force of history. Finally, he contended that the economic foundation was the base from which the superstructure (law, religion, politics, ideology, etc.) rose and upon which it rested.

From this materialistic (economic) interpretation of society and history evolved two basic Marxist interpretations of the interaction of race and class, the orthodox Marxist theory (Cox, 1970; Reich, 1981) and the split labor-market theory (Bonacich, 1972). Orthodox Marxists theory argues that racism is a reflection of the manipulation of workers by the capitalist class to divide them along racial lines and reduce their capacity to struggle against the system. This results in encouraging discrimination against Blacks, arguing their inferiority, use of Blacks as a surplus, marginal low-paid work force, and establishing a privileged better-paid racist white labor force. Thus, racism is a function of class struggle, not an independent variable itself. The split labor-market theory argues that racial antagonism begins in the labor-market split along racial lines when business promotes worker competition to displace higher paid labor. If the labor-market split is along racial lines with whites' being the higher-paid and Blacks being the lower-paid labor, class antagonism is transformed into racial antagonism in which whites fight to neutralize or eliminate occupational competition with Blacks.

Both of these class theories of race fail to perceive that race and class interact dynamically as variables in social conflict and position. Although the orthodox Marxist view blames the capitalist and split labor-market theory places the essential burden on the white worker, there are clearly cases where both white capitalists and white workers join to oppress or discriminate against Blacks and other Third World people. Moreover, sometimes it is done for reasons of race and others times for reasons of class and still at other times for both reasons of race and class. Also, in a racist society the class position of a person is greatly determined by his/her race. This is what Fanon (1968:40) meant when he wrote that in a racist context, i.e., the colony, race is the key determinant.

RACE AND RACISM

Blauner (1972:31) also calls attention to the fact that often in a racist society, racial exploitation and/or control becomes "an end itself, despite its original limited purpose as a means to exploitation and privilege." Finally, Turner (1979:31) argues that racism has become so endemic and historically rooted in U.S. society and its institutions that "it exists apart from and in some cases in spite of, the social attitudes of the people who administer these institutions." Thus, the factor of "covert or institutional racism has a dynamic of its own, despite the vagaries of prejudice and bigotry, real as they are." Given all the above contentions concerning race and class and their interaction and relation, it is clear that racism cannot be reductively translated as a function of class or class struggle. Such a position obscures the complexity and variousness of their interplay and their separate relevance as factors in a racist-capitalist society (Franklin, 1991; Staples, 1987).

Moreover, recent literature argues the persistence of race as a major determinant in life-chances and life-conditions (Franklin, 1997; Franklin, 1993; West, 1993; Bell, 1992, 1987; Hacker, 1992). Hacker (1995:13) notes that even those Blacks "who aspire to careers in white institutions, and emulate white demeanor and diction, find that white America lets them only partly past the door." It is in this context of the historical and continuing denial of racial justice to Blacks and others of color that Derrick Bell (1992:ix) concludes, "racism is an integral, permanent and indestructible component of this society" at least in its present form. There are other positions on race and class, but they will be covered in Chapter 8 on economics. However, it is important to note in conclusion, that one of the reasons many social scientists and others have problems in identifying racism is that their definition is deficient. Marxists and non-Marxists tend to see racism as simply attitudes or ideology rather than as multi-faceted phenomenon and process, involving ideology, structure and practice (Allen, 1974). Thus, it is important to define racism in its multidimensional and interrelated aspects (Dijk, 1993; Miles, 1989).

Racism is essentially a system of denial and deformation of a people's history, humanity and right to freedom based exclusively or pri-

marily on the specious concept of race (Karenga, 1981, 1985). Stripped of all its cultural and pseudo-scientific mystification, *race is a socio-biological category designed to assign human worth and social status, using whites as the paradigm.* Racism, then, which begins with the creation and mystification of race, is social thought and practice which expresses itself in three basic ways, i.e., as: 1) imposition, i.e., conquest and oppression of a people, and interruption, destruction and appropriation of a people's history and productive capacity in racial terms; 2) ideology, i.e., an elaborate system of pseudo-intellectual categories, assumptions and contentions negative to peoples of color and serving as justification of the imposition and reinforcement of the institutional arrangement; and 3) institutional arrangement, i.e., a system of political, economic and social structures which insure white power and privilege over peoples of color. Racism, thus, becomes a continuing problem, not only for social inquiry, but also for the quality of social life and the ongoing quest for human freedom and human flourishing.

6.4   THE ISSUE OF CULTURE

Although the question of culture had been raised during the Harlem Renaissance in the 20's, it was during the 1960's that the Black community became more concerned than ever about the possession, meaning, reappropriation and reconstruction of their culture. The shift away from integration as the main goal of the Black Freedom Movement and the resurgence of Black nationalism brought about a renewed interest in Black culture, its role in life and struggle and a profound and pervasive commitment to revitalize, reconstruct and construct it (Karenga, 2002; Woodard, 1999; Van DeBurg, 1993). Expressive of this thrust were the struggle for Blacks Studies which demanded recognition of the Black contribution to society and the world, the look to Africa for inspiration and models and the proliferation of creative artist groups, study groups, literature and institutions which focused on culture. This thrust was both reactive and proactive, defensive and developmental. It sought not only to halt and reverse the racist attempt to negate Black culture, but also to rebuild and build a system of views and values which aided Blacks in their struggle for liberation and a higher level of human life (Gay and Baber, 1997).

THE DEFICIENCY PARADIGM

Social scientists of varying ideological orientation, i.e., conservative, liberal and Marxist, have argued that Blacks have no real culture, that slavery destroyed it, and that what passed as Black culture was simply a pathological reaction to whites, a duplication of them or an expression of lower-class culture rather than a specific Black culture (Myrdal, 1944; Glazer and Moynihan, 1963; Berger, 1967; Liebow, 1967). As Scott (1998) argues, these deficiency paradigm advocates use the damaged imagery model of Black people in varied but equally injurious ways. Conservatives, he notes, have used the image of the damaged Black psyche to elicit white contempt, while liberals have used it to evoke white pity. Thus, not only does this have implications for "race" relations, but also for public policy. Myrdal (1944:927-930) argued that the Black person is "an exaggerated American" and essentially a "pathological" reaction to whites. Also, Glazer and Moynihan (1963:52) contended that the key to understanding Blacks is to recognize they cannot view themselves as other ethnic groups who have a culture. For the Black person "is only an American and nothing else. He has no values and culture to guard and protect."

In his response to Myrdal, Ralph Ellison (1966:316-317), author of the classic work, *Invisible Man*, stated that Myrdal misjudges Black creative and adaptive vitality. He argues cogently that African Americans could not possibly "live and develop for over three hundred years simply by reacting" as Myrdal and others suggest. On the contrary, he posits that Blacks have made self-conscious and self-constructive efforts which have contributed to American culture and have not simply borrowed from the dominant white culture. Nevertheless, Ellison recognized the dynamic interchange between the cultures of America and the tendency toward coercive homogenization as well as the development of homogenization by processes of what we now call the consumer or market culture. But he urged Blacks to hold on to the best of what they have learned and gleaned from life and struggle in U.S. society.

He (1966:39-40) notes that "our situation is changing rapidly, but so much of what we have gleaned through the harsh discipline of (Black) life is simply too precious to be lost." This need to hold to our culture, he asserts, is especially important concerning those things which define us. He says that there are some "things which we dare not fail to adapt to changed situations lest we destroy ourselves. Times change but these possessions must endure forever – not simply because they define us as a group but because they represent a further instance of man's triumph over chaos." Ellison's challenge mirrored much of the response of Black intellectuals of his time to the paradigm of a culturally deficient people vis-a-vis whites.

But it was the Black Cultural Revolution of the Sixties which not only reaffirmed the beauty and integrity of Black culture, Continental and Diasporan, and its difference from white culture in terms of life goals, worldview and values, but also the need to draw on its African and mass sources to recreate and revitalize it and use it as a weapon in the Black struggle (Karenga, 1967; Gayle, 1971). It is, thus, in this period of dynamic confrontation and change that concepts of cultural hegemony, cultural struggle and cultural recovery and reconstruction would become a central part of the discourse on Black liberation (Semmes, 1992). Two of the most important and influential contributions to this discourse in the 60's were the cultural theories of Harold Cruse (1967, 1968) and Maulana Karenga (1967, 1980, 2002).

THE CRUSIAN PARADIGM

Dr. Harold Cruse

Harold Cruse (1967) in his massive study of culture and politics in Harlem, *The Crisis of the Negro Intellectual*, made a profound contribution to the focus on cultural revitalization and struggle. He maintained that cultural oppression is tightly interlocked with political and economic oppression. For cultural control facilitates political control which in turn insures economic control. Thus, he argued that although culture must be seen as central, the three factors of culture, politics and economics must be welded together into a dynamic synthesis and social strategy.

Cruse (1967:7-8) begins his project with the fundamental assumption that group identity in America defines one's life chances and life possibilities. He contends that there is "a very real dilemma inherent in the (African American's) position" and "this dilemma rests on the fact that America, which idealizes the rights of the individual above everything else, is in reality a nation dominated by the social power of groups, classes, ingroups and cliques – both ethnic and religious." In fact, he continues, "the individual in America has few rights that are not backed up by the political, economic and social power of one group or the other." But given that African Americans are treated according to the power and position of their group, those Blacks "and there are many of them, who have accepted the full essence of the Great American Ideal of individualism, are in serious trouble trying to function in America."

Cruse (1967:454) is especially critical of the culturally *deraciné* Black intellectuals "who have no firm base in the reality of either the black world or the white (even when they *have* achieved recognition....)" If one adds to these, he states, " a large fluctuating contingent who make up the bulk of new aspirants to integrated cultural achievement, the result (is) a rootless class of displaced persons who are refugees from the social poverty of the Black World."

The role of the Black intellectual begins with recognition of the cultural base of power in this country as expressed in the power of three main groups – the white Protestants, the white Catholics and the white Jews. The Black intellectuals must likewise root themselves in their own cultural reality, recovering its rich and varied resources and using them to build and reinforce political and economic power. Indeed, Cruse (1967:12-13) states "as long as the (African American's) cultural identity is in question or open to self-doubts, then there can be no positive identification with the real demands of his political and economic existence." And "further than that, without a cultural identity that adequately defines *himself*, the (African American) cannot even identify with the American nation as a whole." On the contrary, "he is left in the limbo of social marginality, alienated and directionless on the landscape of America...."

Moreover, the need is for the Black intellectual to play a

vanguard role in radical change in America linking their rootedness in culture with the political and economic struggle for
shared power in the country. "For American society," he
(1967:45) states, "the most crucial requirement is a complete
democratization of the national cultural ethos." Criticizing the
white ruling class, he (1967:456) contends that in spite of "their
alleged vows to contribute to fashioning of an American nation
worthy of the high esteem of the rest of the world, so far they
have reneged." In fact, "America is an unfinished nation – the
product of a badly-bungled process of intergroup cultural fusion."
In its self-delusion and racist projects, "it has effectively dissuad-
ed, crippled and smothered the cultivation of a democratic cultural pluralism." Thus, there must be a struggle for cultural
democracy by all ethnic groups. However, given the history of
Black people's commitment to and the intensity of their struggle
for freedom, they should assume a vanguard role in this struggle.
And at the heart of the struggle for freedom and democracy must
be a Black cultural revolution. For he (1967:475) states, "there
can be no real Black revolution without cultural revolution as a
corollary to the scheme of 'agencies for social change'."

Finally, Cruse (1967:455) contends that the "Negro intellectuals" can only end their historical crisis of alternating between
integrationist fantasies and pseudo-nationalist responses when
rejected by whites by stepping forward and guiding the masses in
their historic struggle for liberation and cultural democracy. He
states that:

> The special function of the (African American) intellectual
> is a cultural one. He should take to the rostrum and assail
> the stultifying blight of the commercially deprived white mid-
> dle class who has poisoned the roots of the American ethos
> and transformed the American people in a nation of intel-
> lectual dolts. He should explain the economic and institu-
> tional causes of this American cultural depravity. He should
> tell Black America how and why (Blacks) are trapped in
> this cultural degeneracy, and how it has dehumanized their
> essential identity, squeezed the lifeblood of their inherited
> cultural ingredients out of them, and then relegated them to
> the cultural slums.

And finally, these intellectuals "should tell this brainwashed white America, this 'nation of sheep', this overfed, over-developed, over-privileged (but culturally pauperized) federation of unassimilated European remnants that their days of grace are numbered." And this requires a struggle to expand Black intellectual discourse from "piddling intellectual civil writism and racial integrationism," to issues of cultural, economic and political power and return the institutions of power to the people for the good of the nation as a whole.

THE KAWAIDA PARADIGM

Maulana Karenga (1967, 1980, 1997, 2002) places at the heart of Kawaida philosophy the fundamental contention that the key crisis and challenge in Black life is the cultural crisis and challenge and that Africans must recover the best of their culture and use it to envision a new world and to support the struggle to bring that world into being. Speaking to and in the midst of the Black Power Movement in the 60's, he (1967:16) states that "the revolution being fought now is the revolution to win the minds and hearts of our people." In fact, he (1967:20) maintains that "the battle for the mind (and heart) is the first half of the struggle." Thus, Black people must have a cultural revolution before the political one. For the cultural revolution prepares for and makes possible the people's choice and active commitment to wage a political revolution. "The cultural revolution gives identity, purpose and direction," he argues. It reaffirms their right and responsibility to struggle for freedom and it cultivates in them the will to bring forth the best of what it means to be African and human in the fullest sense.

Recognizing the need, however, for struggle on many fronts, Karenga (1967:25) states that "We must move on every level to get power. We must have an organization that thinks, acts, breathes and sleeps on the question of power." In addition, he links cultural politics and economics, arguing as above that without cultural grounding, an effective political struggle cannot be waged and likewise that "you cannot have political freedom without an economic base." The model posed for this economic base is *ujamaa* – a democratic African socialism which is based on "maximum cooperation" and which "must benefit the maximum amount of the community" (Karenga, 1966:26). In a word, ujamaa requires the principle and practice of shared work and shared wealth.

[*Since the 60's, Kawaida has continued to develop, expanding the range of its intellectual and social concerns and contentions. Below is a brief statement by Maulana Karenga, summarizing some of the major contentions of Kawaida philosophy which build on earlier fundamental assertions of the 60's. It appeared in the* **Black Collegian,** *February 1997, under the title "African Culture and the Ongoing Quest for Excellence: Dialog, Principles, Practice."*]

The beginning of the new century unavoidably evokes concerns and calls for a critical assessment of where we are and to what tasks we should direct our attention and efforts in our ongoing quest for a free and empowered community, a just and good society and a better world. In our assessment we are of necessity directed toward the continuing struggle to free ourselves both socially and culturally. In fact, the two struggles are linked in an unbreakable way. For in order to free ourselves socially, we must build a consciousness, cohesion and sense of specialness in community only culture can give. But in order to bring forth the best of our culture, we must struggle to clear social space for its recovery, reception and development. It is in this context that our organization Us (Us, African people) argued in the Sixties and continues to argue that the key challenge in Black life is the cultural challenge. And this challenge is essentially to break beyond the boundaries of the culture of the established order, recover, discover and bring forth the best of our own culture and effectively address the fundamental questions of our world and our times.

The task, as Us perceived it then and contends now, is to forge and embrace a culture which both prepares the people for the struggle and sustains them in the process of the struggle for a world of human freedom and human flourishing. This meant then and continues to mean selecting and stressing elements of Black culture which represent the best of African and human values, values which protect and promote human life, human freedom and maximum human development. It means also recreating liberation-supportive values, views and practices which were lost, damaged or transformed in the midst of oppression and creating new ways of seeing and approaching the world that reinforce and raise up the people, support and sustain the struggle and point toward the new world we struggle to bring into being.

Key to this process of cultural construction and reconstruction is the *ongoing dialog with African culture. Kawaida*, the philosophy of Us organization, defines this dialog as the constant practice of asking questions and seeking answers from African culture to the fundamental and enduring concerns of the African and human community. At the heart of this project is the continuing quest to free ourselves, live full and meaningful lives and become the best of what it means to be both African and human in the fullest sense of the words. Moreover, it involves an ongoing search for models of excellence and possibilities within our culture by which we speak our own special cultural truth to the world and make our own unique contribution to the forward flow of human history.

To truly dialog with African culture means, first of all, using it as a resource rather than a mere reference. This is the meaning of posing questions and seeking answers within African culture concerning central issues of life and the world. To simply use African culture as a reference is to name things considered important, but never use it to answer questions, solve problems or extract and shape paradigms of excellence and possibility in thought and practice. To dialog with African culture, then, is to constantly engage its texts, i.e., its oral, written and living-practice texts, its paradigms, its worldview and values, its understanding of itself and the world, in an ongoing search for ever better answers to the fundamental questions and challenges of our time.

We must always recognize and respect the fact that our culture comes with its own special way of being human in the world and that this particular African way of being human in the world provides a pathway to the universal. For it represents African peoples' way of engaging the fundamental concerns of humankind. Furthermore, our culture has evolved in the longest of histories and thus has amassed a rich and varied array of ancient and modern knowledge, understanding and wisdom concerning the world. Ours is a history of struggle, creativity, achievement and constant concern for the right, the just and the good. It is a history of ancient wonder and achievement in the Nile Valley, awesome tragedy and destruction in the Holocaust of enslavement and impressive triumph in our constant struggle against overwhelming societal odds against us in modern times. And ours is a history of an ongoing commitment to raise up the good even in the midst of the most horrific evil and to pursue the possible in spite of the catechism of impossibilities repeatedly offered us.

Seven Core Areas of Culture

It is within the context of this rich and most ancient of histories and cultures, that we must constantly search for and bring forth the best of what it means to be African and pose new paradigms of human excellence and possibility. This ongoing search for solutions and models of human excellence and possibilities must occur, Kawaida contends, in every area of human life, but especially in the seven core areas of culture: history; religion (spirituality and ethics); social organization; economic organization; political organization; creative production (art, music, literature, dance, etc.) and ethos, the collective self-consciousness achieved as a result of activity in the other six areas.

History. In the area of history, Us maintains, we must study history to learn its lessons, absorb its spirit of possibility, extract and emulate its models of excellence and possibility and honor the moral obligation to remember. We must measure ourselves in the mirror of the best of our history and constantly ask ourselves how can we use the past as a foundation to inform, expand and enrich our present and future. We must always be conscious of our identity as the fathers and mothers of humanity and human civilization in the Nile Valley, the sons and daughters of the Holocaust of enslavement and the authors and heirs of the Reaffirmation of our Africanness and social justice tradition in the Sixties. Surely this is a challenge for intellectual, social and moral excellence, active opposition to all forms of enslavement and an enduring commitment to cultural rootedness, justice and good in the world.

Religion (Spirituality and Ethics). In the area of religion (spirituality and ethics), our culture has the most ancient of ethical traditions, the oldest ethical, spiritual and social justice texts. We introduced the concept of human dignity and divine image of the human person as early as 2140 B.C.E. (before the

common era) in the sacred *Husia*, in the Book of Kheti. We are
the ones in the earliest of time who spoke to the world saying,
"speak truth, do justice, care for the vulnerable, give food to the
hungry, water to the thirsty, clothes to the naked and a boat to
those without one. Care for the ill, be a staff of support for those
of old age, a father to the orphan, a mother to the timid, a raft
for the drowning and a ladder for those trapped in the pit of
despair. Honor the elders and ancestors, cherish and challenge
the children, maintain a right relation with the environment
and always raise up the good and pursue the possible." This is a
tradition we must neither ignore nor abandon.

SOCIAL ORGANIZATION. Our social organization must be con-
stantly concerned with values and practice that affirm and
strengthen family, community and culture. Certainly, the *Nguzo
Saba*, the Seven Principles of Kawaida, which undergird
Kwanzaa, independent schools and rights of passage, family
maintenance, school retention and numerous other community
development and action programs, are key to this. They are:
Umoja (Unity); *Kujichagulia* (Self-Determination); *Ujima*
(Collective Work and Responsibility); *Ujamaa* (Cooperative
Economics); *Nia* (Purpose); *Kuumba* (Creativity); and *Imani*
(Faith). It is within this framework of communitarian values
that we build a peaceful and harmonious togetherness; respect
our special way of being human in the world; build together in
responsibility the relationships, family, community, society and
world we want to live in; share work and wealth; accept the collective vocation of struggle for freedom, justice, peace and
human flourishing in the world; constantly repair and restore
the world, making it ever more beautiful and beneficial and
maintain our faith in the right and the good by working and
struggling to define, defend and develop them in the world.

ECONOMIC ORGANIZATION. In the area of economics, our culture teaches us the principle of *ujamaa* which in its most expansive sense means shared work and wealth rooted in a profound
sense of kinship with other humans and the environment. It
teaches us to be constantly concerned in our economic practice
with the dignity of the human person, with the well-being of
family and community, the integrity of the environment, and
especially with the vulnerable among us: the poor, the ill, the

aged, the captive, the disabled, the refugee and the stranger. For ours is a consciousness born not only of ancient ethical teaching but also the historical experience of the vulnerability of the "motherless child, a long ways from home" as expressed in our sacred songs.

POLITICAL ORGANIZATION. Our culture teaches us to view politics as a collective vocation to create a just and good society and advance human good in the world. It calls on us to honor our most ancient social justice tradition which, as I noted in the *Million Man March/Day of Absence Mission Statement*, "requires respect for the dignity and rights of the human person, economic justice, meaningful political participation, shared power, cultural integrity, mutual respect for all peoples, and an uncompromising resistance to social forces and structures which deny or limit these."

CREATIVE PRODUCTION. The best of African culture insists that our creative production or art not only be technically sound but also socially purposeful and responsible. It is at its best functional, collective and committing. To be functional, is to self-consciously have and urge social purpose, to inform, instruct and inspire the people and be an aesthetic translation of our will and struggle for liberation and ever higher levels of life. It also means searching for and creating new forms and styles to speak our truth and possibilities. To be collective, Black art must be done for all, drawn and synthesized from all, and rooted in a life-based language and imagery rich in everyday relevance. It must be understandable without being vulgarly simplistic, i.e., so pedestrian and impoverished that it does damage to art as a discipline and to the social message it attempts to advance. And it must celebrate not only the transcendent and awesome, but also the ordinary, teaching the beauty and sacredness of everyday people and their struggles to live full, decent and meaningful lives.

Finally, Black art must be committing, i.e., not simply inform and inspire Blacks, but also commit them to the historical project of liberation and a higher level of human life. To do this, it must demand and urge willing and conscious involvement in struggle and building of a new world and new men, women and children to inhabit it. And it must move beyond protest and teach possibilities, beyond victimization and teach Blacks to dare victory. The best of the Black aesthetic teaches that art, then, must commit us to what we can become and are becoming and inspire us to dare the positive in a world often defined and deformed by the negative.

ETHOS. Finally, our culture provides us with an ethos we must honor in both thought and practice. By *ethos*, we mean *a people's self-understanding as well as its self-presentation in the world through its thought and practice in the other areas of culture*. This cultural self-understanding and self-presentation are best summed up in the conclusion I posed in the *MMM/DOA Mission Statement*. The challenge I posed there is the one I pose here as we move forward in the new millennium. It is above all a cultural challenge. For *culture* is here defined as *the totality of thought and practice by which a people creates itself, celebrates, sustains and develops itself and introduces itself to history and humanity*. And so the challenge of our culture is to come to the tasks before us, "bringing the most central views and values of our faith communities, our deepest commitments to our social justice tradition and the struggle it requires, the most instructive lessons of our history, and a profoundly urgent sense of the need for positive and productive action. In standing up and assuming responsibility in a new, renewed and expanded sense, we honor our ancestors, enrich our lives and give promise to our descendants. Moreover, through this historic work and struggle we strive to always know and introduce ourselves to history and humanity as a people who are spiritually and ethically grounded; who speak truth, do justice, respect our ancestors and elders, cherish, support and challenge our children, care for the vulnerable, relate rightfully to the environment, struggle for what is right and resist what is wrong, honor our past, willingly engage our present and self-consciously plan for and welcome our future."

6.5 THE BLACK FAMILY

At the heart of social organization is the way a people organizes its relationships. In fact, another way to define social organization is as *ways of teaching, structuring, validating, changing and expanding social behavior and relationships*. Thus, an important focus of sociology is on the socialization process, i.e., the value and vision orientation designed to instruct and enhance personal and collective behavior and relationships. Nowhere is this more clear than in the discussion of the Black family (Ladner, 1999; McAdoo, 1996; Sudarkasa, 1995). For if the Black family is the smallest example of the nation, i.e., Black people, its strength and weakness greatly determine the capacity of Black people to achieve the social tasks they pose for themselves (Staples, 1999; Taylor et al, 1997; Jones, 1998).

The assessment of the Black family's strength and weakness pervade social science literature (Reed and Hill, 1993; Parker, 1991; Cheatam and Stewart, 1990; Willie, 1988). In fact, much of the literature, if not most, can be assigned to either one school of thought and research or the other. These two approaches to the Black family may be termed the pathological-pathogenic and the adaptive-vitality approaches. The first is predicated on the assumption that the Black family is either pathological or pathogenic or both. That is to say, it is not only a dysfunctional and sick social unit, but produces sick and dysfunctional members of society.

THE PATHOLOGICAL-PATHOGENIC SCHOOL

The pioneering African American sociologist, E. Franklin Frazier (1939), unintentionally may have helped lay the basis for the pathology school in his research on the Black family. He believed that enslavement, urbanization and racism pre-

Dr. E. Franklin Frazier

vented perpetuation of the African family relations and forms and imposed severe strains on the Black family's ability to function effectively. Thus, it developed negative situational adaptations to handle this legacy of oppression and exploitation. From this, he notes, came the matriarchal character of the Black family with its strong women and ineffective and marginal men; its unstable marriages; the prevailing norm of casual sex, and the loss of folk culture cohesiveness in the urbanization process. However, it is important to note here, as indicated above, that Frazier attributed these problems to social causes and to social policies not to an inherent deficiency of Black people and the community.

Daniel Moynihan (1965), using largely census data, tried to

confirm Frazier's conception by statistics (Scott, 1996). Although Frazier had pointed to the social causes of Black family problems, Moynihan blamed social problems on the Black family. Making a generalized indictment of Black families, he (1965:5) argued that "at the heart of the deterioration of the fabric of (Black) society is the deterioration of the (Black) family." Citing Frazier as if to escape the charge of racist sociology, Moynihan charged that the Black community was plagued by pathological and pathogenic families marked by and conducive to matriarchy, broken and ineffective males, delinquency, economic dependency, poor academic performance, unwed motherhood, etc. A storm of criticism rose against this approach and it was generally muted until the rise of a neo-racism during the Reagan era, when it was revived in similar but more invidious works (Murray, 1984)

THE ADAPTIVE VITALITY SCHOOL

The adaptive-vitality school contends that adaptation by Blacks to socio-economic pressures and limitations must not be seen as pathology, but as strength, i.e., adaptive vitality (Ladner, 1999). Billingsley (1992, 1968), McAdoo (1996), Blassingame (1972), Young, (1970), Hill (1999, 1972), Nobles (1987, 1985, 1978), and Nobles and Goddard, (1984), Staples (1999), Sudarkasa, (1995); McCubbin, (1998), and Staples and Johnson (1993) et al, represent this school. Among the propositions they argue are the following: 1) that the Black family is unique and cannot be fitted into a white formula for analysis; 2) that it was not totally destroyed during enslavement; 3) that it has proved its durability and adaptive vitality in the face of severe oppression, and thus, is a strong and functional social unit, even though it has problems which are socially rooted and reflective of ongoing racial and class oppression.

Staples (1999) notes that one of the major problems with the traditional approaches to the study of the Black family has been their tendency to fit it in a white-middle class formula. He argues that the result of this is that the Black family continues to be defined as a pathological unit whose very functioning sustains the conditions of its oppression and basic problems. Staples and Johnson (1993) also make this contention in another work on the Black family, arguing that the problems of Black families are essentially attributable to social conditions of oppression in which they find themselves. Billingsley (1970, 1992) also criticized white social science for focusing almost exclusively on lower income families and ignoring the majority of stable Black families and for blaming lower-class families for their victimization by society. Although, he concedes lower-class family negatives while praising upper-class positives, he nevertheless argues these negatives are socially-rooted. Moreover, he stresses that many misunderstood features of the Black family are sources of strength and raises questions concerning politically suspect conclusions which have social policy implications.

Although proponents of the adaptive vitality approach do not agree on the degree of African influence on African American culture and family, there is agreement that enslavement did not destroy all. Early studies by DuBois (1969) and Carter G. Woodson (1936), as well as Herskovits (1941) showed a legacy from Africa, as well as from enslavement, in African American culture and social institutions. In the 70's, Blassingame (1972) found African survivals in courtship practices, dance, familial roles, folktales, language, music, names, proverbs, and religious beliefs and practice. Blassingame asserted that it is important to realize that "Whatever the impact slavery had on (Blacks') behavior and attitudes, it did not force them to concentrate all their psychic energy on survival." On the contrary, they showed remarkable adaptive vitality in the system of enslavement in spite of the end of contact with Africa when Africans were no longer forcibly imported. Indeed, the enslaved African "was able to retain many cultural elements and (for a while) an emotional contact with his motherland."

Nobles (1978, 1981) posits that Africanity or Africanness is clearly evidenced in African American families. He (1978:22) cites "the actuality of black kinship bonds and the sense of extended family" as an example of this as well as an egalitarian quality to relationships and a profound commitment to the survival of the family (ethnic group). Moreover, he sees Africanity in Blacks' affective rather than economic approach to family life and their sense of collectivity rather than the individualism which is endemic to European culture. Thus, Nobles (1985) argues that viewing the African American family from an Afrocentric perspective is not only key to understanding them, but also indispensable in assisting them in self-strengthening.

Finally, Sudarkasa (1980, 1981, 1995) asserts that both African and enslavement legacies exist. She (1981:37) states that "just as surely as Black American family patterns are in part an outgrowth of the descent into slavery, so too are they partly a reflection of the archetypical African institutions and values that informed and influenced the behavior of the Africans who were enslaved in America." Also she (1981:39) notes, that although there are "relatively few `traces' of direct *institutional transfer* from Africa to America," there are "numerous examples of the *institutional transformation* from Africa to America." Thus, she tends to support Blassingame's contention that Africans were able to build a viable and creative synthesis out of African and European culture. Sudarkasa essentially poses the concept and strength of consanguinity or blood tie kinship as an enduring Africanism as well as the extended family of which it is an expression. "The extended family networks that were formed during slavery by Africans and their descendants were based on the institutional heritage which Africans had brought with them to this continent," she (1981:45) contends. And the specific forms they assumed depend on the cultural, economic and political circumstances in which Blacks found themselves. Martin and Martin (1985) also identify this extended family tradition and reaffirm its relevance to Black family life.

The proponents of the adaptive-vitality model and approach are concerned also that the Black family be viewed and studied as a distinct institution with its own historical tradition and characteristics, not as a pathological or defective variation on the European theme. Although some make a distinction between *alternative* and *adaptive* strategies and forms developed by Black families to meet the challenges of an oppressive social life, that distinction is not made here. As Sudarkasa (1981:37) has noted, the two characterizations of Black families are not mutually exclusive and represent false dichotomies. For adaptive strategies and behavior contribute to the development of alternative formations as the history of the Black family shows. I have used the term adaptive vitality which is the "ability to adjust structurally and ideologically in confrontation with society without losing one distinct character," to absorb stress and strain and bounce back with vigor (Karenga, 1980:51). It is the ability to push past simple survival and develop continuously. It is in the context of the above clarification that the strengths of Black families arguments by proponents of the adaptive-vitality school are presented and have meaning.

Although Sudarkasa, Staples, Ladner, Billingsley, Nobles and others have listed various strengths of Black families, the classic study on this is Robert Hill's (1972) book of the same title, *The Strengths of Black Families*. He revisited and reaffirmed his earlier findings in his new text, *The Strengths of the African American Families Twenty Five Years Later* (1999). In his earlier text, Hill (1972:3) defines family strengths as "those traits which facilitate the ability of the family to meet the needs of its members and the demands made upon it by systems outside the family unit." Having done this, he (1972:4) lists five strengths which an examination of literature on Black families reveals as having been "functional for their survival, development and stability": 1) strong kinship bonds which is stronger among Blacks than whites and expresses itself by absorption of relatives, especially minors and the elderly in various families; 2) strong work orientation, i.e., "the Black poor still are more likely to work than the white poor"; 3) the adaptability of family roles, i.e., male and female can assume each other's household roles in the event of absence, illness, etc.; 4) high achievement orientation, i.e., the majority of low-income students and their parents have college aspirations; and finally, 5) religious orientation.

HARE'S CAUTIONARY CRITIQUE

In criticism of the adaptive-vitality proponents, Nathan Hare (1976) contends the strength-of-the-family school may have unwittingly created their own negatives while challenging the negatives of the pathology-pathogenesis school. First, he (1976:9) states that strength-of-the-family orientation "prohibits any recognition of pathological consequences of our oppression" and thus, undermines the thrust of corrective action. Secondly, Hare (1976: 10) argues that such an approach "fails to incorporate a power-conflict model appropriate to advocates of social change." Finally, Hare (1976:11) contends that the strength-of-the-family approach helps "make it easier for an oppressive society to ignore the heinous conditions it imposes on the Black family." He stresses that he is not advocating victimology, but he has problems with claiming all is well with the Black world at the expense of social criticism.

Hare's contentions point to a serious dilemma of Black scholarship, i.e., how does one prove strength in oppression without overstating the case, diluting criticism of the system and absolving the oppressor in the process? Likewise, the parallel dilemma is how does one criticize the system and state of things without contributing to the victimology school which thrives on litanies of lost battles and casualty lists, while omitting victories and strengths and the possibilities for change inherent in both Black people and society? The answer to these questions are not easily achieved. The tasks of an emancipatory social science are to develop a critical and balanced analysis which reveals Blacks strengths and weaknesses as well as a prescription for self-conscious action to free themselves and to shape reality into their own image and interest. Such, then, is the central task of an emancipatory Black social science.

6.6   BLACK MALE/FEMALE RELATIONS

WOMANIST/FEMINIST DISCOURSE

One of the most important discourses to evolve in Black Studies and in the academy as a whole is the womanist/feminist discourse (Bambara, 1970; Rodgers-Rose, 1980; Gordon, 1987; Hudson-Weems, 1989, 1993; Collins, 2000). Its significance lies first in the rich, varied and instructive voices women bring to the enduring questions of human life. Secondly, it is valuable for the necessary and rightful critique and corrective it poses for the male-dominant order of things. And thirdly, womanist/feminist discourse is also of great value because as female voice and vision, it cultivates a complementarity with male voice and vision, necessary in the human pursuit of truth and good in the world (Cooper, 1982:60; Karenga, 1998: *Odu Ifa*, 10:2, 248:1).

ANCIENT AFRICAN SOURCES

Although the category womanist has its origin in the 80's (Walker, 1983:xi), womanist discourse as a distinctive voice and vision has its origin in ancient Africa. Tiamoyo Karenga (2000) and Chimbuko Tembo (1996) locate evidence of its origins in the sacred texts of ancient Africa, especially *The Husia* of ancient Egypt and the *Odu Ifa* of ancient Yorubaland (Karenga, 1984, 1998; Abimbola, 1976, 1977, 1997). Karenga, (2000:1) states that "although the term womanism was coined in the early 80's, its origin as a movement and philosophy extend back in time to the continent of Africa and the teachings of our ancestors and runs through the teachings of our foremothers and forefathers in the Diaspora." She notes that it is "a constantly evolving tradition" and has its essential origins and foundation in African *"ethical and spiritual teachings and the resultant practices which affirm the dignity, rights, equality and indispensability of women in all things of importance in the world."* Among these concepts are the Husitic or Maatian concepts which express the equal spiritual, moral and social status of women such as: Divine inclusiveness of the male and female principles without being reduced to either; woman and man as *snn ntr*, the image of God, and thus equal bearers of dignity and divinity; the concept of human (*rmt*) customarily written with male and female characters in hieroglyphs, indicating equal male/female dimensions constitute humanity in its wholeness; and the Sebait, the ethical teachings, which taught the equality of female and male. These basic tents were reflected in social practice and gave the ancient Egyptian woman a status far above women of other ancient societies such as Babylonia, Israel, Greece and Rome (Karenga, 1994; Watterson, 1991; Lesko, 1987).

Drawing from the *Odu Ifa*, Karenga cites other spiritual, moral and social concepts which form a philosophical foundation for womanist thought and practice. She includes: the Ifaic concepts of equal status of women and men as *omo Oludumare*, the offspring of Olodumare, God; the Divine assertion of the indispensability of women to everything of importance in the world (Odu, 10:2); the reaffirmation of this and a Divine command to give women due respect and include them fully if we wish to prosper and succeed in the world (Odu, 248:1); and the equal status and obligation of women and men as divinely chosen ones, *eniyan*, that is to say, those who are given the joint and equal task of bringing good into the world (Odu, 78:1).

EARLY REAFFIRMATION AND RECONSTRUCTION IN THE U.S.

Tembo, (1996) draws a distinction between Alice Walker's (1983:xiff) concept of womanist in terms of its root idea and Kawaida womanism. She (1996:1) states that "Walker cites as the root of her term the word "womanish" which historically speaks essentially to a boundary crossing in age. Therefore, the term is socio-historically limited. It does not speak to *the full range of ways of being an African woman in the world* and does not speak to the long history in which the conception of the African woman evolves in its diversity." On the contrary, she concludes "our use of the term derives from the category *womanly* and refers to our constant concern for discovering and practicing the best of what it means to be an African woman in the world."

In this framework, the origins of womanism, as a spiritual, moral and social project begins in Africa, but it is transformed and assumes its more recent forms in the U.S. beginning during the Holocaust of enslavement. Here the tradition is reconstructed and reforged in a new context of the struggle for freedom from enslavement and sexual exploitation and various other forms of oppression. Also, it is shaped in the struggle for family integrity and maintenance, equal rights, self-definition and respect, justice and reaffirmation of our identity and dignity as a people. These are themes which appear repeatedly in the written and spoken discourse of our early foremothers (Logan, 1999; Lowenberg and Bogin, 1993).

Clearly, Maria Stewart's *Productions of Mrs. Maria Stewart* (1835) and her historic speech in 1832 at the Afric-American Female Intelligence Society represent the earliest womanist documents as well as the earliest example of a womanist, feminist or woman's lecture before a mixed audience on political issues in the U.S. (Richardson, 1979). Stewart posits some of the basic recurring themes of womanism in her works (Lowenberg and Bogin, 1993:183-200). These include reaffirmation of our identity as an African people and the obligation to honor the burden and glory of that history both as women and men. She calls on women to distinguish themselves as the daughters of Africa, saying, "O ye daughters of Africa, awake, awake, arise...distinguish yourselves. Show forth to the world that you are endowed with noble and exalted faculties." She challenges them further to dare struggle and greatness asking "O ye daughters of Africa! What have you done to immortalize your names beyond the grave? What example have ye set before the rising generation? What foundation have you laid for generations yet unborn?" Stewart poses a broad communal and societal project for Black women and anticipates the debates about balancing private and public responsibilities.

Thus, she contends that it is right and necessary for women to strive "both in public and private" to end the injustices imposed on them. Also, she critiques religious restraint on women. suggesting Paul's admonition of silence and submission is not to be observed and saying "did Saint Paul but know our wrongs and deprivations, he would make no objections to our pleading in public for our rights." Stewart also was an abolitionist and struggled against enslavement, posing it as a sin against God and the human person. And finally, she challenges Black men to act politically and confront the established order, and called on both women and men to stand up and "enter the field of action" in the struggle for freedom and justice.

Dr. Anna Julia Cooper

Certainly, no early womanist text is more important and representative than Anna Julia Cooper's, *A Voice From the South* (1892). In this seminal volume, Cooper criticizes racism, sexism and classism and argues that "there is a feminine as well as masculine side to truth, that these are related, not as inferior or superior, not as better or worse, not as weaker or stronger, but as complements — complements in one necessary and symmetric whole." Moreover, Cooper (1892:29) argues against elevation of the personal over the collective saying, "we too often mistake individual honor for race development and are so ready to substitute petty accomplishments for sound sense and purpose." She (1892:134) recognized and noted the dual character of her oppression and possibilities as both Black and woman and the essential role women must play in defining "an ideal manhood and womanhood" free from racist, classist and sexist flaws. Recognizing the need to engage in struggle, she was active along with other women in varied causes for freedom and justice, linking them to the critical struggle of women's liberation (Johnson, 1999). Maintaining that the women's cause in this epoch of crisis and struggle is a universal one which will free not only Africans, but Native Americans and other oppressed peoples, she (1892:144) says "To be a woman in such an age carries with it a privilege and opportunity never implied before. But to be a woman of the (African) race in America and to grasp the deep significance of the possibilities of the crisis is to have a heritage, it seems to me, unique in the ages." Finally, Cooper (1892:71) challenges Black men to build a partnership of equals in love and struggle for liberation and a higher level of human life for "nature never meant the ideals and standards of the world should be dwarfing and minimizing ones, and men should thank us for requiring of them the richest fruits they grow." It is this equal partnership in love and struggle that Afrocentric womanists would later pose as the key and priority focus in male/female relationships and womanist discourse.

POST-60's REASSESSMENT

As mentioned in the chapter on Black History, the 70's marked a flourishing of discourse around the issue of Black male/female relations. The discourse originally rose from within the ranks of activist women who had worked in the Black Freedom Movement of the 60's and who, in looking back on their experiences, remembered painful encounters with sexism, marginalization and disappreciation of their contributions. Writings and narratives by key women in the Black Movement such as Toni Cade Bambara (1970a, 1970b), Frances Beale (1970), Ella Baker (Cantarow, 1987) and Septima Clark (Brown, 1986) bear important witness to these problems. In an essay titled "On the Issue of Roles," Toni Cade (Bambara) (1970b) outlined some of the basic criticisms of sexism in the Movement: 1) assignment of silencing and servile roles to women; 2) focusing on problematic notions of manhood and womanhood rather than progressive concepts of "Blackhood"; and 3) talking revolutionary rhetoric about "picking up the gun" rather than facing "the task of creating a new identity, a (new) self" which synthesized the best of both woman and man "via commitment to struggle."

Inherent in Bambara's concerns is a set of charges and challenges which have consistently informed Black women's discourse concerning men's approaches to male/female relationships and relations. Among the major points of focus are: 1) the tendency to define roles which are unequal, exploitative, oppressive, and unresponsive to the demands of equality, reciprocity and mutual benefit; 2) the tendency to subordinate gender issues to racial (people) issues and using calls to unity to suppress difference, critique and challenge; 3) failing to define the terms and goals of the struggle, so that freedom is a collective project and practice and current relations prefigure the new society and community struggled for; 4) resistance to redefining and reconstructing Black masculinity and Black femininity in and for the liberation struggle; 5) inadequate sensitivity to Black women's pain — current and historical — and the need to bear witness to it and have it acknowledged and ended; and 6) frequent unwillingness to be self-critical and self-corrective and to practice partnership in equality rather than relationship in dominance.

The ongoing dialogue around these issues in the 60's was not always conducted in a full, free, frank and principled manner and it began to take an ominous turn in the 70's. Key developments in this dialogue were the publication and resultant discourse around Ntozake Shange's play, *For Colored Girls Who Have Considered Suicide When the Rainbow is Enuff* (1977) and Michele Wallace's *Black Macho and the Myth of the Super Woman* (1979). Major publications in the Black community such as the *Black Scholar*, *Black Books Bulletin* and *Freedomways* provided ample space for the ongoing debate; and the debate was wide-ranging in the community. Toni Morrison's *The Bluest Eye* (1970) and *Beloved* (1987) and Gloria Naylor's *Women of Brewster Place* (1982) among other works by African American women in the 80's not only continued to express the painful and intense conflict between Black men and women, but also revealed the development of Black women's literature as a major, perhaps the primary, way in which this conflict was defined and pursued. Black men writers like Ishmael Reed in *Reckless Eyeballing* (1986) and Trey Ellis in *Platitudes* (1988) responded strongly to this genre of literature and its negative representation of Black men. Other men, on campus and in the community, joined in the criticism and challenge. Thus, the debate around Wallace's work had essentially yielded a series of issues and a pattern of public and private encounters that would repeat themselves in the 80's and 90's (*Black Scholar*, May/June 1979; Karenga, 1979; Staples, 1979). Such exchanges intensified and expanded in the debate around Alice Walker's *The Color Purple* (1983) and culminated in a very bitter and difficult discourse around the Clarence Thomas-Anita Hill confrontation in 1991 (Chrisman and Allen, 1992; Morrison, 1992; Karenga, 1992). Terri McMillan's *Waiting to Exhale* (1992) however, tends to take a different turn and appeared to many men as a call to responsible and principled partnership between Black women and men rather than the condemnatory project they perceived much of other Black women's literature to be.

As it was possible to glean from Toni Cade Bambara's (1970b) concerns a basic set of charges and challenges posed by Black women concerning men's approaches to male/female relations, it is also possible to extract a similar set of concerns from the discussion by Black male writers and other Black men around Black women's literature. Among the major points of focus are: 1) the tendency towards monolithic and reductive characterizations of Black men; 2) the failure to contextualize the problem and critique race, class and gender relations in the context of oppression; 3) subordination of race, community and collective issues to gender and personal ones rather than linking them in a mutually beneficial way; 4) consciously or unconsciously providing the established order and racists in general with negative images of Black men, women and families which they appropriate and use to their advantage against all; 5) the failure to develop an Afrocentric approach to the question of male-female relations and thus an over-reliance on white feminists for both essential categories and concepts; and 6) the unwillingness to be self-critical and self-corrective, moving from an over-abundant discourse on victimization and oppression to one of agency and the practice of freedom.

DISTINCTIONS AND DELINEATIONS

It is important to note here that within the Black women's study project and the Black Women's Movement in general, there exist two intellectual and political tendencies. The first is the Afrocentric womanist tendency which as Stewart (1992:4) notes "embraces the field's (Black Studies') long-standing cultural nationalist ideology" and focuses on "forging a new partnership between Africana men and women in pursuit of previously articulated intellectual and political objectives." Moreover, this body of scholars and activists consider alliances with white feminists problematic at best and use of their theories and practices inappropriate in defining the Black woman's experience and approaching Black male/female relations. On the contrary, they pose rootedness in Black culture as indispensable to creating the new partnership between women and men, free of racist, classist and sexist assumptions and practices (Tembo, 1996; Gordon, 1987; Hudson-Weems,1989, 1993; Hare and Hare, 1989; Rodgers-Rose and Rodgers,1985; Henry and Foster, 1982).

AFROCENTRIC WOMANISM

Some of the common themes which Afrocentric (Africana, Kawaida) womanists constantly raise and reaffirm are: rootedness in African culture; spiritual and ethical grounding; self-definition; sisterhood; partnership with men based on equality; mutual respect and responsibility; dedication to family and community; and commitment to social activism in the interest of liberation and an expanded realm of human freedom and human flourishing. These major common themes are clearly defined and discussed in Hudson-Weems (1993) *Africana Womanism* and Tembo's (1996) "Kawaida Womanism." Although, as noted above, they appear in various forms and formulations throughout the writings of African-centered womanist scholars and activists.

FEMINIST WOMANISM

The other tendency, which may be called either Black womanist or Black feminist, "elevates feminism to a higher ideological status than cultural nationalism..., tends to be more directly connected to traditional academic disciplines...and, more specifically, they are clustered in the areas of literary criticism and creative writing" (Stewart, 1992). Moreover, they are both critical of and collaborative with white feminists, often building alliances with them, but usually trying to maintain a measure of distinctiveness (Guy-Sheftall, 1995). In fact, the category womanist introduced by Alice Walker (1983:xi) is an expression of this desire for distinction. However their priority focus on gender issues and criticism of race focus often finds them unable to establish a clear distinction conceptually between Black and white feminism (Collins, 2000; 1998; Carby,1987; Christian

1989; Hull, Scott and Smith, 1982). However, Collins (1998) has expressed a need for a distinctiveness and the retention of a theory of social group identity and positioning in spite of critiques of essentializing group identities. She also concedes that some Afrocentric concepts and contentions serve the emancipatory interests of Black women when they are void of male-biased implications.

CHRISTIAN WOMANISM

In addition to Stewart's categorization of the two tendencies in the Black woman's emancipatory project, there is a third tendency, Christian womanism, discussed in Chapter 5 and which grows out of a Christian theological project. This tendency of womanism is above all defined by its rootedness in the Christian tradition, its theological search for place, voice and reaffirmation within that tradition, and its concern for how this religious tradition can speak to critical issues of our time (Cannon, 1995; Douglass, 1999; Grant, 1989; Sanders, 1995; Terrell, 1998; Townes, 1995; Williams, 1993). Although the Christian womanists stress the Black experience in the U.S. as the point of departure for engagement, they are not African centered in the pan-African sense in which Afrocentric womanists root themselves in the whole of African culture – ancient and modern, Continental and Diasporan (Sanders, 1995). Also, like their more secular counterparts, they borrow language and concepts from white feminists, even as they criticize their limitations. This contrasts with the Afrocentric womanists who insist on cultural rootedness and distinctiveness.

6.7   THE QUESTION OF QUALITY RELATIONS

THE SIGNIFICANCE OF THE SUBJECT

Within male/female discourse, quality relationships are clearly both a shared aspiration and a constant source of focus. Their importance to both those involved and the larger community are the subject of much literature (Staples, 1981; Gordon, 1987; Rodgers-Rose, 1985; Aldridge, 1989; Hare and Hare, 1989; hooks, 1990, 1992; Tucker and Mitchell, 1995).

Building on this constantly expanding body of literature, male/female relationships can be seen as a fundamental and enduring concern and has importance for several reasons: 1) they have a species character, i.e, they are indispensable to the maintenance and development of the species; 2) they are a measurement of our humanity, i.e., how far humans are from the animal world; 3) they are a measurement of the quality of social life of any given society, i.e., the treatment of women in relationships and by extension in society becomes, as Toure (1959:72) notes, "...a mirror that reflects the economic and social conditions, the level of political, cultural and moral development of a given country;" 4) they are a measurement and mirror of personal development and identity, i.e., a revelation of who persons really are, and finally; 5) they are, a measurement of a people's capacity for struggle and social construction, for as a fundamental unit of the nation, their strengths and weaknesses determine the nation's capacity to define, defend and develop its interests (Karenga, 1978a; Aldridge, 1989; Rodgers-Rose and Rodgers, 1985).

In an important article on the "Dialectics of Black Male/Female Relationships" in her edited book, *The Black Woman*, La Frances Rodgers-Rose (1980a) provides a discussion of male/female relations that retains its currency and cogency in contemporary discourse on this subject. She (1980b:251) begins by attesting the urgency, complexity and importance of the issue. She says "One of the most complex and pressing issues in the struggle for Black survival is centered in and grows out of the relationship between Black men and women." But she urges us to realize that these relationships must be contextualized if we are to understand them in a critical and useful way.

Dr. La Frances Rodgers-Rose

For "the relationship between Black men and women does not take place in a vacuum." Indeed, they take place in a society which assigns roles, stereotypes and oppresses based on race, and provides research and conclusions based on historical and current mythology and misconceptions of the dominant group. What aggravates these external impositions is that too often many African Americans internalize these negative definitions and stereotypical misconceptions of Black people and Black life. And "to the extent that an individual has internalized these definitions, his/her mode of interaction with the opposite sex will be affected."

Rodgers-Rose (1980b:251) calls for a recognition of the "dialectics of creation and criticism" that should inform and undergird any quality relation. For she (1980b:253) is concerned that internalization of the negative societal conceptions of Black men and women will encourage them to focus on criticism of each other and mutual blame "rather than on the interplay between the critical and creative aspects of any male/female relationship." Finally, she is concerned that research has been essentially focused on the surface area of relationships, like outer status factors of income, education and sexual compatibility rather than deeper issues which shape persons' encounter and their interaction. She (1908b:253-254) contends that these issues revolve around "what attracts people to each other and what people are looking for in intimate relations and what qualities make for viable dialectic relationships." Rodgers-Rose (1980b:260) finds in her research that "Black males and females show that they are concerned with the inner qualities of the individual rather than outward qualities." In fact, she notes that in her study, "even the quality of sexual compatibility does not rank as high as the quality of honesty, understanding, independence and proper manners." Certainly, much work has been done since her study, but it clear that qualities and values of one's mate remains high on the list of what makes a relationship work whether in terms of a dyad or a family (Ladner, 2000; Staples, 1999; Sudarkasa, 1996). Also, Rodgers-Rose's stress on social conditions which affect how relationships are conceived and engaged remains a salient factor in recent studies.

No one can honestly deny that there are substantive problems concerning Black male/female relationships (Tucker and Mitchell-Kernan, 1995; Karenga, 1979). This is true whether one focuses on sexism (hooks, 1990; Collins, 1998) or the scarcity of men (Jackson, 1978), or the games one plays to begin and sustain relationships (Staples, 1981), or the self-destructiveness and racist targeting of Black men (Wilson, 1990; Madhubuti, 1990; Gibbs, 1988; Gary, 1981). For in the final analysis, it is the quality of relations that is a key and continuing question and challenge. And this challenge requires serious and sober reassessment and reconstruction of and by both men and women in order to lay the basis for more proactive and mutually beneficial exchanges and relationships.

However, in discussing the problems of Black male/female relationships, it is important to keep in mind at least four fundamental facts. First, Black male/female relationships like Black families are no more problem ridden or pathological than white families and male/female relationships, but given our moral claims and liberational struggle, we are morally compelled to create a context for maximum human flourishing. Secondly, it is important to recognize that real life unavoidably involves problems and problem-solving. The point, then, is not to be without problems, but to be resourceful in devising solutions. Thirdly, it is important to recognize that not all Black male/female relationships are in turmoil and trouble. However, there are enough relationships in turmoil and trouble and enough persons without relationships to make the question of Black male/female relationships necessary for discussion. Finally, it is of equal importance to realize that any criticism of Black male/female relationships is at the same time and in equal measure a criticism of U.S. society which has shaped them to fit and function "properly" in it. For social conditions create both social consciousness and social conduct and failure to recognize this can lead one to see racial defects where social ones are more real and relevant.

It is this final contention that serves as a key point of departure for any serious analysis of Black male/female relationships. For to say we are products of our social conditions is to say the same thing about our relationships. Analyses of the major problems in Black male/female relationships clearly reveal their social rather than genetic or purely personal basis. Thus, to understand the negatives of our relationships we must understand the negative characteristics of society which have shaped them.

These negatives of U.S. society are defined by and derived from three major structural and value systems: capitalism, racism and sexism. Capitalism *is a socio-economic system defined by private ownership of the means to satisfy human needs and the ruthless and continuous pursuit of profit which turns virtually everything into a commodity, i.e., an object for sale and purchase.* Racism *is a system of denial and deformation of a people's history and humanity and right to freedom based primarily or exclusively on the specious concept of race and racial hierarchies.* Sexism *is the social practice of using gender or sex as the key determinant in establishing, maintaining and explaining unequal, oppressive and exploitative relationships and exchanges.* In other words, it is a system of assumptions and acts, theories and practices which imply and impose unequal, oppressive and exploitative relationships based on gender or sex.

Capitalism, then, turns relationships and parts of relationships into commodities and utilitarian arrangements. Racism engenders self-hate, self-doubt and pathological fixation on the white paradigm. And sexism encourages artificial personal power over women as a substitute for real social power over one's destiny and daily life. The result of these three structural and value strains on Black male/female relationships expresses itself as a transformation of the relationships into what can be best described as connections. A connection is *a short-term or tentative association which is utilitarian and alienated and is designed primarily for the mutual misuse of each other.* A quality relationship on the other hand is *a long-term, stable association defined by its positive sharing and its mutual investment in each other's happiness, well-being and development.*

THE CONNECTIONS

There are four basic connections which plague male/female relationships in the U.S. and by logical extension Black male/female relationships: 1) the cash connection; 2) the flesh connection; 3) the force connection; and 4) the dependency connection (Karenga, 1978a). The cash connection grows out of the commodity character of society. It is informed by several capitalistic assumptions among which are: 1) everything and everyone has a price; 2) anything you can't buy ain't worth having anyhow; 3) what you invest money or material assets in is yours; and 4) money is the measure of and solution to everything.

THE CASH CONNECTION

In such a context, mothers tell their daughters to look for and marry someone who can "take care" of them, as if they were disabled; women sell themselves to men, exchanging sex for economic security and call it marriage; teenage men invest materially in young women with a movie and a Mac burger and demand their bodies in exchange; and men claim the right to rule and ruin the lives of their wives and children on the basis of the money they bring in. Money and material consideration, then, form the basis for the cash connection and diminish the chances for a quality relationship which is conscious of but not ruled by material consideration. It often leads to women collaborating in their own oppression.

THE FLESH CONNECTION

The flesh connection grows out of the pornographic character of society and is defined as an association based purely or predominantly on the pursuit of sex. This connection focuses on the body and all the perverse things one can do with all or selected parts of it. Pornography, as a definite social thought and practice and as the essence and source of the flesh connection, expresses itself in five basic ways: 1) as species alienation, i.e., man or woman alienated from and oblivious of his/her species half; 2) objectification of the species half, turning a natural partner into an object of use and disuse; 3) fragmentation of the body, i.e., hacking the body into usable pieces and rejecting the wholeness of the human personality; 4) brutalization, most viciously expressed in the sadomasochistic vulgarities society at its most violent and alienated level has produced; and 5) a sexual commodity form, i.e., the joining of the cash and flesh connection through the packaging and peddling of the human body.

THE FORCE CONNECTION

A third connection is the force connection which rises out of the violent and oppressive character of society. Historically, men have used their greater physical strength to subdue women and win arguments they would otherwise lose. Moreover, the flesh and force connection merge in the act of rape which is not so much sexual as it is psycho-cultural and physical. For above all, it is an act of domination practiced by husbands, friends and strangers (Karenga, 1978a:15).

Also, there is social or ideological coercion which forces women, through censure and labeling, into roles which degrade and silence. As Vivian Gordon (1987:18,19) notes, "we are all familiar with the denigrating labels which confront the Black woman who strikes out and dares to maintain a valued self; such women are variously viewed to be: domineering, aggressive, probably threatening to the man, bad looking/bad acting women that no man wants." The tragedy, she says is that many Black women have accepted these stereotypes but fortunately "the majority of Black women have managed to maintain positive self-identities". The force connection also expresses itself in economic coercion. This operates on the principle that whoever controls the means to satisfy human needs controls at the same time the humans with those needs.

THE DEPENDENCY CONNECTION

The fourth and final connection which challenges and often denies quality Black male/female relationships is the dependency connection. This connection is the logical and inevitable result of the others. After a woman has been transformed into a commodity, reduced to parts of her body and physically or ideologically whipped into compliance, she can only be dependent. Like all enslaved persons and servants, she becomes a set of reactions to her slaveholder, a defender of his definitions and treatment of her (Ali, 1989; Madhubuti, 1990). Thus, interdependence, a key value in quality relationships, becomes impossible and the connection becomes the model rather than the deviance (Nobles, 1978).

TOWARD SOLUTIONS

Given the seriousness of the problem, it is only logical to ask what is the solution? The solution like the problem has both a personal and social dimension and requires transformation on both levels. Although, one can argue that conditions create consciousness, consciousness and the social practice that it engenders can and often do create conditions. Certainly, capitalism, racism and sexism shape our relationships, but they are systems created and maintained by humans and they can be changed and rebuilt by humans. Without such a proactive conception of human possibility, neither personal nor social change is possible (Hudson-Weems, 1993; Tembo, 1996; Chapman, 1996).

But the struggle to change systems must begin with the struggle of a people to change themselves, i.e, their own views and values and the negative and non-productive ways they have organized and live their daily life. Only then can they self-consciously rebuild their relationships and begin to change the social conditions which deform and deny these relationships.

The solution to deficient relations, then, is rooted in the creation, acceptance and practice of a value system which produces the attitudes and practices necessary to build and sustain quality relationships. Ladner (2000:8ff, 1971:269), Staples (1981:231-232) and Sudarkasa (1996:64ff) argue the need for a value system which rejects and counters the standards of the dominant society. "We must seek other alternative and more viable standards," Ladner (1971:269) asserts. For the U.S. model "which purports to be the exemplary one" is not only negative to Black interest, but also "is in the process of internal destruction, and there is little within it which seems worthy of salvaging." This requires an alternative value system which calls for a redefinition of reality in Blacks' own interest and image, for a new definition of man and woman and the kind of relationship they ought to have.

Real relationships must begin with terms clearly stated, and then grow and are reinforced by common values, common interests and aspirations, quality commitment, support structures, continuous renewal, and common struggle for liberation and a higher level of human life (Karenga, 1980:47-48). For in the final analysis, the call for an end to problematic and deficient relationships, must be a call for an end to the social conditions which created and sustain them. One must begin with a *moral minimum* that cannot be compromised, a set of values which are resistant to revision because they are at the very roots of the relationship. Prohibition against violence; full, free and frank discussion; egalitarian exchange; collective decision-making; and shared responsibility in love and struggle must be a part of that moral minimum, if a relationship is to be real and mutually beneficial. Moreover, it is important that women continue to define and fight for the freedom, equality and the kind of relationships they need and want, that they reconstruct their supportive links with each other and speak their own African truth of what it means to be a woman-in-community. Likewise, men must stand upright, assume a moral posture on the personal and the political level and reconstruct themselves in relationship with and in consideration of women.

It is important to repeat that any solution that evolves must be a collective and community-affirming solution, one that honors the moral demands of equality, mutual respect and reciprocity. It is this conception of person-in-community, being of equal worth, rights and respect that stands at the center of any Afrocentric conception of man/woman relations. Rodgers-Rose (1980:12, 13) in her early work on the Black woman reaffirmed this location and rootedness in community, saying the authors of articles in her book "stress the point that the history and lives of Black women cannot be separated from the history and lives of Black men and Black children." Thus, the need became one of studying and reconstructing relations among them to achieve maximum human flourishing.

Sudarkasa (1996:143ff) urges us "to draw on our heritage as a people" and to embrace "the values of "respect, responsibility, reciprocity, restraint, reverence, reason and reconciliation" which will build and sustain our relationships, families and our people as a whole. Also Vivian Gordon (1987:13) reaffirms the need for this building of relations in the context of building and liberation the Black community, stating that "African women are in a partnership struggle with Black men for the emancipation of their communities." Defining a fundamental aspect of Afrocentric feminism, Clenora Hudson-Weems (1989:187) argues that "The Africana womanist...perceives herself as the companion to the Africana man, and works diligently toward continuing their established union in the struggle against racial oppression." And in *Africana Womanism* (1993), she (1993:61) affirms that "the Africana womanist is...*in concert with males* in the broader struggle for humanity and the liberation of all African people." But the community cannot stifle, cannot impose silence or abusive conformity on women or any of its members. On the contrary, if it stifles voices, it stifles itself and will wither and decay morally and culturally. Maximum freedom is the basis for maximum human flourishing, and social freedom as well as social oppression are ultimately expressed or exposed in the quality of human relations.

This, however, is just a beginning and an outline of possibilities. The realities will be built by those *New Africans* in U.S. society who dare to be other than their immediate and social conditions encourage them to be. Staples (1981:232) has correctly observed that, "Now we stand at the crossroads of a major decision about which way we will proceed to order our lives." The choice is clearly between the continuation of the current social and personal state of things or self-conscious intervention to change it and build a better society and more life-affirming, moral and meaningful relationships. And as Staples concludes, "Whatever the decision may be, we should not be deluded into believing that the consequences are individual ones. The future of the race may be at stake."

STUDY QUESTIONS

1. Define social organization.
2. What are some basic aims of Black sociology as an emancipatory social science?
3. What are the basic characteristics of the ghetto?
4. What are the possible resource structures and some proposed solutions to problems of the ghetto?
5. Discuss the race/class controversy.
6. What is racism? Discuss its three basic aspects.
7. Discuss Kawaida's position on cultural revolution.
8. What are the two basic approaches to the study of the Black family? What are their basic concerns and contentions?
9. What are Hare's contentions about the strength-of-the-family advocates and the problems these pose for a critical and emancipatory social science?
10. Discuss womanist/feminist concerns about Black male/female relationships.
11. Discuss the men's concerns with the womanist/feminist approach to male/female relationships.
12. Define and discuss the differences and commonalities between the Afrocentric womanists and other Black womanists/feminists.
13. What are the reasons male/female relationships are so important?
14. What four fundamental facts must be kept in mind when discussing Black male/female relations?
15. What three structural and value tendencies of U.S. society help shape male/female relations?
16. What are the four basic connections in male/female relations?
17. What are some basic solutions to the problem of male/ female relations?

REFERENCES

Abimbola, Wande. (1976) *Ifá: An Exposition of the Ifá Literary Corpus*, Ìbàdàn, Nigeria: Oxford University Press.

Abimbola, Wande. (1977) *Ifá Divination Poetry*, New York: London, Lagos: Nok Publishers.

Abimbola, Wande. (1997) *Ifá Will Mend Our Broken Ways: Thoughts on Yoruba Religion and Culture in Africa and the Diaspora*, Roxbury, MA: Aim Books.

Aldridge, Delores. (ed.) (1989) *Black Male - Female Relationships: A Resource Book of Selected Materials*, Dubuque, IA: Kendall/Hunt Publishing Co.

Ali, Shaharazad. (1989) *The Blackman's Guide to Understanding the Black Woman*, Philadelphia: Civilized Publications.

Allen, Robert. (1974) *Reluctant Reformers*, Washington, D.C.: Howard University Press.

Anderson, Elijah. (1992) *Streetwise: Race, Class and Change in an Urban Community*, Chicago: University of Chicago Press.

Bambara, Toni Cade. (1970a) "On The Issue of Roles," in *The Black Woman: An Anthology*, Toni Cade Bambara, (ed.) New York: Signet, 101-110.

Bambara, Toni Cade. (1970b) *The Black Woman: An Anthology*, New York: Signet.

Beale, Frances. (1970) "Double Jeopardy: To Be Black and Female," in *The Black Woman: An Anthology*, Toni Cade Bambara, (ed.) New York: Signet, 90-100.

Bell, Derrick. (1987) *And We Are Not Saved: The Elusive Quest for Racial Justice*, New York: Basic Books.

Bell, Derrick. (1992) *Faces at the Bottom of the Well: The Permanence of Racism*, New York: Basic Books.

Benjamin, Lois. (1991) *The Black Elite: Facing the Color Line in the Twentieth Century*, Chicago: Nelson-Hall Publishers.

Berger, Bennett. (1967) "Soul Searching," *Trans-Action*, (June) 54-57).

Billingsley, Andrew. (1970) "Black Families and White Social Science," *Journal of Social Issues*, 26, 3 (Summer) 127-142.

Billingsley, Andrew. (1968) *Black Families in White America*, Englewood Cliffs, NJ: Prentice-Hall, Inc.

Billingsley, Andrew. (1992) *Climbing Jacob's Ladder: The Enduring Legacy of African-American Families*, New York: Simon & Schuster.

Blassingame, John. (1972) *The Slave Community*, New York: Oxford University Press.

Blauner, Robert. (1972) *Racial Oppression in America*, New York: Harper & Row, Publishers.

Bonacich, Edna. (1972) "A Theory of Ethnic Antagonism: The Split Labor Market," *American Sociological Review*, 37 (October), 547-559.

Bottomore, T.B. and Maximilien Rubel. (1964) *Karl Marx: Selected Writings in Sociology and Social Philosophy*, New York: McGraw Hill.

Branch, Taylor. (1988) *Parting the Waters: America in the King Years*, New York: Simon & Shuster.

Brown, Cynthia Stokes. (ed.) (1986) *Ready From Within: Septima Clark and the Civil Rights Movement*, Navarro, CA: Wild Trees Press.

Bullard, Robert. (1990) *Dumping in Dixie: Race, Class and Environmental Quality*, Boulder, CO: Westview Press.

Bullard, Robert and Joe Feagin. (1991) "Racism in the City," in Mark Gottdiener and C.V. Pickvance, (eds.) *Urban Life in Transition*, Newbury Park, CA: Sage Publications.

Carroll, Grace. (1998) *Environmental Stress and African Americans: The Other Side of the Moon*, Wesport, CT: Greenwood.

Cannon, Katie. (1995) *Katie's Cannon: Womanism and the Soul of the Black Community*, New York: Continuum.

Cantarow, Ellen. (1987) *Moving the Mountain: Women Working for Social Change*, Old Westbury, NY: Feminist Press.

Carby, Hazel. (1987) *Reconstructing Womanhood: The Emergence of the Afro-American Woman Novelist*, New York: Oxford University Press.

Carson, Claybourne et al. (1987) *Eyes on the Prize Reader*, New York: Penguin Books.

Chapman, Audrey B. (1996) *Getting Good Loving: How Black Men and Women Can Make Love Work*, New York: Ballantine Publishing.

Cheatam, Harold and James Stewart. (1990) *Black Families: Interdisciplinary Perspectives*, New Brunswick, NJ: Transaction.

Chrisman, Robert and Robert Allen, (eds.) (1992) *Court of Appeal: The Black Community Speaks Out on the Racial and Sexual Politics of Clarence Thomas vs. Anita Hill*, New York: Ballantine Books.

Christian, Barbara. (1989) "But Who Do You Really Belong To Black Studies or Women Studies?" *Women Studies*, 17, 1/2, 17-23.

Clark, Kenneth. (1965) *The Dark Ghetto*, New York: Harper & Row Publishers.

Clay, Phillip. (1981) "Housing and Neighborhoods," in *The State of Black America-1981*, New York: National Urban League.

Clayton, Obie, Jr. (eds.) (1996) *An American Dilemma: Revisited Race Relations in a Changing World*, New York: Russel Sage Foundation.

Collins, Patricia Hill. (2000) *Black Feminist Thought: Knowledge, Consciousness, and the Politics of Empowerment*, London: Routledge.

Collins, Patricia Hill. (1998) *Fighting Words: Black Women and the Search for Justice*, Minneapolis: University of Minnesota Press.

Conyers, James, Jr. and Alva P. Barnett (eds.) 1999) *African American Sociology: A Social Study of the Pan-African Diaspora*, Chicago: Nelson-Hall Publishers.

Cooper, Anna Julia. (1892) *A Voice From the South*, Xenia, OH: Aldine Printing House.

Cox, Oliver C. (1970) *Caste, Class and Race*, New York: Monthly Review Press.

Cruse, Harold. (1967) *The Crisis of the Negro Intellectual*, New York: William Morrow.

Cruse, Harold. (1987) *Plural But Equal: A Critical Study of Blacks and Minorities in American's Plural Society*, New York: William Morrow and Company.

Cruse, Harold. (1968) *Rebellion or Revolution?* New York: William Morrow.

Daniels, Lee (ed.), (1998) *The State of Black America*, New York: National Urban League.

Danziger, Sheldon H. and Peter Gottschalk. (1995) *America Unequal*, Cambridge: Harvard University Press.

Douglas, Kelly Brown. (1999) *Sexuality and the Black Church: A Womanist Perspective*, MaryKnoll, NY: Orbis Books.

Drake, St. Clair and Horace R. Cayton. (1962) *Black Metropolis*, New York: Harper & Row Publishers.

DuBois, W.E.B. (1969) *The Negro American Family*, New York: New American Library.

DuBois, W.E.B. (1967) *The Philadelphia Negro*, New York: Schocken Books.

DuBois, W.E.B. (1959) "The Talented Tenth," in Ulysses Lee, (ed.) *The Negro Problem*, New York: Arno Press and New York Times, pp. 31-76.

DuBois, W.E.B. (1975) *W.E.B. DuBois on Sociology and the Black Community*, (eds.) Dan Green and Edwin Driver, Chicago: University of Chicago Press.

Ellison, Ralph. (1966) *Shadow and Act*, New York: New American Library.

Fanon, Frantz. (1968) *The Wretched of the Earth*, New York: Grove Press.

Farmer, James. (1985) *Lay Bare the Heart: An Autobiography of the Civil Rights Movement*, New York: Arbor House.

Foster, Frances S. (1990) *A Brighter Coming Day: A Frances Ellen Watkins Harper Reader*, New York: The Feminist Press and City University of New York.

Franklin, Donna L. (1997) *Ensuring Inequality: The Structural Transformation of the African American Family*, Columbus: Ohio University Press.

Franklin, John Hope. (1993) *The Color Line: Legacy for the Twenty-First Century*, Columbia: University of Missouri Press.

Franklin, Raymond S. (1991) *Shadows of Race and Class*, Minneapolis: University of Minnesota Press.

Frazier, E. Franklin. (1973) "The Failure of the Negro Intellectual," in Joyce A. Ladner, (ed.) *The Death of White Sociology*, New York: Vintage Books, pp. 52-66.

Frazier, E. Franklin. (1939) *The Negro Family in America*, Chicago: University of Chicago Press.

Frazier, E. Franklin. (1957) *The Negro in the United States*, New York: Macmillan Company.

Garrow, Paul. (1986) *Bearing the Cross: Martin Luther King, Jr. & the Southern Christian Leadership Conference*, New York: Morrow.

Gary, Lawrence E. (ed.) (1981) *Black Men*, Beverly Hills: Sage Publications.

Gates, Henry Louis, Jr. and Cornel West. (1997) *The Future of the Race*, New York: Vintage Books.

Gay, Geneva and Willie L. Baber, (eds.) (1997) *Expressively Black: The Cultural Basis of Ethnic Identity*, Westport, CT: Greenwood Press.

Gayle, Addison. (1971) *The Black Aesthetic*, New York: Doubleday & Co.

Gibbs, Jewelle Taylor. (1988) *Young, Black, and Male in America: An Endangered Species*, Dover: Auburn House.

Glasgow, Douglas. (1981) *The Black Underclass*, New York: Vintage Books.

Glazer, Nathan and Daniel P. Moynihan. (1963) *Beyond the Melting Pot*, Cambridge: M.I.T. and Harvard University Press.

Gordon, Vivian. (1987) *Black Women, Feminism and Black Liberation: Which Way?* Chicago: Third World Press.

Grant, Jacquelyn. (1989) *White Women's Christ and Black Women's Jesus: Feminist Christology and Womanist Response*, Atlanta: Scholars Press.

Guy-Sheftall, Beverly. (ed.) (1995) *Words of Fire: An Anthology of African American Feminist Thought*, New York: New Press, Norton.

Hacker, Andrew. (1995) *Two Nations: Black and White, Separate, Hostile, Unequal*, Revised Edition, New York: Ballantine Publishing Group.

Harding, Vincent. (1987) *Hope and History: Why We Must Share the Story of the Movement*, Maryknoll, NY: Orbis

Hare, Bruce R. (1988) "Black Youth at Risk," in National Urban League *The State of Black America 1988*, New York: National Urban League, Inc.

Hare, Nathan. (1965) "The Challenge of a Black Scholar," in *The Death of White Sociology*, Joyce A. Ladner, (ed.) New York: Vintage Books, pp. 67-78.

Hare, Nathan. (1976) "What Black Intellectuals Misunderstand About the Black Family," *Black World*, (March) 5-14.

Hare, Nathan and Julia Hare. (1989) *Crisis in Black Sexual Politics*, San Francisco: The Black Think Tank.

Henry, C. and F. Foster. (1982) "Black Women's Studies: Threat or Challenge?" *Western Journal of Black Studies*, 6, 1, 15-21.

Herskovits, M. (1941) *The Myth of the Negro Past*, New York: Harper & Row, Publishers.

Hill, Robert. (1999) *The Strengths of African American Families Twenty Five Years Later*, Washington, D.C.: R & B Publishers.

Hill, Robert. (1972) *The Strengths of the Black Family*, New York: Emerson Hall.

Hochschild, Jennifer. (1995) *Facing Up to the American Dream: Race, Class and the Soul of the Nation*, Princeton: Princeton University Press.

hooks, bell. (1990) *Yearning: Race, Gender and Cultural Politics*, Boston: South End Press.

hooks, bell. (1992) *Black Looks: Race and Representation*, Boston: South End Press.

Hudson-Weems, Clenora. (1993) *Africana Womanism: Reclaiming Ourselves*, Troy, MI: Bedford Publishers.

Hudson-Weems, Clenora. (1989) "Cultural and Agenda Conflicts in Academia: Critical Issues for Africana Women's Studies," *Western Journal of Black Studies*, 13, 4, 185-189.

Hull, Gloria, Patricia Bell Scott and Barbara Smith. (eds.) (1982) *All the Women are White, All the Blacks are Men, but Some of Us are Brave*, Old Westbury, NY: Feminist Press.

Jackson, Jacqueline. (1978) "But Where Are the Men?" in *The Black Family: Essays and Studies*, Robert Staples, (ed.) Belmont, CA: Wadsworth Publishing Company, pp. 110-117.

Johnson, Karen A. (1999) *Uplifting the Women of the Race: The Lives, Educational Philosophies and Social Activism of Anna Julia Cooper and Nannie Helen Borroughs*, New York: Garland.

Jones, Reginald, (ed.) (1997) *African American Children, Youth and Parenting*, Hampton: Cobbs and Henry Publications.

Judd, Dennis R. (1999) "Symbolic Politics and Urban Policies: Why African Americans Got So Little from the Democrats," in Adolph Reed, Jr. (ed.), *Without Justice for All: The New Liberalism and Our Retreat from Racial Equality*, Boulder, CO: Westview Press.

Karenga, Maulana. (1997) "African Culture and the Ongoing Quest for Excellence: Dialog, Principles, Practice," *Black Collegian*, (February) 160-163.

Karenga, Maulana. (1985) "The African Intellectual and the Problem of Class Suicide: Ideological and Political Dimensions," in Molefi Kete Asante and Kariamu Welsh Asante (eds.) *African Culture: The Rhythms of Unity*, Westport, CT: Greenwood Press.

Karenga, Maulana. (1978a) *Beyond Connections: Liberation in Love and Struggle*, New Orleans: Ahidiana.

Karenga, Maulana. (1978b) *Essays on Struggle: Position and Analysis*, San Diego: Kawaida Publications.

Karenga, Maulana. (2002) *Kawaida: A Communitarian African Philosophy*, Los Angeles: University of Sankore Press.

Karenga, Maulana. (1980) *Kawaida Theory: An Introductory Outline*, Inglewood: Kawaida Publications.

Karenga, Maulana. (1994) *Maat, The Moral Ideal in Ancient Egypt: A Study in Classical African Ethics.* Unpublished dissertation, University of Southern California, Los Angeles.

Karenga, Maulana. (1995) *Million Man March/Day of Absence Mission Statement,* Los Angeles: University of Sankore Press.

Karenga, Maulana. (1998) *Odu Ifa: The Ethical Teachings,* Los Angeles: University of Sankore Press.

Karenga, Maulana. (1979) "On Wallace's Myths: Wading Thru Troubled Waters," *Black Scholar,* 10, 8 (May/June) 36-39.

Karenga, Maulana. (1981) "The Problematic Aspects of Pluralism: Ideological and Political Dimensions" in *Pluralism, Racism and Public Policy: The Search for Equality,* Edwin G. Clausen and Jack Bermingham, (eds.) Boston: G.K. Hall & Co., pp. 223-246.

Karenga, Maulana. (1967) *The Quotable Karenga,* Clyde Halisi and James Mtume, (eds.) Los Angeles: Saidi Publications.

Karenga, Maulana. (1984) *Selections From The Husia: Sacred Wisdom of Ancient Egypt,* Los Angeles: University of Sankore Press.

Karenga, Maulana. (1982) "Society, Culture and the Problem of Self-Consciousness: A Kawaida Analysis," in *Philosophy Born of Struggle: Anthology of Afro-American Philosophy From 1917,* Leonard Harris, (ed.) Dubuque, IA: Kendall/Hunt; pp. 212-228.

Karenga, Maulana. (1992) "Under the Camouflage of Color and Gender: The Dred and Drama of Thomas-Hill," in Robert Chrisman and Robert A. Allen, (eds.) *Court of Appeal,* New York: Ballantine Books.

Karenga, Tiamoyo. (2000) "A Brief History of Kawaida Womanism," paper presented at the African American Cultural Center, (March), pp. 1-11).

Kluger, Richard. (1976) *Simple Justice: The History of Brown v. Board of Education and Black America's Struggle for Equality,* New York: Knopf.

Ladner, Joyce. (1973) *The Death of White Sociology,* New York: Vintage Books.

Ladner, Joyce. (1999) *The Ties That Bind: Timeless Values for African American Families,* New York: Wiley.

Ladner, Joyce. (1971) *Tomorrow's Tomorrow: The Black Woman,* Garden City, N.Y.: Anchor Books.

Lesko, Barbara. (1987) *The Remarkable Women of Ancient Egypt,* Providence, RI: B.C. Scribe Publications.

Lusane, Clarene, (1997) *Race in a Global Era: African Americans at the Millennium,* Boston: South End Press.

Liebow, Elliot. (1967) *Tally's Corner,* Boston: Little, Brown & Co.

Logan, Shirley. (1999) *We Are Coming, The Persuasive Discourse: Nineteenth Century Black Women,* Carbondale: Southern Illinois University Press.

Lowenberg, Bert James and Ruth Bogin, (eds.) (1993) *Black Women in Nineteenth-Century American Life*, University Park: Pennsylvania State University Press.

Madhubuti, Haki. (1990) *Black Men: Obsolete, Single, Dangerous?* Chicago: Third World Press.

Madhubuti, Haki. (ed.) (1990) *Confusion By Any Other Name*, Chicago: Third World Press.

Madhubuti, Haki. (1980) "Not Allowed to Be Lovers," *Black Books Bulletin*, 6, 4, pp. 48-57, 71.

Martin, E. P. and J. M. Martin. (1985) *The Black Extended Family*, Chicago: University of Chicago Press.

Massey, Douglas S. and Nancy A. Denton. (1994) *American Apartheid: Segregation and the Making of the Underclass*, Cambridge: Harvard University Press.

McAdam, Doug. (1983) *Political Process and the Development of Black Insurgency 1930-1970*, Chicago: Chicago University Press.

McAdoo, Harriette P. (ed.) (1996) *Black Families*, 3rd Edition, Newbury Park, CA: Sage Publications.

McCubbin, Hamilton. (1998) *Resiliency in African American Families*, Newbury Park, CA: Sage Publications.

Miles, Robert. (1989) *Racism*, London: Routledge.

Momemi, Jamshid (ed.). (1986) *Race, Ethnicity and Housing in the United States*, Westport, CT: Greenwood Press.

Morris, Aldon. (1984) *The Origins of the Civil Rights Movement* New York: Free Press.

Morrison, Toni, (ed.) (1992) *Race-Ing Justice, En-Gendering Power: Essays on Anita Hill, Clarence Thomas and the Construction of Social Reality*, New York: Pantheon Books.

Moynihan, Daniel. (1965) *The Negro Family*, Washington, D.C.: Office of Planning and Research, U.S. Dept. of Labor.

Myrdal, Gunnar. (1944) *An American Dilemma*, New York: Harper & Row Publishers.

Nobles, Wade. (1987) *African American Families: Issues, Ideas and Insights*, Oakland: Black Family Institute.

Nobles, Wade. (1985) *Africanity and the Black Family*, 2nd Edition, Oakland: Black Family Institute.

Nobles, Wade. (1981) "African-American Family Life," in, *An Instrument of Culture*, Harriette P. McAdoo, (ed.) Beverly Hills: Sage Publications.

Nobles, Wade. (1978) "Africanity: Its Role in Black Families," in *The Black Family: Essays and Studies*, Robert Staples, (ed.) Belmont, Ca: Wadsworth Publishing Co., pp. 19-25.

Nobles, Wade and L.L. Goddard. (1984) *Understanding the Black Family: A Guide to Scholarship and Research*, Oakland: Black Family Institute.

Parker, Matthew. (1991) *The Black Family: Past, Present and Future; Perspectives of Sixteen Black Christian Leaders*, Grand Rapids: Zondervan Publishing House.

Persuad, Randolph B. And Clarence Lusane. (2000) "The New Economy, Globalisation and the Impact on African Americans," *Race & Class*, 42:21-34.

Pinderhughes, Dianne M. (1988) "Civil Rights and the Future of the American Presidency," in *National Urban League, The State of Black America 1988*, New York: National Urban League, Inc.

Polednak, Anthony P. (1997) *Segregation, Poverty and Morality in Urban American Americans*, Columbus: Ohio University Press.

Poussaint, Alvin P. and Amy Alexander. (2000) *Lay My Burden Down: Suicide and Mental Health Crisis Among African Americans*, Boston: Beacon Press.

Reed, Wornie L. and Robert B. Hill, (eds.) (1993) *Research on the African American Family: A Holistic Perspective*, Westport, CT: Greenwood Press.

Reich, Michael. (1981) *Racial Equality*, Princeton: Princeton University Press.

Richardson, Marilyn, (ed.) (1979) *Maria W. Stewart, America's First Black Woman Political Writer, Essays and Speeches*, Bloomington: Indiana University Press.

Rodgers-Rose, La Frances. (ed.) (1980a) *The Black Woman*, Beverly Hills, CA: Sage Publications.

Rodgers-Rose, La Frances. (1980b) "Dialectics of Black Male/Female Relationships" in *The Black Woman*, La Frances Rodgers-Rose, (ed.) Beverly Hills, CA: Sage Publications.

Rodgers-Rose, La Frances and James T. Rogers. (1985) *Strategies for Resolving Conflict in Black Male and Female Relationships*, Newark: Traces Institute Publications.

Rose, H.M. (1976) *Black Suburbanization*, Cambridge, MA: Ballinger.

Sanders, Cheryl J. (ed.) (1995) *Living in the Intersection: Womanism and Afrocentrism in Theology*, Minneapolis: Fortress Press.

Sawyers, Andrew and Lenneal Henderson. (2000) "Race, Space and Justice: Cities and Their Growth in the 21st Century," in Lee Daniels, (ed.) *State of Black America*, New York: National Urban League.

Scott, Daryl M. (1997) *Contempt & Pity: Social Policy and the Image of the Damaged Black Psyche, 1880-1996*, Chapel Hill: University of North Carolina Press.

Scott, Daryl M. (1996) "The Politics of Pathology: The Ideological Origins of the Moynihan Controversy," *Journal of Policy History*, 8:81-105.

Semmes, Clovis E. (1992) *Cultural Hegemony and African American Development*, Westport, CT: Praeger Publishers.

Sowell, Thomas. (1981a) *Ethnic Minorities*, New York: Basic Books.

Sowell, Thomas. (1981b) *Markets and Minorities*. New York: Basic Books.

Sowell, Thomas. (1975) *Race and Economics*, New York: David McKay Company.

Spear, Allen H. (1967) *Black Chicago*, Chicago: University of Chicago Press.

Springer, Kimberly. (1999) *Still Lifting, Still Climbing: African American Women's Contemporary Activism*, New York: New York University Press.

Staples, Robert, (ed.). (1999) *The Black Family: Essays and Studies*, 6th Ed. Belmont, CA: Wadsworth Publishing Company.

Staples, Robert. (1976) *Introduction to Black Sociology*, New York: McGraw Hill.

Staples, Robert. (1979) "The Myth of Black Macho: A Response to Angry Black Feminist," *Black Scholar*, 10, 6, 24-33.

Staples, Robert. (1987) *The Urban Plantation: Racism and Colonialism in the Post Civil Rights Era*, San Francisco: Black Scholar Press.

Staples, Robert. (1971) "Toward A Sociology of the Black Family: A Theoretical and Methodological Assessment," *Journal of Marriage and Family*, 33, 1 (February) 119-138.

Staples, Robert. (1973) "What is Black Sociology: Towards a of Black Liberation," in *The Death of White Sociology*, (ed) Joyce A. Ladner, New York: Vintage Books, pp. 161-172.

Staples, Robert. (1981) *The World of Black Singles*, Westport, CT: Greenwood Press.

Staples, Robert and Leanore Boulin Johnson. (1993) *Black Families at the Crossroads: Challenges and Prospects*, San Francisco: Jossey-Bass Publishers.

Stewart, James B. (1992) "Reaching for Higher Ground: Toward an Understanding of Black/Africana Studies," *The Afrocentric Scholar*, 1, 1, 1-63.

Sudarkasa, Niara. (1980) "African and Afro-American Family Structure: A Comparison." *Black Scholar*, 11 (November/December) 37-60.

Sudarkasa, Niara. (1981) "Interpreting the African Heritage in Afro-American Family Organization," in *Black Families*, Harriette P. McAdoo, (ed.) Beverly Hills: Sage Publications.

Sudarkasa, Niara. (1995) *The Strength of Our Mothers: African and African American Women and Families*, Trenton, NJ: Africa World Press.

Taylor, Robert J. et al. (1997) *Family Life in Black America*, Newbury Park, CA: Sage Publications.

Tembo, Chimbuko. (1996) "Kawaida Womanism: An Introduction to its Theory and Practice," paper presented at the Annual Cheikh Anta Diop Conference, Temple University (October), pp. 1-15.

Terrell, JoAnn. (1998) *Power in the Blood? The Cross in the African American Experience*. Maryknoll, NY: Orbis Books.

Thomas, June M. and Marsha Ritzdorg, (eds.) 1996) *Urban Planning and the African American Community: In the Shadows*, Newbury Park, CA: Sage Publications.

Tidwell, Billy J. (2000) "Parity, Progress and Prospects: Racial Inequalities in Economic Well-being," in Lee Daniels, (ed.) *State of Black America*, New York: National Urban League, pp. 287-316.

Toliver, Susan D. (1998) *Black Families in Corporate America*, Newbury Park, CA: Sage Publications.

Toure, Sekou. (1959) *Toward Full Re-Africanization*, Paris Présence Africaine.

Townes, Emilie M. (1995) *In a Blaze of Glory: Womanist Spirituality as Social Witness*, Nashville: Abingdon Press.

Tucker, M. Belinda and Claudia Mitchell-Kernan, (eds.) (1995) *The Decline in Marriage Among African Americans: Causes, Consequences and Policy Implications*, New York: Russell Sage.

Turner, James. (1979) "The Political Sociology of Racism and Systematic Oppression: Internal Colonization as a Paradigm for Socio-Economic Analysis," *Studia Africana*, 1,2 (Fall) 294-314.

Tushnet, Mark. (1987) *The NAACP's Legal Strategy Against Segregated Education 1925*, Chapel Hill: University of North Carolina.

Van DeBurg, William. (1993) *New Day in Babylon: The Black Power Movement and African American Culture 1965-1975*, Chicago: University of Chicago Press.

Van Dijk, Teun A. (1993) *Elite Discourse and Racism*, Newbury Park, CA: Sage Publications.

Walker, Alice. (1983) *In Search of Our Mothers' Gardens*, New York: Harcourt Brace Jovanovich.

Wallace, Michelle. (1979) *Black Macho and the Myth of the Superwoman*, New York: Dial Press.

Watterson, Barbara. (1991) *Women in Ancient Egypt*, New York: St. Martin's Press.

West, Cornel. (1993) *Race Matters*, Boston: Beacon Press.

West, Cornel. (1997) *Restoring Hope: Conversations on the Future of Black America*, Boston: Beacon Press.

White, Deborah Gray. (1998) *Too Heavy a Load: Black Women in Defense of Themselves, 1894-1994*, New York: Norton.

Williams, Delores. (1993) *Sisters in the Wilderness: The Challenge of Womanist God-Talk*, Maryknoll, NY: Orbis Books.

Willie, Charles. (1988) "The Black Family: Striving Toward Freedom," in *National Urban League The State of Black America 1988*, New York: National Urban League, Inc.

Willie, Charles. (1979) *The Caste and Class Controversy*, New York: General Hall, Inc.

Willie, Charles. (1970) *The Family Life of Black People*, Columbus, OH: Charles Merrill.

Wilson, Amos N. (1990) *Black-on-Black Violence: The Psychodynamics of Black Self-Annihilation in Service of White Domination*, New York: Afrikan World Infosystems.

Wilson, Amos N. (1992) *Understanding Black Adolescent Male Violence: Its Remediation and Prevention*, Chicago: Afrikan World.

Wilson, Franklin. (1979) *Residential Consumption, Economic Opportunity and Race*, New York: Academic Press.

Wilson, William J. (1978) *The Declining Significance of Race*, Chicago: University of Chicago Press.

Wilson, William J. (1993) *The Ghetto Underclass: Social Science Perspectives*, Newbury Park, CA: Sage Publications.

Wilson, William J. (1998) "Jobless Ghettos: The Disappearance of Work in Segregated Neighborhoods," in Lee Daniels, (ed.), *The State of Black America*, New York: National Urban League.

Wilson, William J. (1996) *When Work Disappears: The world of the New Urban Poor*, New York: Alfred A. Knopf.

Woodard, Komozi. (1999) *A Nation Within A Nation: Amiri Baraka (LeRoi Jones) and Black Power Politics*, Chapel Hill: University of North Carolina Press.

Woodson, Carter G. (1936) *The African Background Outlined*, Washington, D.C.: Association for the Study of Negro Life and History.

Young, Virginia. (1970) "Family and Childhood in a Southern Negro Community," *American Anthropologist*, 72:269-288.

Zegeye, Abebe, Leonard Harris and Julia Maxted, (eds.) 1991) *Exploitation and Exclusion: Race and Class in Contemporary U.S. Society*, New York: H. Zell.

BLACK POLITICS

BLACK POLITICS

CHAPTER 7

7.1 INTRODUCTION

ANCIENT SOURCES

Politics, as activities relating to issues of governance reaches back to the earliest of human societies concerned with creating a context of benefit and obligation of its members (Ki-Zerbo, 1990; Phillipson, 1993). Usually, however, when we think of politics, we envision large units such as cities, states and empires (Mokhtar, 1990). Certainly in Africa we have the first examples of these large units and the earliest writings on governance and associate issues of right, justice, care and responsibility for the poor and vulnerable, ethical leadership, the right to petition for redress and commitment to the rule of law (Karenga, 1994).

INSTRUCTIONS TO THE PRIME MINISTER

One of the oldest documents on ethical standards of governance is the ancient Egyptian text, the Instructions to the Prime Minister (Lichtheim, 1976:21-24; Sethe, 1961, Urk. IV:1086-1093). This text was developed as an ethical standard of governance, which was given to the newly appointed prime minister by the reigning pharaoh. It reflected the ancient Egyptian commitment to Maat, the moral ideal in matters of governance and the expressed goal of creating a just and good society and world. It was also a fundamental source of ethics, along with the Sebait and the Declarations of Virtues, for ancient Egypt's large bureaucracy.

In establishing the Maatian conception of governance and thus the standard by which the prime minister is to conduct the affairs of state, the king (pharaoh) stresses the importance of the office. Speaking to the prime minister in front of the council of state, he says, "be very attentive to the office of the prime minister; watch over all that is done in it. It is the pillar of the entire land." He then goes on to stress due process saying, "see to it that all is done according to the law." In fact, "the security of the official lies in acting according to the rule." Next, the prime minister is instructed to be impartial and fair, "Do not judge unfairly, God abhors partiality. Regard one whom you know like one you don't know, one near you like one far from you. The official who acts like this will succeed in this place." Also, the prime minister is instructed not to be dismissive or inconsiderate of the petitioner and to explain why his/her petition is denied, if it has to be denied. He says, " Do not pass over a petitioner before you consider his petition. When a petitioner is about to petition, you don't dismiss what he says as already said. Deny him only after you let him know the reason you denied him." The king also tells the prime minister, "Do not act arbitrarily where the law is known." Finally, the pharaoh tells the prime minister to always do justice, for this is the essential requirement of the office, saying:

> *Lo, you succeed in performing this office by doing justice (Maat). Lo, justice is what is wanted in the actions of the prime minister. Lo, the prime minister is its (justice) guardian since the beginning of time. Lo, what one says of the prime minister's chief scribe is that he is the 'scribe of justice.' He who does justice for all the people, he is truly the prime minister.*

THE BOOK OF KHUNANUP

Another important contribution to the discourse on governance is the ancient Egyptian social justice text, the Book of Khunanup (Parkinson, 1991; Assmann, 1990; Karenga, 1984:29-35). As Assmann (1990:58) notes, it is the definitive text on Maat and it is also the oldest social justice text in the world. Commonly called the Story of the Eloquent Peasant, it is a social justice narrative in which Khunanup, a peasant, pursues a grievance against a corrupt official and wins. As Kemp (1983:116) states, this reflects the ancient Egyptian recognition of "the need to ensure that the state accommodated the hopes of the ordinary man." In his petitions for redress, Khunanup delivers a treatise on justice and on the obligations of leadership which reveals the moral and social expectations of leadership even from the masses. As Lichtheim (1992:42) states, in this treatise, "[t]he justice due to the common man was most impressively worked out...."

In his discourse on Maat, Khunanup instructs leaders saying: "Speak Maat. Do Maat. For it is mighty. It is great; it endures. Its worth is tested. It leads one to worthiness." Khunanup tells Rensi, the official to whom he is making his petition, that long life and immortality are based on Maatian conduct. Thus he says, "Doing Maat (justice, here) is breath to the nose (t3w pw n fnd irt m3't)." Moreover, Khunanup defines the Maatian leader as one who exhibits care and responsibility, rewards the poor and the vulnerable. He says the Maatian leader is "the father of the orphan, the husband of the widow, the brother of the divorced woman and protective garment for the motherless." Also, he instructs the leader that "The balancing of the land lies in Maat (truth, justice, lawfulness)." Thus, "do not speak falsely for you are great; do not act lightly for you have weight; be not untrue for you are the balance (scales of justice) and do not swerve for you are the standard."

Linking right conduct on earth with eternal life, he urges the leader again to do Maat (justice) saying:

Do justice for the lord of justice
whose justice is justice indeed
Keep away from wrongdoing
When goodness is good, it is truly good
Justice is for eternity
It goes to the grave with one who does it
When he is buried and the earth enfolds him
His name is not erased from the earth
He is remembered because of his goodness
This is a norm of the word of God.

This social justice text, ostensibly used as a text in ancient Egyptian schools, is significant in the study of governance or politics for several reasons. First, it is a critique of leadership by a simple peasant and carries implicitly within it a recognition of the right—whether formal or customary—to engage in such a critique. Secondly, its popularity and use in schools suggests an active tradition of critique and redress of grievance as well as right. Thirdly, the fact that the peasant, Khunanup, wins over an upper class person reinforces the concept and practice of a justice without class bias. Fourthly, as Breasted (1934:183ff) suggests, it is a definition and boast by the officials of a just society with honest officials committed to Maat, an open and viable process for redress of grievances and the triumph of Maat regardless of class. Finally, the text is important because of the valuable contribution it makes to the corpus of political and ethical discourse on the question of the nature and value of justice.

In the text, Khunanup delineates five criteria for a just leader and thereby gives us an important insight into the Maatian concept of social justice. He defines the Maatian leader as: 1) one "without greed"; 2) one "without baseness"; 3) "a destroyer of falsehood"; 4) "an establisher of the right"; and 5) "one who comes at the voice of the caller." The just or Maatian leader for Khunanup is one who does not use his or her office for vulgar self-enrichment, is not mean-spirited, is truthful and intolerant of personal and official deception, establishes and sustains the right and the good, and is responsive to and responsible for the petitioner, the needy and the vulnerable.

From these two classical African texts we can construct an idea of how the ancient Egyptians conceived of what they called governance and we call now politics. Within the framework of their moral ideal Maat, as reflected in these and related texts, governance or politics can be defined as a collective ethical vocation to create and sustain a just and good society and world. By collective vocation, I mean a shared morally compelling commitment to a certain kind of work. And in this case, it is work to create and sustain a just and good society and world. It is this understanding of politics, as a collective ethical vocation to create and sustain a just and good society and world, that has informed the core of African American political practice both in electoral politics and community organization. Thus, this political practice   represents the oldest social justice tradition in the world and offers an important contribution to modern political discourse and practice as both a source of paradigms and possibilities.

7.2 POLITICS IN THE U.S. CONTEXT

In addition to the stress on social justice as a core concern of politics, the emphasis on power as an indispensable element and focus is also made. For without power, social justice is difficult, if not impossible, to achieve. In fact, it is this dual focus on justice and power that has shaped Black political practice in this country from the beginning and reaches its clearest expression in the civil rights and Black Power tendencies within the Black Freedom Movement of the 60's. However, much, if not most, of the literature on politics in the U.S. is about gaining, maintaining and using power. Thus, one of the main ways politics can be defined is as *the art and process of gaining, maintaining and using power.*

However, the question of for what purpose do we seek power remains. And here the best theories of governance suggest that it is primarily in the interest of the people that power should be pursued and governance conducted. And this takes us back to the earliest discourse on governance in the classical African society of ancient Egypt and its stress on Maat (truth, justice, rightness). And as the texts say, this means it must be conducted truthfully, justly and rightly without distinction of class, gender or culture as discussed in chapter 5. One might expect race rather than culture here, but race is a modern concept, classical cultures in Africa and the rest of the world made cultural distinctions, not racial ones. And in ancient Egypt the category of "stranger" represents this cultural distinction. Nevertheless, Maatian ethics requires that the "other", to use a modern term, be treated no differently from the familiar, that officials be impartial and that "one who does justice for all the people, he is truly the prime minister" or the just leader and ruler.

If we combine the two concerns for justice and power, then we can define *politics* as the *art and process of gaining, maintaining and using power to create and sustain a just and good society and world.* Such a definition does not compromise the need for power, but clearly expresses the reason for its pursuit and the purpose of its maintenance and use. This definition also reaffirms the African social justice tradition – Continental and Diasporan, classical and modern - in its concern for "*all the people.*" In addition, it can be argued within this framework that the people's possession of *power* over their destiny and daily lives is a moral necessity, that is a cardinal good and that politics is the process through which that good is pursued and sustained. And it is within this understanding that the pursuit and possession of power as a core value in politics does not overshadow the central purpose for which it is pursued and held, i.e., to create a just and good society and world.

THE ISSUE OF POWER

The centrality of the issue of power in politics is obvious in political science discourse. Whether one uses system-oriented literature (Barker, 1999; Lowi and Ginsberg, 1996) or studies on more progressive and radical structures and processes (Pinderhughes, 1987; McAdam, 1999), the focus is on power, the process of its acquisition, maintenance and utilization. Thus, a key element in politics is *power* which can be defined as *the social capacity of a group to realize its will, in spite of opposition from others* (Karenga, 1980:65). Social capacity is used here to stress both the *collective* and *structural* character of power as well as to indicate that power as a political concept and fact must be achieved in a societal context as opposed to a family or personal context (Walton, 1997; Walters and Smith, 1999).

Social capacity, then, is rooted in collective (group) capacity and is expressed in a group's structural capacity, i.e., its organizational and institutional ability to realize its will – in spite of opposition from others. Also, it is important at this point to make the distinction between *influence* and *power* which are often used interchangeably though technically they are very different. For whereas *power* is *the capacity to act and achieve*, *influence* is simply *the ability to affect*. It is having influence with people in power that often passes in Black leadership circles as having power itself (Salley, 1999; Hamilton, 1993).

It is in the context of these assumptions about the pervasiveness and centrality of power to politics that Jones (1972:8) defines Black politics as "a manifestation of one dimension or extension of the universal struggle for power." This stress on power, then, is the beginning concept in establishing and developing a fundamental framework for the study of Black politics (Keiser, 1997; Gomes and Williams, 1995). However, there are other concepts key to a critical grasp of Black politics as both a study and a social process. These key concepts are *conflict, inter-*

est, change, and *the state* which are also alternative related ways of defining and understanding politics and its central concept, power.

THE PRESENCE OF CONFLICT

The stress on the struggle for power presupposes the real and continuing presence of conflict in society as another basic aspect of politics (Tate, 1993; Morris and Mueller, 1992). As Walton (1972b:1) states, "Politics is born of societal conflict." This conflict is defined not only by the struggle for power but also, as Samuel D. Cook contended, for "values associated with and derived from the possession of power" (Walton, 1972b:xv). In other words, power, although key social value in politics, is sought not simply for itself but for other key values or treasured things, which power can provide and protect, i.e., rights, resources, status, and, of course, the just and good society and world (Walton, 1994). The assumption here then, is that the presence of conflict in society, especially an oppressive one, is normal rather than abnormal and that the most severe forms of conflict are rooted in the struggle for power and the values it provides and protects. Therefore, system theory which poses conflict as abnormal is not so much an analysis as it is a political projection and description of utopia (Parsons, 1951).

SOCIAL INTERESTS

Another key concept of Black politics is interests (Swain, 1994; Clay, 1999). In fact, another way to define power is *a group's capacity to define, defend and develop its interests.* To define them is to articulate and establish them; to defend them to is protect them against challenge and to develop them is to promote and expand them. Interests can be defined as social stakes, claims or concerns (Balbus, 1974). They may be subjective (simply perceived) or objective, i.e., existing independent of perception. In a society divided and defined by race and class, interests and the conflict around them assume a race and class character (Reed, 2000; Reeves, 1997; Perry, 1997; Kinder and Sanders, 1996; Dawson, 1994; Scott, 1980). Thus, another way of viewing social conflict is as the struggle between differing, competing and often antagonistic interests.

SOCIAL CHANGE

A fourth key concept in Black politics is social change which is linked to and rooted in social conflict. The assumption here is that the U.S. political system is defined by contradictory interests not simply by consensus as the pluralists (Apter, 1977; Dahl, 1967) contend. Consensus or universal agreement on values is clearly impossible in a society wracked by severe race and class division. Thus, constraint through coercion becomes a way to institutionalize and regulate interests and conflicts or suppress them. The political struggle to break through constraints and reorder society in a group's interest becomes the key impetus for social change (Jennings, 1992; Gregory, 1998).

RELATIONSHIP TO THE STATE

Finally, it is important in understanding politics to realize that "power in society is *ultimately determined by a people's relationship to the state*" (Karenga, 1980:65). The *state* here is defined as "*the totality of institutions which facilitate governance and insure social control*." Within the general framework of these functions, two sets of institutions stand out as most definitive. These are the institutions of dominance, i.e., coercion (armed forces, police, courts, prisons, etc.) and institutions of political socialization (the educational system, the media and other structures used to advance the ideas and values of those who rule). The instruments of political socialization represent the right and ability to define social reality and the instruments of domination represent the power of the state to make its definition stick. Given this awesome power of the state, and the fact that ultimately power is determined by a group's relationship to the state, an essential political question is how does one check, challenge, seize control of or effectively participate in the exercise of state power (King, 1997)?

Walton (1985; 1972b:2-4), however, is correct in his criticism of the exclusive or predominant emphasis on electoral politics in the study of Black politics. The early political studies of Gosnell (1967) and Wilson (1960) in Chicago, Ladd's (1969) study of Black leadership in two North Carolina cities, and the readings on the Black electorate on the national level by Bailey (1967) all reflect this unbalanced focus on electoral politics.

However, power and the struggle for it, which are key elements of politics, are much more multidimensional than electoral activity (Nelson, 2000; Pinderhughes, 1992).

AREAS OF POLITICAL POWER

Essentially there are eight areas or bases of political power: 1) key positions in government; 2) voting strength; 3) community control; 4) economic capacity; 5) community organization; 6) possession of critical knowledge; 7) coalition and alliance; and 8) coercive capacity (Preston, et al, 1987). Key positions in government at the national, state or local levels places a group in the position to determine or share in the determination of public policy. These positions may be appointed (cabinet members, advisors, bureaucratic positions) or elected (Congresspersons, mayors, council persons, etc.). Voting strength is key to electing one's own representatives or allies or in penalizing or threatening penalty. Community control is translated as command of an authority over the economic, political and cultural institutions and processes of the community as a result of community organization, institutional penetration and development. Economic capacity is transformed into political power through financing campaigns and lobbies, control of a city's economics, determining public opinion through control of the media, and buying votes and/or officials.

Community organization means a highly mobilized, organized political force which makes possible all the others (Guinier, 1998; Morris and Mueller, 1992). For if power is collective and structural capacity, organization of the people itself is the *sine qua non* of this. Another source of power is the possession of critical knowledge, especially given the social tendency toward specialized knowledge. Possession of such knowledge whether in science, technology, finance or politics makes processes and structures dependent on the possessors and often puts the possessors at the very center of the social power process. Coalitions and alliances are also ways to create and augment power. Effective unity strengthens weak groups and increases the power of strong ones.

Finally within the state, the ultimate negative power is coercive power, the capacity to impose one's interest, to physically factor out opposition under the cover of law, to raise class or race will and interest to the status of law and to establish authority through the strength of the gun. If the ultimate power is state power, state power is above all rooted in control of the coercive apparatus, i.e., army, police, etc. There is, however, the alternative power of violence, i.e., urban guerilla strikes, revolt and revolution against the state or social disruption in other forms.

Below is a discussion of three basic areas and expressions of Black politics. Each represents Blacks' struggle to define, defend and develop their interests as a people in and outside of government. Hopefully, the discussion of these will give added meaning to Mervyn Dymally's (1972:21) statement that:

> *Because of the Black man's (and woman's) situation which is radical by any definition, and because of the nature of American politics, which is moderate to conservative by any definition, the Black man (and woman) in America has been condemned to seek radical ends within a political framework which was designed to prevent sudden and radical social and economical changes.*

The radicalness of the situation is not always by choice, but by the fact that Blacks' social location - in terms of both race and class - is such that an effective end to their oppression must and will require the fundamental restructuring of society, i.e., its power and status relations. The history of Blacks in the U.S. offers ample proof of this contention and their future will undoubtedly reaffirm it.

7.3   PARTY POLITICS

RATIONALE

The rationale for party politics begins with the fact that a party is the key political structure in the acquisition and exercise of state power (Walton, 1972a; Shea and Green, 1994; Klinkner, 1994). By definition, a *party*, revolutionary or system-oriented, "*is a political structure specifically designed to seize, control or effectively participate in state power*" (Karenga, 1980:66). Within the framework of the party's focus on the exercise of state power, African Americans, like other party members and/or supporters, seek to use the party to achieve their group and personal interests (Key, 1962). Among the perceived benefits of participation in Democratic and Republican party politics are: 1) a vital, even if tenuous, link to state power; 2) a vehicle through which one's interests are represented, i.e., advanced and protected; 3) a means of becoming one's own group representative, i.e., an elected or appointed official; 4) an opportunity to determine or help determine public policy; 5) a share of party patronage (appointments, jobs, funds, etc.).

In addition to participation in the two-party system, African Americans have also participated in non-Black third parties such as the Socialist, Progressive, Communist, Populist, Liberty and Peace and Freedom parties, and the Reform Party of Ross Perot (Walton, 1994:282-293; Walton, 1969). Although these parties did not usually win and had little or no patronage to offer, Blacks supported them for various other reasons, as Walton (1972a) notes. These include: 1) dissatisfaction with the two dominant parties' level of lack of commitment to Black interests; 2) a sense of exclusion and alienation from the two major parties, as in Southern racist branches; 3) perception that opportunities to voice and fight for Black interests exist in alternative parties; 4) the public policy appeal of third parties; and 5) strong recruitment efforts by third parties.

Finally, Black parties have also emerged as an alternative to the two-party system (Walton, 1972a). Given the fact that Black parties are third parties, they tend to rise for similar reasons as other third parties. Frye (1980:5) states that "independent Black parties tend to rise when (1) Black participation in one or the other party is denied," or (2) when "political leaders decide that aspects of their social, political and economic grievances cannot or will not be met by existing parties." He cites the founding of the Mississippi Freedom Democratic Party and the National Democratic Party of Alabama as examples of the first; and the founding of the United Citizens Party in South Carolina and the Lowndes County Freedom Organization in Alabama as examples of the latter. In addition, to these reasons for formation, Black parties also rise as a result of: 1) increased levels of Black consciousness; 2) the desire for an independent politics which not only wins a share of the political power, but also makes a statement concerning their capacity for independent action; and 3) perception that party-building and electoral activities are ways of politically educating, mobilizing and organizing the masses of Blacks around vital issues (Walters, 1989: Chapter 6).

THE REPUBLICAN EXPERIENCE

The first electoral activity of African Americans was in the context of the Republican party in the Reconstruction era, 1865-1877 (DuBois, 1935; Foner, 1988). During Reconstruction, Blacks joined the Republican party in great numbers and held various offices on the national, state and local levels. The reasons for the Black affiliation with the Republican party were both by choice and the political situation in the U.S. at the time. First, Blacks joined and supported the Republican party because it was the party of Lincoln and represented to them the party of emancipation. Secondly, the Republicans put forth legislation in the interest of Black people, i.e., the 13th, 14th and 15th Amendments. Thirdly, Republicans actively recruited Blacks and financed their campaigns in an effort to build a Black electorate in their struggle with the Democrats (Franklin, 1961; Foner, 1993). Finally, the Democratic party was closed to Blacks, thus, eliminating an alternative option. Morris (1975:19), in discussing Republican motivation for involvement of Blacks, cites three basic reasons: 1) their desire to solidify Republican control by developing a solid base of support among Blacks in the South; 2) their desire to punish the South by imposing a strong Black electorate on it; and 3) the struggle between the legislative and executive branches, with each needing to prove its predominance. In such a context, Morris concludes, Blacks and Republicans entered into a mutually beneficial relationship which, however, was short-lived.

The decisive year was 1876 when Republican presidential candidate, Rutherford B. Hayes, agreed to withdraw federal troops and adopt a hands-off policy toward the South in exchange for Southern electoral votes needed to win the election. This "Compromise of 1877" led to massive violence against Blacks at the hands of white terrorist societies such as the Ku Klux Klan and to a division of the party into two factions, the lily-white Republicans and the Black and Tan Republicans

(Walton, 1975). Thus, in their efforts to accommodate white racists, Republicans lost the Black electorate which began to transfer to the Democratic Party in 1932 with the election of Franklin D. Roosevelt.

Not until the late 1970's did Republicans make a significant effort to challenge the Democratic monopoly on the Black vote and to reinvolve Blacks in the Republican party process (Karenga, 1978a). Their strategy had two basic aims: 1) to win a significant share of the Black vote in various elections, and failing to do this 2) to minimize the size and effect of the Democrats' share.

In 1978, it looked as though Republicans would at least make significant inroads in the Democratic monopoly on the Black vote, given the rise of a new middle class with interests which seemed to coincide with some Republican positions. As an indication of their seriousness in wooing Blacks, the GOP appropriated monies for recruitment and campaign finance for suitable Black candidates and invited leaders like Jesse Jackson of PUSH and Benjamin Hooks of the NAACP to open the dialogue on possible mutually beneficial cooperation.

However, beginning in 1980 with the election of Ronald Reagan and the ascendancy of the New Right, the push seemed to have been de-emphasized. Blacks voted overwhelmingly Democratic in that election even when other ethnic and interest groups shifted (Williams and Morris, 1981). Reagan, being a model conservative and the symbol of the New Right's ascendancy was not sensitive to or mindful of Black needs and interests. In fact, he set about cutting the budget and advancing negative policy in areas most detrimental to Blacks, other peoples of color and the poor (Barker, 1987:30-31; Dalleck, 1984). Given this, it was difficult for either Black or white Republicans to seriously suggest a reinvolvement of Blacks in the party.

During the Bush campaign to succeed Reagan, the Republicans continued to engage in political behavior designed to alienate and even antagonize Blacks rather than include them. He continued to push to achieve one of the New Right's key goals which was to reverse the gains in the 60's, especially the social welfare and social action programs. George Bush, his successor, followed in his footsteps showing a similar mean-spiritedness toward the poor and vulnerable, cutting federal funds for cities in half, terminating some family programs, urban redevelopment and the construction of public housing.

George W. Bush, who succeeded Bill Clinton, came to office under the cloud of a suspect election. He lost the popular vote, but, with help from a ruling by the U.S. Supreme Court to stop a recount in Florida, won the electoral vote. Many voters, especially Blacks and Latinos but also Jews, felt they were denied their right to vote by Florida's use of an outdated system and various disqualifying practices. Also, there was evidence of officials placing obstacles in the way of voters of color, including a reported substantial police presence near the polls which, of course, had a negative effect on many Black and Latino voters' participation.

Nevertheless, even if all this had transpired and the Republicans had not turned out to exhibit so much of what is called now "social meanness" in their brutal attacks on social welfare programs and questioning elections, there still would have been formidable problems for the Republicans to overcome in their quest for Black support. Among these are: 1) the historical tendency of Blacks to vote Democratic regardless; 2) the ideological orientation of the Republican Party which stands for objectives and principles opposite to Black interests, i.e., its stands against social welfare, government intervention and African liberation movements; and 3) the conservative internal resistance to courting Blacks and making the kind of concessions this requires with no guarantee of positive results (Walters, 1989).

THE DEMOCRATIC EXPERIENCE

It was during the Franklin D. Roosevelt administration beginning in 1932 that Black support for the Democratic party began (Frymer, 1999; Judd, 1999). Before this, African Americans were repelled by the open racism advocated and practiced by the party. The Democratic party not only opposed the vote for Blacks, but used terror and violence against them to discourage their voting. But during the New Deal era, the Roosevelt administration drew Blacks to the party through relief and public work programs which benefited Blacks and later through Roosevelt's anti-discrimination measures. Roosevelt also reinforced his position with Blacks by creating the "Black Cabinet," an advisory group of skilled Blacks, and by issuing Executive Order 8802 which created a Fair Employment Practice

Commission and banned discrimination in industries with federal contracts. Since the Roosevelt administration, Blacks have maintained a steadfast loyalty to the Democratic party even though Roosevelt and subsequent presidents did not always live up to their commitment or even promise Blacks substantial gains.

It is in recent times with the presidency of Bill Clinton that this "electoral capture," as Frymer (1999:7ff) notes, has been dramatically apparent. In spite of African Americans' support of Clinton in overwhelming numbers, he did not reciprocate (Klinkner, 1999). He came to office arguing a New Liberalism which made its goal the putting of distance between the New Democratic Party and the old one in the latter's identification with the working class, the poor and people of color. In 1992, he not only staged a fight with Jesse Jackson over remarks about Sista Souljah at a Rainbow Coalition meeting, but he also denounced the Los Angeles Revolt and linked it to the discredited theories of dependency and culture of poverty in the African American neighborhood. He put forward an Omnibus Crime Bill which expanded the death penalty, added funding for new prisons and challenged the civil rights of citizens and noncitizens with his so-called anti-terrorism legislation. His Welfare Reform Act left welfare to states and the racism that often informs their decisions, and it required essentially dead-end and demeaning work for welfare recipients without providing adequate training, transportation and child care for them to do the work. Clinton also waffled on affirmative action and left in place a grossly unequal sentencing policy for crack cocaine and Blacks and powdered cocaine and whites. Playing to the loyal liberal crowd, he held a national conversation on race as a substitute for initiating substantive policies against racism. In spite of all this, African Americans remained loyal. Walters (1975) has continuously called attention to this impolitic loyalty for the Democratic party, arguing that in a situation where the African American vote is expected and delivered, there is no leverage. Such a blind and impolitic loyalty is clearly disadvantageous to Blacks in the political arena and it becomes important to raise the question of why the persistence.

From available evidence, it seems that Blacks' party identification with the Democrats persists for several reasons. First, the Democrats have historically tended to be more favorable to socio-economic issues facing Blacks. Secondly, the party had been supportive of civil rights since the Roosevelt administration. Thirdly, the factor of group cohesiveness tends to reinforce existing patterns once they are established. Fourthly, socialization into a given party tends to persist. Finally, the Republican party offers no real alternative given its stance on socio-economic and civil rights issues (Morris, 1975; Barker and McCorry, 1976).

Although Morris (1975), Barker and McCorry (1976) and Williams (1979) saw early indicators of rising independent registration and voting, later evidence does not suggest a substantial shift in party participation patterns (Walters, 1989). In fact, in the 1980 presidential election, Blacks gave their vote to Jimmy Carter overwhelmingly in spite of their severe criticism of him (Karenga, 1977). Also, in spite of shifts by Jews, labor and others to Reagan, Williams and Morris (1978: 227ff) had suggested that the consequence of this vote might be an impetus to a more sophisticated and pragmatic approach to party politics. But in the Bill Clinton election of 1992 and 1996 and in the run by Al Gore in 1999, the percentages of African American votes for the Democratic candidates were consistently high despite Clinton's and the Democratic Party's retreat from the liberal state (Lusane, 1994; Lashley and Jackson, 1994). This is not to say that the shift in allegiance to the Democratic Party will not come, but only to emphasize its difficulty and the need for a new and bolder politics than traditional approaches suggest (Walters, 1988; Strickland, 1972).

BLACK PARTY INITIATIVES

Black Party initiatives have been on both the national and state levels, but the most successful efforts have been on the state level (Frye, 1980; Walton, 1972a). Moreover, these parties have been two basic types - parallel and independent parties (Walton, 1972a:80-81). Black party initiatives began as early as 1904 with the founding of the National Liberty Party. In that year, delegates from 36 states met in a national convention in St. Louis and developed a platform dedicated to complete enfranchisement and the restoration of Black civil rights which were lost after the Compromise of 1877 (Walton, 1972a:51). This party, however, was short lived and in its place rose a series of non-partisan political organizations, beginning with the National Negro American Political League in 1908 and culminating in the National Negro Congress in 1936.

INDEPENDENT PARTIES

The 60's saw the rise of three independent Black parties: 1) the African American Party in Alabama (1960); 2) the National Civil Rights Party (1963); and 3) the Freedom Now Party (1964). However, the electoral activity of these parties was also minimal and unsuccessful and they too eventually faded from the political scene. Although Walton, considers the Peace and Freedom party a Black party, its integrated character and predominant white membership contradict this classification. Moreover, even he (1972b:128) states that "it was a coalition of Black militants and white liberals," i.e., between the Panthers and their white allies, an arrangement which clearly pushes it outside any meaningful definition of Black.

PARALLEL PARTIES

Also, the 60's saw the rise of four major parallel Black parties: 1) the Mississippi Freedom Democratic Party (MFDP) (1964); 2) the Lowndes County Freedom Organization or the Black Panther Party of Alabama (1966); 3) the National Democratic Party of Alabama (NDPA) (1968); and 4) the United Citizen's Party of South Carolina (1969) (Walton, 1927a). The MFDP led the way and left valuable lessons for subsequent parallel parties. It taught the method and possibilities of challenge to the established parties at national conventions, the value of using elections to dramatize basic issues and politically educate the masses, and the possibilities and problems of being a parallel party (McLemore, 1971; Walton, 1972a:Chapter 3). The NDPA has clearly been the most successful Black party in terms of both votes received and offices won (Frye, 1980; Walton, 1972a:1957). Although it declined in the late seventies, it too, by both achievements and losses, left valuable lessons on the problems and possibilities of Black parties in the political arena.

THE NATIONAL BLACK INDEPENDENT POLITICAL PARTY

The most recent example of the Black party thrust was the founding of the National Black Independent Political Party (NBIPP) in 1980 (Holmes, 1999; Walton, 1989:148ff). The ideological origins of the party are rooted in the National Black

Political Convention held in Gary in 1972 (Smith and Walters, 1996; Gilliam, 1975:Chapter 6). William Strickland (1972) who helped develop a National Black Political Agenda at Gary which set forth political goals for African Americans, summed up the basic concerns for a new Black politics and a new party to initiate this process and give it an ongoing practical expression. He (1972:25-26) argued that the point was not to create just any party and certainly not the kind "that white folks have or talk about." Nor could it be one which is "simply an electoral party" or "simply a party that is dedicated to jobs and patronage or the election of individuals as a first concern." What was needed, Strickland posited, was a party which self-consciously strove to "advance the interests of the Black masses" and was fundamentally concerned with institution-building and institutional control, the assumption of power and ultimately the shaping of the destiny and daily lives of Black people. Without such a bold and multidimensional approach, i.e., electoral and non-electoral politics, he concluded, the party would be neither new nor viable.

Thus although the Gary Convention did not produce a mandate for a new party, it did raise and thoroughly discuss the question. Moreover, it did produce a mandate for a new politics and a National Black Political Assembly (NBPA). Daniels (1980:3) who served as chairman of NBPA and later of NBIPP posed the "principal role" of NBPA as "the shaping, projecting and institutionalization of an independent progressive Black politics of social transformation, economic democracy and self-determination." It is thus out of such a mandate, structure and political focus that the Black party emerged (Elam, 1981a; Marable, 1980).

NBIPP did not assume an electoral significance on the national or state level, but it did have some local victories, i.e., in northern California. Thus, its relevance resides not so much in its achievements, but in the multidimensionality and ambitiousness of its goals and the possibilities suggested by these. As all third parties, NBIPP had general and specific problems (Walton, 1969). Among these were: 1) building bases in local communities and a viable effective national structure; 2) developing a financial base; 3) developing non-material incentives in the absence of monies and patronage and in furtherance of a new politics; 4) building and maintaining an effective unity among the diverse tendencies in it, especially avoiding the disruptive struggles between nationalists and Marxists which has undermined so many other Black united efforts; and 5) making significant and ongoing gains which demonstrate its viability and possibilities (Walters, 1988:148ff).

Daniels (1971) argues that there are both socio-psychological and structural constraints on Black party building. Among the former are Black "feelings of inferiority and of political inefficacy," a negative definition of politics, previous party identification and belief in integration. The structural constraints include the institutionalized co-optation process which absorbs real and potential Black challengers; single member districts which prohibit a numerical minority from winning; rigid built-in qualifying rules; and gerrymandering of political districts. In addition and reinforcement of the above problems and constraint, I (1980:71) have also posed the following constraints: political underdevelopment of the Black community; ideological hegemony of the system which argues that only two parties are viable and realistic; fear of penalty, i.e., loss of benefits from the Democratic or Republican party; fear of failure; and lack of an historical model which worked well for a considerable time.

But in spite of these constraints and problems, Black party advocates still argue that the Black party is both possible and necessary. For if a party is impossible, they argue, then so is liberation and an effective relation to state power. In fact, Cruse (1974:10) has summed up their position quite well in his assertion that "if such a party is premature, then so is all talk of 'revolution' and "if an independent Black political party is unwise and unfeasible so is revolution unwise and unfeasible." In a word, if the party is key to state power, those without one can never hope to ever seize control or effectively participate in it.

7.4 THE JACKSON CAMPAIGNS

Of all the electoral campaigns Blacks have waged, won and lost, none has captured their imagination and cultivated their sense of history as the Jesse Jackson campaigns. Doug Wilder's winning the governorship of Virginia and the mayoral victory of David Dinkins of New York both in 1989 were seen as milestones (McCormick and Jones, 1993). As John Jacobs

(1990:4) described these events, they "were another step in the long process of removing America's racial barriers, indicators that we have come a long way as a nation since the 1965 Voting Rights Act" (see also Holden, 1990). Also Harold Washington's skillfully achieved victory as Mayor of Chicago in 1983 became another indicator of electoral progress and the possibilities of principled democratic leadership (Starks and Preston, 1990; Preston, 1987).

But it was Jesse Jackson whose historical campaigns, the first major and wide-reaching campaigns by an African American, captured the hearts and minds of African Americans on a national scale and in a special way (Henry, 1991; Collins, 1986; Karenga, 1984; Walters, 1989; Barker, 1988). In spite of his critics, Jackson's campaigns were important not only to the Black community but to the country (Reed, 1986; Faw and Skelton, 1986; Landess and Quinn, 1985).

The significance of the Jesse Jackson campaigns revolves around and is rooted in several factors. First, Jackson redefined the racial parameters of U.S. politics. He was the first African American or person of color to mount a major campaign which in the second run garnered over seven million votes. He thus confronted the system with an anomaly reflected in his media treatment in which white reporters and commentators continued to ask "What does Jesse want?" even though he was clearly running for the presidency. At the same time, it caused a kind of cognitive dissonance for some whites; it was a politically motivating boundary crossing for African Americans and others.

Secondly, Jesse reopened the social justice dialog missing since the Sixties, again crossing boundaries, especially in the first campaign and moving beyond the safe center of standard politics (Henry, 1991; Walters and Barker, 1989; Barker, 1988). He spoke to such issues as homelessness, the oversized military budget at the expense of social programs, the inner city problematic, the farm problems of monopoly and foreclosure, and peace and justice in the Middle East (Hatch, 1988; Jackson, 1987). Thirdly, in raising these and other critical issues, Jackson reaffirmed the African American legacy of setting the moral and progressive agenda. (Cavanaugh and Foster, 1984; Collins, 1986; Henry, 1991).

Fourthly, Jackson opened the party process for people of color and other marginalized persons and reaffirmed the value and vision of the democratic process (Barker, 1988; Cavanaugh and Foster, 1984). It can be argued that it was this opening and involvement that made possible the gains for African Americans and others formerly marginalized (Collins, 1986). Fifthly, Jackson contributed to the redefinition of relations between the African American community and the Democratic Party. Ronald Walters (1989) argues that Jackson was successful in his attempt to increase Black leverage by refusing to build an independent campaign and then bargaining (Henry, 1991:132). He thus never really developed the Rainbow coalition as an independent option (Collins, 1986).

Sixthly, Jackson's significance rests in his reaffirmation of the value of electoral politics (Henry, 1991; Walters and Barker, 1989). The campaign proved to be an important way to raise critical issues and to mobilize and organize people around their own interest. Finally, Jackson laid the basis for a new coalition politics. Charles Henry contends that Jackson's campaign in California and his impressive showing among Latinos, Asians and whites as well as Blacks (reflects his understanding of coalition politics, in which three concepts are crucial: interest, reciprocity and leverage." Jackson, Henry continues, "believes that America's rejected hold the keys to progressive political change." And thus, their interest must be respected and reciprocity rather than domination must be a central principle." Jackson posited that a Rainbow Coalition based on such principles can, in fact, exercise effective leverage on national politics.

7.5   BLACK ELECTED OFFICIALS

In the early seventies, a prevalent assumption rose that mass political struggle was somewhat passé and that electoral politics was the key to power and the future (Tate, 1993; Barker, 1999). In fact, Conyers and Wallace (1976:6) stated that "...the presence of Blacks in elected government positions...is not only a manifestation of the Black community's political advance but a principal guarantee that advance will continue." Such faith is perhaps understandable but easily an overstatement. As Holden (1973:193) observed, "the electoral process is neither sufficient in itself nor has any politically sophisticated population regarded it as sufficient by itself." He states that

"The basic rationale for electoral politics, insofar as policy is concerned, is that desirable policies will emerge when there is a clear identity between the interests and values of the elected and of those who elect them." But he notes, "This rationale also required, of course, that those elected come into command of the appropriate public resources." Moreover, it presupposes a strong enough political force to assume command or at least share in it (Banks, et al, 1996).

LIMITATIONS AND CONSTRAINTS

There have been many studies on the limitations of the electoral process and on the various constraints imposed on Black elected officials or BEO's (Swain, 1993; Barker, 1994; Rich, 1996). Speaking in general, Michael Preston (1978:196-197) lists eight basic constraints: 1) lack of "permanent political machinery"; 2) lack of "tradition and power"; 3) "little economic clout"; 4) tendency of votes to be taken for granted by Democrats; 5) "lack (of) power to implement program or policies"; 6) limited influence because of the structure of government and fragmentation; 7) reluctance of national policy makers "to deal with the issues of Blacks and the poor", and 8) "minority status in a majority culture and the race variable." He notes that these eight constraints are in addition to the obvious fact of limited numbers and their inheriting long-term problems which have plagued the country for over two hundred years.

In his important study of Black politics in Gary and his subsequent study with Meranto on electing Black mayors in Gary, St. Louis and Cleveland, as well as his latest study of politics in Boston and London, William Nelson (1972, 1977, 2000) also found constraints on BEO's inside and outside the Black community. Among those internal are the low-level of political mobilization in the Black community, its position as an economic colony, its competition over resources, it "mosaic" of ideological positions and approaches, "social class tensions" and a pervasive distrust of Black leadership and alienation from the political system (Nelson and Meranto, 1977). In terms of political alienation, they advance Gamson's (1971) theory of "stable unrepresentation" in which they argue that Blacks occupy a status essentially outside the area of political decision-making on a more or less permanent basis. Walters (1988, 1999:107) argues similarly when he states that there is "a flow in the rules of political legitimacy for elections or decisions based on the firm principle of majority rule because of the existence of groups which are outside the process of consent." In such a context, these groups, i.e., Blacks and other people of color, are a "permanent minority" in power and status regardless of numbers in the system where racism restricts the sharing of power and wealth in an egalitarian and meaningful way.

Moreover, as Nelson and Meranto (1977:382) asserted in their study, "the election of a Black mayor does not automatically mean that the colonized position of the Black community will be significantly changed." For "constraints placed on the administrative authority of Black mayors by a host of economic, political, social and psychological factors make it impossible for their administrations to effectively satisfy the quest for Black liberation," i.e., material, education and cultural benefits which "would encourage the development rather than the oppression of Black people." Among these constraints are: white racist resistance, bureaucratic obstruction, the political need to represent all the people, the tendency toward over-dependence on the federal government for the limited urban reform resources available, inability to successfully challenge the hold of the economic elite (especially corporations) on the decision-making process of the cities and finally, the "inability to attack the fundamental character of the economic and the political order" (Nelson and Meranto, 1977:385).

In another work, Nelson (1987:195) argues that in spite of a new Black politics, "the key assumption that the movement for social and economic freedom is always progressive has not been substantiated by the pattern of political activity occurring in many Black communities over the past two decades." He argues that political activities can either support or change the established order. And it is his assumption that "in the 70's and 80's, Black political activities in local communities have been heavily weighted toward the maintenance of existing social, economic and political arrangements." This he attributes to a problem of theory and practice, i.e., the abandonment of "theories of political independence and self-determination" which characterized the quest for freedom and social justice in the 60's. In their place a vulgar pragmatism of traditional power structures has emerged (Jennings, 1992).

Finally, Georgia Persons (1993a) has posed the problematic "race-neutral" cross-over politics which changes the process of Black politics from "system-challenging action" to emphasis on the positive symbolism of race." In such a process "an opportunity to embrace demonstrably the principles of full participatory equality for Americans regardless of race; for Blacks it provides major symbolic gratification and necessary opportunities to take pride in the achievements of Blacks to more and higher offices."

FUNCTIONS OF BEO'S

In spite of these new developments and continuing constraints, there are studies which show the value of BEO's and of Black participation in the electoral process. Cole (1976), in his early study of BEO's in New Jersey, found several important functions Black BEO's serve. First, they are able to formulate and influence the formulation of policies which affect Black life. This is, of course, more effective on the local level where voting blocs along racial lines are not often found. Secondly, Black BEO's are instrumental in the increasing number and level of Black appointments to governmental positions. Thirdly, they tend to influence white associates' sensitivity to Black issues and interests as well as demonstrate to whites their capacity to govern. Fourthly, Cole argues, Black BEO's provide a necessary link between government and Black citizens white BEO's could not possibly provide. And finally, he contends that Black BEO's serve an important function as a role model for the Black community, demonstrating Black capacity to govern and challenge the concept of white superiority and their monopoly on government. In addition, Gill (1997) found the participation of African American women in Congress of great historical significance, not only in breaking down barriers, but also in terms of leadership in critical issues. Walters (1999) also reaffirms both the necessity and value of Black elected officials.

In sum then, as I (1980:76) have argued elsewhere, BEO's have the following positive functions: 1) introduce and advance African American interests on the level of law, policy, appropriation, allocation, etc.; 2) expose contradictions and criticize the established order from a position of "legitimacy"; 3) create and propose alternatives to the existing order; 4) make appropriate alliances and coalitions; 5) serve as a symbol of the possibility of

Black political power; 6) monitor use of social wealth and struggle for Blacks' just share; and finally 7) gain historical experience in electoral politics which could be transferred to building a Black party.

7.6   INTEREST GROUP POLITICS

As Barker and McCorry (1976:207) contend, "Interest groups are a dominant feature of American life." This is true and necessary because of the conflicting and competing interests which, as mentioned above, shape and define U.S. life. An interest group may be defined as a group organized to define, defend and advance common claims and/or stakes in society, i.e., common interests. Interest groups realize that "political organization and political power are inextricably intertwined" and that "an unorganized mass of people can have little impact on the governmental allocation of social and economic values" (Bailey, 1968:27). Moreover, interest groups tend to be aware that organizational power not only means the ability to help shape government policy, but also private policy, i.e., that of other groups and organizations, enterprises, institutions and persons. Finally, interest groups, in this case Black ones, embrace Prestage's (1968:460) contention that "any meaningful gains for Blacks will come as a result of demands, supported by evidence of Blacks' willingness to cause great inconvenience to the community at large if these legitimate demands are ignored.

Black interest groups use varying strategies and tactics to achieve their goals or policy objectives. Essentially, strategies are broad plans for the achievement of goals and tactics are specific methods of action used to carry out the strategy. Interest group tactics include electoral participation, i.e., voting, campaigning, donations, etc., influencing public opinion, verbal protests, lobbying governmental and non-governmental sources, negotiations, litigation, threats, mass action, i.e., strikes, demonstrations, marches, etc., disruption, violence and focus on internal development. Black interest group strategies can be categorized according to their goals and the methods used to achieve them. Given this, there are three major interest groups strategies among African Americans: liberal, conservative and radical.

LIBERAL STRATEGY

The liberal strategy is reflected in the leadership offered by such middle-class groups as the Urban League and NAACP, but it is prevalent among many sectors of Black people. This strategy, like the leadership which proposes and pursues it, is characterized by several factors (Walters and Smith, 1999; Smith and Walters, 1996). Among these are: 1) assumption that the system is flawed but salvageable; 2) stress on integration; 3) focus on goal pursuance through non-confrontational means where possible, i.e., litigation, elections, lobbying, etc.; 4) rejection of violence; 5) reliance on white political and financial support; 6) strong reliance on government intervention; 7) general confusion of influence with power, i.e., personal persuasion with structural capacity; and 8) focus on minimal goals rather than maximum goals, i.e., jobs vs. ownership, participation in major parties vs. building a Black one, etc. (Bailey, 1968; Thompson, 1963).

Out of these basic dimensions of liberal strategy, three seem to pose more problems than others. First, is the over-emphasis on what Pinderhughes (1980) calls electoral lobbying, i.e., attempts to use the Black vote in sanction or support in order to affect decision makers. Pinderhughes sees this as problematic in that the liberal interest groups do not yet have the ability to organize or direct the vote as effectively as is needed. Thus, Stone's (1970) and others' suggestion to use the Black vote as a swing vote becomes impossible even if the election were close enough to allow it.

Moreover, such a heavy focus on electoral lobbying and the attendant posing of it almost as a panacea, has caused liberal Black interest groups to abandon the mass action tactics which served them so well in the past. In fact, the assumption developed is that these methods are passé and less than sophisticated. The expression used to advance this position is "Blacks must move from protest to politics" (Tate, 1993). This seems to suggest protest and the pressure which accompanies it are not politics, but rather some unclassified or unsophisticated kind of action.

Secondly, liberal Black interest groups rely heavily on white philanthropic support and are thus vulnerable to its political pressure. In such a position, independence is also threatened by the belief that whites are indispensable for Black success as well as by the patron-recipient relation which Hamilton (1979) rightly criticizes. Such positions clearly damage initiative and make self-determination highly problematic, if not impossible. Finally, liberal Black interest groups face the problem of over-reliance on governmental support. One can easily see the positive role government intervention has played in the Black struggle for rights and development during Reconstruction, and the Civil Rights era. But one can also see the vulnerability of over-reliance on government in the "benign neglect" of the Nixon administration or even the last years of the Carter administration when it was clear that even a favorable administration might be unable to act in Black interests, if the political climate is against it and if interest groups who are more powerful oppose Black interests or simply push their own at Blacks' expense (Karenga, 1977; Reed, 1999; Frymer, 1999).

CONSERVATIVE STRATEGY

Although the liberal strategy was temporarily challenged by the Black Power Movement, it reigned unchallenged in the civil rights era and resurged in the early Seventies. However, it now faces a challenge from Black conservatism (Eisenstadt, 1998; Marable, 1997). Black conservative interest-group strategy is defined by: 1) opposition to government intervention and regulation on behalf of Blacks; 2) distaste for mass action tactics; 3) emphasis on individual self-reliance and achievement; 4) stress on group self-help; 5) tendency to blame Blacks for their social problems; 6) a belief in the free-enterprise system as it was, i.e., without its current monopoly and with chances for Black and white miraculous success stories (Fairmont Papers, 1980); Sowell, 1981). Among the Black conservative strategists are Thomas Sowell, an economist at the Hoover Institute; Martin Kilson, a political scientist at Harvard University; Walter Williams, an economist at George Mason University in Virginia; J.A.Y. Parker, president of Lincoln Institute and the Educational Foundation in Washington; syndicated columnist and commentator Armstrong Williams; and Shelby Steele, an English professor, specializing in race matters at the Hoover Institute. Furthermore, in the general context of the shift to a more conservative politics in the U.S., there is a significant increase in Black elected officials who are Republic and conservatives.

The conservative strategy clearly mirrors the philosophy of Booker T. Washington who rejected Black protest, stressed economic developments and power and argued the need for self-help. Likewise, the liberal counter to this adds the DuBoisian dimension to the debate with his emphasis on protest, political rights and the government's obligation to facilitate and insure the freedom, justice and equality for all. Although the conservatives do not have the historical record or structural capacity the liberals enjoy, the current conservative character of U.S. politics tend to give them an increased relevance they would otherwise lack (Palmer, 1999; Faryna and Stetson, 1997).

As I (1982:18-20) have argued elsewhere, this increased relevance is based on several factors. First, Black conservatives are tied to the party in power - politically and/or philosophically - and will thus benefit in stature and influence from that position, i.e., in appointments, resource allocation and consultation. Secondly, Black conservatives benefit from the country's shift to the right. In addition to patronage from the Administration, Congressional support is more likely as well as private support from "resource-rich white conservatives who have never been comfortable with the Black Civil Rights Leadership" (Daniels, 1981:21). Thirdly, given their philosophical and political link with the Administration and the general rightward shift, they will probably be considered more "media worthy" and thus be given more time to introduce and argue their position.

Fourthly, their relevance as an oppositional strategy to liberal strategy dominance will be more apparent the more they are used: to lessen the charge of racism by their inclusion at some level in policy decisions; to support and justify public policies negative to Black interests; and to break the monopoly on Black leadership which liberal interest groups usually enjoy. The irony of this is that liberal Administrations and other liberal whites used Black liberals for similar purposes, i.e., to push and justify their version of what the social order and social policy should be.

THE RADICAL STRATEGY

Radical interest group strategy includes a wide range of tendencies within the African American Movement. Unlike the liberal strategy, it begins with the assumption that the system is not only flawed but also indeed of broad and fundamental change. Secondly, it focuses on confrontation with the established order. Also, it seeks power rather than influence. And it is oriented toward a fundamental reordering of social forces with preference for the masses. Finally, it tends to work outside the system rather than within it, focusing on organization, mobilization and education of the masses. Radical interest-group strategy includes nationalist, pan-Africanist and socialist themes and formations.

NATIONALISM

Nationalism has many tendencies within it (Van DeBurg, 1996; Carmichael and Hamilton, 1992; Pinkney, 1976). However, as a liberational project, *nationalism is social thought and practice centered in the concept and conviction that African Americans are a distinct people with a distinct personality and they have the right an responsibility to unite in order to gain the structural capacity to define, defend and develop their interests* (Karenga, 1980:15). It expresses itself in three basic ways. It is first a redefinition of reality, a redefining of the world in Black images and interests, i.e., from an Afrocentric perspective. Secondly, it is a social corrective, i.e., a thrust to build alternative structures, which check the deprivation and deformation of European institutions and house and advance Black aspirations and interest. Finally, nationalism is a collective vocation, a call and active commitment to liberate Black people, restore them to their traditional greatness and "make African presence both powerful and permanent throughout the world." It is this last aspect of collective vocation which points to the link between nationalism and Pan-Africanism.

PAN-AFRICANISM

There are two basic kinds of Pan-Africanism - continental and global (Walters, 1997). Continental Pan-Africanism is essentially thought and practice directed toward the liberation and unity of the African continent (Ajala, 1973; Padmore, 1971). Global Pan-Africanism is essentially thought and practice directed toward the liberation, unity and mutual support of African peoples throughout the world (Walters, 1997; Garvey, 1977; Chrisman and Hare, 1974). African Americans are essentially global Pan-Africanists, but among them are two tendencies. The first tendency accepts and works within the general framework of the definition above and is represented by groups as diverse as TransAfrica, the Black lobby for Africa and the Caribbean, the National Association of Kawaida Organizations (NAKO), the RNA and Us. In fact, much of African Americans' concern with U.s. foreign policy is due to linkage with and concern for African (Plummer, 1997; McKelvy, 1994). However, African American international interest is wide-ranging and motivated by many factors (Henry, 2000; Stanford, 1997; Henderson, 1995). The second tendency argues not only for the unity and liberation of Africa, but also the return of all Africans to the Continent. It is represented most definitively by the All African People's Revolutionary Party which sees nationalism as a component part and a beginning level of Pan-Africanism (Carmichael, 1971).

SOCIALISM

Also, the radical strategy includes a socialist dimension, either as a separate thrust or as a component part of nationalism (Cruse, 1967; Allen, 1970; McAdam, 1999). Moreover, some socialists see nationalism as a state in socialist development (Boggs, 1974) and some nationalists see socialism as a contribution to nationalist development (Karenga, 1980). The socialist strategy seeks, above all, to organize the worker into a self-conscious social force n order to transform society in the interests of the working masses. It is internationalist in scope and calls for workers of the world to recognize common interests and unite to protect and advance them (see also the next chapter under socialism).

SUMMARY

Given these qualifications, the radical interest-group strategy is defined by: 1) profound alienation from and what Barker and McCorry (1976:217) call "low-integration" into the established political system; 2) call and struggle for fundamental change in the economic and political structure of society; 3) willingness to use any means necessary to achieve ultimate goals; 4) preference for confrontational and mass action politics; 5) focus on the Black masses as the ultimate power with simultaneous stress on the role of a Black vanguard to organize, educate and lead them; 6) stress power, self-development and self-determination; 7) emphasis on history, heritage and the distinctness this expresses; and 8) emulation of and solidarity with African and other Third World peoples and struggles.

The radical interest groups include among others the RNA, All African People's Revolutionary Party (AAPRP), NAKO, the NOI, Us, Council for Independent Black Institutions (CIBI), and Institute of Positive Education (IPE). Once SNCC, CORE, the East, Ahidiana, and the Panthers were included in this category, but these groups have either disbanded or like CORE, been transformed into less than radical models. For a review of these and other radical groups ideologies, tactics and achievements, see Civil Rights and Revolts in Chapter 2. The problems radical interest groups face are many. First, they face the severe and sustained hostility of the system reserved for those who challenge its legitimacy. Secondly, they are actively opposed by the established liberal and conservative interest groups who consider their strategy rhetoric, irrational and negative to their and Black interests. Thirdly, except for possibly the NOI, they lack the financial resources available to the liberal and the conservative groups. Fourthly, they have less institutionalized bases than the liberals and conservatives. Fifthly, they are upstaged by the liberals in their thrust for mass leadership. However, in crisis and with the continuing failure of the liberals to produce resources or viable plans, they get the opportunity to advance alternatives and win greater respect. Finally, the radical interest groups have not yet firmly established the kind of viable working alliance that the liberals had in the Sixties with its Big Six leadership grouping, i.e., SNCC, CORE, SCLC, NUL, NAACP and NALC and now have in the National Black Leadership Forum.

The radical interest groups have built numerous collective leadership groups, but they have been disbanded, become alternative projects or transformed into a single organization after a period of time. The African American Leadership Forum and the National MMM/DOA Organizing Committee during the Million Man March/Day of Absence and the Black United Front are examples of this respectively (Madhubuti and Karenga,

1996). Recently, initiatives for such a collective leadership approach were taken up around discussions and planning for the state of the Black world Conference in 2001. Given the essentiality of such a structure of combined strength and resources and collective planning, it can be safely argued that their success or failure in building it, determine their ability to achieve the objectives they have set for themselves. Also, key to their success will be the development of an intellectual vanguard which can give both a critical and substantive theoretical and practical dimension to their strategy with both rooted in the social reality of U.S. society (Strickland, 1975; Cruse, 1967). Without such a theoretical and practical rootedness in U.S. social reality their thought and practice will be less than effective and the alternative strategies will reign unchecked and unchallenged. Even worse, the alternative to building internally and calling on Blacks to develop and use their own resources instead of depending on external sources will be reduced by critics to rhetoric and denied its deserved status as a viable and critical alternative.

7.7   COALITIONS AND ALLIANCES

Another key concern and problem of Blacks politics is the problem of coalition (Alex-Assensoh, 2000; Frymer, 1999). Central to the problem is the definition, character and results of those coalitions. As Carmichael and Hamilton (1992:59-60) noted, "all too frequently, coalitions involving Black people have been only at the leadership level, dictated by terms set by others, and for objectives not calculated to bring major improvements in the lives of the Black masses. "Historically, Black middle class leadership, i.e., the liberal interest group leadership, has been dependent on white coalition partners - Jewish and Gentile - for financial, legal and political support. In fact, there is or seems to be a basic assumption among this leadership that Blacks would not have come as far as they have, if it were not for whites of goodwill. Such a conception is problematic on at least three levels and speaks to the crisis which currently plagues Black middle class leadership. First, it has been an underlying theme for misconceptions created about Black/white coalitions. Secondly, it has led to a confusion of patronage with coalition. And thirdly, it has tended to encourage denial and reductive translation of Blacks' contribution to their own struggle.

Two of the coalitions on which Blacks have relied heavily are the Jewish and Democratic coalitions (Salzman and West, 1997; Frymer, 1999). These coalitions have produced their share of misconceptions and at the same time revealed the nature of the problem of coalitions faced by Blacks, especially the Black middle class leadership. The misconceptions which surround coalitions are many. Carmichael and Hamilton (1992:58ff) have cited three myths of coalitions which are important to understanding their weakness and unworkability. Agreeing with and incorporating some of their contentions, I have developed five misconceptions of coalitions which clearly create a problem for the coalition in which Black middle class leadership involved itself.

MISCONCEPTIONS

First, there is a clear misconception that the basis of coalition is long-term common interests and principles rather than short-term specific goals. This is a confusion between alliance and coalition. Alliance is a long-term ongoing unity based on common interests and common basic principles, whereas a coalition is a short-term working association based on specific short-term goals. Failure to make and observe this basic distinction has crated situations in which Blacks have assumed too much about their relationship with their more powerful coalition partners and left themselves vulnerable to joint actions not mutually beneficial and to withdrawal of expected support at crucial time. The Andrew Young affair with the Jews and Carter's poor performance in behalf are good examples (Fuller, 1969; Karenga, 1977).

A second misconception is that common goals on one level or in one area is bases for unity in another. For example, Jews might support Blacks against one kind of racism (neo-Nazi or KKK attacks) but opposes them in correctives for racism (Affirmative action). Thirdly, there is a misconception that moral unity - assumed or real - is a substitute for unity around concrete goals and self-interests. This is clear in the case of the assumed Black/Jewish unity based on common or similar suffering. But no unity is automatic, neither political nor personal; each one must be build around concrete goals and interests which change or disappear and therefore, must be reinforced and renewed or replaced by others.

A fourth misconception is that a genuine coalition between the powerful and the powerless (or clearly less powerful) is always possible, rather than always problematic and often pure patronage politics. In fact, one of the problems of the Jewish and Democratic coalitions is that they often deteriorate into patronage politics, i.e., dependence by Blacks on Jewish and Democratic patrons who may be unable or unwilling at various times, to give the largesse or support Blacks request or need (Hamilton, 1979; Frymer, 1999). And the problem is that Blacks cannot effectively penalize or reward these partners in any significant way to compel compliance. The Jewish withdrawal of support from SNCC and CORE as they transformed into Blacks power structures and their opposition to affirmative action are examples of the disenchantment and disengagement without penalty from coalition partners. So are the Democratic Party's unwillingness to support fully Black social justice and social welfare goals under Carter and their unwillingness and inability to produce under Reagan.

In such a coalition, the less powerful partner can lessen or eliminate such politically unhealthy arrangements in three basic ways. It can: (1) unite with other less powerful partners in the coalition to increase its power; (2) build other coalitions to offset negative effects of the problematic one; and (3) shelter no misconception about the problems of coalitions between the powerful and clearly less powerful. Black middle class leadership does not seem to have achieved any of these alternative options.

A final misconception about coalitions is that coalition action is a substitute for a people's or group's own initiative. Such a misconception leaves a group hopelessly and slavishly dependent on forces outside its control and often beyond its influence. There is, in fact, no substitute for the structural capacity to define, defend and develop one's interest. For regardless how numerous or sincere one's allies are, a people that cannot save itself is lost forever.

BLACK-JEWISH RELATIONS

The Black/Jewish coalition is a classic study in the problems of coalitions and there is abundant literature on its history and how it was/is conceived by both African Americans and Jews

(Salzman and West, 1997; Lerner and West, 1996; Lerner, 1995; Berman, 1994). Not only does it reflect commitment to the misconceptions which characterize coalitions in general, it also carries its own particular myths or misconceptions held mainly by its Black members. Among these are first, the myth that Jews are not white in spite of visual reality, self-definition and social acceptance of this fact. A second myth is the Jews are Blacks' best friend, a myth which (Cruse (1967:467) argues is misphrased. It would be far more accurate to say, he states, that "certain Jews have been best friends of certain (Blacks) which in any case is nothing unusual." Thirdly, there is a myth of moral affinity between Blacks and Jews based on similar suffering - historical and current.

These myths suggest or seek to foster a unity and commonality of interests that do not exist and thus produce a political practice and thought based on false premises problematic to African American interests. The first myth seeks to redefine Jews into the Third World to achieve unity through a contrived similarity. The second makes a claim more true for the Black middle class leadership than the Blacks masses and the third assumes an automatic unity and commonality of interest and implies that moral affinity, if it exists, can substitute for concrete interests and goals as a basis for a viable coalition.

As Isaacs (1974:160-181) and Weisbord and Stein (1970) pointed out in earlier works, concrete differences of interests and goals not only separate Blacks and Jews, but also often place them in active opposition to each other. The Andrew Young Affair; affirmative action; the 1966 new York City referendum on a civilian review board; the fight over the Forest Hills housing project in Queen, New York; and the struggle for Black community control in Brooklyn's Ocean-Hill Brownsville School District, and most recently the conflict around Jesse Jackson and especially Farrakhan, all clearly reflect this. This is due to the fact that Jewish power, wealth, social achievement and status and white skin privilege objectively give them a different set of priorities and interests that Blacks whose race and general class character assigns them a marginal and subordinate role and status in the social process. (Shorris, 1982).

THE DEMOCRATIC COALITION

Since Roosevelt's New Deal in the 30's, Blacks have aligned themselves with the Democratic Party (Walters, 1988; Frymer, 1999; Judd, 199). But the alliance was never of equals or semi-equals. On the contrary, like the other alliances, it was essentially a question of patronage, an alignment based on influences not power, and thus, subject to the interests and aspirations of the persons who control it. The party, as a political structure, after all is out to win votes and to do so will no doubt cater to the cutback, cut-off and trim-down attitudes dominant now among white voters. Black middle class leadership finds itself, then, locked into the Democratic Party, with no structural or financial ability to significantly reward or punish it in order to induce it into compliance with the demands of Black interest. Moreover, it has developed no party alternative either with the Republican Party or through the building of a national Black independent party.

As mentioned above, there was talk in 1978 of Blacks moving in significant numbers to the Republican Party as a way of increasing their bargaining power and political options, but as also noted above, nothing serious has come of it. There is not current strategy to enter or construct or benefit the proposed relationship with the Republicans, to pressure the Democrats or demand and get from each party a minimum set of legislative and financial concessions. It could well be that both will decide Blacks are dispensable, that given their overall structural incapacity to reward or punish with organized, self-conscious voting or financial and campaign labor contributions, they are neither needed nor worthy of serious consideration. This obviously presents a practical problem for Black middle class leadership which count so much on the Democratic coalition and talked so much about the Republican option.

INTERNAL ALLIANCES

Although coalition and alliance are used interchangeably in most political science literature, I would like to maintain the difference. Essentially, alliances are internal first and then among others whose long term goals and principles coincide or mesh with those of African Americans. These are usually other peoples of color. Two examples of internal alliances are the Black Leadership

Forum among the liberal middle class leadership and the early National Black Untied Front among the radical leadership.

The Black leadership Forum, formed in 1977, is a national alliance of 16 Black civil rights groups and leaders. The Forum focuses on political and economic issues vital to Blacks and tries to influence public policy in support of Black interests. To achieve this, members meet and lobby with presidents and Congresspersons and make joint position statements. However, it is not well-known or visibly active in the daily problems confronting Blacks as was the Big Six (Walters and Smith, 1999).

The National Black United Front, as noted in Chapter II, was founded in 1980 and has regional and local networks. Unlike the BLF, NBUF is visibly involved in the daily struggles of Black people. It is dedicated to "defense of social service programs and civil rights laws; the fight against the upsurge in racist violence, and opposition to the imperialist war danger" (Elam, 1981b:5). It is also engaging in political education, mass rallies, demonstrations, strikes, and boycotts as well as various expressions of support for continental African and Third World Liberation struggles. However, in recent years, it is more a single leadership organization although it still has national representation.

ALLIANCES WITH PEOPLES OF COLOR

The second kind of alliance has been established at various times with various peoples of color, most notably Puerto Ricans in the East and Mexicans in the Southwest. In late 1978, Blacks and Latinos formed a coalition called "Working Committee on Concerns of Hispanics and Blacks" to ensure that the two constituencies "not bear the brunt of a restrictive economic, social and political climate" (Williams, 1979:74). Participating in the formation of this coalition were Black, Puerto Rican, Mexican and Cuban organizations. Clearly, there is a special and critical need for the building of Black-Brown alliances, although African American alliances with Native Americans and Asians are also important (Stewart, 1996; Karenga, 1997) This is important not simply because of the increasing numbers of Latinos, but essentially because the question of shared power is central to creating a just and good society. Such an ongoing and mutually beneficial alliance will require a new discourse of ethnic relations which talks not simply of Black and white, but of all five groups – Africans, Native Americans, Latinos, Asians and Europeans. Such a discourse must inform a public philosophy, public policy and overall political practice based on an *ethics of sharing* (see below).

As I (Karenga, 1980:77, 1997) have argued elsewhere, there are concrete bases for alliances among peoples of color growing out of their situational similarity in that they are oppressed and exploited on the bases of race and class. In order for such alliances to work, however, clear principles of unity must be established and observed. Among these should be: 1) mutual respect for each people's political, economic and cultural interest;) non-interference in each other's internal affairs; 3) a clear conception of each other's interests; 4) independent power bases; 5) a clear conception of possibilities and problems in unity; 6) clear and concrete goals around which to unify; 7) a clear statement and agreement on principles of cooperation; and 8) a clear statement and agreement on methods of cooperation and struggle" (Karenga, 1980:77-78). Although acceptance and agreement on these principles will not eliminate all obstacles and problems to Third World alliances, it will lay a necessary basis for them. It will require, as noted above, a new discourse, public philosophy and political practice. And it will also require a moral leadership committed to providing a moral vision based on an *ethics of sharing* directed toward building a just and good society and world, mobilizing and organizing the peoples of the various communities in a cooperative political practice to achieve this.

Henry (1980:230) notes that although there are admittedly obstacles confronting such alliances, they nevertheless "appear to be less formidable than those facing Black-white coalitions..." Moreover, given the existence of over 50 million Blacks and Latinos in the U.S., the importance of exploring and building such an alliance is clear and compelling. For if the essence of politics is power and power rests in structural capacity, an alliance becomes a way not only to increase one's own strength, but to deprive the opposition of an ally. This is especially true in an oppressive and conflict-laden society where competing sides seek allies constantly and neutrality is objectively supportive of the established order. For it deprives smaller power blocs of possible added strength and spares the established order a united challenge from the oppressed. Black politics, then, as argued at the beginning, has been and must remain multi-dimensional in both theory and practice. After all, given the multidimensional character of the problem of liberation and a higher level of human life, anything less would certainly be unsuccessful.

7.8   THE POLITICS AND ETHICS OF REPARATIONS

One of the most engaging political and ethical issues in this period of the ongoing struggle for justice by African Americans is the issue of reparations (Obadele, 2000; Eustace and Obadele, 2000; Chokwe, Obadele and Taifa, 2000; Robinson, 2000; Westley, 1998; Verdun, 1993). It has seized the minds of so many different segments of African peoples – Continental and Diasporan – and has become a fundamental issue around which much political discourse, globalization and organization are occurring. The issue of reparations was a key item on the social policy agenda in the *Million Man March/Day of Absence Mission Statement* (Karenga, 1995) and was a central topic at the World Conference Against Racism held in Durban, South Africa, August 31-September 7, 2001. The history of the issue goes back to the Holocaust of enslavement, with Africans petitioning for reparations to return to Africa and to rebuild their lives after the enslavement. The struggle continued after enslavement with claims made by the Nation of Islam, the Self-Determination Committee and various other groups from the 60's. But in the most recent struggle for reparations, no group has been more consistent and active than the National Coalition of Blacks for Reparations in America (N'COBRA), founded in 1987 (Lumumba, Obadele and Taifa, 1993). In the text *Reparations Yes!*, articles and documents by the authors lay out the essential N'COBRA position as evidenced in their text's subtitle, *The Legal and Political Reasons Why New Afrikans – Black People in the United States – Should Be Paid Now For the Enslavement of Our Ancestors and for War Against us **After** Slavery.*

Chokwe, Obadele and Taifa are veterans in the Republic of New Africa's (RNA) struggle for self-determination and thus, these core arguments grow in great part out of the writings of Imari Obadele, chairperson of the People's Center Council of the RNA and its major theorist, as well as from wide-ranging discussions within the RNA about the liberation and self-determination of African people (Obadele, 2000, 1989, 1975; Obadele and Henry, 1998). Also, it is important to note that African American women have been very active in the leadership of this movement. A recent publication titled *Eight Women Leaders of the Reparations Movement, USA* (Eustace and Obadele, 2000) pays special tribute to Queen Mother Audley Moore, founder of the Reparations Committee of Descendants of U.S. Slaves, Inc.; Dorothy Benton-Lewis, national co-chair; Adjoa Aiyetoro, first national co-chair and chair, Legal Strategies Committee; Johnita Scott Obadele, former co-chair of N'COBRA and co-chair, Commission on Membership and Organizational Development; Kupenda Olusegun, co-chair, Commission on Membership and Organizational Development; JoAnn Watson, co-chair, Detroit Chapter and public liaison director on Reparations for Detroit Congressman John Conyers, author of the H.R. 40 bill on reparations; and Erline Arikpo, founder of the Chicago chapter.

Essentially, Obadele (Lumumba, Obadele and Taifa, 1993:24) argues for reparations for both activities and atrocities carried out against African people during and after the Holocaust of enslavement by the U.S. government with conscious and unconscious support of the white population. This, for him is key, given that some reparations advocates would leave out the claim of reparations for the Holocaust. The case for reparations begins with what he terms *the war against Africans* during enslavement, the monstrous treatment and the capture and forced transfer of African people from their homeland. For him reparations means: 1) compensation for *damages*; 2) compensation and measures for *rehabilitation*; 3) compensation and measures for *repatriation* of those Africans who wish to return; 4) compensation and measures for those who choose to practice *self-determination* in or outside the U.S.; and 5) removal of all barriers to the *free exercise of the human rights* of African people in the U.S.

[In continuing contribution to this discourse on reparations, I presented a paper on the "The Ethics of Reparations: Engaging the Holocaust of Enslavement" at the Annual N'COBRA Conference at Southern University, Baton Rouge, June 22-23, 2001. Below is its essential content.]

The struggle for reparations for the Holocaust of enslavement of African people is clearly one of the most important struggles being waged in the world today. For it is about fundamental issues of human freedom, human justice and the value we place on human life in the past as well as in the present and future. It is a struggle which, of necessity, contributes to our regaining and refreshing our historical memory as a people, remembering and raising up the rightful claims of our ancestors to lives of dignity and decency and to our reaffirming and securing the rights of their descendants to live free, full and meaningful lives in our times.

But this struggle, like all our struggles, begins with the need for a clear conception of what we want, how we define the issue and explain it to the world and what is to be done to achieve it. The struggle for reparations begins with the definition of the horrendous injury to African people which demands repair. To talk of reparations is first to identify and define the injury, to say what it is and is not, and to define its nature and its impact on the one(s) injured. Unless this is done first and maintained throughout the process, there is no case for reparations only an incoherent set of claims without basis in ethics or law.

This is why the established order works so hard to define away the historical and ongoing character of the injury. This is especially done in two basic ways. First, the injury is distorted and hidden under the category of "slave trade". The category "trade" tends to sanitize the high level of violence and mass murder that was inflicted on African peoples and societies. If the categorization of the Holocaust of enslavement can be reduced to the category of "trade," two things happen. First, it becomes more of a *commercial* issue rather than a *moral* issue. And secondly, since trade is the primary focus, the mass murder or genocide can be and often is conveniently understood and accepted a simply "collateral damage."

A second attempt of the established order to deny the horrendous nature of the injury of the Holocaust of enslavement and its essential responsibility for it, is to claim collaboration of the victims in their own victimization. Here, it is morally and factually important to make a distinction between collaborators *among* the people and the people themselves. Every people faced with conquest, oppression and destruction has had collaborators among them, but it is factually inaccurate and morally wrong and repulsive to indict a whole people for a holocaust which was imposed on them and was aided by collaborators. Every holocaust had collaborators: the Native Americans, Jews, Australoids, Armenians and Africans. No one morally sensitive claims Jews are responsible for their holocaust based on the historical evidence of Jewish collaborators. How then are Africans indicted for the collaborators among them? Although there are other ways the established order seeks to undermine the factual and moral basis of the African claim for reparations, these two approaches are indispensable to its efforts. And thus, they must be raised up and rejected constantly, for they speak to the indispensable need to define the injury to African people and to maintain control of it.

Us has maintained since the Sixties concerning European cultural hegemony, one of the greatest powers in the world is to be able to define reality and make others accept it even when it's to their disadvantage. And it is this power to define the injury of holocaust as trade and self-victimization and make Africans accept it, that has dominated the discourse on enslavement in America. Our task it to reframe the discourse and initiate a new national dialog on this. We have argued that the injury just be defined as holocaust (see above, chapter 4, section on the Holocaust of enslavement) By *holocaust* we mean *a morally monstrous act of genocide that is not only against the people themselves, but also a crime against humanity*. The Holocaust of enslavement expresses itself in three basic ways: the morally monstrous destruction of human life, human culture and human possibility.

In terms of the destruction of human life, estimates run as high as ten to a hundred million persons killed individually and collectively in various brutal and vicious ways. The destruction of culture includes the destruction of centers, products and producers of culture: cities, towns, villages, libraries, great literatures (written and oral), and great works of art and other cultural creations as well as the creative and skilled persons who produced them. And finally, the morally monstrous destruction of human possibility involved redefining African humanity to the world, poisoning past, present and future relations with other peoples who only know us through this stereotyping and thus, damaging the truly human relations among peoples. It also involves lifting Africans out of their own history making them a footnote and forgotten casualty in European history and thus limiting and denying their ability to speak their own special cultural truth to

the world and make their own unique contribution to the forward flow of human history. It is here that the issue of stolen
labor and ill-gotten gains which is seen as important to the legal
case can be raised. For in removing us from our own history,
enslaving us and brutally exploiting our labor, this process limited and prevented us from building our own future and living the
lives of dignity and decency which is our human right.

At this point, it is important to stress the role of *intentionality* in the Holocaust. Again, discussion of the Holocaust as a
commercial project often leads to an understanding of the massive violence and mass murder as intended collateral damage.
Thus, to frame it rightfully as a *moral issue* rather than a commercial one, we must use terms of discourse which speak not only
to the human costs, but to the element of intentionality. It is in
this regard that Us maintains that *maangamizi*, the Swahili term
for Holocaust, is more appropriate than its alternative category
maafa. For maafa which means calamity, accident, ill luck, disaster, or damage does not indicate intentionality. It could be a natural disaster or a deadly highway accident. But *maagamizi* is
derived from the verb *angamiza* which means to cause destruction, to utterly destroy and thus carries with it a sense of intentionality. The "ma" prefix of the word, suggests an amplified
destruction and thus speaks to the massive nature of the
Holocaust.

Clearly, it is issues like these, and the ones discussed below
which require an expanded communal, national and international dialog, which precedes and makes possible a final decision
on the definition and meaning of the Holocaust, and the morally and legally compelling steps which must be taken to repair this
horrendous past and ongoing injury. Regardless of the eventual
shape of the evolved discourse and policy on reparations, there
are five essential aspects which must be addressed and included
in any meaningful and moral approach to reparations. They are:
1) public admission; 2) public apology; 3) public recognition; 4)
compensation; and 5) institutional preventive measures against
the recurrence of holocaust and other similar forms of massive
destruction of human life, human culture and human possibility.

First, there must be *public admission* of the Holocaust committed against African people by the state and its *ruling
race/class*, white people. This, of course, must be preceded by a
public discussion or national conversation in which whites over-

come their acute denial of the nature and extent of injuries inflicted on African people and concede that the most morally appropriate term for this utter destruction of human life, human culture and human possibility is holocaust.

Secondly, once there is public discussion and concession on the nature and extent of the injury, then there must be a *public apology*. One of the reasons we rejected the one-sentence attempt to get a congressional apology is that it was premature and did not allow for discussion and admission of holocaust. In addition, as the injured party, Africans must initiate and maintain control of the definition and discussion of the injury. No one would suggest or contemplate Germans superceding Jewish initiatives and claims concerning their holocaust, nor Turks seizing the initiative in the resolution of the Armenian holocaust claims. The point here is that Africans must define the framework for the discussion and determine the content of the apology. And, of course, the apology can't be for "slave trade," or simply "slavery"; it must be an apology for committing holocaust. Moreover, the state must offer it on behalf of its white citizens. For the state is the crime partner with corporations in the initiation, conduct and sustaining of this destructive process. It is the state which maintained and supported the system of destruction with law, army, ideology and brutal suppression. Thus, it must offer the apology for the Holocaust committed.

Thirdly, public admission and public apology must be reinforced with *public recognition* through institutional establishment, monumental construction and educational instruction through the school and university system and the media, directed toward teaching and preserving memory of the horror and meaning of the Holocaust of enslavement, not only for Africans and this country, but also for humanity as a whole. Here it is important to note that the first holocaust memorial should have been for Native Americans who suffered the first holocaust in this hemisphere. And we must address their holocaust concerns and claims, as a matter of principle and with the understanding that until and unless they receive justice in their rightful claims, the country can never call itself a free, just or good society.

Fourthly, reparations also requires compensation in various forms. Compensation can never be simply financial or monetary payoffs, either individually or collectively. Nor should the movement for reparations be reduced to simply a quest for compensation without addressing the other four aspects. Indeed, compensation itself is a multidimensional demand and option and may involve not only money, but land, free health care, housing, free education from grade school through college, etc. But whether we choose one or all, we must have a communal discussion about the forms of compensation we want, and then make the choice. Moreover, compensation as an issue is not simply compensation for lost labor, but for the comprehensive injury – the brutal destruction of human lives, human cultures and human possibilities.

Finally, reparations requires that in the midst of our national conversation, we must discuss and commit ourselves to continue the struggle to establish measures to prevent the reoccurrence of such massive destruction of human life, human culture and human possibility. This means that we must see and approach the reparations struggle as part and parcel of our overall struggle for freedom, justice, equality and power in and over our destiny and daily lives. In the final analysis, this requires the bringing into being a just and good society and the creation of a context for maximum human freedom and human flourishing. Indeed, it is only in such a context that we can truly begin to repair and heal ourselves, our injuries, return fully to our own history, live free, full, meaningful and productive lives and bring into being the good world we all want and deserve to live in.

7.9 AN ETHICS OF SHARING: A PUBLIC POLICY INITIATIVE

INTRODUCTION

At the beginning of this chapter, I put forth the proposition that politics, at its best, is a collective ethical vocation to create and sustain a just and good society and world. What I want to do in this last section is to raise and engage the question of what ethical vision and social practice are necessary to carry this project to a successful conclusion. To accomplish, this I will suggest a framework for a public policy initiative directed toward creating a national discourse on the just and good society and world and the social vision and practice central to their realization. In doing this, I want to reaffirm the importance of African Americans self-consciously playing their historical and ongoing role as a *moral and political vanguard* in this country. This piece is essentially to provoke critical thought about African Americans' political practice, their self-understanding and self-assertion in society and the world and the vanguard role they can and must play to honor their ancient and ongoing social justice tradition and to bring about a just and good society and world. This will lead to a discussion of an ethics of sharing as the core of the collective ethical vocation.

SELF-UNDERSTANDING AND SELF-ASSERTION

The quality of our life in our community and the country depends decisively on our *self-understanding* and our *self-assertion* as a people. Indeed, how we see ourselves dictates how we assert ourselves in the world in terms of both our aspirations and sense of what is possible. Thus, the first struggle of a people who dares to achieve liberation and a higher level of life is to understand themselves in such a way that their self-conception compels and sustains a practice that leads to the realization of their highest aspirations. African Americans have, at their best, understood themselves as a decisive *moral and political vanguard* of this country. Indeed, we have defined ourselves as such in a historical practice that not only expanded the realm of freedom in this country, but inspired and informed other marginalized, oppressed and struggling peoples in this country and the world. In this country and around the world, other peoples struggling for freedom, for the right and for the good have borrowed our moral vision and our moral vocabulary, sang our songs of freedom and posed our struggle as a model of the human struggle for liberation and ever higher levels of human life.

However, conservative social forces have attempted to undermine this identity and to redefine our self-understanding and other's understanding of us from that of a critical moral and political vanguard for this country to the pathological and pathogenic source of many, if not most, of its central problems. Our challenge is to reaffirm our central identity in a vision and practice that not only improve and expand our lives as a community, but at the same time pose a central vision for a new public philosophy and policy for this country with implications for the world, self-consciously directed toward improving the human condition and enhancing the human future.

PUBLIC PHILOSOPHY AND DISCOURSE

Our task then is to reestablish a *collective ethical vocation* for our community which is not only the basis of our self-understanding and self-assertion but also contributes definitively to a new and expanded public philosophy and discourse on the just and good society in a global context. In a word, we must initiate and sustain a public discourse which produces policies and practices with a substantive ethical character as distinct from the current almost exclusive focus on procedures of right and justice.

Our central model is the Black Freedom Movement (1955-1975) which was not only a struggle for rights and procedures but for the reaffirmation of human dignity; not only a means to achieve equal rights but a process of empowerment and deepening our self-understanding as agents of change, who are uncompromisingly committed to expanding the realm of human freedom and human flourishing, in a word, a *moral and political vanguard* for the country and in a larger sense, the world. The need, then, is to recover this history and all that represents the best of what it means to be both African and human and to use it as a framework and foundation to radically improve the conditions of the present and enhance the possibilities of the future.

The public philosophy we propose then must be self-consciously *ethical* as distinct from the essentially *procedural*. For it is not simply laws we seek to be used to declare the end of racism or statistics which show economic growth in spite of obvious human poverty, but rather *access, opportunity* and *results* that emerge from reflection, discussion and action rooted in a profound concern with achieving the good life and an ethical understanding of the conditions for human freedom and human flourishing in society and the world.

Within the African ethical tradition, ancient and modern, there are four fundamental and overarching principles and goals which ground and guide our pursuit of the good life and the ongoing struggle to create the conditions for maximum human freedom and human flourishing. And thus, we must initiate and sustain a national thinking, discourse and practice which are self-consciously rooted in and reflective of a profound and ongoing commitment to these fundamental and overarching principles and goals. And they are: (1) the dignity and rights of the human person; (2) the well-being and flourishing of family and community; (3) the integrity and value of the environment; and (4) the reciprocal solidarity and cooperation for mutual benefit of humanity. In order to uphold these principles and achieve these goals in society and the world, we must create a public philosophy discourse and practiced rooted in an *ethics of sharing*, i.e., the moral thought and practice of: (1) shared status; (2) shared knowledge; (3) shared space; (4) shared wealth; (5) shared power; (6) shared interests; and (7) shared responsibility. This reaffirms the central African ethical understanding that the greatest goods are and must be a shared good. Indeed, the good of freedom, justice, equality, love, friendship, sisterhood, brotherhood and even life itself are all shared goods. Thus, an ethics of sharing is essential, in fact, indispensable.

SHARED STATUS

Shared status is the fundamental principle of human and social relations and speaks to the mutual commitment to the dignity of the human person, not as an abstraction but as a *person-in-community*, a community which is fundamental to a person's self-understanding and self-assertion in the world. It embraces the basic principle that each culture is a unique and equally valuable way of being human in the world. It requires equal status of each person and people as human beings and citizens, who are equal in dignity, rights, opportunity and respect in both principle and practice. As mutual respect and recognition, it rejects all concepts and practices of superiority and inferiority of persons and peoples and upholds the principle of equal human and social worth for all.

SHARED KNOWLEDGE

The principle of shared knowledge speaks to the human and social need for knowledge for development and human flourishing. We understand access to knowledge or quality education in the broadest sense as a fundamental human right. Moreover, the central role of knowledge in determining the quality of life and the possibilities of meaningful participation in society in economic, political and cultural terms require a sharing of the highest level and most current knowledge. Without this access, other critical social goods remain at best severely diminished and at worst impossible. The need, then, is for knowledge for "a living" and for life, i.e., for the conception and achievement of maximum human flourishing.

SHARED SPACE

The principle of shared space requires a meaningful recognition that sharing the country means sharing space with other citizens and immigrants in an equitable and ethical way. It speaks to an immigration policy without race, class, religious or any other irrational and immoral biases; urban, neighborhood and housing policies that preserve and expand public spaces (parks, libraries, schools, town halls, community centers, etc.) which cultivate meaningful interaction and mutually beneficial exchanges; and an environmental policy that respects the integrity of the environment and avoids the gross choice of economic development in spite of environmental blight. Here we engage the need to reverse the privatization of public wealth and space, to restrain corporate private claims on the environment, which is a human resource and responsibility, and to alter the isolation of suburbs from urban areas and the separatist seclusion of wall-off enclaves and gated communities that challenge the concepts of shared space and common good.

SHARED WEALTH

The principle of shared wealth is one of an equitable distribution of wealth. It is based on the understanding that the right to a life in dignity includes the right to a decent life, a life in which people have the basic necessities of food, clothing, shelter, health care, physical and economic security and education. And this in turn requires a sharing of wealth which makes these things possible. This principle also speaks to the need to care for the vulnerable and to aid the poor in their struggle to reduce and end poverty. It reaffirms the right to economic initiative which includes *ownership* as well as *employment*. It also upholds the right of workers to just wages, adequate benefits, safe working conditions, just treatment on the job and in separation, unionization and meaningful participation in decisions which affect them, the country and the world.

This principle also reaffirms the right and responsibility to engage in purposeful and productive work, as far as we are able, as essential to the dignity and self-respect of persons. Moreover, the principle of shared wealth calls for corporate, governmental and people responsibility in insuring human rights and the integrity of the environment in the areas of production, ownership, consumption, distribution, investment, trade and development, especially in an era of the globalization of wealth and power concentrated in ever fewer hands and structures. It affirms that shared wealth remains an essential way of increasing beneficiaries of economic growth and expansion, promoting democratic decision-making in the economic process, and laying the ground for cooperative activities and shared interests in other areas.

SHARED POWER

The central concern of the principle of shared power is the right of self-determination, the principle and practice of self-governance, the need for meaningful and effective participation in decisions that affect and determine our destiny and daily lives. This principle speaks to the need for the capacity to define, defend and develop our interests and realize our will in the context of cooperative efforts toward the common good. It distinguishes the possession of *power*, the ability to achieve ends and *influence*, the ability to affect those who hold power. The principle of shared power also speaks to the need for effective representation and substantive presence in critical social space, especially political, economic and cultural space, as distinct from symbolic placement.

SHARED INTERESTS

The principle of shared interests stresses the need for common ground in the midst of our diversity. It assumes that whatever our differences, a moral minimum number of common interests must undergird and inform our common efforts. It begins with our mutual commitment to the dignity and rights of the human person, the well being and flourishing of family and community, the integrity and value of the environment and the reciprocal solidarity and cooperation for mutual benefit of humanity. It extends to and includes the explicit commitment to the struggles for freedom, justice, equality, peace and other good in the world. In other words, it includes our common interests in achieving engaged and empowered communities, a just and good society and a good and sustainable world.

SHARED RESPONSIBILITY

The principle of shared responsibility speaks to the need for an active commitment to collective responsibility for building the communities, society and world we want and deserve to live in. It stresses active engagement in reconceiving and reconstructing our communities, society and the world in a more human image and interest. It calls on us *personally* and *collectively* to study, reflect, discuss and act together around the critical issues facing us, for ourselves, history and the future. It requires constant moral assessment of policies and practices in terms of how they affect human life and human development, respect the environment, and leave a worthy legacy for future generations. And it emphasizes the need for us to recognize both the significance and urgency of our shared active responsibility. For as it is written, "every day is a donation to eternity and even one hour is a contribution to the future."

STUDY QUESTIONS

1. What are two major ancient sources for political discourse?
2. Discuss the ideas of each and their relevance to modern political discourse.
3. What is politics? Discuss some of its core concepts.
4. What are eight areas of power?
5. What is the rationale for party politics?
6. Discuss the Democratic party experience.
7. Discuss the Republican party experience.
8. Discuss the Black party initiatives in terms of problems and possibilities.
9. Cite and discuss constraints on BEO's.
10. What are some of the valuable functions BEO's serve in spite of constraints?
11. Discuss the significance of the Jackson campaigns?

12. What is an interest group and what are three basic Black interest group strategies?
13. What are some misconceptions about coalitions?
14. Discuss two basic coalitions Blacks have been in and the problems of each.
15. Discuss two kinds of alliance giving examples of each.
16. What are the requirements for effective alliances?
17. What are four overarching principles and goals of the African ethical tradition key to the pursuit of politics as an ethical vocation?
18. Discuss the ethics of sharing and its role as a basis for a just and good society.

REFERENCES

Ajala, Adekunle. (1973) *Pan-Africanism: Evolution, Progress and Prospects*, New York: St. Martin's Press.

Alex-Assenoh, Yvette M. (2000) *Black and Multiracial Politics in America*, New York: New York University Press.

Allen, Robert. (1970) *Black Awakening in Capitalist America*, Garden City, NY: Doubleday.

Apter, David. (1977) *Introduction to Political Analysis*, Cambridge, MA: Winthrop Publishers, Inc.

Baily, Harry, Jr. (1968) "Negro Interest Group Strategies," *Urban Affairs Quarterly*, 4, 1 (September).

Baily, Harry, Jr. (ed.) (1967) *Negro Politics in America*, Columbus, OH: Charles Merrill Books.

Balbus, Isaac. (1974) "The Concept of Interest in Pluralist and Marxian Analysis," in Ira Katznelson, et al, (eds.), *Politics and Society*, New York: David McKay Co., Inc. pp. 278-304.

Banks, Manley et al. (1996) "Transformative Leadership in the Post-Civil Rights Era: The 'War on Poverty' and the Emergence of African American Municipal Political Leadership," *Western Journal of Black Studies*, 20, 173-87.

Barker, Lucius J. (1999) *Black Electoral Politics: Participation, Performance, Promise*, New Brunswick, NJ: Transaction Publications.

Barker, Lucius J. (1994) "Limits of Political Strategy: A Systematic View of the African American Experience," *American Political Science Review*, 88, 1-18.

Barker, Lucius U. (1988) *Our Time Has Come*, Urbana: University of Illinois Press.

Barker, Lucius J. (1987) "Ronald Reagan, Jesse Jackson and the 1984 Presidential Election: The Continuing American Dilemma of Race," in Michael Preston et al (eds.), *The New Black Politics*, New York: Longman.

Barker, Lucius J. and Mack H. Jones. (1994) *African Americans and the Political System*, Paramus: Prentice Hall PTR.

Barker, Lucius J. and Jesse McCorry, Jr. (1976) *Black Americans and the Political System*, Cambridge, MA: Winthrop Publishers, Inc.

Berman, Paul. (1994) *Blacks and Jews: Alliances and Arguments*, New York: Delacorte.

Boggs, James. (1974) *Revolution and Evolution in the Twentieth Century*, New York: Monthly Review Press.

Breasted, James. (1934) *The Dawn of Conscience*, New York: Charles Scribners Sons

Carmichael, Stokely. (1971) *Stokely Speaks*, New York: Vintage Books.

Carmichael, Stokely and Charles V. Hamilton. (1992) *Black Power: The Politics of Liberation in America*, New York: Vintage Books.

Cavanaugh, Thomas and Lorn Foster. (1984) *Jesse Jackson's Campaign: The Primaries and Caucuses*, Washington, DC: Joint Center for Political Studies.

Chrisman, Robert and Nathan Hare. (1974) *Pan-Africanism*, Indianapolis: Bobbs-Merrill Co., Inc.

Clay, William L. (1999) *Just Permanent Interest*, New York: Harper Trade.

Cohen, Cathy. (1999) *The Boundaries of Blackness: AIDS and the Breakdown of Black Politics*, Chicago: University of Chicago Press.

Cole, Leonard. (1976) *Blacks in Power*, Princeton, NJ: Princeton University Press.

Collins, Sheila D. (1986) *The Rainbow Coalition: The Jackson Campaign and the Future of U.S. Politics*, New York: Monthly Review Press.

Conyers, James and Walter Wallace. (1976) *Black Elected Officials*, New York: Russell Sage Foundation.

Cruse, Harold. (1967) *Crisis of the Negro Intellectual*, New York: William Morrow.

Cruse, Harold. (1974) "The National Black Convention at Little Rock," *Black World*, 24, 1 (November) 4-21.

Dahl, Robert. (1976) *Pluralist Democracy in America*, Chicago: Rand McNally.

Dalleck, Robert. (1984) *Ronald Reagan: The Politics of Symbolism*, Cambridge: Harvard University Press.

Daniels, Johnnie. (1971) "The Development of an Independent Black Political Party," *African American Studies*, 2, pp. 95-105.

Daniels, Lee A. (1981) "The New Black Conservatives," *New York Times Magazine* (October 4) Section 6:20, 54, 58.

Daniels, Ron. (1980) "The National Black Assembly," *Black Scholar* 11, 4 (March/April) 32-41.

Dawson, Michael C. (1994) *Race and Class in African American Politics*, Princeton: Princeton University Press.

Drake, St. Clair. (1971) "The Social and Economic Status of the Negro in the United States," in Edward Greenbert et al (eds.), *Black Politics*, New York: Holt, Rinehard and Winston.

Drake, W. Avon and Robert D. Halsworth. (1996) *Affirmative Action & the Stalled Quest for Black Progress*, Champaign: University of Illinois Press.

DuBois, W.E.B. (1935) *Black Reconstruction in America: An Essay Toward a History of the Part Which Black Folk Played in the Attempt to Reconstruct Democracy in America, 1860-1880*, New York: Russell & Russell.

Dymally, Mervyn. (1972) "The Black Man's Role in American Politics," in *Black Political Life in the United States*, Lenneal Henderson, Jr., (ed.), San Francisco: Chandler Publishing Company.

Eisenstadt, Peter, (ed.), (1998) *Black Conservatism: Essays in Intellectual and Political History*, New York: Garland Publishing.

Elam, Frank. (1981a) "NBIPP: Problems and Prospects," *Guardian*, (October) 7ff.

Elam, Frank. (1981b) "NBUF Action Plan Targets Budgets Cuts, Racism, War," *Guardian*, (July 15) 5.

Eustace, Linda Allen and Imari A. Obadele. (2000) *Eight Women Leaders of the Reparations Movement, USA*, Baton Rouge: Malcolm Generation Inc.

The Fairmont Papers, Black Alternatives Conference. (1980) San Francisco: Institute for Contemporary Studies (December).

Faryna, Stan G. and Brad Stetson, (eds.) (1997) *Black and Right: The Bold New Voice of Black Conservatives in America*, Westport, CT: Greenwood Press.

Faw, Bob and Nancy Skelton. (1986) *Thunder in America*, Austin: Texas Monthly Press.

Foner, Eric. (1988) *Reconstruction: America's Unfinished Revolution, 1863-1877*, New York: Harper & Row.

Frye, Hardy. (1980) *Black Parties and Political Power*, Boston: G.K. Hall & Co.

Frymer, Paul. (1999) *Uneasy Alliances: Race and Party Competition in America*, Princeton: Princeton University Press.

Fuller, Hoyt. (1969) "Black Leadership and the Black-Jewish Debacle," *First World*, 2, 3.

Gamson, William. (1971) "Stable Unrepresentation in American Society," in *Black Politics*, Edward S. Greenberg, et al, (eds.), New York: Holt, Rinehard and Winston.

Garvey, Marcus. (1977) *Philosophy and Opinions of Marcus Garvey, I & II*, New York: Atheneum.

Gill, La Verne M. (1997) *African American Women in Congress*, Piscataway: Rutgers University Press.

Gilliam, Reginald, Jr. (1975) *Black Political Development*, Port Washington, New York: Dunellen Publishing Company, Inc.

Gosnell, Harold (1967) *Negro Politicians: The Rise of Negro Politics in Chicago*, Chicago: University of Chicago Press.

Guinier, Lani. (1998) *Lift Every Voice: Turning A Civil Rights Setback Into a New Vision of Social Justice*, New York: Simon and Schuster.

Guinier, Lani. (1994) *The Tyranny of the Majority*, New York: Free Press.

Hamilton, Charles. (1979) "The Patron-Recipient Relationship and Minority Politics in New York City," *Political Science Quarterly*, 95, 2, pp. 211-227.

Hamilton, Charles. (1993) "Promoting Priorities: African American Political Influence in the 1990's" in Janet Dewart, (ed.), *The State of Black America*, New York: National Urban League, pp. 59-69.

Hatch, Robert. (1988) *Beyond Opportunity*, Philadelphia: Fortress.

Henderson, Errol Anthony. (1995) *Afrocentrism and world Politics: Towards A New Paradigm*, Westport, CT: Praeger.

Henry, Charles. (1980) "Black-Chicano Coalitions: Possibilities and Problems," *Western Journal of Black Studies*, 4, 4 (Winter) 222-231.

Henry, Charles. (1982) "Black Neo-Conservatism," a paper presented at the Annual Meeting of the National Conference of Black Political Scientists, New Orleans, LA. (April 21-24).

Henry, Charles. (2000) *Foreign Policy and Black (Inter) National Interest*, Albany: State University of New York Press.

Henry, Charles. (1991) *Jesse Jackson: The Search for Common Ground*, Oakland, CA: Black Scholar Press.

Holden, Matthew, Jr. (1973) *The Politics of the Black Nation*, New York: Chandler Publishing Company.

Holden, Matthew, Jr. (1990) "The Rewards of Daring and the Ambiguity of Power: Perspectives on the Wilder Election of 1989," in Janet Dewart, (ed.), *The State of Black America, 1990*, New York: National Urban League, pp. 121-142.

Isaac, Stephen. (1974) *Jews and American Politics*, Garden City, NY: Doubleday.

Jackson, Jesse. (1987) *Straight From the Heart*, Garden City, NY: Doubleday.

Jacobs, John. (1990) "Black America, 1989: An Overview," in Janet Dewart, (ed.), *The State of Black America, 1990*, New York: National Urban League, pp.1-8.

James, T.G.H. (1984) *Pharaoh's People*, Chicago: University of Chicago Press.

Jennings, James. (1992) *The Politics of Black Empowerment: The Transformation of Black Activism in Urban America*, Detroit: Wayne State University Press.

Jones, Mack. (1972) "A Frame of Reference for Black Politics," in *Black Political Life in the United States*, Lenneal Henderson Jr. (ed.), San Francisco: Chandler Publishing Co., pp. 7-20.

Judd, Dennis R. (1999) "Symbolic Politics and Urban Policies: Why African Americans Got So Little From the Democrats," in Adolph Reed, (ed.), *Without Justice For All: The New Liberalism and Our Retreat From Racial Equality*, Boulder, CO: Westview Press, pp. 123-150.

Karenga, Maulana. (1978a) "Blacks and the GOP: The Newest Deal," *In These Times*, 2, 46 (October 11-16) 16.

Karenga, Maulana. (1977) "Carter and His Black Critics: The Dialogue and Its Lessons," *Black Scholar*, 9,3 (November) 52-54.

Karenga, Maulana. (1982) "The Crisis of Black Middle-Class Leadership," *Black Scholar*, 13,6 (Fall) 16-36.

Karenga, Maulana. (1978b) *Essays on Struggle: Position and Analysis*, Inglewood, CA: Kawaida Publications.

Karenga, Maulana. (1984) "Jesse Jackson and the Presidential Campaign: The Invitation and Oppositions of History," *Black Scholar*, 15, 5 (September/October) 57-71.

Karenga, Maulana. (1980) *Kawaida Theory: An Introductory Outline*, Inglewood, CA: Kawaida Publications.

Karenga, Maulana. (1994) *Maat, The Moral Ideal in Ancient Egypt: A Study in Classical African Ethic*, unpublished dissertation, University of Southern California, Los Angeles.

Karenga, Maulana. (1995) *Million Man March/Day of Absence Mission Statement*, Los Angeles: University of Sankore Press.

Karenga, Maulana. (1984) *Selections From The Husia: Sacred Wisdom of Ancient Egypt*, Los Angeles: University of Sankore Press.

Kemp, Barry. (1983) "Old Kingdom, Middle Kingdom and Second Intermediate Period c. 2686-1152 BC," in B.G. Trigger et al, (eds.), *Ancient Egypt, A Social History*, Cambridge: Cambridge University Press, pp. 71-82.

Key, V.O. Jr. (1962) *Politics, Parties and Pressure Groups*, New York: Thomas Y. Crowell Company.

Ki-Zergo, J. (1981) *General History of Africa, I: Methodology and African Prehistory*, Paris/London: UNESCO/Heinemann.

Kinder, Donald R. and Lynn M. Sanders. (1996) *Divided By Color*, Chicago: University of Chicago Press.

Klinkner, Phillip. (1999) "Bill Clinton and the Politics of the New Liberalism," in Adolph Reed, (ed.), *Without Justice For All: The New Liberalism and Our Retreat From Racial Equality*, Boulder, CO: Westview Press, pp. 11-28.

Klinkner, Phillip. (1994) *The Losing Parties: Out-Party National Committee, 1956-1993*, New Haven, CT: Yale University Press.

Ladd, Everett. (1969) *Negro Political Leadership in the South*, New York: Atheneum.

Landass, Thomas and Richard M. Quinn. (1985) *Jesse Jackson and the Politics of Race*, Ottowa, IL: Jameson Books.

Lashley, Marilyn E. and Melanie N. Jackson, (eds.) (1994) *African Americans and the New Policy Consensus: Retreat of the Liberal State? 347*, Westport, CT: Greenwood Publishing.

Lerner, Michael. (1995) *Blacks and Jews, Let the Healing Begin*, New York: Putnam.

Lerner, Michael and Cornel West. (1996) *Jews & Blacks, A Dialog on Race, Religion & Culture in America*, New York: Dutton/Plume.

Lichtheim, Miriam. (1976) *Ancient Egyptian Literature, Volume II*, Berkeley: University of California Press.

Lichtheim, Miriam. (1992) *Maat in Egyptian Autobiographies and Related Studies*, Friburg, Gottingen: Universitäts-Verlag.

Lowi, Theodore and Benjamin Ginsberg. (1996) *American Government*, New York: W.W. Norton.

Lumumba, Chokwe, Imari A. Obadele and Nkecha Taifa. (1993) *Reparations Yes! The Legal and Political Reasons Why New Afrikans – Black People in the United States – Should Be Paid Now for the Enslavement of Our Ancestors and for War Against Us After Slavery*, 3rd Edition, Baton Rouge: House of Songhay.

Lusane, Clarence. (1994) *African Americans at the Crossroads: The Restructuring of Black Leadership & the 1992 Elections*, Cambridge: South End Press.

Lusane, Clarence. (1997) *Race in the Global Era: African Americans and the Millenium*, Boston: South End Press.

Marable, Manning. (1997) *Black Liberation in Conservative America*, Boston: South End Press.

Marable, Manning. (1980) *From the Grassroots*, Boston: South End Press.

McAdam, Doug. (1983) *Political Process and the Development of Black Insurgency 1930-1970*, Chicago: Chicago University Press.

McCormick, Joseph and Charles E. Jones. (1993) "The Conceptualization of Deracialization: Thinking Through the Dilemma," in Georgia A. Persons, (ed.), *Dilemmas of Black Politics*, New York: Harper Collins College Publishing, pp. 66-84.

McLemore, Leslie B. (1971) "Mississippi Freedom Democratic Party," *Black Politician*, 3,2 (October) 19-22.

Mokhtar, G. (ed.) (1990) *General History of Africa: Ancient Civilizations of Africa, Volume II*, Paris: UNESCO.

Morris, Aldon D. and Carol McClurg Mueller. (1992) *Frontiers in Social Movement Theory*, New Haven, CT: Yale University Press.

Morris, Milton. (1975) *The Politics of Black America*, New York: Harper & Row Publishers, Inc.

Muhammad, Silas. (n.d.) *Reparations Petition: For United Nations Assistance Under Resolution 1503 (XLVIII) on Behalf of the African-Americans in the United States of America*, Hampton, VA: United Brothers and Sisters.

Mumford, Clarence J. (1996) *Race and Reparations: A Black Perspective for the Twenty-First Century*, Trenton, NJ: Africa World Press.

Nelson, William E., Jr. (2000) *Black Atlantic Politics: Dilemmas of Political Empowerment in Boston and Liverpool*, Albany: State University of New York Press.

Nelson, William E., Jr. (1972) *Black Politics in Gary: Problems and Prospects*, Washington, DC: Joint Center for Political Studies.

Nelson, William and Philip Meranto. (1977) *Electing Black Mayors*, Columbus, OH: Ohio State University Press.

Obadele, Imari A. (1989) *America: The Nation State*, Washington, DC: House of Songhay.

Obadele, Imari A. (1975) *Foundations of the Black Nation*, Detroit: House of Songhay.

Obadele, Imari A. and Laurence G. Henry. (1998) *America, The Nation State: The Politics of the United States From A State-Building Perspective*, Baton Rouge: Malcolm Generation, Inc.

Padmore, George. (1971) *Pan-Africanism or Communism*, Garden City, NY: Doubleday.

Palmer, Barbara Jean C. (1999) *Black Conservatives*, Boca Raton, FL: Ide House, Inc.

Parsons, Talcott. (1951) *The Social System*, New York: Free Press.

Phillipson, David W. (1993) *African Archaeology*, 2nd Edition, Cambridge: Cambridge University Press.

Pinderhughes, Dianne M. (1980) "The Limits of Electoral Lobbying," a paper presented at the Annual Meeting of the National Conference of Black Political Scientists, Atlanta, Ga. (March 19).

Pinderhughes, Dianne M. (1992) "Power and Progress: African American Politics in the New Era of Diversity," in Janet Dewart, (ed.), *The State of Black America*, New York: National Urban League, pp. 265-280.

Pinderhughes, Dianne M. (1987) *Race and Ethnicity in Chicago Politics*, Urbana: University of Illinois Press.

Pinkney, Alphonso. (1976) *Red, Black and Green: Black Nationalism in the United States*, New York: Cambridge University Press.

Plummer, Brenda. (1997) *Rising Wind: Black Americans and U.S. Foreign Affairs, 1935-1960*, Chapel Hill: University of North Carolina Press.

Prestage, Jewel. (1968) "Black Politics and the Kerner Report: Concerns and Directions," *Social Science Quarterly*, 49, 3 (December) 453-464.

Preston, Michael. (1978) " Black Elected Officials and Public Policy," *Policy Studies Journal*, (Winter) 196-201.

Preston, Michael et al (eds.) (1987) *The New Black Politics: The Search for Political Power*, New York: Longman.

Reed, Adolph, Jr. (1986) *The Jesse Jackson Phenomenon*, New Haven: Yale University Press.

Reed, Adolph, (ed.) (1999) *Without Justice For All: The New Liberalism and Our Retreat From Racial Equality*, Boulder, CO: Westview Press.

Reeves, Keith. (1997) *Voting Hopes or Fears? White Voters, Black Candidates and Racial Politics in America*, New York: Oxford University Press.

Rich, Wilbur C. (1996) *Black Mayors and School Politics: The Failure of Reform in Detroit, Gary and Newark*, New York: Garland Publishing.

Robinson, Pearl T. (1982). "Black Political Power - Upward or Downward," in *The State of Black America*, James Williams, (ed.), New York: National Urban League.

Robinson, Randall. (2000) *The Debt: What America Owes to Blacks*, New York: Dutton.

Salley, Columbus. (1999) *Black 100: The Ranking of the Most Influential African Americans, Past & Present*, Secaucus, NJ: Carol Publishing Group.

Salzman, Jack and Cornel West. (1997) *Struggles in the Promised Land: Toward a History of Black-Jewish Relations in the United States*, New York: Oxford University Press.

Scott, Joseph W. (1980) "Capitalism, Socialism and Libertarianism: Race, Class and Power in the Black American Experience," *Western Journal of Black Studies*, 4,2 (Summer) 78-83.

Sethe, Kurt, (ed.) (1961) *Urkunden der 18. Dynastie*, Berlin: Akademie-Verlag.

Shea, Daniel M. and John G. Green, (eds.) (1994) *The State of Parties: The Changing Role of Contemporary American Party Organizations*, Lanham: Rowman & Littlefield Publishers.

Shorris, Earl. (1982) "The Jews of the New Right," *Nation*, 234, 18 (May 8) 543, 557-561.

Smith, Robert C. and Ronald W. Walters. (1996) *We Have No Leaders: African Americans in the Post-Civil Rights Era*, Albany: State University of New York Press.

Sorauf, Frank. (1976) *Party Politics in America*, Boston: Little, Brown & Company.

Sowell, Thomas. (1981) *Ethnic Minorities*, New York: Basic Books.

Stanford, Karin L. (1997) *Beyond the Boundaries: Reverend Jesse Jackson in International Affairs*, Albany: State University of New York Press.

Starks, Robert and Michael Preston. (1990) "Harold Washington and the Politics of Reform in Chicago: 1985-1987," in Rufus Browning, Dale Rogers Marshall and William Tabb, (eds.), *Racial Politics in American Cities*, New York: Longman, pp. 88-107.

Steinberg, Stephen. (1999) "Occupational Apartheid in America: Race, Labor Market, Segregation and Affirmative Action," in Adolph Reed, (ed.), *Without Justice For All: The New Liberalism and Our Retreat From Racial Equality*, Boulder, CO: Westview Press, pp. 215-233.

Stewart, James B. (1996) " Developing Black and Latino Survival Strategies: The Future of Urban Areas in Lee Daniels, (ed.), *The State of Black America*, New York: National Urban League, pp.

Stone, Chuck. (1970) *Black Political Power in America*, New York: Dell Publishing Company.

Strickland, William. (1975) "Black Intellectuals and the American Social Scene," *Black World*, 25,1 (November) 4-10.

Strickland, William. (1972) "The Gary Convention and the Crisis of American Politics," *Black World*, 21,12 (October) 18-26.

Swain, Carol. (1994) *Black Faces, Black Interests*, Cambridge: Harvard University Press.

Swain, Carol. (1993) "Black Mayors: Urban Decline and the Underclass," *Journal of Black Studies*, 24, 16-28.

Tate, Katherine. (1993) *From Protest to Politics: The New Black Voters in American Elections*, Cambridge: Harvard University Press.

Thompson, Daniel. (1963) *The Negro Leadership Class*, Englewood Cliffs, NJ: Prentice Hall, Inc.

Van DeBurg, William L. (ed.) (1996) *Modern Black Nationalism: From Marcus Garvey to Louis Farrakhan*, New York: New York University Press.

Verdun, Vincene. (1993) "If the Shoe Fits Wear It: An Analysis of Reparations to African Americans," *Tulane Law Review*, 67,3 (February) 597- 668.

Walters, Ronald W. (1989) *Black Presidential Politics in America: A Strategic Approach*, Albany: State University of New York Press.

Walters, Ronald W. (1980) "Black Presidential Politics in 1980: Bar gaining or Begging?" *Black Scholar*, 11, 4 (March/ April) 22-31.

Walters, Ronald W. (1999) "Color-Blind Redistricting and the Efficiency of Black Representation," in Lee Daniels, (ed.), *The State of Black America*, New York: National Urban League, pp. 107-135.

Walters, Ronald W. (1997) *Pan Africanism in the African Diaspora: An Analysis of Modern Afrocentric Political Movements*, Detroit: Wayne State University Press.

Walters, Ronald W. (1975) "Strategy for 1976: A Black Political Party" *Black Scholar*, 7 (October).

Walters, Ronald W. and Lucius Barker, (eds.) 1989) *Jesse Jackson's 1984 Presidential Campaign*, Urbana: University of Illinois Press.

Walters, Ronald W. and Robert C. Smith. (1999) *African American Leadership*, Albany: State University of New York Press.

Walton, Hanes, Jr. (1972a) *Black Political Parties*, New York: Free Press.

Walton, Hanes, Jr. (1972b) *Black Politics*, Philadelphia: J.B. Lippincott Co.

Walton, Hanes, Jr. (1975) *Black Republicans*, Metuchen, NJ: The Scarecrow Press.

Walton, Hanes, Jr. (1985) *Invisible Politics: Black Political Behavior*, Albany: State University of New York Press.

Walton, Hanes, Jr. (1969) *The Negro in Third Party Politics* Philadelphia: Dorrance & Co.

Weisbord, Robert and Arthur Stein. (1970) *Bittersweet Encounter: The African American and the American Jew*, Westport, CT: Negro Universities Press.

Westley, Robert. (1998) "Many Billions Gone: Is It Time to Reconsider the Case for Black Reparations?" *Boston College Law Review*, (December) 429-476.

Williams, Eddie. (1979) "Black Political Participation in 1978, *The State of Black America*, New York: National Urban League.

Williams, Eddie and Milton Morris, (1981) "The Black Vote in a Presidential Election year," *The State of Black America*, New York: National Urban League.

Williams, Rhonda M. (1999) "Unfinished Business: African American Political Economy During the Age of Color-Blind Politics," in Lee Daniels, (ed.), *The State of Black America*, New York: National Urban League, pp. 137-151.

Willingham, Alex. (1981) "The Place of the New Black Conservatives in Black Social Thought: Groundwork for the Full Critique," unpublished paper, Philadelphia, PA., (October).

Willingham, Alex. (1999) "The Voting Rights Movement in Perspective," in Adolph Reed, (ed.), *Without Justice For All: The New Liberalism and Our Retreat From Racial Equality*, Boulder, CO: Westview Press, pp. 235-254.

Wilson, James Q. (1960) *Negro Politics*, New York: Free Press.

BLACK ECONOMICS

BLACK ECONOMICS

CHAPTER 8

8.1   INTRODUCTION

*E*conomics is generally defined as the study and process of produc-*
ing, distributing (or exchanging) and consuming goods and serv-
ices. However, such a definition hides, in part, the fact of how
economics penetrates every aspect of social life. Whether one
talks of poverty, income, jobs, housing, class, race, gender, education, religion, the arts or social status, all at one level imply
and necessitate a concern with economics (Boston, 2001, 2000;
Alexis, 1999; Malveaux, 1999). Even the major ideologies and
social systems of today which compete for the minds of peoples,
i.e., capitalism, socialism, nationalism, etc., have been shaped in
significant part by important economists of the past, i.e., Adam
Smith, Karl Marx, and John Maynard Keynes, etc. (Heilbroner,
1972; Fusfeld, 1977). Moreover, it would be relatively impossible
and certainly unwise and irregular for national leaders to make
political decisions without economic considerations.

LINKS BETWEEN POLITICS AND ECONOMICS

In fact, politics and economics are unavoidably linked on
several levels. First, wealth and power are mutually engendering
and supportive. The possession of one implies and leads to the
possession of the other. Likewise, the lack of one implies the lack
of the other. Secondly, those with power and wealth tend to
strive to monopolize both. Thirdly, those with wealth and power
tend to shape society in their own image and interests at the
expense of those without it, especially Blacks and other peoples
of color whose relative possession of both wealth and power are

at low levels. It is thus difficult to imagine corporations not having political power, i.e., significant and greater control and influence over public policy, especially as it relates to their own interests. Finally, the struggle for distributive justice or an egalitarian distribution of social wealth is both an economic and a political struggle. In fact, the decision of who gets what and how much is both an economic and political decision, made by those whose wealth and political power enable them to control directly or indirectly the decision-making process.

THE CONCEPT OF POLITICAL ECONOMY

It is this interrelatedness of politics and economics which prompts some Black and radical economists to insist that the science of economics is best categorized as *political economy* (Boston, 2001; Andrews, 1999; Hogan, 1984). As the staff of the *Review of Black Political Economy* explained in their inaugural issue (Spring/Summer, 1970), the term seems a more accurate one. For it "includes within its scope the political realities of economic relations" and thus describes "the necessary focus of Black economic development." Moreover, given the political dimension of economics, "for Black people to affect any significant alteration in their economic position, they will first be obliged to develop a sound political strategy." And as Alexis (1999:54) states, "the remedy to the economic plight of blacks is not to be found in economic activity alone. Until and unless blacks achieve some degree of effective political power (i.e. command over institutions –public and private—that establish the rules of the game and determine the payoffs) they will continue to suffer from second-class economic citizenship."

Political economy, then, can be defined as the study of the interrelationship between politics and economics and the power relations they express and produce. It focuses not simply on the economic process, but also on economic policy and the race and class interests and value judgments this suggests. Thus, the study of Black economics, of necessity, includes a study of the politics which shape economics in both positive and negative ways. This will become clear as the problems and solutions posed are discussed.

8.2   POLITICAL ECONOMIC STATUS

THE COLONIAL ANALOGY

The ghettoization of the African American community is both an economic and political reality as argued in Chapter 6 (Wilson, 1993; Sugrue, 1998; Hirsch, 1998)). Even allowing for class differences, the general state of political and economic subordination is obvious and unarguable. The only question is the character and process of the subordination. The race and class character and process of the exploitation and oppression of the Black community has been summed up by many as domestic colonialism. As early as 1962, in an article reprinted in a later book, Harold Cruse (1968) used the category "domestic colonialism" to discuss Black-white relations in the U.S. society. He (1968:77) argued that "from the beginning (the African-American) has existed as a colonial being...The only fact which differentiates the (African-American's) status from that of a pure colonial status is that his position is maintained in the "home country" in close proximity to the dominant racial group." Kenneth Clark (1964) argued the colony analogy two years later using the political, economic and social structure of Harlem to demonstrate it. Although, he (1965) did not pursue the analogy in *Dark Ghetto*, he used the category and most of his analysis pointed to the same conclusion.

Two years later, Stokely Carmichael and Charles Hamilton (1967:6ff) advanced the internal colony analogy in their book on Black power. Admitting that "the analogy is not perfect," they argued that regardless of the difference between the classical colony and the ghetto, there are still enough significant similarities to justify calling the ghetto an internal colony. Among these similarities are: 1) economic exploitation of the colony as a cheap supply of labor and a captive market; 2) external control of the colony by the ruling country, usually by indirect rule through political puppets; and 3) the socio-psychological results of racist humiliation and assignment of Blacks to "subordination, inferior status in society." Robert Allen (1970) also discussed the Black community in terms of the internal colony analogy. He (1970:7ff) maintained that "Black communi-

ties are victims of white imperialism and colonial exploitation."
Colonialism, he suggested, can be defined as direct and overall
subordination, administration, economic exploitation and cultural destruction of a nation, people or country by another whose
power is enshrined in law and backed by coercive bodies, i.e.,
armies and police. Thus, he concludes, the status of the Black
population in the United States shows a striking similarity to
this colonial situation.

Allowing for limitation of the analogy, one still is unavoidably struck by the political oppression and economic exploitation
of the Black community which stand at the heart of any form of
colonialism. The ghetto economy stands out at the center of
urban poverty (Massey and Denton, 1993). Its unemployment is
so high that if it occurred in the overall economy, it would be
defined as symptomatic of a depression. Its labor is superexploit-
ed in both racial and class terms, being employed mainly in the
low-wage sector of the economy and with unequal power in
unions in spite of proportional representation (Harris, 1982).

Moreover, the ghetto economy is marked by a continuous
drain of financial, physical and human resources (Wilson, 1989,
1996). The savings are placed in financial institutions whose
loans are primarily made to enterprises outside the inner city.
The ghettos's annual purchasing power is spent mainly outside
the ghetto. As Andrew Brimmer (1982:30) had noted that Black
firms have been losing ground to white firms for Black consumer
dollars since 1969 with a decline of about 13.5% to 7%. "In 1969
receipts of Black firms were equal to 13.5 percent of total Black
income. By 1980 the share was down to 8.9 percent, and his projection for 1990 was a decline to 7 percent. Furthermore, products sold in the ghetto and outside it are made outside the ghetto, most of the businessmen live outside the ghetto, and the
enterprises which service the retail business, i.e., wholesale, ship-
ping, advertising, etc., also are located outside the ghetto"
(Browne, 1971).

Finally, there is a lower level of repairs and renewal of physical plants in the ghetto, and better educated Blacks with higher
salaries tend to move out, thus, depriving the ghetto of persons
whose education, income, and initiatives would be valuable to
its revitalization and organized efforts to free itself (Watkins,
2001). It is in such a context of oppression, exploitation and relative powerlessness and segregate isolation, that the colonial

analogy seems to be the definitive one (Tabb, 1970; Fusfeld, 1970; Browning, Marshall and Tabb, 1984; Katz, 1993; Massey and Denton, 1994).

8.3   DATA OF ECONOMIC DISADVANTAGE

Summing up this situation, David Swinton (1990, 1991, 1992) has argued that the African American community is above all marked by *economic disadvantage* in varied and essential ways. In his reports to the National Urban League on the economic *State of Black America*, Swinton (1992:61) states that "in comparison to Americans of European descent, African Americans experience substantially lower economic status throughout the income distribution." Moreover, he continues, "as we have noted on several occasions, relatively well-off Blacks are much less well off than well-off whites, and relatively poor Blacks are much poorer than poor whites." He concludes saying "all standard measures of central tendency have consistently revealed the relatively low economic status of the population as a whole." Recent data confirms that this disadvantage remains essentially in place, despite claims of Black advancement and the touted boom in the U.S. economy since 1992. Persuad and Lusane (2000) concede that there has indeed been an economic surge, but caution that it has not eliminated the disadvantages and inequalities of persons categorized and confined by belonging to the wrong race, class or gender. They (Persuad and Lusane, 2000) note that:

> It is correct, as the US administration and the ideologues of capital note, that there has been a economic recovery since 1992. The features of the recovery that have benefited both capital and in some ways, some workers can be identified and delineated. They include, in measurable terms, a balanced budget and budget surplus; upsurge of the stock market; expansion of the GNP; low inflation; low interest rates; growth in home ownership; and declining unemployment."

However, "it is through the prisms of class, gender and race that a more genuine characterization can be seen."

INCOME INEQUALITY

Swinton (1992:74) found a clear pattern of inequality between Blacks and whites. He noted that, "African American per capita income in 1990 was $9,017 compared to $15,265 for whites." This translates as Blacks having "only 59.1 percent as much income per capita as whites had during 1990." Moreover, data showed the Black male median income to be $12,868 for 1990 compared to white male income of $21,170. This equals only 60.8 percent of white male median income. The Black female median income of 1990 was $8,328 compared to $10,317 of the white female's median income or 85 percent. In more recent studies, Conley (1999), Rodgers (1999) and Persuad and Lusane (2000) found a continuing inequality. Conley (1999:11) reports that "in 1997, the median income for Black females was 55 percent that of whites ($26,522 compared to $47,023)." And that "in this same year twenty-six percent of Black families lived under the poverty line whereas only 6 percent of white families did so."

POVERTY RATES

Swinton (1992:88) also found that "income disadvantages for Blacks lead directly to higher rates of poverty." In 1990, 31.9 percent of Blacks were in poverty as compared to 10.7 percent of whites. This means that "for Blacks 9.8 million persons were in poverty, up by 500 thousand over 1989." This picture is made bleaker by the fact that the rate of poverty among Black children was 44.8 percent compared to 15.9 percent for white children. Thus over 44 out of every 100 Black children are in poverty compared to 16 of every 100 white children. This picture of child poverty is explained in part and at the same time made more severe by the fact that over 50 percent of all persons living in female-headed Black families (6,005,000) lived in poverty compared to 30 percent of persons in white female-headed households. Female-headed Black families were 45 percent of all Black families compared to 12 percent of white families. Swinton (1992:91) concludes that "the problem of female-headed poverty is of much larger magnitude for Blacks." Finally, Swinton (1992:95) states that 13 percent of the African American community received public assistance (6.5 percent) or supplemental security income (5.3 percent) compared to 3.33 percent of the white population.

Again, more recent data show a continuing trend. Persuad and Lusane (2000:28) note that:

"While 600,000 African Americans fell out of the poverty categories between 1996 and 1997, 26.5 per cent of that population still live in poverty. In other words, despite the tremendous economic upsurge (of the US economy), 9.1 million African Americans were still living in poverty in 1997. The US (Latino) population does not fare much better. Thus, while 400,000 also came out of the poverty category between 1996 and 1997, an astonishing 27.1 per cent still live below the poverty line. Regardless of the overall decline in poverty for both groups, the rate is still twice as high as that for whites, which is 11 per cent.

In terms of data on African American children in poverty, Persuad and Lusane (2000:29) argue that "there is a clear cut racial dimension as well as to the situation of children." In fact, "in 1996, while 10 percent of white children lived in poverty, 40 percent of Black children and 40 percent of (Latino) children did so." Moreover, they point out that "the infant mortality rate for children in 1996 was 14.2 per 1,000 live births, or more than double the 6 per 1,000 for white infants." In addition, Watkins (2001:72) points out that "by 1995, 63 percent of all Black children were in female-headed households and 46 percent of Black female-headed households were in poverty."

Conley (1999:6) posits that "in the current state of race in America, it may help to view racial inequality in the context of the life course, starting with birth." And what one sees here is disadvantage at the very start of Black life. "Black infants for example are much more likely than white infants to be born with low or very low birth weight...the primary cause of death among Black infants." Moreover, "half of all African American children under the age of six live in poverty, three times greater than the portion in the white community. Finally, Persuad and Lusane (2000:28) call our attention to the fact that the reality of poverty is undoubtedly greater than it appears in statistics because of the questionable and conservative understanding of poverty. They state that, "it is important to note that the definition of poverty is extremely conservative and has been challenged by a wide number of progressive economists. A family of four, for example must subsist on less than $16,400, or a family of three on $12,802, for them to be considered in the official poverty count."

EMPLOYMENT STATUS

The economic disadvantage of the African American community appears also in employment data and labor market trends (Wilson, 1996). Employment for Blacks fluctuates between 54.1 and 55.7 percent. The low employment rate is higher than the historical average and "is primarily due to the increasing participation and employment of Black women" (Swinton, 1992:97ff). The "employment rates for Black women have risen from mid-40 percent range to 54 percent of the (African American community) over the past two decades." However, Williams (1999:146) found that "Black women lost earning ground to white women in the 1980s and early 1990s" even in the service economy which had generated what is terms "women's work." Overall, Bound and Dresser (1998) reported an erosion of the relative employment and earnings of African American women. Casserly (1998) finds a similar problematic and discusses the persistence of African American women's persisting poverty and susceptibility to poverty in spite of educational investments by African American women. Overall unemployment fluctuates also and ranges between 11.8 and 13.1 percent for the Black community as a whole. For the first three quarters of 1991, the unemployment rate average was 12.4. Conley (1999:11) reports that "in 1994, the unemployment rates for Blacks was 13.9 percent, whereas it was only 6.2 percent for whites...."

The past two decades have yielded data of high unemployment among Black men, Black women and Black teenagers. "Adult Black men have had unemployment rates above 10 percent for every year since 1980 and adult Black women have had unemployment rates above 10 percent in every year except 1989 and in 1990 when their employment rate was 9.8 percent" (Swinton, 1992:102). Moreover, "the lowest unemployment rate experienced by Black teenagers since 1980 was 31.1 percent in 1990." The unemployment rate of Black teenagers, however, fluctuates between 30 and 50 percent and there is the likelihood it will rise higher given the fact they will "comprise an increasing proportion of the youth population; and probably will continue to be concentrated in areas of limited job opportunities" (Anderson, 1982:5). Furthermore, it is assumed that Black youth unemployment will be more difficult to reduce due to increased competitions for jobs and the problems of preparation (Freeman and Holzer, 1986; Wilson, 1996).

There are several reasons offered for Black unemployment: low educational levels and lack of job skills, the recurring recession, unwillingness to take menial jobs; displacement, the move of industry from the central city; shutdowns in industries where Blacks are in heavy numbers; lack of viable social networks and above all, continuing discrimination (Williams, 1999; Rodgers, 1999; Wilson, 1989; Jaynes and Williams, 1989:315-324). In his analysis of racism, Alexis (1999, 1980) challenges Becker's (1957) often quoted study on discrimination for its focus on personal rather than collective discrimination and the problem this poses for employment. He (1980:338) argues that Becker's focus on personal discrimination fails to see that "discrimination is against Blacks as a group, not as individuals" and that hiring or not hiring is a political decision as well as an economic one. In what he calls the "malice-envy approach," the economic discriminator (employer, employee, government or consumer) interprets the relative well-being of Blacks as a decrease in his/her own welfare. Blacks are thus viewed as opponents and under such competitive conditions, the white employer "might be willing to reduce (his/her) own welfare, if by doing so, (he/she) could reduce the welfare of (his/her) competitor by more." Given this political aspect of economic discrimination, Alexis maintains that the "remedy to the economic plight of Blacks is not to be found in economic activity alone." Thus, "until and unless Blacks achieve some degree of effective power, (i.e., command over institutions - public and private - that establish the rules of the game and determine the payoffs) they will continue to suffer from second-class economic citizenship."

The problem of preparation indeed remains a problem of employment. Brimmer (1982:32) predicted correctly in the 80's that science and technology with heavy reliance on computers would be the area of the fastest growing occupations. Thus, he stated, "if Blacks are to get a fair share of the new jobs, they will have to accelerate and upgrade their basic preparation in mathematics and communication skills." Secondly, Brimmer argued that the private sector will expand more rapidly than the public sector. He also projected that this decline will cost Blacks jobs given their large share of public jobs.

Not only will most of the jobs be in the private sector, he predicted correctly, but they will demand a high degree of skill. In fact, corporate requirements for entry and promotion are the typical skills needed as Brimmer suggested they would be. For many of these professional and managerial positions are in production, marketing, distribution and financial controls (i.e. accounting). Clearly, Black preparation is necessary to be eligible for these positions. But whether they will get them depends upon not only on their availability, but also the willingness of firms to hire Blacks. Without a concern for the problems of the economy and the problems of discrimination in it, job possibilities are not a realistic assumption.

Nevertheless, as Margaret C. Simms of the Joint Center for Political and Economic Studies argues, "the key to creating a productive work force is quality education and training" (McCoy, 1992:202). For "increased real incomes are closely related to education." She maintains that for Blacks, especially higher educational levels are associated with greater employment. As other African American economists, she advocates a comprehensive strategy for improving the productivity of the U.S. workforce which will, of necessity, include African Americans. She notes that such a comprehensive strategy "will provide: adequate preparation of new entrants to the labor force; the upgrading of low-skilled workers; and the retraining of adult workers for new jobs and improved technology."

OCCUPATIONAL DISTRIBUTION

Swinton (1991:62) found that African Americans are further disadvantaged by unfavorable occupation distribution. "Employed Black males (are) only about half as likely as white males to be employed in managerial, sales or professional occupations, and only about three-quarters as likely to be employed as technicians or craft workers." These occupational categories are the top-paying ones for males and, of course, Blacks are restricted in these areas and highly represented in the lowest paying occupational categories (Steinberg, 1999). Similarly, Black women were less likely to be employed in the top paying jobs. "In 1990 40.8 percent of white women and only 28.1 percent of Black women were employed in these good jobs" (Swinton, 1992:106). On the other hand, "37.3 percent of Black women compared to 22.9 percent of white women were more likely to be employed in household or other service, laborer and operative occupations." Also, Conley (1999:11) found that "in 1997, only 16 percent of employed African Americans held professional or managerial jobs, compared to 31 percent of employed whites." He notes that "(by) contrast, Black workers are overrepresented in the service sector, with its lower wages: 26 percent of employed African Americans worked in the service industries in 1997, while only 15 percent of their white counterparts held jobs in this sector.

Finally, although education is noted as central to the possibility of better paying jobs, Swinton (1992:114) argues that in general "racial inequality does not decline with education." For both males and females, racial inequality in wages are about the same across educational levels. "For females, racial inequality increased slightly with education up to a college degree (whereas) females with four years of college have equal wages."

Darity and Myers (1992:136-137) list several factors for earning inequality: 1) increase in female-headed families who earn less; 2) "the continued decline in the relative earnings and educational prospects of young Black males"; 3) the unevenness of educational gains within the Black community; and 4) a continuing gap between Blacks and whites in higher education. For example, "in 1990 46 percent of whites had some college education compared to only 37 percent of Blacks."

WEALTH

Clearly one of the most important developments in the study of the economic disadvantage of African Americans is work on Black-white wealth inequality as distinct from income (Anderson, 1994; Oliver and Shapiro, 1995; Conley, 1999). Key to this discussion is first the distinction between "wealth and other traditional measures of economic status...for example, income occupation and education" (Oliver and Shapiro, 1995:2). Oliver and Shapiro define wealth as "a stock of assets owned at a particular time." It is "what people own." And it "signifies the command over financial resources that a family has accumulated over its lifetime along with those resources that have been inherited across generations." It is the possession of wealth that creates access, opportunities, stature, a high standard of living and allows transfer of significant resources to one's children.

According to Oliver and Shapiro (1995:4-5), three main factors have impeded African Americans' accumulation of wealth: 1) "racialization of state policy"; 2) "economic detour"; and 3) the "sedimentation of racial inequality." Racialization of state policy refers to state policy which impaired the ability of African Americans to benefit from government sponsored opportunities to acquire wealth and other policies which blocked them in their attempts to acquire it. This begins with enslavement and continues through segregation to the racism of today. Anderson (1994) makes a similar argument. Economic detour refers to all the obstacles African Americans encounter in society which diminish or deny their ability to establish and maintain businesses. Sedimentation of racial inequality refers to "the cumulative effects of the past which have seemingly cemented Blacks to the bottom of society's economic hierarchy."

Oliver and Shapiro (1995) dramatically illustrate the distinction between income and wealth by noting that although half of the top 10 income earners in the U.S. are Black, there are virtually no Blacks among the wealthiest 400 Americans. Even in terms of income, Blacks earn an average of less than 60% of white household income, but middle class Blacks have only 15% of the wealth level of middle class whites. Overall African Americans have only 60% of white income and one-twelfth of white wealth. Moreover, 61% of Black households have no assets compared to 25% of white households.

Conley (1999) builds on Oliver and Shapiro's work. He (1999:5) notes that "at all income, occupational and educational levels, Black families on the average have drastically lower levels of wealth than similar white families...." And although he puts greater emphasis on class location and opportunities in come cases, as the determinant of wealth, he concedes that "(i)n contemporary America, race and property are intimately linked and form the nexus for the persistence of Black-white inequality." As a solution to this gross inequality, Conley (1999:152) proposes a two-pronged policy. He states that the first "policy possibility involves shifting race-based affirmative action from areas of education and occupation to a focus on asset inequality." And secondly, he proposes "shifting to a class-based affirmative action policy rather than a race-based one, including net worth as the definition of class."

Conley's study, while well-received in many quarters, suffers from some problematic aspects. First, there is a question of whether his measurement of the impact of childhood family wealth on later life outcomes is representative enough to establish validity. Although his pool is 5,000 families, his working sample is 1,285 and out of this only 143 are Black, i.e., approximately 11.1 percent. In the multivariate analysis, his sample of Blacks may be even smaller, but these figures are not reported. Likewise, his framework is limited by his study of only 18 to 30-year olds. If his race-class framework were expanded, it would raise the question of whether race would matter more to older or younger persons. This becomes especially important in terms of his stress on wealth generation which comes from equity in homes. For in large part, it is racial discrimination which causes Blacks to have less home equity than whites. Thus, concentrating on a younger group limits his ability to explore this factor.

Thirdly, Conley, while making an important contribution to the race/class debate on the side of class, tends to under-emphasize the interrelatedness of race and class. In fact, he himself, concedes that wherever there is a class disadvantage, it is tied also to race. This interrelationship of race and class varies across sectors, affecting accumulation and outcomes in various degrees and ways depending upon various contexts and related conditions.

Finally, although he discusses past and current initiatives designed to increase the accumulation of assets among African Americans, in terms of his own research, he does not take up the question of its implication for a race-based affirmative action. As Drake and Hollsworth (1996) argued in their study of Richmond's set aside program, affirmative action can be both important and limited in its impact on the larger African American community. But it is embraced by the majority of African Americans as a major, just and necessary policy initiatives to correct injustices of the past and present and provide needed opportunities for wealth accumulation. That he failed to address the implications of his research findings for race-based affirmative action policy not only reflects his preference for class-based solutions, but also suggests his privileging of class in such a way that reflects on the quality of his work.

8.4   PROBLEMS OF RACE AND CLASS

Again, the race/class question is central to the discussion of African American life, especially in economics (Alexis, 1999; Conley, 1999; Wilson, 1996; Oliver and Shapiro, 1995). The race and class question serves as a problem for Black economics on two levels. First, both race and class are the bases of Black exploitation and oppression. And secondly, the development of sharp class divisions among Blacks tend to impede an overall solution to the problem of Black economic development (Turner, 1976). In fact, the interpretation of the source of and solution of Black oppression can end up as a class focused interpretation rather than an overall Black one.

For example, one could take the interpretations of Thomas Sowell (1975, 1981a, 1981b). Sowell essentially argues that race is not as important a factor as often suggested and that the attitudes and skills of Blacks may be as important to social achievement and social status as racism. Moreover, he maintains that demographics rather than racism explain differences in income among ethnic groups. Thus, the source of Blacks differential income can be found for example in the fact of age, i.e., they are disproportionately younger and still climbing the income ladder, and in the fact of residence, i.e., they live more often in the South where wages are usually lower. He also rejects affirmative action as insulting treatment and gratuitous government intervention in an admittedly flawed though essentially workable system. Finally, Sowell argues that racism, where it exists, can be explained by economic motivations and interests and that once racism becomes economically unprofitable, racists will no longer practice it. Therefore, he argues that market forces are much more effective mediators of racial inequities than non-market forces like the collective Black struggle and government intervention.

Much of the criticism of Sowell has been ad hominem and unworthy of repetition. But his argument tends to support and dovetail William Wilson's ideas which will be covered below. Thus, criticism of Wilson's contentions will for the most part answer Sowell's. However, it is important to note that Sowell, like Wilson, tends to blame the victim, overlook or minimize the active force and result of racism, and while blaming Blacks for defective attitudes and habits, seems reluctant to indict racist attitudes and practices of whites. Moreover, his contention that racism ends when it is no longer profitable is not always true. Reich (1981:311-312) argues in his work that although "racism works against most whites economic interest, it is being reinforced today" by a series of social, cultural and personal factors. Brimmer (1997:2) notes that "the disparate treatment of Blacks cost the American economy about $241 billion in 1993."

Certainly, one of the most provocative works in recent sociological literature is William Wilson's (1978) *The Declining Significance of Race*. Wilson's work while attempting to de-emphasize the significance of race also points to the problem of uneven development among Blacks and the accompanying class divisions. Essentially, Wilson argues that race has declined in significance and been replaced by class as the key determinant affecting life-chances and institutional access in U.S. society. He contends that this shift on the basis of social stratification is due to government intervention and support, the current predominance of service industries (transportation, government and social service, public utilities, finance, social welfare, etc.) over productive industries (manufacturing, mining, etc.), and the substitution of class characteristics for racial ones as criteria for employment. Moreover, he maintains that this declining significance of race has created a new middle class insensitive to "lower" class Black needs and is increasingly used by the whites to control Blacks in the working class and underclass. Furthermore, he (1978:152) argues that "the traditional racial struggles for power and privilege have shifted away from the economic sector and are now concentrated in the sociopolitical order."

The arguments against Wilson's thesis are numerous and cogent and Wilson, himself, found it necessary to clarify further his ideas in a more recent work (Willie, 1979; Pinkney, 1984; Wilson, 1987). First, Wilson's use of the advancing middle class as in index of the declining significance of race is impoverished data, showing not that the race has declined, but suggesting that racism against the middle class has declined. Furthermore, Black and white middle class incomes are still not the same and evidence of "catching up" does not eliminate the fact that significant differences still exist. Also, there are not enough Blacks in these new positions or significant power positions to claim such a momentous event as the decline of the significance of race. They are not in ownership positions or significantly represented in high level management. And even when they arrive, they continue to suffer severe discrimination (Benjamin, 1991). Finally, it could be argued that allowing certain sectors of the Black middle class access to new status is also based on race and a political calculation. For it tends to legitimize and reinforce the system and win it new Black allies which, even Wilson admits, can and may be used against the interests of the Black masses.

Secondly, Wilson concentrated only on the narrow data of income increase to prove his thesis as if income increase were an inclusive category of the various forms of racism. A modicum of acquaintance with the various open and convert expressions of racism tends to disprove such a contention. Thirdly, he commits a gross conceptual error by attempting to separate the economic arena from the socio-political one. A holistic conception of society shows that all areas of society interact, and policies in one area tend to affect and often determine conditions and behavior in others. Affirmative action legislation had impact on the economic and educational spheres. And the Supreme Court decision outlawing segregation, *Brown vs. Board of Education*, affected virtually every area of social life (Kluger, 1977).

Fourthly, Wilson's contention that the discrimination against the Black poor is only because of their low level of education and few marketable skills, overlooks the fact that it is racism which imposed this condition on them and continues to exclude them (Harris, 1982; Cotton, 1988). Thus, a system which is responsible for inadequate acquisition of education and skills by Blacks and other peoples of color cannot escape the charge of racism simply by saying that their lack of qualifications is the reason for their occupational rejection. Finally, Wilson's position suggests that now Blacks are responsible for their non-access and non-achievement, as if wealth and power were equitably distributed and equally available. This personalization of blame for social evils could be and perhaps already is being used as a justification for an end to public and private policies and programs designed to end racist and socio-economic inequities in U.S. society.

Regardless of Wilson's flawed interpretation of the declining significance of race, his charge of increasing class division and middle class insensitivity to the interests of the Black masses requires discussion. For if he and others are correct, then rather than being a resource for Black liberation and economic development, the Black middle class will serve the opposite function of retarding development and the struggle for a higher level of social life (Wilson, 1987).

8.5   THE MIDDLE CLASS

The middle class is continuously the focus of much social science literature as evidence of progress, a source of hope, a caricature or diminished version of its Euroamerican model, and an enraged, unrewarded, and misunderstood supporter of the system among other things, (Cose, 1993; Feagin, 1994; Banner-Haley, 1994; Collins-Laury, 1996; Pattillo-McCoy, 1999). The problematic character of the middle class was first raised extensively by E. Franklin Frazier (1962) in his classic work, *Black Bourgeoisie*. In it, he posed the middle class as essentially living in a world characterized by make-believe, self-hate, conspicuous consumption, rejection of the Black masses and the fruitless and frustrating quest for white status and acceptance.

Nathan Hare (1965), a student of Frazier, reinforced Frazier's view of the middle class in his book, *Black Anglo Saxons*, which posed "aping of the white man as their overriding concern." Cruse (1967:312) in his seminal work on the Black intellectual also reinforced Frazier's stress on the theme of personal self-interest of the middle class, arguing that "No matter how you view it, the integration movement is run by the middle class who, even when they are militant and sometimes radical, twist the meaning of integration to suit their own aspirations." If these assessments are correct, then, the problem of class division and distance become not simply a problem of economics, but also a problem of politics. For if middle class interests are pushed at the expense of the masses of Blacks, then, rather than being a resource in terms of capital and leadership for economic development, the middle class will become an obstacle in both the political and economic sense.

The above claims do not go without challenge. There is evidence to suggest that the claims of a growing middle class are exaggerated and must be seen in the light of several related facts. First, although "professionals and mangers" is the standard census category for middle class, it also includes modest status jobs as dental technicians and night managers, along with doctors, lawyers and other traditional professionals. Moreover, growth in the professional occupations is concentrated at the lower end of the income scale with technicians, counselors and health technologists. Pattillo-McCoy (1999:27) stated that the great increase in middle class persons is also related to the increase in sales and clerical workers. Secondly, Anderson (1982:7) noted many of these occupational gains were in the public sector in social welfare. This public sector concentration makes the Black middle class highly vulnerable to the current administration's reduction-in-force policy which calls for heavy layoffs at social service agencies which employ large numbers of Blacks. In addition, Oliver and Shapiro (1995:92-93) notes that "an accurate and realistic appraisal of the economic footing of the Black middle class reveals its precariousness, marginality and fragility." They state that "the case for this characterization rests not only on an inspection of the resources available to the Black middle class, but on the relative position of the latter with respect to the white middle class."

In addition, Robert Hill (1978) argues that the advocates of the new middle class are confusing "middle income" with "middle class." "(I)ncome only indicates how much money a person has, while class helps determines how that money is spent." In a word, a class is not simply defined by income but by wealth, status, "styles of life, living standards, values and beliefs." Also Hill (1980:40) contends that although middle class classifications usually include all persons holding white collar jobs or moving into higher status jobs, movement into higher status jobs do not necessarily mean higher paying jobs. In fact, he (1980:37) states, "only a small minority of Black white collar workers have middle class incomes." He concludes that instead of a spectacular growth of the Black middle class, one has statistics that show 25% of Blacks belong to the middle class as compared to 50% of whites.

Finally, in terms of middle class insensitivity, the argument can be made that leadership of the civil rights movement and their constant struggle to maintain gains of the 60's contradict the insensitivity and selfishness suggested by Frazier and reinforced by those after him (Morris, 1984; Pattillo-McCoy, 1999). Moreover, it can be argued that a distinction must be made between the radical or socially-conscious and active segment of the middle class and the "system-oriented" sector. The former, it can be said, led the struggle, and the latter served the traditional role of buffer between the masses and the rulers of society. The radicals, Amilcar Cabral (1969:110) argues, has committed "class suicide" and identified with the aspirations of the masses whereas the "system-oriented" members have thrown their lot in with society's rulers. The problem, then, becomes one of how to initiate and sustain the process which radicalizes a significant sector of the middle class and causes them to assume the "Talented Tenth" role of leadership DuBois (1969) and others posed for them. Working for this community consciousness is, of course, the fact that in spite of middle-class advancement, racism still restricts their movement and reminds them of their limitations in a racist society (Benjamin, 1991; Landry, 1987).

8.6   The "Underclass"

The problem of class also figures in the ongoing discourse around the question of the *underclass* (Glasgow, 1981; Wilson, 1987, 1996). Douglas Glasgow (1981:3,5) offered one of the earliest studies of this group and defined underclass as "a permanently entrapped population of poor persons, used and unwanted...unemployed, welfare dependent and without sufficient income to secure a decent quality of life." Such an entrapped sector of the population, Glasgow maintains, not only poses a threat to the broader social order, but more importantly to the safety, survival and development of the African American community. For such a state of things creates not only the potential and reality of violence turned inward and crime, but also diminishes the life chances of those so trapped.

William J. Wilson (1987, 1996) has also contributed important studies of this class which he calls "the truly disadvantaged." He (1987:8) defines the underclass as "...the most disadvantaged segments of the Black urban community, that heterogeneous grouping of families and individuals who are outside the mainstream of the American occupations system." Defining this class more extensively, he goes on to say that " included in this group are individuals who lack training and skills and either experience long-term unemployment or are not members of the labor force, individuals who are engaged in street crime and other forms of aberrant behavior, and families that experience long term spells of poverty and/or welfare dependency."

Wilson sees the evolution of this class as being shaped by both internal and external factors in a context of both historic and contemporary discrimination. These factors include: 1) the flow of migrants which created a large concentration of the disadvantaged; 2) the increasing number of young people among inner city residents which is associated with major problems, i.e., out-of-wedlock births, crime, female-headed households and welfare dependency; 3) structural changes in the economy "such as the shift from goods-producing to service-producing industries, the increasing polarization of the labor market into low-wage and high-wage sectors; technological innovations and the relocation of manufacturing industries out of the central cities" to the suburbs and low-wage foreign countries (Wilson, 1987:45); and 4) concentration of poverty in the inner city which as a result of middle class exodus creates both extreme social isolation and an institutional inability to effectively intervene in community problems or build on role models of possibility and achievement. In his newer work, he (1996) argues that this situation is also aggravated by the moving into the inner city of large numbers of poor people in general, thus adding to the already existing concentration of poverty.

Moreover, Wilson argues that key to the solution of the problem of the underclass is to first concede its existence and problematic character and then develop a comprehensive public policy to solve it. He (1987:163) concludes that this comprehensive program must be one "that combines employment policies with social welfare policies and that features universal as opposed to race or group specific strategies." This would include stress on generation of a tight labor market, industrial competitiveness, increased skills for the labor force and social welfare policies of child support, family allowance and child care. His stress on the universal programs rather than race-specific ones is called a "hidden agenda" which will appeal to the larger public while simultaneously solving specific problems of the disadvantaged in a general framework.

There are arguments against both the identification of an underclass and Wilson's "hidden agenda" strategy to solve problems of the underclass. First, the term underclass is rejected as stigmatizing and indicting ghetto residents. It is argued that not only does such conceptualization of problems give racist categories with which to indict ghetto residents, but it also tends to blame the victims of the system rather than the system (Katz, 1986). A second problem with the term is its tendency toward imprecision, lumping together different peoples with different problems for different reasons and with differing capacities to solve them. Thirdly, such a formulation can easily deny or diminish the importance of racism in the very factors Wilson cites as shaping the formation of the underclass.

Fourthly, it is argued that underclass arguments are uncomfortably close to the culture of poverty arguments which stress the interconnection between cultural traditions, family history and individual character and values (Auletta, 1982:Chapter 2). These conservatives who argue these tend to see the situation of the underclass self-perpetuating and a reflection of the pathological character of both the subculture and the persons who compose it (Murray, 1984; Gilder, 1981). Although Wilson clearly rejects this stress on cultural tradition, family history and individual values and instead stresses structural factors which shape the formation and maintenance of the class, it is argued that focus on the problems of the group rather than society's oppressive character still leave open the door for racist manipulation (Feagin, 1998:1129).

Finally, Wilson's approach to solving the problems associated with the underclass has been questioned. The issue revolves around his "hidden agenda" strategy which suggests that one must disguise the real and greater needs of the poor and vulnerable and offer advantaged groups a public policy proposal which is universal and caters to their moral insensitivity to the truly disadvantaged. As I (Karenga, 1992:70) have argued "the question is: do we cater to the advantaged group's insensitivity to issues involving the poor and vulnerable by disguising or hiding our real agenda and offering them similar benefits or do we challenge them to grow morally and recognize and respond positively to the priority of the poor and the vulnerable?" To search for

common ground in public policy, as Wilson suggests, is imperative, but to find or fashion it at the expense of the disadvantaged
is both morally untenable and politically counterproductive.

8.7   THE PROBLEM OF BUSINESS

The problem of economic development is also tied to the
problems of Black business. Although Frazier's (1962)
contention that Black business was a "social myth" was extremely harsh, one cannot disagree that it has certainly found itself
fragile and marginal to the larger economy (Brimmer, 1998;
Swinton, 1992; Coles, 1975; Tabb, 1970). According to Brimmer
(1998:19), "in 1992 (the last year for which official Census
Bureau figures are available), there were 621,000 Black-owned
firms in the United States, accounting for 3.599 percent of the
total of 17.3 percent" for the entire country. Moreover, "black
firms had sales and receipts of $32.2 billion in that year, repre-
senting 0.969 percent of the $3.3 trillion reported by all firms."
Measured against corresponding figures of 1987, with 424,000
Black firms with sales of $19.8 billion, there was a slight decline
in their ownership of firms, but an increase in share of sales. Still,
however, Brimmer (1998:20) notes that "these figures yielded
Disparity Indexes of 26.9 percent in 1992 compared with 32.07
percent in 1987. Consequently, over the five-year period, the
overall position of Black-owned businesses deteriorated somewhat." These figures indicate one of the problems of Black businesses, undercapitalization, which tends to insure smallness,
inefficiency, and prevents managerial competence and often
leads to failure.

Secondly, Black businesses, in spite of some diversification,
are essentially concentrated in personal service as in the past.
Black Enterprise's 1992 Top 100 Black Businesses report (June,
1992) reaffirms this. Thus, the essential process of production
escapes them and is not a fundamental part of government or private proposals for Black economic development. Thirdly, as mentioned above, Black businesses are losing in the grossly unequal
competition for Black consumer dollars. Fourthly, low-level of
managerial competence continues to plague Black businesses.
Most are self-owned and too small to hire any other employee, let
alone skilled managers which insure correct business decisions.

However, Brimmer (1998:20) contends that actually Black businesses are beginning to grow slightly in size. But he concedes that "nevertheless Black-owned businesses are continuing to play a very modest role in the American economy."

Fifthly, Blacks businesses essentially operate in a restricted market which is marked by small savings, high debt, low income, high unemployment and an environment shunned by possible large investors although the top 100 Black firms do not have these problems to the same degree (McCoy, 1992). Finally, the shift in the politics and economics of the country to the right with a focus on the rich at the expense of the poor and stress on less government assistance to the Black community in general and Black businesses in particular had an ill effect on Black business. For government assistance had been an important source not only of loans but also of support for affirmative action contracts for Black business and hiring (Lee, 1982).

The *Black Enterprise*'s assessment of Black businesses' future in the 90's links it to a variety of continuing practices. In order to sustain growth and avoid following on the fatality list, Black businesses would have to, among other things: 1) acquire increased amounts of capital from other sources than the government; 2) diversify and work to get a greater share of the approximately $265 billion income of Blacks; 3) locate in industries such as telecommunications, cable, high technology and manufacturing; 4) engage in collective community planning; and 5) participate in building political bases among Blacks through service, donation and investment which come back in higher levels of Black support as consumers, investors, and partners in political and economic development of the Black community (Brimmer, 1998; Swinton, 1992).

8.8 SOLUTIONS

Given the severity of the political-economic problems of the inner city, the question of what is to be done and who is to do it are necessarily raised. Three basic resource structures are identified as fundamental to reduce the gross inequities between Blacks and whites and to overcome the severe economic problems of the inner cities: 1) government; 2) the private sector; and 3) the Black community itself (Barnett and Hefner, 1976; Williams, 1982; Karenga, 1980; Jaynes and Williams, 1989; Swinton, 1990, 1991, 1992; Anderson, 1994; Wilson, 1996, 1999).

GOVERNMENT INTERVENTION

Governmental intervention and assistance are proposed for four basic reasons (Franklin and Norton, 1987; Wilson, 1996; Watkins, 2001). First, the problems are of dimensions beyond the means of any one or combination of community structures. Secondly, the problems are socially-rooted and the result of racist discrimination and the government is obligated to assist in providing necessary correctives for these problems. Thirdly, Blacks helped create the social wealth of America and deserve an equitable share of it, not in the sense of sympathetic welfare, but in the sense of *distributive justice*, i.e., that share which is rightly theirs by their contribution and by just reasoning. Finally, it is objectively in the interest of the whole society to solve these problems, for as long as they remain unsolved, their negative effect will impact on the larger society also. For example, acquisition crime, generational poverty, socially incompetent members of society, and violently aggressive alienation all merit societal attention.

THE PRIVATE SECTOR

Secondly, the private sector is proposed because 1) there is a sense that businesses, especially larger corporations have drained and exploited the community and thus, owe it support in its revitalization efforts; 2) that businesses will benefit in tax credits, public relations, and even make a profit on their investment in the ghetto; and 3) they too should be concerned about the negative impact of unsolved ghetto problems on the larger society.

THE COMMUNITY

Undoubtedly the most important resource structure, however, in solving Black problems is the Black community itself. Regardless of external goodwill, a people must initiate and lead the struggle for its own liberation. However, this necessitates the structural capacity - an institutional and organizational network

- to wage such a struggle. As noted above, one of the greatest, if not the greatest, problems Blacks face is structural incapacity to define, defend and develop their interests. This, therefore, must be a priority. Each year in its *State of Black America*, the National Urban League gives recommendations for the struggle for Black freedom, justice and equality, placing heavy emphasis on governmental intervention and assistance. However, the tasks proposed and the struggle to be waged presupposes and necessitates a self-conscious organized people to execute them. After all, one cannot expect the government to respond simply because recommendations are published or verbally proposed yearly. The government is a political structure, organized around the holding, using and respect of power. Thus, Blacks must politically educate and organize themselves and become a self-conscious social power with which to reckon.

Often, it is pointed out that the problems of the ghetto are too large and deep-rooted for Blacks to solve and that talk of community self-help is utopian. There are several things wrong with this "reasoning" which are immediately observable. First, no one offers such a position to Jewish or Gentile communities or any other communities of color except the African American community. Secondly, as noted above, resources from the government or others still require organization, knowledge of policy, collective strategy and the power to have an impact on policy. Thirdly, given Black structural incapacity, the government and the private sector are not likely to run to the rescue with the immediately necessary resources, as history as shown. Moreover, given the shift to the right in and out of government, the unlikelihood of this is even greater. Fourthly, given the above reality, it would seem sensible and contributive to survival and development if Blacks developed structures which even on a limited scale helped improve conditions of the ghetto.

Finally, Blacks have already built structures to deal with their deprivations imposed by discrimination; the point, then, would be how to expand and strengthen them. And here again, the Sixties provide a model, as I have argued in chapter 4. For not only were structures built to provide services, politically educate and organize the community, pressure was also put on the system to produce legislation, judicial decisions and programs which improved conditions in a significant way. The problem often faced is the one of dismissing Black strategies that do not produce the maximum goals or results and making alternative suggestions that theoretically produce maximum gains, but practically are less than effective or realistic. It is obvious that these three resource structures must be tapped and utilized for whatever gains are possible. But it is equally obvious that without a *structural base* of its own, the Black community will not only be unable to effectively demand from government and the private sector what is rightfully theirs, but will also be unable to provide for itself what is possible in the meantime. Black history is full of examples of Black self-help and struggle to win their rightful share of social wealth and social space. Not to honor this history by continuing it, seems not only an avoidable loss, but also an irrational and self-defeating position.

PROPOSALS

In terms of proposals for each resource structure, several recommendations for government and the private sector (businesses) are most often quoted (Barnett and Hefner, 1976; Williams, 1982; Franklin and Norton, 1987; Simms, 1989; Brimmer, 1998).

GOVERNMENT DIRECTED

ECONOMIC RECOMMENDATIONS. Economically, recommendations for the state and federal governments are: 1) continued and reinforced employment training programs; 2) more federal government revenue for domestic programs and less for an inflated defense budget; 3) less layoffs of government workers which affect Blacks, other peoples of color and women disproportionately; 4) perception of federal business programs for peoples of color as economic programs rather than social welfare programs and improvement of delivery services to them; 5) encouragement of majority-owned and operated businesses to assist and use services of businesses of peoples of color; 6) encouragement of employment and training of Blacks by private industry and small and medium business through tax incentives, wage subsidies, work study, etc.; 7) rejection of altered minimum wage for youth; 8) serious efforts toward full employment; 9) a reduction of budget cuts which affect monies and services vital to Blacks, other peoples of color and the poor; and 10) continued application and support of Affirmative Action. A recent addition to these proposals is the demand for reparations for the Holocaust of enslavement (Lumumba, Obadele and Taifa, 1993; Robinson, 2000; America, 1999; also see extended discussion of reparations in chapter 7).

POLITICAL RECOMMENDATIONS. Politically, government, especially federal, is asked to: 1) resume and reinforce its traditional defense of civil rights; 2) monitor white terrorist and racist organizations like the Klan and neo-nazi groups; 3) appoint qualified Blacks in the government structure; 4) support the Voting Rights Act; and 5) oppose reapportionment and redistricting schemes that dilute Black voting power or dissolve districts represented by Blacks.

EDUCATIONAL RECOMMENDATIONS. Educationally, government should: 1) oppose the voucher education system which is detrimental to public education; 2) increase support for historically Black colleges; 3) continue federal resources for quality education for the disadvantaged; and 4) insist that post-secondary institutions receiving federal monies maintain effective affirmative action programs for faculty and students.

PRIVATE SECTOR. DIRECTED

STANDARD RECOMMENDATIONS. Standard recommendations for the private sector are: 1) location of plants in the inner city; 2) job training and employment for Blacks; 3) use of Black business services and products; 4) provision of resources to insure expansion of alternative educational programs; and 5) continued application and support of affirmative action. As in the proposals to government, demands for corporations to pay reparations for the Holocaust of enslavement are now being put forth (see chapter 7).

EXPANDED RECOMMENDATIONS. In the policy agenda section of the *Million Man March/Day of Absence Mission Statement*, the proposals were rooted and framed in a larger vision of a just and good society and world. It began with a call on the corporate world to demonstrate *corporate responsibility* in the community, society and the world by recognizing and responding rightfully to the tremendous social cost its activities often lead to, i.e., deteriorating and dangerous working conditions, massive layoffs, harmful products projected as beneficial, environmental degradation, deindustrialization, corporate relocation and disinvestment in social structures and development (Karenga, 1995:13-15). Thus the statement calls on corporations:

1. to practice a corporate responsibility that requires and encourages efforts to minimize and eventually eliminate harmful consequences which persons, communities and the environment sustain as a result of productive and consumptive practices;

2. to respect the dignity and interest of the worker in this country and abroad, to maintain safe and adequate working conditions for workers, provide adequate benefits, prohibit and penalize racial and gender discrimination, halt displacement and dislocation of workers, encourage organization and meaningful participation in decision-making by workers, and halt disinvestment in the social structure, deindustrialization and corporate relocation;

3. to reinvest profits back into the communities from which it extracts profits, to increase support for Black charities, contribute more to Black education in public schools and traditional Black universities and colleges, and to Black education in predominantly white colleges and universities; to open facilities to the community for cultural and recreational use and to contribute to the building of community institutions and other projects to reinvest in the social structure and development of the Black community;

4. to provide expanded investment opportunities for Black people; engage in partnership with Black businesses and business persons; increase employment of Black managers and general employees; conduct massive job training among Blacks for work in the 21st century; and aid in the development of programs to halt and reverse urban decay; and finally,

5. to show appropriate care and responsibility for the environment; to minimize and halt pollution, deforestation and depletion of natural resources, and the destruction of plants, animals, birds, fish, reptiles and

insects and their natural habitats; and to rebuild wasted and damaged areas and expand the number, size and kinds of areas preserved.

These proposals were made with the understanding that the Black community is located in a larger political and human context and that in order to solve its problems it must engage and contribute to the solution of problems that affect society and the world. This is especially important in an era of globalism in which U.S. corporations have spread across the world with a new technological capacity but with the standard notion that they have no social responsibility except to maximize profit within the rules of an open and competitive market through cutting costs, maximizing benefits and constantly increasing technological efficiency (Lusane, 1997).

COMMUNITY DIRECTED

In terms of the Black community, is clear as stated above, that their primary focus must be on building the *structural* capacity to define, defend and develop their interests. This essentially means building an organizational, institutional and enterprise network that not only provides social services, but politically organizes and educates the community to its interests and possibilities (Steward, 1984; Anderson, 1994; Kikazi, 1997). This requires strengthening existing structures and building new ones, building economic enterprises on the individual and cooperative level, alternative educational institutions, Black united fronts for collective planning and actions, and eventually, a Black political party which is dedicated exclusively to organizing Blacks for political power and effectively participating in the exercise of state power. Below are broad strategies for community economic development.

BROAD STRATEGIES

There are obviously several eclectic approaches to Black economic development which are initiated and controlled by Blacks (Coles,1975; Cash and Oliver,1975; Browne,1976; America,1977; Woodson, 1987; Wilson, 1987; Simms, 1989; Brimmer, 1998; Haynes, 1999; Alexis, 1999; Watkins, 2001).

Approaches can also be defined by their rootedness in or advocacy of three broad developmental strategies: capitalism, socialism and cooperative economics. Although it is theoretically possible to combine these developmental strategies, advocates of each usually tend to praise one and condemn or severely question the others. However, cooperative economic and socialist strategies are often linked and capitalist advocates have been known to tolerate parallel cooperative strategies. The discussion below seeks to give the basic contentions of each of these strategies with explanatory comments where warranted.

BLACK CAPITALISM

Black capitalism which gained popularity as a strategy during the Nixon Administration attempted to reduce the "perceived cycle of Black dependency" on governmental intervention. The alternative was to expand Black ownership which would stress private efforts, profit pursuit and free marketism for Blacks using the model of capitalism on a societal level (Cross, 1969). Black capitalism as a strategy contains several basic principles which define it and also lay the basis for its criticism (Brimmer and Terrell, 1971).

First, it argues that increase in Black private ownership and control will enhance Black independence and pride, employ Blacks and help ease unemployment, increase the availability of services for the community and expand the wealth in the community. Secondly, Black capitalism argues for market protectionism that would shield Black enterprises form competition with larger more competitive outside enterprises. Thirdly, it advocates Black self-help and solidarity which would support Black business and benefit from its expansion. Fourthly, Black capitalism demands subsidization from the dominant society, i.e., government and the private sector. Subsidization may take the form of loans, grants, property, equipment or training and is seen as a contribution to capital formation as well as a moral and economic debt U.S. society owes Blacks for long-term discrimination and deprivation.

Criticism of Black capitalism is severe and from many quarters. First, Boggs (1970) argues that it is an irrational strategy which poses itself as a collective strategy, but is in fact a class strategy to further enrich a few at the expense of the many.

Secondly, Allen (1970) and Zweig (1972) argue that the political economy of subsidization is negative to Black self-determination and will mean creation of a manipulated class still dependent on outside sources. Thirdly, Ofari (1970) calls attention to the fact that the strategy is overweighed toward service rather than *production*, the key process in economics. And finally, Brimmer and Terrell (1971), as well as Ofari, point to its nonviability given the small amount of capital available to Black enterprises, their low expansion possibility, low efficiency, marginal existence, high mortality rate, and restricted and problematic market, i.e., the ghetto economy.

SOCIALISM

Black advocates of socialism see Black capitalism as a myth and hindrance to serious Black economic development and political emancipation (Ofari,1970; Allen,1971; Davis, 1987). Their focus is essentially on Black labor rather than Black capital. As Harris (1978:14) argues, "Blacks cannot be adequately understood except as an integral part of the capital labor relation as a whole in U.S. capitalism." Given the fact that the Black working class is approximately 90% of the Black population, a strategy which does not focus on problems and possibilities of Black labor is both deficient and self-deluding.

Secondly, Black socialists argue that regardless of the temporary and partial measures that Blacks institute for economic betterment, a real and full solution depends on the transformation of society from capitalism to socialism. Given this reality, Black socialists argue for greater stress on the political dimensions of the economic process, and stress the need for organizing Black workers and the Black community into a self-conscious political force which challenges and transforms the established order (Alkalimat and Johnson,1974).

Fourthly, the Black socialist strategy involves seizure of power and institution of: 1) collective ownership and control of the productive apparatus; 2) an egalitarian distribution of wealth; 3) a planned economy; 4) a political and economic democracy; and 5) an end to class, race and sexual alienation (Karenga, 1980:61). Essentially this is seen as a long-range strategy, and the organization of the Black workers (and the Black community) as a fighting force for democratic rights, higher

wages, better work and living conditions and greater participation in political and economic decision-making are posed as
immediate goals.

This stress on the working class, especially by orthodox
Marxists, however, often poses a problem for a specifically Black
solution. For not only does it tend to play down racism as a simple function of capitalism (Harris,1978), but it also ends up with
no ethnic-specific program for Blacks - only for workers in general. Thus, as Browne (1976:153) contends, given Marx's and
Lenin's failure to "directly address the unique situation in which
American Blacks find themselves...there are very real limits on
the extent to which that analysis speaks to our racial situation,
irrespective of how eloquently it may dissect our economic
dilemma." Moreover, the failure of communism to establish
humanistic societies and the collapse of the Soviet Union and
communism in Eastern Europe have made both communists and
socialists reevaluate the problematics of possibilities of socialist
society, especially in a multicultural context (Davis, et al, 1987).

COOPERATIVE ECONOMICS

As Ofari (1970:89) states, the theory and practice of cooperative economics has an early history in the mutual aid societies
in northern Black communities which pooled resources and dedicated themselves to social service and community development.
Stewart (1984) has also written concerning the challenge of
building a cooperative economy and the lessons which evolve
from the Black experience in this ongoing historical project. The
idea of cooperative economics among African Americans, however, was eventually submerged with the emergence of a Black
elite which developed a capitalist merchant class orientation
(Harris, 1936). But in 1940, DuBois (1968) had proposed a comprehensive theoretical framework and rationale for cooperative
economics as a viable and necessary alternative to capitalism.

He (1968:216-219) stressed the need for a communal, Black-
focused solution which would emphasize and establish: 1) social
ownership; 2) strong family and group ties; 3) consumer unions;
4) economic planning; 5) socialized medicine; 6) cooperative
organization of Black professionals for social service; 7) the elimination of private profit; 8) a Black controlled educational system; and 9) the essentiality of collective self-reliance. This solu-

tion he called "a cooperative commonwealth," a communal social system which built new relations among Blacks and gave them the internal strength to resist the corrupting influence of capitalism and the collective values necessary for cooperative community development.

Although DuBois' program was never implemented, it did yield an important model and since the '60's cooperatives have been posed as an important model of Black economic development, especially in the South (Marshall and Godwin, 1971). Over one hundred were formed during the '60's in the South and ninety of those were organized in the Federation of Southern Cooperatives. Although they have been resisted by hostile forces, they nevertheless have provided food, jobs, and capital otherwise unobtainable and have thus helped raise the overall standard of living among the rural population.

Ofari (1970:89), though a socialist, admits that in spite of its problems, the Black cooperative proposal is "by far the most positive proposal that has been offered." Likewise, Allen (1970) who is also socialist, concedes the limitations of cooperative economics, but maintains that given the distance of the socialist revolution and the problems of integrating into a capitalist economy, a transitional program of cooperative economics is necessary." Led by an independent Black party, this transitional program, he (1970:278) states, should involve "a struggle to create an all encompassing, planned communal social system on a national scale and with strong international ties."

Hayes and Nembhard (1999) argue for a cooperative economic strategy for the revitalization of current socio-economic urban conditions. They (1999:48) are concerned that "the cooperative enterprise can be the cornerstone of a progressive revitalization strategy, but to date this model has been left out of the debate." Actually, it is left out of the debates on national policy for African Americans by government and many intellectuals, but in the nationalist community, it is standard policy (Karenga, 1980). Hayes and Nembhard (1999:63-64) summarize the benefits of cooperative economic development in the following way: 1) it "provides employment and educational opportunities"; 2) cooperative models have "generated revenues and capital for sustainable economic growth"; 3) "cooperatives are competitive"; 4) "cooperative organization contributes to the development of community members, through provision of employment, quality

goods and services and a commitment to community building";
and 5) "accumulated wealth is returned to the community and
cooperative members in the form of lower prices, dividends and
safety (material and non-material forms)."

Finally, as I (1980:62-64) have argued elsewhere, *ujamaa*
(cooperative economics) proves its value and validity in that it:
1) aids in increasing capital capacity necessary for economic
development; 2) increases the beneficiaries, unlike Black capitalism; 3) teaches the value for shared social wealth, egalitarian-
ism, collective work and decision-making, the priority of the person over profit and the centrality of the community; and 4)
establishes cooperative thought and practice which can be transferred to other areas, i.e., political struggle and social construction (see also Kawaida, chapter 6). Again, then, it is clear that
politics and economics are unavoidably linked and any strategy
for one must have as a major focus concern for the other.

STUDY QUESTIONS

1.   Define economics.
2.   Discuss the relation between politics and economics and why political econo-
     my is a more accurate word for economics.
3.   Discuss the political economic status of the ghetto as an internal colony.
4.   Discuss the data of Black economic disadvantage.
5.   Discuss the intersection of race and class.
6.   Discuss Sowell's and Wilson's contentions and arguments against racial inter-
     pretation of disadvantage
7.   Discuss the status and problematic of the middle class.
8.   What are some basic problems of Black business?
9.   Discuss the three basic resources bases for Black economic development and
     the rationale for each.
10. Discuss the policy agenda for engaging corporations in the MMM/DOA Mission
     Statement.
11. What are the basic principles and criticism of Black capitalism?
12. What are the basic contentions and objectives of socialism?
13. What were DuBois' cooperative economic proposals?
14. What are the arguments for cooperative economics?

REFERENCES

Abramovitz, Mimi and Ann Withorn. (1999) "Playing by the Rules Welfare Reform and the New Authoritarian State," in Adolph Reed, (ed.) *Without Justice for All: The New Liberalism and Our Retreat from Racial Equality*, Boulder, CO: Westview Press.

Alexis, Marcus. (1999) "The Economics of Racism," *Review of Black Political Economy*, 26, 3 (Winter) 51-76.

Alexis, Marcus. (1980) "Race and Social Organization: An Economic Perspective," *Review of Black Political Economy*, 10,4 (Summer) 334-353.

Alkalimat, Abdul H. and Nelson Johnson. (1974) *"Toward the Ideological Unity of the African Liberation Support Committee,"* a position paper, South Carolina (June-July).

Allen, Robert L. (1970) *Black Awakening in Capitalist America*, Garden City, NY: Anchor Books.

America, Richard. (1977) *Developing the Afro-American Economy*, Lexington, MA: Lexington Books.

America, Richard. (1995/1996) "Reparations and the Combative Advantage of Inner Cities," *Review of Black Political Economy*, 24, 2/3 (Fall/Winter) 193-206.

America, Richard. (1999) "Reparations and Public Policy," *Review of Black Political Economy*, 26, 3 (Winter) 77-83.

Anderson, Bernard C. (1982) "Economic Patterns in Black America," in James D. Williams, (ed.) *The State of Black America, 1982*, New York: National Urban League, pp. 1-32.

Anderson, Elijah. (1992) *Streetwise: Race, Class and Change in an Urban Community*, Chicago: University of Chicago Press.

Andrews, Marcellus. (1999) *The Political Economy of Hope and Fear: Capitalism and the Black Condition in America*, New York: New York University Press.

Auletta, Ken. (1982) *The Underclass*, New York: Random House.

Barnett, Marguerite and James Hefner. (1976) *Public Policy for the Black Community*, New York: Alfred Knopf Publishing.

Banner-Haley, Charles P. (1994) *The Fruits of Integration: Black Middle Class Ideology and Culture*, Jackson: University of Mississippi Press.

Becker, Gary. (1957) *The Economics of Discrimination*, Chicago: University of Chicago Press.

Benjamin, Lois. (1991) *The Black Elite*, Chicago: Nelson-Hall Publishers.

Boggs, James. (1970) "The Myth and Irrationality of Capitalism," *Review of Black Political Economy*, 1, 1 (Spring/ Summer) 27-35.

Boston, Thomas D. (1998) *Affirmative Action and Black Entrepreneurship*, New York: Routledge.

Boston, Thomas D. (1996) *A Different Vision: African American Economic Thought*, New York: Routledge.

Boston, Thomas D. (ed.) (2001) *Leading Issues in Black Political Economy*, Piscataway: Transaction Publishers.

Bound, John and Laura Dresser. (1998) "The Erosion of the Relative Earnings and Employment of Young African American Women During the 1980's," in Irene Brown, (ed.), *African American and Latina Women At Work: Race, Gender and Economic Inequality*, New York: Russell Sage.

Brimmer, Andrew F. (1997) "The Economic Cost of Discrimination Against Black Americans," in Thomas D. Boston, (eds.), *A Different Vision: Race and Public Policy, Volume 2*, London: Routledge, pp. 1-13.

Brimmer, Andrew F. (1982) "Economic Growth and Job and Job Opportunities: The Long-Term Outlook," *Black Enterprise*, 12, 7 (February) 32.

Brimmer, Andrew and Henry S. Terrell. (1971) "The Economic Potential of Black Capitalism," *Black Politician*, 2, 4 (April) 19-23, 78-88.

Browne, Robert S. (1976) "The Black Community and Contemporary Economic Dynamics," *Review of Black Political Economy*, 6, 2 (Winter) 145-160.

Browne, Robert S. (1971) "Cash Flow in a Ghetto Economy," *Review of Black Political Economy*, (Winter/ Spring).

Browning, Rufus, Dale R. Marshall and David H. Tabb. (1984) *Protest is not Enough: The Struggle of Blacks and Hispanics for Equality in Urban Politics*, Berkeley: University of California Press.

Cabral, Amilcar. (1969) *Revolution in Guinea*, New York: Monthly Review Press.

Carmichael, Stokely and Charles Hamilton. (1967) *Black Power*, New York: Random House.

Carnoy, Martin. (1996) *Faded Dreams: Politics and Economics of Race in America*, New York: Cambridge University Press.

Carroll, Grace. (1998) *Environmental Stress and African Americans: The Other Side of the Moon*, Westport, CT: Greenwood.

Cash, William L., Jr. and Lucy R. Oliver (eds). (1975) *Black Economic Development*, Ann Arbor: University of Michigan Press.

Casserly, Catherine M. (1998) *African-American Women and Poverty: Can Education Alone Change the Status Quo?* New York: Garland Publishing.

Clark, Kenneth. (1965) *Dark Ghetto*, New York: Harper & Row.

Clark, Kenneth. (1964) *Youth in the Ghetto*, New York: Haryou Associates.

Coles, Flournoy A. (1975) *Black Economic Development*, Chicago: Nelson Hall.

Conley, Dalton. (1999) *Being Black, Living in the Red: Race, Wealth and Social Policy in America*, Berkeley: University of California Press.

Cose, Ellis. (1993) *The Rage of the Privileged Class*, New York: HarperCollins.

Cotton, S. (1988) "Discrimination or Favoritism in the U.S. Labor Market: The Cost to a Wage Earner of Being Female and Black and the Benefit of Being Male and White," *American Journal of Economic Sociology*, 47, (January) pp. 15-28.

Cross, Theodore L. (1969) *Black Capitalism*, New York: Atheneum.

Cruse, Harold. (1967) *The Crisis of the Negro Intellectual*, New York: William Morrow & Co.

Cruse, Harold. (1968) *Rebellion or Revolution*, New York: William Morrow & Co.

Darity, William Jr. and Samuel Myers, Jr. (1992) "Racial Earnings Inequality into the 21st Century," in Billy Tidwell (ed.) *The State of Black America*, New York: National Urban League, pp. 119-139.

Davis, Mike. et al (1987) *The Year Left 2, Towards a Rainbow Socialism*, Lorder: Verse.

Drake, W. Avon and Robert Hollsworth. (1996) *Affirmative Action and the Stalled Quest for Black Progress*, Urbana: University of Illinois Press.

DuBois, W.E.B. (1968) *Dusk of Dawn*, New York: Schocken Books.

DuBois, W.E.B. (1969) "The Talented Tenth," in Ulysses Lee, (ed.), *The Negro Problem*, New York: Arno Press and The New York Times, pp. 31-76.

Feagin, Joe. (1996) "Facing Up to the American Dream: Race, Class and the Soul of the Nation," (Review), *American Political Science Review*, 90, 2 (June) 429-430.

Feagin, Joe. (1994) *Living With Racism: The Black Middle-Class Experience*, Boston: Beacon Press.

Feagin, Joe. (2001) *"Social Justice and Sociology: Agendas for the Twenty-First Century,"* *American Sociological Review*, 66 , 1 (February).

Feagin, Joe. (1997) "Turning Back: The Retreat from Racial Justice in American Thought and Policy," (Review) *African American Review*, 31, 2 (Summer) 313.

Feagin, Joe. (1998) "When Work Disappears: The World of the New Urban Poor," (Review) *American Journal of Sociology*, 103, 4 (January) 1129.

Franklin, John H. and Eleanor Holmes Norton. (1987) *Black Initiative and Governmental Responsibility*, Washington, DC: Joint Center for Political Studies.

Frazier, E. Franklin. (1962) *Black Bourgeoisie*, New York: Collier Books.

Frazier, George MacDonald. (1998) *Race for Success*, New York: William Morrow.

Freeman, Richard and Harry Holzer. (1986) *The Black Youth Employment Crisis*, Chicago: University of Chicago Press.

Fusfeld, Daniel. (1977) *The Age of the Economist*, Chicago: Scott, Foresman and Co.

Fusfeld, Daniel. (1970) "The Basic Economics of the Urban and Racial Crisis," *The Review of Black Political Economy*, 1, 1 (Spring/Summer) 58-83.

Gilder, George. (1981) *Wealth and Poverty*, New York: Basic Books.

Glasgow, Douglas. (1981) *The Black Underclass*, New York: Vintage Books.

Hacker, Andrew. (1992) *Two Nations, Black and White, Separate and Hostile*, New York: Macmillan.

Hare, Nathan. (1965) *The Black Anglo-Saxons*, New York: Marzani and Munsell, Inc.

Harris, Abram. (1936) *The Negro as Capitalist*, Philadelphia: American Academy of Political Science.

Harris, Donald J. (1978) "Capitalist Exploitation and Black Labor: Some Conceptual Issues," *Review of Black Political Economy*, 8, 2 (Winter) 134-151.

Harris, William H. (1982) *The Harder We Run*, New York: Oxford University Press.

Haynes, Curtis, Jr. (1994) "A Democratic Cooperative Enterprise System: A Response to Urban Decay," *Ceteris Paribus*, 4, 2 (October).

Haynes, Curtis, Jr. and Jessica Gordon Nembhard. (1999) "Cooperative Economics–A Community Revitalization Strategy," *Review of Black Political Economy*, 27, 1 (Summer) 47-72.

Heilbroner, Robert. (1972) *The Worldly Philosophers*, New York: Oxford University Press.

Hill, Robert B. (1980) "Black Families in the 70's." in James D. Williams, (ed.), *The State of Black America, 1980*, New York: National Urban league, Inc., pp. 29 -58.

Hill, Robert B. (1981) "The Economic Status of Black Americans." James D. Williams, (ed.), *The State of Black America, 1981*, New York: National Urban League, Inc.

Hill, Robert B. (1978) *The Illusion of Black Progress*, Washington, D.C: National Urban League Research Department.

Hirsch, Arnold R. (1998) *Making Second Ghetto*, Chicago: University of Chicago Press.

Hogan, Lloyd. (1984) *Principles of Black Political Economy*, London: Routledge and Kegan Paul.

Jackson, John L. (2001) *Harlemworld: Doing Race and Class in Contemporary Black America*, Chicago: University of Chicago Press.

Jaynes, Gerald D. and Robin Williams, Jr. (eds.) (1989) *Common Destiny: Blacks and American Society*, Washington, DC: National Academy Press.

Karenga, Maulana. (1992) "African Americans and the Reconstruction of Social Policy." *Harvard Journal of African American Public Policy*, Vol. I, pp. 55-74.

Karenga, Maulana. (1980) *Kawaida Theory: An Introductory Outline*, Inglewood, CA: Kawaida Publications.

Katz, Michael B. (1986) *In the Shadow of the Poorhouse*, New York: Basic Books.

Katz, Michael B. (1993) *the Underclass Debate: Views From History*, Princeton: Princeton University Press.

Keating, W. Dennis. (1994) *The Suburban Racial Dilemma: Housing and Neighborhoods*, Philadelphia: Temple University Press.

Kikazi, Kilolo. (1997) *African American Economic Development and Small Business Ownership*, New York: Garland Publishing.

Kluger, Richard. (1977) *Simple Justice*, New York: Vintage Books.

Landry, Bart. (1987) *The New Black Middle Class*, Berkeley, University of California.

Lee, Elliot. (1982) "The BE Board of Economics Look at the Future" *Black Enterprise*, 12,11 (June) 191-200.

Lusane, Clarence. (1997) *Race in the Global Era: African Americans at the Millenium*, Boston: South End Press.

Malveaux, Julianne. (1999) *Wall Street, Main Street and the Side Street: A Mad Economist Takes a Stroll*, Los Angeles: Pine One Publications.

Mandle, Jay R. (1992) *Not Slave, Not Free: The African American Economic Experience Since the Civil War*, Durham: Duke University.

Marshall, Ray and Lamond Godwin. (1971) *Cooperatives and Rural Poverty in the South*, Baltimore: The John Hopkins Press.

Mason, Patrick L. (ed.) (2000) *African Americans, Labor and Society: Organizing for a New Agenda*, Detroit: Wayne State University Press.

Massey, Douglass S. and Nancy A. Denton. (1994) *American Apartheid: Segregation and the Making of the Underclass*, Cambridge: Harvard University Press.

McCoy, Frank. (1992) "A Decade in Review," *Black Enterprise* 22, 11 (June) 195-202.

Morris, Aldon. (1984) *The Origins of the Civil Rights Movement: Black Communities Organizing for Social Change*, New York: The Free Press.

Murray, Charles. (1984) *Losing Ground: American Social Policy 1950-1980*, New York: Basic Books.

Ofari, Earl. (1970) *The Myth of Black Capitalism*, New York: Monthly Review Press.

Oliver, Melvin L. (1996) *Black Wealth White Wealth: A New Perspective on Racial Inequality*, New York: Routledge.

Oliver, Melvin L. and Thomas M. Shapiro. (1995) *Black Wealth/White Wealth: A New Perspective on Racial Inequality*, London: Routledge.

Pattillo-McCoy, Mary. (1999) *Black Picket Fences: Privilege and Peril Among the Black Middle Class*, Chicago: University of Chicago Press.

Persaud, Randolph B. and Clarence Lusane. (2000) "The New Economy, Globalization and the Impact of African Americans," *Race and Class*, 41, 1 (September) 21-34.

Pinkney, Alphonso. (1984) *The Myth of Black Progress*, Cambridge: Cambridge University Press.

Reed, Adolph, (ed.) (1999) *Without Justice for All: The New Liberalism and Our Retreat from Racial Equality*, Boulder, CO: Westview Press

Reich, Michael. (1981) *Racial Equality*, Princeton, NJ: Princeton University Press.

Rodgers, William M. (1999) "A Critical Assessment of Skills Explanations of White-White Employment and Wage Gaps," *The State of Black America, 1999*, New York: National Urban League.

Simms, Margaret C. (1989) *Black Economic Progress: An Agenda for the 1990's*, Washington, DC: Joint Center for Political Studies.

Sowell, Thomas. (1981a) *Ethnic Minorities*, New York: Basic Books.

Sowell, Thomas. (1981b) *Markets and Minorities*, New York: Basic Books.

Sowell, Thomas. (1975) *Race and Economics*, New York: David McKay.

Steinberg, Stephen. (1999) "Occupational Apartheid in America: Race, Labor Market Segmentation and Affirmative Action," in Adolph Reed, (ed.) *Without Justice for All: The New Liberalism and Our Retreat from Racial Equality*, Boulder, CO: Westview Press

Stewart, James (1984) "Building a Cooperative Economy: Lessons from the Black Experience," *Review of Social Economy*, XVII, pp. 360-268.

Sugrue, Thomas J. (1998) *The Origins of the Urban Crisis: Race and Inequality in Postwar Detroit*, Princeton: Princeton University Press.

Swinton, David H. (1992) "The Economic Status of African Americans: Limited Ownership and Persistent Inequality," in Billy Tidwell (ed.) *The State of Black America*, New York: National Urban League, pp. 61-117.

Swinton, David H. (1991) "The Economic Status of African Americans: 'Permanent' Poverty and Inequality," in Janet Dewar (ed.), *The State of Black America*, New York: National Urban League, pp. 25-75.

Swinton, David H. (1990) "Economic Status of Black Americans During the 80's: A Decade of Limited Progress," in Janet Dewar (ed.), *The State of Black America*, New York: National Urban League, pp. 25-52.

Tabb, William K. (1970) *The Political Economy of the Black Ghetto*, New York: W.W. Norton and Company.

Turner, James. (1976) "Implications of Class Conflict and Racial Cleavage for the U.S. Black Community," *Review of Black Political Economy*, 6, 2 (Winter) 133-144.

Waldinger, Roger. (1999) *Still the Promised City? African-Americans and New Immigrants in Postindustrial New York*, Cambridge: Harvard University Press.

Watkins, Celeste. (2001) "A Tale of Two Classes: The Socio-Economic Divide Among Black Americans Under 35," *State of Black America*, New York: National Urban League.

Williams, James D. (ed.) (1982) *The State of Black America, 1982*, New York: National Urban League, Inc.

Williams, Rhonda M. (1999) "Unfinished Business: African American Political Economy During the Age of 'Color-Blind' Politics," *The State of Black America*, New York: National Urban League.

Willie, Charles. (1979) *The Caste and Class Controversy*, New York: General Hall, Inc.

Wilson, William J. (1978) *The Declining Significance of Race*, Chicago: University of Chicago Press.

Wilson, William J. (1993) *The Ghetto Underclass: Social Science Perspectives*, Thousand Oaks: Sage Publications.

Wilson, William J. (1996) *When Work Disappears: The World of the New Urban Poor*, New York: Vintage Books.

Woodson, Robert. (ed.) (1987) *On the Road to Economic Freedom*, Washington, DC: Regency Gateway.

Zweig, Michael. (1972) "The Dialectics of Black Capitalism," *Review of Black Political Economy*, 2 (Spring) 25-37.

BLACK CREATIVE
PRODUCTION

BLACK CREATIVE PRODUCTION

CHAPTER 9

9.1 INTRODUCTION

DEFINING ART

Although the category, creative production, can be used more generally to include various other forms of creative work, it will focus in this chapter on Black Art, Music and Literature. These are definitive of Black aesthetic creations and can, for the purpose of this chapter, be categorized as Black Arts, or Art in the general sense. The sense of an overall interrelatedness of art is evident in the anthology, *Call and Response*, which links literature, music and the performing arts (Hill, 1998). By *Art*, then, I mean *"cultural production informed by standards of creativity and beauty and inspired by and reflective of a people's life-experiences and life-aspirations"* (Karenga, 1980:80). The focus here is on the collective base of art, for as Evans (1979:37) contends concerning Black art, "...it is Black art because it is saturated in the experience and behavior patterns of the people for who it is created and because its substance is functional."

DuBois (1925) also stressed the collective source of Black art in his discussion of its social origin. He (1925:53) stated that even though Black art has both a personal and universal aspect, these are "combined with a certain group compulsion...meaning that the wishes, thoughts and experiences of thousands of individuals influence consciously and unconsciously the message of the one who speaks for all." This "social compulsion", DuBois continues, was shaped by Black experience in enslavement and emancipation, and the struggle Blacks waged to liberate themselves and strive upward. In a word, it rises out of a culture in which a people are creating themselves, celebrating, sustain and developing themselves and introducing themselves to history and humanity (Powell, 1997; Stuckey, 1994).

It is this struggle for freedom, dignity and self-definition in a hostile and challenge-filled world, then, that shaped Black art and gave it its relevance and reality. Black art, therefore, "as an expression of Black life experiences and aspirations, is the conscious and unconscious aesthetic contribution of Black people to their struggle to rescue and reconstruct their history and humanity in their own image and interest" (Karenga, 1980:80). Thus, Alain Locke (1969:266), a key figure in the Harlem Renaissance of the 1920's, argued for the development of an African-American mode of artistic expression which spoke directly to the Black need for self-expression in their own terms. "We ought and must have a school of (Black) art," he asserted, "a local and racially representative tradition." The impetus and inspiration for this, he maintained, would come from Blacks' recognition, respect and use of their African heritage. This stress on the use of Africa as a rich and ancient source of culture and creativity is also made by Kariamu Welsh-Asante (1993) and others.

THE BLACK AESTHETIC

Although this question was raised and debated during the Harlem Renaissance and after, it received its most critical and enthusiastic attention during the Sixties in the debate revolving around the Black aesthetic (Gayle,1971). The Black aesthetic had two distinct but interrelated meanings. First, it was used to mean a distinctive mode of aesthetic expression by which Black art could be identified. Secondly, it meant a criteria by which Black art could not only be judged in terms of its creativity and beauty, but also in terms of its social relevance.

If one combines these two interrelated definitions, the *Black aesthetic* can be defined as *a distinctive mode of artistic expression and a distinctive standard by which Black art can be identified and judged in terms of its creativity and beauty as well as its social relevance.* From the debate around this question which continues even now, two schools evolved, *the detached-art school* and *the committed-art school.* Writers such as Ellison (1966) and Redding (1966) argued the primacy of art rather than race or politics, suggesting art was universal and personal but not Black. They asserted that the artist does a disservice to himself/herself and his/her profession by being overly concerned with race and politics.

Langston Hughes, Richard Wright and the creative artists and critics of the 60's all argued against such a view. Hughes (1970:262) stated that he was "ashamed for the Black poet who says `I want to be a poet not a (Black) poet', as though his own racial world were not as interesting as any world." Also, he expressed shame for the Black artist who paints sunsets instead of Black faces "because he fears the strange un-whiteness of his features." Wright, as Gayle (1970:xiii) notes, "argued, in essence, that conditions in America had not changed to the degree that the (African-American) could desert the race question, engage in an art for art's sake endeavor or wander free in the sunny utopia of abstraction in an attempt to desert the harsh reality of being Black in the twentieth century."

In the 60's Hoyt Fuller, Larry Neal, Mari Evans, Haki Madhubuti (Don L. Lee), Carolyn Rodgers, Rhonda Davis, Addison Gayle, Amiri Baraka, Sonia Sanchez, Woodie King, Ron Milner, Dudley Randall, this author and others contributed to the discussion and definition of the Black aesthetic (Gayle 1971). Neal (1971:272; also Gates and McKay, 1997:1959ff) posited essential contentions of the committed-art school when he rejected "any concept of the artist that alienates him from the community," posed Black art as "the aesthetic sister of the Black Power concept" and argued that the Black artist's primary duty is to speak to the spiritual and cultural needs of Black people. Moreover, the *Negro Digest* (later named the *Black World*), under the editorship of Hoyt Fuller (1971) who helped establish it in 1967, ran over a year of continuous commentary and discussion on the Black aesthetic from September 1968 through November 1969. In the January 1968 issue, a wide spectrum of views was presented on the question of the Black aesthetic. Most of these commentaries reaffirmed the need for Blacks to create and employ an aesthetic in their own image and interest.

In the 70's, the discussion continued. Elizabeth Catlett (1975:13) reaffirmed the need for art being linked to Black strug-gle, stating that "only the liberation of Black people will make the real development of Black art possible. Therefore, it is to our advantage as artists as well as Blacks to lend all our strength to the struggle." She notes that art "...will not create authentic social change, but it can provoke thought and prepare us for change, even helping in its achievement. For art can tell us what we do not see consciously, what we may not realize, and that there are other ways of seeing things-maybe opposite ways."

John Killens (1975:46) also reemphasized that culture and literature were weapons for liberation and "words are the writer's ammunition." And Madhubuti (Lee) (1972:39) continued his stress on the social role of art and the artist, and the need to develop a people-focused art stating that "To be able to define one's self from a historically and culturally accurate base and to follow through in your work; keeping the best interest of your history and culture in mind is to-actually-give direction to the coming generations." In addition, Evans (1979:37) reaffirmed the political character and role of Black art, contending that "It is political since its intent is to speak to the Black community about the quality of life in that community and the ramification of individual responsibility for the community both within and outside the systems of the larger society.

Finally, Chestyn Everett (1975:34,35) reasserts the need for respect of Black tradition. For any art "which denies *tradition* removes the necessary cultural cohesion of the form, sensibilities and integrity" of the art itself. Artists, he continues, "enrich themselves and their works when they bring to themselves and to their writing a clear perspective and appreciation for the *cultural and historical tradition* of Black life and (art). The need, then, is to "advance the best of this tradition and `standing on the shoulders of our forefathers' set our rainbow in the sky!

It is in the context and support of the commitment-art school, that I (Karenga, 1971, 1980:34ff;) offered suggestions for a Black aesthetic, first in the *Black World* series of commentaries and afterward in an outline of *Kawaida Theory*. Essentially, I (1980:84ff) argued that "for Black Art to truly be in the image and interest of Black people to whom it owes its existence and inner thrust, it must be informed, inspired and judged by social criteria as well as an aesthetic criteria." This social criteria which evolved within the framework of Kawaida philosophy was based on: 1) the tradition role of art in African society; 2) the discussions by advocates of the commitment-art school during and before the 60's; and 3) a Kawaida perception of the demands of Black life and struggle (Ransaw, 1979).

Therefore, I (1980:84ff) contended that for Black art to be real and relevant it had to have three basic characteristics, i.e., it had to be functional, collective and committing. For art to be functional is to be useful. And if art is not useful, it is by definition, useless. To be *functional*, art must self-consciously have and urge social purpose, inform, instruct and inspire the people and be an unashamed partisan for them. "In a word, to be functional, Black art must be an aesthetic translation of our will and struggle for liberation and a higher level of life," searching for and creating new forms and styles to speak our truth and possibilities. To be *collective*, Black art must be done for all, drawn and synthesized from all, and rooted in a life-based language and imagery rich in everyday relevance. It must be understandable without being vulgarly simplistic, that is, so pedestrian and impoverished that it does damage to art as a discipline and to the social message it attempts to advance.

Finally, Black art must be *committing*. It must not simply inform and inspire Blacks, but also commit them to the historical project of liberation and a higher level of human life. To do this, "it must demand and urge willing and conscious involvement in struggle and building of a new world and new men, women and children to inhabit it". And it must move beyond protest and teach possibilities, beyond victimization and teach Blacks to dare victory. Art, then, "must commit us to what we can become and are becoming and inspire us to dare the positive in a world defined and deformed by the negative.

Moreover, "committing art is nationally self-conscious art, i.e., consciously a fundamental contribution to the definition, defense and development of the national Black community." This is not to deny art's human character, but to endow it with a concrete human reality by giving it a people-specific expression. For "our art, like our lives, is great not because it's defined as more human than Black, but because we have explored the richness of our own life experience and aspirations and discovered and offer life-lessons from which the whole world can benefit - not only aesthetically, but culturally in the wide sense of the word." It is in the framework of these assumptions that the following summaries of Black artistic achievement are offered and explained. This also maintain the stated thrust of this text to present a proactive and positive view of African American life and struggle in its current and historical unfolding.

9.2   BLACK ART

THE CONTINENTAL AFRICAN DIMENSION

African American art has its origins in Africa where art and artistic production, like religion, manifested itself in all aspects of communal life. African art was functional as well as aesthetic, being created for and used in various religious and social activities (Lewis, 1994; Blauer and Laurbe, 2001; Blackman, 2000; Patton, 1998; Adler and Barnard, 1992; Drewal and Pemberton, 1990; Niangoran-Bouah, 1984; Gillon, 1984; Porter, 1970 Smith, 1981). African artists were carvers in wood, ivory and bone, sculptors in stone, clay, bronze, gold and iron, and created one of the oldest and most skilled traditions of functional and aesthetic art in the history of humankind (Locke, 1936; Butcher, 1956 McLeod, 1980, Wilkinson, 1992). Although there is continuing controversy over how much of the African artistic tradition was transferred to the U.S., the fact cannot be denied that there are clear evidences of the African motif in early African American art (Porter, 1943; Dover, 1960; Thompson, 1983).

Even though enslavers often condemned and destroyed Black art to destroy Black communication and culture, enslaved Africans nevertheless produced impressive works of art (Driskell, 1976:12ff). These included not only personal art objects, but public works as Samella Lewis (1978:9ff) asserts. Among the personal art objects, Robert F. Thompson (1969) lists ceramics, basketry, earthenware, grave decorations, wood carvings and weavings. Examples of these are in the works of Elsa Fine (1973:12ff) and David Driskell (1976:12ff). James Porter (1943) contends that the Janson House, built on the Hudson River in 1712 for a Dutch patron, exhibits a clear African motif in its construction and ornamentation, i.e., hand forged hinges and detailed-work fireplace. He also cites their art work in silver, gold and iron. Driskell (1976:22ff) shows remarkable similarities between African and African American art and architecture, among which are wrought iron balconies in New Orleans, plantation houses in African motif, a cylindrical quarter for enslaved Africans in Virginia which resemble Tembu houses in South Africa, and carved mantels with an African mask motif in North Carolina.

In addition, there is impressive evidence of African building and masonry skill in the Chapel of Cross in Chapel Hill, N.C., the Virginia State Capital building, the Torrence House of Mecklingburg County, the Harvey Castle near New Orleans, St. Andrew's Episcopal Church in Prairieville, Ala., and the famous Melrose plantation, near Natchitoches, LA. (Dozier, 1974; Newton, 1977). James Newton concludes that there were at least 90 different areas of arts and craft in which African Americans exhibited skillful workmanship.

PROFESSIONAL EMERGENCE

Samella Lewis (1978:12-13) marks the emergence of the professional artist before Emancipation with painters Scipio Moorhead and G.W. Hobbs in the 1770's, and Josua Johnston who "was the first artist of Black ancestry to gain public recognition in the United States as a portrait painter." After these were Julien Hudson (active 1830-40); Robert Douglass (1809-87); an abolitionist and painter, Patrick Henry Reason (1817-50); an engraver, William Simpson (active 1854-72); and later Robert Duncanson, Edward Bannister, Grafton Brown and Nelson Primus.

Edmonia Lewis (1843-1900) was the first Black woman in the U.S. to gain widespread recognition as an artist and the first Black to gain national reputation as a sculptor. Her *Forever Free*, a Black couple looking upward with broken chains, is in Howard University's Gallery of Art. Also, one of the most impressive early Black artists was Henry O. Tanner (1859-97), famous for his oil on canvas pieces such as *Banjo Lesson* and *The Thankful Poor*. However, having suffered much from racism, Tanner went to Paris and although he helped young Black artists who came to Paris, he refused to return to the U.S. and establish the Black Art School Alain Locke advocated.

THE HARLEM RENAISSANCE

The Harlem Renaissance produced race and socially conscious artists who reached back to Africa and the Black masses for a distinctive Black motif (Marks, 1999; Powell, 1997). As mentioned above, Locke (1968:267) had challenged Black artists to turn to their "ancestral arts of Africa" in order to develop a race art. He argued that if African art had influenced Pablo Picasso, Modigliani, Matisse and other white artists, it was surely "not too much to expect...its influence upon the culturally awakened (Black) artist of the present generations." Three artists in particular - Palmer Hayden, Archibald Motley, Jr., and Aaron Douglass - focused on developing styles that reflected the Black aesthetic.

Hayden in his *Fetiche et Cleurs* (Fetish and Flowers) used African print to emphasize Africanness and later painted subject matter which stressed the life and custom of the Black masses as in *John Henry on the Right, Stem Drill on the Left* and *The Janitor Who Paints*. Motley also used African and African American themes. *His Old Snuff Dipper, The Barbecue* and *Chicken Shack* are clear examples of his focus on Black life. Douglass was a "pioneer Africanist", using the ancestral legacy to develop an original style which "combined modernism and Africanism in an astonishing (and original) synthesis" (Driskell, 1976:62). Focusing on the beauty and strength of Black life, he employed geometric figures reflecting an African motif in his illustrations for Locke's (1968) *The New Negro* and James Weldon's Johnson's *God Trombones* and in his major work, a series of murals for the Countee Cullen branch of the New York library which portrayed the history of African Americans.

POST RENAISSANCE

Hale Woodruff also reflected a race and social consciousness in his art. In 1939, he painted a series of three socially conscious oil on canvas pieces entitled *The Amistad Murals* in honor of the Amistad Mutiny. This creation for Talladega College in Alabama, reflects the influence of socially-conscious Mexican muralists Jose C. Orozco, Diego Rivera, and David Siquieros on him and other Black artists during the 30's and 40's (Lewis, 1978:67-68). Richmond Barthe (b.1901) is clearly one of African Americans' leading sculptors. His sculptural figures are technically immaculate and graceful and focus on Black life, strength and dignity. Among these are *Blackberry Woman, Wetta, African Dancer*, and the *Negro Looks Ahead*. He also produces two marble reliefs, *Exodus* and *Dance*.

The 40's continued the tradition of race and socially conscious art, and mural art stood out as a major mode of expression. This, as mentioned before, was influenced by the Mexican muralists Rivera, Orozco and Siquieros, but also Lewis (1978:110) notes, "mural art is a major aspect of African architectural tradition". Charles Alston was one of the most important Black muralists during this time. Using a cubist style, his mural, *Magic and Medicine* for the Harlem Hospital in 1937, depicts a contrast between African and American life, the former being nature-oriented and warm, and the later, mechanical and cold. Alston also produced with Hale Woodruff a joint mural documenting Black contributions to the founding of California for Golden State Mutual Life Insurance Company of Los Angeles. Alton's panel is *Exploration and Colonization* (1527-1850) and Woodruff's is *Settlement and Development* (1850-1949).

Charles White is by all estimates one of the most gifted race and socially conscious Black artists. Early in his art he announced that he was interested in the social role and function of art and sought to express it in his own. He showed Black people in various roles in history as worker, soldier, mother, father, scientist, civic leader, and musician. Drawing from the muralists school, his works are monumental, bold and defiant. Some of his most famous murals are *Five Great American Negroes* and *The Contribution of the Negro to American Democracy*. His lithographs, *Frederick Douglass* and *Harriet Tubman*, and his crayon *Mother and Child* are also impressive pieces.

James Porter, who wrote *Modern Negro Art*, and was appointed head of Howard University's art department and art gallery in 1953, also painted. Essentially between 1954 and 1964, he painted African and African American themes and as an art critic and art historian, he, like Alain Locke, played a vital role in the early establishment and development of Black art (Lewis, 1978:102).

Lois Mailou Jones and Elizabeth Catlett were two important Black women artists during this period. Although Jones at first painted the French countryside in an earlier period, she evolved into a self-conscious Black artist, visited 11 African countries and incorporated African imagery in her subsequent painting. Her *Moon Mask* from her African series reflects this consciousness. Catlett, a sculptor and printmaker, was involved in the

Civil Rights Movement as a student and teacher, and assigned art a social role in the struggle against oppression. Some of her strongest works are *Black Unity*, in honor of Pan-Africanism; her lithograph *Negro Es Bello* (Black is Beautiful), a gentle rendition of the profile of a Black child; and *Malcolm Speaks For Us*, a strong linocut in her series on Black heroes.

THE SIXTIES AND BEYOND

The Sixties and Seventies saw an impressive growth of race conscious and socially conscious art (Thompson and Randall, 1998). The Black Arts Movement of the 60's, which demanded that art serve Black people and their struggle, recruited many artists who reflected in their art not only a commitment to their heritage but also a commitment to use their medium to support and achieve Black liberation. Murals again became a way to make art serve and express the people. Among these are *Mural at Massachusetts* in Boston by Dana Chandler and Gary Rickson, Eugene Edna's *Howard University Mural*, John Outerbridge's *Something From Nothing* in Compton, California, Dana Chandler's *Knowledge is Power: Stay in School* in Boston, and in Chicago, William Walker's *Peace and Salvation Wall*, Mitchell Caton's *Universal Alley Wall* and *Wall of Respect* by Eugene Edna, William Walker, Jeff Donaldson and other members of the Organization of Black American Culture, a group of artists and community workers dedicated to bringing art to Black people.

Paintings with Black themes of struggle, repression and daily life are also found in the works of David Hammonds, Cliff Joseph, Faith Ringgold, Alvin Hollings, Benny Andrews, Milton Johnson, Joe Overstreet, Daniel Johnson, Ben Jones, Murray De Pillars, Malcolm Bailey, Ernest Trove, Lovett Thompson, Ernie Barnes and Mikelle Fletcher. Herman Kofi Bailey's *Unity*, Varnette Honeywood's *Gossip in the Sanctuary*, David Driskell's *Shango Gone*, John Bigger's *The Time of Edge*, *Nigeria* and *Web of Life "Ananse"*, Jacob Lawrence's *The Worker*, Vernell DeSilva's *Chicago Pool Hall* and *Harriet Tubman* and Murray De Pillars' *People of the Sun* are definitive period pieces also.

Mixed media assemblages include Noah Purifoy's *Sir Watts*, Bettye Ann Saar's *Nine Mojo Secrets*, John Outterbridge's *Shoeshine Box*, and Kay Brown's *Take It Now*. In sculpture, Margaret Burrough's *Head* and Doyle Foreman's *Corner* with their African projections stand out. And in graphic processes, Ruth Waddy's *The Key*, Jeff Donaldson's *Victory in the Valley of Eshu*, and Carol Ward's *Foloyan* are strong examples of African and African American focus. Examples of these and all others listed above can be found in Lewis (1978), Driskell (1976) and Fine (1973).

9.3   BLACK MUSIC

AFRICAN ORIGINS

The African origins and character of Black music are well-documented (Southern, 1971; Meadows, 1979; Maultsby, 1979; Caldwell, 1997; Floyd, 1996). Not only did Africans bring songs and dances but also brought and reconstructed musical instruments played in Africa such as the banjo, the balafone (xylophone), the musical bow, flutes, the elephant tusk horn, a kind of bagpipe, types of clarinets (dududen), trumpets made of wood and ivory, gongs, rattles, castanets, the quill or panpipes, the sansa or thumb piano and, of course, the drum (Kebede, 1995). Harold Courlander (1963) gives a detailed discussion of Africa-derived instruments played by African Americans. Moreover, as Meadows (1979:185) notes "the performance practices, melodies, rhythms, and aesthetic musical practices of today's Black Americans are only a mirror of the practices of their African forefathers and mothers."

None of this means that Africans in the U.S. did not borrow from their new environment for they did (Levine, 1977). But as Maultsby (1979:200-21) states, "these elements were recycled through the concepts and aesthetic principles that defined the musical tradition of the Africans." For example, melodies, rhythms, texts, and tempos were changed and shouts, calls, words, clapping, foot stomping and body movements were added to give them an African character. The first music Blacks sang in the U.S., then, were songs from Africa. These included war songs and holiday songs in their own languages. However, fearing rebellions and plots, the enslavers moved to prohibit both African song and languages as well as instruments like drums which could be used for communication.

THE SPIRITUALS

Following African tradition, early African Americans distinguished many different types among their songs according to how they were used (Southern, 1971:175). Given the religiousness of Africans, the largest number of songs in the ante-bellum or pre-Civil War period were religious songs or spirituals (Reagan, 2001; Cruz, 1999; Jones, 1999, Cone, 1992). DuBois (1969) in 1903 was the first scholar to pay deserved attention to the beauty and significance of the spirituals. He saw these "sorrow songs" of enslaved and disappointed Africans as a message to the world in their expression of "faith in the ultimate justice in the world."

There are three basic approaches to the interpretation of the spirituals, i.e., that they are: 1) essentially social; 2) essentially religious; and 3) a synthesis of both the social and religious. John Lovell (1969) and Mark Fisher (1953) see them as essentially expressions of social strivings and struggle whose themes are: 1) the desire for freedom, justice and penalty for the oppressor; 2) criticism of the existing order; and 3) coded messages of escape, meetings and struggle. "Go Down Moses," "Swing Low Sweet Chariot," "Oh Freedom, Oh Freedom," "Before I'd Be A Slave I'd Be Buried In My Grave," "If I Had My Way I'd Tear This Building Down," "Oh Mary Don't You Weep, Don't You Mourn," "My Lord Delivered Daniel," and "No More Auction Block For Me," etc., are examples of these.

Secondly, Howard Thurman (1947) and Benjamin Mays (1968) saw the spirituals as essentially religious. Thurman (1947:12) contended that "The clue to the meaning of the spirituals is to be found in religious experience and spiritual discernment." He saw them as a religious expression of the enslaved African's struggle to maintain his/her dignity, personality and human spirit and transcend the context dedicated to their destruction. Mays (1968:21) argues that the spirituals are rooted in the "compensatory idea, that God will bring His own out victoriously in the end." The compensatory aspect, then, is rooted in a religious force and outcome not social ones.

Finally, James Cone (1972) sees the need of a synthesis for the two interpretations. He (1972:20) contends that "no theological interpretation of the Black spirituals can be valid that ignores the cultural environment that created them." The enslaved African found him/herself in a violent and brutal and dehumanizing environment and he/she offered both social and religious resistance. Spirituals, then, Cone concludes are a religious expression of resistance. It is reinforcement of identity and dignity, an expression of the use of religion as a "source of strength in a time of trouble" and "a vibrant affirmation of life and its possibilities in an appropriate aesthetic form" (Cone, 1972:32-33).

SONGS OF WORK AND LEISURE

Work songs, as Eileen Southern (1971:177) notes, grew out of work activity in the fields, in prison, on roads, on the waterfront, on railroads, and other work sites. Essentially, this was not only psychic relief from tedium, but also depicted graphically the worker's situation and built on a sense of shared responsibility and fate (Roberts, 1974:140ff). Especially relevant were heroic work songs like "John Henry" which showed Blacks defeating "white society on its own terms" by smashing its expectations and the stereotypes, by insisting that their lives transcend the traditional models and roles established for them and their people by the white majority" (Levine, 1977:420).

Southern (1971:182) also list dance songs and play songs often called "fiddle songs", "devil songs", etc. As the names suggest, these were recreational songs. In addition, there were also narrative songs, satirical songs and field and street cries. All these reflected Blacks' aesthetic expression created in the midst of giving beauty and color to a hostile and challenge-filled world.

THE BLUES

It is important to stress here how each kind of Black music, both religious and secular, reaffirmed and reinforced the functional, collective and committing character of Black art forms. All truly African art was/is rooted in and reflective of life-situations, aspirations and possibilities. Thus, Black music, as an art form, expresses these characteristics also. This is clear also in blues which began to take form in the late nineteenth century and "by the twentieth century had become a major form of Black expression" (Maultsby, 1979:203).

James Cone (1972:112) argues that the blues are secular spirituals; secular in their focus on this world and the body and spiritual in that "they are impelled by the same search for the truth of the Black experience." According to Amiri Baraka (Jones, 1963:18), "the immediate predecessors of Blues were the African American...work songs which had their origins in West Africa." Maultsby contends that blues is rooted in both secular and religious musical traditions, citing the training blues singers had in church, their singing of both hymns and blues, the tendency to call on the Lord while expressing deep sorrow, etc.

Blues, then, is rooted in the totality of the Black experience in the U.S. and the historical and social burden of being Black in a racist society which this implied, i.e., exploitation and oppression, loss of love, "hard rows to hoe," bad news and worse dreams, drinking and loving hard, resignation, reaffirmation and above all durability (Handy, 1941; Van Rijn, 1996). In an earlier article on Black art, I (Karenga, 1971) criticized blues as being essentially focused on resignation, but as my critics have rightly observed, blues is much more multidimensional than that (Neal, 1972).

Thus, blues speaks of: Black beauty; woman so good looking "make a bulldog break his chain and a snail to catch a train;" being down and out, "sometimes I feel like nothing, somethin, th'owed away, Then I get my g'itar and play the blues all day;" defiant dignity, "I'd rather drink muddy water, sleep in a hollow log, dan stay in this town and be treated like a dirty dog;" sexual betrayal, "went out this morning left my gate unlatched, come back home, found that boy in my potato patch;" plea bargaining, "come back baby, please don't go, cuz the way I love you baby, you'll never know," and social criticism, "Uncle Sam ain't no woman, but he sure can take yo' man. Boys der got'em in the service, doin something I cain' understand."

Some of the more important names in blues are William C. Handy, considered the "Father of the Blues," who first published "Memphis Blues" in 1912 and in 1914 published "St. Louis Blues" which made blues a household word around the world; Ma Rainey, the first professional blues singer considered "Queen of the Blues," Billie Holiday; John Lee Hooker; Leadbelly; Muddy Waters; Blind Lemon Jefferson; B.B. King; Bobby Blue Bland; Nina Simone; Lightnin Hopkins; Aaron T-Bone Walker;

"Sonny Boy" Williamson; Bessie Smith; Alberta Hunter; Josh White; and Ray Charles (Frayer, 1998; Awmiller, 1996).

RAGTIME

Ragtime, like blues and spirituals, was another early manifestation of distinct African American music (Metis, 1966, Lems-Dwrokin, 1991; Hasse, 1985)Because it was associated primarily with the piano, it evolved after enslavement when Blacks had access to the instrument. It was especially designed for Black consumption and was played by Black musicians anonymously and known in eating places, saloons, riverside dives, honky tonk spots and later clubs. Ragtime composers were many. Among the earliest were Irving Jones and Cris Smith. Others were Scott Joplin, the "King of Ragtime", whose music was made popular in the 1970's by the movie *The Sting*; Thomas Turpin, "Father of St. Louis Ragtime;" Joe Jordan; Eubie Blake; James Scott; Scott Hayden and Louis Chauvin.

GOSPEL MUSIC

Gospel music rose out of the late 19th century and early 20th century folk church as opposed to the 20th century middle class church (Reagan, 2001, 1993; Blue, 2001; Harris, 1992; Williams-Jones, 1975; Helibut, 1975). Essentially, it is created in a context of individual and collective spontaneity, improvisation for church service and are thus called "church songs". Methodist minister, Charles Albert Tindley, the pioneer Gospel song creator, wrote his first songs in the early 1900's. And Thomas Dorsey, another pioneer, contributed to the Gospel idiom "a ragtime, boogie woogie piano style, his blues-based melodies, harmonies and an interest in religious spirit and faith" (Maultsby, 1979:204). To this instrumentation, chants, calls, hand clapping and foot stomping were added in the free creativity and expression characteristic of folk environments. Some of the most notable gospel singers are Mahalia Jackson, James Cleveland, Clara Ward, Marion Williams, Rosetta Thorpe, Sallie Maetin, Mother Smith, Bessie Griffin, Golden Gate Quartet, the Sensational Nightingales, the Dixie Humming Birds, Ruth David and the Staple Singers.

THE EMERGENCE OF JAZZ

Southern (1971:374) states that "the fusion of blues and rag-time with brass band and syncopated dance music resulted in a music called Jazz, a music with its own characteristics". Jazz start-ed in New Orleans with pioneers like King Oliver and his Creole Band; Jelly Roll Morton and his Red Hot Peppers; Louis Satchmo Armstrong with his Hot Five and Hot Seven, and clar-inetist John Dodds. From New Orleans, jazz moved in the 1920's to the Chicago Southside (Conyers, 2001; Lee, 1999; Seymour, 1996). In addition, big bands like those of Chuck Webb, Jimmie Lunceford, Cab Calloway, Erskine Hawkins, Lionel Hampton, Count Basie and Duke Ellington also emerged in the 20's.

With jazz several styles developed. Among them were: swing in the 30's associated with Duke Ellington and big bands; bop in the early 40's which evolved into hard bop or soul jazz in the 50's represented by Dizzie Gillespie, Thelonius Monk, Kenny Clark, Charlie Christian, Lester Young, Jimmy Blanton, Charlie Parker, Bud Powell, Miles Davis, Earl Hines, Max Roach, Art Blakey, Horace Silver, Nat and Cannonball Adderly, Sonny Rollins; avant garde in the late 50's exemplified by Ornette Colman, John Coltrane, Cecil Taylor, Charles Mingus and Eric Dolphy. In addi-tion, Sun Ra, Pharaoh Saunders, Albert Ayler, Don Ayler, Marian Brown and Archie Shepp have shown impressive originality.

There are obviously too many Black musicians to be listed in this short overview, but it is important to mention musical greats like jazz singers Ella Fitzgerald, Billie Holiday, King Pleasure, Joe Williams, Sarah Vaughn, Arthur Prysock and pianists Fats Waller, Errol Garner, Hazel Scott and trumpeter Donald Byrd.

RHYTHM AND BLUES

Rhythm and Blues emerged during the 1940's and 1950's, but reached its height in the 1960's (Vernon, 1999; Caldwell, 1996). Essentially an urban product, it reflected a self-conscious identity, cohesiveness and focus on love, combining elements of pop, gospel and blues traditions. In the 60's, rhythm and blues became "Soul" music, a further indication of its identification with the Black Power thrusts of the 60's. Stress was placed on distinctiveness from white music, Black self-respect and self-cel-ebration of soul. This is, by far, the most popular music among

Blacks although it is constantly challenged by white attempts to absorb and dilute it and deprive it of its distinctiveness as in the case of disco.

Some of the classic rhythm and blues artists and songs from the 60's were James Brown , "Mr. Soul," *I'm Black and I'm Proud*; Aretha Franklin " Ms. Soul," *Respect*; Otis Redding, *Sitting on the Dock of the Bay*; Chuck Berry; The Four Tops; Curtis Mayfield; The Impressions, *We're A Winner*; Marvin Gaye and Tammy Terrell, *Ain't No Mountain High Enough*; The Supremes, *Love is Like An Itchin In My Heart*; Gladys Knight and the Pips; The Temptations, *My Girl*; *Message From A Black Man*; Al Green, *Let's Stay Together*; Sam Cooke, *Change Gon' Come*; Smokey Robinson, *I'll Try Something New*; Nina Simone, *Young, Gifted and Black*; Ray Charles, Les McCann and others. (Current artists are assumed to be familiar to the student so there is little need to list them.)

Given the influence music has on Black life, there is a continuous discussion on how to make it better serve the interests of Blacks. This question becomes especially urgent in terms of rhythm and blues and which has not only lost its social consciousness for the most part but is losing its distinctiveness as Black music (George, 1988). One cannot help but notice the contrast between the race and socially conscious quality music of the 60's and the insipid, socially irresponsible, raw sex-focused music of today. What one is witnessing, as disco most vividly showed during the 1970's and negative rap is currently showing, is the merciless drive of the music industry to make money, reducing all music to a homogenized packageable sound, regardless of its effect on social life, aesthetics or a rich Black heritage (Byrd, 1978). In the early 20's, Locke (1969:45) had argued Black music had become "tarnished with commercialism and the dust of the marketplace," and that Black musicians were "in commercial enslavement to the Schylocks of Tin Pany Alley and in artistic bondage to the cash of...dance halls and vaudeville stages." If this were true then, it is obviously even more so now (Byrd, 1978; Ashborne, 1977).

Few artists are strong or politically conscious enough to oppose the tide of commercialism and create the race- and socially-conscious model and music which so marked the 60's. Paul Robeson stands as a model in the past of the socially conscious artist who excelled aesthetically and refused to compromise politically (Dent, 1976). Most recently, Terry Callier "Be A Believer", "African Violet" and "Martin Street Martin", and especially Gil Scott-Heron stand out as models of artists who have a high level of aesthetic achievement and social consciousness. As Kalamu ya Salaam (1982:12) states, "Scott-Heron represents the most socially conscious element of (the message-music) tradition." His hits - among which are *The Revolution Will Not Be Televised; The Bottle*, an attack on alcoholism; *We Almost Lost Detroit*, a criticism of nuclear power; and *Angel Dust*, an appeal to youth to avoid it - all demonstrate a commendable aesthetic and socially conscious quality.

THE CHALLENGE OF RAP

This concern for socially conscious music led African Americans in the 70's to embrace and support reggae for its social commentary and criticism and then turn to socially conscious rap to celebrate community and reaffirm the necessity of the struggle (George, 1988:188ff; Spencer, 1991; Eure and Spade, 1991; Kitwana, 1994; Conyers, 2001)). Although rap emerges in the 70's, it is in the 80's that it becomes a wide-spread definitive statement of new Black music (Lemmel, 2000; Ayazi-Hashjin, 1999; Caldwell, 1996). Ronald Stephens (1991) is correct, however, to put the origins of rap back even further within the context of Black musical history as well as the African cultural tradition of Nommo or oratory (Asante, 1987:59ff; Toop, 1984:19; Smitherman, 1973). The form clearly evolves in the tradition of oratorical modes such as "signifying" and "playing the dozens" as well as "rapping" in both the sense of political discourse and romantic "programming", in a word, the sense of skilled word use to achieve given ends.

In music, artists like King Pleasure, Eddie Vinson and Joe Williams created modes of singing-talking that already prefigures rap in the pre-60's period. Later, the Last Poets and Gil Scott-Heron in the 60's and 70's continued the tradition adding to it their own unique contribution (Williams, 1992). Thus, as Ceola Ross Baber (1984:104) notes, "Master rappers of today are keeping alive and visible the tradition of African American artistry in communication, like all those unnamed Blacks who toasted B'rer Rabbit, Stagolee, or some other fictitious character; like the authors and lyrics who have praised Black perseverance in poem and song; and like all the average Black Americans who speak poetically and poignantly of their experiences, and who give rhythm and sense to their daily existence through music of rhyming speech."

Rap, then, evolved from an ancient tradition passing through modern forms of that tradition and emerging in night clubs and the streets of New York in the mid-seventies. Names of major figures include D.J. Hollywood, Kurtis Blow, Eddie Cheebu, D.J. Lovebug, Starsky, Junebug Starski, Grandmaster Flash and the Furious Five, Africa Bambaataa, Melle Me, Whodini and Russell and Joey. Rap gets its definitive push on the national and international scene with Sylvia and Joe Robinson's recording of the Sugar Hill Gang's "Rapper's Delight" in 1979, which sold over 2 million copies. From this point on, Rap becomes a major and engaging African American music form.

It is important here to note that there are various schools of rap music defined by their self-definition and lyrical stress (Powell, 1991). The first kind is a teacher-rap or nation-conscious rap which stresses social consciousness, social commitment and struggle (Eure and Spady, 1991). This includes rap by KRS-One, Arrested Development, Def Jef, Poor Righteous Teachers, X-Clan, Sistah Souljah, Queen Latifah, Kool Moe Dee, Prince Akeem, Boogie Down Productions, and perhaps the premier nation-conscious group, Public Enemy, as well as many others. A second major form of rap is "gangsta rap" represented by rappers like NWA, Ice Cub, Ice T and BWA. Thirdly, there is a player/lover rap represented by LL Cool J, Salt n Pepa et al. Fourthly, there is porno rap as reflected in the lyrics of 2 Live Crew et al. Although these are the major forms of Rap, there are other forms which can be categorized differently, and even these forms are not always clear cut. On the contrary, they often overlap and resemble each other.

Rap, unlike any music before it, initiates a passionate discourse of supporters and critics. Essentially this is because of its dual character and mixed messages and its relevance to both youth culture and the Black musical tradition (Kitwana, 1994; *Black Collegian*, 1990). Rap's relevance begins with its providing a much-needed challenge to the crossover tendency of many Black artists such as Prince and Michael Jackson (George, 1988). This tendency included denial of Blackness, servile attempts to appeal to white audiences through both alteration of music and physical features and claiming a desperate and vague universality which denied African authenticity. This created the basis for white co-optation of Black music in sound and market, and the initiation of a trend which Nelson George calls "the death of rhythm and blues." And, although rhythm and blues did not die, it was for a brief period rendered less vigorous. Ironically, however, as crossover artists abandoned their rootedness in Black music, white artists, especially those from Britain, began to sing Black music, reviving old songs and making them popular. Also, rap artists while often denying their debt to predecessors in rhythm and blues (R & B), nevertheless added depth and color to their rap by using R & B music as background (Conyers, 2001; Corio and Goldman, 1999).

Rap's relevance then begins with its reaffirming the creativity and distinctiveness of Black music. Moreover, it carved out a space for independent Black artists and companies though eventually most succumbed to capitalist co-optation. Thirdly, rap rebuilt an eroding sense of community among Black youth, spoke to them in a special way and at its best, i.e., nation-consciousness rap, contributed in a significant way to conscious raising. Fourthly, rap helped build an equally eroding sense of community among Black musicians who, since the introduction of mechanization of music, began to lose both the opportunity and ability to build community along the model of the earlier jazz community which was so interactive, mutually supportive and creatively challenging. Fifthly, rap's relevance lies also in its reintroducing in its nation-consciousness form a political discourse in African American music which was missing since the sixties. It thus became a way to both criticize and understand U.S. society.

Rap, however, because of its varied forms brings mixed messages which divides its history into both the relevant and positive and the problematic and negative (Dyson, 1996). The first problem rap poses is its sexist character (Peterson-Lewis, 1991). It demeans the Black woman, reducing her to her genitals and an objectified instrument of male gratification, and preaches violent domination of the woman. Moreover, closely related to this is the widespread vulgar character of `gangsta' and porno rap, rejecting all boundaries under the amoral observation that people want it. Thirdly, `gangsta' and porno rap are too often violent in a vulgarly individualistic way, pretending strength by symbolically claiming the power to destroy, injure, and maim. Also, such rap is also extremely nihilistic, tending to destroy and dominate rather than propose creative or life affirming solutions. Fourthly, these negative forms of rap offer an easy vocabulary and image to stereotype Blacks and give license to racists to use anti-Black images and vocabularies. It is, at this level, the height of self-disrespect, and self-mutilation, reducing oneself to mindless sexual and physical beings and calling each other and oneself the "n_" word, the "b_" word, "ho's," "nasty," "freaks," etc.

Also, negative forms of rap pretend a *sui generis* origin for rap, dismissing a rich cultural history and drawing generational lines so typical of the European society these rappers claim to reject. Finally, even political Rap has a tendency to claim a knowledge it does not have, a link with struggle it does not demonstrate, and a political relevance it still must prove. The point is that a song is not a revolution, and as Gil Scott-Heron says, "the revolution will not be televised," nor will it be the result of a song or series of songs. In the final analysis, Sekou Toure is instructive. For he says, "to take part in the African revolution, it is not enough to write a revolutionary song; you must make the revolution with the people. If you make it with the people, the songs will come by themselves and of themselves" (quoted in Frazier, 1968:167). What rap offers, then, is a promise and this promise can only be realized in positive social practice.

The continuing need then is for the *cultivation* and *support* of the positive in rap and in every other from of African American music. For, in the final analysis, a people saves itself from social danger and disintegration or there is no hope for it. Moreover, Blacks are for the most part Black artists' main customers and have the capacity to give or withhold support. Thus, if the records and concerts of negative artists were not bought or attended, raw sex, sexist labeling and assaults on Black women, the reductive translations of love, and other negatives could not survive. And in place of much of the current music which has neither socially or aesthetically redeeming value, a music marked by race and social consciousness and solid aesthetic quality can and will re-emerge, and a rich distinctive Black heritage will be preserved and expanded. The success of such a project, however, will depend upon the success of the revival of the cultural and political development and struggles which characterized the Sixties. For without a cultural struggle to transform consciousness and the political struggle to acquire control of

Black destiny and daily life, neither Black music nor Black lives will be shaped in their own image and interest.

9.4   BLACK LITERATURE

THE EARLY PERIOD I

Black literature does not begin with written aesthetic expressions but with oral ones. Although some African literature was written, much of it was not and still none of what was written was brought by enslaved Africans when they were brought to the Americas (Hill, 1998; Gates and McKay, 1997). Debate still rages on how much oral literature survived from Africa but every serious writer concedes a significant amount of African survivals (Courlander, 1976; Dorson, 1965). Moreover, as Arna Bontemps and Langston Hughes (1958) noted, in addition to Africanization, there was a parallel process of Americanization which translated as Africans modifying characters and themselves to reflect more accurately their new experience in the U.S. Thus, the African animals - jackal, hare, tortoise and hyena - are translated in an American environment as the fox, rabbit, turtle or terrapin and wolf.

African American folklore is often associated with animal stories like B'rer Rabbit, made familiar to American audiences through Joel Chandler Harris' collection and publication of them in his *Uncle Remus: His Songs and Sayings* and Walt Disney who made them into a movie, *Song of the South*. But as Sterling Brown (1970) contends, it is important to note that there are many more kinds of folklore than the animal stories. Zora Neale Hurston (1935) in her collection, *Mules and Men*, Charles Chestnutt in the *Conjure Woman* (1889), Arthur Huff Fauset, Thomas Talley, and J. Mason Brewer all give an idea of the rich variousness of Black folklore.

From the above, several kinds of folklore emerge: 1) animal stories; 2) legendary hero stories; 3) human trickster stories; 4) exaggeration stories; 5) why stories; and 6) tales of satire. In animal stories, there is the theme of weakness overcoming strength through intelligence, skill and cleverness. B'rer Rabbit, B'rer Squirrel and other small animals outwit the larger slower ones. In legendary men stories, like those of Stagolee, African Americans are posed as defiant and rebellious or in colloquial terms "a bad, crazy 'n__' that don't take no 's_' from nobody, Black or white". In the ones like John Henry, they are posed as beating the white man at his own game, breaking stereotypes and winning against all odds. The human trickster is ol' John that outwits the white man playing on his ego - saying, "I went on the red light cuz the whites were going on the green and I knew then it wasn't for me." The exaggeration stories in Hurston's collections have mosquitos sing like alligators, eat up the cow and then ring the bell for the calf; or a man so fast he shoots at a deer, runs and catches the deer and holds the dar till the bullet hits it. "Why stories" give explanations of the origin of the world, races, division of labor, etc. And tales of satire lampoon the enslaver and white man, in general, who figure with a crooked pencil that "ought's a ought, figger's a figger, all for de white man, none for de 'n_'. "

Although blues, spirituals and work songs can be considered folklore also, their treatment in the music section will be considered sufficient. It is important to note here that folklore though originally oral, took on a written form in the works of Charles Chestnutt, Paul Lawrence Dunbar, Earnest Gaines, George Henderson, Langston Hughes, Zora Neal Hurston, Claude McKay, Jean Toomer, Margaret Walker, Sarah Wright, J. Mason Brewer, Arthur Huff Fauset, Thomas Talley, et al.

THE EARLY PERIOD II

A second early period of Black written literature began in 1746 with Lucy Terry's (1730-1821) poem on a Native American raid in Massachusetts which was the first known piece of literature by an African American (Whitlow, 1974:15). After her came Jupiter Hammond, poet and essayist and Phyllis Wheatley, who wrote the first Black book of poems by an African in English, *Poems on Various Subjects, Religious and Moral* (1773). Narratives of enslaved Africans by Briton Hamon in 1760 and Oladah Equiano (Gustavus Vassa) in 1789 followed with Equiano's narrative being the most popular and detailed on life in Africa and during enslavement. These early writings are marked by a "redeemed Christian" mentality which is racially self-effacing and apologetic for enslavement, seeing it as God's way of rescuing them from savagery.

THE 1800'S

The 1800's marks a third period and the rise of what is commonly called "protest" literature, i.e., the speaking out strongly against the established state of things - enslavement, oppression, exploitation, racism. It is set in the midst of the revolts by enslaved Africans and other forms of resistance like abolitionism. Thus, almost all Black writers who published during this period wrote in the spirit of protest (Whitlow, 1974:29). George Moses Horton's (1797-1883) *Hope of Liberty*, James Whitefield's *America and Other Poems*, Lucy Delany's *From Darkness Cometh the Light or Struggles for Freedom*, and Frances Harper's *Poems on Miscellaneous Subjects* all indict the slave system for its injustice and brutality. Also, in this period autobiographies were written by Frederick Douglass (1817-1895), *Life and Times*, a brilliantly well-written autobiography with strong political content by Harriet Jacobs, *Incidents in the Life of a Slave Girl*; and by William Wells Brown, *The Narrative of William Wells Brown*. Also, Brown wrote three novels and three plays. The first novel *Clotel: or the President's Daughter* was written in 1853 and was the first Black novel. The earliest novel by a Black woman was *Our Nig; or Sketches from the Life of a Free Black* (1859) written by Harriet Wilson. Other novelists were Frank Webb, *The Garies and Their Friends*; Frances Harper, *Iola Leroy*, which criticizes the failure of Reconstruction and the racism which followed; and Martin Delaney, *Blake*. Delaney also wrote a major political work, *The Condition, Elevation, Emigration and Destiny of the Colored People of the United States*. Also included in this period is the classic womanist writing of Anna J. Cooper, *A Voice From the South* (1892).

THE PRE-HARLEM RENAISSANCE PERIOD

The pre-Harlem Renaissance period begins with publication of poetry by one of Afro-America's most gifted poets, Paul Lawrence Dunbar. Dunbar is well-known for his poetry in African American idiom like "When Malindy Sings", "The Antebellum Sermon" and "Keep A Plugging Away". Dunbar also wrote short stories and a novel. His works were, however, consciously unpolitical to accommodate the fact that his main audience was white. The Black middle class was embarrassed by his use of folk language instead of standard English.

Charles Chestnutt is known for his *Conjure Woman and Other Tales*, based on folklore heard in North Carolina and narrated by Uncle Julius, a shrewd African who was formerly enslaved, and now manipulates his employer with these tales. Chestnutt also wrote short stories and three novels. James Weldon Johnson spans two main periods in African American literature. He wrote his novel, *Autobiography of An Ex-Colored Man* in 1912, *God's Trombones, Seven Negro Sermons* in verse in 1927, *Black Manhattan*, an excellent study of Black culture in 1930 and his autobiography *Along This Way* in 1933. His poetic sermon "The Creation" is considered a classic. Also Johnson wrote the Black National Anthem, "Lift Every Voice and Sing" along with his brother, John Rosamond Johnson. Ida B. Wells joined literature with political activism, writing essays critical of lynching and racism in general. She is most known for he essays *Southern Horror* and *A Red Record*. W.E.B. DuBois wrote in this period also. In addition to his social and political writings, he wrote five novels and a volume of poetry. His most known piece during this period was his *Souls of Black Folk* in 1903. Finally, Pauline Hopkins wrote four novels and many short stories in this period. Her first novel was *Contending Forces* (1900). She was also founding editor of the *Colored American Magazine*, the first monthly magazine dedicated to African American art and literature, with a readership extending to China, Hawaii, Manila and the West Indies (Carby, 1987:125ff).

THE HARLEM RENAISSANCE

The Harlem Renaissance was one of Black writers' most prolific period (Bontemps, 1972; Huggins, 1979; Watson, 1995). It was a time when Harlem became the capital of Black America (Schoener, 1995); Blacks looked to their African roots for revitalization; Marcus Garvey issued the call for Black pride and power and the rescue and reconstruction of Africa (Garvey, 1977); and Alain Locke (1969), the main interpreter of the Renaissance, announced the coming into being of the "New Negro". In fact, Garvey's and Locke's influence on the Harlem Renaissance cannot be overestimated. Garvey's ideological and political push for respect, African heritage and race pride, coincided with Locke's stress on the need for examination and use of the African ancestral legacy. And although Garvey was misunderstood and often maligned by the writers of this period, it is safe to assume he and his movement are significantly responsible for their stress on Black culture and consciousness (Martin, 1983).

Locke's *The New Negro* is a classic and his most known work, but he wrote and edited other works on Black culture, i.e., *Four Negro Poets*, *The Negro in Art*, and *The Negro and His Music*. Claude McKay was one of the most militant writers of the Renaissance. His "If We Must Die" in 1917 which calls for Blacks not to die like dogs but fight the "murderous cowardly pack" is definitive and is considered by some to be the beginning of the Renaissance. His *Home to Harlem* is also well-known. Jean Toomer's *Cane*, a collection of prose and poems; Countee Cullen's collection of poems, *Cooper Sun*; Nella Larsen's novel *Quicksand*; and Langston Hughes classic poem, "The Negro Speaks of Rivers", his dozen books of poetry and two autobiographies, *The Big Sea* and *I Wonder as I Wander*, stand out as definitive of the period. Also included in this period is Jessie Fauset's *There is Confusion* and *Plum Bun*. Later, she would also write *The Chinaberry Tree* and *Comedy American Style*.

The Depression of 1912 marked the slowing of the prolific writing of the Renaissance. New writers emerged such as Zora Neal Hurston, *Mules and Men* (folktales), three novels and a satire on America race relations, *Jonah's Gourd Vine*, *Their Eyes Were Watching God*, *Tell My Horse*, *Moses*, *Man of the Mountain* and *Dust Tracks on a Road* (autobiography); and Arna Bontemps' three novels, *Black Thunder*, *Drums at Dusk* and *God Sends Sunday*.

In the period of 1940-1960, Richard *Wright* stands out as a giant with his classic novel *Native Son* and his autobiography *Black Boy*. He established a school of writing called Urban Realism, a rough unadorned exposure and critical depiction of urban Black life. Among the writers who were included in this school were Chester Himes, *If He Hollers Let Him Go*, and Ann Petry, *The Street*. Ralph Ellison's work *Invisible Man* (1952), is another Black classic in which he poses Blacks as invisible in a racist society and in search of a solid identity. James Baldwin is a multitalented essayist, novelist and playwright of this period. Among his works are the novel, *Go Tell It On the Mountain* (1953); an essay, *The Fire Next Time* (1963); a play, *The Amen Corner* (1967); and his novel *Just Above My Head* (1982).

Gwendolyn Brooks emerged in this period also. She was obviously one of the most gifted poets in the U.S. Having won the Pulitzer Prize for Poetry for her collection *Annie Allen* in 1940. She was the first Black to receive the award. Moreover, she wrote *Maud Martha*. Margaret Walker is known for her classic poem *For My People* and her novel *Jubilee*. Her poem, written in free verse, is a praise poem to the life, struggle, adaptive vitality, durability, strength and achievement of Blacks. It is also a call for struggle and a new social order. Robert Hayden has published five volumes of poems, among which are *A Ballad of Remembrance* and *Words in the Mourning Time*. Lorraine Hansberry's play, "A Raisin in the Sun", was a successful Broadway production and marked a high point in critical achievement and recognition for Black drama.

THE SIXTIES

The Sixties is considered by many a Second Black Renaissance (Bigsby, 1979). It produced and was produced by both literary and political diversity and multiplicity. It was, as argued in chapter 4, Blacks' most significant decade in terms of self-conscious goals and achievements. The Harlem Renaissance was, in part, fostered by white patrons and declined with their withdrawal after the Crash of 1929. But the Sixties was self-generating, self-determining and self-sustaining. Its literary personalities are often known in political as well as literary circles, for the decade demanded a merging of the political and the literary. Larry Neal, Askia M. Toure, Ishmael Reed, Amiri Baraka, Sonia Sanchez, Nikki Giovanni, Mari Evans, Etheridge Knight, A.B. Spellman, Johari Amini, June Jordan, Quincy Troupe, Lucille Clifton, Stanley Crouch, Joe Goncalves (Dingaan), Carolyn Rodgers, Yusef Iman, Ed Bullins, James Randall, Stephany, Conrad Rivers, Eugene Redman, Haki Madhubuti and Kalamu ya Salaam are but a few examples of Black socially conscious writers (Randall, 1971). Many of the above wrote poetry, drama and prose.

Definitive of this period are Sonia Sanchez's *We a BaddDDD People*; Amiri Baraka's *Black Magic Poetry 1961-67* and *Four Revolutionary Plays*; Johari Amini's *Black Essence*; Haki Madhubuti's *We Walk The Way of the New World*; June Jordan's

Who Look at Me; Ishmael Reed's *Yellow Back Radio Broke-Down*; Ed Bullins *New Plays From the Black Theatre*; Larry Neal's and Leroi Jones' (Baraka) *Black Fire*; Mari Evans' *I'm A Black Woman*, Etheridge Knight's *Poems from Prison*; Nikki Giovanni's *Black Feeling Black Talk*; and John Williams' *The Man Who Cried I Am*.

THE SEVENTIES

The Seventies saw the emergence of Alice Walker whose credits include novels, *Meridian,* poetry, *Revolutionary Petunia,* and short stories, *In Love and In Struggle*; novelists Toni Morrison who had then written four novels and whose *Song of Solomon* won the Best Novel of the Year Award in 1977; and a long list of Black poetesses and poets which have published in the Black literature issues of the Black Scholar, `71, `75, `78 and `81. Notable also are the poetry of Sonia Sanchez, *I've Been A Woman*, Mari Evan's *Night Star*; Lucille Clifton's *Ordinary Woman*; Bell's, Parker's and Guy-Sheftalls, *Sturdy Black Bridges: Visions of Black Women in Literature*; Gwen Brooks' anthology of new Chicago poets, *Jump Bad*; Maya Angelou's *I Know Why the Caged Bird Sings*; Kalamu ya Salaam's *Revolutionary Love;* and Eugene Redmond's *Drum Voices: The Mission of African American Poetry.*

Although these writings do not have the self-conscious urgency and fire of the 60's, they, nevertheless, like the literature of the 60's and other periods, speak the truth of Black people, i.e., their hopes, aspirations, love and constant struggle to have a full and free life. Thus, by teaching beauty in the midst of ugliness and strength and durability under stress and strain, they inspire and teach possibilities which, as argued at the outset, is the fundamental function of African American literature.

THE EIGHTIES AND NINETIES

Literature in the 80's and 90's is marked by several distinguishing features. The first of these is the overwhelming predominance of works by and about Black women. This surge begins in the 70's and reaches its height in the 80's. In the 80's this process seems to seems to be defined by Alice Walker's *The Color Purple* (1982) which won a Pulitzer Prize and initiated a rather passionate discourse which ran the gamut of topics from the quality of Black male-female relations to the political use of the book by the dominant society to indict the Black community and reaffirm its racist conceptions and practices. Drawing both avid supporters and critics, the book nevertheless was a kind of literary omen of both the predominant women-focused character of the coming literature and the larger society's interest in or preference for publishing it (Nunez and Green, 1999; Sandi, 1998; Gates, 1998; Roses, 1997).

Other notable works were Toni Morrison's *Beloved* (1987) which also received a Pulitzer Prize; Gloria Naylor's *Women of Brewster Place* (1982), Ntozake Shange's *Betsy Brown* (1985); Paule Marshall's *Praise Song for the Widow* (1983); Sonia Sanchez's *Home Girls and Hand Grenades* (1984) *Under a Soprano Sky* (1987), *Wounded in the House of a Friend* (1995) and *Shake Loose My Skin* (1999); June Jordan's *Passion: New Poems, 1977-1980* (1980) and *Living Room: New Poems 1980-1984* (1985); Audre Lorde's *Chosen Poems: Old and New* (1982) and *Our Dead Behind Us* (1986); Sherley Anne Williams *Dessa Rose* (1986); Maya Angelou's *All of God's Children Need Travelling Shoes* (1986), *The Heart Of A Woman* (1987), and *A Brave And Startling Truth* (1995); and Rita Dove's *The Yellow House on the Corner* and *Thomas and Beulah* (1986) for which she won a Pulitzer Prize and became the only Black woman since Gwendolyn Brooks' award to win the Pulitzer Prize for Poetry. Pearl Cleage's *Looking Like Crazy One Sunday Morning* and Lucille Clifton's *Good Woman* (1987) and *Blessing the Boats* (2000) for which she received the National Book Award. Certainly notable also is Henry Louis Gates, Jr.'s editing of the *Schomburg Library of Nineteenth Century Black Women Writers* (1988), a thirty-volume set of prominent texts by Black women from 1890-1910.

Finally, among women writers of this period, no one emerged as quickly and distinctively as Terry McMillan. Her *Waiting to Exhale* became both a tremendous commercial success and a major literary achievement which, while resembling other major women writers' approach, differed in significant ways. First, McMillan, although critical of Black male-female relations as Walker, Naylor, Shange, et al, nevertheless maintained an open-textured posture toward reconciliation and reconstruction. Secondly, her women characters were more self-critical and her criticism of Black men appeared more as a challenge to them to

self-correct than a condemnation. Thirdly, she writes in a popular style and thus created a mass reading audience which differed
from the academic style and audience many other Black women
writers cultivated.

Black men continued to write, of course, but were less
prominent and less published, causing some authors and critics
to suggest the publishing industry was both interested in and
hostile to works by and about Black men. Nevertheless, impor-
tant works by Black men did emerge. Among these were John
Edgar Wideman's *Brothers and Keepers* (1984); August Wilson's
Fences (1985) for which he won a Pulitzer Prize and *The Piano
Lesson* (1990); Ishmael Reed's *Reckless Eyeballing* (1986), *Airing
Dirty Laundry* (1993) and *The Reed Reader* (2000); Henry Dumas'
Goodbye Sweetwater (1988); Jay Wright's *The Double Invention of
Komo* (1980); Haki Madhubuti's *Earthquakes and Sunrise Missions*
(1984), *Killing Memory, Seeking Ancestors* (1987), *Say that the
River Turns: The Impact of Gwendolyn Brooks* (1987), *Groundwork*
(1996) and *Heartlove* (1998); Etheridge Knight's *Born of a
Woman: New and Selected Poems* (1980), and Walter Mosely's
Devil in a Blue Dress (1997) and *Black Betty* (1997). Worthy of
note also are the anthologies by Terry McMillan, *Breaking Ice*
(1990); Henry Louis Gates, Jr. *Reading Black, Reading Feminist*
(1990); and Frank McGill, *Master Plots of African American
Literature* (1992); Henry Louis Gates and Nellie McKay, *Norton
Anthology of African American Literature* (1997); and Patricia
Higgin Hill, *Call and Response, The Riverside Anthology of the
Afro-American Literary Tradition* (1998).

A second defining characteristic of the Eighties and early
Nineties is the continuing expansion of African American liter-
ary criticism. This includes both a general criticism as well as a
specific womanist or Black woman's criticism. Among works in
this genre are: Mari Evans' *Black Women Writers: A Critical
Introduction* (1984); Gloria Wade-Gayles' *No Crystal Stair:
Visions of Race and Sex in Black Women's Fiction* (1984); Barbara
Christian's *Black Feminist Criticism: Perspectives on Black Women
Writers* (1985); Hazel Carby's *Reconstructing Womanhood: The
Emergence of the Afro-American Woman Novelist* (1987); Henry
Louis Gates, Jr.'s *Figures in Black: Words, Signs and the `Racial' Self*
(1987) and *Loose Cannons: Notes on Cultural Wars* (1992);
Charles Johnson's *Being and Race: Black Writing Since the 1970's*
(1988); Houston Baker, Jr.'s and Patricia Redmond's *Afro-

American Literary Study in the 1990's (1989); Fred Lee Hord's *Reconstructing Memory: Black Literary Criticism* (1991); Houston Baker Jr.'s, *Workings of the Spirit: The Poetics of Afro-American Women's Writing* (1991); and Toni Morrison's *Playing in the Dark* (1992); (Gates, Appiah and Naylor, 1999).

A third feature of the writing of this period is a tendency for the authors to distance themselves from the long literary tradition of social engagement as a member of the African American community. This problematic distancing is achieved in several ways. First, there is a tendency to privilege the vaguely universal and human at the expense of the particular and the African. This is done first in the spirit and language of deconstructionism with critiques of racial essentialism and calls for focus on the specificity of the texts which is supposed to "reveal a depth and range of culture details far beyond the economic exploitation of Blacks by whites" (Gates, 1992:101). From these "close readings of the text," it is argued, "one learns to invent oneself and the other and rejects the preconstituted racial self." For Gates (1992:151) the project of the new generation of writers "is about affinities, unburdened by an ideology of descent; it speaks about blackness without blood" and sees race as a trope, i.e., a mere problematic figure of speech.

A second mode of distancing and creating what Trey Ellis calls "a new Black aesthetic" is to privilege gender over racial or ethnic concerns. Such a posture while giving necessary voice to Black women can and often does treat gender concerns as exclusive of and often hostile to ethnic concerns. In fact, appeals to ethnicity are often seen as ways to stifle women voices and equate the race with men, as an important text states in its title, *All the Women are White, All the Blacks are Men, But Some of Us are Brave*, (Hull, Scott, Smith, 1982). And as Deborah McDowell (1989:59) contends, focus on race "is often almost tantamount to focus on maleness." Thus, she advocates a women's literature free from race conscious concerns and transcending social and linguistic boundaries. It is important to note that all women writers do not separate race and gender struggle, but those who do, contribute to the transformation of the tradition of engaged literature.

A third way of distancing from the historical tradition of an engaged Black literature is to declare literature and text exempt from the burden of history and community and essentially an individual author's context for invention and reinvention of self, a self no longer "shocked," "surprised" or "enraged" by racism as Trey Ellis states (McMillan, 1990:xxi). Self-focus is privileged here over collective concerns or self-in-community. For these writers, speaking deconstructionist language, the self is fluid, ambiguous, contradictory and hardly a candidate for the unchanging essence of race or ethnicity. Loyalties and relationships to various social groups are ambiguous, complex and constantly shifting. What is key, then, is not the community or group, but "self."

Deborah E. McDowell (1989:55) notes that "...Afro-American literary criticism has finally seen the beginnings of a paradigm shift, one that has extended the boundaries and altered the terms of inquiry." She goes on to say that "falling in step with recent developments in contemporary critical theory, some critics of Afro-American literature have usefully complicated some of our most common assumptions about self, and about race as a meaningful category in literary study and critical theory." This paradigm shift, of course, is not only in literary criticism, but also in the literature itself. And thus, "self," in the making and constantly in transition and contradiction, becomes the replacement for the person-in-community, and one who is socially conscious and committed to liberation and a higher level of human life. According to this argument, the focus on struggle is limited and limiting. Indeed, the self must have no boundaries, no fixed identities and thus cannot be concerned with defense of cultural borders it does not recognize, nor with ethnic loyalties it does not feel compelled to maintain.

A final development in the literature of the 80's and early 90's is the assumption of a relevance for literature equal or even superior to social science in understanding the Black experience. Many writers and their supporters have argued that literature can and often does yield a more accurate portrait of Black life than the social sciences. Such a claim can best be seen in the discourse around *The Color Purple* which became a text that, for many, offered a more accurate assessment of the Black family than the works of sociologists such as Harriet McAdoo, Nathan and Julia Hare, Robert Staples, Andrew Billingsley et al.

Moreover, in major universities this same text becomes for various interrelated reasons, the central text to explain Black culture and history in multicultural classes. Thus literature, even as fiction and personal imagination, is used as an alternative to a social scientific understanding of Black life rather than as a contribution to a holistic understanding of it. In other words, personal subjectivity is privileged over social science study and a novel or short story becomes the most important and, at times, only way one understands Black life.

This privileging of literature over social science data takes place in a context where humanities discourse in general becomes more important and frequent than discussion of real life. In such a context of privileging humanities, history is reduced to a Rap song, relationships to imaginative revelations of a novel or short story, and the complexity and achievement of a world historical man reduced to the banality of a comedic movie. This is clearly a problematic deserving a creative solution. For although one can easily concede the importance of literature to life, given its personal and subjective character, it cannot serve as an alternative to an objective study of life nor as a substitute for the social struggle to enrich and expand it. A sociology of this problematic development suggests that its life and tenure fit well within the interests and ideology of the established order. For emphasis on the personal at the expense of the social, and discussion of literature rather than its source, i.e., concrete life, is less likely to pose a threat to the existing social power and wealth relations. In fact, such discourse is by its own definition detached from its social source, and instead rooted and developed essentially in and through the text itself. Such a discourse, then, is not a social analysis but rather the imaginative product of authors and audiences constantly reinventing themselves in the context of ambiguity, contradiction and shifting loyalties.

In such a context, art is no longer a reflection of life, it becomes its surrogate or substitute. And discourse on literature becomes a myth of social action relieving its participants of the responsibility of seeking social solutions. In their place one seeks personal understanding and personal gratification. The point, therefore, is not to heal the world, but to heal oneself, not to concern oneself with the issues of human flourishing in community but of personal expansion and enjoyment in the context of shifting loyalties and ambiguous and contradictory callings.

The problematic posed by such a paradigm shift in African American literature is clearly one worthy and demanding of further discourse. it is, thus, is posed here to provoke and expand the discussion, not to close or avoid it.

STUDY QUESTIONS

1.   What is art?
2.   What is the Black aesthetic and what are the two schools which developed around the issue? Discuss their views.
3.   What is the Kawaida social criteria for art? Discuss the three criteria.
4.   Give examples of African art survivals.
5.   Discuss the artists of the Harlem Renaissance period and of the 40's.
6.   Discuss some of the main Black women artists.
7.   What are the main themes of Black art in the 60's and 70's?
8.   What are three basic approaches to interpretations of the spirituals?
9.   Discuss the multidimensionality of the blues as a reflection of the Black experience.
10.   Discuss the origin of gospel and ragtime and some of the pioneers.
11.   Discuss the evolution of jazz and the different styles.
12.   What are the origins of rhythm and blues and the problems it poses?
13.   What are the several forms of African American folklore?
14.   Discuss the evolution of African American literature from narratives through the 70's including themes and focus.
15.   What are the relevances and problematic aspects of rap?
16.   Discuss fundamental developments in the literature of the 80's and 90's.
17.   What are some basic aspects of the new aesthetic among some African American writers.

REFERENCES

Adler, Peter and Nicholas Barnard. (1992) *African Majesty: The Textile Art of the Ashanti and Ewe*, London: Thames and Hudson.

Asante, Molefi K. (1987) *The Afro-centric Idea*, Philadelphia: Temple University Press.

Ashburne, Michael R. (1977) "Black Music: A Financial Perspective", *Western Journal of Black Studies*, 1, 4 (December) 263-269.

Awmiller, Craig. (1996) *This House on Fire: The Store of Blues*, Danbury: Franklin Watts Inc.

Ayazi-Hashjin, Sherry. (1999) *Rap & Hip Hop: The Voice of a Generation*, New York: Rosen Publishing Group.

Baber, Ceola Ross. (1984) "The Artistry of Artifice of Black Communication," in Geneva Gay and Willie Baber (eds.) Expressively Black: The Cultural Basis of Ethnic Identity, New York: Praeger.

Bigsby, C.W.E. (1980) *The Second Black Renaissance*, Westport, CT: Greenwood Press.

Black Collegian. (1990) "Rap Music, Positive or Negative? Passing Fad or Cultural Force? Censored or Uncensored? 21, 2, (November-December 181-183).

Blauer, Ettagale and Jason Laurbe. (2001) *African Art*, Chicago: Heinemann Library.

Blue, R. (2001) *The History of Gospel Music*, Broomall: Chelsea House Publishers.

Bontemps, Arna and Langston Hughes. (1958) *The Book of Negro Folklore*, New York: Dodd, Mead.

Brown, Sterling A. (1970) "Negro Folk Expression" in *Black Expression*, (ed.) Addison Gayle, Jr., New York: Weybright and Talley.

Butcher, Margaret J. (1956) *The Negro in American Culture*, New York: Knopf.

Byrd, Donald. (1978) "Music Without Aesthetics: How Some Non-Musical Forces and Institutions Influence Change in Black Music", *The Black Scholar* (July-August 2-5).

Caldwell, Hansonia. (1996) *African American Music: A Chronology, 1619-1995*, Los Angeles: Ikoro Commons.

Caldwell, Hansonia. (1997) *An Educator's Resource Manual, Volume I: African American Music, A Chronology, 1619-1995*, Los Angeles: Ikoro Commons.

Campbell, Mary S. (1994) *Harlem Renaissance: Art of Black America*, New York: Harry N. Abrams.

Carby, Hazel. (1987) *Reconstructing Womanhood: The emergence of the Afro-American Woman Novelist*, New York: Oxford University Press.

Catlett, Elizabeth. (1975) "The Role of the Black Artist", *The Black Scholar*, 6, 9 (June) 10-14.

Cone, James. (1972) *The Spirituals and the Blues*, New York: The Seabury Press.

Conyers, James L., Jr. (2001) *African American Jazz & Rap: Social and Philosophical Examinations of Black Expressive Behavior*, Jefferson: McFarland & Companyh.

Corio, David and Vivien Goldman. (1999) *Visions of the Groove: Connections Between Afrobeats, Rhythm & Blues, Hip Hop and More*, New York: St. Martin's Press.

Courlander, Harold. (1963) *Negro Folk Music, U.S.A.* New York: Columbia University Press.

Courlander, Harold. (1976) *A Treasury of American Folklore*, New York: Crown Publishers, Inc.

Cruz, Jon. (1999) *Culture on the Margins: The Black Spiritual and the Rise of American Cultural Interpretation*, Princeton: Princeton University Press.

Dent, Roberta Y. (ed.) (1976) *Paul Robeson Tributes and Selected Writings*, New York: Paul Robeson Archives, Inc.

Dorson, Richard M. (1965) *American Negro Folktales*, Greenwich, CT.: Fawcett.

Dover, Cedric. (1960) *American Negro Art*, Connecticut: New York Graphic Society.

Dozier, Richard K. (1974) "Black Architects and Craftsmen", *Black World* (May) 5-7.

Drewal, Henry J. and John Pemberton. (1990) *Yoruba: Nine Centuries of African Art & Thought*, New York: Harry N. Adams.

Driskell, David C. (1976) *Two Centuries of Black American Art*, New York: Los Angeles County Museum of Art and Alfred A. Knopf.

DuBois, W.E.B. (1925) "The Social Origins of American Negro Art", *Modern Quarterly*, 3, 1 (October-December) 53-55.

DuBois, W.E.B. (1969) *The Souls of Black Folk*, New York: The New American Library.

Ellison, Ralph. (1966) *Shadow and Act*, New York: Signet Books.

Eure, Joseph D. and James Spady. (1991) *Nation Conscious Rap*, New York: PC International Press.

Evans, Mari. (1979) "Political Writing as Device", *First World*, 2, 3:34-39.

Everett, Chestyn. (1975) "Tradition in Afro-American Literature", *Black World*, 25, 2 (December) 20-25.

Fanon, Frantz. (1968) *The Wretched of the Earth*, New York: Grove Press.

Fine, Elsa H. (1973) *The Afro-American Artist*, New York: Holt Rinehart and Winston.

Fisher, Mark M. (1953) *Negro Slave Songs in the United States*, New York: Citadel Press.

Floyd, Samuel A., Jr. (1996) *The Power of Black Music: Interpreting Its History from Africa to the United States*, New York: Oxford University Press.

Frayer, James. (1998) *The Blues is a Feeling: Voices & Visions of African-American Blues Musicians*, Shorewood: Midwest Traditions.

Fuller, Hoyt W. (1971) "Introduction: Towards a Black Aesthetic", in *The Black Aesthetic*, (ed.) Addison Gayle, Jr., Garden City: Doubleday.

Garvey, Marcus. (1977) *Philosophy and Opinions*, New York: Atheneum.

Gates, Henry Louis. (1998) *Afro-American Women Writers*, New York: Macmillan.

Gates, Henry Louis. (1992) *Loose Canons: Notes on the Culture Wars*, New York: Oxford University Press.

Gates, Henry Louis and Kwame Anthony Appiah. (1999) *Gloria Naylor: Critical Perspectives Past and Present*, New York: Harper Trade.

Gates, Henry Louis and Nellie Y. McKay, (eds.) (1997) *North Anthology of African American Literature*, New York: W.W. Norton.

Gayle, Addison, Jr. (ed.) (1971) *The Black Aesthetic*, Garden City: Doubleday.

Gayle, Addison, Jr. (1970) *Black Expression*, New York: Weybright and Talley.

George, Nelson. (1988) *The Death of Rhythm and Blues*, New York: Pantheon Books.

Gillon, Werner. (1984) *A Short History of African Art* New York: Viking Penguin.

Handy, W.C. (1941) *Father of the Blues: An Autobiography*, New York: Macmillan.

Harris, Michael. (1992) *The Rise of the Gospel Music of Thomas Andrew Dorsey in the Urban Church*, New York: Oxford University Press.

Hasse, John Edward. (ed.) (1985) *Ragtime, Its History, Composers and Music*, London: Macmillan.

Heilbut, Tony. (1975) *The Gospel Sound*, Garden City: Anchor Books.

Hill, Patricia Liggins, (ed.) (1998) *Call and Response, The Riverside Anthology of the African American Literary Tradition*, Boston: Houghton Mifflin Company.

Huggins, Nathan I. (1979) *Harlem Renaissance*, New York: Oxford University Press.

Hughes, Langston. (1970) "The Negro Artist and the Racial Mountain", in *Black Expression*, (ed.) Addison Gayle Jr., New York: Weybright Talley.

Hull, Gloria, Patricia Bell Scott and Barbara Smith, (eds.) 1982) *All Women Are White, All Blacks Are Men, But Some of Us Are Brave*, Old Westbury, NY: Feminist Press.

Jones, Arthur C. (1993) *Wade in the Water: The Wisdom of the Spirituals*, Maryknoll: Orbis Books.

Jones, Leroi (Amiri Baraka). (1963) *Blues People*, New York: William Morrow,

Karenga, Maulana. (1971) "Black Cultural Nationalism", in *The Black Aesthetic*, (ed.) Addison Gayle, Jr., Garden City: Doubleday.

Karenga, Maulana. (1980) *Kawaida Theory: An Introductory Outline*, Inglewood, CA: Kawaida Publications.

Kebede, Ashenafi. (1995) *Roots of Black Music: The Vocal, Instrumental & Dance Heritage of Africa and Black America*, Trenton, NJ: Africa World Press.

Killens, John O. (1975) "The Image of Black Folk in American Literature", *The Black Scholar*, 6, 9 (June) 45-52.

Lee, Jeanne. (1999) *Jam! The Story of Jazz Music*, New York: Rosen Publishing Group.

Lems-Dworkin, Carol. (1991) *Africa in Scott Joplin's Music*, Evanston: C Lems-Dworkin Publications.

Levine, Lawrence W. (1977) *Black Culture and Black Consciousness*, New York: Oxford University Press.

Lewis, Samella. (1994) *African American Art and Artists*, Berkeley: University of California Press.

Lewis, Samella. (1978) *Art: African American*, New York: Harcourt Brace Jovanovich.

Locke, Alain. (1969) *The Negro and His Music*, New York: Arno Press, New York Times.

Locke, Alain. (1936) *Negro Art*, Washington, D.C.: Association in Negro Folk Education.

Locke, Alain. (1968) *The New Negro*, New York: Atheneum.

Lommel, Cookie. (2000) *History of Rap Music*, Broomall: Chelsea House Publishers.

Lovell, John. (1969) "The Social Implications of the Negro Spiritual", in *The Social Implications of Early Negro Music in the United States*, (ed.) Bernard Katz, New York: Arno Press.

Madhubuti, Haki (Don L. Lee). (1972) "The Achievement of Gwendolyn Brooks", *The Black Scholar*, 3, 10, (Summer) 32-41.

Marks, Carole L. and Diana Edkins. (1999) *The Power of Pride: The Man & Women Who Embodied the Spirit of the Harlem Renaissance*, New York: Crown Publishing Group.

Martin, Tony. (1983) *Literary Garveyism: Garvey, Black Arts and the Harlem Renaissance*, Dover, MA: The Majesty Press.

Maultsby, Portia K. (1979) "Influences and Retentions of West African Musical Concepts in U.S. Black Music", *Western Journal of Black Studies*, 3, 3 (Fall) 197-215.

Mays, Benjamin. (1968) *The Negro's God*, New York: Atheneum.

McDowell, Deborah. (1989) "Boundaries: Or Distant Relations and Close Kin," in Houston Baker, Jr. and Patricia Redmond, (eds.) *Afro-American Literary Study in the 1990's*, Chicago: University of Chicago Press, pp. 51-70.

McLeod, Malcolm. (1980) *Treasure of African Art*, New York: Abbeville Press.

Meadows, Eddie S. (1970) "African Retentions in Blues and Jazz", *Western Journal of Black Studies*, 3, 3 (Fall) 180-185.

Metis, Frank. (1996) *At Your Fingertips: Boogie, Marches & Ragtime*, New York: Music Sales..

Neal, Larry. (1972) "The Ethos of the Blues", *The Black Scholar*, 3, 10 (Summer) 42-48.

Neal, Larry. (1971) "Some Reflections on the Black Aesthetic", in *The Black Aesthetic*, (ed.) Addison Gayle, Jr., Garden City: Doubleday.

Newton, James E. (1977) "Slave Artisans and Craftsmen: The Roots of Afro-American Art", *The Black Scholar*, 9, 3 (November) 35-44.

Niangoran-Bouah, G. (1984) *The Akan World of Gold Weights: Abstract Design Weights*, Abidjan, Ivory Coast: Les Nouvelles Editions Africaines.

Nunez, Elizabeth and Brenda M. Greene, (eds.) (1999) *Defining Ourselves: Black Writers in the 90s*, New York: Peter Lang Publishing.

Patton, Sharon F. (1998) *African-American Art*, New York: Oxford University Press.

Porter, James. (1970) "African Art From Prehistory to Present," in Joseph S. Roucek and Thomas Kiernam, (eds.) *The Negro Impact on Western Civilization*, New York: Philosophical Library, pp. 467-487.

Porter, James. (1943) *Modern Negro Art*, New York: Dryden Press.

Powell, Catherine. (1991) "Rap Music: An Education with a Beat from the Street," *Journal of Negro Education*, 60, 3 (Summer) 245-259.

Powell, Richard J. (1997) *Black Art & Culture in the 20th Century*, London: Thames & Hudson.

Powell, Richard J., et al. (1997) *Rhapsodies in Black: Art of the Harlem Renaissance*, Berkeley: University of California Press.

Randall, Dudley. (1971) *The Black Poets*, New York: Bantam Books.

Ransaw, Lee A. (1979) "The Changing Relationship of the Black Visual Artist to His Community", *Black Art*, 3,3:44-56.

Reagan, Bernice J. (1993) *We'll Understand It Better By & By: Pioneering African American Gospel Composers*, Washington: Smithsonian Institution Press.

Redding, J. Saunders. (1966) "The Negro Writer and American Literature," in Herbert Hill, (ed.) *Anger and Beyond*, New York: Harper & Row.

Roberts, John Storm. (1974) *Black Music of Two Worlds*, New York: William Morrow.

Roses, Lorraine E. (1997) *Harlem Renaissance & Beyond: Literary Biographies of 100 Black Women Writers, 1900-1945*, Cambridge: Harvard University Press.

Russell, Sandi. (1998) *Render Me My Song: African-American Women Writers from Slavery to the Present*, San Francisco: Harper.

Salaam, Kalamu ya. (1982) "Hit Records in an Old Tradition", *In These Times*, (May 19-25) 21.

Schoener, Allon (ed.) (1995) *Harlem on My Mind: Cultural Capital of Black America, 1900-1968*, New York: New Press.

Seymour, Gene. (1996) *Jazz: The Great American Art*, Danbury: Franklin Watts Inc.

Smith, L.A. (1981) *Art and Architecture of Ancient Egypt*, New York: Penguin.

Smitherman, Geneva. (1973) "The Power of Rap: The Black Idiom and the New Black Poetry," in *Twentieth Century Literature*, 19,4 (October).

Southern, Eileen. (1971) *The Music of Black Americans*, New York: W.W. Norton.

Spencer, Jon Michael, (ed.) (1991) "The Emergency of Black and the Emergence of Rap," in Special Issue of *Black Sacred Music*, Durham: Duke University Press.

Stephens, Ronald J. (1991) "Three Waves of Contemporary Rap Music," in Jon Spencer (ed.) *The Emergency of Black and the Emergence of Rap*, Durham: Duke University Press.

Stuckey, Sterling. (1994) *Going Through the Storm: The Influence of African American Art in History*, New York: Oxford University Press.

Thompson, Julius E. (1998) *Dudley Randall, Broadside Press and the Black Arts Movement in Detroit, 1960-1995*, Jefferson: McFarland & Co.

Thompson, Robert F. (1969) "African Influence on the Art of the United States", *Black Studies in the University*, Robinson, A.L. (eds.) New Haven: Yale University Press, 122-70.

Thompson, Robert F. (1983) *Flash of the Spirit*, New York: Random House.

Thurman, Howard. (1947) *The Negro Spiritual Speaks of Life and Death*, New York: Harper & Row.

Van Rijn, Guido. (1996) *Roosevelt's Blues: African-American Blues & Gospel Songs on FDR*, Jackson: University Press of Mississippi.

Vernon, Paul. (1999) *African-American Blues, Rhythm & Blues, Gospel & Zydeco on Film & Video, 1926-1997*, Brookfield: Ashgate.

Welsh-Asante, Kariamu (ed.) (1993) *The African Aesthetic: Keeper of the Tradition*, Westport, CT: Greenwood.

Wade-Gayles, Gloria. (1984) *No Crystal Stair: Visions of Race and Sex in Black Women's Fiction*, New York: The Pilgrim Press.

Whitlow, Roger. (1974) *Black American Literature*, Totowa, NJ: J.J. Littlefied, Adams & Co.

Wilkinson, Richard (1992) *Reading Egyptian Art*, London: Thames and Hudson, Ltd.

Williams, Todd (Ty.) (1992) "The Last Poets and Gill Scott-Heron are Pioneers of Rhythm and Spoken Word," in *The Source*, (May) 42-44, 59.

Williams-Jones, Pearl. (1975) "Afro-American Gospel Music: A Crystallization of the Black Aesthetic", *Journal of the Society for Ethnomusicology*, XIX (September).

BLACK PSYCHOLOGY

BLACK PSYCHOLOGY

CHAPTER 10

10.1 INTRODUCTION

All science is ultimately systematic study and knowledge to enhance humans' grasp of and effective encounter with themselves and their environment. *Psychology is essentially the science that systematically studies behavior in its relationship to the complexity of mental, emotional, physical and environmental factors which shape it.* As a person-focused discipline, psychology stands out as a key science in this historical project of overall human understanding of self, society and the world. For at its most relevant level, it not only focuses on the structure and functioning of the human personality, but equally important, points to the possibilities of its unlimited expansion and thus the realization of a higher level of human life on the *personal* and *social* level (Parham, White and Ajamu, 2000; Jones, 1991; Azibo, 1996; Karenga, 1978). Although there is a tendency to include the study of animal behavior as part of the definition of psychology (Kagan and Haveman, 1976), I have purposely omitted it in order to maintain focus on the human personality as the core and motive force of psychological study. In fact, even the study of animal behavior in psychology is only relevant in its use to deepen and expand understanding of human behavior. Otherwise, such study of animals is better defined as zoology rather than psychology.

(Jones, 1991; Burlew et al, 1992; Kambon, 1998; Harrell, 1999) The concerns of Black psychology revolve around the development of a discipline which not only studies the behavior of Black persons, but seeks to transform them into self-conscious agents of their own mental, emotional and social liberation. This is achieved through: 1) a severe critique and rejection of white psychology, in terms of its methodology, conclusions and the ideological premises on which it rests; 2) provision of Afrocentric models of study, prevention and treatment; and 3) self-conscious intervention in the social struggle to achieve and insure conditions of well-being and wholeness for African persons and people and a context of maximum human freedom and human flourishing in the world.

10.2 HISTORICAL ORIGINS

Clearly, one can point to the ancient African origins for some of the concepts of psychology which we use today (Akbar, 1994; Nobles, 1980, 1986; Karenga, 1999). Moreover, African-centered psychology is, of necessary, rooted in the best of African cultural concepts and practices. But Black psychology as a formal discipline emerges in the African American context of oppression, resistance and self-confirming practices rooted in our historical memory and our ongoing capacity as a people to create realms of meaning, beauty and freedom regardless of context.

Thus, Black psychology has its origins in the 1920's when Francis Sumner became the first Black Ph.D. in psychology in 1920, and subsequently Blacks began to publish research to disprove racists charges of Black inferiority, to push for stronger departments of psychology in Black schools, and to attempt to provide better psychological services to the Black community (Guthrie, 1976). It gained greater strength as an educational thrust when in 1938 Herman Canady of West Virginia State College began to organize Black professionals interested in psychology. Although he was unable then to organize an independent Black psychologists association, he did establish a Black psychologists' caucus within the American Teachers Association, the main professional structure for Black educators. Among the goals they set for themselves were: 1) to promote the teaching and application of psychology, especially in Black schools; 2) to stimulate study, research and exchange; and 3) to set up qualifications for teachers of psychology and assist Black institutions in training and selecting psychologists (Guthrie, 1976:115ff).

However, it was not until the 1960's as Jackson (1979:27) notes, "that Afro-American psychologists made a concerted and sustained effort to expand their concerns into a distinct system of thought and not until the 70's that publications appeared in the form of a Black Psychology". In the 60's, the resurgence of Black nationalism, and its Black Power expression, encouraged and demanded Black caucuses within traditionally white-controlled and white-oriented professional organizations as well as independent Black organizations. In 1968 the Association of Black Psychologists (ABP) was founded in the midst of criticism of the American Psychological Association (APA) for its limited vision and conscious and unconscious support of the racist character of American society.

Pledging themselves "to the realization that they are Black people first and psychologists second", the ABP vowed not to "ignore the exploitation of the Black community" and expressed urgent concern "about its role and that of the APA in Black people's struggle for dignity and equality in this country" (Williams, 1974:11-12). The suggestion that the APA had a role in the Black struggle and the subsequent 10-point program for correctives of the APA's thought and practice shows that Black psychologists were still in transition toward an Afro-centric psychology. However, in 1974 when Williams wrote a brief history of the ABP, it was his assessment that traditional psychology was out and Black psychology coming into being. "Black psychologists", he (1974:24) asserted, "have finally broken the symbiotic relationship with white psychology." Black psychology must now, he continued, "be about the business of setting forth new definitions, conceptual models, test theories, normative behavior, all of which must come from the heart of the Black experience."

10.3 THREE MAJOR SCHOOLS: DELINEATIONS

The history of the Association of Black Psychologists reflects the consolidation and development of distinct but overlapping schools of Black psychology. These are the traditional, reformist and radical schools. Although these approximate Jackson's (1979) reactive, inventive and innovative categories of Black psychology components, I find the categories "inventive" and innovative" close enough in redefinition to warrant alternative categories. Thus, I have offered "reformist" and "radical" as alternative categories. It is important to state here that I suggest no pejorative meaning to reform or the reformist school. I recognize it as a transitional and middle posture between the traditional and the radical schools and as having exhibited necessary and significant development from the traditional school. Moreover, the reformist school not only often borrows from the radical school, but also often leads to the assumption of a radical posture.

The traditional school is defined by: 1) its defensive and/or reactive posture; 2) its lack of concern for the development of a Black psychology and its continued support of the Eurocentric model with minor changes; 3) its concern with changing white attitudes; and 4) its being essentially critical without offering substantive correctives (Guthrie, 1970).

The reformist school represents a period of historical evolution as well as a current posture. It maintains some of the concern for white attitudes and behavior, but focuses more on change in public policy than on simply attitudinal change. Furthermore, this school begins to advocate an Afro-centric psychology but still combines it with traditional focus on appeal for change that would ostensibly benefit Blacks and whites and thus U.S. society (Thomas, 1971; Cross, 1971).

The radical school makes no appeal to whites and directs their attention instead to Black people in terms of analysis, treatment and transformation. Moreover, they insist on and are developing a psychology that has its roots in the African worldview which is opposite of and opposed to the European worldview (Jackson, 1982; King, et al, 1976; Baldwin, 1998). Moreover, the members of this school are socially conscious theorists and practitioners who advocate self-conscious participation of Black psychologists and Black people in the transformation of social reality through cultural and political struggle. This, of course, is in the Fanonian tradition which influenced many of them (Fanon, 1968, 1967).

10.4 Schools, Models and Methodologies

The Traditional School

Kenneth Clark

Kenneth Clark, who is the first and only Black to be president of the APA, early established himself with the citation of his work on the damaging effects of segregation by the U.S. Supreme Court in its historical *Brown vs. Board of Education* (1954) decision. The author of several books and articles, his work, *The Dark Ghetto: Dilemma of Social Power* (1965) stands out as a seminal work on the sociology and psychology of the ghetto. In chapter IV of his book, entitled the "Psychology of the Ghetto", he essentially gives a "traditional" analysis of segregation. He (1965:63) argues that "racial segregation, like all other forms of cruelty and tyranny, debases all human beings-those who are its victims, those who victimize, and in quite subtle ways those who are merely accessories."

The victims, Blacks, are essentially portrayed with little or no strengths, i.e., as fantasy-oriented, sexually excessive, matriarchal, irresponsible, etc. However, Clark does not attribute these negatives to Black inferiority, but to an insensitive and brutally segregated society which imposes these patterns of thought and behavior on Blacks. Clark argues that social (white) insensitivity is "a protective device" and criticizes some of its "primitive examples", i.e. labeling of Blacks as inferior and "subhuman persons who cause and perpetuate their own difficulties" (1965:75-76).

In addition, he criticizes those social scientists whose "preoccupation with trivia...leads to the irrelevance of much of social science research", and "detached professionalism", which, in reality, is a false objectivity and masked insensitivity. And finally, he (1965:77, 80) criticizes the "professional perspective which constricts social vision to the impulses, strengths and weakness of the individual 'client' as if these can be isolated from the injustices and pathologies of his life." Such a detached and alleged objectivity, he concludes, serves "not to enlarge truth but to constrict it."

WILLIAM GRIER AND PRICE COBBS

William Grier and Price Cobbs are best known for their work, *Black Rage*. Although it was written in a popular style, it nevertheless reflects some of the basic contentions of the traditionalist school. Like Clark, Grier and Cobbs are concerned with whites knowing what they're doing to Blacks in order to change their attitudes and behavior. Concerned with the implication of the mutual racial hostility, they (1968:2) assert that "if racist hostility is to subside and if we are to avoid conflict on a nationwide scale, information is the most desperate commodity of our time." And, they continue, "of all the things worth knowing, none is more important than that all Blacks are angry" - in a word enraged.

Having established the fact of Black rage, Grier and Cobbs then set out to explain its origins and expressions. They establish the effects of what they call the shadows of the past, i.e., slavery, arguing that through this oppression and its sequel, "The psyche of Black men has been distorted". But, they assert "their genius is that they have survived" through adaptations of both positive and negative dimensions (1968:31). Unwilling and/or unable to see significant distinctness in Black life, they (1968:29) contend that "the psychological principles first understood in the study of white men are true, no matter what the man's color." And they (1968:86) maintain that "all that is uniquely (Black) found its origins on these shores, and provides a living document of Black history in America."

In what seems to be a contradiction to the denial of Black uniqueness, Grier and Cobbs then set down some principles of a "Black norm" which they claim distinguishes Black psychological postures from others but which are essentially a list of unsubstantiated and self-indicting negatives (1968:149ff). Among these are: 1) Blacks' understandable and necessary cultural paranoia; 2) their cultural depression and cultural masochism rising out of "sadness and intimacy with misery"; and 3) cultural antisocialism, i.e., disrespect for white laws which are designed to protect whites not Blacks. They (1968:124) conclude their "dismal tone is deliberate" in an attempt to stir the feelings of the reader to the "depression and hopelessness" Blacks feel daily.

ALVIN POUSSAINT

Poussaint's major work is his *Why Blacks Kill Blacks*. In his work, he covers a series of topics including Black Power, Black suicide, Black sexuality, and suggestions to white parents on how to raise their children free of prejudice. Criticizing the racial and socio-economic bias of traditional white psychiatry, Poussaint (1972:49ff) shows sensitivity to Black "suspicion of its concepts and practice" and their tendency to label it the "white man's psychology." He (1972:51) states that not only have white psychiatrists preferred to treat members of their own race and class, but their "short-sighted training...has made it impossible for them to distinguish deviant behavior from what is in fact *different* behavior." In this regard, he (1972:54) argues for "understanding special cultural adaptations or interests" of Blacks, if white psychiatrists are to be effective clinicians. For he (1972:55) believes that "despite obvious handicaps, some white psychiatrists are sensitive to the Black experience and have helped all types of Black patients."

In his chapter on "Why Blacks Kill Blacks", Poussaint (1972:69-70) begins by criticizing deficient modeling of Blacks as "culturally deprived" and "socially disadvantaged" and "culturally paranoid." These labels would fit the racist more than the Black, he argues. Likewise, the "creation of self-serving theories by some white academicians" about how Blacks hate themselves is not only exaggerated, but "another subtle attempt to maintain the oppressor's false sense of superiority." In fact, "it is likely," he maintains, "that whites have more self-hate and insecurity than we do, since they need racism to maintain a sense of self."

Recognizing, however, that there are negatives among Blacks and that crime and violence by Blacks against each other is a serious problem, he posits several reasons for it. Among these are: 1) the American cultural experience that teaches "crime and violence as a way to success and manhood;" 2) the fact that "Americans respect violence and often will not respond to just demands except through violence" as with the revolts; 3) the sense of power violence gives the oppressed; and 4) dehumanizing transformation in incarceration which perpetuates the cycle of violence. Poussaint, however, rushes to say, that regardless of the blame white society must shoulder for the Black condition, Blacks, in the final analysis, must move to intervene in and transform their own lives and life-conditions. This essentially means development of community programs which check the negatives and the development of "deep self-love that ends the self-defeating behavior among ourselves."

Poussaint, however, has apparently moved beyond his early traditionalist approach and has explored incorporation of Afrocentric methodology. In his latest book, co-authored with Amy Alexander, Poussaint (Poussaint and Alexander, 2000) turns his attention to unraveling the puzzle and problem of suicide among African Americans. They note that although in the past, in spite of racism and poverty, the African American community had consistently experienced a low rate of suicide, in the years between 1980-1995, suicides among Black youth increased 114 percent. They discuss historical, cultural, social and institutional factors which underlie this dramatic increase. In doing this, Poussaint and Alexander are very critical of the white medical establishment and its damaging approach to Black mental health. In addition, they introduced what they call "post-traumatic slavery syndrome" and the legacy of hopelessness, self-hatred, despair and self-destruction the Holocaust of enslavement left in its wake. It is a parallel discussion made earlier by Na'im Akbar (see below). They also call for a national dialog to deal with this problem and the development of "culturally sensitive" diagnoses and treatment which would involve an exploration and incorporation of Afrocentric communitarian models of treatment. This is a notable and interesting development and represents a developing and mutually beneficial collegial exchange between the schools of Black psychology.

THE REFORMIST SCHOOL

CHARLES THOMAS

Charles Thomas is one of the founders and first co-chairpersons of the ABP and was instrumental in shaping the early moves of Black psychology from the negatives of the traditional school. He and others of the school stand as bridges between the traditional and radical school, attempting a synthesis of the social and discipline criticism of the traditional school and the demands for and development of new models and professional engagement from the radical schools. Thomas' book *Boys No More* and subsequent articles represent this attempt toward synthesis.

Thomas (1979, 1971) begins by assigning Black psychologists the fundamental task of "instructive intervention" which leads to change in Black attitudes, self-mastery, social competence and personal fulfillment. He asserts that social scientists have an ethical responsibility for changing the Black condition "by defining, defending and developing information systems that will give Blacks increased socio-political power" (1979:7). Thus, he rejects the simple treatment-centered therapy and urges community engagement for the psychology.

Secondly, Thomas (1974) argues the significance of the Ethnocentrism factor. By ethnocentrism or ethnicity, he means, focus and pride in one's bio-social identity - in this case, one's Blackness. For Thomas, ethnicity not only provides the "frame of reference...for the development of countervailing social forces and institutions, it encourages self-activated behavior and breaks down patterns of self-hate and self-denial." Thomas contends that within the context of Black oppression, four major social roles were generated to meet it: "hybrid or bad n—s, conformists or good (African Americans), marginalists or white middle class (African Americans) and rebels, or Black 'militants'." Each group not only represents a search for identity but except for the last one, they also represent "modes of escape which are ineffective." This is so, for the flight from oneself essentially means a flight from one's humanity. Ethnicity as a proactive alternative, then, poses and cultivates "the renewed thrust toward self-esteem, environmental mastery, definition of self in terms of potential and a variety of other concerns around intervention or prevention of pathological cognition..."

Also, Thomas (1978:11ff) is concerned about the damage done by white or other social scientists who "have confused knowledge about a people with knowledge of a people." The first is superficial learning from without and imposing a conceptual framework; the latter is learning from within the group and sharing its conceptual framework. The bio-socialists who deny cultural differences, the cultural pathologists who are "preoccupied with the victim of oppression rather than with oppressive institutions," and the integrationists which limit social options on the assumption that Blacks "ought to be white or placed in situations where they can be treated as if white," all fit in this category of deficient and damaging social science.

Finally, Thomas (1978, 1971) poses deficient-deficit modeling as a major problem of Black psychology as well as for Blacks in terms of its implications for public policy and self-actualization. Examples of this are terms such as minority, and all its variations, i.e., minority status, culture, etc., disadvantaged, culturally deprived African American, etc. He (1978:21-22) states that "if 'Blackness' came into existence as a healthy support state, it cannot be logically used as a symptomatology of maladaptive behavior." The need, then, is for imaginative cross cultural conceptual models which press for para-cultural (equal rather than sub-cultural) frames of reference.

JOSEPH WHITE

Although Joseph White has written and co-authored other articles and books (White, 1984; White and Parham, 1990; Parham, White and Ajamu, 2000) his "Toward A Black Psychology," written in 1970, is seen a seminal contribution in the early criticism of and move from the traditional school of psychology and the subsequent creation of a Black psychology. In fact, he (1991:5) begins his article, reprinted in *Black Psychology* (Jones, 1991), arguing that "it is very difficult, if not impossible to understand the life styles of Black people using the traditional theories developed by white psychologists to explain white people." Furthermore, "when these traditional theories are applied to the lives of Blacks folks, many incorrect, weakness-dominated, and inferiority-oriented conclusions come about." Responding to the various social forces vying for the hearts and minds of African Americans in the midst of the Black Freedom Movement, White (1991:5) takes the stand that "regardless of what black people ultimately decide about the questions of separation, integration, segregation, revolution or reform, it is vitally important that we develop, out of the authentic experience of Black people in this country, an accurate, workable theory of Black psychology."

White maintains that traditional psychology's use of "an Anglo middle-class frame of reference" gives it a distorted view of the adaptive vitality of Black children and the Black family. Instead of a correct and positive view, hypotheses of cultural deprivation and matriarchal families are advanced. His contention is that a Black frame of reference is necessary which will enable Black psychologists and others "to come up with more accurate and comprehensive explanations" of Black life, as well as enable them "to build the kinds of programs within the Black world which capitalize on the strengths of Black people" (White, 1991:8).

He also argues "that not all traditional white psychology theory is useless." The existentialists' stress on pain and struggle as unavoidable and the self-theorists' stress on understanding one's experiential background to understand a person are examples of useful theories. The need, then, in building a Black psychology is to incorporate what is useful and reject the rest. White (1991:13) argues the value of Black/white dialogue and exchange in encounter groups, suggesting they give whites a better chance to experience Blackness "outside the protective setting of the group."

Again, like Poussaint's, the expansion of the intellectual horizon and theoretical engagement of Joseph White has blurred lines between classifications and suggests a definite move beyond membership in his former school of psychology. His joint work with Parham and Ajamu on the *Psychology of Blacks: An African Centered Perspective* (2000) indicates in the subtitle a clear move into the African-centered or radical school. Among the tenets and themes of Afrocentric psychology that they reaffirm are the imperative of multicultural approaches to the discipline of psychology; the centrality in Black psychology of the African worldview in preventive and therapeutic treatment modalities; the responsibility and value of social advocacy to contribute to the shaping of public policy on mental health; and the commitment to the liberation of the whole person and community – mentally, spiritually and socially.

WILLIAM CROSS

Concerned with the prevalence and negatives of Western thought and science and the need for "psychological liberation under conditions of oppression," William Cross (1971:13) offered a model suggesting the stages persons go through in the process of the "Negro-to-Black conversion". In a subsequent article, comparing this model to one Thomas developed, he

(1980) terms these models of "nigrescence", i.e., the process of becoming Black. The first state of nigrescence is the *pre-encounter* (or prediscovery) stage in which the person is out of touch with himself/herself racially and the "the person's world-view is dominated by Euro-American determinants" causing him/her to act in ways which degrade and deny Blackness (Cross 1971:15ff).

The second or *encounter* (discovery) stage involves a shocking personal or social event which pushes the person past his/her old conceptions of Black and Black conditions to an intense search for Black identity. The third stage is one of *immersion-emersion*. In the first phase of immersion-emersion, there is an intense involvement in being and demonstrating Blackness and rejection and condemnation of white people and culture. In the second phase, there is a levelling off and emergence from either/or and racist positions and the oversimplified aspects of Blackness, as well as acceptance of white humanity. Stage four is one of *internalization*, a sense of security, receptivity to discussion, and action and resolution of the conflict between the old and the new. The final state is *internalization-commitment* in which one "becomes the new identity and pro-Black attitudes become more expansive, open and less-defensive."

In focusing in on and criticizing Blacks for high levels of racial identity and severe rejection of whites and white values in the immersion phase, Cross seems to demonstrate again the reformist school's concern for relations with whites. This is not to say or imply that this represents servility, but to make the point that this is clearly an issue the radical school would neither raise, be concerned with, nor agree with. On the contrary, the radical school would see questioning of white humanity and total rejection of their values as positive.

In later work, however, Cross (1991) revised his original theory of nigrescence in order to bring it in line with new discoveries in his research. He begins his revision by noting that understanding Black mental health is more complex than his original theory of nigrescence suggested. Such complexity begins with recognition of the fact that any identity change is mixed, not pure and thus involves carryovers from previous identity, transformation of old into new and incorporation of things new. Also Cross argues that given the distinction between personal identity and group identity or reference group orientation, one can be mentally healthy without the need to relate strongly to a distinct cultural group. Finally, he contends that the aspects of the personality remain stable and healthy even while ideologies are changing thus revealing a greater diversity of attitudes, behaviors and possibilities than he first suggested. Thus, he (1991:xiv) maintains that at the heart of the identity conversion in the 60's "was not so much the dynamics of self-hatred as the metamorphosis of a Eurocentric worldview into an Afrocentric one."

Cross, like others, has continued to develop from his original position. He has engaged research by and with Parham and Helms (Cross, Parham and Helms, 1991) and with others and revised parts of his original theory, developing a new model of ego-identity development. In his new model, he allows for more flexibility and variation in his states of nigresence, delineating various ways in which African Americans embrace and internalize their culture and its concepts of identity and their relationship to others.

THE RADICAL SCHOOL

NA'IM AKBAR

Na'im Akbar's (1994, 1991, 1981, 1976, 1974) critique of the traditional psychology model begins with the historical fact that African Americans have been victims of intellectual as well physical oppression. "Intellectual oppression," he asserts (1981:18), "involves the abusive use of ideas, labels and concepts geared toward the mental degradation of a people." And, he states, "there is no area in which mental or intellectual oppression is more clearly illustrated than...the area of mental health judgement." In such a context not only are white oppressors' sanity not questioned, but Black mental health is not linked with the social conditions which shaped it.

The white oppressor, Akbar (1981:18,49) states, uncertain as to "what constituted a normal human being" established a kind of "democratic sanity" model of mental health. This was a kind of "majority rule" application to mental health judgement, i.e. insane behavior was determined "on the basis of the degree to which it deviated from the majority's behavior in a given context." This approach had the tragic consequence of judging sane and competent "entire communities of raving inhuman lunatics...because the majority of people in that particular context either participated in the questionable behavior or refused to question (it)." It is, Akbar maintains, clearly necessary to raise questions about the mental health standards and mental competence of a people who enslaved, terrorized and murdered numerous non-hostile peoples throughout the world.

Secondly, Akbar (1981:20) criticizes white scientists for "acquiring great scholarly renown for documenting deficits of Afro-Americans," a pathology perspective based on the norm and context of the people who uphold the "democratic sanity" standard. Thirdly, he (1981:20) criticizes Black traditionalists like Clark and Grier and Cobbs for "following the lead of Caucasian scholars in both conceptualizing and analyzing problems." He especially criticizes Grier and Cobbs for their "guide to the neurotic Negro", *Black Rage*, and their overgeneralization and use of the pathology model in it. Moreover, he concludes that the traditional school: 1) equates mental health with imitation of white middle class behavior; 2) assumes similarity of sources of Black and white behavior; and 3) assumes "democratic sanity" standards are "reflective of human standards documented by thousands of years of human history."

Fourthly, he argues that these and other traditional psychologists fail to take into consideration "two essential variables in determining the adequacy of human behavior"; 1) the historical antecedents or determinants of the behavior; and 2) the effects of inhuman conditions on the human being. As a result of these failures, there are attempts to eliminate or diminish many behaviors in African Americans "which are essential to their survival and development."

Having critiqued the traditional school, Akbar defines mental health in proactive terms as a state "reflected in those behaviors which foster mental growth and awareness (i.e., mental life)." Mental illness, then, is posed as reflected in "ideas and forces within the mind that threaten awareness and mental growth." It also can mean from an extended self concept, disorders reflected in "behaviors or ideas which threaten the survival of the collective self," i.e., one's people. Given these definitions, one can understand the reasoning of an insane parasitic people which justified domination as a mode of survival and the reasoning of the dominated people which poses liberation as a mode of survival and development.

Finally, within the framework of his definitions, Akbar (1981) poses four kinds of disorders which threaten Black life and development, i.e., "anti-life forces." These are the alien-self disorder, a socialization to be other than oneself on a race, class and sex level; the anti-self disorder, which expresses "overt and covert hostility towards the group of one's origin and thus one's self"; the self-destructive disorder, a destructive retreat from reality, i.e., drugs, etc.; and organic disorders, physiological, neurological or biochemical malfunctions. He (1982:25) concludes noting that these four disorders, it must be remembered, all emanate from "a psychopathic society typified by oppression and racism," a situation which must be changed for Blacks to "realize the full power of their human potential."

In a work on Black men, Akbar (1991) offers an analysis of the problematic of maleness and the challenge of manhood. He explains this as a process concerning, "the transformation of African consciousness" (Akbar, 1991:3). For him, the essence of the transformation is moving from the biologically bound in both the physical and mental sense. This requires, first, external discipline then internal discipline. "The thing that moves us from the male to the boy is discipline and that frees the boy from being slave to his male" (Akbar, 1991:18). Likewise that which transforms a boy into a man is knowledge. "Consciousness is a natural possibility or potential, but it must be tended and guided in order for it to develop properly."

Manhood for Akbar (1991:32) which is at first defined by discipline and then knowledge, is also expressed by self-definition. "Men must define themselves. It is their definitions that give them power." Finally, Akbar (1991:61) argues that manhood must ultimately be grounded in a proactive spirituality. "In order to establish authority over our lives, you must call upon that ruling force of 'will power' within your make-up. That will be the representative of the 'Divine Kingship' within our being...You can do it once you begin to utilize the power that is naturally yours. You are the ones who first came into human mastery," therefore, he concludes, "you can do it again."

KOBI K. KAMBON (JOSEPH BALDWIN)

Within the context of his contribution to Black psychology, Kobi Kambon (1998; Baldwin, 1992, 1980, 1976) focuses on the function of definitional systems in liberation and oppression. Definitional systems are key, he (Baldwin, 1980:96) posits, for they "determine how we experience (perceive and respond to) the variations phenomena that characterize the ongoing process of everyday existence." Moreover, the definitional system or worldview represents the ideological or philosophical base of a social system or a people and thus determines the meanings or values a people attach to their experience including their experience of themselves and how they will react.

The problem, however, arises, Kambon argues, when an alien worldview is imposed on and/or accepted by people, leaving the people at the mercy of definitions negative to their image and interests. Such is the case of Blacks under white domination. According to Baldwin, race, i.e., biogenetic commonality, "constitutes the principal binding condition underlying the evolution of definitional systems which "in their most basic fundamental nature have a 'racial character'."

Given this, what passes and is pushed as a universal worldview turns out to be nothing more than a European definitional system. This system is not only diametrically opposed to Black interests, but reinforces a distorted reality in the image and interest for the Europeans. Thus, African Americans "operate in a space dominated primarily by a definitional framework which does not and cannot give legitimacy to our African social reality" (1980:108). Complicating resistance to this state of things, Kambon (Baldwin, 1980:101) contends is that the "Europeans control the formal process of social reinforcements," i.e., economics and political power. This gives them power to impose their "definitions and the experiential confirmations on the experiences of Black people in society."

Although there has been some Black resistance to this imposition, it has "not necessarily been of a highly conscious form," that is to say, "it has not generally taken the form of a carefully planned or necessarily intentional collective resistance" (Baldwin, 1980:106). Thus, if Blacks are to liberate themselves and validate and expand their own African definitional system and social reality, "*conscious, collective resistance* is ultimately required." This of necessity requires a "clear frame of reference from which to ultimately examine the psychological nature of (Black) oppression" (Baldwin, 1980:107). This in turn demands a Black psychology, Kambon concludes, which not only explains the "ongoing process of psychological genocide," but contributes to a critical understanding of Euro-American society by which African people can "ultimately achieve the fullness of psychological and physical liberation from it."

Continuing his concern with the distinctness of a worldview for the African person, Kambon (Baldwin, 1992) develops an Africentric theory of the Black personality. Essentially he argues that a healthy functioning African personality has a bio-genetic tendency to affirm rather than deny Black life, makes group a priority, including survival of culture and institutions and engages in activities that promote this survival as well as the dignity and mental health of Black people.

He (Baldwin,1992:41) also makes four critical "assumptions about the nature of the African personality which derive from an Africentric approach." They are : 1) a bio-genetically or innately determined character of the personality; 2) the intrapsychic integrity of the personality which cannot be separated or analyzed from the context of the whole; 3) the social or collective character of the personality and the need to understand it in a "social-collective context"; and 4) the racial distinctiveness of the personality which is affirmed in its own context and negatively affected outside of it. Finally, Baldwin identifies two major psychological components of the core African personality: 1) The African Self-Extension Orientation (ASEO); and 2) African Self-Consciousness (ASC) which derives from the ASEO and engages it in a mutually interactive process.

In his latest work developed as a textbook, Kambon, (1998) takes up again and expands at length on some of the fundamental issues in African-centered psychology. These are framed under the broad rubrics of: 1) the historical foundations of African psychology; 2) paradigmatic foundations and issues; 3) recent historical and contemporary expressions; and 4) concepts and issues in the discipline. It is a sweeping and densely packed work seeking, as he (1998:7) notes, not simply "the imparting of psychological information from the cultural perspective of "African people," but the "laying out of the foundation for their psychological recovery process in the aftermath of the African Holocaust." Kambon's contribution to this begins with exploring the Kemetic foundations of Black psychology. He then continues defining the period of the Holocaust of enslavement and its devastating and continuing impact, critiques African and

European paradigms and ends with a discussion of modalities of recovery and a call for more think tanks and activist intellectuals to facilitate this historic project.

LINDA JAMES MYERS

The key concepts in Linda James Myers' (1992, 1988, 1987) contribution to an Afrocentric psychology are "optimality" and "suboptimality." Her thrust is to define and implement, as a critical framework for understanding and achieving maximum mental health, a theory of psychology rooted in and reflective of African culture. This begins with a definition of the optimal Afrocentric belief system. For Myers such an Afrocentric worldview is characterized by at least three basic concepts: 1) holistic-spiritual/unity; 2) communalism; and 3) proper consciousness. For Myers (1988:12) this optimal worldview first of all "assumes that reality is spiritual and material." Thus, the first aspect of it is a spiritual/material unity. This arises from the concept of the unity of being thru assumption that "all is spirit individually and uniquely expressed" (Myers, 1988:19). When one adheres to this principle, she states, one "loses the sense of the individualized ego/mind and experiences the harmony of collective identity of being one with the source of all good"(Myers, 1988:12).

Secondly, the African worldview is communalistic. It originates from the concept of the extended self. "Self in this instance is extended to include all the ancestors, the yet unborn, all nature and the entire community" (Myers:1988:12). Thirdly, Myers argues that proper consciousness or self-knowledge is another aspect of the Afrocentric worldview. She states that "the role of consciousness is primary in this conceptual system; in fact consciousness is identifiably that permeating essence or pervasive energy and spirit." This centrality is reflected in African concepts of Maat (truth); Mdw Ntr (divine speech); and Nommo (word power).

Myers contrasts this African worldview to the Eurocentric worldview with the former representing an optimal psychology and the latter a suboptimal psychology. The latter is racist, sexist, materialist and ultimately unworkable. Its fatal flaw is the socialization of its adherents to seek the key values in life, i.e. self-worth, peace, happiness, etc. through externals. But the reality is "identity and self-worth are intrinsic" and peace and happiness are generated from within. This in turn requires self-realization of the spirit within.

Secondly, she (1988:14) asserts that "the suboptimal conceptual system oppresses all its adherents. It makes the racist/sexist the oppressor acting out and projecting the negativity and insecurity he/she feels within." The oppressed however, are "doubly oppressed" when they absorb, "adapt and assimilate the conceptual system of the oppressor." In the end they suffer from all kinds of mental health and social problems.

Myers (1992:6) also defines the suboptimal or Eurocentric worldview in terms of its tendency to fragment and segment not only reality but peoples (racism) and genders (sexism). Although racism is clearly a problem for the African American community, "sexism is a serious problem that we have not as a people really addressed or solved" (Myers, 1992:8) It is her contention that "in a suboptimal/fragmented culture like this one, womanhood and motherhood (the central role of woman) are disdained rather than revered." But she (Myers 1992:9) notes "In a patriarchal society, anything feminine is inferior." Moreover, "In a sexist environment, women tend to hate themselves", Myers states, and they tend to "think that men are superior just like many Blacks (in a racist society) tend to think whites are superior."

The need then is to come into African consciousness "to begin forging a relationship with ourselves so that we can come into right relationship with our counterpart." She (1988:15) concludes, arguing that Black intervention in their liberation from oppression is key and compelling in the struggle for an optimal psychology and a positive social context. The "charge then is to learn more about our choices through increased awareness of the nature of that which is us" and then act accordingly (Myers, 1988:15).

WADE NOBLES

Clearly Wade Nobles (1986, 1985, 1980, 1976) is a pioneer and most quoted in the area of using African philosophy as a foundation for Black psychology. In his seminal essay on the subject, Nobles (1980:23) begins by arguing that Black psychology is more than the psychology of the underprivileged, the ghettoized or the enslaved and more than the "darker" dimension of general psychology. In a word, "Its unique status," "is derived not from the negative aspect of being Black in white America," he argues, "but rather from the positive features of basic African philosophy which dictates the values, customs, attitudes and behavior of Africans in Africa and the New World."

Nobles argues that what we have here is a commonality of consciousness based on guiding beliefs, an ethos which is at the core of African philosophy. This ethos determines two operational orders - the notion of oneness with nature and the survival of one's people. Given its distinctiveness from the white ethos and its place at the center of African philosophy, African philosophy easily and effectively serves as the foundation for Black psychology. A study of African philosophy shows several fundamental themes which not only explain African philosophy, but also African (Black) psychology.

First, one sees the rootedness of philosophy in religion. Religion, in turn, was life-practice, not sect or church or Sunday or proselytizing. "Traditional Africans made no distinction between the act and the belief" (1980:25). Secondly, the notion of unity of humans with God and the whole universe is key to African philosophy. A third key concept is the concept of time which is/was essentially "a composition of events" in two dimensions, the past and present, which are experienced rather than calculated. A fourth fundamental concept is that of death and immortality through recognition and remembrance. A final concept is one of kinship or collective unity which created a sense of collective identity, i.e., an extended self.

What this explanation of African philosophical themes does is demonstrate a distinctiveness of philosophy and psychology. The point now, Nobles (1980:31) contends is to "'prove' that Africans living in the Western world and in contemporary times still have or maintain an African philosophical definition." Thus, there is a need for demonstration of links and ways Blacks express an African perception of reality. Nobles argues that several Africanisms did survive slavery and contemporary times. The first is the stress on the survival of the people which expressed itself in a mentality and structures like benevolent societies and the church. Also the idea of a man being inseparable, one with nature and the community is a surviving Africanism. Oral tradition in the form of folktales, the dozens, rappin, etc., have also survived. Finally, the concept of time as phenomenal, potential and flexible rather than mathematical as expressed in CP time is also a surviving Africanism. These, Nobles (1980:35) states, are some examples which demonstrate a distinctiveness of Black consciousness rooted in and reflective of African philosophy. "The task of Black psychology, (then), is to offer an understanding of the behavioral definitions of African philosophy and to document what, if any, modifications it has undergone during particular experiential periods" in the U.S.

FRANCES CRESS WELSING

Frances Cress Welsing, (1991,1980,1970) a noted psychiatrist, advances one of the most controversial and discussed theories in the area of Black psychology, "The Cress Theory of Color-Confrontation and Racism (White Supremacy)." Welsing builds on the contentions of Neeley Fuller in his *Textbook of Victims of White Supremacy (1969)*. Fuller essentially argued that: 1)white supremacy was the only functional racism; 2) all Third World people are victims of it; 3) racism is not merely an individual or institutional phenomena, but a universal system of domination; and 4) that European theories and systems of political and economic organization are designed to establish, insure and expand white domination.

Having accepted these essential contentions. Welsing developed them further and advanced other ones. First, she (1970:5) argued that the white supremacy drive is in fact like other neurotic drives for superiority or domination "founded upon a deep and pervading sense of inadequacy and inferiority." Secondly, she contends that the basis for this neurotic disorder is found in the "quality of whiteness (which) is indeed a genetic inadequacy or a relative genetic deficiency, state or disease based upon the genetic inability to produce the skin pigments of melanin which are responsible for all skin coloration."

Whiteness as the absence of color or "the very absence of any ability to produce color" is the minority in the world given that "the massive majority of the world's people are not so afflicted." Thus, the color normality in the majority throws light on the abnormality of the colorless minority. Moreover, given that "color always annihilates phenotypically and genetically speaking, the non-color, white," and given their numerical minority status, whites are faced with the constant fear of genetic extinction (1970:6). Therefore, Welsing continues, "an uncontrollable sense of hostility and aggression developed defensively which has continued to manifest itself throughout the entire historical epoch of mass confrontations of the whites with (people of color)."

Welsing contends that this "sense of numerical inadequacy and genetic color inferiority" led whites not only to dominate, destroy and deform peoples of color, but also to alienation and self-hatred as well as defense mechanisms to handle these feelings. Among these are: 1) repression of the inadequacy inferiority feeling by denying it; 2) discrediting and despising Black and other colors of skin; 3) sun tanning and making up to acquire color; 4) elaborating myths of white genetic superiority as with Jensen's and other racist theories; 5) projection of their hate and sexual desires on peoples of color, pretending it is they who hate and lust after white; 6) obsessive focus on the body, yet alienated from sex because of inability to produce color; 7) dividing peoples of color into factions to make them minorities; and 8) imposing birth control on peoples of color to limit or reverse their majority number. Welsing (1970:10) concludes that if peoples of color are armed with the above insights, this will indeed reduce their vulnerability to manipulation, messages of white supremacy and contribute to their psychological liberation from the white racist ideology which so dominates their lives.

In a later work, Cress-Welsing (1991) reaffirms her theories in earlier literature adding emphasis in two basic areas: decoding symbols of white supremacy and the crisis in male/female relations. She (1992:xi) states that there are many symbols "in the system of white supremacy that reveal its roots in the struggle for white survival." These include the cross, the gun, smoking objects, boxing, paper money and various sizes and colors of balls, etc. Cress-Welsing (1991:54) contends that "the process of decoding a power system and its culture is a necessary first step to achieve behavioral mastery over that system/culture." And she concludes "the attainment of such mastery is an essential step in the process of total liberation for the victims who wish to end that oppression and regain their self-respect and mental health." Without this, there is a failure to understand the system which is being confronted, low levels of self and group consciousness and respect and the pervasive presence of mental illness.

Cress-Welsing (1992:277) also turns attention to the crisis in Black male/female relationships. She argues that most discus-

sions on the subject focus on the wrong issue. The key to understanding Black male/female relationships is analysis of "the
white supremacy dynamic" which puts "disproportionate pressure on Black males (and) ...produces a grave imbalance
between the Black male and female, even though both are vic-
timized by white supremacy." The thrust is to incapacitate Black
males in a white struggle for survival so that the "Black female
must confront a white male-dominated power system alone"
(Cress-Welsing, 1991:278). But, Black males and females can
defeat this, if they together "take up the struggle for justice
against white supremacy" as "their number one priority." For in
this move they are strengthened and "are united in a common
effort against injustice and simultaneously, they express the
strongest possible statement about respect and love for themselves as individuals" (Cress-Welsing, 1991:280).

AMOS WILSON

Focusing on the psychological development of the Black
child, Amos Wilson (1991,1981,1978), contributes to the projects of defining the tasks and parameters of Black psychology.
Wilson (1981:8) argues as Nobles and others, that an understanding of the psychology of Blacks - adults and children,
demands that the study of Blacks begin in Africa, not in slavery.
Moreover, he (1981:10) argues that Black psychology must be
extremely careful about the application of European based psychology and the use of its models. In fact, he suggests white psychology does not even adequately explain white people who
"seem bent on destroying themselves as well as the rest of the
world."

Drawing on the growing interest in melanin and its proper-
ties in the early 1980's, Wilson (1981:10) contends that the
study of melanin is important in the study of Black people.
Arguing that the history of Blacks are in their genes, he suggests
Black superiority in the areas of mental development, neurological functioning and psychomotor development of the Black
child which are all related to the possession of a high level of
melanin. Melanin, he contends, is not simply a coloring agent,
but "an integral part of the body system itself operating in the
brain." In fact, the ability of the Black child to survive and the
comparative long life of Blacks are related to their Blackness.

Wilson (1981:12) is also concerned that Blacks have been reduced to use only one side of their brain. This right side, he states "processes information...deals with the world in a holistic fashion and (also) processes music and art." The left side is the analytical side which develops technology, mathematics and so forth. But "the side of the brain an individual uses is determined by experience," therefore, if we look at the history and experience of Blacks in America, we see essentially that the European has rewarded Blacks for using the right brain," i.e., singing, dancing, music and sports. On the other hand, because whites "are afraid of intellectually assertive Black people," Blacks are discriminated against and discouraged from using the left side of the brain, i.e., the linguistic and analytical. The need is thus for a balance, for "the ultimate human being is the one who can balance between the use of both sides of the brain."

Finally, Wilson (1981:12) maintains that one of the major problems of Black child development "is determining how we can maintain the intellectual and psychological advance that nature has give our children." It is here, he states, that we see the inadequacy of white child psychology for "the issues and questions that the Black psychologist must address are distinctively different." This essentially demands the development of an educational psychology and methodology directed toward "the reconstruction of the personality and the orientation of our children" (Wilson, 1981:13).

Such a thrust would be directed toward educational and cultural change which not only stimulates the brain, but teaches children how to think, not simply prepares them for jobs but also facilitates and encourages high levels of self-development and service to their people. For "Blacks who are not conscious of their Blackness, who have no sense of destiny, and then go through (white systems of education) ultimately end up serving their own oppressors and become a means of oppressing their own people." Therefore, Black liberation depends on an educational system for Black children based on a psychological model which builds on and develops Black strength in order "to create an intelligent, independent thinking, interpretive and critical person committed to working tirelessly in the interest of Black people."

In a later work, Wilson (1992) also discusses the social psychology of violence among young Black men. It is his (1992:2) contention that Black male adolescent criminality is the principle outcome of three things: 1) white-on-Black violence since enslavement; 2) the deliberate creation of white American-dominated racist society; and 3) "unrelenting and collective ego defensive and political economic needs for white America to criminalize, denigrate and degrade Black America." Moreover, he states that he is not arguing that Blacks have no responsibility in this problem. Rather he is arguing that white America sets the context and sustains it. But he (1991:31) argues that "such a regime can only hold sway over African Americans and Africans in general as long as their consciousness and identity are not African centered." The need then, is to bring that consciousness to them in order to end their destructive alienation from self and community and enable them to escape the criminality and anti-social conduct which plagues them.

BOBBY WRIGHT

Although Wright (1981, 1975) has written other pieces in Black psychology, his fundamental and most-known work is *The Psychopathic Racial Personality*. In this essay, he poses whites as the mortal danger to Black people and seeks to analyze their behavior to demonstrate this. The urgency of such an analysis, he suggests, is due to the fact that this period in history is critical to Blacks' future. Using the analogy of a bullfight in which the bull finally stops charging the cape blindly, sees the "matador" and faces "the moment of truth," he (1975:3) argues that "this is indeed Blacks' moment of truth and it is time for them to look at the matador".

According to Wright, European "matadors" have for hundreds of years held up various banners to distract and delude Black people, i.e., "such concepts as democracy, capitalism, Marxism, religion and education." But now these banners, Wright contends, have been reduced to one - genocide, as evidenced in the development of genetic, chemical, electrical, surgical and other behavioral control strategies. This emerges from the fact that due to technological development and the world-wide struggle for resources, "Blacks are now a threat and a liability to the white race." It is in such a context that the understanding of the white "matador" becomes imperative.

Wright (1975:3) states at the outset that the basic premise of his work "is that in their relationship with the Black race

Europeans (whites) are psychopaths." Moreover, he states that this "behavior reflects an underlying biologically transmitted proclivity with roots deep in their evolutionary history." He defines a psychopath as "one who is constantly in conflict with others...unable to experience guilt, completely selfish and callous and has total disregard for the rights of others."

Expanding his analysis, Wright focuses on evidence of behavior traits which he reasons proves his contentions and demands Black consideration. He (1975:5) asserts that key to understanding the psychopathic personality is its "almost complete absence of ethical or moral development and an almost total disregard for appropriate patterns of behavior." This is expressed in the fact that whites have "historically oppressed, exploited and killed Black people - all in the name of their God Jesus...and with the sanction of the churches"(Wright, 1975:6). The activities of the Ku Klux Klan, a white Christian organization, and the Pope blessing Italian planes and pilots on their way to bomb Ethiopia, without provocation, are cited as examples.

Secondly, Wright maintains, the psychopath is also defined by the lack of "concern or commitment except to their own interests" and becoming indignant and angry when they are exposed or questioned. The unkept promises of the 1960's by whites and their attitude toward Black liberation and progress are examples of this. Also, Wright argues that "the psychopath is usually sexually inadequate with a very limited capacity to form interpersonal relationships." This is exhibited in whites in their constant projection of excessive sexuality on Blacks, although it is they "who streak, mate swap, participate in orgies, etc."

Fourthly, the psychopath has a marked "inability to accept blame (or) to learn from previous experience." Whites "never accept blame for Blacks environmental conditions which is clearly the result of white oppression" (1975:7). Instead, Blacks are held responsible. Also, attempts to sensitize and change them fail because of their inability to feel guilt. Finally, the psychopath rejects authority and discipline. Even when their own laws are the authority, they reject them, if it is not in their interests, as Blacks "who seek legal solutions to their problems" discover (1975:8).

Given this kind of adversary, "the inevitable question is what should Blacks do?" (1975:9). First, Wright suggests that Blacks must cast aside illusions that a psychopathic oppressor can provide strategies of liberation for those they oppress. Secondly, Blacks must recognize the oppressors as waging war against them and respond in equal measure. And finally, he (1975:11) states that they should seek the "answer to Blacks' problems in the works and lives of Black heroes" and heroines "whose minds have moved past the psychopath's imposed boundaries and have begun to blaze new paths towards Black's rendezvous with destiny."

10.5 ETHOS

The stress on the radical restructuring of the consciousness of Black people and persons by Black psychologists finds its logical parallel and support in the Kawaida contentions concerning the need for a proactive and positive ethos among African Americans (Karenga, 1980:Chapter VIII). Kawaida defines ethos "as the sum of characteristics and achievements of a people which define and distinguish it from others and gives it its collective self-consciousness and collective personality" (Karenga, 1980:90). Put another way, "the ethos of a people is often called its national or ethnic character which is not only defined by itself, but also assumed by others."

Now, ethos, or a people's self-consciousness and self-definition is defined by their thought and practice in at least the other six fundamental areas of culture, i.e., history, religion, social organization, economic organization, political organization and creative production. This means essentially that we know ourselves and are known by what we have done and do. And from our knowledge of self and others' knowledge or perception of us, we acquire our self-concept. Thus, the Africans' or ancient Egyptian's contribution to the establishment of the major disciplines of human knowledge defines them in their own eyes as well as the world's. Moreover, the Moorish African contribution to the civilization of Europe, the African contribution to the Olmec civilization and African Americans' contribution to the social and cultural wealth of the U.S. and its political liberation and development, all indicate sources of positive self-consciousness and self-definition.

The achievement of a positive ethos lies then in historical and current struggle and achievement. The struggle can be seen as an ongoing struggle of humans, in this case Blacks, to realize themselves. In Kawaida philosophy, self-realization has a double meaning, i.e., to know and to produce oneself. To know oneself is to grasp the essences of one's past, one's present and especially one's future possibilities and thereby know who you are by what you have done and thus what you are capable of doing and becoming based on past achievement and current conditions. To produce oneself, is to create oneself through struggle against natural and social oppositions and through knowledge of what and who you can and ought to be. Thus, self-knowledge and self-production are at the heart of ethos and are clearly linked. For as a people struggles to overcome basic oppositions, then, it creates and defines itself and informs the world of its difference and distinctiveness, i.e., its ethos. Thus, a people comes into being and knows itself by its achievements; and through its efforts to become and know itself, it achieves.

Given this, it is a fundamental Kawaida contention that a people whose sense of achievements are minor or whose knowledge of its history and the possibilities it suggests is deficient, develops a self-consciousness of similar characteristics. Moreover, in a social context which defines and deforms a people's capacity to realize itself, the problem of self-consciousness is not simply a problem of thought, but also a problem of practice (Karenga, 1982). For the demand to end a deficient consciousness must be joined to a demand to eliminate the conditions which caused it. This is why Black psychologists advocate the social intervention model of psychology advanced by Fanon (1967:11) who argued mental health demanded a solution on both the subjective (mental) and objective (social) level.

In conclusion, then, the problem of self-consciousness is solved in the process of solving the social problems which cause it. This essentially means that through *study, work* and *struggle, building and becoming*, Blacks' real self, hidden under layers of false roles and identities imposed by the dominant society, will emerge. Through these self-conscious efforts and the resultant achievements in the various areas of human thought and practice as well as the model of work and liberational struggle Africans in America establish, they will, as I (Karenga, 1980:114) stated, transform themselves into a distinct self-realized and "self-conscious historical personality, proud of its past, challenged by the present and inspired by the possibilities of the future."

STUDY QUESTIONS

1. Define psychology stressing the reasons for its human focus.
2. Give historical summary of the development of Black psychology.
3. What are the defining aspects of the traditional school of Black psychology?
4 What are some defining aspects of the reformist school of Black psychology?
5. What are some defining aspects of the radical school of Black psychology?
6. Discuss critically the contentions of the traditional psychologists presented.
7. Discuss critically the contentions of the reformist psychologists presented.
8. Discuss critically the contentions of the radical psychologists presented.
9. Define and discuss the Kawaida conception of ethos.
10. Discuss the link between self-consciousness, social achievement and social struggle.

REFERENCES

Akbar, Na'im (Luther X Weems). (1974) "Awareness: The Key to Black Mental Health," Journal of Black Psychology, 1, 1 (August) 30-37.

Akbar, Na'im. (1994) *Light From Ancient Africa*, Tallahassee: Mind Productions.

Akbar, Na'im. (1981) "Mental Disorder Among African Americans," *Black Books Bulletin*, 5, 2:18-25.

Akbar, Na'im. (1976) "Rhythmic Pattern in African Personality," in Lewis King, et al, (eds.) *African Philosophy, Assumption & Paradigms for Research on Black Persons*, Los Angeles: Fanon Center Publication, pp. 175-189.

Akbar, Na'im. (1991) *Visions for Black Men, Nashville, TN: Winston-Derek Publishers, Inc.*

Azibo, David, (ed.) (1996) *African Psychology in Historical Perspectives and Related Commentary*, Trenton, NJ: Africa World Press.

Berlew, A. Kathleen Hoard, W. Curtis Banks, Harriet Pipes McAdoo and Daudi Ajani ya Azibo. (1992) *African American Psychology*, Newbury Park, CA: Sage Publications.

Clark, Kenneth. (1965) *Dark Ghetto*, New York: Harper & Row.

Cross, William E., Jr. (1980) "Models of Psychological Nigrescence: A Literature Review," in Reginald L. Jones, (ed.) *Black Psychology*, New York: Harper & Row.

Cross, William E. Jr. (1991) *Shades of Black: Diversity in Africa-American Identity*, Philadelphia: Temple University Press.

Cross, William E. Jr., (1971) "The Negro-To-Black Conversation Experience," *Black World*, (July) 13-27.

Cross, William E. Jr., Thomas Parham and Janet E. Helms. (1991) "The Stages of Black Identity Development: Nigresence Models," in Reginald L. Jones, (ed.), *Black Psychology*, 3rd Edition, Berkeley, CA: Cobbs & Henry Publishers, pp. 319-338.

Fanon, Frantz. (1967) *Black Skin, White Masks*, New York: Grove Press.

Fanon, Frantz. (1968) *The Wretched of the Earth*, New York: Grove Press.

Grier, William H. and Price M. Cobbs (1968) *Black Rage*, New York: Bantam Books.

Guthrie, Robert V. (1970) *Being Black*, San Francisco: Canfied Press.

Guthrie, Robert V. (1976) *Even the Rat Was White*, New York: Harper & Row.

Harrell, Camara Jules P. (1999) Manichean Psychology: *Racism and the Minds of People of African Descent*, Washington, DC: Howard University Press.

Jackson, Gerald G. (1982) "Black Psychology: An Avenue to the Study of Afro-Americans," *Journal of Black Studies*, 12, 3 (March) 241-261.

Jackson, Gerald G. (1979) "The Origin and Development of Black Psychology Implications for Black Studies and Human Behavior," *Studia Africana*, 1, 3 (Fall) 270-293.

Jones, Reginald. (1991) *Black Psychology*, 3rd Edition, Hampton, VA: Cobb & Henry.

Kagan, Jerome and Ernest Havemann. (1976) *Psychology*, New York: Harcourt Brace Jovanovich.

Kambon, Kobi. K. (Baldwin, Joseph) (1998) *African-Black Psychology in the American Context: An African-Centered Approach*, Tallahassee: Nubian Nation Publications.

Kambon, Kobi K. (Baldwin, Joseph) (1992) *The African Personality in America: An African-Centered Framework*, Tallahassee, FL: Nubian Nation Publications.

Kambon, Kobi K. (Baldwin, Joseph). (1976) "Black Psychology and Black Personality: Some Issues for Consideration," *Black Book Bulletin*, 4, 3:6-11.

Kambon, Kobi K. (Baldwin, Joseph). (1980) "The Psychology of Oppression," in Molefi K. Asante and Abdulai S. Vandi, (eds.), *Contemporary Black Thought*, Beverly Hills: Sage Publications, pp. 95-110.

Karenga, Maulana. (1978) "Chinese Psycho-Social Therapy: A Strategic Model for Mental Health," *Psychotherapy: Theory, Research and Practice*, 15, 1 (Spring) 101-107.

Karenga, Maulana. (1980) *Kawaida Theory: An Introductory Outline*, Inglewood, CA: Kawaida Publications.

Karenga, Maulana. (1982) "Society, Culture and the Problem of Self-Consciousness: A Kawaida Analysis," in Leonard Harris, (ed.), *Philosophy Born of Struggle*, Dubuque, IA: Kendall/Hunt.

Karenga, Maulana. (1999) "Sources of Self in Ancient Egyptian Autobiographies: A Kawaida Articulation," in James Conyers, Jr. (ed.), *Black American Intellectualism and Culture: A Social Study of African American Social and Political Thought*, Stamford, CT: JAI Press, Inc.

King, Lewis M. et al (eds.) (1976) *African Philosophy*, Los Angeles: Fanon Center Publication.

Myers, Linda James. (1988) *Understanding an Afrocentric World View: Introduction to an Optimal Psychology*, Dubuque, IA: Kendall/Hunt.

Nobles, Wade W. (1980) "African Philosophy: Foundations for Black Psychology," in Reginald L. Jones, (ed.), *Black Psychology*, York: Harper & Row, 23-26.

Nobles, Wade W. (1985) *Africanity and the Black Family: The Development of a Theoretical Model*, Oakland: Black Family Institute Publications.

Nobles, Wade W. (1986) *African Psychology: Toward Its Reclamation, Reascension and Revitalization*, Oakland: Black Family Institute.

Nobles, Wade W. (1976) "Black People in White Insanity: Issues for Black Community Mental Health," *Journal of Afro-American Issues*, 4, 1:21-27.

Parham, Thomas, Joseph White and Adisa Ajamu. (2000) *The Psychology of Blacks: An African Centered Perspective*, 3rd Edition, Upper Saddle River, NJ: Prentice Hall.

Poussaint, Alvin F. (1972) *Why Blacks Kill Blacks*, New York: Emerson Hall Publishers.

Poussaint, Alvin F. and Amy Alexander. (2000) *Lay My Burden Down: Unraveling Suicide and the Mental Health Crisis Among African Americans*, Boston: Beacon Press.

Thomas, Charles W. (1971) *Boys No More*, Beverly Hills: Glencoe Press.

Thomas, Charles W. (1978) "The Need for an Ethnically Specific Social Science," lecture, Tuskegee Institute, Tuskegee, Alabama, April 27.

Thomas, Charles W. (1974) "The Significance of the E(thnocentrism) Factor in Mental Health," *Journal of Non-White Concerns in Personal Guidance*, 2, 2.

Thomas, Charles W. (1979) "The Social Significance of Research," paper presented at Howard University Mental Health Research and Development Center, May 1-3.

Welsing, Frances Cress. (1980) "The Concept and the Color of God and Black Mental Health," *Black Books Bulletin*, 7, 1:27ff.

Welsing, Frances Cress. (1970) *The Cress Theory of Color Confrontation and Racism (White Supremacy)*, Washington, D.C.: C-R Publishers.

White, Joseph. (1991) "Toward a Black Psychology," in Reginald L. Jones, (ed.) *Black Psychology*, New York: Harper & Row, pp. 5-13.

White, Joseph L. and Thomas A. Parham. (2000) *The Psychology of Blacks: An African-American Perspective*, 3rd Edition, Englewood Cliffs, NJ: Prentice Hall.

Williams, Robert. (1974) "A History of the Association of Black Psychologists: Early Formation and Development," *Journal of Black Psychology*, 1, 1 (August) 7-24.

Wilson, Amos N. (1978) *The Development Psychology of the Black Child*, New York: Africana Research Publications.

Wilson, Amos N. (1981) "The Psychological Development of the Black Child," *Black Books Bulletin*, 7, 2:8-14.

Wilson, Amos N. (1992) *Understanding Black Adolescent Male Violence*, New York: Afrikan World Infosystems.

Wright, Bobby E. (1981) "Black Suicide: Lynching by Any Other Name is Still Lynching," *Black Books Bulletin*, 7, 2:15-17.

Wright, Bobby E. (1975) *The Psychopathic Racial Personality*, Chicago: Third World Press.

REASSESSMENT
AND
REAFFIRMATION

REASSESSMENT AND REAFFIRMATION

CHAPTER 11

11.1 INTRODUCTION

This concluding chapter has as its essential content an ongoing dialog conducted in Black Studies/Africana Studies departments and programs, discipline journals, web site and e-mail exchanges, intercampus and on-campus presentations and in papers and forums at meetings of Black Studies professional organizations. It is a dialog that the discipline is having and must have with itself about its mission, meaning and methodology. Therefore, this chapter is both a review and reassessment, a revisiting of things engaged in the prior chapters and a contribution to the ongoing discipline dialog about the direction, function and future of the discipline. The intention is not only to share this contribution, but to invite exchange by the questions it raises and the contentions it offers. The chapter or dialog begins with a review of the discipline's initial assumptions about its role and relevance and ends with a reaffirmation of the early and ongoing social mission of the discipline.

THE EARLY SELF-UNDERSTANDING OF THE DISCIPLINE

As an emerging discipline, Black Studies sheltered the assumption that the Black experience clearly represented a truth worth knowing, but also one worth living and offering as a paradigm for human liberation and a higher level of human life. Conceiving of intellectual emancipation as a prerequisite and parallel support for political emancipation, Black studies advocates posed the discipline as a fundamental site of engagement in the struggle to expand the realm of freedom in society as well as the academy. Informing its self-understanding was the stance that the pursuit and possession of knowledge must never simply be based on the principle of *knowledge for knowledge sake*, but essentially on the principle of *knowledge for human sake*. In other words, it challenged both student and faculty to always ask in the pursuit and possession of knowledge, how can this knowledge improve the human condition and enhance the human prospect? Given that African people are the subject and substance of Black studies, the challenge was always and remains one of recovering, reconstructing and posing paradigms from the rich and ancient resource of Black culture in order to frame and answer these questions. Moreover, Africana studies is continuously concerned with the conditions and possibilities of Black life and with the ongoing task of enhancing Black people's capacity to critically grasp their inherent possibilities for freedom and flourishing and to self-consciously bringing these into being both as a distinct people and as fundamental part of society and the world (Karenga, 1997).

11.2 REVIEW OF THE DEVELOPMENTS

The discipline of Africana/Black Studies has, of necessity, undergone a series of significant changes since its inception. These changes, as might be anticipated, are the result of both the internal developmental dynamics of the discipline itself and its sharing and responding to similar challenges of other disciplines posed by a changing academy, society and world (Conyers, 1997; Hall, 1999; Karenga, 2000a). As I have indicated in chapter 2, five of the most important developments are: (1) professional organizations of the discipline; (2) the methodology of Afrocentricity; (3) Black women studies; (4) multicultural studies; and (5) classical African studies. The National Council for Black Studies, the preeminent professional organization of the discipline, has been very instrumental in providing forums, models, advisors and scholars for development of curriculum, programs of assessment, service learning, community linkage, and international exchange. These initiatives have not only brought scholars together in mutually beneficial exchanges, but has helped to expand the discipline as well as move it toward a flexible standardization in vital areas (*Afrocentric Scholar*, 1993, 1992). The African Heritage Studies Association has also played a similar role in the development of the discipline.

Clearly, one of the most important developments in Black Studies is the emergence of Afrocentricity as a major conceptual framework within the discipline. A methodological initiative put forth by Molefi Asante (1990, 1998), professor of African American Studies at Temple University and founder of the first Ph.D. Africana Studies program, Afrocentricity quickly became a major focus and framework for discourse in Black Studies, the academy and society. It has invigorated academic and public discourse and posed challenges of methodology, pedagogy and research to the discipline itself and the academy as a whole. Black women studies has also been essential to the discipline's development and the maintenance of its self-understanding as a liberatory project which offers moral critique and corrective for constraints on human freedom and human flourishing. The development of Black women studies as an integral and indispensable part of Black Studies reaffirms this position, enriches and expands Black Studies discourse and research and reflects the discipline's capacity to constantly rethink its scope and content, and to reconstruct itself in ever more valuable and vital ways (Gordon, 1987; ; Hudson-Weems, 1994; Aldridge, 1997; Collins, 2000).

Multicultural studies actually were initiated with and through the struggles for Black Studies with its critique of and demand for an end to a monocultural and Eurocentric education. Our contention, then and now, was and is that a quality education is, of necessity, a multicultural education and that comparative engagement in analysis and understanding can only enrich our learning and teaching experience (Bowser, et al, 1995; Karenga,1995a; Reed, 1997). Classical African studies (ancient Egyptian, Nubian, Yoruba, Ashanti and other cultures of antiquity) has brought an expanded and enriched understanding and exchange to the Black Studies project. It has provided an ancient and instructive point of departure for framing and pursuing critical issues, reaffirming the centrality of African history to the history of humanity and human civilization and providing useful and expansive paradigms of human excellence and human possibility (Diop, 1982; Karenga, 1984, 1994, 1999; Obenga, 1992).

11.3 THE REQUIREMENT OF REASSESSMENT

It is in this context of ongoing development that Africana Studies, like every project of value and vision, is rightfully compelled to engage regularly and with sufficient rigor in sustained and sober reflection on its achievements and unfinished business, its theoretical and empirical possibilities, its self-understanding as an academic and social practice and its rootedness and relevance in an era of increasing possibilities and contradictions (Karenga, 2000a; Hall, 1999; Conyers, 1997, Stewart, 1997). The point here is to look back and face forward in an ongoing effort to understand and engage the world in new and meaningful ways from an African-centered standpoint. And it is also to raise and pursue this self-questioning and quest within the core self-understanding of the discipline as a self-conscious project directed, not only toward a critical grasp of the world, but also toward improving the human condition and enhancing the human prospect (Karenga, 1988).

At such a point of critical engagement in consideration of the state and future of the discipline, it is useful to remember and bring into focus the ancient Yoruba teaching on the appropriate posture for such a serious and sustained undertaking. The ancient Yoruba sacred text, *Odu Ifa* (1:1), says:

> *Let us not engage the world hurriedly.*
> *Let us not grasp at the rope of wealth impatiently.*
> *That which should be treated in a mature manner,*
> *Let us not deal with it in a state of uncontrolled passion.*
> *When we arrive at a cool place,*
> *Let us rest fully.*
> *Let us give continuous attention to the future.*
> *Let us give deep consideration to the consequences*
>   *of things.*
> *And this, because of our eventual passing*
> *(Karenga, 1999:1).*

So we are charged here, then, not to approach a serious matter hurriedly, impatiently or irrationally. On the contrary, we are to approach the matter calmly and in a manner that reflects adequate pause and mature judgment. Also, in our deliberations, we are charged rightly with the responsibility of giving "continuous attention to the future" and "deep consideration to the consequences of things." This critical and measured approach and its depthful and future-focused thrust are in the interest of leaving a worthy legacy, given the reality and consequences of "our eventual passing" and our implicit obligation to the generations who come after us.

A DuBOISIAN PERSPECTIVE

Always open to fruitful engagement, the writings of W.E.B. DuBois also offer us an instructive parallel concern with the developmental demands of an evolving discipline. In an essay written at the end of the nineteenth century, DuBois (Foner, 1982:102) noted that the development of sociological study was then at a critical period "...without settled principles and guiding lines and subject ever to the pertinent criticism; what, after all has been accomplished?" His response to this was to reason that the answer to the question of accomplishment is found in the scholarly commitment and realization that "the phenomena of society are worth the most careful and systematic study, and whether or not this study may eventually lead to a systematic body of knowledge deserving the name of science, it cannot in any case fail to give the world a mass of truth worth the knowing."

As I read DuBois' advice, it is counsel to a developing discipline to welcome "pertinent criticism," accept the need of constant assessment and realize that key to the relevance of its work is the rigor of its research, the meticulous and systematic character of its studies. For, as he argues, it is through such criticism, i.e., external challenge and self-questioning, and through rigorous research that we produce and give to the world "a mass of truth worth knowing." From an African-centered standpoint, we must read this "mass of truth worth knowing" as a body of knowledge which contributes in a real and meaningful way to improving the condition and enhancing the future of our community, society and the world. Indeed, it is within this understanding that the concept of the dual mission of Africana Studies, academic excellence and social responsibility, evolved (Hare, 1969). The central question here, then, becomes one of how do we continue to understand in new and various ways this project, and how do we honor the implications of this mission to create, sustain and constantly develop a discipline defined not simply by its academic presence and discourse, but also by its self-conscious linking in thought and practice the campus with the community, and intellectual grounding with social engagement (Hare, 1972).

As has been noted, Africana Studies came into being as an agency of change in the academy and community, as a key participant in the challenge to the university to reconceive and reconstruct itself. We challenged not only its intellectual project, but also its structure and functioning as an agent of the established order, rather than as an agent of human development. It is Africana studies which first issued the intellectual obituary of the Eurocentric project and raised the concept of relevance in education (Hare, 1975). And it is Africana Studies that revitalized and expanded the challenge to what counted as knowledge, and rejected the imposition of a Eurocentric canon through the Afrocentric initiative (Asante, 1990). Now, Africana studies is challenged by its own history, that is to say, to honor its legacy through continued development. It also must continue to develop and expand in the interest of consistently providing the *relevant* and *quality* education which it demanded at its founding. That is why Africana Studies must continuously engage in critical self-questioning concerning things "achieved and undone," things still to be thought out and transformed, the quality of its practice and the central mission, meaning and methodology of its project.

THE DOGON MODEL OF KNOWLEDGE ACQUISITION

To pursue this project of critical self-questioning, I would like to employ the African, in this case the Dogon, concept of knowledge acquisition which is posed as a continuous *becoming-in-thought-and-practice* at ever higher levels. The knowledge process for the Dogon is conceived as a continuous *becoming-in-thought-and-practice* because "It forms or models the individual at the same time he is assimilating the knowledge it offers" (Griaule and Dieterlen, 1986:70). The point here is that our quest for and production of knowledge is part and parcel of our self-formation as scholars and of the shaping of the discipline. And it is thus key to our self-understanding and self-assertion in the world as both scholars and a discipline to proceed with our project in the most meticulous and measured ways, so that the rigor and range of our process, constantly yield the quality products our self-understanding as a discipline demands. The Dogon conception that the production and possession of knowledge at ever higher levels is central to our constantly becoming and our ongoing self-formation is useful, then, in its offering a framework for an open-textured developmental process, both for scholars in the discipline and the discipline itself.

The Dogon posit four fundamental stages of knowledge which are directed toward understanding the story of the world and one's place and responsibility in it. The first level of knowledge is called *giri-so* or "fore-word." It consists of basic facts and descriptive explanations. This is also called "first knowledge." The second stage of knowledge is *benne-so* or the "side-word" and involves a deeper encounter with the given, categorization and the search for meaning. The third stage in the Dogon knowledge process is *bolo-so* or the "back-word," which is directed toward comparison and linking of parts into a meaningful and instructive whole. And the final stage is *so-dayi*, "the clear word" which "concerns itself with the edifice of knowledge in its ordered complexity" and its application in practice in the assumption of responsibility in and for the world.

The categorization of the stages of knowledge as fore-word, back-word, side-word, and clear-word suggest a multidimensional and holistic approach to knowledge. It requires looking at its various dimensions, analyzing each, comparing and linking them within a holistic framework and then extracting a clear conception from both the product and the process. It is clear that these *stages* of knowledge are at the same time *kinds* of knowledge and it is in this way I wish to approach them. These kinds of knowledge, thus, may be categorized as: (1) giri-so, descriptive knowledge; (2) benne-so, analytic knowledge; (3) bolo-so, comparative knowledge; and (4) so-dayi, active knowledge. It is within this framework that I will delineate and discuss some current challenges and possibilities of Africana Studies. And I will do this from a *Kawaida* perspective, that is a critical cultural perspective, which privileges tradition, requires reason and insists on practice in both the grasping of knowledge and its proving its ultimate value (Karenga, 2000b; 1997). Kawaida is a philosophy of culture and social change which has as one of its central tenets the assumption that culture is the ground of self-understanding and self-realization and that it requires and rewards dialogue with it, as I will discuss below. Inherent in this presentation is the assumption that each general stage of development of Africana Studies, must of necessity identify, engage and resolve a series of specific problematics which serve as a subset of challenges within the larger framework of the four overarching challenges I pose here. Moreover, I pose all the challenges here as also possibilities, for in the midst of every structural and processual challenge is the possibilities of growth and change, as well as failure, digression and decline.

11.4 GIRI-SO, DESCRIPTIVE KNOWLEDGE

THE QUESTION OF CULTURE

The initial and ongoing challenge for Africana studies is to continue to define itself in ways that reaffirm its original and fundamental mission and yet reflect its capacity and commitment to continuously extend the range of its concerns to deal with new problematics and new understandings within the discipline and within an ever-changing world. Within the National Council For Black Studies (NCBS), we have consistently maintained that the mission of Black Studies is a dual one – academic excellence and social responsibility. The first focus was/is to reaffirm and insure our commitment to the highest level of intellectual production as scholars and to a similar profound intellectual grounding for our students. And the second focus was/is to reaffirm our commitment to the principle and practice of social responsibility and our dedication to cultivating in our students a similar commitment. But in spite of this generally accepted and explicit dual focus, there has always been a third implicit focus which undergirds and informs both our emphasis on academic excellence and social responsibility. This invisible but unavoidably present element is *cultural grounding* which was not included in the explicitly stated mission and motto of NCBS, although implicitly it is always present.

From its very inception, Black Studies/Africana Studies has stressed the Black or African character, i.e., the cultural character, of its project. In fact, it was a fundamental point of our criticism of the white or European educational system that it lacked an adequate presence and presentation of the African or Black experience as well as the experience of other peoples of color. Inherent in this criticism was the concern that the cultural representation of African people in the educational process exhibit accuracy in fact, competence in interpretation and an adequacy of African presence in appropriate places. Furthermore, in the NCBS community, culture is constantly identified as an indispensable element in both the conception and practice of the Black Studies discipline. And no Black Studies scholar denies the centrality of culture to the Africana Studies project. For African culture is literally the ground of our intellectual project, the indispensable source of our identity, purpose and direction as a discipline and a people. It is from African culture – Continental and Diasporan – that we draw the data, the intellectual and practical paradigms to frame, establish and pursue the Africana Studies project. And it is because of our considered judgment that African people have *a culture that offers a unique and valuable way of being human in the world and one worthy of study in its own right* that we demanded and struggled to bring Black Studies into being as a discipline.

Moreover, my courses and *IBS* are organized around my understanding of Black Studies as a holistic project and thus a cultural one. It is within this understanding that I define Black Studies as the critical and systematic study of the multidimensional aspects of Black thought and practice in their current and historical unfolding. This stress on the many-sidedness of Black thought and practice, joined with concern for historical and current unfolding, points towards emphasis on a holistic approach. This context of wholeness, in turn, points to the Kawaida concept of *culture*, which is *the totality of thought and practice by which a people creates itself, celebrates, sustains and develops itself, and introduces itself to history and humanity.* As noted above, This activity occurs in at least seven basic areas: (1) history; (2) religion (spirituality and ethics); (3) social organization; (4) economic organization; (5) political organization; (6) creative production (art, music, literature, dance, theatre); and (7) ethos. These areas of culture translate in Black Studies as core areas of focus and core courses in the discipline.

Political, economic and social organization are posited as politics, economics and sociology; creative production is taught in its various distinct areas and ethos is covered in psychology. But in any case, Black Studies is clearly about Black culture and Black people's initiative and experience within that culture as well as within the world. Most Black Studies programs and departments, then, have some version of these seven subject areas or sub-fields as core course areas. It, thus, becomes important to introduce the student to these seven core subject areas in the introductory course as a foundation for the various other courses which they will take in the discipline and which will also fit within the framework of African intellectual and social culture – continental and diasporan. So, it is clear that culture is the foundation and framework for the Africana Studies project and has been from the inception of Black Studies as a discipline, the hub and hinge on which the project turns. The need, then, is to add *cultural grounding* as a third fundamental focus in the discipline's mission. And it is with this understanding that I offered this category of mission in chapter 1.

RETHINKING THE SOCIAL DIMENSION

But in *reshaping* and *reaffirming* the mission, we also need, perhaps, to rethink the category "social responsibility" and ask ourselves whether the concept of responsibility speaks to the level of active commitment we seek to cultivate and reaffirm in faculty and students. It is an open and ongoing question, but it is clear that one of the defining distinctions some of us make between ourselves as activist scholars or activist intellectuals and the *nouveau venu* or recently arrived public intellectuals is that we are more concretely engaged. Our role, we argue, is not to explain Black people to the established order or its various kinds of members as, we reason, they are doing. It is rather to produce and use knowledge in the service of our people and the world. And this ultimately means that *we seek to play an active role in developing public philosophy and policy* and *to engage in social practices which aid in both understanding the world and changing it in profound and promising ways.* This is, at one level, certainly related to a broad concept of social responsibility. But on a deeper level, such an activist intellectual position calls for a more concrete intervention which is, perhaps, better captured in the concept of *social engagement.* For social engagement involves both active commitment and meaningful intervention. Thus, the triple focus and thrust of the Africana Studies mission might be better defined as: *cultural grounding, academic excellence,* and *social engagement.*

REAFFIRMATION OF OVERARCHING GOALS

Within the context of these three fundamental foci and commitments of its mission, the Africana Studies project, as indicated in chapter 1, is informed by five overarching goals: (1) the critical and persistent search for truth and meaning in human history and social reality from an African vantage point; (2) a depthful intellectual grasp and appreciation of the ancient, rich, varied and instructive character of the African initiative and experience in the world and of the essential relevance of African culture as a unique and valuable way of being human in the world; (3) a rigorous intellectual challenge and alternative to established-order ways of viewing social and human reality; (4) a moral critique and social policy correctives for social constraints on human freedom and development, especially those rooted in race, class and gender considerations; and (5) cultivation of commitment and contribution to the historical project of creating the truly multicultural, democratic and just society and good world based on mutual respect of the rights and needs of persons and peoples, mutual cooperation for mutual benefit and shared responsibility for building the good world all humans want and deserve to live in (*Odu Ifa*, 78:1).

SOME FUNDAMENTAL OBJECTIVES

In realizing these overarching goals, some of the fundamental objectives of Africana Studies are: (1) to provide students with a critical integrated overview of the origins, scope and relevance of the discipline, its seven core subject areas, its academic, cultural and social mission and its major research issues and schools of thought; (2) to enhance critical thinking through engaging the oppositional propositions and thinking in the discipline which challenge established-order ways of approaching the world; (3) to engage historical and current events as a mode of cultivating and expanding the capacity for critical analysis and social ethical concern for the human condition and the human prospect from within an African cultural and intellectual framework; (4) to heighten awareness of the role of race, class and gender in human community and exchange; and (5) to use the African initiative and experience in the world to cultivate critical appreciation of diversity as both an engaging problematic and a rich resource of human community, human exchange and human self-understanding. Again, it is in this process of faculty and student collaboration and exchange that both they and the discipline develop and produce what the Dogon understand as a constant becoming in thought and practice at ever higher levels.

A DEFINITIVE LITERATURE

Finally, Africana Studies is of necessity challenged to continue to define itself through its ongoing intellectual production of a defining and definitive basic literature. For as I (1988:399) have noted, "a discipline is by definition a self-conscious organized system of research and communication in a defined area of inquiry and knowledge . . . ." And the product of this research is a literature which is the basic source of what James Stewart (1984) calls "a coherent intellectual enterprise." Moreover, as James Turner (1984:xviii) has argued, "Black Studies is a conceptual paradigm that principally tells us like other academic discourse what counts as facts and what problems of explanation exist." But we cannot effectively posit "what counts as facts" if there is no literature which adequately assembles them. And we cannot delineate "what problems of explanation exist," if the discipline must depend on those outside it to provide its central library or basic literature. So the challenge of giri-so here is to continue to produce a constantly expanding body of literature which assembles basic definitive facts and explanations of the discipline and makes them available for discipline discourse and development. For it is in this process that boundaries of the discipline are delineated, essential content is identified, and indispensable and definitive explanations are provided. It is here too that discipline language and essential paradigms are introduced and the subject areas delineated (Turner, 1984; Stewart, 1992; Karenga, 1993).

But to do this Black Studies scholars must avoid certain pit-falls, such as exclusive focus on developing grand theories of social life, superficial reference to areas of inquiry outside their scope, failing to bring forward the lessons of the past in the interest of the present and the future and interpreting the demands of descriptive knowledge as the need for statements of faith rather than presentations of facts. The collection of facts is often tedious and never-ending and in no way compares to heady discourse that passes as theoretical insight or to the cata-loging of injustices and urgent and often misconceived calls for survival. But it is a noble, necessary, even indispensable enter-prise and no discipline is either conceivable or possible without this. True, one can always borrow literature from scholars in other disciplines for intellectual diversity, but not for intellectu-al grounding. For a discipline must justify itself in its own terms and by its own research and intellectual production. And litera-ture is an indispensable product and expression of this.

11.5 BENNE-SO, ANALYTIC KNOWLEDGE

The descriptive knowledge of a discipline is by definition first knowledge or beginning knowledge. It thus requires critical explanation, a below-the-surface search for relevance and mean-ing which results in benne-so, knowledge at an analytical level. The fact that Africans introduced the concept of human dignity in the *Book of Kheti* in ancient Egypt in 2140 B.C.E is clearly rel-evant as a reference. But it is more meaningful as a point of departure for moral philosophy which establishes both the con-textual and theoretical origins of such a concept and explores its value as an expression of African ethical discourse about what it means to be human (Karenga, 1994:597ff). This is why it is imperative that Black Studies scholars challenge students and colleagues to engage African culture as a perennially fruitful resource rather than as an ungrounded and convenient reference.

DIALOGING WITH AFRICAN CULTURE

And so if we are to use Black culture as a resource rather than a simple reference, then the process of analysis must begin, as noted above, with a dialogue with this culture. In fact, there is no greater challenge to Africana Studies than that it move from simple description of Black life and culture to an African-centered analysis of its meaning in the most insightful and incisive ways. In a word, the essential and ongoing challenge it is to engage African culture in dialogue. By dialogue, here, I mean intellectual engagement of the texts, thought and practices of the culture, to ask the texts questions and extract its answers with analytical incisiveness. By texts I mean oral, written and living-practice texts, i.e., those texts whose lessons are the lived lives of the people whether they wrote or not. Within this framework, the living-practice text of Harriet Tubman is instructive. It is a narrative which has as its central focus her decision to free herself and then share the good of freedom with others. Her report of her reasoning that freedom was a good to be shared shows her redefining freedom from an act of individual escape to a collective act of self-determination in community. In this single yet instructive act and in what Quarles (1988) calls her "unlikely," yet extraordinary leadership, she enriches our modern discussion on the personal and collective nature of freedom, our moral responsibility to significant others and the grounds and delimitations of a morality of sacrifice. And there are clearly numerous others who "specialize in the wholly impossible" and leave similarly instructive legacies (Hines, King and Reed, 1996).

It is important to note that this process of analytically engaging African texts – oral, written and living-practice texts, is, of necessity, distinguished from the word wizardry, hyperabstraction and deconstructionism which shape and inform so much of current humanities discourse. In such a context there is a deconstructionist tendency to expose the defective rather than raise up paradigms of possibility. In the process, so-called subversive discourse on texts becomes an alternative to subversive thought about social change and new and improved ways of being human in the actual world. The language of subversion is borrowed from a tradition of radical social thought and practice, but talk of "transgression," "boundary crossing" and the like is at best a gentle rattling of the bars of the conceptual prisons society has constructed as part of its edifice of oppression and domination. At worst, it is little more than flights of linguistic fantasy, a diversionary discourse of individualistic self-indulgence which leaves the paradigms of possibility unengaged and the actual social borders and barriers in tact and unconfronted.

THE RESOURCE OF CULTURE

The approach of this text is essentially an Afrocentric cultural approach rooted in *Kawaida* philosophy. Kawaida philosophy defines itself as an *ongoing synthesis of the best of African thought and practice in constant exchange with the world* (Karenga, 1997). It poses culture as the fundamental framework and way of being human in the world and maintains that as persons in general and intellectuals in particular, we must constantly dialogue with African culture, asking it questions and seeking from it answers to the fundamental and enduring concerns of humankind. Among these fundamental questions are: What constitutes the good life? How do we create the just and good society? What are our obligations to each other as fellow human beings and fellow citizens? How do we establish and maintain a rightful relationship with the environment? How do we define and secure the dignity and rights of the human person and the well-being and flourishing of community? And what are some essential ways we might improve the human condition and enhance the human prospect? Through this process of posing questions of enduring human concern and seeking answers within the framework of our culture and in constant exchange with the world, we discover the rich and varied resources in African cultures. And these resources not only provide the basis for reflective problematics indispensable to the educational enterprise, but also aid us in our ongoing efforts to bring forth paradigms and propositions of the best of what it means to be African and human in the fullest sense.

This dialogue with African culture requires that Africana Studies scholars ask at every critical juncture of research, writing and discourse, the crucial question of what does Africa, i.e., African people and African culture, have to offer in efforts toward understanding and improving the human condition and enhancing the human prospect. The dialogue or ongoing conversation with African culture becomes even more significant when one realizes that Europe continues for the most part to monologue with itself and to offer a curriculum which is often little more than one long self-congratulatory narrative about itself in every discipline. Indeed, it has never dialogued in any meaningful sense with Africa or for that matter with any other people of color. By meaningful dialogue I mean engaging African culture as a valuable site and source for generating and providing *reflective problematics*, that is to say, problems of thought, practice and experience which form the foundation and framework for the educational and intellectual enterprise.

THE RETURN TO ANCIENT EGYPT

Even that part of Africa called Egypt (Kemet) was not engaged in dialogue by Europe. In spite of Egypt's gifts to Europe and ancient Israel, and indeed the world, there is no real or relevant discussion in the established order curriculum of ancient Egypt's literature, philosophy, ethics, and other contributions to humanity, using its own texts, i.e., the words, expressed ideas and concerns of its own people (El-Nadoury, 1990; Diop, 1981, 1974; Harris, 1971). Instead, Egypt was relegated to mythological and monumental reference, archaeological study and museum placement. Even at the height of European romantic fascination with Egypt outlined by Bernal (1987), it was never more than an idealized reference. This was, in great part, due to the fact that by the time modern Europe "discovered" or "rediscovered" Egypt, it had already chosen ancient Greece and ancient Israel as the undisputed sources of its fundamental paradigms of knowledge and religion. For paradigms of knowledge, it chose ancient Greece; and for paradigms of religion, it chose ancient Israel. Certainly, a dialogue with ancient Egypt would have made these paradigms more problematic, given their debt to ancient Egypt and thus their contradictory claim to uniqueness and exclusivity. Therefore, ancient Egypt's rich and expansive ethics and spirituality were hidden under biblical myths of its being a land of bondage for ancient Israel, its scientific achievements rendered irrelevant by the need to see ancient Greece as the source of all substantive science and its relationship to Africa denied by geographical and cultural redefinition of it as a part of the Middle East or Western Asia (Obenga, 1992; Karenga, 1994). This is why Diop's posing Egypt as a classical source of paradigms is so important. For as he (1981:10ff) says, it is not his assertion of the fact of the Blackness of Egypt that is so important, but that he made it an intellectually and scientifically operational fact. Thus, he challenged Africana Studies scholars to dialogue with Egypt to extract *ancient paradigms* which point toward *modern possibilities* and ways of building a new body of human sciences and humanities and of renewing African culture. It is in this spirit and understanding that Africana Studies scholars began to introduce ancient Egyptian studies in the departmental curriculum and to explore ancient Egyptian studies as a rich resource in the ongoing developmental thrust of the discipline (Karenga, 1993: 49-56).

SANKOFA REVISITED

Here the right approach to the Akan intellectual and cultural challenge of *sankofa* must be correctly grasped and interpreted. For the sankofa call to "go back and retrieve it" is not a call to make our history a mere point of descriptive facts and references but an intellectual project of recovery of essential data and a critical analysis of issues of truth and meaning concerning the African initiative and experience in the world. As noted above in chapter 3, Niangoran-Bouah (1984:210) states, *Sankofa* literally means "come back, seek and take or recover." He reads the *Sankofa* ideogram, a bird reaching back with its beak into its feathers, as "a symbol representing the quest for knowledge and the return to the source." Niangoran-Bouah further states that the ideogram implies that the resulting knowledge "is the outcome of research, of an intelligent and patient investigation."

As an Afrocentric methodological practice of historical recovery, then, sankofa is not simply the collection of data but also a critical analysis of meaning from an African centered standpoint (Keto, 1995). In its most expansive understanding and definition, sankofa contains three basic elements and processes: (1) an ongoing quest for knowledge, that is to say, a continuing search for truth and meaning in history and the world; (2) a return to the source, to one's history and culture for grounding and models in one's unique cultural way of being human in the world; and (3) a critical retrieval and reclaiming the past, especially the hidden, denied and undiscovered truths of the African initiative and experience in the world. By critical retrieval I mean an analytical approach to things encountered, a below-the-surface grasping for deeper and larger meanings that routine competence cannot provide. And I use critical reclaiming in its meaning of extracting the valuable from the midst of the waste which surrounds it, i.e., the racist falsification and intellectually deficient interpretations of African history and culture.

This refers to a critical process which self-consciously distinguishes itself from the deconstructionist janitorial model of history. In such a model writers or researchers become little more than janitors of history, constantly searching for stench, stain and peeling paint in the lives of great or notable men and women and revealing it as the central meaning of these persons' lives and work. Such diligent but misguided searches for dirt and debris fit well within the racist reading of Black history. For racism from its inception has had as its central goal the spurious revelation and specious proof of how weak and unworthy Africans are. Thus, any African contribution to such a project only adds to the racist deformation and denial of African history and culture. It does not, as some scholars claim, aid us in our understanding of persons in all their complexity. It is little more than deconstructionist bias to argue that the meaning of a great person's life is understood by concentration on her weaknesses rather than the strength displayed in models of human excellence and human achievement which he or she offers. After all, we know and learn lessons of human possibility, not from the weaknesses of the great and notable, but from their triumph over them.

11.6 BOLO-SO, COMPARATIVE KNOWLEDGE

REVISITING AFROCENTRIC METHODOLOGY

The comparative mode of knowing is central to Africana Studies and is a fundamental feature of Afrocentric methodology. As I have (1995a:45) argued above and elsewhere, "Afrocentricity can be defined as a methodology, orientation and quality of thought and practice rooted in the *cultural image* and *human interest* of African people." To be rooted in the cultural image of African people is to be grounded in the views and values of Africans and in the practices that both evolve from and inform those views and values. And to be rooted in the human interests of African people is to be anchored in the highest of

African views and values and just claims on life and society that we share with other peoples and that represent the best of what it means to be African and human in the fullest sense. These values will, of necessity, include a profound commitment to truth, justice, freedom, human dignity, community, mutual respect, shared good and other fundamental principles which give foundation and framework for bringing, sustaining and enhancing good into the world in all its aspects – spiritual/ethical, natural and social.

It is at this point that it becomes clear that Afrocentricity, as a culturally rooted approach to understanding and engaging the world, contains both a *particular* and *universal* dimension. It begins as a centering of oneself in one's own culture, dialoguing with it and bringing forth a particular and useful insight and discourse to the multicultural project. This initiative is, of necessity, grounded in the considered assumption that the rich, varied, ancient and complex character of African culture is a critical resource in understanding and engaging the world. And it is in the process of such a culturally rooted exchange with the other peoples of the world that the African person and scholar discover common ground with other peoples and cultures which can be cultivated and developed for mutual benefit and deeper insight into the human condition and human prospect.

ENGAGING THE WORLD

It is also in this context that the comparative method finds fertile ground both on a national and global level. It is important to note here that a comparative method does not hide or minimize variation or difference. It simply focuses on similarities as more fundamental in understanding factors that shape ethnic, national and global communities. Thus, the Africana Studies scholar will want to know not only how the fundamental factors of race, class and gender intersect as modes of domination and resistance, but also to understand differential responses and modes of engagement of various peoples and persons with these national and global systems of oppression. S/he will recognize that though these factors of race, class and gender can be understood critically on an ethnic or national level, they are at one level better treated as trans-ethnic and transnational or global processes. It is within this understanding of different levels of comparison from the ethnic to the national and eventually to the global that Malcolm X (1982), Mary McLeod Bethune (1974) and Marcus Garvey's (1977), among others, insisted that we see ourselves as a people, not in isolation and marginal, but in a national and global context, indeed as a *world historical people*.

In such a national and global conception of ourselves as a key people in a key country and world community, we develop a more critical understanding of the particular historical trajectory of African people and their role in the forward flow of human history. We are able to locate ourselves within the major movements for human liberation and understand in new and meaningful ways how the African American Liberation Movement —both its Civil Rights and Black Power dimension – impacted not only this country but also peoples in struggle for freedom and human rights all over the world. For it not only expanded the realm of freedom in this country, but also inspired and informed the movements of other oppressed and marginalized groups – other peoples of color, women, seniors and the disabled, et al and posed a paradigm of possibility and struggle for peoples all over the world. Indeed, these groups and peoples of the Americas, Africa, Asia, Latin America and the Middle East (Western Asia) have borrowed from and built on our moral vision and moral vocabulary, sung our songs of freedom and posed our struggle as a central and instructive model of the struggle for human liberation.

In addition, there is a pressing need for an increase in comparative studies of the ethnic cultures of the U.S. as *cultures of resistance*, comparative gender studies, including comparative studies of womanist and feminist approaches to understanding and engaging the world, and comparative holocaust studies, with special attention to the Holocaust of African enslavement and the Native American Holocaust as paradigms for subsequent morally monstrous acts of genocide in both the physical and cultural sense. And certainly, there is a wide range of promising lines of intellectual pursuit in comparative studies in the ancient classical civilizations of Africa, Native America, Asia and the Pacific Island cultures with their rich, varied and complex understandings of the divine, natural and the social.

The comparative method, then, allows for and encourages studies of movements, institutions, peoples, cultures and other social formations in a cross-cultural, trans-national and historical framework, examining the interplay, interconnections and interrelationships between societies, cultures and peoples as well as the intersection of factors which shape them and inform relations of power and social change, especially factors of race, class and gender. In such a thrust, the Africana Studies scholar offers not only a critique of existing established order conceptions of the world, but also a multicultural and African-centered paradigm which provides a significant contribution to alternative ways of viewing and engaging the world, thus enriching and expanding the discipline (Henderson, 1995, Schiele, 2000).

11.7 SO-DAYI, ACTIVE KNOWLEDGE

CLASSICAL FOUNDATIONS

If, as we've argued, knowledge in an African centered understanding and context is never simply knowledge for knowledge sake but always knowledge for human sake, indeed for the sake or good of the world, then, Africana Studies finds its ultimate fulfillment in its contribution to improving the condition of the world and enhancing its prospect in the social and natural realms. This Afrocentric understanding of the role and ultimate value of knowledge is rooted and reaffirmed in the reading of both the ancient Egyptian sacred text, *The Husia* (Karenga, 1984) and the Yoruba sacred text, the *Odu Ifa* (Karenga, 1999). In *The Husia*, knowledge acquisition, or in the Kemetic phraseology, "the constant searching after truth, justice and rightness in the world (ph̲r m-s3 M3ʿt) in the interest of continuously improving the world (srwd̲ t3), and making it more beautiful and beneficial than it was when we inherited it, is an ethical obligation. In fact, the ancient Africans of Kemet called humans *rhyt*, possessors of knowledge, a designation which defines not only an essential element in understanding our humanity, but also that which is equally essential in realizing our humanity in its fullest and most flourishing forms.

In the *Odu Ifa* (78:1), we are told that humans are divinely chosen to bring good into the world and that the first criteria for a good world is full knowledge of things (Bmòtán ohun gbogbo) and that the first criteria for achieving the good world is wisdom – moral, intellectual and practical – adequate to govern the world (ogbón tí ó pò tó eyí tí a lè fise àkóso ayé). If we are to continuously dialogue with our culture and constantly bring forth the best of what it means to be African and human, this is undoubtedly an excellent point of departure. For in both Kemetic and Yoruba culture, the ultimate value of knowledge lies in its role in bringing and increasing good into the world, making it more beautiful and beneficial than we inherited so that the legacy we leave to future generations is worthy of us as an African people.

SOCIAL ENGAGEMENT

HARE'S CONCERN FOR THE SOCIAL MISSION

An African-centered understanding of Africana Studies, of necessity, translates as *social engagement*. In fact, it challenges us to reaffirm our commitment to the activist conception of the role and responsibility of the African intellectual which requires the acquisition, production and use of knowledge in the service of the community and world. Even in the early years of the formation of Black Studies, Nathan Hare, organizer of the first Black studies program and a leading activist intellectual of the period, expressed concern about Black Studies becoming a pale image of its former self. He (1972:34) noted that the tendency toward dilution and diversion from the original social and academic mission of Black Studies came from without and within. College and university administrators, he stated, were dissolving and encouraging the dissolution of links between the community and Black Studies departments and programs and had been partially successful "in restricting Black Studies to culture and the humanities and to the mere study of Blackness." By this he meant restricting Black Studies to a narrow concept of culture and cultural studies. In this he had already anticipated the current university preference for engagement with the abstract problems of literature rather than the concrete problems of life.

Also, Hare reminded us that such disengagement from the life and struggle of the Black community was in contradiction to the mission and ultimate meaning of Black Studies – a project not simply to understand the world, but also to change it in ways that improved the lives and enhanced the future of the masses. Indeed, he (1972:33) argued that "Black Studies was (essentially) a mass movement and mass struggle based on the notion that education belongs to the people and the idea is to give it back to them." Within this framework, he continued, "most crucial to Black Studies, Black education, aside from its ideology of liberation, would be the community component of its methodology." This means that doing Black Studies is both an intellectual and practical activity and project. In a recent interview, Hare (2001:25-26) argues that Black intellectuals must focus on bringing forth knowledge of our past in service of our present and future, and developing a "balance between focus on information and implementation." He concludes, reminding us that "the African approach to education...is always practical and involves the collective."

CRITICAL ISSUES

Such a commitment to social engagement as a fundamental element of Black Studies practice leads, of necessity, to taking up the critical issues of our times and contributing to development of ethical social policies and practices to address these. Building on those issues cited in the social policy agenda of the *Million Man March/Day of Absence Mission Statement* (Karenga, 1995b), these critical issues include: the ongoing struggle in the interest of human freedom, dignity and justice; enhanced economic development based on economic discipline and cooperative practices; an independent politics and increased engagement of the masses; reaffirmation of and strengthening of the family and male/female relations based on principles of equality; mutual respect and shared responsibility; reparations; affirmative action; care and active responsibility in the AIDS crisis; struggle against police abuse, government suppression and the industrialization of prisons; support of the freedom of all political prisoners; organizing against drugs; expanded support for public and independent schools; elimination of negative media images and practices; strengthening community organization; protection of the environment; mutually supportive alliances with other peoples of color; and standing in solidarity with other African peoples in their struggles to free themselves, harness their material resources and live full, free and meaningful lives.

In conclusion, the wide-ranging and ongoing character of these problems call for cultural, intellectual and practical engagement of the most profound and enduring quality. Such a self-conscious commitment is captured in the conclusion of the *Million Man March/Day of Absence Mission Statement* (Karenga, 1995:22). It says:

> We stand in Washington conscious that its a pivotal point from which to speak to the country and the world. And we come bringing the most central views and values of our faith communities, our deepest commitments to our social justice tradition and the struggle it requires, the most instructive lessons of our history, and a profoundly urgent sense of the need for positive and productive action. In standing up and assuming responsibility in a new, renewed and expanded sense, we honor our ancestors, enrich our lives and give promise to our descendants. Moreover, through this historic work and struggle we strive to always know and introduce ourselves to history and humanity as a people who are spiritually and ethically grounded; who speak truth, do justice, respect our ancestors and elders, cherish, support and challenge our children, care for the vulnerable, relate rightfully to the environment, struggle for what is right and resist what is wrong, honor our past, willingly engage our present and self-consciously plan for and welcome our future.

If we are to conceive and build the just society and good world, we all want and deserve to live in, and if Black Studies is to honor its mission in its fullest form, such an emancipatory conception of our responsibility as teacher, students and activist intellectuals is both central and mandatory to our project.

STUDY QUESTIONS

1. Discuss Black Studies' self-conception at its emergence as a discipline.
2. Review the key developments in the discipline since its early period and discuss their relevance.
3. Discuss the value of reaffirmation of the beginning of the Black Studies mission and critical reassessment as an ongoing need. What is DuBois' contribution to our understanding of this need?

4. What are the four stages in the Dogon concept of knowledge acquisition? What do they mean literally and how are they used here?
5. Discuss the cultural grounding aspect of the Black Studies mission, its value and contribution to the Black Studies project.
6. Discuss the rethinking of the concept of social responsibility, comparing it with the concept of social engagement.
7. Review and discuss the five overarching goals of Black Studies.
8. Discuss some of the fundamental objectives of Africana Studies within these goals.
9. Discuss the significance of an ongoing dialog with African culture in the discipline. How is it a resource in addressing fundamental questions of human life? What are some of these questions?
10. Discuss Europe's failure to dialog with African culture, especially ancient Egypt. What are some reasons for this?
11. Discuss the concept of sankofa. What are its three basic elements and processes? Discuss the difference between the critical retrieval of the sankofa process and the deconstructionist janitorial model of doing history.
12. Discuss the particular and universal dimension of Afrocentric methodology. How does this inform comparative analysis? What are some promising subjects for comparative studies?
13. What are Dr. Hare's concerns about the transformation and possible loss of the initial social dimension of the Black Studies project?
14. Discuss some of the critical, current and ongoing issues that Black Studies must engage intellectually and practically as part of its cultural, academic and social mission.

REFERENCES

Afrocentric Scholar, 2, 1 (May 1993); 1, 1 (May 1992).

Aldridge, Delores. (1997) "Womanist Issues in Black Studies: Toward Integrating Womanism in Africana Studies," in James Conyers, Jr. (ed.), *Africana Studies*, Jefferson, NC: McFarland and Company, Inc., pp. 143-54.

Asante, Molefi. (1990) *Kemet, Afrocentricity and Knowledge*, Trenton, NJ: African World Press.

Asante, Molefi. (1998) *The Afrocentric Idea*, Philadelphia: Temple University Press.

Bernal, Martin. (1987) *Black Athena: The Afro-Asiatic Roots of Classical Civilization*, Vol. 1, London: Free Association Press.

Bethune, Mary McLeod. (1974) *The Legacy of Mary McLeod Bethune*, Washington, D.C.: The National Education Association.

Bowser, Benjamin, Terry Jones and Gale Auletta Young, (eds.). (1995) *Toward the Multicultural University*, Westport, CT: Praeger.

Conyers, Jr., James. (1997) *Africana Studies: A Disciplinary Quest for Both Theory and Method*, Jefferson, NC: McFarland and Company, Inc..

Cooper, Anna Julia. (1988) *A Voice From the South*, New York: Oxford University Press.

Diop, Cheikh Anta. (1974) *The African Origins of Civilization: Myth or Reality*, Westport, CT: Lawrence Hill & Co.

Diop, Cheikh Anta. (1981) *Civilisation ou Barbarie*, Paris: Presence Africaine, English translation, *Civilization or Barbarism*, Brooklyn, NY: Lawrence Hill, 1991.

El-Nadoury, R. (1990) "The Legacy of Pharaonic Egypt," in G. Mokhtar (ed.), *General History of Africa, Volume II, Ancient Civilizations of Africa*, Berkeley: University of California Press, pp. 103-118.

Foner, Philip S. (1982) *W.E.B. DuBois Speaks, Speeches and Addresses 1890-1919*, New York: Pathfinder Press.

Garvey, Marcus. (1977) *Philosophy and Opinions of Marcus Garvey*, Volume I and II, Amy Jacques Garvey (ed.), New York: Atheneum.

Gordon, Vivian. (1987) *Black women, Feminism and Black Liberation: Which Way?* New York: William Morrow.

Griaule, Marcel and Germaine Dieterlen. (1986) *The Pale Fox*, Chino Valley, AZ: Continuum Foundation.

Hall, Perry A. (1999) *In the Vineyard: Working in African American Studies*, Knoxville, TN: University of Tennessee Press.

Hare, Nathan. (1969) "What Should be the Role of Afro-American Education in the Undergraduate Curriculum?" *Liberal Education* 55 (March) 42-50.

Hare, Nathan. (1972) "The Battle of Black Studies," *Black Scholar* 3 (May) 32-37.

Hare, Nathan. (1975) "A Black Paper: The Relevance of Black Studies," *Black Collegian* 6 (September/October) 46-50.

Hare, Nathan. (2001) "Facing the Challenges of Black Manhood, An Interview," *African Business and Culture*, 2, 15:24-27.

Henderson, Earl. (1995) *Afrocentrism and World Politics: Towards a New Paradigm*, Westport, CT: Praeger.

Hill-Collins, Patricia. (2000) *Black Feminist Thought: Knowledge, Consciousness and the Politics of Empowerment*, New York: Routledge.

Hine, Darlene, Wilma King and Linda Reed (eds.) (1996) *"We Specialize in the Wholly Impossible": A Reader in Black Women's History*, Brooklyn, NY: Carlson Publishing.

Hudson-Weems, Clenora. (1993) *Africana Womanism: Reclaiming Ourselves*, Troy, MI: Bedford Publishers, Inc.

Karenga, Maulana. (1984) *Selections from the Husia: Sacred Wisdom of Ancient Egypt*, Los Angeles: University of Sankore Press.

Karenga, Maulana. (1988) "Black Studies and the Problematic of Paradigm: the Philosophical Dimension," *Journal of Black Studies* 18, 4 (June) 395-414.

Karenga, Maulana. (1993) *Introduction to Black Studies*, Los Angeles: University of Sankore Press.

Karenga, Maulana. (1994) *Maat, The Moral Ideal in Ancient Egypt: A Study in Classical African Ethics*, 2 vols., Ph.D. Dissertation, University of Southern California.

Karenga, Maulana. (1995a) "Afrocentricity and Multicultural Education: Concept, Challenge and Contribution," in Benjamin Bowser, Terry Jones and Gale Auletta Young (eds.), *Toward the Multicultural University*, Westport, CT: Praeger, pp. 42-61.

Karenga, Maulana. (1995b) *The Million Man March/Day of Absence: Mission Statement*, Los Angeles: University of Sankore Press.

Karenga, Maulana. (1997) *Kawaida Theory: A Communitarian African Philosophy*, Los Angeles: University of Sankore Press.

Karenga, Maulana. (1999) *Odu Ifa: The Ethical Teachings*, Los Angeles: University of Sankore Press.

Karenga, Maulana. (2000a) "Black Studies: A Critical Assessment," in Manning Marable (ed.), *Dispatches from the Ebony Tower: Intellectuals Confront the African American Experience*, New York: Columbia University Press, pp.162-170.

Karenga, Maulana. (2000b) "Society, Culture and the Problem of Self-Consciousness: A Kawaida Analysis," in Leonard Harris (ed.), *Philosophy Born of Struggle: Anthology of Afro-American Philosophy from 1917*, Dubuque, IA: Kendall/Hunt Publishing Company, pp. 136-151.

Keto, Tsehloane. (1995) *Vision, Identity and Time: The Afrocentric Paradigm and Study of the Past*, Dubuque, IA: Kendall/Hunt Publishing Company.

Obenga, Theophile. (1992) *Ancient Egypt and Black Africa, A Student's Handbook for the Study of Ancient Egypt in Philosophy, Linguistics and Gender Relations*, London: Karnak House.

Quarles, Benjamin. (1988) "Harriet Tubman's Unlikely Leadership," *Black Leaders of the Nineteenth Century*, Urbana: University of Illinois Press.

Reed, Ishmael. (ed.) (1997) *MultiAmerica: Essays on Cultural Wars and Cultural Peace*, New York: Viking Penguin.

Schiele, Jerome H. (2000) *Human Services and the Afrocentric Paradigm*, New York: Haworth Press.

Stewart, James. (1984) "The Legacy of W.E.B. DuBois For Contemporary Black Studies," *Journal of Negro Education* 53, 296-311.

Stewart, James. (1997) "Reaching for Higher Ground: Toward an Understanding of Black/Africana Studies," in James Conyers, Jr. (ed.), *Africana Studies*, Jefferson,NC: McFarland and Company, Inc., pp. 108-129.

Takaki, Ronald. (1993) *A Different Mirror: A History of Multicultural America*, Boston: Little, Brown and Company.

Turner, James. (1984) *The Next Decade: Theoretical and Research Issues in Africana Studies*, Ithaca: Africana Studies and Research Center, Cornell University.

Photo Credits

Cover: Ancient Egyptians – KIPAS Archives; Frederick Douglass – Photographs and Prints Division, Schomburg Center for Research in Black Culture, The New York Public Library, Astor, Lenox and Tilden Foundations; Harriet Tubman, Paul Collins; MFDP Delegation, George Ballis/Take Stock. **Text:** Kawaida Institute of Pan-African Studies Archives, 6, 7; Photographs and Prints Division, Schomburg Center for Research in Black Culture, The New York Public Library, Astor, Lenox and Tilden Foundations, 9; Courtesy, Spelman College Archives, Atlanta, Georgia, 11; Us Archives, 12; Courtesy of Dr. Nathan Hare, 15; Courtesy of Dr. Bertha Maxwell Roddy, 43; Courtesy of Dr. Molefi Asante, 45; Courtesy of Third World Press, 51; Courtesy of Dr. Barbara Wheeler, 51; African American Cultural Center, 62; Photographs and Prints Division, Schomburg Center for Research in Black Culture, The New York Public Library, Astor, Lenox and Tilden Foundations 148, 149, 152, 166, 173, 175; George Ballis/Take Stock, 185; Photographs and Prints Division, Schomburg Center for Research in Black Culture, The New York Public Library, Astor, Lenox and Tilden Foundations, 186; Photograph by Seba Tiamoyo Karenga, 191; Us Archives, 193; Photograph by Tiamoyo Karenga, 194; Us Archives, 195; Third World Press, 198; Courtesy of the New Black Panther Vanguard, 199; Courtesy of Dr. Imari Obadele, 200; Photograph by Tiamoyo Karenga, 209; Photographs by David Barnes, 211, 215; Courtesy of Dr. La Frances Rodgers Rose, 332.

INDEX